France

Vintage	Médoc/Gra...				...ace
2008	5–8	5–8			
2007	5–7	6–7	8–9	8–9	6–8
2006	7–8	7–9	8–9	8–9	6–8
2005	9–10	9–10	8–10	8–10	8–9
2004	7–8	7–9	5–7	6–7	6–8
2003	5–9	5–8	7–8	6–7	6–7
2002	6–8	5–8	7–8	7–8	7–8
2001	6–8	7–8	8–10	7–9	6–8
2000	8–10	7–9	6–8	6–8	8–10
99	5–7	5–8	6–9	7–10	6–8
98	5–8	6–9	5–8	5–9	7–9
97	5–7	4–7	7–9	4–7	7–9
96	6–8	5–7	7–9	7–10	8–10
95	7–9	6–9	6–8	5–9	6–9
94	6–8	5–8	4–6	5–8	6–9
93	4–6	5–7	2–5	5–7	6–8
92	3–5	3–5	3–5	4–8	5–7
91	3–7	2–7	2–5	6–8	3–5
90	8–10	8–10	8–10	7–8	7–9

France continued

Vintage	Burgundy			Rhône	
	Côte d'Or red	Côte d'Or white	Chablis	Rhône (N)	Rhône (S)
2008	7–9	7–8	7–8	6–7	5–7
2007	7–8	8–9	8–9	6–8	7–8
2006	7–8	8–10	8–9	7–8	7–9
2005	7–9	7–9	7–9	7–8	6–8
2004	7–8	7–8	7–8	6–7	6–7
2003	6–7	6–7	6–7	5–7	6–8
2002	7–8	7–8	7–8	4–6	5–5
2001	6–8	7–9	6–8	7–8	7–9
2000	7–8	6–9	7–9	6–8	7–9
99	7–10	5–7	5–8	7–9	6–9
98	5–8	5–7	7–8	6–8	7–9
97	5–8	5–8	5–8	7–9	5–8
96	6–8	7–8	5–10	5–7	4–6
95	7–9	7–9	6–9	6–8	6–8

Beaujolais 08, 07, 06, 05. Crus will keep. **Mâcon–Villages** (white). Drink 08, 07, 05. **Loire** (Sweet Anjou and Touraine) best recent vintages: 07, 05, 02, 97, 96, 93, 90, 89, 88, 85; Bourgueil, Chinon, Saumur–Champigny: 06, 05, 04, 02, 00, 99, 97. **Upper Loire** (Sancerre, Pouilly–Fumé): 08, 07, 06 **Muscadet** 08 DYA.

Hugh Johnson's Pocket Wine Book 2010

Edited and designed by Mitchell Beazley, an imprint of Octopus Publishing Group Limited, 2–4 Heron Quays, London E14 4JP.

An Hachette Livre UK Company
www.hachettelivre.co.uk

Distributed in the USA and Canada by Octopus Books USA: c/o Hachette Book Group USA, 237 Park Avenue, New York, NY 10017

First edition published 1977
Revised editions published 1978, 1979, 1980, 1981, 1982, 1983, 1984, 1985, 1986, 1987, 1988, 1989, 1990, 1991, 1992, 1993, 1994, 1995, 1996, 1997, 1998, 1999, 2000, 2001, 2002 (twice), 2003, 2004, 2005, 2006 (twice), 2007, 2008, 2009

ISBN (UK): 978 1 845 33501 4

ISBN (US): 978 1 845 33529 8

General Editor **Margaret Rand**
Commissioning Editor **Becca Spry**
Project Editor **Jo Wilson**
Editor **Deirdre Headon**
Proofreader **Theresa Bebbington**
Art Director **Pene Parker**
Art Editor **Yasia Williams-Leedham**
Designer **Colin Goody**
Production Manager **Peter Hunt**

Printed and bound in China

Picture credits

1 Shutterstock/5am Media; 3, Shutterstock/Nicola Spasenoski; 4, Shutterstock/Johan Kalen; 6, Octopus Publishing/Adrian Pope; 305 Stockfood/Hans-Peter Siffert; 307, 308, 310 Photolibrary/Cephas Picture Library/Andy Christodolo; 311 Alamy/Bon Appetit; 312 Photolibrary/Cephas Picture Library/Kevin Judd; 313 Alamy/Russell Kord; 317 Octopus Publishing/Jason Lowe; 318 Shutterstock/Luiz Claudio Ribeiro; 319 Shutterstock/guentermanaus; 320 Shutterstock/Licia Rubinstein

MITCHELL BEAZLEY

HUGH JOHNSON'S

POCKET WINE BOOK

2010

GENERAL EDITOR MARGARET RAND

Acknowledgments

This store of detailed recommendations comes partly from my own notes and mainly from those of a great number of kind friends. Without the generous help and cooperation of innumerable winemakers, merchants, and critics, I could not attempt it. I particularly want to thank the following for help with research or in the areas of their special knowledge:

Geoff Adams
Sarah Ahmed
Helena Baker
Nicolas Belfrage MW
Philipp Blom
Jim Budd
Michael Cooper
Rupert Dean
Michael Edwards
Sarah Jane Evans MW
Rosemary George MW
Caroline Gilby MW
Robert Gorjak
James Halliday

Annie Kay
Chandra Kurt
James Lawther MW
Konstantinos Lazarakis
  MW
John Livingstone-
  Learmonth
Nico Manessis
Adam Montefiore
Jasper Morris MW
Shirley Nelson
Margaret Rand
Ulrich Sautter
Eleonora Scholes

Stephen Skelton MW
Paul Strang
Marguerite Thomas
Larry Walker
Simon Woods
Philip van Zyl

Contents

Front endpaper: Quick reference vintage charts

Back endpaper: A little learning / the right temperature

Agenda 2010

The wine world has gone mad. Or, at least, parts of it have; and Britain is one of those parts. Here, where connoisseurship has always rubbed shoulders with simple boozing, but where everyone has known the difference, wine is under attack by a government intent on demonizing the drinking of wine with dinner. In France there is an even more egregious folly: a serious attempt to reintroduce elements of Prohibition, or at least to discourage us from drinking, or even talking about, wine.

I am talking, of course, about France and the oddly named Loi Evin, a law named after the minister who dreamt it up. The French government's aim (says the Minister now in charge) is to "harmonize" the laws discouraging the enjoyment of wine throughout Europe. When the world has more pressing problems on its mind, I'm afraid there is a chance they might succeed.

Those of us who love wine must be clear about what it is we cherish and why. We argue that wine, its properties, traditions, varieties, and indeed its effects, are a part of European culture and identity as important as any other. It is as much our right to enjoy them as it is to walk our streets or fish our rivers. And it is our duty to conserve such a cultural asset for the future.

The insidious argument coming from the French government is that wine is "a harmful product causing addiction". Most remarkably, the minister wishes "to give consumers back their freedom of choice"; stolen from them, he claims, by the seductions of wine and its cultural heritage. Freedom from culture? Goering wanted that, didn't he? "Whenever I hear the word culture," the quote goes, "I reach for the safety catch of my revolver."

The French government hopes to persuade the managers of Europe that its citizens have been robbed of their power to decide. What has robbed them? Addiction "caused" by wine. But what proportion of its consumers are so affected? Scarcely any is the answer. There was a time (but you have to be 60 years old to remember it) when French workmen were wedded to their wine-bottles. Six litres of red a day was not extraordinary on building sites. Consumption crashed in the 1960s and 70s. Today France's alcohol consumption is lower than Britain's.

And then there is the European Union, which is currently engaging in an act of breathtaking stupidity aimed, you would think, at destroying the whole culture of European wine selection, discrimination and choice. The cult of EU-niformity has gone mad.

What the EU has done is announce, with no fanfare at all, that appellation contrôlée and its equivalents are to be abolished. This enormous and detailed structure, to which new member states have to tailor their existing wine regimes, and which in old member states is the reflection of a way of understanding wine that influences every wine-producing country in the world, is to go. The announcement was made just like that, in August 2008.

The new system, the EU declared, would be in place within 12 months: by August 2009. It announced this with a perfectly straight face. The EU seemed to believe that it was really going to happen. By the time you read this we will know more; but at the time of writing the picture, across Europe, is one of baffled inaction.

The new system is not a new invention: it's merely that which already applies to food. Instead of AC there'll be Appellation d'Origine Protegé (AOP); Italy's DOC will be replaced by Denominazione di Origine Protetta (DOP), and the same will happen in Spain, Hungary, Germany, Bulgaria and everywhere else. Lower down the range Vin de Pays, IGT and all the rest will be replaced by IGP (Indication Geographique Protegé). That seems straightforward, but what will happen to France's VDQS wines is less obvious: will they be promoted up or demoted down? There is supposed to be a parallel process of rationalization, with France's 470 AC regions and Italy's 470 denominations, for example, being reduced in number – to 182 in Italy's case.

How this will work is far from clear. Of the countries contacted, only France's INAO (Institut National des Appellations d'Origine) was able to field a coherent reply which was, basically, don't hold your breath. Is it possible that the new codes of production will be ready by August 2009 – just look at Bordeaux and the legal wars that have broken out with attempts to reclassify crus bourgeois and Graves crus classés. The message is: tamper with the status quo and somebody will send you a writ.

Some reorganization would not be a bad thing. Appellation contrôlée is a weary old warhorse, used cynically by many a producer intent merely on ticking boxes. (Think of the nastiest Champagne – to take a wine at random – you've ever drunk, and wonder how it got the AC.) It is not, and should not be taken to be, a guarantee of quality. It preserves in aspic the attitudes and practices of earlier years while its strictures are not impossible to evade for those who want to do so badly enough.

Perhaps we should be content with this: with, on the one hand, some wines that are a disgrace to their AC, in return for, on the other hand, growers who will bend (all right, break) the rules because that way they believe they give us better quality. Perhaps it's altogether too English to think that the rules should be correct in the first place. Because we can be sure that when European wine producers do get around to filling that large pit dug by the Eurocrats, the main substance they will use is fudge.

Does anyone believe, meanwhile, that all this would be of any benefit to consumers? Wine represents an infinitely complex culture of its own. Those (they may not be many, but they are serious) who have trained and honed their appreciation and their palates on the distinctions between, for example, the appellations of the Côte d'Or will not be happy with a new set of rules changing a system that has taken centuries to create. The chances are, in fact, that they will simply ignore them, or find a way of getting round them. It takes many sea-miles to turn round a tanker.

To conclude: in a year when money is short, Britain is chastising us, France is pussyfooting with the notion of prohibition, and Europe is about to tear up the appellations that guide our enjoyment, we need to be sure of our priorities. As inheritors of something so rich and life-enhancing as the world of wine we need to act in its defence. The range of wines this book describes is an artefact like no other: the product of a passion shared by individuals, interpreted by individuals, and enjoyed by individuals in almost as many countries as play football. The best way to defend it is to explore, to enjoy and to share it. To your health!

The memory lingers on...
In this edition I have indicated within entries 200 or so of the wines I remember having specially (and in some cases regularly) enjoyed over the past 12 months (that is mid '08–'09). It can be no guide to the future, but with so many alternatives on offer one has to start somewhere, and fragrant memories seem the best place. Lest anyone mistake these for "The World's 200 Best Wines" let me restate my fixed position: taste is personal. I like what I like – and so should you. The wines are indicated within entries in this way: *Clos de Chênes*.

How to use this book

The top line of most entries consists of the following information:

Aglianico del Vulture Bas r dr (s/sw sp) ★★★ 96' 97 98 99' 00 01' 02 (03)

❶ Wine name and the region the wine comes from.

❷ Whether it is red, rosé or white (or brown/amber), dry, sweet or
sparkling, or several of these (and which is most important):

r	red
p	rosé
w	white
br	brown
dr	dry*
sw	sweet
s/sw	semi-sweet
sp	sparkling

() brackets here denote a less important wine

* assume wine is dry when **dr** or **sw** are not indicated

❸ Its general standing as to quality: a necessarily rough-and-ready
guide based on its current reputation as reflected in its prices:

★	plain, everyday quality
★★	above average
★★★	well known, highly reputed
★★★★	grand, prestigious, expensive

So much is more or less objective. Additionally there is a subjective rating:

★ etc   Stars are coloured for any wine which in my experience is usually
especially good within its price range. There are good everyday wines
as well as good luxury wines. This system helps you find them.

❹ Vintage information: which of the recent vintages can be recommended; of
these, which are ready to drink this year, and which will probably improve with
keeping. Your choice for current drinking should be one of the vintage years
printed in bold type. Buy light-type years for further maturing.

00 etc	recommended years that may be currently available
96' etc	vintage regarded as particularly successful for the property in question
97 etc	years in bold should be ready for drinking (those not in bold will benefit from keeping)
98 etc	vintages in colour are those recommended as first choice for drinking in 2010. (See also Bordeaux introduction, p.84.)
(02) etc	provisional rating

The German vintages work on a different principle again: see p.143.

Other abbreviations

DYA	drink the youngest available
NV	vintage not normally shown on label; in Champagne, means a blend of several vintages for continuity

CHABLIS properties, areas or terms cross-referred within the section

Châteaux Aiguilloux type so styled within entries indicates wine
(mid '08–'09) especially enjoyed by Hugh Johnson

Vintage report 2008

The summer of 2008 was the time when the hills of Provence were so swathed in grey cloud as to look not unlike Scotland; when the chill on the Montagne de Reims got into the bones, and when one German grower, dismounting from his tractor, said that really he was quite enjoying spraying his vines against mildew and rot. He simply imagined that it was his bank manager he was attacking with fungicides...

In Europe the summer was almost universally cool, damp and disease-prone. Which doesn't mean that it was a dreadful year: vines are resistant and will seize any spell of good weather to put on some speed. Sometimes this good weather didn't arrive until September; in the Mosel it didn't happen until the first week of November, which is pushing it a bit.

Australia faced quite different challenges. Many regions had started the summer with low water reserves and ever-increasing restrictions on water use. The drought, however, wasn't universal: the Hunter Valley was getting more rain than it had had for years.

In the event, predictions of a vintage of half the usual size proved over-pessimistic: quantities were down, but not by that much. And quality was good, for those who picked before the three weeks of very, very hot weather that hit South Australia in March, and did nothing at all for the quality of the remaining grapes. The following spring the Aussies were still speaking of this heat with awe: up in the 30s°C at night, and with hardly any difference in temperature between night and day.

Over in Chile things weren't this hot, and in Argentina they weren't especially hot at all. Argentina had heavy rain in February and autumn frosts in April. But quality is good in both countries. South Africa was more inconsistent: cool, wet weather alternating with heat spikes. And in New Zealand it was rain at vintage time in many regions. But not in Central Otago. Pinot Noir fans can relax in the expectation of excellent wines.

There were more heat spikes in California: growers don't really like heat spikes because what they like is nice even ripening, with sugar levels in balance. Heat spikes are liable to send balance all over the place. However, things calmed down in time for the harvest, and in Oregon and Washington it was a good, unexcitable season, with good quality, and no signs of unwelcome temperament on the part of the weather.

This, of course, is just what Europe would have liked. All that greyness and damp got a little depressing after a bit. The Champenois were preparing to write the vintage off as a not-very-charming ingredient of non-vintage blends. But then September managed two weeks of warm sunshine, and the crop was saved. The relief in Reims and Epernay was palpable. As it was in Beaune and Bordeaux. In Burgundy it looks as though Chablis came off well, with the Côte d'Or patchier; in Bordeaux there are some excellent wines.

The word from the Mosel is that it's a year for good Kabinetts rather than for anything of higher Prädikat, although these will be good where selection has been rigorous. Max Ferd. Richter reports that good harvest weather only arrived in the first week of November, and that they were doing up to three passes in the vineyards just to eradicate unhealthy grapes. In Austria whites have done better than reds: expect pure fruit and crisp acidity. There were few botrytis wines but some Icewines, picked in a period of cold that began on 28 December. "A frosty farewell to the vintage," they call it. Quite so.

A closer look at 2007

This was the year of the Great Cool in much of Europe. A perfectly beautiful spring was followed by a perfectly horrible summer, which in turn was saved in the nick of time by a good September. Nature does love a bit of brinkmanship.

The relief that a bit of sunshine brought in Bordeaux and Burgundy might have brought a rush of blood to the head, though: the wines are good, but they're mostly not sensational. In Burgundy the reds are juicy, soft and forward: good wines for drinking, and good restaurant wines. In Bordeaux the reds were more up and down, though with more homogeneity on the Right Bank than on the Left. Whites in both regions were very good, however: lovely Chablis, pretty good Côte d'Or, lovely dry white Bordeaux, excellent Sauternes. Graves and Pessac-Léognan in particular are looking very good: sleek, harmonious white wines, with a little more unevenness in Graves. But how we see any of them in the long term is going to depend on what the world economy does and what the Euro does against other currencies. The vintage of 2005 was the year of the massive price hike in Bordeaux; if prices for the 2008s fall then 2007 will be left out on a limb. What might happen is that the château-owners release only a little of the 2008 vintage *en primeur*, perhaps at reduced prices, and sit on the rest in the hope of better times. Well, we're all hoping for better times.

Better times and better weather. The south of Europe had a generally better summer than the north, and the Rhône has produced a memorably good vintage of balanced, lively, deep wines which are looking a far better bet than Bordeaux, for anybody wanting to buy something good. And down in Provence the seriousness with which they're taking rosé these days is paying off: 2007 produced some beautiful pale, delicate wines with good structure and mineral core, and they'll be repeating the feat every year. They're taking everything seriously there now, so take a look at the reds as well: lovely complex, deep wines. The prices are pretty amazing, but that's what happens if you have a tame tourist market.

The vintage was excellent, in fact, all across the south of France: certainly in the eastern parts, and even right across to the southwest, there are beautifully balanced, ripe wines. And in Germany the 2007s are simply glorious. From just about every region they are pure, concentrated and ripe. They're giving immediate pleasure now, but there will be no problem with keeping them.

A safe pair of brands...

Even the most ardent of wine critics finds it impossible to keep up with the many new wines being launched each month. With the help of friends of this guide from around the world, we've put together a selection of the new and nearly-new brands that are currently available, often in innovative packaging. Some travel little beyond their native countries, while others are aimed at an international audience.

France

Arrogant Frog A brand from the Languedoc created by go-ahead Frenchman Jean-Claude Mas that is making waves in many countries, including Australia. The name may be tongue-in-cheek, but the wines – a chewy, Bordeaux-esque Cabernet/Merlot and a fresh, citrus Chardonnay/Viognier – manage to be both fun and serious at the same time.

Chamarré The idea here was to create a user-friendly French brand. The packaging is slightly old-fashioned, while the wines, though not offensive, offer little beyond soft, gentle fruit.

French Rabbit This range of Pinot Noir, Chardonnay, Cabernet Sauvignon and Merlot from French winemaker Boisset stands out not so much for its flavour as for its presentation. The wines come in 250ml, 500ml and 1-litre recyclable juice carton-style containers.

HobNob This selection of varietal Vins de Pays (Pinot Noir, Shiraz, Chardonnay and Merlot) from Beaujolais guru George Duboeuf is proving a big hit in the US and parts of Asia, thanks to its clean packaging and fresh if rather simple flavours.

Italy

Via Collina A promising new label from Guy Anderson, creator of the Fat Bastard brand. The aim of the range is to provide good value examples of authentic Italian wines, and the initial releases, among them a smoky, young Dolcetto di Diano d'Alba and a solid, peppery Aglianico del Vulture are impressive.

Germany

Relax Riesling This is an authentic, vibrant, off-dry young white with a touch of the sweet'n'sour, but you have to look closely to discover that it comes from Germany (courtesy of Schmitt Söhne). It is available in both a striking blue glass bottle (750 ml) or a similarly stylish 375ml aluminium bottle called a "junior". A Relax Cool Red and a rosé, both made from Dornfelder, are also available.

Spain

Spanish Quarter The target audience for this new brand from Spain's largest winemaker, the Codorníu group, is younger wine drinkers who are looking to experiment. First releases are a zippy Chardonnay/Albariño blend and a cherry-like Cabernet Sauvignon/Tempranillo

Torres Viña Sol The Parellada-based white version of this wine from the renowned Catalan producer has existed for many years, but has recently been joined by a fleshy Garnacha/Cariñena rosé and a bright, juicy Tempranillo red.

Wild Pelican One is an addition to the growing number of wines now available in a single-serving sized can (hence the name). Wild Pelican has a range of three wines: a Tempranillo from Cariñena in Spain, a Western Cape Chenin Blanc, and a Grenache/Shiraz rosé from Languedoc-Roussillon.

Portugal

Mateus Sparkling Rosé Most people will be familiar with regular Mateus in its distinctive squat bottle. This is a new, fully sparkling version made from the Baga grape from Bairrada in Portugal. Surprisingly good it is too, with a bready edge to its apple and raspberry fruit.

Pink Elephant This Portuguese rosé, made from Alfrocheiro, Touriga Nacional, Castelão and Cabernet Sauvignon, has been specially developed to partner curries and other spicy foods. It works well in such a role but also isn't bad by itself too, in a zesty, strawberry-ish fashion.

USA

Fish Eye One of a growing number of wines aimed at younger Americans, with the accent on eye-catching labels and an absence of complicated winespeak. The range of six varietal wines is available both in bottles and as bag-in-box.

3 Blind Moose Aimed at younger wine drinkers, this Californian range from wine giant Canandaigua is about more than just packaging. Cabernet Sauvignon is the pick of a quartet that also includes Chardonnay, Merlot and Pinot Grigio.

Chile

Espíritu de Chile This joint venture between the Aresti winery and German company Racke International is proving to be a hit in many countries, with a competent range of wines, including some more ambitious Gran Reserva bottlings. An Espíritu de Argentina also exists.

Fairhills Arguably the leading brand of fair trade wines has now added Chilean wine to its selection from South Africa and Argentina. Quality is good throughout, with the pick of the range being the tangy, creamy Chardonnay and honest, smoky Bonarda from Argentina.

Australia

Kid You Not A new and striking label from the latest generation of the Brown family of Brown Brothers fame in Victoria, Australia. The first releases are a rich, mealy Viognier/Roussanne, and a blend spicy, berry-rich blend of Tempranillo and Graciano.

Pink Piccolo Picking up on the trends for sparkling wine, rosé and individual servings, Pink Piccolo is a 200ml bottle of Australia's Yellowglen Rosé made from Chardonnay, Pinot Noir and Shiraz. Not the most complex of wines, but it does exactly what it should do with juicy, fruity style.

India

Château d'Ori A new estate in the Indian province of Nashik, northeast of Mumbai, that is making a splash (and not just in its home country) with its rich, juicy, New-World-style reds. Another label from Nashik to watch for is the Seagram-owned Nine Hills and its Cabernet Sauvignon in particular.

Grape varieties

In the past two decades a radical change has come about in all except the most long-established wine countries: the names of a handful of grape varieties have become the ready reference to wine. In senior wine countries, above all France and Italy, more complex traditions prevail. All wine of old prestige is known by its origin, more or less narrowly defined, not just the particular fruit-juice that fermented.

For the present the two notions are in rivalry. Eventually the primacy of place over fruit will become obvious, at least for wines of quality. But for now, for most people, grape tastes are the easy reference-point – despite the fact that they are often confused by the added taste of oak. If grape flavours were really all that mattered this would be a very short book.

But of course they do matter, and a knowledge of them both guides you to flavours you enjoy and helps comparisons between regions. Hence the originally Californian term "varietal wine" – meaning, in principle, from one grape variety.

At least seven varieties – Cabernet Sauvignon, Pinot Noir, Riesling, Sauvignon Blanc, Chardonnay, Gewurztraminer and Muscat – taste and smell distinct and memorable enough to form international categories of wine. To these you can add Merlot, Malbec, Syrah, Sémillon, Chenin Blanc, Pinots Blanc and Gris, Sylvaner, Viognier, Nebbiolo, Sangiovese, Tempranillo. The following are the best and/or most popular wine grapes.

Grapes for red wine

Agiorgitiko (St George) Versatile Greek (Nemea) variety with juicy damson fruit and velvety tannins. Sufficient structure for serious ageing.

Baga Bairrada grape. Dark and tannic. Great potential but hard to grow.

Barbera Widely grown in Italy, at its best in Piedmont, giving dark, fruity, often sharp wine. Fashionable in California and Australia; promising in Argentina.

Blaufränkisch Mostly Austrian; can be light and juicy but at best (in Burgenland) a considerable red. LEMBERGER in Germany, KEKFRANKOS in Hungary.

Brunello Alias for SANGIOVESE, splendid at Montalcino.

Cabernet Franc, alias Bouchet (Cab Fr) The lesser of two sorts of Cabernet grown in Bordeaux but dominant (as "Bouchet") in St-Emilion. The Cabernet of the Loire, making Chinon, Saumur-Champigny, and rosé. Used for blending with CABERNET SAUVIGNON, etc., or alone, in California, Australia and South Africa.

Cabernet Sauvignon (Cab Sauv) Grape of great character: spicy, herby, tannic, with characteristic blackcurrant aroma. The first grape of the Médoc; also makes most of the best California, South American, East European reds. Vies with Shiraz in Australia. Its wine almost always needs ageing; usually benefits from blending with e.g. MERLOT, CABERNET FRANC, SYRAH, TEMPRANILLO, SANGIOVESE etc. Makes aromatic rosé.

Cannonau GRENACHE in its Sardinian manifestation: can be very fine, potent.

Carignan In decline in France. Needs low yields, old vines; best in Corbières. Otherwise dull but harmless. Common in North Africa, Spain, and California.

Carmènere An old Bordeaux variety now extremely rare in France. Widely used in Chile where until recently it was often mistaken for MERLOT.

Cinsault/Cinsaut Usually bulk-producing grape of S France; in S Africa crossed with PINOT NOIR to make PINOTAGE. Pale wine, but quality potential.

Dolcetto Source of soft seductive dry red in Piedmont. Now high fashion.

Gamay The Beaujolais grape: light, very fragrant wines, at their best young. Makes even lighter wine in the Loire Valley, in central France, and in

Switzerland and Savoie. Known as "Napa Gamay" in California.

Grenache, alias Garnacha, Cannonau Useful grape for strong and fruity but pale wine: good rosé and *vin doux naturel* – especially in the South of France, Spain, and California – but also the mainstay of beefy Priorato. Old-vine versions are prized in South Australia. Usually blended with other varieties.

Grignolino Makes one of the good everyday table wines of Piedmont.

Kadarka, alias Gamza Makes healthy, sound, agreeable reds in East Europe.

Kékfrankos Hungarian BLAUFRÄNKISCH; similar lightish reds.

Lambrusco Productive grape of the lower Po valley, giving quintessentially Italian, cheerful, sweet and fizzy red.

Lemberger See BLAUFRÄNKISCH. Württemberg's red.

Malbec, alias Côt Minor in Bordeaux, major in Cahors (alias Auxerrois) and the star in Argentina. Dark, dense, tannic wine capable of real quality.

Merlot Adaptable grape making the great fragrant and plummy wines of Pomerol and (with CABERNET FRANC) St-Emilion, an important element in Médoc reds, soft and strong (and à la mode) in California, Washington, Chile, Australia. Lighter but often good in North Italy, Italian Switzerland, Slovenia, Argentina, South Africa, New Zealand etc.. Grassy when not fully ripe.

Montepulciano A good central-eastern Italian grape, and a Tuscan town.

Morellino Alias for SANGIOVESE in Scansano, southern Tuscany.

Mourvèdre, alias Mataro Excellent dark aromatic tannic grape used mainly for blending in Provence (but solo in Bandol) and the Midi. Enjoying new interest in, for example, South Australia and California.

Nebbiolo, alias Spanna and Chiavennasca One of Italy's best red grapes; makes Barolo, Barbaresco, Gattinara, and Valtellina. Intense, nobly fruity, perfumed wine but very tannic: improves for years.

Periquita Ubiquitous in Portugal for firm-flavoured reds. Often blended with CABERNET SAUVIGNON and also known as Castelão.

Petit Verdot Excellent but awkward Médoc grape, now increasingly planted in Cabernet areas worldwide for extra fragrance.

Pinot Noir (Pinot N) The glory of Burgundy's Côte d'Or, with scent, flavour, and texture that are unmatched anywhere. Makes light wines rarely of much distinction in Switzerland and Hungary. Improving in Germany and Austria. But now also splendid results in California's Sonoma, Carneros, and Central Coast, as well as Oregon, Ontario, Yarra Valley, Adelaide Hills, Tasmania, New Zealand's South Island and South Africa's Walker Bay.

Pinotage Singular South African grape (PINOT NOIR X CINSAUT). Can be very fruity and can age interestingly, but often jammy. Good rosé.

Primitivo Southern Italian grape making big, rustic wines, now fashionable because genetically identical to ZINFANDEL.

Refosco In northeast Italy possibly a synonym for Mondeuse of Savoie. Deep, flavoursome and age-worthy wines, especially in warmer climates.

Sagrantino Italian grape found in Umbria for powerful cherry-flavoured wines.

Sangiovese (or Sangioveto) Main red grape of Chianti and much of central Italy. Aliases include BRUNELLO and MORELLINO. Interesting in Australia.

Saperavi Makes good, sharp, very long-lived wine in Georgia, Ukraine etc. Blends very well with CAB SAUV (e.g. in Moldova).

Spätburgunder German for PINOT N. Quality is variable, seldom wildly exciting.

St-Laurent Dark, smooth and full-flavoured Austrian speciality. Also in the Pfalz.

Syrah, alias Shiraz The great Rhône red grape: tannic, purple, peppery wine which matures superbly. Important as Shiraz in Australia, and under either name in California, Washington State, South Africa, Chile, and elsewhere.

Tannat Raspberry-perfumed, highly tannic force behind Madiran, Tursan, and other firm reds from Southwest France. Also rosé. Now the star of Uruguay.

Tempranillo Aromatic fine Rioja grape, called Ull de Llebre in Catalonia, Cencibel in La Mancha, Tinto Fino in Ribera del Duero, Tinta Roriz in Douro, Aragonez in southern Portugal. Now Australia, too. Very fashionable; elegant in cool climates, beefy in warm. Early ripening.

Touriga Nacional Top port grape grown in the Douro Valley. Also makes full-bodied reds in south Portugal.

Zinfandel (Zin) Fruity adaptable grape of California (though identical to PRIMITIVO) with blackberry-like, and sometimes metallic, flavour. Can be structured and gloriously lush, but also makes "blush" white wine.

Grapes for white wine

Albariño The Spanish name for North Portugal's Alvarinho, making excellent fresh and fragrant wine in Galicia. Both fashionable and expensive in Spain.

Aligoté Burgundy's second-rank white grape. Crisp (often sharp) wine needs drinking in 1–3 years. Perfect for mixing with cassis (blackcurrant liqueur) to make "Kir". Widely planted in East Europe, especially Russia.

Arinto White central Portuguese grape for crisp, fragrant dry whites.

Arneis Aromatic, high-priced grape, DOC in Roero, Piedmont.

Blanc Fumé Occasional (New World) alias of SAUVIGNON BLANC, referring to its smoky smell, particularly from the Loire (Sancerre, Pouilly). In California used for oak-aged Sauvignon and reversed to "Fumé Blanc". (The smoke is oak.)

Bourboulenc This and the rare Rolle make some of the Midi's best wines.

Bual Makes top-quality sweet madeira wines, not quite so rich as malmsey.

Chardonnay (Chard) The white grape of Burgundy, Champagne and the New World, partly because it is one of the easiest to grow and vinify. All regions are trying it, mostly aged (or, better, fermented) in oak to reproduce the flavours of burgundy. Australia and California make classics (but also much dross). Italy, Spain, New Zealand, South Africa, New York State, Argentina, Chile, Hungary and the Midi are all coming on strong. Morillon in Austria.

Chasselas Prolific early-ripening grape with little aroma, mainly grown for eating. AKA Fendant in Switzerland (where it is supreme), Gutedel in Germany.

Chenin Blanc (Chenin Bl) Great white grape of the middle Loire (Vouvray, Layon, etc). Wine can be dry or sweet (or very sweet), but with plenty of acidity. Bulk wine in California, but increasingly serious in S Africa. See also STEEN.

Clairette A low-acid grape, part of many southern French blends.

Colombard Slightly fruity, nicely sharp grape, makes everyday wine in South Africa, California, and Southwest France. Often blended.

Falanghina Ancient grape of Campanian hills revived to make excellent dense aromatic dry whites.

Fiano High quality grape giving peachy, spicy wine in Campania, S. Italy.

Folle Blanche High acid/little flavour make this ideal for brandy. Called Gros Plant in Brittany, Picpoul in Armagnac. Also respectable in California.

Furmint A grape of great character: the trademark of Hungary both as the principal grape in Tokáj and as vivid, vigorous table wine with an appley flavour. Called Sipon in Slovenia. Some grown in Austria.

Garganega Best grape in the Soave blend. Top wines, esp sweet ones, age well.

Gewurztraminer, alias Traminer (Gewurz) One of the most pungent grapes, spicy with aromas like rose petals and grapefruit. Wines are often rich and soft, even when fully dry. Best in Alsace; also good in Germany (Gewürztraminer), East Europe, Australia, California, Pacific Northwest and New Zealand.

Grauburgunder See PINOT GRIS.

Grechetto or Greco Ancient grape of central and south Italy noted for the vitality and stylishness of its wine.

Grüner Veltliner Austria's favourite. Around Vienna and in the Wachau and

Weinviertel (also in Moravia) it can be delicious: structured, dry, peppery and lively. Excellent young, but the best age five years or so.

Hárslevelü Other main grape of Tokáj (with FURMINT). Adds softness and body.

Kéknyelü Low-yielding, flavourful grape giving one of Hungary's best whites. Has the potential for fieriness and spice. To be watched.

Kerner Most successful of recent German varieties, mostly RIESLING X SILVANER, but in this case Riesling x (red) Trollinger. Early-ripening, flowery (but often too blatant) wine with good acidity. Popular in Pfalz, Rheinhessen, etc.

Laski Rizling Grown in northern Italy and Eastern Europe. Much inferior to Rhine RIESLING, with lower acidity, best in sweet wines. Alias Welschriesling, Riesling Italico, Olaszrizling (no longer legally labelled simply "Riesling").

Loureiro The best and most fragrant Vinho Verde variety in Portugal.

Macabeo The workhorse white grape of north Spain, widespread in Rioja (alias Viura) and in Catalan cava country. Good quality potential.

Malvasia A family of grapes rather than a single variety, found all over Italy and Iberia. May be red, white, or pink. Usually plump, soft wine. Malvoisie in France is unrelated.

Marsanne Principal white grape (with ROUSSANNE) of the northern Rhône (e.g. in Hermitage, St-Joseph, St-Péray). Also good in Australia, California, and (as Ermitage Blanc) the Valais. Soft full wines that age very well.

Moschofilero Good, aromatic pink Greek grape. Makes white or rosé wine.

Müller-Thurgau (Müller-T) Dominant in Germany's Rheinhessen and Pfalz and too common on the Mosel. It was thought to be a cross between RIESLING and Chasselas de Courtellier, but recent studies suggests otherwise. Soft aromatic wines for drinking young. Makes good sweet wines but usually dull, often coarse, dry ones. Should have no place in top vineyards.

Muscadelle Adds aroma to white Bordeaux, esp Sauternes. In Victoria as 'Tokay' it is used (with MUSCAT, to which it is unrelated) for Rutherglen Muscat.

Muscadet, alias Melon de Bourgogne Makes light, refreshing, very dry wines with a seaside tang round Nantes in Brittany.

Muscat (Many varieties; the best is Muscat Blanc à Petits Grains.) Widely grown, easily recognized, pungent grapes, mostly made into perfumed sweet wines, often fortified (as in France's *vins doux naturels*). Superb in Australia. The third element in Tokáj Aszú. Rarely (e.g. Alsace) made dry.

Palomino, alias Listán Makes all the best sherry but poor table wine.

Pedro Ximénez, alias PX Makes very strong wine in Montilla and Málaga. Used in blending sweet sherries. Also grown in Argentina, the Canaries, Australia, California and South Africa.

Petit (and Gros) Manseng The secret weapon of the French Basque country: vital for Jurançon; increasingly blended elsewhere in the Southwest.

Pinot Blanc (Pinot Bl) A cousin of PINOT NOIR, similar to but milder than CHARDONNAY: light, fresh, fruity, not aromatic, to drink young. Good for Italian spumante. Grown in Alsace, northern Italy, south Germany, and East Europe. Weissburgunder in Germany.

Pinot Gris (Pinot Gr) Best in Alsace for full-bodied whites with a certain spicy style. In Germany can be alias Ruländer (sweet) or GRAUBURGUNDER (dry); the work horse Pinot Grigio Italy, where it is newly popular for rosé. Also found in Hungary, Slovenia, Canada, Oregon, New Zealand...

Pinot Noir (Pinot N) Superlative black grape used in Champagne and elsewhere (e.g. California, Australia) for white, sparkling, or very pale pink "vin gris".

Riesling (Ries) Making its re-entrance on the world-stage . Riesling stands level with Chardonnay as the world's best white wine grape, though diametrically opposite in style. Chardonnay gives full-bodied but aromatically discreet wines; Riesling offers a range from steely to voluptuous, always positively perfumed, and with more ageing potential than Chardonnay. Germany makes the greatest Riesling in all styles. Its popularity is being revived in S Australia, where this cool-climate grape does its best to ape Chardonnay. Holding the middle ground, with forceful but still steely wines, is Austria, while lovers of light and fragrant, often piercingly refreshing Rieslings have the Mosel as their exclusive playground. Also grown in Alsace (nowhere else in France), Pacific Northwest, Ontario, California, New Zealand and S Africa.

Roussanne Rhône grape of finesse, now popping up in California and Australia. Can age well.

Sauvignon Blanc (Sauv Bl) Makes distinctive aromatic grassy wines, pungent in New Zealand, often mineral in Sancerre, riper in Australia; good in Rueda, Austria, north Italy, Chile's Casablanca Valley, and South Africa. Blended with Semillon in Bordeaux. Can be austere or buxom (or indeed nauseating).

Savagnin The grape of *vin jaune* of Savoie: related to TRAMINER?

Scheurebe Spicy-flavoured German RIES X SILVANER (possibly), very successful in Pfalz, especially for Auslese. Can be weedy: must be very ripe to be good.

Semillon (Sem) Contributes the lusciousness to Sauternes and increasingly important for Graves and other dry white Bordeaux. Grassy if not fully ripe, but can make soft dry wine of great ageing potential. Superb in Australia; New Zealand and S Africa promising.

Sercial Makes the driest madeira (where myth used to identify it with RIESLING).

Seyval Blanc (Seyval Bl) French-made hybrid of French and American vines. Very hardy and attractively fruity. Popular and reasonably successful in eastern States and England but dogmatically banned by EU from "quality" wines.

Steen South African alias for CHENIN BLANC, not used for better examples.

Silvaner, alias Sylvaner Germany's former workhorse grape. Rarely fine except in Franken – where it is savoury and ages admirably – and in Rheinhessen and Pfalz, where it is enjoying a renaissance. Good in the Italian Tyrol; sadly declining in popularity in Alsace. Very good (and powerful) as Johannisberg in the Valais, Switzerland.

Tocai Friulano North Italian grape with a flavour best described as "subtle". Now to be called plain Friulano.

Tokay Supposedly Hungarian grape in Australia and a table grape in California. The wine Tokay (Tokáj) is FURMINT, HARSLEVELU and MUSCAT.

Torrontes Strongly aromatic, MUSCAT-like Argentine speciality, usually dry.

Trebbiano Important but mediocre grape of central Italy (Orvieto, Soave etc.). Also grown in southern France as Ugni Blanc, and Cognac as St-Emilion. Mostly thin bland wine; needs blending (and more careful growing).

Ugni Blanc (Ugni Bl) See TREBBIANO.

Verdejo The grape of Rueda in Castile, potentially fine and long-lived.

Verdelho Madeira grape making excellent medium-sweet wine; in Australia, fresh soft dry wine of great character. Worth trying elsewhere.

Verdicchio Potentially good dry wine in central-eastern Italy.

Vermentino Italian, sprightly with satisfying texture and ageing capacity.

Vernaccia Name given to many unrelated grapes in Italy. Vernaccia di San Gimignano is crisp, lively; Vernaccia di Oristano is sherry-like.

Viognier Ultra-fashionable Rhône grape, finest in Condrieu, less fine but still aromatic in the Midi. Good examples from California and Australia.

Viura See MACABEO.

Welschriesling See LASKI RIZLING.

Wine & food

Food these days is becoming almost as complicated as wine. We take Japanese for granted, Chinese as staple, look to Italian for comfort and then stir the pot with this strange thing called Fusion Rules. Don't try to be too clever; wine you like with food you like is safest.

Before the meal – apéritifs

The conventional apéritif wines are either sparkling (epitomized by Champagne) or fortified (epitomized by sherry in Britain, port in France, vermouth in Italy, etc.). A glass of white or rosé (or in France red) table wine before eating is presently in vogue. It calls for something light and stimulating, fairly dry but not acidic, with a degree of character; rather Riesling or Chenin Blanc than Chardonnay. Sauvignon Blanc has become a cliché.

Warning: Avoid peanuts; they destroy wine flavours. Olives are too piquant for many wines; they need sherry or a Martini. Eat almonds, pistachios, cashews or walnuts, plain crisps or cheese straws instead.

First courses

Aïoli A thirst-quencher is needed for its garlic heat. Rhône, sparkling dry white; Provence rosé, Verdicchio. And marc or grappa, too, for courage.

Antipasti Dry or medium white: Italian (Arneis, Soave, Pinot Grigio, Prosecco, Vermentino); light but gutsy red (Dolcetto, Franciacorta, young Chianti).

Artichoke vinaigrette An incisive dry white: New Zealand Sauv Bl; Côtes de Gascogne or a modern Greek; young red: Bordeaux, Côtes du Rhône.
    with hollandaise Full-bodied slightly crisp dry white: Pouilly-Fuissé, Pfalz Spätlese, or a Carneros or Yarra Valley Chard.

Asparagus A difficult flavour for wine, being slightly bitter, so the wine needs plenty of its own. Sauv Bl echoes the flavour. Semillon beats Chard, especially Australian, but Chard works well with melted butter or hollandaise. Alsace Pinot Gr, even dry Muscat is good, or Jurançon Sec.

Aubergine purée (Melitzanosalata) Crisp New World Sauv Bl e.g. from South Africa or New Zealand; or modern Greek or Sicilian dry white. Or try Bardolino red or Chiaretto. Baked aubergine dishes can need sturdier reds: Shiraz, Zin.

Avocado with seafood Dry to medium or slightly sharp white: Rheingau or Pfalz Kabinett, Grüner Veltliner, Wachau Ries, Sancerre, Pinot Gr; Sonoma or Australian Chard or Sauv Bl, or a dry rosé. Or Chablis Premier Cru.
    with mozzarella and tomato Crisp but ripe white with acidity: South African Chenin Blanc, Soave.

Bouillabaisse Savoury dry white, Marsanne from the Midi, Rhône or Australia, Corsican or Spanish rosé, or Cassis, Verdicchio.

Carpaccio, beef Seems to work well with most wines, inc reds. Top Tuscan is appropriate, but fine Chards are good. So are vintage and pink Champagnes.
    salmon Chard or Champagne.
    tuna Viognier, California Chard or New Zealand Sauv Bl.

Caviar Iced vodka. Champagne, if you must, full-bodied (e.g. Bollinger, Krug).

Ceviche Australian Ries or Verdelho, New Zealand Sauv Bl.

Charcuterie Young Beaujolais-Villages, Loire reds such as Saumur, New Zealand or Oregon Pinot N. Young Argentine or Italian reds. Bordeaux Blanc can work well too, as can light Chard like Côte Chalonnaise.

Chorizo Austrian Ries, good white Graves, Grüner Veltliner

Crostini Morellino di Scansano, Montepulciano d'Abruzzo, Valpolicella, or a dry Italian white such as Verdicchio or Orvieto.

Crudités Light red or rosé: Côtes du Rhône, Minervois, Chianti, Pinot N; or fino sherry. For whites: Alsace Sylvaner or Pinot Blanc.

Dim-Sum Classically, China tea. For fun: Pinot Grigio or Ries; light red (Bardolino or Loire). NV Champagne or good New World fizz.

Eggs See also Soufflés. These present difficulties: they clash with most wines and can ruin good ones. But local wine with local egg dishes is a safe bet. So ★→★★ of whatever is going. Try Pinot Bl or not too oaky Chard. As a last resort I can bring myself to drink Champagne with scrambled eggs.

quail's eggs Blanc de Blancs Champagne.

seagull's (or gull's) eggs Mature white burgundy or vintage Champagne.

oeufs en meurette Burgundian genius: eggs in red wine calls for a glass of the same.

Escargots Rhône reds (Gigondas, Vacqueyras), St-Véran or Aligoté. In the Midi, very good Petits-Gris go with local white, rosé or red. In Alsace, Pinot Bl or the dry Muscat.

Fish terrine Pfalz Ries Spätlese Trocken, Grüner Veltliner, Chablis Premier Cru, Clare Valley Ries, Sonoma Chard; or manzanilla.

Foie gras Sweet white. In Bordeaux they drink Sauternes. Others prefer a late-harvest Pinot Gr or Ries (inc New World), Vouvray, Montlouis, Jurançon Moelleux or Gewurz. Tokáj Aszú 5 puttonyos is a Lucullan choice. Old dry amontillado can be sublime. With hot foie gras, mature vintage Champagne. But not on any account Chard or Sauv Bl.

Goat's cheese, warm Sancerre, Pouilly-Fumé or New World Sauv Bl.

chilled Chinon, Saumur-Champigny or Provence rosé. Or strong red: Ch Musar, Greek, Turkish, Australian sparkling Shiraz.

Guacamole California Chard, Sauv Blanc, dry Muscat or NV Champagne. Or Mexican beer.

Haddock, smoked, mousse or brandade A wonderful dish for showing off any stylish full-bodied white, inc Grand Cru Chablis or Sonoma, South African or New Zealand Chard.

Ham, raw or cured See also Prosciutto. Alsace Grand Cru Pinot Gr or good, crisp Italian Collio white. With Spanish *pata negra* or *jamon*, fino sherry or tawny port. See also Ham, cooked.

Herrings, raw or pickled Dutch gin (young, not aged) or Scandinavian akvavit, and cold beer. If wine essential, try Muscadet.

Mackerel, smoked An oily wine-destroyer. Manzanilla sherry, proper dry Vinho Verde or Schnapps, peppered or bison-grass vodka. Or good lager.

Mayonnaise Adds richness that calls for a contrasting bite in the wine. Côte Chalonnaise whites (e.g. Rully) are good. Try NZ Sauv Bl, Verdicchio or a Spätlese trocken.

Mezze A selection of hot and cold vegetable dishes. Sparkling is a good all-purpose choice, as is rosé from the Languedoc or Provence. Fino sherry is in its element.

Mozzarella with tomatoes, basil Fresh Italian white, e.g. Soave, Alto Adige. Vermintino from the coast. Or simple Bordeaux Blanc. See also Avocado.

Oysters, raw NV Champagne, Chablis Premier Cru, Muscadet, white Graves, Sancerre or Guinness. Or even light, cold Sauternes.

cooked Puligny-Montrachet or good New World Chard. Champagne is good with either.

Pasta Red or white according to the sauce or trimmings:

cream sauce Orvieto, Frascati, Alto Adige Chard.

meat sauce Montepulciano d'Abruzzo, Salice Salentino, Merlot.

pesto (basil) sauce Barbera, Ligurian Vermentino, New Zealand Sauv Bl, Hungarian Furmint.

seafood sauce (e.g. vongole) Verdicchio, Soave, white Rioja, Cirò, Sauv Bl.

tomato sauce Chianti, Barbera, south Italian red, Zin, South Australian Grenache.

Pastrami Alsace Ries, young Sangiovese or Cab Fr.

Pâté

  chicken liver Calls for pungent white (Alsace Pinot Gr or Marsanne), a smooth red like a light Pomerol, Volnay or New Zealand Pinot N, or even amontillado sherry.

  duck pâté Châteauneuf-du-Pape, Cornas, Chianti Classico, Franciacorta.

  fish pâté Muscadet, Mâcon-Villages, Australian or South African Chard (unoaked).

  pâté de campagne A dry white ★★: good vin de pays, Graves, Fumé Blanc.

Peperonata Dry Australian Ries, Western Australia Sem or New Zealand Sauv Bl. Tempranillo or Grenache.

Pipérade Navarra rosado, Provence or Southern French rosés. Or dry Australian Ries. For a red: Corbières.

Pizza Any ★★ dry Italian red. Or Rioja, Australian Shiraz or southern French red.

Prawns, shrimps, or langoustines Fine dry white: burgundy, Graves, New Zealand Chard, Washington Ries, Pfalz Ries, Australian Ries – even fine mature Champagne. ("Cocktail sauce" kills wine, and in time, people.)

Prosciutto (also with melon, pears or figs) Full dry or medium white: Orvieto, Lugana, Sauv Bl, Grüner Veltliner, Tokay Furmint, white Rioja, Australian Sem, or Jurançon Sec.

Quiches Dry full-bodied white: Alsace, Graves, Sauv Bl, dry Rheingau; or young red (Tempranillo, Periquita), according to ingredients.

Risotto Pinot Gr from Friuli, Gavi, youngish Sem, Dolcetto or Barbera d'Alba.

  with fungi porcini Finest mature Barolo or Barbaresco.

  with mushrooms Cahors, Madiran, Barbera, or New World Pinot N.

Salade niçoise Very dry, ★★, not too light or flowery white or rosé: Provençal, Rhône, or Corsican; Catalan white; Fernão Pires, Sauv Bl.

Salads As a first course, any dry and appetizing white wine.

  Caesar salad Spanish or southern French rosé; Italian neutral, crisp whites. NB Vinegar in salad dressings destroys the flavour of wine. If you want salad at a meal with fine wine, dress the salad with wine or a little lemon juice instead of vinegar.

Salami Barbera, top Valpolicella, genuine Lambrusco, young Zin, Tavel or Ajaccio rosé, Vacqueyras, young Bordeaux, Chilean Cab Sauv, Argentine Malbec.

Salmon, smoked A dry but pungent white: fino (esp manzanilla) sherry, Alsace Pinot Gr, Chablis Grand Cru, Pouilly-Fumé, Pfalz Ries Spätlese, vintage Champagne. If you must have a red, try a lighter one such as Barbera. Vodka, schnapps or akvavit.

Soufflés As show dishes these deserve ★★★ wines.

  cheese Red burgundy or Bordeaux, Cab Sauv (not Chilean or Australian), etc. Or fine white burgundy.

  fish Dry white: ★★★ Burgundy, Bordeaux, Alsace, Chard, etc.

  spinach (tougher on wine) Mâcon-Villages, St-Véran, or Valpolicella. Champagne can also be good with all textures of soufflé.

Tapas Perfect with fino sherry, which can cope with the wide range of flavours in both hot and cold dishes.

Tapenade Manzanilla or fino sherry, or any sharpish dry white or rosé.

Taramasalata A rustic southern white with personality; not necessarily Retsina. Fino sherry works well. Try white Rioja or a Rhône Marsanne. The bland supermarket version submits to fine delicate whites or Champagne.

Tortilla Rioja crianza, fino sherry, or white Mâcon-Villages.

Trout, smoked Sancerre, California or South African Sauv Bl. Rully or Bourgogne Aligoté, Chablis or Champagne. Light German Riesling Kabinett.

Vegetable terrine Not a great help to fine wine, but Chilean Chard makes a fashionable marriage, Chenin Blanc such as Vouvray a lasting one.

Whitebait Crisp dry whites: Greek, Touraine Sauv Bl, Verdicchio or fino sherry.

Fish

Abalone Dry or medium white: Sauv Bl, Côte de Beaune blanc, Pinot Gr, Grüner Veltliner. Chinese style: vintage Champagne.

Anchovies, marinated The marinade will clash with pretty well everything. Keep it light, white, dry, and neutral.

   in olive oil, or salted A robust wine: red, white or rosé – try Rioja.

Bass, sea Weissburgunder from Baden or Pfalz. Very good for any fine/delicate white, e.g. Clare dry Ries, Chablis, white Châteauneuf-du-Pape. But strengthen the flavours of the wine according to the flavourings of the fish: **ginger, spring onions** more powerful Ries; **porcini** top Alsace Pinot Bl.

Beurre blanc, fish with A top-notch Muscadet-sur-lie, a Sauv Bl/Sem blend, Chablis Premier Cru, Vouvray or a Rheingau Ries.

Brandade Chablis Premier Cru, Sancerre Rouge or New Zealand Pinot N.

Brill Very delicate: hence a top fish for fine old Puligny and the like.

Cod, roast good neutral background for fine dry/medium whites: Chablis, Meursault, Corton-Charlemagne, cru classé Graves, Grüner Veltliner, German Kabinett or dry Spätlesen, or a good lightish Pinot N.

Crab Crab and Riesling are part of the Creator's plan.

   Chinese, with ginger and onion German Ries Kabinett or Spätlese Halbtrocken. Tokay Furmint, Gewürz.

   cioppino Sauv Bl; but West Coast friends say Zin. Also California sparkling.

   cold, dressed Alsace, Austrian or Rhine Ries; dry Australian Ries or Condrieu.

   softshell Chard or top-quality German Ries Spätlese.

   Thai crabcakes Pungent Sauv Bl (Loire, South Africa, Australia, New Zealand) or Ries (German Spätlese or Australian).

   with black bean sauce A big Barossa Shiraz or Syrah. Even Cognac.

   with chilli and garlic Quite powerful Ries, perhaps German Grosses Gewächs.

Curry A generic term for a multitude of flavours. Ries is a good bet. Or Sauv Bl.

Eel, smoked Ries, Alsace or Austrian according to the other ingredients. Or fino sherry, Bourgogne Aligoté. Schnapps

Fish and chips, fritto misto, tempura Chablis, white Bordeaux, Sauv Bl, Pinot Bl, Gavi, fino, montilla, Koshu, tea; or NV Champagne and Cava.

Fish baked in a salt crust Full-bodied white or rosé; Rioja, Albariño, Sicily, Côtes de Lubéron or Minervois.

Fish pie (with creamy sauce) Albariño, Soave Classico, Alsace Pinot Gr or Ries.

Haddock Rich dry whites: Meursault, California Chard, Marsanne or Albariño.

Hake Sauv Bl or any fresh fruity white: Pacherenc, Tursan, white Navarra.

Halibut As for turbot.

Herrings, fried/grilled Need a white with some acidity to cut their richness. Rully, Chablis, Bourgogne Aligoté, Greek, dry Sauv Bl. Or cider.

Kedgeree Full white, still or sparkling: Mâcon-Villages, South African Chard, . Grüner Veltliner, or (at breakfast) Champagne.

Kippers A good cup of tea, preferably Ceylon (milk, no sugar). Scotch? Dry oloroso sherry is surprisingly good.

Lamproie à la Bordelaise 5-yr-old St-Emilion or Fronsac. Or Douro reds with Portuguese lampreys.

Lobster, richly sauced Vintage Champagne, fine white burgundy, cru classé

Graves, California Chard or Australian Ries, Pfalz Spätlese.

cold NV Champagne, Alsace Ries, Chablis Premier Cru, Condrieu, Mosel Spätlese, Penedès Chard, or a local fizz.

Mackerel, grilled Hard or sharp white: Sauv Bl from Touraine, Gaillac, Vinho Verde, white Rioja or English white. Or Guinness.

with spices White with muscle : Austrian Ries, Grüner Veltliner, German Grosses Gewächs.

Monkfish Often roasted, which needs fuller rather than leaner wines. Try New Zealand Chard, New Zealand/Oregon Pinot N or Chilean Merlot.

Mullet, red A chameleon, adaptable to good white or red, especially Pinot N.

Mullet, grey Verdicchio, Rully or unoaked Chard.

Mussels Muscadet-sur-lie, Chablis Premier Cru, Chard.

stuffed, with garlic See Escargots.

Paella, shellfish Full-bodied white or rosé, unoaked Chard.

Perch, sandre Exquisite fishes for finest wines: top white burgundy, Alsace Ries Grand Cru or noble Mosels. Or try top Swiss Fendant or Johannisberg.

Salmon, seared or grilled Pinot N is the fashionable option. Merlot or light claret not bad. Or fine white burgundy: Puligny- or Chassagne-Montrachet, Meursault, Corton-Charlemagne, Chablis Grand Cru; Grüner Veltliner, Condrieu, California, Idaho or New Zealand Chard, Rheingau Kabinett/Spätlese, Australian Ries.

fishcakes Call for similar (as for above), but less grand, wines.

Sardines, fresh grilled Very dry white: Vinho Verde, Muscadet, or modern Greek.

Sashimi If you are prepared to forego the wasabi, sparkling wines will go. Or Washington or Tasmanian Chard, Chablis Grand Cru, Rheingau Ries English Seyval Bl. Otherwise, iced sake, fino sherry, or beer. Trials have matched 5-putt Tokáj with fat tuna, sea urchin and anago (eel).

Scallops An inherently slightly sweet dish, best with medium-dry whites.

in cream sauces German Spätlese, Montrachet, or top Australian Chard.

grilled or seared Hermitage Blanc, Grüner Veltliner, Entre-Deux-Mers, vintage Champagne, or Pinot N.

with Asian seasoning New Zealand, Chenin Blanc, Verdelho, or Gewurz.

Shellfish Dry white with plain boiled shellfish, richer wines with richer sauces.

with plateaux de fruits de mer: Chablis, Muscadet, Picpoul de Pinet, Alto Adige Pinot Blanc.

Skate/raie with brown butter White with some pungency (e.g. Pinot Gr d'Alsace), or a clean straightforward wine like Muscadet or Verdicchio.

Snapper Sauv Bl if cooked with Oriental flavours; white Rhône or Provence rosé with Mediterranean flavours.

Sole, plaice, etc.: plain, grilled, or fried Perfect with fine wines: white burgundy or its equivalent.

with sauce According to the ingredients: sharp dry wine for tomato sauce, fairly rich for creamy preparations.

Sushi Hot wasabi is usually hidden in every piece. German QbA trocken wines, simple Chablis, or NV brut Champagne. Or, of course, sake or beer.

Swordfish Full-bodied dry white of the country. Nothing grand.

Tagine, with couscous North African flavours need substantial whites to balance – Austrian, Rhône – or crisp, neutral whites that won't compete. Preserved lemon demands something with acidity. Go easy on the oak.

Trout, grilled or fried Delicate white wine, e.g. Mosel (especially Saar or Ruwer), Alsace Pinot Bl.

Tuna, grilled or seared Generally served rare, so try a red: Cab Fr from the Loire, or Pinot N. Young Rioja is a possibility.

Turbot Serve with your best rich dry white: Meursault or Chassagne-Montrachet,

Corton-Charlemagne, mature Chablis or its California, Australian or New Zealand equivalent. Condrieu. Mature Rheingau, Mosel or Nahe Spätlese or Auslese (not trocken).

Meat, poultry, game

Barbecues The local wine: Australian, South African, Argentina are right in spirit.

Asian flavours (lime, coriander, etc.): rosé, Pinot Gr, Ries.

Chilli: Shiraz, Zin, Pinotage, Malbec.

Middle Eastern (cumin, mint): crisp dry whites, rosé.

Oil, lemon, herbs: Sauv Bl.

Red wine: Cab, Merlot, Malbec, Tannat.

Tomato sauces: Zin, Sangiovese.

Beef, boiled Red: Bordeaux (Bourg or Fronsac), Roussillon, Gevrey-Chambertin, or Côte-Rôtie. Medium-ranking white Burgundy is good, e.g. Auxey-Duresses. Or top-notch beer. Mustard softens tannic reds, horseradish kills everything – but can be worth the sacrifice.

roast An ideal partner for fine red wine of any kind. See above for mustard.

stew Sturdy red: Pomerol or St-Emilion, Hermitage, Cornas, Barbera, Shiraz, Napa Cab Sauv, Ribera del Duero or Douro red.

Beef Stroganoff Dramatic red: Barolo, Valpolicella Amarone, Cahors, Hermitage, late-harvest Zin – even Moldovan Negru de Purkar.

Boudin Blanc Loire Chenin Bl, especially when served with apples: dry Vouvray, Saumur, Savennières. Mature red Côtes de Beaune, if without apple.

Boudin Noir (blood sausage) Local Sauv Bl or Chenin Bl – especially in the Loire. Or Beaujolais Cru, especially Morgon. Or light Tempranillo.

Cabbage, stuffed Hungarian Cab Fr/Kadarka; village Rhônes; Salice Salentino, Primitivo and other spicy southern Italian reds. Or Argentine Malbec.

Cajun food Fleurie, Brouilly, or New World Sauv Bl. **with gumbo:** amontillado.

Cassoulet Red from southwest France (Gaillac, Minervois, Corbières, St-Chinian or Fitou) or Shiraz. But best of all Beaujolais Cru or young Tempranillo.

Chicken/turkey/guinea fowl, roast Virtually any wine, including very best bottles of dry to medium white and finest old reds (especially burgundy). The meat of fowl can be adapted with sauces to match almost any fine wine (e.g. *coq au vin* w. red or white burgundy). Sparkling Shiraz with strong, spicy stuffing.

Chicken Kiev Alsace Ries, Collio, Chard, Bergerac rouge.

Chilli con carne Young red: Beaujolais, Tempranillo, Zin, Argentine Malbec.

Chinese food

Canton or Peking style Rosé, or dry to medium-dry white – Mosel Ries Kabinett or Spätlese trocken – can be good throughout a Chinese banquet. Gewürz often suggested but rarely works (but brilliant with ginger), yet Chasselas and Pinot Gr are attractive alternatives. Dry or off-dry sparkling (especially Cava) cuts the oil and matches sweetness. Eschew sweet/sour dishes but try St-Emilion ★★, New World Pinot N, or Châteauneuf-du-Pape with duck. I often serve both white and red wines concurrently during Chinese meals. Champagne becomes a thirst quencher.

Szechuan style Verdicchio, Alsace Pinot Bl, or very cold beer.

Choucroute garni Alsace Pinot Bl, Pinot Gr, Ries, or beer.

Cold roast meat Generally better with full-flavoured white than red. Mosel Spätlese or Hochheimer and Côte Chalonnaise are very good, as is Beaujolais. Leftover cold beef with leftover vintage Champagne is bliss.

Confit d'oie/de canard Young tannic red Bordeaux, California Cab Sauv and Merlot, and Priorato cut richness. Alsace Pinot Gr or Gewürz match it.

Coq au vin Red burgundy. In an ideal world, one bottle of Chambertin in the dish, two on the table.

Duck or goose Rather rich white: Pfalz Spätlese or off-dry Alsace Grand Cru. Or mature gamey red: Morey-St-Denis, Côte-Rôtie, Bordeaux, or Burgundy. With oranges or peaches, the Sauternais propose drinking Sauternes, others Monbazillac or Ries Auslese. Mature weighty vintage Champagne is good, too, and handles red cabbage surprisingly well.

  Peking See Chinese food.

  wild duck Big-scale red: Hermitage, Bandol, California or South African Cab Sauv, Australian Shiraz – Grange if you can afford it.

  with olives Top-notch Chianti or other Tuscans.

Frankfurters German, NY Ries., Beaujolais, light Pinot N. Or Budweiser (Budwar).

Game birds, young, plain-roasted The best red wine you can afford.

  older birds in casseroles Red (Gevrey-Chambertin, Pommard, Santenay or Grand Cru St-Emilion, Napa Valley Cab Sauv or Rhône).

  well-hung game Vega Sicilia, great red Rhône, Château Musar.

  cold game Mature vintage Champagne.

Game pie, hot Red: Oregon Pinot Noir.

  cold Good quality white burgundy, cru Beaujolais, or Champagne.

Goulash Flavoursome young red: Hungarian Kékoportó, Zin, Uruguayan Tannat, Morellino di Scansano, young Australian Shiraz.

Grouse See Game birds – but push the boat right out.

Haggis Fruity red, e.g. young claret, young Portuguese red, New World Cab Sauv or Malbec, or Châteauneuf-du-Pape. Or, of course, malt whisky.

Ham, cooked Softer red burgundies: Volnay, Savigny, Beaune; Chinon or Bourgueil; sweetish German white (Rhine Spätlese); Tokaj Furmint or Czech Frankovka; lightish Cab Sauv (e.g. Chilean), or New World Pinot N. And don't forget the heaven-made match of ham and sherry. See ham, raw or cured.

Hamburger Young red: Australian Cab Sauv, Chianti, Zin, Argentine Malbec, Tempranillo. Or full-strength colas (not 'Diet').

Hare Jugged hare calls for flavourful red: not-too-old burgundy or Bordeaux, Rhône (e.g. Gigondas), Bandol, Barbaresco, Rib del Duero, Rioja Reserva. The same for saddle, or for hare sauce with pappardelle.

Indian dishes Medium-sweet white, very cold: Orvieto abboccato, South African Chenin Bl, Alsace Pinot Bl, Torrontes, Indian sparkling, Cava or NV Champagne. Or emphasize the heat with a tannic Barolo or Barbaresco, or deep-flavoured reds such as Châteauneuf-du-Pape, Cornas, Australian Grenache or Mourvèdre, or Valpolicella Amarone.

Kebabs Vigorous red: modern Greek, Corbières, Chilean Cab Sauv, Zin, or Barossa Shiraz. Sauv Bl, if lots of garlic.

Kidneys Red: St-Emilion or Fronsac: Nuits-St-Georges, Cornas, Barbaresco, Rioja, Spanish or Australian Cab Sauv, top Alentejo.

Lamb, roast One of the traditional and best partners for very good red Bordeaux – or its Cab Sauv equivalents from the New World. In Spain, the partner of the finest old Rioja and Ribera del Duero Reservas.

  cutlets or chops As for roast lamb, but a little less grand.

Liver Young red: Beaujolais-Villages, St-Joseph, Médoc, Italian Merlot, Breganze Cab Sauv, Zin, Tempranillo, Portuguese Bairrada.

  calf's Red Rioja crianza, Salice Salentino Riserva, Fleurie.

Meatballs Tangy medium-bodied red: Mercurey, Crozes-Hermitage, Madiran, Morellino di Scansano, Langhe Nebbiolo, Zin, Cab Sauv.

  spicy Middle-Eastern style Simple, rustic red.

Moussaka Red or rosé: Naoussa from Greece, Sangiovese, Corbières, Côtes de Provence, Ajaccio, New Zealand Pinot N, young Zin, Tempranillo.

Osso buco Low tannin, supple red, such as Dolcetto d'Alba or Pinot N. Or dry Italian white such as Soave and Lugana.

Oxtail Rather rich red: St-Emilion, Pomerol, Pommard, Nuits-St-Georges, Barolo or Rioja Reserva, Ribera del Duero, California or Coonawarra Cab Sauv, Châteauneuf-du-Pape, mid-weight Shiraz.

Paella Young Spanish wines: red, dry white or rosé: Penedès, Somontano, Navarra or Rioja.

Pigeon Lively reds: Savigny, Chambolle-Musigny; Crozes-Hermitage, Chianti Classico, Argentine Malbec, or California Pinot. Or try Franken Silvaner Spätlese. See also Squab.

Pork, roast A good rich, neutral background to a fairly light red or rich white. It deserves ★★ treatment – Médoc is fine. Portugal's suckling pig is eaten with Bairrada Garrafeira, Chinese is good with Pinot N.

Pot au feu, bollito misto, cocido Rustic red wines from the region of origin; Sangiovese di Romagna, Chusclan, Lirac, Rasteau, Portuguese Alentejo or Yecla and Jumilla from Spain.

Quail Carmignano, Rioja Reserva, mature claret, Pinot N.

Rabbit Lively medium-bodied young Italian red or Aglianico del Vulture; Chiroubles, Chinon, Saumur-Champigny, or Rhône rosé.
    with prunes Bigger, richer, fruitier red.

Satay Australia's McLaren Vale Shiraz, or Alsace or New Zealand Gewürz.

Sauerkraut (German) Lager or Pils. (But see also Choucroute garni.)

Sausages See also Charcuterie, Frankfurters, Salami. The British banger requires a young Malbec from Argentina (a red wine, anyway), or British ale.

Shepherd's pie Rough-and-ready red seems most appropriate, e.g. Sangiovese di Romagna, but beer or dry cider is the real McCoy.

Steak
    au poivre A fairly young Rhône red or Cab Sauv.
    filet or tournedos Any red (but not old wines with Béarnaise sauce: top New World Pinot N or Californian Chard is better).
    Fiorentina (bistecca) Chianti Classico Riserva or Brunello. The rarer the meat, the more classic the wine; the more well done, the more you need New World, fruit-driven wines. Argentina Malbec is the perfect partner for steak Argentine style, i.e. cooked to death.
    Korean Yuk Whe (the world's best steak tartare) Sake.
    tartare Vodka or light young red: Beaujolais, Bergerac, Valpolicella.
    T-bone Reds of similar bone structure: Barolo, Hermitage, Australian Cab Sauv or Shiraz.

Steak and kidney pie or pudding Red Rioja Reserva or mature Bordeaux.

Stews and casseroles Burgundy such as Chambolle-Musigny or Bonnes-Mares if fairly simple; otherwise lusty full-flavoured red: young Côtes du Rhône, Toro, Corbières, Barbera, Shiraz, Zin, etc.

Sweetbreads A grand dish, so grand wine: Rhine Ries or Franken Silvaner Spätlese, Alsace Grand Cru Pinot Gr, or Condrieu, depending on sauce.

Tagines These vary enormously, but fruity young reds are a good bet: Beaujolais, Tempranillo, Sangiovese, Merlot, Shiraz.

Tandoori chicken Reisling or Sauv Bl, or young red Bordeaux or light north Italian red served cool. Also Cava and NV Champagne.

Thai dishes Ginger and lemongrass call for pungent Sauv Bl (Loire, Australia, New Zealand, South Africa) or Ries (Spätlese or Australian).
    coconut milk Hunter Valley and other ripe, oaked Chards; Alsace Pinot Bl for refreshment; Gewürz or Verdelho. And, of course, Cava or NV Champagne.

Tongue Good for any red or white of abundant character, especially Italian. Also Beaujolais, Loire reds, Tempranillo, and full dry rosés.

Tripe Red (eg Corbières, Roussillon) or rather sweet white (eg German Spätlese). Better: Western Australian Sem/Chard, or cut with pungent dry white such as

Pouilly-Fumé or fresh red such as Saumur-Champigny.

Veal, roast A good neutral background for any fine old red which may have faded with age (eg a Rioja Reserva) or a German or Austrian Ries or Vouvray, or Alsace Pinot Gr.

Venison Big-scale reds, including Mourvèdre, solo as in Bandol, or in blends. Rhône, Bordeaux or California Cab Sauv of a mature vintage; or rather rich white (Pfalz Spätlese or Alsace Pinot Gr). With a sharp berry sauce, try a German Grosses Gewächs Riesling, or a New World Cab Sauv.

Vitello tonnato Full-bodied whites, especially Chard; or light reds (eg Valpolicella) served cool.

Wild boar Serious red: top Tuscan or Priorat.

Vegetarian dishes (see also First courses)

Baked pasta dishes Pasticcio, lasagne and cannelloni with elaborate vegetarian fillings and sauces: an occasion to show off a grand wine, especially finest Tuscan red, but also claret and burgundy. Also Gavi from Italy.

Cauliflower cheese Crisp aromatic white: Sancerre, Ries Spätlese, Muscat, English Seyval Bl, or Schönburger.

Couscous with vegetables Young red with a bite: Shiraz, Corbières, Minervois; or well-chilled rosé from Navarra or Somontano; or a robust Moroccan red.

Fennel-based dishes Sauv Bl: Pouilly-Fumé or one from New Zealand; English Seyval Bl or young Tempranillo.

Grilled Mediterranean vegetables Brouilly, Barbera, Tempranillo, or Shiraz.

Lentil dishes Sturdy reds such as southern French, or Zin or Shiraz.

Mushrooms (in most contexts) Fleshy red, eg Pomerol, California Merlot, Rioja Reserva, top Burgundy, or Vega Sicilia. On toast , your best claret. Ceps/porcini are best for Ribera del Duero, Barolo or Chianti Rufina, or top claret: Pauillac or St-Estèphe.

Onion/leek tart Fruity off-dry or dry white: Alsace Pinot Gr or Gewürz, Canadian or New Zies Ries, English whites, Jurançon, Australian Ries. Or Loire red.

Peppers or aubergines (eggplant), stuffed Vigorous red wine: Nemea, Chianti, Dolcetto, Zin, Bandol, Vacqueyras.

Pumpkin/squash ravioli or risotto Full-bodied fruity dry or off-dry white: Viognier or Marsanne, demi-sec Vouvray, Gavi, or South African Chenin.

Ratatouille Vigorous young red: Chianti, New Zealand Cabernet , Merlot, Malbec, Tempranillo; young red Bordeaux, Gigondas, or Coteaux du Languedoc.

Spanacopitta Valpolicella; Greco di Molise, or white Sicilian.

Spiced vegetarian dishes See under Indian dishes, Thai dishes.

Watercress, raw This makes every wine on earth taste revolting. Soup is slightly easier, but doesn't require wine.

Desserts

Apple pie, strudel or tarts Sweet German, Austrian, or Loire white, Tokáji Aszú, or Canadian Ice Wine.

Apples, Cox's Orange Pippins Vintage port (and sweetmeal biscuits).

Bread-and-butter pudding Fine 10-yr-old Barsac, Tokáji Azsú or Australian botrytized Sem.

Cakes and gâteaux See also Chocolate, Coffee, Ginger, Rum. Bual or Malmsey madeira, oloroso or cream sherry.

Cheesecake Sweet white: Vouvray, Anjou, or fizz – refreshing, nothing special.

Chocolate Generally only powerful flavours can compete. Bual, California Orange Muscat, Tokay Azsú, Australian Liqueur Muscat, 10-yr-old tawny port; Asti for light, fluffy mousses. Experiment with rich, ripe reds: Syrah, Zin, even sparkling Shiraz. Banyuls for a weightier partnership. Médoc can match bitter black chocolate. Or a tot of good rum.

Christmas pudding, mince pies Tawny port, cream sherry, or liquid Christmas pudding itself, Pedro Ximénez sherry. Asti or Banyuls.

Coffee desserts Sweet Muscat, Australia Liqueur Muscats, or Tokáji Aszú.

Creams, custards, fools, syllabubs See also Chocolate, Coffee, Ginger, and Rum. Sauternes, Loupiac, Ste-Croix-du-Mont, or Monbazillac.

Crème brûlée Sauternes or Rhine Beerenauslese, best madeira or Tokáji. (With concealed fruit, a more modest sweet wine.)

Crêpes Suzette Sweet Champagne, Orange Muscat or Asti.

Fruit

> **blackberries** vintage port.
>
> **dried fruit (and compotes)** Banyuls, Rivesaltes, Maury.
>
> **flans and tarts** Sauternes, Monbazillac, sweet Vouvray or Anjou.
>
> **fresh** Sweet Coteaux du Layon or light sweet Muscat.
>
> **poached, i.e. apricots, pears, etc.** Sweet Muscatel: try Muscat de Beaumes-de-Venise, Moscato di Pantelleria, or Spanish dessert Tarragona.
>
> **salads, orange salad** A fine sweet sherry or any Muscat-based wine.

Ginger flavours Sweet Muscats, New World botrytized Ries and Sém.

Ice-cream and sorbets Fortified wine (Australian liqueur Muscat, Banyuls); sweet Asti or sparkling Moscato. Pedro Ximenez, Amaretto liqueur with vanilla; rum with chocolate.

Lemon flavours For dishes like Tarte au Citron, try sweet Ries from Germany or Austria, or Tokay Aszú; very sweet if lemon is very tart.

Meringues Recioto di Soave, Asti or Champagne doux.

Mille-feuille Delicate sweet sparkling white, such as Moscato d'Asti or demi-sec Champagne.

Nuts Finest oloroso sherry, madeira, vintage or tawny port (nature's match for **walnuts**), Tokáji Aszú, Vin Santo or Setúbal Moscatel.

Orange flavours Experiment with old Sauternes, Tokáji Aszú or California Orange Muscat.

Panettone Jurançon moelleux, late-harvest Ries, Barsac, Tokáji Aszú.

Pears in red wine A pause before the port. Or try Rivesaltes, Banyuls or Ries Beerenauslese.

Pecan pie Orange Muscat or liqueur Muscat.

Raspberries (no cream, little sugar) Excellent with fine reds which themselves taste of raspberries: young Juliénas, Regnié.

Rum flavours (baba, mousses, ice-cream) Muscat – from Asti to Australian liqueur, according to weight of dish.

Strawberries and cream Sauternes or similar sweet Bordeaux, Vouvray moelleux or Jurançon Vendange Tardive.

Strawberries, wild (no cream) Serve with red Bordeaux (most exquisitely Margaux) poured over.

Summer pudding Fairly young Sauternes of a good vintage.

Sweet soufflés Sauternes or Vouvray moelleux. Sweet (or rich) Champagne.

Tiramisú Vin Santo, young tawny port, Muscat de Beaumes-de-Venise, Sauternes, or Australian Liqueur Muscat.

Trifle Should be sufficiently vibrant with its internal sherry.

Zabaglione Light-gold marsala or Australian botrytized Sem, or Asti.

Wine & cheese

The notion that wine and cheese were married in heaven is not borne out by experience. Fine red wines are slaughtered by strong cheeses: only sharp or sweet white wines survive. Principles to remember, despite exceptions, are first: the harder the cheese the more tannin the wine can have. And second: the creamier the cheese is the more acidity needed in the wine. Cheese is classified by its texture and the nature of its rind, so its appearance is a guide to the type of wine to match it. Individual cheeses mentioned below are only examples . I try to keep a glass of white wine to drink with my cheese.

Fresh, no rind – cream cheese, crème fraîche, Mozzarella
   Light crisp white – Simple Bordeaux Blanc, Bergerac, English unoaked whites; or rosé – Anjou, Rhône; or very light, very young, very fresh red such as Bordeaux, Bardolino, or Beaujolais.

Hard cheeses, waxed or oiled, often showing marks from cheesecloth – Gruyère family, Manchego and other Spanish cheeses, Parmesan, Cantal, Comté, old Gouda, Cheddar and most "traditional" English cheeses
   Particularly hard to generalize here; Gouda, Gruyère, some Spanish, and a few English cheeses complement fine claret or Cab Sauv and great Shiraz/Syrah wines. But strong cheeses need less refined wines, preferably local ones. Sugary, granular old Dutch red Mimolette or Beaufort are good for finest mature Bordeaux. Also for Tokáj Aszú. But try white wines too.

Blue cheeses Roquefort can be wonderful with Sauternes, but don't extend the idea to other blues. It is the sweetness of Sauternes, especially old, that complements the saltiness. Stilton and port, preferably tawny, is a classic. Intensely flavoured old oloroso, amontillado, madeira, marsala, and other fortified wines go with most blues.

Natural rind (mostly goat's cheese) with bluish-grey mould (the rind becomes wrinkled when mature), sometimes dusted with ash – St-Marcellin
   Sancerre, Valençay, light fresh Sauv Bl, Jurançon, Savoie, Soave, Italian Chard, lightly oaked English whites.

Bloomy rind soft cheeses, pure white rind if pasteurized, or dotted with red: Brie, Camembert, Chaource, Bougon (goat's milk 'Camembert')
   Full dry white burgundy or Rhône if the cheese is white and immature; powerful, fruity St-Emilion, young Australian (or Rhône) Shiraz/ Syrah or Grenache if it's mature.

Washed-rind soft cheeses, with rather sticky orange-red rind – Langres, mature Epoisses, Maroilles, Carré de l'Est, Milleens, Munster
   Local reds, especially for Burgundy cheeses; vigorous Languedoc, Cahors, Côtes du Frontonnais, Corsican, southern Italian, Sicilian, Bairrada. Also powerful whites, especially Alsace Gewurz and Muscat.

Semi-soft cheeses, grey-pink thickish rind – Livarot, Pont l'Evêque, Reblochon, Tomme de Savoie, St-Nectaire
   Powerful white Bordeaux, Chard, Alsace Pinot Gr, dryish Ries, southern Italian and Sicilian whites, aged white Rioja or dry oloroso sherry. But the strongest of these cheeses kill most wines.

Food and finest wines

With very special bottles the wine guides the choice of food rather than the other way around. The following suggestions are based largely on the gastronomic conventions of the wine regions producing these treasures, plus much diligent research. They should help bring out the best in your best wines.

Red wines

Red Bordeaux and other Cabernet Sauvignon-based wines (very old, light and delicate: eg pre-1959, with exceptions such as 45)
   Leg or rack of young lamb, roast with a hint of herbs (but not garlic); entrecôte; roast partridge or grouse, sweetbreads; or cheese soufflé after the meat has been served.

Fully mature great vintages (eg Bordeaux 59 61 82) Shoulder or saddle of lamb, roast with a touch of garlic, roast ribs, or grilled rump of beef.

Mature but still vigorous (eg 89 90) Shoulder or saddle of lamb (inc kidneys) with rich sauce. Fillet of beef marchand de vin (with wine and bone-marrow). Avoid Beef Wellington: pastry dulls the palate.

Merlot-based Bordeaux (Pomerol, St-Emilion) Beef as above (fillet is richest) or well-hung venison.

Côte d'Or red burgundy Consider the weight and texture, which grow lighter/more velvety with age. Also the character of the wine: Nuits is earthy, Musigny flowery, great Romanées can be exotic, Pommard renowned for its four-squareness. Roast chicken, or capon, is a safe standard with red burgundy; guinea-fowl for slightly stronger wines, then partridge, grouse, or woodcock for those progressively more rich and pungent. Hare and venison (chevreuil) are alternatives.

    great old burgundy The Burgundian formula is cheese: Epoisses (unfermented). A fine cheese but a terrible waste of fine old wines.

    vigorous younger burgundy Duck or goose roasted to minimize fat.

Great Syrahs: Hermitage, Côte-Rôtie, Grange; or Vega Sicilia Beef, venison, well-hung game; bone-marrow on toast; English cheese (especially best farm Cheddar) but also hard goat's milk and ewe's milk cheeses such as England's Berkswell and Ticklemore.

Rioja Gran Reserva, Pesquera... Richly flavoured roasts: wild boar, mutton, saddle of hare, or whole suckling pig.

Barolo, Barbaresco Risotto with white truffles; pasta with game sauce (eg pappardelle alla lepre); porcini mushrooms; Parmesan.

White wines

Very good Chablis, white burgundy, other top-quality Chards White fish simply grilled or meunière. Dover sole, turbot, halibut are best; brill, drenched in butter, can be excellent. (Sea bass is too delicate; salmon passes but does little for the finest wine.)

Supreme white burgundy (Le Montrachet, Corton-Charlemagne) or equivalent Graves Roast veal, farm chicken stuffed with truffles or herbs under the skin, or sweetbreads; richly sauced white fish or scallops as above. Or lobster or wild salmon.

Condrieu, Château-Grillet or Hermitage Blanc Very light pasta scented with herbs and tiny peas or broad beans.

Grand Cru Alsace: Riesling Truite au bleu, smoked salmon or choucroute garni. **Pinot Gris** Roast or grilled veal. **Gewurztraminer** Cheese soufflé (Münster cheese). **Vendange Tardive** Foie gras or Tarte Tatin.

Sauternes Simple crisp buttery biscuits (eg Langues-de-Chat), white peaches, nectarines, strawberries (without cream). Not tropical fruit. Pan-seared foie-gras. Experiment with blue cheeses.

Supreme Vouvray moelleux, etc. Buttery biscuits, apples, or apple tart.

Beerenauslese/Trockenbeerenauslese Biscuits, peaches, greengages. Desserts made from rhubarb, gooseberries, quince, or apples.

Tokáj Aszú (5–6 puttonyos) Foie gras is thoroughly recommended. Fruit desserts, cream desserts, even chocolate can be wonderful. But so is the naked sip.

Great vintage port or madeira Walnuts or pecans. A Cox's Orange Pippin and a digestive biscuit is a classic English accompaniment.

Old vintage Champagne (not Blanc de Blancs) As an apéritif, or with cold partridge, grouse or woodcock.

France

**More heavily shaded areas are the
wine-growing regions**

The following abbreviations
are used in the text:

Al	Alsace
Beauj	Beaujolais
Burg	Burgundy
B'x	Bordeaux
Champ	Champagne
Lo	Loire
Prov	Provence
Pyr	Pyrenees
N/S Rh	North/South Rhône
SW	Southwest
AC	*appellation contrôlée*

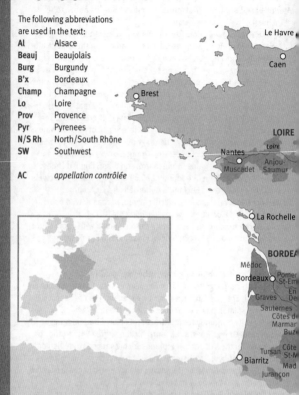

How is France placed to deal with these difficult times? It's a question we could ask of any wine region. French growers share factors such as high labour costs with most wine-producing countries; exchange rates, likewise, can be a problem for anybody and everybody.

France's great advantage, and her great disadvantage, is her history. She has been a leading wine producer for so long that to despise her wines is a quick and easy sign of modernity; to drink them to the exclusion of all others is an equally facile sign of conservatism, middle age – you name it. The truth is that if we were coming to France afresh we'd be bowled over. The variety! The interest! The eccentricities! And the solid good value and reliability of many of the wines. Bordeaux's become too expensive? Try the Rhône. Burgundy's too hard to understand? Drink Pinot Noir from New

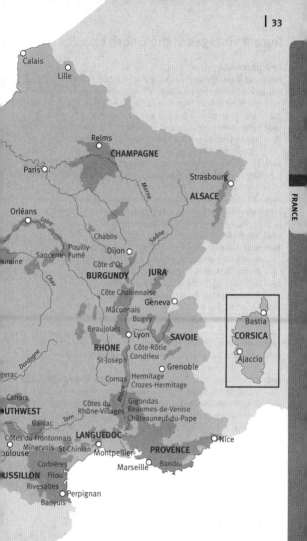

Zealand and California – and then come back to Burgundy. Riesling from Australia not quite complex enough? Try Riesling from Alsace.

France is also good at reinventing itself. Take Provence rosé. For years it's been notorious as overpriced tourist fuel, sold cynically by producers who are barely answerable to their customers. Well, forget it. There are research projects going ahead into terroir, the ideal grape varieties, you name it. And the wines are delicious: firm, mineral and elegant.

But the prices – well…

France entries also cross-refer to Châteaux of Bordeaux section.

Recent vintages of the French classics

Red Bordeaux

Médoc/red Graves For some wines bottle age is optional: for these it is indispensable. Minor châteaux from light vintages need only two or three years, but even modest wines of great years can improve for 15 or so, and the great châteaux of these years can profit from double that time.

2008 Quality compromised by another indifferent summer. Yields down due to poor fruit set, mildew and frost in places. Late-season sunshine helped, results better than expected.

2007 A miserable summer with a huge attack of mildew spelled a difficult year. Late-season sunshine offered some hope. Variable from one estate to the next. Be selective.

2006 Cab Sauv had difficulty ripening. Good colour and alcohol. Be selective.

2005 Perfect weather conditions throughout the year. Rich, balanced, long-ageing wines from an outstanding vintage.

2004 Mixed bag, but top wines good in a classic mould.

2003 Hottest summer on record. Cab Sauv can be tremendous (St-Estèphe, Pauillac). Atypical but rich, powerful wines at best (so keep), unbalanced at worst (already drinking).

2002 Saved by a dry, sunny Sept. Later-ripening Cab Sauv benefited most. Some good wines if selective. Drink now–2018.

2001 A cool Sept and rain at vintage meant Cab Sauv had difficulty in ripening fully. Some fine fresh wines to drink now–2015.

2000 Superb wines throughout. Start tentatively on all but the top wines.

1999 Vintage rain again diluted ripe juice, so-so wines to drink now–2010.

1998 Good (especially Pessac-Léognan), but the Right Bank is clearly the winner this year. Drink now–2015.

1997 Uneven flowering and summer rain were a double challenge. Top wines still of interest, but the rest have faded.

1996 Cool summer, fine harvest. Good to excellent. Drink now–2020.

1995 Heatwave and drought; saved by rain. Good to excellent. Now–2015.

1994 Hopes of a supreme year; then heavy vintage rain. The best good, but be careful. Drink now.

1990 A paradox: a drought year with a threat of over-production. Its results are magnificent. To 2015.

1989 Early spring, splendid summer. Top wines classics of the ripe, dark kind: elegance, length. Some better than 1990. Small chx uneven. To 2020.

Older fine vintages: 88, 86 85 82 75 70 66 62 61 59 55 53 49 48 47 45 29 28.

St-Emilion/Pomerol

2008 Similar conditions to the Médoc. Late harvest into Nov. Tiny yields helped quality which is surprisingly good.

2007 Same pattern as the Médoc. Huge disparity in picking dates (up to five weeks). Extremely variable.

2006 Rain and rot at harvest. Earlier-ripening Pomerol a success but St-Emilion and satellites variable.

2005 Same conditions as the Médoc. An overall success.

2004 Merlot often better than 2003 (Pomerol). Good Cab Fr. Variable.

2003 Merlot suffered in the heat, but exceptional Cab Fr. Very mixed. Some over-extraction again. Top St-Emilion on the plateau good.

2002 Problems with rot and ripeness; some over-extraction. Modest to good.

2001 Less rain than Médoc during vintage. Some powerful Merlot, sometimes better than 2000. Drinking now–2015.

2000 Similar conditions to Médoc. Less kind to Merlot, but a v.gd vintage.

1999 Careful, lucky growers made good wines, but rain was again a problem.

1998 Earlier-ripening Merlot largely escaped the rain. Some excellent wines.

1997 Merlot suffered in the rain. Only a handful of wines still of interest.

1996 Cool, fine summer. Vintage rain. Less consistent than Médoc. Now–2015.

1995 Perhaps even better than Médoc/Graves. Now–2015.

1994 Good, especially Pomerol. Drink now.

1990 Another chance to make great wine or a lot of wine. Now–2015.

1989 Large, ripe, early harvest; an overall triumph. To 2020.

Older fine vintages: 88, 85 82 71 70 67 66 64 61 59 53 52 49 47 45.

Red Burgundy

Côte d'Or Côte de Beaune reds generally mature sooner than bigger wines of Côte de Nuits. Earliest drinking dates are for lighter commune wines – eg Volnay, Beaune; latest for biggest wines of, eg Chambertin, Romanée. Even the best Burgundies are more attractive young than equivalent red Bordeaux.

2008 Fine wines from those who avoided fungal diseases oidium and mildew, disaster for others. Pick and choose carefully.

2007 Small crop of attractive, perfumed wines for the medium term.

2006 An attractive year, better in Côte de Nuits (less rain); some rot problems in Côte de Beaune but there are some gems.

2005 The best for a generation, potentially outstanding wines everywhere. Must be kept, however tempting.

2004 Good, except where hail has caused significant damage. Can be herbaceous. Start drinking.

2003 Reds coped with the heat better than the whites. Muscular, rich wines. Best wines outstanding, others short and hot.

2002 Middleweight wines of great class with an attractive point of freshness. Best still to keep.

2001 Just needed a touch more sun for excellence. Good to drink now.

2000 Gave more pleasure than expected but drink up now.

1999 Big, ripe vintage; good colour, bags of fruit, steely tannins. Start drinking, but save the best.

1998 Ripe fruit but dry tannins. Those in balance look good now.

1997 Time to finish up these attractive wines from a sunny year.

1996 Fine summer and vintage. Top wines must be kept. 2008–2020.

1995 Small crop, potentially fine but not yet showing its expected class.

1994 Compromised by vintage rain. Drink up.

1993 Impressive fruit to balance the tannins in Côte de Nuits; mostly drying out in Côte de Beaune.

Older fine vintages: 90 88 85 78 71 69 66 64 62 61 59 (all mature).

White Burgundy

Côte de Beaune Well-made wines of good vintages with plenty of acidity as well as fruit. Will improve and gain depth and richness for some years – up to ten. Lesser wines from lighter vintages are ready for drinking after two or three.

2008 Small crop but some will be rich and flavoursome.

2007 Big crop – those who picked late did very well.

2006 Plentiful crop of charming, aromatic wines – 1992-plus. Start drinking.

2005 Small but outstanding crop of dense, concentrated wines.

2004 Promising for aromatic, balanced wines. Now showing their paces.

2003 Hot vintage; all but the best are falling over fast.

2002 Stylish wines, starting to show very well.

2001 Sound but anonymous. Drink soon.

2000 A big crop of ripe, healthy grapes. Drink now.

1999 Generous vintage of good, well-balanced wines mostly fully mature.

1998 Difficult year for white. Chassagne was successful. Drink up rapidly.

1997 Attractive plump wines now passing their best.

1996 Not developing as well as hoped. Over-acidic.

1995 A potentially great vintage, diluted in places. Ready to drink.

The white wines of the Mâconnais (Pouilly-Fuissé, St-Véran, Mâcon-Villages) follow a similar pattern, but do not last as long. They are appreciated more for their freshness than their richness.

Chablis *Grand cru* Chablis of vintages with both strength and acidity can age superbly for up to ten years; *premiers crus* proportionately less.

2008 A small crop of powerful, juicy wines, which ripened well in a sunny Sept.

2007 Brilliant *grand cru* and *premier cru* where not damaged by hail. Basic Chablis more modest.

2006 An early harvest of attractive, aromatically pleasing wines.

2005 Small but outstanding crop of dense, concentrated wines.

2004 Difficult vintage, with mildew a problem. Not for keeping.

2003 Small crop of ripe wines, but acidity is low and balance in question.

2002 Delicious wines in most cases developing well.

2001 Too much rain. Relatively weak. Drink up.

2000 A great vintage for Chablis. Keep the *grands crus*, drink the rest.

1999 Attractive but now want drinking up.

1998 Cool weather and some hail. Wines fair to good: not for long keeping.

1997 Another fine vintage; *grands crus* excellent now.

Beaujolais 08: Tough going with widespread hail. **07:** attractive but without the heart of a really great year. **06:** tricky vintage with some rot compromising the fruit. **05:** concentrated wines. **04:** light, some weak, some pretty. **03:** too much heat on the grapes, some excellent. **02:** drink up fast. **01:** very good if picked before rain. **00:** excellent, but drink up. **99:** splendid, rich, and deep. Older wines should be finished.

Southwest France

2008 Cold and wet spring, with much hail and rot, followed by cool June and July. Augt through to the end of the season sunny and warm, raising hopes for a fine year. Quantities severely down.

2007 Not quite as bad as feared. Whites fared better than reds, esp the sweets. The styles are all on the light side, with quantities down.

2006 A capricious and variable summer. Some wines may be better than expected. Tip: taste before you buy.

2005 Best year of the decade so far. Uniformly very good.

2004 Better than usual acidity suggests keeping potential. Excellent in Jurançon and Madiran. Middling elsewhere.

2003 The Ribena year. Small quantities of unbalanced wines, heavy in sweet fruit and alcohol, but often with stalky tannins. Drink up.

2002 For those who prefer elegance and finesse to brute force. Good Cahors, Madiran, and Jurançon (late pickers).

The Midi

2008 A similar year to 2007, with a wet spring and cool weather during flowering, but sufficient sunshine to produce some elegant wines from unstressed vines.

2007 A damp spring and a cooler than average summer, with a fine Sept

producing some beautifully balanced wines, with some ageing potential.
2006 Fine results from the best winemakers.
2005 A beautifully balanced year, with sunshine and rain at the right times throughout the region.
2004 Marked by Aug storms and a fine Sept. Wines are elegantly balanced, with lower alcohol than 2003 or 2001.
2003 The year of the heatwave. Many fine wines from skilled winemakers.
2002 Varies widely from AC to AC, and grower to grower. Good in the Minervois; diluted in Pic St-Loup.

Northern Rhône

2008 Low-key vintage after all the weather problems. The top names have made small amounts of directly fruited red wines that will drink well within 8–10 years max, a shade better than expected. A good year for the whites.
2007 The best sites, the best growers at Hermitage, Côte-Rôtie, Cornas, St-Joseph have produced very good wines, with stylish fruit, life of 18+ years. The whites are good, mixing early appeal with depth for the future.
2006 Big, healthy crop with wines showing plenty of clear fruit and sound stuffing. Are improving and evolving well, esp at Côte-Rôtie. Good acidity in robust whites, heady Condrieu wines.
2005 An exceptional vintage, with wonderful Syrah, tight flavours and long ageing potential for Hermitage, Cornas and the fullest Côte Rôties. St-Joseph reds have v. bright fruit. Whites are full – gd for mid-term drinking.
2004 Mid-weight, mid-term year, with Côte-Rôtie showing well over time; best reds are from top v'yds. Superb whites.
2003 A half-sized crop. Intense sun gave cooked "southern" flavours. Best reds show genuine richness, and are coming together. 25+ yrs for best.
2002 Dodgy due to heavy rain. Stick to best growers. Drink up red St-Josephs, small grower Côte-Rôtie. Hermitage, Cornas until 2015–18. Good whites, esp Condrieu.
2001 Reds ageing well, now stylish, fresh. Top yr at Côte-Rôtie. Often v.gd whites.
2000 Reds simpler than 1999 and 2001, less bright fruit, quite warm with a gentle richness. Some stewed flavours. Hermitage good in parts, Cornas did well, Côte-Rôtie variable. Good Condrieu, sumptuous.
1999 Very successful. Delicious, likely to live long. More balance than the 1998s. Great heart and harmony. Ace Côte-Rôties. Sound whites.
1998 Big, robust vintage. More overt tannins than 1999, but have fused well, with rich, oily textures, now on a second, gamey phase of life. Good Marsanne-based whites.

Southern Rhône

2008 A bad summer meant a tiny crop, reds that have some fruit but lack body. Gigondas helped by altitude, later ripening. Comparisons with 2002 in the air. Côtes du Rhône/Villages – avoid mass-market wines, choose only top domaine names. Whites will be good.
2007 Very good, an early-drinking vintage. Abundant, sweet fruit is the vintage imprint. Grenache-only wines can lack tannin but drink sumptuously. Exceptional Châteauneuf-du-Pape from top names. V.gd at Gigondas. Côtes du Rhônes are fat and good. Openly fruited, aromatic whites.
2006 Good; some very good wines. Quite rich Châteauneuf-du-Pape reds, starting to tighten. More open than the 2005s, less sweet and plush than the 2007s. Good Vacqueyras, Gigondas, best Villages such as Cairanne. Drink up the Côtes du Rhônes, then Lirac, Villages. Good, full whites, ideal for food.

2005 Very good. Strong, compact wines, esp from top sites and old vines. Will age well – 20+ years for top Châteauneufs. Tannins need leaving until 2010, eg Gigondas. Whites best drunk young.

2004 Good, but variable. Sinew and fresh, mineral flavours in Châteauneufs will suit European palates. Gigondas not always rounded. Be patient. Good fresh whites, will age well.

2003 At last this vintage is gaining balance. Chunky, potent wines, with jam and date/raisin flavours from the best, eg Châteauneuf – better than Gigondas, Vacqueyras. Not all balanced, but end tannins starting to fuse. Best wines can live a long time. Go for the best names, best areas.

2002 Drink up. Nature's payback: 66 cm of rain in a day. Simply fruited, early reds, acceptable whites. Gigondas did best.

2001 Excellent classic vintage. Complex reds, lots of life ahead, be patient for top areas. Cracking Châteauneufs showing well after 9 years.

2000 Tasty, open wines, led by fruit. Not a long-lived year. Go for leading names. Gigondas may edge Châteauneuf in quality. Best reds are singing now.

1999 Very good, underestimated wines from the best names. Some wines advancing quickly, others have fine, clear fruit. Châteauneuf reds have moved up a gear with age, with interesting variety. Good Gigondas, Lirac.

1998 Very good, but not the complete blockbuster as first thought. Big, warm, Grenache-led wines, emerging into a more integrated middle age after a mineral, funky stage. Some Châteauneufs have evolved fast, can be hollow in mid-palate.

Champagne

2008 Possibly the best vintage for 20 years in the making. Harvest in perfect "Champenois" weather – warm days and cool nights – has shaped classic wines of good maturity and textbook acidity across every district and all three grape varieties. Potentially very great.

2007 Selected wines from GRAND CRU villages where top growers picked later under sunny Sept skies will make goodish Champagnes. Otherwise a mixed bag after cold wet summer.

2006 Topsy-turvy growing season but fine Sept: made for ripe, expressive wines, esp Pinot Noir. Could be underrated by some houses.

2005 Not a great year overall in Champagne: a bit hot for real class, wines lacking dash and verve, also some pockets of rot. Vintage wines though from Bollinger and Jacquesson.

2004 Exactly what was needed. Record bumper crop giving Champagnes of classic finesse and "tension". Vintage year.

2003 Torrid, difficult year. Wines lack acidity and typicity. Roederer looks best.

2002 Undoubtedly a great, graceful year for superb Pinot Noir and sumptuous Chardonnay. Best released vintage of early 21st century.

2000 Not a great vintage year, but now showing forward, charming fruit and character ideal for drinking in 2009/10.

1999 Ripe, showy wines, ready soon. Grandstanding Dom Pérignon. Against the odds, some exceptional Champagnes (Pol Roger, Gimmonet, Paillard).

1998 Best are classic wines, some superior to 96, esp Chard *cuvées* of Pol Roger and Billecart-Salmon. Great Clicquot Grande Dame and Gosset Celebris.

Older fine vintages: 96 95 90 89 88 85 82

The Loire

2008 Once again saved by fine Sept and Oct. Cool year, dry after May. Small harvest, especially Muscadet – early April frost and hail in Pouilly and Sancerre. Very healthy grapes – with high acidity. Very promising reds and

dry whites, sweets hit by wet November.
2007 Very difficult summer – mildew rife. Vintage saved by fine Sept and Oct. Producer's name crucial. Fine but often austere dry whites and good Anjou sweets. Reds for early drinking.
2006 Challenging vintage in which only the conscientious succeeded. Dry whites fared well, reds nearly as attractive. Not great for sweet whites.
2005 Excellent across the board. Buy without fear, though some reds quite tannic. The sweet wines are more likely to be the product of shrivelled grapes than noble rot.
2004 Huge crop. In general better for reds than whites. Few or no sweet wines in Vouvray/Montlouis. Anjou's whites fewer and less sweet than usual.
2003 Heatwave vintage. Wines are big and supple, some flaccid, some not. Will they last? Jury is still out. Excellent year for sweet wines.
2002 Best since 97 – wonderful balance. Vivid fruit and vibrant acidity in the dry whites. Some fine sweet Chenins. Where yields were kept low, the reds are juicy with good colour.

FRANCE

Alsace

2008 A cool but dry Aug and good Sept shaped a healthy vintage of dry, crisp wines – a pleasing antidote to the over-sweet style of late.
2007 As throughout France, hot spring, cold, wet summer but sunny autumn weather allowed picking of healthy, ripe grapes. Promising.
2006 Hottest recorded July followed by coolest Aug. Top producers like Faller and Kuehly made subtle, fine Ries.
2005 A large crop of healthy grapes harvested after an Indian summer. Ripe and well-balanced wines of character, minerality and strength.
2004 Growers who picked early and kept yields low produced classic wines. Subtle year, especially for Ries.
2003 Earliest harvest since 1893. Small crop of variable wines. Best are ripe, but with low acidity (hence acidification allowed for the first time ever).
2002 Better than most of France. As in Champagne, some beautiful, supple wines – lots of personality, class, complete.
2001 Well-balanced wines, good but not great.
2000 Superb – probably best since 90. Very good for Vendanges Tardives and Sélections des Grains Nobles.

Abel-Lepitre Middle-rank CHAMPAGNE house. V.gd BRUT Millésimé **98** 99 00 02 04. Excellent BLANC DE BLANCS Cuvée 134 (blend of two gd yrs).
Abymes Savoie w ★ DYA Hilly area nr Chambéry; light, mild Vin de Savoie AC from Jacquère grape has alpine charm. SAVOIE has many such *crus*.
Agenais SW France r p w ★ DYA VDP of Lot-et-Garonne, rapid burst of gd independents alongside co-ops, esp DOMS Lou Gaillot and Campet.
Aligoté DYA Fresh, thirst-quenching secondary grape from Burgundy with own appellation at BOUZERON. Base wine for apéritif *crème blanc* CASSIS (Kir).
Alliet, Philippe Lo r w ★★→★★★ Top-quality Chinon and one of the Loire's leading producers. Best CUVÉES include barrel-aged Coteau du Noire and VIEILLES VIGNES and a recent hill v'yd L'Huisserie. Also a small amount of white.
Aloxe-Corton Burg r w ★★→★★★ 96' 97 98 99' 02' 03 05' 06 Village at north end of CÔTE DE BEAUNE famous for 2 GRANDS CRUS: CORTON (red), CORTON-CHARLEMAGNE (white). Village wines are lighter but to try.
Alquier, Jean-Michel Midi r w Leading FAUGÈRES producer. White Marsanne/Grenache Bl blend; also Sauvignon VDP red CUVÉES Maison Jaune and ageworthy Les Bastides.
Alsace Al w (r sp sw) ★★→★★★★ 00' 02' 04 05 06 07 08 The sheltered east slope

of the Vosges Mts makes France's Rhine wines: aromatic, fruity, full-strength, mostly dry and expressive of variety. Sugar levels vary widely: dry wines now easier to find. Much sold by variety (Pinot Bl, Ries, Gewurz). Matures well (except Pinot Bl, MUSCAT) 5–10 yrs; GRAND CRU even longer. Gd quality and value CRÉMANT. Formerly feeble Pinot N improving fast. See VENDANGE TARDIVE, SELECTION DES GRAINS NOBLES.

Why do Alsace wines vary so much?
Partly because of the complex and richly varied geology of the region, most wine villages have at least 5 different types of soil. You'll find chalk and limestone, sandstone and schist, clay, loess, even volcanic sediment – each fabulous terroir tailor-made for finest Riesling, MUSCAT, PINOT GRIS, and Gewurz. Five soils or more, plus 4 grape varieties, plus umpteen different altitudes and exposures, equals enormous variety. Sweetness is another variable; too much so for comfort.

Alsace Grand Cru W ★★★→★★★★ 90' 95 96 97 98 99 00' 02' 04 05 06 07 08 AC restricted to 51 (KAEFFERKOPF added in 2006) of the best-named v'yds (approx 1,600 ha, 800 in production) and 4 noble grapes (Ries, PINOT GR, Gewurz, MUSCAT) mainly dry, some sweet. Controversial classification now widely respected. They repay several yrs in bottle.

Amiel, Mas Midi r w sw ★★★ The key MAURY DOMAINE. Warming CÔTES DU ROUSSILLON Carerades red, white Altaïr, vin de liqueur Plénitude from Maccabeu. Vintage and cask-aged VDNs. Prestige 15 yrs a star.

Amirault, Yannick Lo r ★★→★★★ Meticulous, first-rate producer of both BOURGUEIL and ST-NICOLAS DE BOURGUEIL. Top cuvées inc La Petite Cave and Les Quartiers in BOURGUEIL, and Malagnes and La Mine in ST-NICOLAS.

Ampeau, Robert Burg ★★★ Exceptional grower and specialist in MEURSAULT and VOLNAY; also POMMARD. Unique in releasing only long-matured bottles.

André, Pierre Burg ★★ NÉGOCIANT at Ch Corton-André, ALOXE-CORTON; 5 ha of v'yds in and around CORTON plus wide range from purchased grapes. Significant improvement since purchase by Ballande Group in 2003.

d'Angerville, Marquis Burg ★★★★ One of Volnay's superstar DOMS with brilliant PREMIER CRUS Clos des Ducs (MONOPOLE), Champans, and Taillepieds. Quality rising yet further of late.

Arlaud Burg ★★→★★★ MOREY-ST-DENIS estate with CHARMES-CHAMBERTIN, CLOS DE LA ROCHE etc. Fine wine at all levels in relatively modern style.

Anjou Lo p r w (sw dr sp) ★→★★★★★ Both region and umbrella Loire AC covering Anjou and SAUMUR. Many styles: Chenin Bl-based dry whites range from light quaffers to potent agers; juicy reds incl rich Gamay; juicy Cab Fr-based Anjou rouge; and structured ANJOU-VILLAGES; also strong, dry SAVENNIÈRES; luscious COTEAUX DU LAYON Chenin Bl; dry sweet rosé, and sparkling.

Anjou-Coteaux de la Loire Lo w s/sw sw ★★→★★★ 02 03 04 05 07 (08) Tiny westernmost Anjou AC for sweet whites made from Chenin Bl that tend to be less rich but nervier than COTEAUX DU LAYON. Esp Doms du Fresche, Musset-Roullier, Ch de Putille.

Anjou-Villages Lo r ★→★★★ 02 03 04 05' 06 07 (08) Superior central ANJOU AC for reds (Cab Fr, but a few pure Cab Sauv). Quality tends to be high and prices reasonable, esp Dom de Brize, Dom Philippe CADY, Clos de Coulaine, Philippe Delesvaux, Dom les Grandes Vignes, Ogereau, Ch Pierre-Bise. Sub-AC Anjou-Villages-Brissac covers the same zone as Coteaux de l'Aubance; look for Bablut, Dom de Haute Perche, Montigilet, Richou, Rochelles, Ch de Varière.

Appellation Contrôlée (AC or AOC) Government control of origin and production (not quality) of all the best French wines.

Apremont Savoie w ★★ DYA One of the best villages of SAVOIE for pale, delicate whites, mainly from Jacquère grapes, but recently inc CHARD.

Arbin Savoie r ★★ Deep-coloured lively red from MONDEUSE grapes, rather like a gd Loire Cab Sauv. Ideal après-ski. Drink at 1–2 yrs.

Arbois Jura r p w (sp) ★★→★★★ Various gd and original light but tasty wines; speciality is VIN JAUNE. On the whole, DYA except excellent VIN JAUNE.

l'Ardèche, Coteaux de r p (w) ★→★★ Hilly area W of Rhône, plenty of gd activity. New DOMS; fresh reds, some oaked; Viognier (eg Mas de Libian, Chapoutier) and Marsanne. Best from pure Syrah, Gamay, Cab Sauv (Serret). Powerful Burgundian-style CHARD Ardèche by LOUIS LATOUR; Grand Ardèche mature vines, but oaked. DOMS du Colombier, Durand, Favette, Flacher, Mazel, Vigier.

Ariège SW r ★ 05 06 08 Growing VDP from nr the Pyrenees. Note esp DOM des Coteaux d'Engravies. Will keep. Not often seen outside the region.

l'Arlot, Domaine de Burg ★★★ Leading exponent in CÔTE DE NUITS of whole-bunch fermentation. Wines pale but aromatic and full of fruit. Best v'yds ROMANÉE-ST-VIVANT and NUITS-ST-GEORGES, esp Clos de l'Arlot.

Armagnac SW The alternative to cognac, and increasingly popular – certainly chez moi; tasty, rustic, and peppery. New AC for young white (colourless) Armagnac. Table wines: CÔTES DE GASCOGNE, GERS, TERROIRS LANDAIS.

Armand, Comte Burg ★★★ Sole owner of exceptional Clos des Epeneaux in POMMARD, as well as other v'yds in AUXEY and VOLNAY. On top form since 1999.

Aube Southern extension of CHAMPAGNE. Now known as Côte des Bar.

Aujoux, J-M Beauj Substantial grower/merchant of BEAUJOLAIS. Swiss-owned.

Auxey-Duresses Burg r w ★★→★★★ 99' 02' 03 05' 06 07 Second-rank (but v. pretty) CÔTE DE BEAUNE village: affinities with VOLNAY, MEURSAULT. Best examples (red) COMTE ARMAND, HOSPICES DE BEAUNE (CUVÉE BOILLOT), LEROY, Prunier; (white) COMTE ARMAND, Fichet, LEROY (Les Boutonniers).

Avize Champ One of the top Côte des Blancs villages. All CHARD.

Aÿ Champ One of the best Pinot N-growing villages of CHAMPAGNE.

Ayala Revitalized Aÿ-based CHAMPAGNE house, owned by BOLLINGER. Fine BRUT Nature Zéro Dosage and racy Rosé. Excellent Prestige Perle d'Ayala (**99**) 02).

Bandol Prov r p (w) ★★★ 96 97 98 99 00 01 02 03 04 05 06 07 Small coastal AC; PROVENCE's best. Long-lasting oak-aged reds mainly from Mourvèdre; elegant rosé from young vines, and a splash of white from Clairette, Ugni Blanc, and occasionally Sauvignon. Stars include DOMS Lafran Veyrolles, La Suffrène, TEMPIER, Chx Pibarnon, Pradeaux, Mas de la Rouvière.

Banyuls Pyr br sw ★★→★★★ One of the most original VDNS, mainly Grenache (Banyuls GRAND CRU: over 75% Grenache, aged for 2 yrs+). Vintage style resembles ruby port but far better are RANCIOS, aged for yrs in large casks. Think fine old tawny port. Best: DOMS du Mas Blanc (★★★), la Rectorie (★★★), Vial Magnères, at 10–15 yrs old.

Barrique The BORDEAUX (and cognac) term for an oak barrel holding 225 litres. Barrique-ageing to flavour almost any wine with oak was craze in late 1980s, with some sad results. Current oak prices should urge discretion.

Barsac B'x W SW ★★→★★★★ 83' 86' 88' 89' 90' 95 96 97' 98 99' 01' 02 03' 05' 07' (08) Neighbour of SAUTERNES with similar superb golden wines from lower-lying limestone soil; generally less powerful with more finesse. Repays long ageing. Top: CLIMENS, COUTET, DOISY-DAËNE, DOISY-VÉDRINES.

Barthod, Ghislaine Burg ★★★→★★★★ Impressive range of archetypal Chambolle-Musigny. Marvellous poise and delicacy yet with depth and concentration. Les Cras, Fuées, and Beauxbruns best.

Barton & Guestier BORDEAUX négociant now part of massive Diageo group.

Bâtard-Montrachet Burg w ★★★★ 92 93 95 96 97' 99' 00 02' 03 04' 05' 06' 07 12-ha GRAND CRU downslope from Le MONTRACHET itself. Rich, fat wines, sometimes four-square. Also worthy siblings Bienvenues-B-M and Criots B-M. Seek out: BOILLOT, BOUCHARD PÈRE & FILS, CARILLON, DROUHIN, GAGNARD, LATOUR, DOM LEFLAIVE, MOREY, Pernot, Ramonet, SAUZET.

Baudry, Domaine Bernard Lo r p w ★★→★★★ Superb CHINON in every style, from Chenin Bl-based whites to Cab Fr-based rosés and excellent CHINON CUVÉES of red, from juicy Les Granges to structured Clos Guillot and Croix Boissées.

Baumard, Domaine des Lo ★★→★★★★ Leading family producer of ANJOU wine, esp Chenin Bl-based whites, inc SAVENNIÈRES (Clos St Yves, Clos du Papillon) and QUARTS DE CHAUME. Baumard makes CRÉMANT de Loire and a tangy VIN DE TABLE from Verdelho. The Loire's brave screwcap pioneer.

Béarn SW r p w ★→★★ w p DYA r **05 06** (08) Pyrenean wine from MADIRAN and JURANÇON producers. Also from DOM ★★ Lapeyre/Guilhémas and Béarn Co-op.

Beaujolais r (p w) ★ DYA The most basic appellation of the huge Beaujolais region, producing 5million cases a yr. Some from the hills can be excellent.

Beaujolais Primeur (or Nouveau) The Beaujolais of the new vintage, made in a hurry (often only 4–5 days' fermenting) for release at midnight on the third Wednesday in Nov. Ideally soft, pungent, fruity, and tempting; too often crude, sharp, too alcoholic. More of an event than a drink.

Beaujolais-Villages r ★★ **05' 06 07 08** Wines from better (northern) half of BEAUJOLAIS; should be much tastier than plain BEAUJOLAIS. The 10 (easily) best villages are the *crus*: FLEURIE, ST-AMOUR, JULIÉNAS, CHÉNAS, MOULIN-À-VENT, CHIROUBLES, MORGON, REGNIÉ, CÔTE DE BROUILLY, BROUILLY. Of the 30 others the best lie around Beaujeu. *Crus* cannot be released EN PRIMEUR before 15 Dec. Best kept until spring (or considerably longer).

Beaumes-de-Venise S Rh br r (p w) ★★03 04 05' 06 07' for reds. DYA for MUSCAT. Often viewed as France's leading dessert MUSCAT; from SE CÔTES DU RHÔNE; can be honeyed or muskily aromatic, peach/apricot flavoured, lingering (eg DOMS Beaumalric, Bernardins, Coyeaux, Durban, JABOULET, Pigeade (v.gd), VIDAL-FLEURY, CO-OP). Midweight, slightly austere, heavy reds, best ripe yrs 07 03 (Ch Redortier, DOM Cassan, du Fenouillet, Durban, Les Goubert) leave for 2–3 yrs. Own AC since 04 vintage. White and rosé are CÔTES DU RHÔNE.

Beaumont des Crayères Champ Bijou Côte d'Epernay co-op making excellent Pinot Meunier-based Grande Réserve NV and v. fine Fleur de Prestige 98' 00 02 04. Exceptional CHARD-led Cuvée Nostalgie **98'**. Fleur de Rosé 02 03 04.

Beaune Burg r (w) ★★★ **02' 03** 05' 07 08 Historic wine capital of Burgundy and home to many merchants: BOUCHARD, CHAMPY, DROUHIN, JADOT, LATOUR as well as HOSPICES DE BEAUNE. No GRAND CRU v'yds but sound PREMIERS CRUS: *eg*, Cras, Grèves, Teurons, Cent Vignes, Clos du Roi, Bressandes for red and an increasing amount of white, of which Drouhin's CLOS DES MOUCHES stands out.

Becker, Caves J Al ★→★★ An organic estate, progressively biodynamic. Stylish, well-balanced wines inc exceptional MUSCAT GRAND CRU Froehn.

Bellet Prov p r w ★★★ The local wine of Nice;expensive, original but unknown in city. White is best, with unexpected ageing potential. A few small producers, esp Ch de Bellet, Clos St Vincent, Les Coteaux de Bellet, Ch de Crémat.

Bellivière, Domaine de Lo r w sw ★★→★★★ Eco-friendly grower: precise Chenin Bl in JASNIÈRES and COTEAUX DU LOIR and eye-opening Pineau d'Aunis.

Bergerac Dordogne r w p dr sw ★→★★★ **02 04 05'** 06 (08) Gd-value look-alike Bordeaux neighbour using B'x grape varieties. Top properties include ★★★ Dom l'Ancienne Cure, Clos des Verdots, Les Hauts de Caillevel, Ch Masburel, *La Tour des Gendres*, Jonc Blanc, Les Marnières. Otherwise ★★ Chx Belingard-Chayne, Clos de la Colline, Les Eyssards, Les Fontenelles, Grinou, de la Mallevieille, Les Miaudoux, le Paradis, Pion, le Raz, Thénac. See also MONBAZILLAC, MONTRAVEL, PÉCHARMANT, ROSETTE, SAUSSIGNAC.

Bertrand, Gérard Midi r p w ★★ One of biggest v'yd owners in South, with 325 ha;

Villemajou in CORBIÈRES *cru* Boutenac, Laville-Bertou in MINERVOIS LA LIVINIÈRE, l'Hospitalet in LA CLAPE, l'Aigle in LIMOUX, and VDP d'Oc.

Besserat de Bellefon Epernay house specializing in gently sparkling CHAMPAGNES (old "crémant" style). Now owned by Boizel Chanoine group. Better quality.

Beyer, Léon ★★→★★★ ALSACE specialist: v. fine, intense, dry wines often needing 10 yrs+ bottle age. Superb Ries. Comtes d'Eguisheim, but no mention on label of GRAND CRU PFERSIGBERG, its originating v'yd. Gd Gewurz.

Bichot, Maison Albert Burg ★★→★★★ Dynamic merchant and owner/distributor of LONG-DEPAQUIT (CHABLIS), Clos Frantin, and more. Quality on the rise.

Billecart-Salmon Family CHAMPAGNE house makes exquisite long-lived wines, vintage CUVÉES progressively fermented in wood. Superb Clos St-Hilaire BLANC DE NOIRS (**96' 98**), NF Billecart (98 99 00) and top BLANC DE BLANCS (98' 99 00).

Bize, Simon Burg ★★★ Patrick B has developed this fine SAVIGNY DOM over 20 yrs to include LATRICIERES-CHAMBERTIN, CORTON-CHARLEMAGNE and some fine inexpensive whites alongside v.gd range of Savigny PREMIERS CRUS.

Blagny Burg r w ★★→★★★ (r) **99' 02' 03'** 05' 07 08 Austere reds sold as Blagny; fresh whites, mostly PREMIER CRU, (legally) borrow names of neighbouring MEURSAULT and PULIGNY. AMPEAU, LATOUR, Matrot, Martelet-Cherisey are gd.

Blanc de Blancs Any white wine made from white grapes only, esp CHAMPAGNE. An indication of style, not of quality.

Blanck, Paul & Fils ★★→★★★ Grower at Kientzheim, ALSACE, producing huge range of wines. Finest from 6 ha GRAND CRU Furstentum (Ries, Gewurz, PINOT GR) and GRAND CRU SCHLOSSBERG (Ries). Also gd Pinot Bl.

Blanc de Noirs White (or slightly pink or "blush") wine from red grapes.

Blanquette de Limoux Midi w sp ★★ Gd-value creamy fizz from nr Carcassonne; claims older history than CHAMPAGNE. Basic Mauzac much improved by CHARD Chenin Bl and, more recently, Pinot N, esp in newer AC CRÉMANT DE LIMOUX. Large co-op with Sieur d'Arques label works well for AC. Also Rives-Blanques, Martinolles.

Blaye B'x r w ★→★★ **01 03 04 05'** (06) As of 2000, designation for top, concentrated reds (lower yields, longer ageing, etc) from PREMIÈRES CÔTES DE BLAYE. Also declining AC for simple dry whites. More change from 2007 vintage.

Boillot Burg Interconnected Burgundy growers. Look for Jean-Marc (POMMARD) ★★★ for fine oaky reds and whites, Henri (VOLNAY) ★★★, Louis (CHAMBOLLE, married to GHISLAINE BARTHOD) ★★→★★★, and the late Pierre (MEURSAULT) ★★.

Boisset, Jean-Claude Burg The biggest Burgundy merchant, based in NUITS-ST-GEORGES. Owner of Bouchard-Aîné, Lionel Bruck, F Chauvenet, Delaunay, Jaffelin, Morin Père & Fils, de Marcilly, Pierre Ponnelle, Thomas-Bassot, Vienot, CELLIER DES SAMSONS (BEAUJOLAIS), Moreau (CHABLIS), and a share in MOMMESSIN. Involved in projects in Canada, California, Chile, Uruguay, and the Languedoc. Used to be fairly dire; Boisset label now resurrected. From 1999 own v'yds separated as DOM DE LA VOUGERAIE (★★★).

Boizel One of CHAMPAGNE's surest values: brilliant, aged BLANC DE BLANCS NV and prestige Joyau de France (**95 96 98 00**) Joyau Rose (**00**). Also Grand Vintage BRUT (**98 99 00** 02) and CUVÉE Sous Bois.

Bollinger Great individualistic CHAMPAGNE house, on a roll in recent vintages (viz. Grande Année 97, Grande Année Rosé 99). Luxury wines: RD (**88' 90 95 96**), VIEILLES VIGNES Françaises (**98 99**) from ungrafted Pinot N vines, La Côte aux Enfants, AŸ (**97 99 02**). See also LANGLOIS-CH.

Bonneau du Martray, Domaine Burg w r ★★★★ (w) ★★ (r) TWO GRANDS CRUS made to highest standard – exemplary, long-lived (10+ yrs) Corton-Charlemagne

Words within entries marked like this *Alter Ego de Palmer* indicate wines especially enjoyed by Hugh Johnson over the past 12 months (mid '08–'09).

and significantly improved if overpriced red CORTON.

Bonnes-Mares Burg r ★★★→★★★★ 90' 91 93 95 96' 97 98 99' 00 02' 03 05' 06 07 08 GRAND CRU (15ha) between CHAMBOLLE-MUSIGNY and MOREY-ST-DENIS. Sturdy long-lived wines, less fragrant than MUSIGNY; to rival CHAMBERTIN. Best: DUJAC, Groffier, JADOT, ROUMIER, DOM des Varoilles, DE VOGÜE, VOUGERAIE.

Bonnezeaux Lo w SW ★★★→★★★★ 88 89' 90' 95' 96' 97' 02 03' 04 05' (07) 08 Magnificently rich, almost everlasting sweet Chenin Bl. QUARTS DE CHAUME top site in COTEAUX DU LAYON. Esp: Chx de Fesles, la Fresnaye, DOMS les Grandes Vignes, du Petit Val (Goizil), Ferme de la Sansonnière.

Bordeaux B'x r w (p) ★→★★ 01 03 05' Catch-all AC for generic Bordeaux. Mixed quality, but can be great value when gd. Most brands are in this category.

Bordeaux Supérieur B'x r ★→★★ 00' 01 03 04 05' Superior denomination to above. Higher minimum alcohol, lower yield, and longer ageing. 75% of production bottled at the property, the reverse of AC Bordeaux.

Borie-Manoux Admirable BORDEAUX shipper, CH-owner. CHX inc Batailley, BEAU-SITE, Croix du Casse, DOM de L'EGLISE, HAUT-BAGES-MONPELOU, TROTTEVIEILLE.

Bouchard Père & Fils Burg Back among the top NÉGOCIANTS since bought by HENRIOT in mid-1990s and development of new winery on edge of BEAUNE. Brilliant whites and exciting reds, esp BEAUNE, VOLNAY, POMMARD.

Bouches-du-Rhône Prov r p w ★ VDP from Marseille environs. Warming reds from southern varieties, plus Cab Sauv, Syrah, and Merlot.

Bourgeois, Henri Lo ★★→★★★ 02 03 04 05 06 07 Top-quality, leading SANCERRE grower/merchant in Chavignol. Also POUILLY-FUMÉ, MENETOU-SALON, QUINCY (CH), COTEAUX DU GIENNOIS (CH), and VDP. Top wines include MD de Bourgeois, La Bourgeoise, Jadis, Sancerre d'Antan. See also Clos Henri (r, w) in Marlborough, New Zealand.

Bourgogne Burg r w (p) ★★ (r) 05' 06 07 08 (w) 05 06 07 08 Catch-all AC, with higher standards than basic BORDEAUX. Light, often gd flavour, best at 2–4 yrs. Top growers make bargain beauties from fringes of CÔTE D'OR villages; do not despise. BEAUJOLAIS *crus* (except REGNIÉ) may be labelled Bourgogne.

Bourgogne Grand Ordinaire r (w) ★ DYA Who invented this crazy name for the most basic of Burgundy? Usually Gamay for red, CHARD, Aligoté or occasionally Melon de Bourgogne for white.

Bourgogne Passe-Tout-Grains r (p) ★ Age 1–2 yrs. The name suggests you can put any grape in, but in fact it must be a mix of Pinot N (minimum 33%) and Gamay. Can be fun from CÔTE D'OR DOMAINES.

Bourgueil Lo r (p) ★★→★★★(★) 96' 02 03 04 05' 06 07 (08) Burly, full-flavoured TOURAINE reds and big, fragrant rosés based on Cab Fr. Good vintages can age 15 yrs. Esp AMIRAULT, Audebert, DOM de la Butte, DOM de la Chevalerie, Delaunay, Druet, Lame Delisle Boucard. See ST-NICOLAS-DE-BOURGUEIL.

Bouscassé, Domaine SW ★★★ 95' 98' 00 01 02 04 05' (06) Alain Brumont's home base in MADIRAN making just as sturdy wines as his CH MONTUS.

Bouvet-Ladubay Lo ★→★★★ Major sparkling SAUMUR house purchased by Indian beer company United Breweries in 2006. Best is the barrel-fermented Cuvée Trésor – both white and rosé. Wide range of sparklers including BRUT zero, sweet and a red. Also still wines mainly from ANJOU-SAUMUR.

Bouzereau Burg ★★→★★★ Family in MEURSAULT making gd whites at gd prices and reds. Jean-Baptiste, son of Michel B, and Vincent B are the 2 best producers.

Bouzeron Burg w ★★ CÔTE CHALONNAISE AC specifically for ALIGOTÉ though they don't tell you so on the label any more. Age 1–2 yrs or more from de Villaine.

Bouzy Rouge Champ r ★★★ 90 95 96 97 99 02 Still red of famous Pinot N village. Like v. light Burgundy, but can last well in sunny vintages.

Brocard, J-M Burg ★★→★★★ One of the recent success stories of Chablis with a fine range of wines at all levels. Also on offer: a range of BOURGOGNE Blancs from different soil types (Kimmeridgian, Jurassic, Portlandian).

Brouilly Beauj r ★★ 05' 06 07 08 Biggest of the 10 *crus* of BEAUJOLAIS: fruity, round, refreshing wine, can age 3–4 yrs. Ch de la Chaize is largest estate. Top growers: Michaud, DOM de Combillaty, DOM des Grandes Vignes.

Brumont, Alain SW ★★★ Once, and some say still, the clear leader in MADIRAN. Specialist in highly extracted and oaked 100% Tannat wines, eg Le Tyre. Flagship wines: *Ch Montus*, DOM BOUSCASSÉ, and gd-value Torus brand. Also big range of VDPS, some varietals, some blends.

Brut Term for the dry classic wines of CHAMPAGNE.

Brut Ultra/Zéro Term for bone-dry wines in CHAMPAGNE back in fashion.

Bugey Savoie r p w sp ★→★★ DYA VDQS for light sparkling, still, or half-sparkling wines from Roussette (or Altesse) and CHARD (gd). Best from Montagnieu; also Rosé de Cerdon, mainly Gamay.

Burguet, Alain Burg ★★→★★★★ Compact VIGNERON for outsize GEVREY-CHAMBERTIN.

Buxy Burg w Village in AC MONTAGNY with gd co-op for CHARD and Pinot N.

Buzet SW r (w p) ★★ 04 05 06 (08) New leadership at the co-op is already bringing more excitement to this appellation, esp from its single properties (eg Ch de Gueyze, and improving, prize-winning Mazelières). Local character from (independent) ★★★ DOM du Pech, ★★ Chx du Frandat, Tournelles.

Cabardès Midi r (p w) ★→★★ 01 02 03 04 05 06 07 08 B'x Cab and Merlot meet MIDI Syrah and Grenache for original blends. Best is DOM de Cabro; also Jouclary, Font Juvenal. Ch Pennautier is largest.

Cabernet d'Anjou Lo p s/sw ★ Traditionally sweet but more often demi-sec, often derided, rosé enjoying renaissance. Can be ageworthy. Ch FIERRE BISE, Dom de Bablut, Cady, Clau de Nell, les Grandes Vignes, Ogereau, de Sauveroy.

Cabrières Midi p (r) ★★ DYA COTEAUX DU LANGUEDOC. Traditionally full-bodied rosé; also sound reds mainly from village co-op.

Cady, Domaine Lo r p s w ★★→★★★ A reliable and excellent ANJOU grower of everything from dry whites to off-dry rosés, to lusciously sweet COTEAUX DU LAYON and CHAUME.

Cahors SW r ★→★★★ 90' 95' 96 98 00 01' 02 04 05' 06 (08) All-red AC based on Malbec (at least 70%). Nearly as many styles as growers (200); fruity, easy wines from ★★ Maison Vigoroux Pigmentum, Ch Latuc, DOM Boliva; more traditional from ★★★ *Clos de Gamot* (esp Cuvée Vignes Centenaires), ★★ Coutale, Chx du Cayrou, La Coustarelle, La Caminade, Gaudou, Les Ifs, DOMS de la Bérengeraie, de Cause, Paillas, Pineraie, Les Rigalets, Savarines (organic); more New World style from Ch Lagrézette, ★★★ Chx du Cèdre, Lamartine, Clos Triguedina, ★★ Ch Eugénie; better control of oak and gentler vinification from cult ★★★ DOM Cosse-Maisonneuve.

Cairanne S Rh r p w ★★→★★★★ 98' 01' 03 04' 05' 06' 07' One of 2 top CÔTES DU RHÔNE-VILLAGES: full, with prominent fruit, some flair, esp DOMS D & D Alary, Ameillaud, Brusset, Escaravailles, Grosset, Hautes Cances, l'Oratoire St-Martin, Présidente, Rabasse-Charavin, Richaud, Perrin et Fils. Improving, food-friendly, robust whites.

Canard-Duchêne CHAMPAGNE house. Inexpensive; improving with ALAIN THIÉNOT.

Canon-Fronsac B'x r ★★→★★★ 95 96 98 00' 01 03 05' 06 Full tannic reds of improved quality from west of POMEROL. Try Chx Barrabaque, Cassagne Haut-Canon La Truffière, La Fleur Caillou, Gaby, Grand-Renouil, Haut-Mazeris, Lamarche Canon Candelaire, Pavillon, Moulin-Pey-Labrie, Vrai Canon Bouché.

Caramany Pyr r (w) ★ Theoretically superior AC for CÔTES DU ROUSSILLON-VILLAGES.

Carillon, Louis Burg ★★★ Sensibly priced and consistently fine PULIGNY producer, esp Combettes, Perrières, Referts.

Cassis Prov w (r p) ★★ DYA Fashionable sailing village east of Marseille with reputation for dry whites based on CLAIRETTE and Marsanne. Delicious with bouillabaisse (eg DOM de la Ferme Blanche, Clos Ste Magdeleine, Clos d'Albizzi). Growers fighting rearguard action with property developers. Do not confuse with cassis: blackcurrant liqueur from Dijon.

De Castellane BRUT NV; BLANC DE BLANCS; BRUT (**99 00 02** 04); Prestige Florens de Castellane (**98 99** 02). Traditional Epernay CHAMPAGNE house. Fair quality: better for vintage wines like CUVÉE Commodore Brut (**98**).

Cathiard Burg ★★★ Brilliant VOSNE-ROMANÉE producer on top form since late 1990s. Perfumed, sensual wines are charming young but will age.

Cave Cellar, or any wine establishment.

Cave coopérative Wine-growers' co-op winery; over half of all French production. Usually well run, well equipped, and wines gd value for money.

Cazes, Domaine Midi r p w sw ★★ Large family producer in ROUSSILLON. VDP pioneer, with Merlot and Cab Sauv, esp for brand Le Canon du Marechal and Le Credo, also CÔTES DU ROUSSILLON-VILLAGES and gd aged RIVESALTES.

Cellier des Samsons ★ BEAUJOLAIS/MÂCONNAIS co-op which has 2,000 grower-members. Wines widely distributed; now owned by BOISSET.

Cérons B'x w dr sw ★★ 97' 98 99' 01' 02 03' 05' 07 (08) Tiny neighbour of SAUTERNES. Less intense wines, eg Chx de Cérons, Chantegrive, Grand Enclos.

Chablis Burg w ★★→★★★ 05' 06' 07 08 At best magical mineral wine from N of Burgundy, but too much anonymous CHARD now made. Usually without oak.

Chablis Grand Cru Burg w ★★★→★★★★ 95' 96' 98 99 00' 02' 03 05' 06' 07 Small block of 7 v'yds on steep slope on right bank of Serein. Needs age for minerality and individual style to develop. V'yds: Blanchots, Bougros, Clos, Grenouilles, Preuses, Valmur, Vaudésir. Clos and Vaudésir best.

Chablis Premier Cru Burg w ★★★ 99 00' 02' 03 05' 06 07 08 Technically second-rank but at best excellent; more typical of CHABLIS than its GRANDS CRUS. Can outclass more expensive MEURSAULT and other CÔTE DE BEAUNE. Best v'yds include Côte de Léchet, Fourchaume, Mont de Milieu, Montée de Tonnerre, Montmains, Vaillons.

Chambertin Burg r ★★★★ 88 89 90' 91 93 95 96' 97 98 99' 00 01 02' 03' 05' 06 07 08 13-ha (or 28-ha including Clos de Bèze) of Burgundy's most imperious wine; amazingly dense, sumptuous, long-lived and expensive. Not everybody up to standard but try from BOUCHARD PÈRE & FILS, Charlopin, Damoy, DROUHIN, LEROY, MORTET, Prieur Rossignol-Trapet, ROUSSEAU, TRAPET.

Chambertin-Clos de Bèze Burg r ★★★★ 88 89 90' 91 93 95 96' 97 98 99' 00 01 02' 03 05' 06 07 08 May be sold under the name of neighbouring CHAMBERTIN. Similarly splendid wines, maybe more accessible in youth. 15 growers, inc CLAIR, Damoy, DROUHIN, Drouhin-Laroze, FAIVELEY, Groffier, JADOT, ROUSSEAU.

Chablis

There is no better expression of the all-conquering CHARD than the full but tense, limpid but stony wines it makes on the heavy limestone soils of Chablis. Chablis terroir divides into three quality levels (four including Petit Chablis) with great consistency. Best makers use little or no new oak to mask the precise definition of variety and terroir: Barat, Bessin*, Billaud-Simon*, Bouchard Père & Fils, Boudin*, J-M Brocard, J Collet*, D Dampt, R & V Dauvissat*, J Dauvissat, B, D et E, and J Defaix, Droin, Drouhin*, Duplessis, Durup, Fèvre*, Geoffroy, J-P Grossot*, Laroche, Long-Depaquit, Dom des Malandes, L Michel, Picq*, Pupillon, Raveneau*, G Robin*, Servin, Tribut, Vocoret. Simple unqualified "Chablis" may be thin; best is PREMIER or GRAND CRU. The co-op, La Chablisienne, has high standards (esp Grenouille*) and many different labels (it makes one in every three bottles). (* = outstanding)

Chambolle-Musigny Burg r ★★★→★★★★ 90' 93 95' 96' 98 99' 01 02' 03 05' 06 07 08 CÔTE DE NUITS village (170 ha): fragrant, complex, but never heavy wine. Best v'yds: Amoureuses, (BONNES-MARES), Charmes, Cras, Fuées, MUSIGNY. Growers to note: Amiot-Servelle, BARTHOD, Digoia-Royer, DROUHIN, Groffier, Hudelot-Noëllat, JADOT, MUGNIER, RION, ROUMIER, DE VOGÜÉ.

Champagne Sparkling wines of Pinots N and Meunier and/or CHARD, and its region (34,000 ha, 145 km east of Paris); made by *méthode traditionnelle*. Bubbles from elsewhere, however gd, cannot be Champagne.

Champagne – expanding the vineyards

Cynicism! Greed! Stupidity! The poor (well, not that poor) Champenois couldn't get it right. So many accusations were flying about, so much indignation about the proposed expansion of the Champagne v'yd that not everybody stopped to think. The Champenois were, we were told, blatantly going all out to produce quantity at the expense of quality. But in truth, the proposed new sites are not new at all, being often located in fine, suitable hillsides that produced good wine in the 19th century, but which were abandoned after *phylloxera*. A greater danger is that Champagne will be made by arable farmers who don't understand wine. The new v'yds will come on stream in 2018–2020. If the big houses have any sense (and any spare cash) they'll get in sharpish to rent the land.

Champs-Fleuris, Domaine des Lo r w p sw ★★→★★★ Exciting 34-ha DOM. Top-notch SAUMUR Blanc; SAUMUR-CHAMPIGNY; fine CRÉMANT, pretty rosé, and, when vintage warrants, succulent COTEAUX DU SAUMUR called CUVÉE SARAH.

Champy Père & Cie Burg ★★→★★★ Oldest négociant in BEAUNE, rejuvenated by Meurgey family (also brokers DIVA). Range of v. well-chosen wines.

Chandon de Briailles, Domaine Burg ★★★ Small estate at SAVIGNY making light, fragrant PERNAND-VERGELESSES, Ile de Vergelesses, gd CORTON red and white.

Chanson Père & Fils Burg ★→★★★ Old grower-négociant at BEAUNE (45 ha). Esp BEAUNE Clos des Fèves, PERNAND-VERGELESSES Les Caradeux, SAVIGNY, CORTON. Fine quality now.

Chapelle-Chambertin Burg r ★★★ 90' 91 93 95 96' 98 99' 01 02' 03 05' 06 A 5.2-ha neighbour of CHAMBERTIN. Wine more "nervous", less meaty. V.gd in cooler yrs. Top producers: Damoy, JADOT, Rossignol-Trapet, Trapet.

Chapoutier N Rh ★★→★★★★★ Old family grower, also merchant of big-bodied red and white Rhônes; biodynamic. Note low-yield special CUVÉES CHÂTEAUNEUF Barbe Rac, Croix de Bois (r), *Côte-Rôtie La Mordorée*, HERMITAGE: L'Ermite, Le Pavillon (r), L'Ermite, CUVÉE de l'Orée, Le Méal (w). Also ST-JOSEPH Les Granits (r, w). V.gd traditional Marsanne N Rhône whites, some reds extracted. Reliable, gd-value Meysonniers Crozes. New holdings in BANYULS, COLLIOURE, COTEAUX DU TRICASTIN, COTEAUX D'AIX-EN-PROVENCE, RIVESALTES promising. Also Australian joint ventures, esp DOMS Tournon and Terlato & Chapoutier.

Chardonnay As well as a white wine grape, also the name of a MÂCON-VILLAGES commune. Hence Mâcon-Chardonnay.

Charmes-Chambertin Burg r ★★★ 90' 93 95 96' 98 99' 01 02' 03 05' 06 07 08 30 ha inc neighbour MAZOYÈRES-CHAMBERTIN of mixed quality. Best has intense, ripe, dark-cherry fruit and fragrant finish. Try Bachelet, DROUHIN, DUGAT, DUJAC, LEROY, Perrot-Minot, ROTY, ROUMIER, ROUSSEAU, VOUGERAIE.

Chassagne-Montrachet Burg w r ★★→★★★★★ (w) 99 00 02' 04 05' 06' 07 08 Large village at south end of CÔTE DE BEAUNE. Soil more suited to reds, but they can be over-tough. Clos St Jean best red. More planted to white now, which can be brilliant in best spots: Caillerets, La Romanée, etc. Shares GRANDS CRUS MONTRACHET and BÂTARD-M with PULIGNY, plus all of Criots-B-M. Best growers:

Champagne growers to watch in 2010

Edmond Barnaut Bouzy. Complex, fine CHAMPAGNES mainly from Pinot N culminate in first-rate Sélection Ultra BRUT, GRAND CRU (98 99 02) and delicious COTEAUX CHAMPENOIS Rosé.

Louise Brisson Ace Côte de Bar (Aube) estate. Top CUVÉE Fût de Chêne (99 00 02).

Claude Cazals Exciting extra-BRUT BLANC DE BLANCS (99) and exceptional Clos Cazals (96 ★★★★ 98).

Richard Cheurlin One of best grower-winemakers of the Aube. Rich but balanced Carte d'Or and vintage-dated CUVÉE Jeanne (98 02).

Pierre Cheval-Gatinois Aÿ. Impeccable producer of mono-CRU CHAMPAGNES and excellent still Aÿ COTEAUX CHAMPENOIS (99 02).

Collard-Picard Rising Marne Valley and Côte des Blancs DOM. Impressive CUVÉE Prestige from all 3 CHAMPAGNE grapes, two gd vintages and part oak-fermented.

Pierre Gimonnet Leading Côte des Blancs grower at Cuis. V. dry CUVÉE Gastronome ideal with oysters, and complex Le Fleuron from old vines.

Henri Giraud Grower-merchant making exceptional Pinot-led CHAMPAGNE. Excellent Prestige CUVÉE Fut de Chene (93 95 96 98'). Getting expensive.

Larmandier-Bernier Vertus; top BLANC DE BLANCS grower-maker, esp Terre de Vertus Non Dosé (03 04) and Cramant VIEILLES VIGNES (02 04).

David Léclapart Talented biodynamic grower in Trépail, known for feisty all-CHARD CHAMPAGNES (excellent CUVÉE Apôtre) and respectable COTEAUX CHAMPENOIS rouge.

José Michel Fresh yet mature Carte Blanche NV. Also excellent BLANC DE BLANCS (00 02) and vintage (00 02).

V. Testulat Great value Epernay DOMAINE and merchant. First-rate BLANC DE NOIRS and elegant Paul Vincent Vintage (99 02).

COLIN, GAGNARD, MOREY families, Ch de la Maltroye, Pillot, Niellon, Ramonet.

Château Means an estate, big or small, gd or indifferent, particularly in Bordeaux (see Chx of Bordeaux). In France, château tends to mean, literally, castle or great house. In Burgundy, "DOMAINE" is the usual term.

Château d'Arlay ★→★★★ Major Jura estate; 65 ha in skilful hands. Wines include v.gd VIN JAUNE, VIN DE PAILLE, Pinot N, and MACVIN.

Château de Beaucastel S Rh r w ★★★★ 78' 79 81' 83 85 86' 88 89' 90' 94' 95' 96' 97 98' 99' 00' 01' 03' 04 05' 06 07' Leading, dynamic CHÂTEAUNEUF estate, also with thriving merchant business, and own Gigondas DOM des Tourelles (from 2008). Deep, complex wines, drink first 2 yrs or from 7–8 yrs; unusual grape mix inc ⅓ Mourvèdre. Have softened in recent yrs. Top-grade 60% Mourvèdre Hommage à Jacques Perrin red. Wonderful old-vine Roussanne: keep 5–25 yrs. Excellent CÔTES DU RHÔNE Coudoulet de Beaucastel red (lives 8+ yrs). Perrin et Fils CAIRANNE, RASTEAU, VINSOBRES v. solid quality. V.gd organic Perrin Nature CÔTES DU RHÔNE (r w) GIGONDAS. (See also Tablas Creek, California.)

Château du Cèdre SW r ★★★ 01' 02 04 05' 06 08 Leading exponent of modern CAHORS. Esp Le Prestige more quick-maturing than top growths. Also delicious white VDP from Viognier.

Château de la Chaize Beauj r ★★★ Magnificent, recently restored château which is home to leading 98-ha BROUILLY estate.

Château-Chalon Jura w ★★★ Not a château but AC and village. Unique dry, yellow, sherry-like wine (Savagnin grape). Develops flor (see Port, Sherry & Madeira) while ageing in barrels for minimum 6 yrs. Ready to drink when bottled (62-cl clavelin bottle), but ages almost forever. A curiosity.

Château Fortia S Rh r (w) ★★ 78' 81' 88 90 95' 96' 97 98' 99 00' 01 03' 04' 05' 06' 07' Traditional 30-ha CHÂTEAUNEUF estate with small château. Owner's father, Baron Le Roy, launched France's AC system in 1920s. Better form, better fruit clarity recently, inc special Le Baron (lots of Syrah) and whites.

Château Fuissé Burg w ★★→★★★ Substantial producer with some of the best terroirs of POUILLY-FUISSÉ. Esp Les Clos, Combettes. Also négociant lines.

Château-Grillet N Rh w ★★ 91' 95' 98' 00' 01' 04' 05 06 07 Single 3.6-ha terraced granite amphitheatre of Viognier; one of France's smallest ACs. Overpriced, but recent revival. Subtle, takes 3+ yrs to open up. Decant

Châteaumeillant Lo r p ★→★★ DYA A small VDQ area (98 ha) S of Bourges in Georges Sand country. Gamay and Pinot N for light reds, gris and rosés. Look for: Chaillot and Geoffrenet-Morval.

Château de Meursault Burg r w ★★ 61-ha estate owned by PATRIARCHE; gd v'yds and wines in BEAUNE, MEURSAULT, POMMARD, VOLNAY. Cellars open to public.

Château Mont-Redon S Rh r w ★★→★★★ 78' 85 88 89 90 94' 95' 97' 98' 00 01' 03' 04' 05' 06' 07' Gd 100-ha CHÂTEAUNEUF estate. Fine red, always best 6+ yrs, gains complexity; fresh, early-drinking white that can age, too. Also high-grade red LIRAC (mainly Grenache).

Château Montus SW r ★★★ 90' 95' 98' 00 01' 02 04 05' 06 (08) ALAIN BRUMONT's flagship MADIRAN property still produces some of top wines in SW despite fearsome competition. Needs long ageing.

Château La Nerthe S Rh r w ★★★ 78' 81' 88' 90' 95' 96' 97 98' 99' 00 01 03 04' 05' 06' 07' V.gd 90-ha CHÂTEAUNEUF estate. Smoothly composed modern-style wines, special CUVÉES the delicious, full Cadettes (r) and oaked Beauvenir (w). Takes 5 yrs to show. Also run v.gd Prieuré Montézargues Tavel, gd DOM de la Renjarde CÔTES DU RHÔNE. Ch Signac CHUSCLAN.

Châteauneuf-du-Pape S Rh r (w) ★★★ 78' 81' 83 85 86 88 89' 90' 94 95' 96 98' 99' 00 01' 03' 04' 05' 06' 07' 3,200 ha nr Avignon with core of 30 DOMS for v. fine wines (quality varies over remaining 90). Mix of up to 13 red, white varieties led by Grenache, Syrah, Mourvèdre, Counoise. Best are dark, strong, v. long-lived, gd value from smaller names. (Too) many, too expensive Prestige wines (old vines, new oak). Whites fresh, fruity, or rather sturdy, heavy, best can age 15 yrs. Top growers include: CHX DE BEAUCASTEL, FORTIA, Gardine, MONT-REDON, LA NERTHE, RAYAS, Vaudieu; DOMS de Beaurenard, Bois de Boursan, Bosquet des Papes, Les Cailloux, Chante Cigale, Charbonnière, Charvin, Font-de-Michelle, Grand Veneur, Marcoux, Pegaü, Roger Sabon, VIEUX TÉLÉGRAPHE, Vieille Julienne, Henri Bonneau, Clos du Mont-Olivet, CLOS DES PAPES, Clos St-Jean, Cuvée du Vatican, P Usseglio, Vieux Donjon.

Château Pierre-Bise Lo r p w ★★→★★★★ Terroir specialist COTEAUX DU LAYON, inc Chaume, QUARTS DE CHAUME, and SAVENNIÈRES, esp Clos de Grand Beaupréau and ROCHE-AUX-MOINES. V.gd Anjou-Gamay, ANJOU-VILLAGES, and ANJOU Blanc.

Château Rayas S Rh r (w) ★★★→★★★★★ 78' 79 81' 85 86 88' 89 90' 93 94 95' 96' 98' 99 00 01 03 04' 05' 06' Back-to-form, v. traditional, one-off 12-ha estate in CHÂTEAUNEUF. Soft, subtle, complex red fruits, its Grenache ages superbly. Traditional-style white Rayas once more v.gd over 15+ yrs. Gd-value second wine: Pignan. V.gd Ch Fonsalette, CÔTES DU RHÔNE. All need decanting. Also gd Ch des Tours VACQUEYRAS.

Château Simone Prov r p w ★★→★★★★ Historic estate where Winston Churchill painted Mont St-Victoire. Virtually synonymous with AC PALETTE nr Aix-en Provence. Warming stylish reds; white repays bottle ageing. Full-bodied rosé.

Château de Villeneuve Lo r w Top SAUMUR grower. Wonderful Saumur Blanc (esp Les Cormiers) and SAUMUR-CHAMPIGNY (esp VIEILLES VIGNES, Grand Clos). Superb Coteaux de Saumur in 2003.

Châtillon-en-Diois Rh r p w ★ DYA Small, ordinary AC east of middle Rhône in pre-

Alps. Just adequate, lean, mainly Gamay reds; white (some ALIGOTÉ) often made into sparkling CLAIRETTE DE DIE.

Chave, Gérard and Jean-Louis N Rh r w ★★★★ First-class HERMITAGE family DOM. 9 hillside sites. Rich, textured, long-lived wines, esp white (mainly Marsanne), also v.gd occasional VIN DE PAILLE. Improving DOMAINE ST-JOSEPH red, fruity J-L Chave brand ST-JOSEPH Offerus, a select merchant HERMITAGE red and white.

Chavignol SANCERRE village with famous steep v'yds, Les Monts Damnés and Cul de Beaujeu. Clay-limestone soil gives full-bodied, mineral wines that age 7–10 yrs (or longer); esp from Boulay, BOURGEOIS, Cotat, and DAGUENEAU.

Chénas Beauj r ★★★ 05' 06 07 08 Smallest BEAUJOLAIS CRU, one of the weightiest; neighbour to MOULIN-À-VENT and JULIÉNAS. Growers inc Benon, Champagnon, Charvet, Ch Chèvres, DUBOEUF, Lapierre, Robin, Trichard, co-op.

Chevalier-Montrachet Burg w ★★★★ 89' 92 95 96 97 99' 00' 01 02' 04 05' 06' 07 08 Just above MONTRACHET geographically, just below in quality, though still capable of brilliant, long-lived, mineral wines. Best sectors are Les Demoiselles (JADOT, LATOUR) and La Cabotte (BOUCHARD). Other top growers: Colin-Deleger, Dancer, LEFLAIVE, Niellon, Ch de Puligny.

Cheverny Lo r p w ★→★★ 05' 06 07 08 Loire AC nr Chambord. Pungent dry white from Sauv Bl and CHARD. Also Gamay, Pinot N, or Cab Sauv. Richer, rarer, and more ageworthy *Cour-Cheverny* uses local Romorantin grape only. Sparkling use CRÉMANT de Loire and TOURAINE ACS. Esp Cazin, Clos Tue-Boeuf, Gendrier, Huards, Oisly & Thésée; DOMS de la Desoucherie, du Moulin.

Chevillon, R Burg ★★★ Delicious, approachable NUITS-ST-GEORGES with v'yds in the best sites, esp Les St-Georges, Cailles, Vaucrains, Roncières.

Chidaine, François Lo dr sw w sp ★★★ Producer of ambitious, v. pure, v. precise Montlouis. In 2002 took over CLOS Baudoin (formerly Prince Poniatowski), making similarly styled VOUVRAY. Concentrates on dry and DEMI-SEC styles. AC TOURAINE in Cher Valley. Biodynamic producer.

Chignin Savoie w ★ DYA Light, soft white from Jacquère grapes for alpine summers. Chignin-Bergeron (with Roussanne grapes) is best and liveliest.

Chinon Lo r (p w) ★★→★★★ 89' 90' 95 96' 97 02 03 04 05' 06 07 08 Juicy, light to rich TOURAINE Cab Fr. Drink young; top vintages from top growers can age 10+ yrs. Increasing amount of taut dry Chenin Bl. Best inc: ALLIET, BAUDRY, Baudry-Dutour; Chx de la Bonnelière, de Coulaine, DOM de la Noblaie, de Noire, Charles Pain.

Chiroubles Beauj r 05' 06 07 08 Gd but tiny BEAUJOLAIS CRU next to FLEURIE; fresh, fruity, silky wine for early drinking (1–3 yrs). Growers include Bouillard, Cheysson, DUBOEUF, Fourneau, Passot, Raousset, co-op.

Chorey-lès-Beaune Burg r (w) ★★ 99' 02' 03 05' 06 07 08 Source of inexpensive Burgundy north of BEAUNE. Try from TOLLOT BEAUT or Ch de Chorey (Germain).

Chusclan S Rh r p w ★→★★ 05' 06' 07' CÔTES DU RHÔNE-VILLAGES with steady co-op. Soft textured reds, sound, lively reds. Labels include CUVÉE de Marcoule, Seigneurie de Gicon. Also gd Ch Signac (more tannin, can age) and special CUVÉES from André Roux. Drink most young.

Clair, Bruno Burg ★★→★★★ Leading MARSANNAY estate. v.gd wines from there and GEVREY-CHAMBERTIN (esp CLOS DE BÈZE), FIXIN, MOREY-ST-DENIS, SAVIGNY.

Clairet V. light red wine. BORDEAUX Clairet is an AC. Try Chx Fontenille, Penin.

Clairette Traditional white grape of the MIDI. Its low-acid wine was a vermouth base. Improvements in winemaking produce easy-drinking glassfuls.

Clairette de Bellegarde Midi w ★ DYA Obscure AC nr Nîmes: dry white.

Clairette de Die Rh w dr s/sw sp ★★ NV Locally popular dry or (better) semi-sweet, interesting character. Traditional, sweetly fruited, MUSCAT-flavoured sparkling wine from pre-Alps in east Rhône; or straight dry CLAIRETTE, can age 3–4 yrs. Gd before Sunday lunch. Achard-Vincent, A Poulet, J-C Raspail.

Clairette du Languedoc Midi w ★ DYA A rare white AC of the MIDI. Original identity was soft and creamy; now some oak-ageing and even late-harvest wines.

Clape, La Midi r p w ★★→★★★ *Cru* of note in AC COTEAUX DU LANGUEDOC. In line for own AC. Warming spicy reds from sun-soaked hills between Narbonne and the Med. *Tangy, salty whites age surprisingly well.* Gd: Chx l'Hospitalet, Moyau, La Négly, Pech-Céléyran, Pech-Redon, Rouquette-sur-Mer, Ricardelle, Anglès, Mas du Soleila.

Clape, Auguste and Pierre N Rh r (w) ★★★→★★★★ 95' 97 98' 99' 00 01' 02 03' 04' 05' 06' 07' Supreme 5+ ha Syrah central v'yd at CORNAS, many old vines. Traditional reds, need 6+ yrs. Epitome of unspoilt, relaxed winemaking, always gd in lesser vintages. Gd CÔTES DU RHÔNE, ST-PÉRAY.

Climat Burgundian word for individually named v'yd, eg MEURSAULT Tesson.

Clos A term carrying some prestige, reserved for distinct (walled) v'yds, often in one ownership (esp Burgundy and ALSACE).

Clos de Gamot SW ★★★ 85 89 90' 95 96 98' 00 01 02 04 05' 06 (08) 400-yr-old estate. Ultra-traditional, long-lived benchmark wines. Top ★★★★ CUVÉE Vignes Centenaires (made best yrs only) is outstanding. Micro-*cuvée* ★★★★ Clos St Jean just becoming available.

Clos des Lambrays Burg r ★★★ 90' 95 99' 00 02 03 05' 06 07 08 GRAND CRU v'yd (6 ha) at MOREY-ST-DENIS. A virtual monopoly of the DOM du Clos des Lambrays, in recent yrs more severe in selecting only the best grapes.

Clos des Mouches Burg r w ★★★ Splendid PREMIER CRU BEAUNE v'yd, largely owned by DROUHIN. Whites and reds, spicy and memorable – and consistent. Little-known v'yds of the same name exist in SANTENAY and MEURSAULT too.

Clos des Papes S Rh r w ★★★★ 98' 99' 00' 01' 03' 04' 05' 06' 07' V.gd, stylish 32-ha (18 plots) CHATEAUNEUF estate Avril-family-owned for centuries. Complex, nuanced red (mainly Grenache, Mourvèdre, drink from 6 yrs) and classy white (5–15 yrs), both reward patience.

Clos de la Roche Burg r ★★★ 90' 91 93' 95 96' 98 99' 01 02' 03 05' 06 07 08 Arguably the finest GRAND CRU of MOREY-ST-DENIS, arguably with as much grace as power. Best: Amiot, BOUCHARD, DUJAC, LEROY, H Lignier, PONSOT, ROUSSEAU.

Clos du Roi Burg r ★★★ The best v'yd in GRAND CRU CORTON and a PREMIER CRU v'yd in BEAUNE.

Clos Rougeard Lo r (sw) ★★★★ Small, influential DOM – benchmark SAUMUR-CHAMPIGNY fine SAUMUR BL, and, when possible, luscious COTEAUX DE SAUMUR.

Clos St-Denis Burg r ★★★ 90' 91 93' 95 96' 98 99' 01 02' 03 05' 06 07 08 GRAND CRU at MOREY-ST-DENIS (6.4 ha). Splendid sturdy wine growing silky with age. Growers include: Arlaud, Bertagna, DUJAC, and PONSOT.

Clos Ste-Hune Al w ★★★★ Greatest Ries in ALSACE (00 02' 04). V. fine, initially austere; needs 5–10+ yrs ageing. A TRIMBACH wine from GRAND CRU ROSACKER.

Clos St-Jacques Burg r ★★★ 90' 91 93 95' 96' 98 99' 01 02' 03 05' 06 07 08 6.7-ha hillside PREMIER CRU in GEVREY-CHAMBERTIN with perfect southeast exposure. Five excellent producers: CLAIR, ESMONIN, Fourrier, JADOT, ROUSSEAU; powerful, velvety reds often ranked above many GRANDS CRUS.

Clos de Tart Burg r ★★★★ 90' 95 96' 99' 02' 03 05' 06 07 08 GRAND CRU at MOREY-ST-DENIS. Now first-rate and priced accordingly.

Clos de Vougeot Burg r ★★★ 90' 91 93' 95 96' 98 99' 01 02' 03' 05' 06 07 A 50-ha CÔTE DE NUITS GRAND CRU with many owners. Occasionally sublime. Maturity depends on grower's philosophy, technique, and position. Top growers include Ch de la Tour, DROUHIN, ENGEL, FAIVELEY, GRIVOT, GROS, Hudelot-Noëllat, JADOT, LEROY, LIGER-BELAIR, MÉO-CAMUZÉT, MUGNERET, VOUGERAIE.

Coche-Dury Burg ★★★★ Superb 11.5-ha MEURSAULT DOM led by Jean-Francois Coche and son Raphael. Exceptional whites from ALIGOTÉ to CORTON-CHARLEMAGNE and very pretty reds, too. Hard to find.

Colin Burg ★★★ Leading CHASSAGNE-MONTRACHET and ST-AUBIN family, several members of the next generation succeeding either Marc Colin (Pierre-Yves) or Michel Colin-Deleger (Bruno, Philippe).

Collines Rhodaniennes N Rh r w ★→★★ Exciting Rhône VDP, with character, gd value, gd growers. Also young-vine CÔTE-RÔTIE. Mainly red, mainly Syrah (best), also Merlot, Gamay. Some Viognier (best), CHARD. Reds: Barou, Bonnefond, Chatagnier, J-M Gérin, Jamet (v.gd), Jasmin, Monier, S Ogier. Whites: Barou, Cuilleron, Perret (v.gd), G Vernay.

Collioure Pyr r w ★★ The table-wine twin of BANYULS with most producers making both. Gutsy red wines from steep terraces overlooking the Med. Also rosé and, since 02, white, based on Grenache Blanc. Top growers: Le Clos des Paulilles, DOMS du Mas Blanc, de la Rectorie, La Tour Vieille, Vial-Magnères, Madeloc.

Comté Tolosan SW r p w ★ Mostly DYA VDP. Includes some nice surprises, a multitude of sins, and the whole of the southwest. ★★★ Ch de Cabidos for varietals from Petit Manseng grapes. ★★ DOM DE RIBONNET (Christian Gerber, south of Toulouse) for experimental use of non-indigenous grape varieties.

Condrieu N Rh w ★★★ 01' 03 04' 05 07 (08) Full-bodied, fragrant white of character and price from home of Viognier. Can be outstanding, but rapid growth of v'yd (now 125 ha; 75 growers) has made quality variable (except marvellous 04); often too much oak, alcohol. Best: CHAPOUTIER, Y Cuilleron, DELAS, Gangloff, GUIGAL, F Merlin, A Perret, C Pichon, ROSTAING, G Vernay (esp supreme, long-lived Coteau de Vernon), F Villard.

Corbières Midi r (p w) ★★→★★★ 00 01 02 03 **04** 05 06 07 The biggest AC of the LANGUEDOC, with *cru* of Boutenac. Wild scenery dominated by Mont Tauch and Mont d'Alaric. Wines like the scenery: sun-soaked and rugged. Best estates inc Chx Aiguilloux, la Baronne, de Cabriac, Lastours, des Ollieux, Les Palais, de la Voulte Gasparet, DOMS du Grand Crès, de Fontsainte, du Vieux Parc, de Villemajou, Villerouge. Co-ops: Camplong, Embrès-et-Castelmaure, Tuchan.

Cornas N Rh r ★★→★★★ 78' 83' 85' 88' 89' 90' 91' 94' 95' 96 97' 98' 99' 00' 01' 01' **02** 03' **04** 05' 06' 07' Sturdy, mineral-edged Syrah from 105-ha v'yds south of HERMITAGE. Needs to age 5–15 yrs; more can be drunk after 4 yrs now. Top: Allemand, Balthazar (traditional), CLAPE (benchmark), Colombo (new oak), Courbis (modern), DELAS, J & E Durand, JABOULET (esp St-Pierre CUVÉE), V Paris (promising), Tardieu-Laurent (modern), DOM du Tunnel, Voge (oak).

Corsica (Vin de Corse) r p w ACS Ajaccio, PATRIMONIO, better *crus* Coteaux du Cap Corse, Sartène, and Calvi. VDP: Ile de Beauté. Original light, spicy reds from Sciacarello and more structured wines from Nielluccio; gd rosés; tangy, herbal whites from Vermentino. Top growers: Abbatucci, Antoine Arena, Clos d'Alzeto, Clos Capitoro, Gentile, Yves Leccia, Montemagni, Peraldi, Vaccelli, Saperale, Fiumicicoli, Torraccia.

Corton Burg r (w) ★★★ 90' 91 93 95 96' 98 99' 01 02' 03' 05' 06 07 08 160 ha classified as GRAND CRU, which only a few Corton v'yds such as CLOS DU ROI, Bressandes, Rognets actually deserve. These have weight and structure, others make appealing, softer reds. Look for d'Ardhuy, CHANDON DE BRIAILLES, Dubreuil-Fontaine, FAIVELEY, Camille Giroud, MÉO-CAMUZET, de Merode, TOLLOT-BEAUT. Occasional whites, eg HOSPICES DE BEAUNE.

Corton-Charlemagne Burg w ★★★★ 92' 95 96 99' 00' 02' 03 04 05' 06 07 08 SW and W exposure of hill of Corton, plus a band round the top, all more suited to white wines. Intense minerality and great ageing potential, often insufficiently realized. Top growers: BONNEAU DU MARTRAY, COCHE-DURY, FAIVELEY, HOSPICES DE BEAUNE, JADOT, P Javillier, LATOUR, ROUMIER, VOUGERAIE.

Costières de Nîmes S Rh r p w ★→★★ 03 04 05 06 07 SW of CHÂTEAUNEUF red with spicy fruit and body; best will age, are gd value. Main names: Chx de Campuget, Grande Cassagne, Mas Neuf, Mourgues-du-Grès, Nages, d'Or et des Gueules, Roubaud, de la Tuilerie; Mas des Bressades; DOMS de la Patience, Tardieu-Laurent, du Vieux Relais. Best reds substantial: 6–8 yrs. Some stylish whites (inc oaked Roussanne).

Coteaux d'Aix-en-Provence Prov r p w ★★→★★★ Sprawling AC from hills N of Aix and on plain around Etang de Berre. A fruit salad of grape varieties, both Bordelais and MIDI. Reds are best, esp from Chx Beaupré, Calissanne, Revelette, Vignelaure; les Bastides, la Realtière, les Béates, du Ch Bas. See also COTEAUX DES BAUX-EN-PROVENCE.

Coteaux d'Ancenis Lo r p w (sw) ★ Generally DYA VDQS (220 ha) – right bank of the Loire, east of Nantes. Chiefly for dry, DEMI-SEC, and sweet Chenin Bl whites plus ageworthy Malvoisie; also light Gamay, Cab Fr, and Cab Sauv reds and rosés. Esp Génaudières, Guindon.

Coteaux de l'Aubance Lo w sw ★★→★★★★ 89' 90' 95' 96' 97' 02 03 04 05' 07' (08) Small AC for sweet whites from Chenin Bl. Nervier less sumptuous than COTEAUX DU LAYON except when SÉLECTIONS DES GRAINS NOBLES. Often gd value. Esp Bablut, Haute-Perche, Montgilet, Ch. Princé, Richou, Rochelles.

Coteaux des Baronnies S Rh r p w ★ DYA Rhône VDP hills nr Nyons. Syrah, Cab Sauv, Merlot, CHARD, plus traditional grapes. Direct reds, from gd altitudes, also Viognier. DOMS du Rieu-Frais and Rosière worth a try.

Coteaux des Baux-en-Provence Prov r p ★★→★★★ 00 01 03 04 05 06 From the bauxite outcrop of the Alpilles topped by village of Les Baux. AC in own right for red and pink. White is COTEAUX D'AIX. Best estate is Trévallon, Cab Sauv/Syrah blend, but VDP, for lack of Grenache. Also Mas des Dames, DOM Hauvette.

Coteaux de Chalosse SW r p w ★ DYA, VDP from unusual local grapes. Co-op now merged with Tursan. Mainly found in local restaurants and épiceries.

Coteaux Champenois Champ r w (p) ★★★ DYA (whites) AC for non-sparkling CHAMPAGNE. Vintages follow those for CHAMPAGNE. Not worth inflated prices.

Coteaux du Giennois Lo r p w ★ DYA Small appellation (196 ha) north of POUILLY. Scattered v'yds – Cosne to Gien. Light, potentially powerful red: blend of Gamay and Pinot N; Sauv Bl like a junior SANCERRE. Best: Emile Balland, BOURGEOIS, Paulat, Villargeau.

Coteaux de Glanes SW France r ★★ DYA Lively, gd-value VDP from upper Dordogne features the Ségalin grape. All from 8-grower co-op. Mostly drunk in local restaurants but well worth trying.

Coteaux du Languedoc Midi r p w ★★→★★★ 00 01 02 03 04 05 06 07 A sprawling AC from Narbonne to Nîmes, with various *crus* and sub-divisions. Newer names are GRÈS DE MONTPELLIER, TERRASSES DU LARZAC, and PÉZENAS. Lots of new estates demonstrating exciting potential of the MIDI. Will disappear as larger AC LANGUEDOC, created 2007, gradually becomes established.

Coteaux du Layon Lo w s/sw ★★→★★★★ 89 90 95 96 97 02 03 04 05 07 Heart of ANJOU: sweet Chenin Bl; lush with admirable acidity, almost everlasting. New SÉLECTION DES GRAINS NOBLES. Seven villages can add name to AC. Top ACS: BONNEZEAUX, QUARTS DE CHAUME, Chaume. Growers: Baudouin, BAUMARD, Delesvaux, des Forges, DOM Les Grands Vignes, Guegniard, DOM de Juchepie, Ogereau, Papin (CH PIERRE-BISE), Jo Pithon, Ch la Fresnaye.

Coteaux du Loir Lo r p w dr sw ★→★★★ 02 03 04 05' 07 (08) The Loir is a northern tributary of the Loire. Small but dynamic region north of Tours, inc JASNIÈRES. Potentially fine, apple-scented Chenin Bl, Gamay, peppery Pineau d'Aunis that goes well with pungent cheeses. Top growers: DOM DE BELLIVIERE, Le Briseau, Fresneau, Gigou, Les Maions Rouges, Robinot, de Rycke.

Coteaux du Lyonnais Beauj r p (w) ★ DYA Junior BEAUJOLAIS. Best EN PRIMEUR.

Coteaux de Pierrevert Prov r p w ★ Cool area producing quaffable wines from high v'yds nr Manosque. DOM la Blaque, Ch Régusse, Ch Rousset. AC since 1998.

Coteaux du Quercy SW r ★→★★★ 02 04 05' (06) S of CAHORS VDQS, queuing for AC.

Cab Fr-based wines from ★★ Dom du Merchien, ★ Doms de la Combarade, de Guyot, de Lafage, Lagarde. Worthy ★ co-op.

Coteaux de Saumur Lo w sw ★★→★★★ Sweet Chenin Bl. A tradition revived since 1989 – resembles COTEAUX DU LAYON but less rich, more citric. Esp DOM DES CHAMPS FLEURIS/Retiveau-Retif, CLOS ROUGEARD, Régis Neau, Vatan.

Coteaux et Terrasses de Montauban SW r p ★→★★ DYA ★★ Dom de Montels (who invented this appellation single-handed) and ★ Dom de Biarnès.

Coteaux du Tricastin S Rh r p w ★→★★ 05' 06' 07' Fringe mid-Rhône AC, hit by bad nuclear-plant publicity 2008, lacks depth of quality. Best inc Doms de Bonetto-Fabrol, Grangeneuve (esp VIEILLES VIGNES), de Montine (gd white), St-Luc, and Ch La Décelle (inc white CÔTES DU RHÔNE).

Coteaux Varois-en-Provence Prov r p w ★→★★ 00 01 02 03 04 05 06 07 Sandwiched between COTEAUX D'AIX and CÔTES DE PROVENCE. Gd source of warming reds and fresh rosés; deserves better reputation. Try Chx *Routas*, la Calisse, Miraval, Dom les Alysses, du Deffends.

Coteaux du Vendômois Lo r p w ★→★★ DYA Marginal Loire AC west of Vendôme (149 ha). The most characteristic wines are VINS GRIS from Pinot d'Aunis grape, which also gives peppery notes to red blends. Whites based on Chenin Bl. Producers: Patrice Colin, Doms du Four à Chaux, J. Martellière, Cave du Vendôme-Villiers.

Côte de Beaune Burg r w ★★ →★★★★ Used geographically: the south half of the CÔTE D'OR. Applies as an AC only to top of hill above BEAUNE itself.

Côte de Beaune-Villages Burg r ★★ 05' 07 08 Regional appellation for lesser wines of classic area. Cannot be labelled "Côte de Beaune" without either "Villages" or village name added. Red wines only.

Côte de Brouilly Beauj r ★★ 05' 07 08 Flanks of the hillside above BROUILLY provide one of the richest BEAUJOLAIS *cru*. Try from J-P Brun or Ch Thivin.

Côte Chalonnaise Burg r w sp ★★ V'yd area between BEAUNE and MÂCON. See BOUZERON, GIVRY, MERCUREY, MONTAGNY, RULLY. Alias "Région de Mercurey".

Côte de Nuits Burg r (w) ★★→★★★★ Northern half of CÔTE d'Or. Mostly red wine.

Côte de Nuits-Villages Burg r (w) ★★ 02' 03 05' 06 07 08 A junior AC for extreme N and S ends of CÔTE DE NUITS; well worth investigating for bargains. Single v'yd versions beginning to appear.

Côte d'Or *Département* name applied to the central and principal Burgundy v'yd slopes: CÔTE DE BEAUNE and CÔTE DE NUITS. Not used on labels.

Côte Roannaise Central Fr r p ★→★★ 03 05' 06 07 08 Small AC (220 ha) on the high granite hills W of Roanne, NW of Lyon. Silky, focused Gamay. DOMS du Fontenay, Lapandéry, des Millets, du Pavillon, Serol, Vial.

Côte-Rôtie N Rh r★★★→★★★★ 78' 83' 85' 88' 89' 90' 91' 94' 95' 97 98' 99' 00 01' 03' 04 05' 06' 07' Finest, most Burgundian Rhône red, from S of Vienne, mainly Syrah, sprinkle of Viognier. Rich, aromatic, complex softness and finesse with age (esp 5–10+ yrs). Top growers: Barge (traditional), Bernard, Bonnefond (oak), Bonserine, Burgaud, CHAPOUTIER, Clusel-Roch, DELAS, Duclaux, Gaillard (oak), J-M Gérin (oak), GUIGAL, Jamet, Jasmin, Ogier (oak), Rosiers, ROSTAING, VIDAL-FLEURY (La Chatillonne).

Côtes d'Auvergne Central Fr r p (w) ★→★★ Generally DYA Small VDQS (412 ha). Mainly Gamay, though some Pinot N and CHARD. Best reds improve 2–3 yrs. Best villages: Boudes, Chanturgue, Châteaugay, Corent, Madargues. Producers: Cave St-Verny, DOM de Peyra (sells wines as VDP), Sauvat.

Côtes de Bourg B'x r w ★→★★ 99 00' 01 02 03 04 05' AC for earthy red and white from east of the Gironde. Steady quality. Top Chx: Brûlesécaille, Bujan, Falfas, Fougas, Garreau, Guerry, Haut-Guiraud, Haut-Maco, Haut Mondésir, Macay, Mercier, Nodoz, *Roc de Cambes*, Rousset, Sociondo.

Côtes du Brulhois SW r p (w) ★→★★ 04 05' 06 (08) Nr Agen. Promising independents Le Bois de Simon, Ch la Bastide, Clos Pountet, DOMS Coujétou-Peyret and des Thermes.

Côtes de Castillon B'x r ★→★★★ **98 99 00' 01 02 03 04 05'** Flourishing region east of ST-EMILION; similar wines. Ageing potential; much recent investment. Label changes from 08 vintage. Top chx: de l'A, d'Aiguilhe, Belcier, Cap de Faugères, la Clarière-Laithwaite, Clos l'Eglise, Clos Les Lunelles, Clos Puy Arnaud, Joanin Bécot, Poupille, Robin, Veyry, Vieux Ch Champs de Mars.

Côtes de Couchois Burg ★→★★ 05' 07 08 Sub-district of Bourgogne Rouge at southern end of CÔTE D'OR v'yds. Powerful reds, on the tannic side. Best grower: Alain Hasard.

Côtes de Duras Dordogne r w p ★→★★★ **05 06** (08) BORDEAUX satellite. Top include newcomers ★★★ DOMS Chator, Mouthes-les-Bihan, Petit Malromé, and Chx Condom Perceval, also more established ★★ des Allegrets, du Grand Mayne, Lafon and de Laulan. Co-op (Berticot) could do better.

Côtes du Forez Lo r p (sp) ★ DYA Loire AC (146 ha) nr St Etienne for Gamay reds and rosés. Main producer Les Vignerons Foréziens, also Verdier et Logel.

Côtes de Francs B'x r w ★★ **98 00' 01 03 04 05'** Fringe BORDEAUX from east of ST-EMILION. Mainly red but some white: tasty and attractive. Reds can age a little. New AC from 08 vintage. Top CHX: Charmes-Godard, Francs, Laclaverie, Marsau, Pelan, La Prade, PUYGUERAUD.

Côtes de Gascogne SW w (r p) ★ DYA VDP. Huge production of v. popular wines led by Plaimont co-op and Grassa family (Ch de Tariquet). Also DOMS d'Arton, des Cassagnoles, de Jöy, de Laballe, de Lauroux, de Magnaut, Millet, Papolle, Pellehaut, St Lannes, Sancet, de San Guilhem, Ch Monluc. Also from MADIRAN growers, notably BRUMONT.

Côtes du Jura r p w (sp) ★ DYA Many light tints/tastes. Arbois more substantial.

Côtes de Montravel Dordogne w dr sw ★★ **97' 01' 03' 04 05' 06** (08) Part of BERGERAC; traditionally medium-sweet, now less common. MONTRAVEL SEC is dry, HAUT-MONTRAVEL is sweet.

Côtes de Provence Prov r p w ★→★★★ r **01 03 04 05** 06 07 (p w DYA) Large AC mainly known for rosé; enjoying big leap in quality, thanks to investment. Satisfying reds and herbal whites. STE-VICTOIRE a sub-zone, as well as Fréjus from 07. La Londe and St Tropez coming soon. Leaders inc *Castel Roubine*, Commanderie de Peyrassol, DOMS Bernarde, de la Courtade, Léoube, Gavoty, Ott with Ch de Selle and Clos Mireille, des Planes, Rabiéga, Richeaume, Rimauresq. See COTEAUX D'AIX, BANDOL.

Côtes du Rhône S Rh r p w ★→★★ **05 06 07'** Basic, vast-volume Rhône AC mainly Grenache, also Syrah. Best drunk young, even as PRIMEUR. Wide quality variations, Vaucluse area best: some heavy over-production. 2008 tricky, so stick to small DOMAINES.

Côtes du Rhône-Villages S Rh r p w ★→★★ **01' 04' 05' 06' 07'** Hearty wine from 7,700 ha, inc 18 best southern Rhône villages. Usually reliable, sometimes delicious and v.gd value. Red core is Grenache, with Syrah, Mourvèdre support. Improving whites, often with Viognier, Roussanne added to CLAIRETTE, Grenache blanc – gd with food. See BEAUMES-DE-VENISE, CAIRANNE, CHUSCLAN, LAUDUN, RASTEAU, ST-GERVAIS, SABLET, SÉGURET. New villages from 2005: MASSIF D'UCHAUX, PLAN DE DIEU, PUYMÉRAS, SIGNARGUES. Gd value, quality eg Chx Fontségune, Signac, DOMS Cabotte, Deforge, Grand Moulas, Grand Veneur, Jérome, Montbayon, Rabasse-Charavin, Renjarde, Romarins, Ste-Anne, St Siffrein, Saladin, Valériane, Vieux Chêne, Mas Libian, Cave Estézargues, Cave Rasteau.

Côtes du Roussillon Pyr r p w ★→★★★ **01 02 03 04 05** 06 07 08 East Pyrenees AC, covers v'yds of Pyrénées-Orientales behind Perpignan. Dominated by co-ops, notably Vignerons Catalans. Red is best, predominantly from Carignan.

> **Top Côtes du Rhône producers:** Chx Courac, La Couranconne, l'Estagnol, Fonsalette, Grand Moulas, Haut-Musiel, Hugues, Montfaucon, St-Estève, Trignon (inc Viognier); Co-ops CAIRANNE, Chantecotes (Ste-Cécile-les-Vignes), Puyméras, Rasteau, Villedieu (esp white); Cave Estézargues, Doms La Bouvade, Bramadou, Charvin, Combebelle, Coudoulet de Beaucastel (r), Cros de la Mûre, M Dumarcher, Espigouette, Ferrand, Gourget, Gramenon, Janasse, Jaume, Perrin, Réméjeanne, Romarins, St-Siffrein, Soumade, Vieille Julienne, Vieux Chêne; DELAS, DUBOEUF, GUIGAL, JABOULET.

Côtes du Roussillon-Villages Pyr r ★★ 02 03 04 05 06 07 08 28 villages form best part of region. Dominated by Vignerons Catalans. Best labels: Cazes Frères, DOMS des Chênes, la Cazenove, Gauby (also characterful white VDP), Piquemal, Seguela, Ch de Jau, Mas Crémat.

Côtes du Roussillon des Aspres Pyr First vintage of AC 2003 for reds only. Similar to basic CÔTES DU ROUSSILLON. Rarely found outside area. Based on Grenache Noir, Carignan, Syrah, and Mourvèdre.

Côtes de St-Mont SW r w p ★★ (r) 05' 06 08 (p w) DYA Gers VDQS still patiently awaiting AC status. Created from nothing by *Producteurs Plaimont*, the most successful co-op in the southwest. Gd red from DOM des Maouries. Same grapes as MADIRAN (but with more emphasis on *fer servadou*) and PACHERENC.

Côtes du Tarn SW r p w ★ DYA VDP overlaps GAILLAC; same growers but also ★★ DOM d'en Segur (does not produce GAILLAC AC).

Côtes de Thongue Midi r w ★★ (DYA p w) Dynamic VDP from HÉRAULT. Intriguing blends in preference to single varietals. Reds will age. DOMS Arjolle, les Chemins de Bassac, Coussergues, la Croix Belle, Magellan, Monplézy, Montmarin, des Henrys.

Côtes de Toul E France (Lorraine) p r w ★ DYA V. light wines; mainly VIN GRIS.

Côtes du Vivarais S Rh r p w ★ 06' 07' DYA 700 ha across several hilly Ardèche villages west of Montélimar; AC in 1999. Improving simple CUVÉES, strong Syrah fruit; more robust, oak-aged reds. Note: Mas de Bagnols.

Coulée de Serrant Lo w dr sw (★★★) 95 96 97 98 99 00 02 03 04 05 07 (08) A 6.4-ha Chenin Bl v'yd at SAVENNIÈRES. High priest of biodynamics, Nicolas Joly's wines now below par and fail to match the theory. Decant 2 hrs before drinking – don't chill. Old vintages can be sublime.

Courcel, Dom Burg ★★★ Leading POMMARD estate – top PREMIER CRU Rugiens.

Crémant In CHAMPAGNE meant "creaming" (half-sparkling). Since 1975, an AC for quality classic-method sparkling from ALSACE, Loire, BOURGOGNE, and most recently LIMOUX – often a bargain. Term no longer used in CHAMPAGNE.

Crépy Savoie w ★★ DYA Light, soft, Swiss-style white from south shore of Lake Geneva. Crépitant has been coined for its faint fizz.

Crozes-Hermitage N Rh r w ★★ 99' 01' 03' 05 06 07 Around Hermitage hill: extensive Syrah v'yds (1,355 ha), mix hill/plain. Should be fruity, early-drinking (2–5 yrs). A minority are local; many are technical wines. Gd: Belle, Y Chave, Ch Curson, Darnaud, DOMS Bruyères, du Colombier, Combier, des Entrefaux (oak), Hauts-Chassis, Mucyn, Murinais, du Pavillon-Mercurol, de Thalabert of JABOULET, *Chapoutier*, *Delas* (Tour d'Albon, LE CLOS v.gd). Drink white early.

Cuve close Short-cut method of making sparkling wine in a tank. Sparkle dies away in glass much quicker than with *méthode traditionnelle* wine.

Cuvée Wine contained in a *cuve*, or vat. A word of many uses, inc synonym for "blend" and first-press wines (as in CHAMPAGNE); in Burg interchangeable with *cru*. Often just refers to a "lot" of wine.

DRC The wine geek's shorthand for DOM DE LA ROMANÉE-CONTI.

Dagueneau, Didier Lo ★★★→★★★★ Best producer of POUILLY-FUMÉ by far and a master of stunningly pure SAUV BL. Died in plane crash Sept 08. Son Benjamin now in charge. Top CUVÉES: Pur Sang, Silex and ungrafted Asteroide. Also SANCERRE with small v'yd in Chavignol.

Dauvissat Burg ★★★ Great CHABLIS producer using old methods for extraordinary long-lived Chablis. Cousin of Ravenau. Best: Forest, Preuses, Les Clos.

Degré alcooolique Degrees of alcohol, ie per cent by volume.

Deiss, Domaine Marcel ★★ High-profile grower at Bergheim, ALSACE. Favours blended wines from individual v'yd sites. Gewurz and Ries SCHOENENBOURG are his best wines. Now biodynamic.

Delamotte BRUT; Blanc de Blancs (**99 02** 04); CUVÉE Nicholas Delamotte. Fine small CHARD-dominated CHAMPAGNE house at Le Mesnil. Managed with SALON by LAURENT-PERRIER. *Excellent vintage Blanc de Blancs* (**99 02**).

Delas Frères N Rh ★→★★★ Consistent, gd quality N Rhône house with CONDRIEU, CÔTE-RÔTIE, HERMITAGE v'yds. Top wines: CONDRIEU (Clos Boucher), CÔTE-RÔTIE Landonne, HERMITAGE M de la Tourette (r, w), Les Bessards (v.gd, long life). Owned by ROEDERER.

Demi-sec Half-dry: in practice more like half-sweet (eg of CHAMPAGNE).

Deutz Brut Classic NV; Rosé NV; Brut (**98 99 00 02**). Top-flight Amour de Deutz CHARD CUVÉE (**99**). One of top small CHAMPAGNE houses, ROEDERER-owned. V. dry, classic wines. Superb CUVÉE William Deutz (**96 98** 02).

Domaine (Dom) Property, particularly in Burgundy and rural France. See under name, eg TEMPIER, DOMAINE.

Dom Pérignon CUVÉE **90' 95 96 98' 99** 00 02; Rosé **98 99** 02' Luxury CUVÉE of MOËT & CHANDON, named after legendary cellarmaster who first blended CHAMPAGNE. Astonishingly consistent quality and creamy character, esp with 10–15 yrs bottle-age. Late-disgorged oenothèque vintages back to 59.

Dopff & Irion ★→★★★ 17th-c ALSACE firm at Riquewihr now part of PFAFFENHEIM. MUSCAT Les Amandiers, Gewurz Les Sorcières. Also gd CRÉMANT D'ALSACE.

Dopff au Moulin ★★★ Ancient top-class family wine house at Riquewihr, ALSACE. Best: Gewurz GRANDS CRUS Brand, Sporen; Ries SCHOENENBOURG; Sylvaner de Riquewihr. Pioneers of ALSACE CRÉMANT; gd CUVÉES: Bartholdi, Julien.

Dourthe, Vins & Vignobles BORDEAUX merchant with wide range and quality emphasis: gd, notably Chx Belgrave, LE BOSCQ, LA GARDE. Beau-Mayne, Pey La Tour, and Dourthe No 1 are well-made generic BORDEAUX. Essence concentrated, modern.

Drappier, André Outstanding family-run AUBE CHAMPAGNE house. Pinot-led NV, BRUT Zéro, Rosé Saignée, Signature BLANC DE BLANCS (**02 04**), Millésime d'Exception (**02** 04), superb prestige CUVÉE Grande Sendrée (**99 02** 04).

Drouhin, J & Cie Burg ★★★→★★★★ Deservedly prestigious grower (61 ha) and merchant. Cellars in BEAUNE; v'yds in BEAUNE, CHABLIS, CLOS DE VOUGEOT, MUSIGNY, etc, and Oregon, USA. Best include (white) Beaune-Clos des Mouches, CHABLIS LES CLOS, CORTON-CHARLEMAGNE, PULIGNY-MONTRACHET, Les Folatières (red) GRIOTTE-CHAMBERTIN, MUSIGNY, GRANDS-ECHÉZEAUX.

Duboeuf, Georges ★★→★★★★ Most famous name of the BEAUJOLAIS, proponent of nouveau. Huge range of CUVÉES and *crus*, but is the lustre fading?

Death of a legend

In Sept 2008 DIDIER DAGUENEAU, the Loire's most famous winemaker, was killed when his small plane crashed near Angoulême. He was a huge influence in many parts of France, except, ironically, in his own backyard of POUILLY, where his criticisms often infuriated his fellow producers.

Duclot Bordeaux NÉGOCIANT; top-growth specialist. Linked with J-P MOUEIX.

Dugat Burg ★★★ Cousins Claude and Bernard (Dugat-Py) both make excellent, deep-coloured wines in GEVREY-CHAMBERTIN under their respective labels.

Dujac, Domaine Burg ★★★→★★★★ Gower (Jacques and Jeremy Seysses) at MOREY-ST-DENIS with v'yds in village and BONNES-MARES, ECHÉZEAUX, GEVREY-CHAMBERTIN. *Splendid long-lived wines inc white.* Other top v'yds: VOSNE-ROMANÉE Malconsorts, CLOS DE BÈZE purchased in 2005. Also NÉGOCIANT for village wines as Dujac Fils & Père. Also venture in COTEAUX VAROIS.

Dulong Bordeaux merchant making unorthodox Rebelle blends. Also VDP.

Durup, Jean Burg ★★→★★★ One of the biggest CHABLIS growers with 152 ha. Sold under various names such as DOM de l'Eglantière and Ch de Maligny.

Duval-Leroy Dynamic Côte des Blancs CHAMPAGNE house. 200 ha of family-owned v'yds source of gd Fleur de Champagne NV, fine Blanc de CHARD (**99 00** 02), and excellent prestige Femme de Champagne (**96'**). New single village/v'yd bottlings. *Even half-litre bottles.*

Echézeaux Burg r ★★★ 90' 93 96' 97 99' 02' 03 05' 06 07 08 GRAND CRU (37.7 ha) next to CLOS DE VOUGEOT. Middling weight but can have exceptionally intricate flavours and startling persistence. Best from Arnoux, DRC, DUJAC, ENGEL (now Eugenie), GRIVOT, Lamarche, ROUGET.

Ecu, Domaine de l' Lo dr w r ★★★ 89 90 95 96 97 02 03 04 05 06 07 08 Guy Bossard is a superb producer of biodynamic MUSCADET (esp mineral-rich CUVÉE Granite) and Gros Plant inc sparkling, plus excellent Cab Fr. Tiny production 07 and 08.

Edelzwicker Al w ★ DYA Blended light white. Delicious Ch d'Ittenwiller (05).

d'Eguisheim, Cave Vinicole ★★ V.gd ALSACE co-op for excellent value: fine GRANDS CRUS Hatschbourg, HENGST, Ollwiller, Spiegel. Owns Willm. Top label: WOLFBERGER. Best: Grande Réserve, Sigillé, Armorié. Gd CRÉMANT and Pinot N.

Engel, R Burg ★★★ Top grower of CLOS DE VOUGEOT, ECHÉZEAUX, GRANDS-ECHÉZEAUX, and VOSNE-ROMANÉE in elegant, savoury style until tragic early death of Philippe E. Resurrected as DOM d'Eugénie from 06 vintage by new owner François Pinault (CH LATOUR). Expect richer wines designed for richer people.

Entraygues et du Fel SW r p w DYA ★ Fragrant VDQS. Diminutive appellation almost in Massif Central. Zinging white ★★ DOM Méjannassère and Laurent Mousset's red and rosé, esp red La Pauca (would keep).

Entre-Deux-Mers B'x w ★★→★★★ DYA Improved dry white BORDEAUX from between rivers Garonne and Dordogne (aka E-2-M). Blends of Sauv Bl, Sem and Muscadelle. Best Chx BONNET, Castenet Greffier, Fontenille, Landereau, Marjosse, Nardique-la-Gravière, Sainte-Marie, *Tour de Mirambeau*, Toutigeac.

Esmonin, Sylvie Burg ★★★ Rich dark wines from fully ripe grapes, esp. since 2000. Notable GEVREY-CHAMBERTIN vv and CLOS ST-JACQUES.

L'Etoile Jura w dr sp (sw) ★★ Sub-region of the Jura known for stylish whites, inc VIN JAUNE, similar to CH-CHALON; gd sparkling.

Faiveley, J Burg ★★→★★★★ Family-owned growers and merchants at NUITS-ST-GEORGES. V'yds (120 ha) in CHAMBERTIN-CLOS DE BEZE, CHAMBOLLE-MUSIGNY, CORTON, MERCUREY, NUITS and recent acquisitions in MEURSAULT and PULIGNY. Look for more succulent wines under new generation.

Faller, Théo/Domaine Weinbach Al ★★→★★★★★ Founded by Capuchin monks in 1612, now run by Colette Faller and 2 daughters. Outstanding wines now often drier, esp GRANDS CRUS SCHLOSSBERG (Ries), Furstentum (Gewurz). Wines of great character and elegance. Now biodynamic.

Faugères Midi r (p w) ★→★★ 02 03 04 05 06 07 Leading LANGUEDOC *cru*. Warming spicy reds from Syrah, Grenache, Carignan, plus Cinsault and Mourvèdre. AC in 1982 for red and 2004 for white, from Marsanne, Roussanne, and Rolle. Drink DOMS Jean-Michel Alquier, Estanilles, Ollier-Taillefer, Mas d'Alézon.

Fessy Beauj ★★ BEAUJOLAIS merchant Henry F now owned by LOUIS LATOUR.

Fèvre, William Burg ★★★ CHABLIS grower with biggest GRAND CRU holding DOM de la Maladière (18 ha). Outstanding since bought by HENRIOT in 1998.

Fiefs Vendéens Lo r p w ★→★★★ Mainly DYA VDQS for easy-drinking wines from the Vendée close to Sables d'Orlonne. Range of varieties: CHARD, Chenin Bl, Sauv Bl, Melon (whites), Grolleau *Gris*, Cab Fr, Cab Sauv, Gamay, Negrette, and Pinot N for reds and rosés. Top CUVÉES, esp from Michon/DOM St-Nicolas, are serious and ageworthy. Also Coirier, Ch Marie du Fou.

Fitou Midi r w ★★ 01 02 03 04 05 06 07 Powerful red, from hills south of Narbonne as well as coastal v'yds. The MIDI's oldest AC, for table wine, created in 1948, 11 months' barrel-ageing and benefits from bottle-age. Co-op at Tuchan a pacesetter among co-ops. Experiments with Mourvèdre. Gd estates include Ch de Nouvelles, DOM Bergé-Bertrand, Lérys, Rolland.

Fixin Burg r ★★★ 99' 01 02' 03 05' 06 07 08 Worthy and undervalued northern neighbour of GEVREY-CHAMBERTIN. Sometimes splendid reds. Best v'yds: Clos de la Perrière, Clos du Chapitre, Clos Napoléon. Growers include CLAIR, FAIVELEY, Gelin, Guyard and revitalized Manoir de la Perrière.

Fleurie Beauj r ★★★ 05' 07 08 The best BEAUJOLAIS *cru* for immediate pleasure. Brilliantly perfumed, silky, racy strawberry fruit. Top sites include La Madone, Les Moriers. Look for Chapelle des Bois, Chignard, Depardon, Després, DUBOEUF, Ch de Fleurie, Métras, the co-op.

Floc de Gascogne SW r w Locally invented Gascon answer to PINEAU DES CHARENTES. Unfermented grape juice blended with ARMAGNAC.

Fronsac B'x r ★→★★★ 95 96 98 00' 01 03 05' 06 Hilly area west of ST-EMILION; one of the best-value reds in B'x. Top chx: DALEM, *La Dauphine*, Fontenil, La Grave, Haut-Carles, Mayne-Vieil, *Moulin-Haut-Laroque*, Richelieu, *La Rivière*, La Rousselle, Tour du Moulin, Les Trois Croix, La Vieille Cure, Villars. See also CANON-FRONSAC.

Frontignan Midi golden sw ★★ NV Small AC outside Sète for sweet fortified MUSCAT. Experiments with late-harvest unfortified wines. Quality steadily improving. Leaders: Chx la Peyrade, de Stony.

Fronton SW r p ★★ 05' 06 (08) Red fruits, violets, liquorice associated with these wines earn them the nickname "BEAUJOLAIS of Toulouse". Gd growers include DOMS de Caze, Joliet, du Roc; Chx Baudare, Bellevue-la-Forêt, Boujac, Cahuzac, Cransac, Plaisance.

Gagnard, Jean-Noel Burg ★★★ At the top of the Gagnard clan. Beautifully expressive GRAND CRU, PREMIER CRU, and village wines in CHASSAGNE-MONTRACHET. Also cousins Blain-Gagnard, Fontaine-Gagnard.

Gaillac SW r p w dr sw sp ★→★★★ Mostly DYA except oaked reds 05' 06 (08). Also sweet whites 05' 06 07 (08). ★★★ PLAGEOLES, DOMS ★★ d'Arlus, Cailloutis, Causse-Marines, La Chanade, d'Escausses, Gineste, Larroque, Long Pech, Mayragues, de Ramaye, Rotier, Salmes, Sarrabelle, Ch Bourguet. Gd all-rounders ★★ DOMS de Labarthe, Mas Pignou, La Vayssette.

Garage *Vins de garage* are (usually) BORDEAUX made on a v. small scale. Rigorous winemaking, but a bottle costs much the same as a full service.

Gard, Vin de Pays du Languedoc ★ The Gard département by mouth of the Rhône is important source of sound VDP production, inc Coteaux Flaviens, du Pont du Gard, SABLES DU GOLFE DU LION, Vaunage. Duché d'Uzès an aspiring AC.

Gauby, Domaine Gérard Midi r p w ★★★ Pioneering ROUSSILLON producer. White VDP Côtes Catalanes Calcinaires; Combe Ginestre; red CÔTES DU ROUSSILLON-VILLAGES, Muntada, Les Calcinaires. First vintage 1985: "c'est moi, l'histoire" (of the estate). Also associated with VDP Le Soula. Dessert wine: Le Pain du Sucre; biodynamic.

Gers SW r w p ★ DYA VDP indistinguishable from nrby CÔTES DE GASCOGNE.

Gevrey-Chambertin Burg r ★★★ 90' 93 96' 98 99' 01 02' 03 05' 06 07 08 Village containing the great CHAMBERTIN, its GRAND CRU cousins and many other noble v'yds (*eg* PREMIERS CRUS Cazetiers, Combe aux Moines, Combottes, CLOS ST-JACQUES. Growers include Bachelet, L Boillot, BURGUET, Damoy, DROUHIN, DUGAT, ESMONIN, FAIVELEY, Geantet-Pansiot, Harmand-Geoffroy, JADOT, LEROY, MORTET, Rossignol-Trapet, ROTY, ROUSSEAU, SÉRAFIN, TRAPET, Varoilles.

Gigondas S Rh r p ★★→★★★ 78' 89' 90' 95' 98' 99' 00' 01' 02 03' 04' 05' 06' 07' Robust, authentic neighbour to CHÂTEAUNEUF. Lots of flavour, chewy, sometimes peppery, mostly Grenache. Genuine local character in many. Try: Ch de Montmirail, St-Cosme, Clos du Joncuas, P Amadieu, DOM Boissan, Bouïssière, Cassan, Espiers, Goubert, Gour de Chaulé, Grapillon d'Or, les Pallières, Raspail-Ay, Roubine, St-Gayan, Santa Duc, Tourelles, des Travers, Perrin. Rosés often too heavy.

Ginestet Go-ahead BORDEAUX négociant. Quality controls for grape suppliers. Principal brands G de Ginestet, Marquis de Chasse, Mascaron.

Girardin, Vincent Burg r w ★★→★★★ Quality grower in SANTENAY, now dynamic merchant, specializing in CÔTE DE BEAUNE ACS. Inc DOM Henri Clerc in Puligny. Modern, oak and fruit style.

Givry Burg r (w) ★★ 03 05' 06 07 08 Underrated CÔTE CHALONNAISE village: light, tasty, typical Burgundy from eg, Joblot, LATOUR, Lumpp, Sarazin, THÉNARD.

Gorges et Côtes de Millau SW r p w ★ DYA Improving VDQS country wines: red best. Gd co-op at Aguessac. Growers inc ★★ DOM Du Vieux Noyer.

Gosset Old small CHAMPAGNE house at AŸ. Traditional wine esp Grand Millésime (**99 02**). Gosset Celebris (**98 99 00** 02) is finest CUVÉE. V.gd Celebris Rosé (**03**).

Gouges, Henri Burg ★★★ Pierre and Christian G make sterling NUITS-ST-GEORGES from a range of PREMIER CRU v'yds. Try Vaucrains, Les St Georges or Chaignots.

Grand Cru One of top Burgundy v'yds with its own AC. In ALSACE one of the 51 top v'yds covered by ALSACE GRAND CRU AC, but more vague elsewhere. In ST-EMILION, 60% of the production is covered by the ST-EMILION GRAND CRU AC.

Grande Champagne The AC of the best area of Cognac. Nothing fizzy about it.

Grande Rue, La Burg r ★★★ 90' 93 95 96' 99' 00 02' 03 05' 06 07 08 Narrow strip of VOSNE-ROMANÉE GRAND CRU (since 1991). MONOPOLE of DOM Lamarche now starting to make fine wines again.

Grands-Echézeaux Burg r ★★★★ 78' 88' 90' 93 95 96' 97 99' 00 02' 03 05' 06 07 08 Superlative 8.9-ha GRAND CRU next to CLOS DE VOUGEOT. Wines not weighty but aromatic. Viz: DRC, DROUHIN, ENGEL, GROS.

Grange des Pères, Domaine de la Midi r w ★★★ VDP de l'HÉRAULT. Cult estate neighbouring MAS DE DAUMAS GASSAC, set up by Laurent Vaillé for first vintage 92. Red from Syrah, Mourvèdre, Cab Sauv; white Roussanne 80% plus Marsanne, CHARD. Original wines; well worth seeking out.

Gratien, Alfred and **Gratien & Meyer** ★★→★★★ BRUT NV; BRUT 97' 98 00 02. Superb Prestige CUVÉE Paradis BRUT and Rosé (blend of fine yrs). Excellent quirky CHAMPAGNE house, now German owned. Fine, v. dry, lasting barrel-fermented wine incl The Wine Society's house CHAMPAGNE. Fine vintage CUVÉE (**98**). Gratien & Meyer is counterpart at SAUMUR. (Gd CUVÉE Flamme.)

Graves B'x r w ★→★★ 00 01 04 05' Region south of BORDEAUX city with soft earthy red; dry minerally white more consistent. Top chx: ARCHAMBEAU, CHANTEGRIVE, *Clos Floridene*, Crabitey, l'Hospital, Léhoul, St-Robert CUVÉE Poncet Deville, Venus, Vieux Ch Gaubert, Villa Bel Air.

Graves de Vayres B'x r w ★ DYA Small AC within E-2-M zone. Consumed locally.

Grès de Montpellier Midi r p w Recently recognized sub-zone of AC COTEAUX DU LANGUEDOC covering v'yds in the hills behind Montpellier, inc St-Georges d'Orques, La Méjanelle, St-Christol, St-Drézery. Try Clavel, Terre Megère, St Martin de la Garrigue.

Griotte-Chambertin Burg r ★★★★ 88' 90' 93 95 96' 97 99' 00 02' 03 05' 06 07 08 Small GRAND CRU next to CHAMBERTIN. Less weight but brisk red fruit and ageing potential, at least from DUGAT, DROUHIN, PONSOT.

Grivot, Jean Burg ★★★ →★★★★ Huge improvements at this VOSNE-ROMANÉE DOM in the past decade. Superb range topped by GRANDS CRUS CLOS DE VOUGET, ECHEZEAUX, RICHEBOURG.

Gros, Domaines Burg ★★★→★★★★ Fine family of VIGNERONS in VOSNE-ROMANÉE comprising (at least) DOMS Jean, Michel, Anne, Anne-Françoise Gros, and Gros Frère & Soeur. Wines range from HAUTES CÔTES DE NUITS to RICHEBOURG.

Gros Plant du Pays Nantais Lo w ★ DYA Decidedly junior VDQS cousin of MUSCADET; sharper, lighter. From Gros Plant (Folle Blanche in COGNAC). Best great with oysters but v'yds diminishing rapidly. Try: Batard, Ch de la Preuille.

Guffens-Heynen Burg ★★★★ Belgian MACON and POUILLY-FUISSÉ grower. Tiny quantity, top quality. Also NÉGOCIANT operation for rest of Burgundy as VERGET.

Guigal, Ets E N Rh ★★→★★★★ High-profile grower-merchant: 31-ha CÔTE-RÔTIE, plus CONDRIEU, CROZES-HERMITAGE, HERMITAGE, ST-JOSEPH. Merchant: CONDRIEU, CÔTE-RÔTIE, CROZES-HERMITAGE, HERMITAGE, South Rhône. Owns DOM de Bonserine, VIDAL-FLEURY. Top CÔTE-RÔTIE La Mouline, La Landonne, La Turque aged for raised 42 months in new oak, a break with local tradition to please (esp) American palates; all reds are big volume. Standard wines: gd value, reliable, esp red, white, rosé CÔTES DU RHÔNE. Also full oaky CONDRIEU La Doriane, sound HERMITAGE white.

Hautes-Côtes de Beaune/Nuits Burg r w ★★ r 05' 06 07 08 w 05' 06' 07 08 ACS for the villages in the hills behind the CÔTE DE BEAUNE. Attractive, lighter reds and whites for early drinking. Best: Cornu, Devevey, Duband, GROS, Jacob, Jayer-Gilles, Mazilly. Also useful large CO-OP nr BEAUNE.

Haut-Médoc B'x r ★★→★★★ 95 96 98 00 01' 02 03 04 05' 06 07 Big AC. Source of gd-value, minerally, digestible wines. Some variation in soils and wines; sand and gravel in south, so finer; heavier clay and gravel farther north, so sturdier. Includes five classed growths (eg LA LAGUNE).

Haut-Montravel Dordogne w sw ★★★ 97' 00 01 03 05 06' (07) (08) Locally much-appreciated sweet AC having a quiet revival. Best are Chx Moulin Caresse, Puy-Servain-Terrement, Roque-Peyre, DOM de Libarde.

Haut-Poitou Lo w r ★→★★ DYA VDQS Reds, whites, rosés, and sparkling from numerous grape varieties. Best are Sauv Bl and Gamay, esp from Cave du Haut Poitou (linked with DUBOEUF). Top individual producer: Ampelidae.

Heidsieck, Charles Brut Réserve NV; BRUT 95 96 00 02; Rosé 02 Major Reims CHAMPAGNE house. Excellent Mis en Cave Brut Reserve (97' 01 03). Outstanding Blanc des Millénaires (95' 02) See also PIPER-HEIDSIECK.

Heidsieck Monopole Once illustrious CHAMPAGNE house. Fair quality. Silver Top (2002) best wine.

Hengst Wintzenheim ALSACE GRAND CRU. Excels with top Gewurz from MANN and Joss Meyer; also Pinot-Auxerrois, Chasselas and Pinot N (not GRAND CRU).

Henriot BRUT Souverain NV; BLANCS DE BLANCS de CHARD NV; Brut 95 96 98; Brut Rosé 99 02 Old family CHAMPAGNE house. Fine, fresh, creamy style. Outstanding prestige CUVÉE Les Enchanteleurs (88' 95). Also owns BOUCHARD PÈRE & FILS (since 1995) and FÈVRE.

Hérault Midi Biggest v'yd *département*: 91,800 ha and declining. Inc FAUGÈRES, ST-CHINIAN, PIC ST-LOUP, GRÈS DE MONTPELLIER, PÉZENAS, TERRASSES DU LARZAC among AC COTEAUX DU LANGUEDOC. Source of VDPS of l'Hérault encompassing full quality spectrum, from pioneering to basic. Also VIN DE TABLE.

Hermitage N Rh r w ★★★ →★★★★ 61' 66 78' 83' 85' 88 89' 90' 91' 94 95' 96 97' 98' 99' 00 01' 03' 04 05' 06' 07' Rich, profound, the truest example of Syrah from 133-ha granite-based hill on east bank of Rhône. Both red, white thrive on long ageing over 30 yrs. Abundant, complex white (Marsanne, some Roussanne) best left for 6–7 yrs. Best: Belle, CHAPOUTIER, CHAVE, Colombier, DELAS, Desmeure (oak), Faurie, GUIGAL, Habrard (white), JABOULET, M Sorrel, Tardieu-Laurent. TAIN co-op gd (esp Gambert de Loche).

Hortus, Domaine de l' Midi r p w ★★★ Pioneering producer of PIC ST-LOUP. Also VDP du Val de Montferrand. Elegant wines; reds Bergerie and oak-aged Grande Réserve.

Hospices de Beaune Burg Grand charity auction on third Sunday in Nov, recently revitalized by Christie's. Individuals can now buy as well as trade. Standards should be more consistent but excellent buys among BEAUNE CUVÉES or expensive GRANDS CRUS, eg CLOS DE LA ROCHE, CORTON (red), BATARD-M (white).

Hudelot Burg ★★★ VIGNERON family in CÔTE DE NUITS. Alain H-Noëllat best known but now surpassed by cousin Joel H-Baillet. Daniel Moine-H recently sold out to DOM Pousse d'Or.

Huet Lo ★★★→★★★★ 88 89' 90' 95' 96' 97' 02' 03' 05' 06 07 08 Biodynamic estate in VOUVRAY. Noël Pinguet, Gaston Huet's son-in-law, continues to run the estate. Three single v'yds: Le Haut Lieu, Le Mont, Clos du Bourg. All great agers: look for ancient vintages such as 24, 47, 59 and 64. Also v.gd and ageworthy pétillant.

Hugel & Fils ★★→★★★ Big ALSACE house, making superb late-harvest wines. 3 quality levels: Classic, Tradition, Jubilee. Opposed to GRAND CRU system.

Irancy Burg r (p) ★★ 05' 06 07 08 Formerly BOURGOGNE-Irancy. Light red made nr CHABLIS from Pinot N and local César. Best vintages mature well. Best: Colinot.

Irouléguy SW r p (w) ★★→★★★ 04 05 06 (08) Fashionable Basque wines made to go with rugby football and bull-fighting; less awesome than rival MADIRAN. Tannat-based reds now softened with Cab, to keep 5 yrs. Gd from DOMS Abotia, Ameztia, Arretxea, Bordatho, Brana, Etchegaraya, Ilarria, Mouguy. Excellent co-op, esp white ★★★ Xuri d'Ansa.

Jaboulet Aîné, Paul N Rh Old family firm at TAIN, sold to Swiss investor early 2006, wines now international. Once leading grower of HERMITAGE (esp La Chapelle ★★★), CORNAS St-Pierre, CROZES Thalabert, Roure; merchant of other Rhône wines, notably CÔTES DU RHÔNE Parallèle 45, CÔTES DU VENTOUX, VACQUEYRAS. Modest whites (much Roussanne), drink most young. Prices up a lot, brand fever rising, inc new v. expensive La Chapelle white.

Jacquart BRUT NV; BRUT Rosé NV (Carte Blanche and Cuvée Spéciale); BRUT 00 02 04 Co-op-based CHAMPAGNE brand; in quantity the sixth largest. Fair quality. Luxury brands: Cuvée Nominée Blanc 00 02 04 and Rosé 02 04. Fine Mosaïque BLANC DE BLANCS 02 04 and Rosé 02 04.

Jacquesson Bijou Dizy CHAMPAGNE house. Superb Avize GRAND CRU 96' 98; exquisite vintage wines: white (90 95 96') new *saignée* skin-contact rosé Terre Rouge (03). Corne Bautray, Dizy 02 04, and excellent NV cuvées 728, 729, 730, 731, 732, and 735.

Jadot, Louis Burg ★★→★★★★ High performance merchant house across the board with significant v'yd holdings in CÔTE D'OR and expanding fast in MÂCON and BEAUJOLAIS; esp POUILLY FUISSE (DOM Ferret) and MOULIN-À-VENT (Ch des Jacques, Clos du Grand Carquelin). Mineral whites as gd as structured reds.

Jasnières Lo w dr (sw) ★★→★★★ 97 02 03 05 06 07 08 VOUVRAY-like wine (Chenin Bl), both dry and off-dry from a tiny but v. dynamic v'yd north of Tours. Top growers: L' Ange Vin, Aubert la Chapelle, DOM de BELLIVIÈRE, Le Briseau, Freseneau, Gigou, Les Maions Rouges, Ryke.

Jobard, François Burg ★★★ Small MEURSAULT DOM; classic, slow-evolving wines. Will son Antoine change things? Look out also for nephew Remi Jobard's more modern-style wines.

Joseph Perrier Cuvée Royale Brut NV; Cuvée Royale BLANC DE BLANCS NV; Cuvée

Royale Rosé NV; Brut **99 00 02** Excellent smaller CHAMPAGNE house at Chalons with gd v'yds in Marne Valley. Supple fruity style; top prestige Cuvée Joséphine **96 98 02**.

Josmeyer ★★→★★★ ALSACE house specializing in fine, elegant, long-lived organic wines in a dry style. Superb Ries GRAND CRU HENGST. Also v.gd wines from lesser varietals, esp Auxerrois.

Juliénas Beauj r ★★★ **05' 06 07 08** Leading *cru* of BEAUJOLAIS: vigorous, fruity wine to keep 2–3 yrs. Growers inc Chx du Bois de la Salle, des Capitans, de Juliénas, des Vignes; DOMS Bottière, du Chapon, Monnet, Michel Tête, co-op.

Jurançon Pyr w sw dr ★→★★★ (sw) 97' 03 **04' 05' 06 07 (08)** (dr) **03' 04' 05** 06 Success story from Pau in Pyrenean foothills. Production of dry and sweet wines increasing every yr. Growers: DOMS Bellegarde, Bordenave, Bru-Baché, Capdevielle, Castéra, Cauhapé, Guirouilh, Jolys, Lapeyre, Larredya, Nigri, Clos Thou, de Souch, Uroulat, Bellevue, Cabarrouy, Vignau-la-Juscle. Also co-op esp gd for dry white.

Kaefferkopf Al w dr (sw) ★★★ Since 2006 the 51st GRAND CRU of ALSACE at Ammerschwihr. Permitted to make blends as well as varietal wines.

Kientzler, André ★★→★★★ Small, v. fine ALSACE grower at Ribeauvillé. V.gd Ries from GRANDS CRUS Osterberg and Geisberg and wonderfully aromatic Gewurz from GRAND CRU Kirchberg. Also v.gd Auxerrois and sweet wines.

Koehly, Christian ★★★ Front-rank ALSACE grower at Rodern. Top Ries from GRAND CRU Altenberg de Bergheim and v.gd PINOT GR GC Gloeckelberg. Exceptional late-picked wines esp in 02. Now biodynamic.

Kreydenweiss, Marc ★★→★★★ Fine ALSACE grower: 12 ha at Andlau, esp for PINOT GR (v.gd GRAND CRU Moenchberg), Pinot Bl, and Ries. Top wine: GRAND CRU Kastelberg (ages 20 yrs); also fine Auxerrois Kritt Klevner and gd VENDANGE TARDIVE. One of first in ALSACE to use new oak – now older casks, too. Gd Ries/PINOT GR blend Clos du Val d'Eléon. Biodynamic.

Krug Grande CUVÉE; Vintage **88 90 95 96 98**; Rosé; Clos du Mesnil (BLANC DE BLANCS) **88 90 96 98**; Krug Collection **76 81 85** Small, supremely prestigious CHAMPAGNE house. Rich, nutty wines, oak fermented: long ageing, superlative quality and soaring price. Great vintages in 96 and 98.

Kuentz-Bas ★→★★★ Alsace Famous grower/merchant at Husseren-les-Chx, esp PINOT GR, Gewurz. Gd VENDANGES TARDIVES. Owned by Caves J-B Adam.

Labouré-Roi Burg ★★→★★★ Reliable old-fashioned merchant with additional strings to its bow – such as dynamic new-generation merchant NICOLAS POTEL.

Ladoix Burg r (w) ★★ **99' 02' 03** 05' **06** 07 08 Village at north end of COTE DE BEAUNE, inc some CORTON and CORTON-CHARLEMAGNE. After years in shadow of ALOXE, now undergoing revival in the hands of Claude Chevalier, Michel Mallard, Sylvain Loichet. Exuberant whites of interest, too.

Ladoucette, de L ★★→★★★ **02 03 04 05 06** 07 08 Largest individual producer of POUILLY-FUMÉ, based at Ch de Nozet with expensive luxury brand Baron de L. Also SANCERRE Comte Lafond, La Poussie; VOUVRAY Marc Brédif.

Lafarge, Michel Burg ★★★★ Top 11.5-ha Volnay estate run by vigorous octogenarian Michel and son Frédéric. *Clos des Chênes*, Caillerets and Clos du Ch des Ducs all outstanding, along with fine BEAUNE and POMMARD.

Lafon, Dom des Comtes Burg ★★★★ Top estate in MEURSAULT, LE MONTRACHET, VOLNAY. Glorious white; extraordinary dark red. Also in the Mâconnais.

Laguiche, Marquis de Burg ★★★★ Largest owner of LE MONTRACHET. Superb DROUHIN-made wines perhaps just below the summit.

Lalande de Pomerol B'x r ★★→★★★ **95 96 98 99 00' 01' 04 05'** 06 07 Northerly neighbour of POMEROL. Wines similar, but less mellow. New investors and younger generation: improving quality. Top chx: des Annereaux, Bertineau-St-Vincent, La Croix-St-André, Les Cruzelles, La Fleur de Boüard, Garraud, Grand

Ormeau, Les Hauts Conseillants, Jean de Gué, Perron (La Fleur), La Sergue, Siaurac, TOURNEFEUILLE.

Landron (Domaines) Lo dr w First-rate producer of organic MUSCADET DE SÈVRE-ET-MAINE with several CUVÉES, bottled by terroir, inc ultra-fresh, unfiltered Amphibolite and ageworthy Fief du Breil and Clos de la Carizière.

Langlois-Château Lo ★★→★★★ A top SAUMUR sparkling (CRÉMANT only) house – BOLLINGER owned. Also still wines, esp exceptional SAUMUR Bl VIEILLES VIGNES.

Languedoc Midi r p w General term for the MIDI and now AC enlarging COTEAUX DU LANGUEDOC to inc MINERVOIS and CORBIÈRES, and also ROUSSILLON. Rules the same as for COTEAUX DU LANGUEDOC, with 5-yr period for name-changing.

Lanson Père & Fils Black Label NV; Rosé NV; BRUT **98' 02** Important improving CHAMPAGNE house now part of Boizel Chanoine group. Long-lived luxury brand: Noble CUVÉE as BLANC DE BLANCS, Rosé and vintage blend (**98**). Black Label recently improved by longer ageing and more reserve wines.

Laroche ★★→★★★★ Important grower and dynamic CHABLIS merchant, inc DOMS La Jouchère, Laroche. Top wines: Blanchots (Réserve de l'Obédiencerie ★★★), CLOS VIEILLES VIGNES. Ambitious MIDI range, DOM La Chevalière and interests in Chile (Viña Punto Alta) and South Africa (l'Avenir).

Latour, Louis Burg ★★→★★★★ Famous traditional family merchant making sound white wines from CÔTE D'OR v'yds, Mâconnais and the ARDÈCHE (all CHARD) and less exciting reds (all Pinot) from CÔTE D'OR and Coteaux du Verdon. Now also owns Henry FESSY in Beaujolais.

Latour de France Pyr r (w) ★→★★ Theoretically superior village in CÔTES DE ROUSSILLON-VILLAGES. Esp Clos de l'Oum, Clos des Fées. Best wines usually VDP des Côtes Catalanes.

Latricières-Chambertin Burg r ★★★ **88' 90' 93 95 96' 99' 00** 02' 03 05' 06 07 08 GRAND CRU neighbour of CHAMBERTIN (6.8 ha). Similar wine but lighter, *eg* from BIZE, Drouhin-Laroze, FAIVELEY, LEROY, Rossignol-Trapet, Trapet.

Laudun S Rh w r p ★★ **05' 06 07'** Village of CÔTES DU RHÔNE-VILLAGES (west bank). Mild reds (lots of Syrah), stylish whites. Agreeable wines from Serre de Bernon co-op. DOM Pelaquié best, esp white. Also Chx de Bord, Courac, DOM Duseigneur, Prieuré St-Pierre.

Laurent-Perrier BRUT NV; Rosé NV; BRUT **99 00 02** Dynamic family-owned CHAMPAGNE house at Tours-sur-Marne. Fine minerally NV; excellent luxury brands: Grand Siècle La cuvée Lumière du Millésime (90 96), CUVÉE Grand Siècle Alexandra BRUT Rosé (02). Also Ultra BRUT.

Lavilledieu-du-Temple SW r p w ★ The co-op has closed its doors but intrepid independents eg DOMS du Rouch and de Gazania continue to carry the torch.

Leflaive, Domaine Burg ★★★★ Among the best white Burgundy growers, at PULIGNY-MONTRACHET. Best v'yds: Bienvenues, CHEVALIER-MONTRACHET, Folatières, Pucelles, and (since 91) Le Montrachet. Also MÂCON from 04. Ever-finer wines on biodynamic principles inc selections from elsewhere in France.

Leflaive, Olivier Burg ★★→★★★★ High-quality négociant at PULIGNY-MONTRACHET, cousin of the above. Reliable wines, mostly white, drink them young.

Leroy, Domaine Burg ★★★★ DOM built around purchase of Noëllat in VOSNE-ROMANÉE in 1988. Extraordinary quality (and prices) from tiny biodynamic yields. Also original Leroy family holdings, DOM d'Auvenay.

Leroy, Maison Burg ★★★★ Bugundy's ultimate négociant-éleveur at AUXEY-DURESSES. Sky-high standards and finest stocks of expensive old wine.

Liger-Belair Burg ★★★→★★★★ Two recently re-established DOMS of high quality. Vicomte Louis-Michel L-B makes brilliantly ethereal wines in VOSNE-ROMANÉE, while cousin Thibault makes plump red wines in NUITS-ST-GEORGES.

Lignier Burg ★→★★★ Family in MOREY-ST-DENIS. Best is Hubert (eg CLOS DE LA ROCHE) but watch Virgile L-Michelot and DOM Lucie & Auguste L.

Limoux Pyr r w ★★ AC for sparkling BLANQUETTE DE LIMOUX or better CRÉMANT de Limoux, also unusual *Méthode Ancestrale*. Oak-aged CHARD for white Limoux AC. Red AC since 2003 based on Merlot, plus Syrah, Grenache, Cabernets, Carignan. Pinot N in CRÉMANT and for VDP. Growers: DOMS de Fourn, des Martinolles, Rives Blanques. Gd co-op: Sieur d'Arques.

Lirac S Rh r p w ★★ 98' 01' 03 04 05' 06' 07 Next to TAVEL. Sound-value red (can age 5+ yrs), recently better fruit and body with raised use of Mourvèdre, more CHÂTEAUNEUF-DU-PAPE owners. More focus on red than rosé, esp DOMS Devoy-Martine, Joncier, Lafond Roc-Epine, Lorentine, Maby (Fermade), André Méjan, de la Mordorée, Rocalière, R Sabon, F Zobel, Prieuré Sainte-Sixte, Chx Bouchassy, Manissy, Mont-Redon, St-Roch, Ségriès. Gd whites (5 yrs).

Listrac-Médoc B'x r ★★→★★★ 95 96 98 00' 01 03 04 05' Neighbour of MOULIS in the southern MÉDOC. Grown-up clarets with tannic grip. Now rounded out with more Merlot. Best chx: CLARKE, Ducluzeau, FONRÉAUD, FOURCAS-DUPRÉ, FOURCAS-HOSTEN, Mayne-Lalande.

Long-Depaquit Burg ★★★ BICHOT-owned CHABLIS DOM inc flagship GRAND CRU brand La Moutonne.

Lorentz, Gustave ★★ ALSACE grower and merchant at Bergheim. Esp Gewurz, Ries from GRAND CRUS Altenberg de Bergheim, Kanzlerberg. Also owns Jerome Lorentz. Equally gd for top estate and volume wines.

Lot SW Important VDP often from CAHORS growers seeking wider market. Also from newly planted surrounding countryside, eg ★★ DOMS de Sully and Belmont.

Loupiac B'x w sw ★★ 96 97' 98 99' 01' 02 03' 05' 07 Across river Garonne from SAUTERNES. Lighter and fresher in style. Top Clos-Jean, Loupiac-Gaudiet, Mémoires, Noble, Ricaud, Les Roques.

Lubéron S Rh r p w →★★ 05 06 07' Name cut from Côtes du Lubéron in 2008. Country wines from 2,500-ha v'yds in far SE of Rhône, depend on modern methods. Many new producers. Star is Ch de la Canorgue. Also: DOM de la Citadelle, Ch Clapier, Fontvert, St-Estève de Neri (improving), Tardieu-Laurent (oak), Cellier de Marrenon, Val-Joanis, LA VIEILLE FERME (W).

Lussac-St-Emilion B'x r ★★ 95 98 00' 01 03 05' Lighter and more rustic than neighbouring ST-EMILION. Co-op the main producer. Top chx: Barbe Blanche, Bel Air, Bellevue, Courlat, la Grenière, Mayne-Blanc, Lussac, Lyonnat.

Macération carbonique Traditional fermentation technique: whole bunches of unbroken grapes in a closed vat. Fermentation induced inside each grape eventually bursts it, giving vivid, fruity, mild wine, not for ageing. Esp in BEAUJOLAIS; now much used in the MIDI and elsewhere, even CHÂTEAUNEUF.

Mâcon Burg r w (p) DYA Sound, usually unremarkable reds (from Gamay), tasty dry (CHARD) whites.

Mâcon-Lugny Burg (r) w sp ★★ 06' 07 08 Leading Mâconnais village. Try Les Charmes from excellent co-op or Genevrières from LATOUR.

Mâcon-Villages Burg w ★★→★★★ 05' 06' 07 08 Catch-all name for better Mâconnais wines, which may also use their own names eg MÂCON-LUGNY, La Roche Vineuse, etc. Quality individual growers emerging. Try Bonhomme, Guillot-Broux, LAFON, Maillet, Merlin, co-ops at Lugny, Prissé, Viré.

Macvin Jura w sw ★★ AC for "traditional" MARC and grape-juice apéritif.

Madiran SW r ★★→★★★ 95' 00 01 02 04 05' (06) (08) Tannat-based hearty red. New fruitier style from joint venture between Plaimont and Crouseilles co-ops; but most need ageing. MONTUS and BOUSCASSÉ best known, but Barrejat, Berthoumieu, Capmartin, Chapelle Lenclos, Clos Bastet, du Crampilh, Labranche-Laffont, Laffitte-Teston, Laplace are worthy rivals. Laplace is now making the wines from Chapelle Lenclos.

Mähler-Besse B'x First-class Dutch NÉGOCIANT in BORDEAUX. Loads of old vintages. Has share in CH PALMER.

FRANCE

Mailly-Champagne Top CHAMPAGNE co-op. Luxury wine: CUVÉE des Echansons.

Maire, Henri ★→★★ The biggest grower/merchant of Jura wines, with half of the entire AC. Some top wines, many cheerfully commercial. Fun to visit.

Malepère Midi r ★ DYA Originally Côtes de la Malepère, now plain Malepère AC for reds that combine BORDEAUX and the MIDI. Fresh reds with a touch of rusticity provide original drinking.

Mann, Albert ★→★★★ Top growers of ALSACE at Wettolsheim: rich, elegant wines. v.gd Pinot Bl Auxerrois and Pinot N, and gd range of GRANDS CRUS wines from SCHLOSSBERG, HENGST, Furstentum, and Steingrubler.

Maranges Burg r (w) ★★ 02' 03' 05' 07 08 CÔTE DE BEAUNE AC beyond SANTENAY (243 ha): one-third PREMIER CRU. Best from Contat-Grange, DROUHIN, GIRARDIN.

Marc Grape skins after pressing; a the strong-smelling brandy made from them.

Marcillac SW r p ★★ DYA Best 3 yrs or so after vintage. AC from 1990. Violet-hued with grassy red-fruit character. DOMS du Cros, Costes, Mioula, Vieux Porche and gd co-op.

Margaux B'x r ★★→★★★★ 89 90' 95 96 98 99 00' 01 02 03 04 05' 06 Largest communal AC in the southern MÉDOC, grouping v'yds from 5 villages, inc Margaux itself and Cantenac. Known for its elegant, fragrant style. Top chx: BRANE-CANTENAC, FERRIÈRE, MARGAUX, PALMER, RAUZAN-SÉGLA.

Marionnet, Henry Lo ★★→★★★ 04 05 06 07 08 Influential TOURAINE grower fascinated by grape varieties. Wines include Sauv Bls (top is Le M de Marionnet) and Gamay, esp the unsulphured Première Vendange, Provignage (from ungrafted Romorantin vines planted 1850), and juicy ungrafted Cot.

Marmande Dordogne r p w ★→★★★ 04 05' 06 (08) Rapidly developing AC formerly Côtes du Marmandais. ★★★ Cult wines from Elian da Ros (Clos Bacquey). V.gd: ★★ de Beaulieu (best need ageing). Also ★ DOM Bonnet et Laborde.

Marne & Champagne CHAMPAGNE house, and many smaller brands, inc BESSERAT DE BELLEFON. Alfred Rothschild brand v.gd CHARD-based wines. Improving quality under Boizel Chanoine ownership.

Marque déposée Trademark.

Marsannay Burg r p r (w) ★★ 02' 03 05' 06 07 08 (rosé DYA) Easy-to-drink wines of all 3 colours. Little of note except reds from gifted producers such as Audoin, Charlopin, CLAIR, Pataille and TRAPET. No PREMIERS CRUS yet, but plans afoot.

Mas, Domaines Paul Midi r p w ★★ Big player in the MIDI; own estates and négociant wine, VDP and AC. Innovative marketing. Known for Arrogant Frog VDP range; also La Forge and Les Vignes de Nicole.

Mas de Daumas Gassac Midi r w p ★★★ 95 96 97 98 99 00 01 02 03 04 05 06 07 Pioneering VDP set an example of excellence in the MIDI, with Cab-based reds produced on apparently unique soil. Quality now rivalled by many, eg neighbouring GRANGE DES PÈRES. Wines include new super-CUVÉE Emile Peynaud, rosé Frizant, delicious, rich, fragrant white blend to drink at 2–3 yrs. VDP status. Intriguing sweet wine: Vin de Laurence (MUSCAT, Sercial).

Massif d'Uchaux S Rh r ★→★★ Southern Rhône Village since 2005, promising zone with able growers, stylish, clear-cut, full wines. Note: Ch St Estève, DOMS La Cabotte, Chapoton, Cros de la Mûre, de la Guicharde.

Maury Pyr r sw ★★ NV red VIN DOUX NATUREL from ROUSSILLON. From Grenache grown on island of schist in limestone hills. Recent improvement, esp at Mas Amiel. RANCIOS age beautifully. Also gd red table wines.

Mazis- (or Mazy-) Chambertin Burg r ★★★ 88' 90' 93 95 96' 99' 00 02' 03 05' 06 07 08 GRAND CRU neighbour of CHAMBERTIN (12 ha); can be equally potent. Best from DUGAT-PY, FAIVELEY, HOSPICES DE BEAUNE, LEROY, Maume.

Mazoyères-Chambertin See CHARMES-CHAMBERTIN.

Médoc B'x r ★★ 98 00' 02 03 04 05' 06 AC for reds in the flatter, northern part of the MÉDOC peninsula. Gd if you're selective. Earthy, with Merlot adding flesh.

Top chx: GREYSAC, LOUDENNE, Lousteauneuf, LES ORMES-SORBET, POTENSAC, Ramafort, Rollan-de-By (HAUT-CONDISSAS), LA TOUR-DE-BY, TOUR HAUT-CAUSSAN.

Meffre, Gabriel ★★ Big southern Rhône estate and merchant at GIGONDAS. Owns mid-range DOM Longue Toque. Recent progress, quality can vary. Also bottles, sells small CHÂTEAUNEUF DOMS. Decent northern Rhône Laurus (new oak) range, esp CROZES-HERMITAGE, ST-JOSEPH.

Mellot, Alphonse Lo r p w ★★→★★★ **02 03 04 05** 06 **07** 08 V. fine range of SANCERRE (white and esp reds) from leading grower: La Moussière (white and red), barrel-fermented CUVÉE Edmond, Génération XIX (red and white), Les Demoiselles and En Grands Champs (red). Since 2005 Les Pénitents in Coteaux Charitois (VDP) CHARD and Pinot N.

Menetou-Salon Lo r p w ★★ **02 03 04 05 06 07 08** Revived and expanding AC (450 ha) SW of SANCERRE; similar wines. Best producers: BOURGEOIS, *Clement* (Dom de Chatenoy), Jacolin, Henry Pellé, Jean-Max Roger, Teiller, Tour St-Martin.

Méo-Camuzet Burg ★★★★ V. fine DOM in CLOS DE VOUGEOT, NUITS-ST-GEORGES, RICHEBOURG, VOSNE-ROMANÉE. Jayer-inspired. Esp VOSNE-ROMANÉE Cros Parantoux. Now also some less expensive négociant CUVÉES.

Mercier & Cie, Champagne BRUT NV; BRUT Rosé NV; Demi-Sec BRUT One of biggest CHAMPAGNE houses at Epernay. Controlled by MOËT & CHANDON. Sold mainly in France. Full-bodied Pinot N-led CUVÉE Eugene Mercier.

Mercurey Burg r (w) ★★→★★★ **99' 02' 03' 05' 06** 07 08 *Leading red wine village* of CÔTE CHALONNAISE. Gd middle-rank Burgundy, include improving whites. Try Ch de Chamirey, FAIVELEY, M Juillot, Lorenzon, Raquillet, de Suremain.

Mesnil-sur-Oger, Le Champ ★★★★ One of the top Côte des Blancs villages. Structured CHARD for v. long ageing.

Méthode champenoise Traditional method of putting bubbles into CHAMPAGNE by refermenting wine in its bottle. Outside CHAMPAGNE region, makers must use terms "classic method" or "*méthode traditionnelle*".

Meursault Burg w (r) ★★★→★★★★ 99' 00' 02' 04 05' **06'** 07 08 CÔTE DE BEAUNE village with some of world's greatest whites: savoury, dry, nutty, mellow. Best v'yds: Charmes, Genevrières, Perrières. Also: Goutte d'Or, Meursault-Blagny, Poruzots, Narvaux, Tesson, Tillets. Producers include: AMPEAU, J-M BOILLOT, M BOUZEREAU, V BOUZEREAU, Boyer-Martenot, CH DE MEURSAULT, COCHE-DURY, Ente, Fichet, Grivault, *P Javillier*, JOBARD, LAFON, Labille-Latour, O LEFLAIVE, LEROY, Matrot, Mikulski, P MOREY, G ROULOT. See also BLAGNY.

Midi Broad term covering Languedoc, Roussillon, and even Provence. A melting-pot; quality improves with every vintage. One of France's most exciting and challenging wine regions. ACs can be intriguing blends; VDP, esp D'OC, are often varietals. Brilliant promise, rewarding drinking.

Minervois Midi r (p w) br sw ★→★★★ **01 02 03 04** 05 06 07 08 Hilly AC region; gd, lively reds, esp Chx Bonhomme, Coupe-Roses, la Grave, Oupia, St Jacques d'Albas, La Tour Boisée, Villerembert-Julien, Clos Centeilles Ste Eulalie, Faiteau; co-ops La Livinière, de Peyriac, Pouzols. See ST-JEAN DE MINERVOIS.

Minervois-La Livinière Midi r (p w) ★→★★★ Quality village, only sub-appellation or *cru* in Minervois. Stricter selection and longer ageing. Best growers: Abbaye de Tholomies, Borie de Maurel, Combe Blanche, Ch de Gourgazaud, Clos Centeilles, Laville-Bertrou, DOMS Maris, Ste-Eulalie, Co-op La Livinière, Vipur.

Mis en bouteille au château/domaine Bottled at the château, property or estate. NB *dans nos caves* (in our cellars) or *dans la région de production* (in the area of production) are often used but mean little.

Moët & Chandon By far the largest CHAMPAGNE house and enlightened leader of v'yd research and development. Now owns 1,500 ha often in the best sites. Improved BRUT NV, recent fine run of BRUT vintages esp **90 95** and an awesome **03**. Impressive CUVÉE DOM PERIGNON. Branches across Europe and New World.

Moillard Burg ★★→★★★ Big firm in NUITS-ST-GEORGES, now sold to Sauvestre of MEURSAULT. Family v'yds now largely sold to DUJAC and de MONTILLE in 2005.

Mommessin, J BOISSET-owned BEAUJOLAIS and MÂCON merchant, better noted for reds than whites. Family still own CLOS DE TART in MOREY-ST-DENIS.

Monbazillac Dordogne w sw ★★→★★★★ 90' 95' 00 01' 02 03' 04 05' 06 (07) (08) Rising standards today make this sweet BERGERAC a serious rival to SAUTERNES. Top producers: L'Ancienne Cure, Clos des Verdots, Tirecul-la-Gravière, and La Grande Maison; Chx de Belingard-Chayne, Le Fagé, Les Hauts de Caillavel, Poulvère, Theulet. Also the co-op's Ch de Monbazillac.

Mondeuse Savoie r ★★ DYA SAVOIE red grape. Potentially gd deep-coloured wine. Possibly same as Italy's Refosco. Don't miss a chance, eg *G Berlioz*.

Monopole A v'yd that is under single ownership.

Montagne-St-Emilion B'x r 95 98 00' 01 03 05' Largest and possibly best satellite of ST-EMILION. Similar style of wine. Top chx: Beauséjour, Calon, La Couronne, Croix Beauséjour, Faizeau, Haut Bonneau, Maison Blanche, Roudier, Teyssier, *Vieux Ch St-André*.

Montagny Burg w ★★ 05' 06' 07 08 CÔTE CHALONNAISE village. Between MÂCON and MEURSAULT, both geographically and gastronomically. Top producers: Aladame, J-M BOILLOT, Cave de Buxy, Michel, Ch de la Saule.

Monthélie Burg r (w) ★★→★★★ 99' 02' 03' 05' 07 08 Little-known VOLNAY neighbour, sometimes almost equal. Best v'yds: Champs Fulliot, Duresses. Fragrant red, esp BOUCHARD PÈRE & FILS, COCHE-DURY, DROUHIN, Garaudet, LAFON, Ch de Monthelie (Suremain).

de Montille Burg ★★★ Hubert de M made long-lived VOLNAY, POMMARD. Son Etienne has expanded DOM with purchases in BEAUNE, NUITS-ST-GEORGES, and potentially outstanding VOSNE-ROMANÉE Malconsorts. Etienne also runs Ch de Puligny. Also Deux Montille (white wines) NÉGOCIANT venture with sister Alix.

Montlouis Lo w dr sw (sp) ★★→★★★ 89' 90' 95' 96' 97' 02 03' 05' 07 08 Sister AC to Vouvray on south side of Loire making similar range of wines from Chenin Bl. 370 ha. Currently one of the Loire's most exciting ACS. Top growers inc Alex-Mathur, Berger, Chatenay, CHIDAINE, Cossais, Damien Delecheneau, Deletang, Moyer, Frantz Saumon, TAILLE-AUX-LOUPS.

Montrachet Burg w ★★★★ 1904 35 47 49 59 64 71 73 79 82 85' 86 89' 90 92' 93 95 96' 97 99 00' 01 02' 03 04 05' 06 07 08 GRAND CRU v'yd (8.01 ha) in both PULIGNY- and CHASSAGNE-MONTRACHET. Potentially the greatest white burgundy: strong, perfumed, intense, dry yet luscious. Top wines: LAFON, LAGUICHE (DROUHIN), LEFLAIVE, Ramonet, ROMANÉE-CONTI. THÉNARD disappoints.

Montravel Dordogne ★★ p dr w DYA (r) 02' 04 05' 06 (08) Now AC for all colours, adjoins and similar to BERGERAC. Gd examples from DOMS De Bloy, de Krevel, chx Jonc Blanc, Laulerie, Masburel, Masmontet, Moulin-Caresse. Separate ACS for semi-sweet CÔTES DE MONTRAVEL, sweet HAUT-MONTRAVEL.

Morey, Domaines Burg ★★★ Various family members in CHASSAGNE-MONTRACHET, esp Bernard, Vincent, inc BÂTARD-MONTRACHET. Also Pierre M in MEURSAULT.

Morey-St-Denis Burg r (w) ★★★ 90' 93 95 96' 97 98 99' 00 02' 03 05' 06 07 Small village with 4 GRANDS CRUS between GEVREY-CHAMBERTIN and CHAMBOLLE-MUSIGNY. Glorious wine often overlooked. Inc Amiot, Arlaud, CLOS DE TART, CLOS DES LAMBRAYS, DUJAC, H Lignier, Perrot-Minot, PONSOT, ROUMIER, ROUSSEAU, Taupenot-Merme.

Morgon Beauj r ★★★ 99' 01 03 05' 06 07 08 Firm, tannic BEAUJOLAIS *cru*, esp from Côte de Py sub-district. Becomes meaty with age. Try, Desvignes, Foillard, Gaget, Lafont, Lapierre, Ch de Pizay.

Mortet, Denis ★★★ Ultra-perfectionist Denis made exceptionally powerful, deep-coloured wines in GEVREY-CHAMBERTIN until his untimely death in early 2006. Son Arnaud looks for more elegance. Try new, successful FIXIN.

Moueix, J-P et Cie B'x Legendary proprietor and merchant of ST-EMILION and POMEROL. Company now run by son Christian. Chx inc LA FLEUR-PÉTRUS, HOSANNA, MAGDELAINE, PÉTRUS, TROTANOY. BELAIR acquired in 2008. Also in California: see Dominus.

Moulin-à-Vent Beauj r ★★★ 96′ 99 03 05′ 07 08 Biggest and potentially best wine of BEAUJOLAIS. Can be powerful, meaty, long-lived; can even taste like fine Rhône or Burgundy. Many gd growers, esp Ch du Moulin-à-Vent, Ch des Jacques, DOM des Hospices, JADOT, Janodet, Merlin.

Moulis B'x r ★★→★★★ 95 96 98 00′ 01 02 03 04 05′ 06 Tiny inland AC in the S MÉDOC, with many honest, gd-value wines. Top chx: Biston-Brillette, Branas, Dutruch Grand Poujeaux, BRILLETTE, CHASSE-SPLEEN, MAUCAILLOU, POUJEAUX.

Mouton Cadet Biggest-selling red BORDEAUX brand. Revamped and fruitier since 2004. Also white, rosé, GRAVES AC and MÉDOC AC.

Mugneret Burg ★★★ Noted family in and around VOSNE ROMANÉE. Mugneret-Gibourg and Dr Georges M best. DOM Mongeard-M no longer what it was.

Mugnier, J-F Burg ★★★→★★★★ Outstanding grower of CHAMBOLLE-MUSIGNY Les Amoureuses and MUSIGNY at Ch de Chambolle. Winery rebuilt to accommodate 9-ha NUITS-ST-GEORGES Clos de la Maréchale since 2004.

Mumm, G H & Cie Cordon Rouge NV; Mumm de Cramant NV; Cordon Rouge 98 00 02 04; Rosé NV Major CHAMPAGNE grower/merchant. Owned by Pernod-Ricard. Improved quality esp in relaunched excellent Cuvée R Lalou 98′.

Muré, Clos St-Landelin ★★→★★★★ One of ALSACE's great names with 16 ha of GRAND CRU Vorbourg, esp fine in full-bodied Ries and PINOT GR. The Pinot N Cuvée "V" (04 05), truly ripe and vinous, is the region's best.

Muscadet Lo w ★→★★★ DYA (but see below) Popular, gd-value, often delicious bone-dry wine from nr Nantes. Should never be sharp, but should always be refreshing. Perfect with fish and seafood. Best are from zonal ACS: MUSCADET-COTEAUX DE LA LOIRE, MUSCADET CÔTES DE GRAND LIEU, MUSCADET DE SÈVRE-ET-MAINE. Choose a SUR LIE.

Muscadet-Coteaux de la Loire Lo w ★→★★★ 04 05 06 07 08 Small MUSCADET zone E of Nantes (best SUR LIE). Esp Guindon, Les Vignerons de la Noëlle.

Muscadet Côtes de Grand Lieu ★→★★ 04 05 06 07 08 Most recent (1995) of MUSCADET's zonal ACS and the closest to Atlantic coast. V. badly hit by frost in 08. Best are SUR LIE from, eg Bâtard,Choblet (DOM des Herbauges), Malidain.

Muscadet de Sèvre-et-Maine ★→★★★★ 01 02 03 04 05 06 07 08 Largest and best of MUSCADET's delimited zones. A safe bet. Top Guy Bossard (DOM DE L'ECU), Bernard Chereau, Bruno Cormerai, Michel Delhommeau, Douillard, Gadais, DOM de la Haute Fevrie, Joseph Landron, Luneau-Papin, Louis Métaireau, Sauvion. Wines from these properties can age beautifully – try 86 or 89.

Muscat Distinctively perfumed and usually sweet wine from the grape of same name, often fortified as VIN DOUX NATUREL. Dry table wine in ALSACE.

Muscat de Lunel Midi golden sw ★★ NV Small AC based on MUSCAT, usually fortified, luscious, and sweet. Some experimental late-harvest wines. Look for DOM de Bellevue, Ch du Grès St Paul.

Spot the Muscadet

Frost hit the MUSCADET v'yds in Apr 08, making bottles of the 08 vintage a rare sight. MUSCADET CÔTES DE GRAND LIEU was the worst affected: the crop was cut by 75%. Overall the yield in MUSCADET was just 22 hl/ha, which is low by any standards. Throughout the Loire, 08 is around 20% down: there was some frost damage in ANJOU, SAUMUR and western TOURAINE; hail in POUILLY and parts of SANCERRE, difficult flowering, and drying E/NE wind of Sept and Oct that saved the vintage, but reduced the volume.

Muscat de Mireval Midi sw ★★ NV Tiny fortified MUSCAT AC nr Montpellier. DOM La Capelle the best.

Muscat de Rivesaltes Midi golden sw ★★ NV Sweet MUSCAT AC wine nr Perpignan. Popularity waning; best from Cazes Frères, Ch de Jau.

Musigny Burg r (w) ★★★★ 85' 88' 89' 90' 91 93 95 96' 98 99' 01 02' 03 04 05' 06 07 08 GRAND CRU in CHAMBOLLE-MUSIGNY (10 ha). Can be the most beautiful, if not the most powerful, of all red Burgundies. Best growers: DROUHIN, JADOT, LEROY, MUGNIER, PRIEUR, ROUMIER, DE VOGÜÉ, VOUGERAIE.

Napoléon Brand name of Prieur family's Vertus CHAMPAGNE house now owned by British wine merchant. Seek out mature vintages 95 96.

Nature "Natural" or "unprocessed" – esp of still CHAMPAGNE.

Négociant-éleveur Merchant who "brings up" (ie matures) the wine.

Nuits-St-Georges Burg r ★★→★★★★ 90' 91 93 95 96' 98 99' 01 02' 03 04 05' 06 07 08 Important wine town: wines of all qualities, typically sturdy, tannic, need time. Best v'yds: Cailles, Vaucrains, Les St Georges south of Nuits; Boudots, Murgers by Vosne; Clos de la Maréchale, Clos St Marc in Prémeaux. Many merchants and growers include: Ambroise, L'ARLOT, J Chauvenet, R CHEVILLON, Confuron, FAIVELEY, GOUGES, GRIVOT, Lechéneaut, LEROY, LIGER-BELAIR, Machard de Gramont, Michelot, MUGNIER, RION.

d'Oc (Vin de Pays d'Oc) Midi r p w ★→★★ Vast regional VDP for LANGUEDOC and ROUSSILLON. Esp single-grape wines and VDP PRIMEURS. Tremendous recent technical advances. Main producers: Jeanjean, VAL D'ORBIEU, DOMS Paul Mas, village co-ops, plus numerous small individual growers. Encompasses the best and the worst of the MIDI.

Orléans Lo r p w ★ DYA Recent (2006) AC 90 ha for whites (chiefly CHARD), *gris*, rosé, and reds (Pinot N and esp Meunier) from small area around Orléans.

Orléans-Clery Lo r ★ DYA 30 ha AC sub-region of AC Orléans for simple Cab Fr reds.

Burgundy: négociants or growers

The merchant houses (négociants) dominated the Burgundian market until the 1980s when an ever-increasing number of individual DOMAINES started bottling their wine themselves – often to a very high standard, but never in great volume. Today the top négociants are intent on increasing their vineyard holdings to guarantee quality supply; while successful domaines can only increase their production by buying-in supplementary grapes. So FAIVELEY and BOUCHARD are the largest v'yd owners on the Côte, while GIRARDIN, H BOILLOT and others are competing with substantial offerings of merchant wines. Don't worry about the distinction any more – as long as the wine is good!

Pacherenc du Vic-Bilh SW Fr w dr sw ★★→★★★ MADIRAN's answer to JURANÇON. Dry (DYA) esp ★★★ CH MONTUS and Cuvée Ericka from Laffitte Teston and sweet (age up to 5 yrs for oaked versions from all good MADIRAN producers). (See MADIRAN for growers).

Paillard, Bruno BRUT Première CUVÉE NV; Rosé Première CUVÉE; CHARD Réserve Privé, BRUT 96' 98. New Vintage BLANC DE BLANCS 95' 96. Superb Nec Plus Ultra prestige CUVÉE (95 96). Youngest grand CHAMPAGNE house. Fine quality. Refined, v. dry style best expressed in BLANC DE BLANCS Réserve Privée and prestige Nec Plus Ultra (90' 96) only now fully mature. Bruno Paillard heads Boizel Chanoine group and owns Ch de Sarrin, Prov.

Palette Prov r p w ★★★ Tiny AC nr Aix-en-Provence. Full reds, fragrant rosés, and intriguing whites, r CH SIMONE, now challenged by Henri Bonnaud.

Pasquier-Desvignes ★→★★ V. old firm of BEAUJOLAIS merchants nr BROUILLY.

Patriarche Burg ★→★★ One of the bigger Burgundy merchants. Cellars in BEAUNE;

also owns CH DE MEURSAULT (61 ha), sparkling Kriter, etc.

Patrimonio Corsica r w p ★★→★★★ Wide range from limestone hills in north CORSICA. Some of island's best. Characterful reds from Nielluccio, intriguing whites from Vermentino. Top growers: Antoine Arena, Clos de Bernardi, Gentile, Yves Leccia, Pastricciola.

Pauillac B'x r ★★★→★★★★ 88' 89' 90' 94 95' 96' 98 99 00' 01 02 03' 04' 05' 06 07 08 Communal AC in the MÉDOC with three first-growths (LAFITE, LATOUR, MOUTON). Famous for its powerful, long-lived wines. Other fine chx include GRAND-PUY-LACOSTE, LYNCH-BAGES, PICHON-LONGUEVILLE, and PICHON-LALANDE.

Pécharmant Dordogne r ★★→★★★ 01' 02 04 05' 06 (08) Inner appellation of BERGERAC making sturdier wines from an iron-based terroir. Best: DOM du Haut-Pécharmant, de l'Ancienne Cure, Les Chemins d'Orient, Clos des Côtes, Ch d'Elle, Renaudie, Terre Vieille, de Tilleraie, de Tiregand. New World style from DOM des Costes. Also gd BERGERAC co-op at Le Fleix.

Pernand-Vergelesses Burg r w ★★★ 99' 02' 03' 05' 06 07 08 Village next to ALOXE-CORTON containing part of the great CORTON-CHARLEMAGNE and CORTON v'yds. Ile des Vergelesses also first rate. Growers: CHANDON DE BRIAILLES, CHANSON, Delarche, Dubreuil-Fontaine, JADOT, LATOUR, Rapet, Rollin.

Perrier-Jouët BRUT NV; Blason de France NV; Blason de France Rosé NV; BRUT 98 Historic CHAMPAGNE house at Epernay, one of first to make dry CHAMPAGNE, once the smartest name of all; now best for respectable vintage wines. De luxe Belle Epoque 96 98 99 02 (Rosé 02) in a painted bottle.

Pessac-Léognan B'x r w ★★★→★★★★ 90' 95 96 98 00' 01 02 04 05' 06 08 AC created in 1987 for the best part of N GRAVES inc all the GRANDS CRUS, HAUT-BRION, LA MISSION-HAUT-BRION, PAPE-CLÉMENT, DOM DE CHEVALIER, etc. Plump minerally reds and B'x's finest dry whites. Some want Pessac to go it alone.

Petit Chablis Burg w ★ DYA Fresh and easy lighter CHABLIS from outlying v'yds. La Chablisienne co-op is gd.

Pézenas Midi r p w COTEAUX DU LANGUEDOC sub-region from v'yds around Molière's town. Try Prieuré de St-Jean-de-Bébian, DOM du Conte des Floris, des Aurelles, Stella Nova.

Pfaffenheim ★→★★ Respectable ALSACE co-op. Style can be a little rustic.

Pfersigberg Eguisheim ALSACE GRAND CRU with two parcels; v. aromatic wines. Gewurz does v. well. Ries, esp Paul Ginglinger, Bruno Sorg, and Léon Beyer Comtes d'Eguisheim. Top grower: KUENTZ-BAS.

Philipponnat NV; Rosé NV; Brut Vintage 99 02 Cuvée 1522 00; Clos des Goisses 85' 91 95 96 98 99 Small CHAMPAGNE house known for well-structured wines and now owned by BOIZEL Chanoine group. *Remarkable single-v'yd Clos des Goisses* and charming rosé.

Picpoul de Pinet Midi w ★→★★ COTEAUX DU LANGUEDOC *cru* and aspiring AC, exclusively from the old variety Picpoul. Best growers: AC St Martin de la Garrigue, Félines-Jourdan, co-ops Pomérols and Pinet. *Perfect with an oyster*.

Pic St-Loup Midi ★→★★★ r (p) 99 00 01 02 03 04 05 06 07 Notable COTEAUX DU LANGUEDOC *cru*, anticipating own AC. Growers: Cazeneuve, Clos Marie, de Lancyre, Lascaux, Mas Bruguière, Mas Mortiès, DOM DE L'HORTUS, Valflaunès.

Pineau des Charentes Strong, sweet apéritif: white grape juice and cognac.

Pinon, François Lo w sw sp ★★★ 89 90 95 96 97 02 03 04 05 06 Eco-friendly producer of v. pure VOUVRAY in all its expressions, inc a v.gd pétillant.

Pinot Gris ALSACE grape formerly called Tokay d'Alsace: full, rich white, a subtler match for foie gras than usual moelleux.

Piper-Heidsieck CHAMPAGNE-makers of repute at Reims. Improved BRUT NV and

To decipher codes, please refer to "Key to symbols" on the front flap of jacket, or "How to use this book" on p.10.

fruit-driven BRUT Rosé Sauvage; BRUT **00 02** 04. V.gd CUVÉE. Sublime DEMI-SEC, rich yet balanced. Old Piper CUVÉE Rare (viz. **79'**) still lovely, as is the 99.

Pithon, Jo (Domaine) Lo w r sw ★★→★★★ 95 **97** 02 **03** 04 05 06 07 (08) Jo Pithon no longer involved. DOM now associated with Ch de Chamboureau (Savennières) with Stéphane Derenoncourt as consultant. Best known for v. fine mineral ANJOU Blanc, SAVENNIÈRES and concentrated COTEAUX DU LAYON. Also substantial reds.

Plageoles, Robert Though partially retired, still the arch-priest of GAILLAC and defender of the lost grape varieties of the Tarn. Amazingly eccentric wines include a rare, big, dry white from the Verdanel grape, a sherry-like VIN JAUNE, an ultra-sweet dessert wine (★★★★ Vin d'Autan) from Ondenc and a rare varietal called Prunelard. Also a pure Mauzac sparkler called Mauzac Nature.

Plan de Dieu S Rh r ★→★★ Southern Rhône village since 2005, robust, heady wines from v. stony, windswept plain. Try: Ch La Courançonne, DOMS Durieu, Espigouette, Vieux-Chêne.

Pol Roger BRUT White Foil renamed BRUT Réserve NV; BRUT **96' 98 99**; Rosé **99**; Blanc de CHARD **98'** ★★★★ Supreme, family-owned Epernay CHAMPAGNE house now with vines in AVIZE joining 85 ha of family v'yds. V. fine floral NV, new Pure BRUT (Zéro Dosage). Sumptuous CUVÉE: Sir Winston Churchill (**96 98 02**).

Pomerol B'x r ★★★→★★★★★ **88 89' 90' 94 95 96 98' 00' 01 04** 05' 06' 08 Next village to ST-EMILION but no limestone; only clay, gravel, sand. Famed for Merlot-dominated, rich, unctuous style. Top chx: LA CONSEILLANTE, L'ÉGLISE-CLINET, L'ÉVANGILE, LAFLEUR, LA FLEUR-PÉTRUS, PÉTRUS, LE PIN, TROTANOY, VIEUX-CH-CERTAN.

Pommard Burg r ★★★ **88' 90' 96' 98 99' 01** 02' 03 05' 06 07 08 The biggest CÔTE D'OR village. Few superlative wines, but many potent, tannic ones to age 10+ yrs. Best v'yds: Epenots, Rugiens. Growers include Comte Armand, Billard-Gonnet, J-M BOILLOT, COURCEL, HOSPICES DE BEAUNE, Huber-Vedereau, LEROY, Machard de Gramont, DE MONTILLE, Ch de Pommard, Pothier-Rieussel.

Pommery BRUT NV; Rosé NV; BRUT **82' 98 00** 02 Historic CHAMPAGNE house; brand now owned by VRANKEN. Outstanding CUVÉE Louise (**89' 90' 96**).

Ponsot Burg ★★→★★★★ Controversial MOREY-ST-DENIS estate. Idiosyncratic high-quality GRANDS CRUS, inc CHAMBERTIN, CHAPELLE-CHAMBERTIN, CLOS DE LA ROCHE, CLOS ST-DENIS.

Portes de la Mediterranée Recent regional VDP from S Rhône/PROVENCE. Simple reds; whites more interesting, inc Viognier. Renamed VDP de Mediterranée.

Potel, Nicolas Burg ★★→★★★★ NÉGOCIANT for delicious, well-priced red wines from BOURGOGNE Rouge to CHAMBERTIN and now a matching range of classy whites. His own DOM in BEAUNE came on stream from 2007.

Pouilly-Fuissé Burg w ★★→★★★ **99' 00' 02' 04** 05' 06' 07 08 The best white of the MÂCON region. Wide range of quality and prices available. Stylistic differences according to location. Wines from Chaintré the softest, Fuissé the most powerful, Vergisson for minerality. Top growers: Barraud, de Beauregard, Bret Bros, Ferret, CH DE FUISSE, Merlin, Ch des Rontets, Saumaize, VERGET.

Pouilly-Fumé Lo w ★→★★★★ **03 04** 05' **06 07** (08) Frequently disappointing white from upper Loire, nr SANCERRE. Best round and full flavoured. Must be Sauv Bl. Top CUVÉES can improve 5–6 yrs. Growers include BOURGEOIS, Cailbourdin, Chatelain, DAGUENEAU, Serge Dagueneau & Filles, Ch de Favray, Edmond and André Figeat, Masson-Blondelet, Redde, Ch de Tracy.

Pouilly-Loché Burg w ★★ 05' 06' 07 08 POUILLY-FUISSÉ's neighbour. Similar, cheaper; scarce. Try Clos des Rocs, Tripoz. Can be sold as POUILLY-VINZELLES.

Pouilly-sur-Loire Lo w ★ DYA Historic but neutral non-aromatic wine from same v'yds as POUILLY-FUMÉ but different grape – Chasselas. Ever-diminishing (only 33 ha). Best from Serge Dagueneau & Filles, Landrat-Guyollot, Michel Redde.

Pouilly-Vinzelles Burg w ★★ 02' 04 05' 06' 07 08 Superior neighbour to POUILLY-LOCHE. Best producers Bret Bros, Valette.

Premier Cru (1er Cru) First-growth in Bordeaux; second rank of v'yds (after GRAND CRU) in Burgundy.

Premières Côtes de Blaye B'x r w ★→★★ 00' 01 03 04 05' Mainly red AC east of the Gironde. Varied but improved quality. Top reds labelled BLAYE as of 2000. More changes from 08 vintage. Best chx: Bel Air la Royère, Gigault CUVÉE Viva, Haut-Bertinerie, Haut-Colombier, Haut-Grelot, Haut-Sociando, Jonqueyres, Mondésir-Gazin, Montfollet, Roland la Garde, Segonzac, des Tourtes.

Premières Côtes de Bordeaux B'x r w (p) dr sw ★→★★ 98 00' 01 03 05' Long, narrow, hilly zone on the right bank of the Garonne opposite the GRAVES. Renamed Côtes de Bordeaux: Cadillac from 08 vintage. Medium-bodied, fresh reds. Quality varied. Best chx, all worth trying: Carignan, Carsin, Chelivette, Grand-Mouëys, Lamothe de Haux, Lezongars, Mont-Pérat, Plaisance, Puy Bardens, Reynon, and Suau.

Prieur, Domaine Jacques Burg ★★★ MEURSAULT estate with amazing GRAND CRU holdings from MONTRACHET to CHAMBERTIN. Part owned by RODET, which has improved quality, but not yet to ★★★★ standard.

Primeur "Early" wine for refreshment and uplift; esp from BEAUJOLAIS; VDP too. Wine sold en primeur is still in barrel for delivery when bottled.

Producteurs Plaimont Scrupulous quality control and clever marketing make this the most vibrant co-op in the southwest and perhaps the whole of France. No CHARD or Merlot here, just a brilliant display of local grape varieties.

Propriétaire récoltant Owner-manager.

Provence See CÔTES DE PROVENCE, CASSIS, BANDOL, PALETTE, COTEAUX DES BAUX-EN-PROVENCE, BOUCHES-DU-RHÔNE, COTEAUX D'AIX-EN-PROVENCE, COTEAUX VAROIS-EN-PROVENCE, PORTES DE LA MEDITERRANÉE, COTEAUX DE PIERREVERT.

Puisseguin St-Emilion B'x r ★★ 98 00' 01 03 05' Satellite neighbour of ST-EMILION; wines firm and solid in style. Top chx: Bel Air, Branda, Durand-Laplagne, Fongaban, Guibot La Fourvieille, La Mauriane, Laurets, Soleil. Also Roc de Puisseguin from co-op.

Puligny-Montrachet Burg w (r) ★★★→★★★★ 92' 95 00 01 02' 04 05' 06' 07 08 Smaller neighbour of CHASSAGNE-MONTRACHET: potentially even finer, more vital and complex wine (apparent finesse can be result of over-production). V'yds: BÂTARD-MONTRACHET, Bienvenues-BÂTARD-MONTRACHET, Caillerets, CHEVALIER-MONTRACHET, Combettes, Folatières, MONTRACHET, Pucelles. Producers: AMPEAU, J-M BOILLOT, BOUCHARD PÈRE & FILS, CARILLON, Ch de Puligny, Chavy, DROUHIN, JADOT, LATOUR, DOM LEFLAIVE, O LEFLAIVE, Pernot, SAUZET.

Puyméras S Rh r w ★ S Rhône Village since 05, based on high v'yds, reliable co-op, modest reds, sound whites. Look for: Cave La Comtadine, Puy de Maupas.

Pyrénées-Atlantiques SW DYA VDP for wines not qualifying for local ACS MADIRAN, PACHERENC DU VIC BILH, TURSAN, or JURANÇON. Esp BRUMONT varietals.

Quarts de Chaume Lo w sw ★★★→★★★★ 89' 90' 95' 96' 97' 02 03 04 05' 07 (08) Miniscule (50 ha), exposed hillside close to Layon devoted to Chenin Bl. Almost everlasting, potent, golden wine with strong mineral undertow. Esp BAUMARD, Branchereau, Yves Guegniard, CH PIERRE-BISE, PITHON, Suronde.

Quatourze Midi r w (p) ★★ DYA Tiny cru of COTEAUX DE LANGUEDOC by Narbonne. Reputation held almost single-handedly by Ch Notre Dame du Quatourze.

Quincy Lo w ★→★★ DYA Small area (224 ha) west of Bourges in Cher Valley. SANCERRE-style Sauv Bl. Worth trying. Growers: Mardon, Portier, Jacques Rouzé, Silice de Quincy, Tatin-Wilk (DOMS Ballandors, Tremblay).

Rancio The most characteristic, lingering and delicious style of VIN DOUX NATUREL, reminiscent of tawny port, in BANYULS, MAURY, RIVESALTES, RASTEAU, wood-aged and exposed to oxygen and heat. Same flavour is a fault in table wine.

Rangen Most southerly GRAND CRU of ALSACE at Thann. 18.8 ha, extremely steep slopes, volcanic soils. Top wines: powerful Ries and PINOT GR from ZIND-HUMBRECHT and SCHOFFIT.

Rasteau S Rh r br sw (p w dr) ★★ 05' 06 07' One of best two CÔTES DU RHÔNE villages – robust, assertive reds, esp Beaurenard, **Cave des Vignerons** (gd), Ch du Trignon, DOMS Didier Charavin, Escaravailles, Girasols, Gourt de Mautens, Rabasse-Charavin, Soumade, St-Gayan, Perrin (gd white, too). Grenache dessert wine VIN DOUX NATUREL improving.

Ratafia de Champagne Sweet apéritif made in CHAMPAGNE of 67% grape juice and 33% brandy. Not unlike PINEAU DES CHARENTES.

Raveneau Burg ★★★ Great CHABLIS producer using old methods for extraordinary long-lived wines. Cousin of Dauvissat. Vaillons, Blanchots, Les Clos best.

Regnié Beauj r ★★ 05' 07 08 Former BEAUJOLAIS VILLAGES turned *cru*. Sandy soil makes for lighter wines than other *crus*. Try Aucoeur, DOM des Braves, DUBOEUF, Laforest, Pechard.

Reine Pédauque, La Burg ★ Name of a barge on canal de Bourgogne and a NÉGOCIANT in BEAUNE and ALOXE-CORTON, now owned by Ballande group.

Reuilly Lo w (r p) ★→★★ 05' 06 07 08 Small AC (186 ha) west of Bourges for Sauv Bl whites plus rosés and VIN GRIS made from Pinot N and/or PINOT GR as well as reds from Pinot N. Best: Claude Lafond, DOM de Reuilly, Sorbe.

Ribonnet, Domaine de SW ★★ Just south of Toulouse, Christian Gerber makes pioneering range of VDP (red, rosé, white) from grapes often not seen in the southwest, eg Marsanne and Roussanne.

Riceys, Rosé des Champ p ★★★ DYA Minute AC in AUBE for a notable Pinot N rosé. Principal producers: **A Bonnet**, Jacques Defrance.

Richeaume, Domaine Prov r ★★ Gd Cab Sauv/Syrah. Organic; a model.

Richebourg Burg r ★★★★ 78' 85' 88' 89' 90' 91 93' 95 96' 97 98 99' 00 01 02' 03 05' 06 07 VOSNE-ROMANÉE GRAND CRU. Powerful, perfumed, expensive wine, among best. Growers: DRC, GRIVOT, GROS, LEROY, LIGER-BELAIR, MÉO-CAMUZET.

Rimage Modern trend for a vintage VIN DOUX NATUREL. For early drinking.

Rion, Patrice Burg ★★★ Premeaux-based DOMAINE with excellent NUITS-ST-GEORGES holdings, esp Clos des Argillières, Clos St Marc, and CHAMBOLLE.

Rivesaltes Midi r w br dr sw ★★ NV Fortified wine made nr Perpignan. A struggling but vibrant tradition. Top producers worth seeking out: Doms Cazes, Sarda-Malet, Vaquer, des Schistes, Ch de Jau. The best are delicious and original, esp old RANCIOS. See MUSCAT DE RIVESALTES.

Roche-aux-Moines, La Lo w SW ★★→★★★ 89' 90' 95' 96' 97' 99 02 03 04 05' 06 07 08 A 33-ha *cru* of SAVENNIÈRES, ANJOU. Potentially powerful, intensely mineral wine; age or drink "on the fruit". Growers include: Le Clos de la Bergerie (Joly), Dom des Forges, CH PIERRE-BISE.

Rodet, Antonin Burg ★★→★★★ Quality merchant based in MERCUREY with individual estates Chx de Chamirey, de Mercey, de Rully and DOMS de la Ferté, Perdrix, and now Dufouleur. Part-owner of DOM PRIEUR in MEURSAULT. Also interests in LANGUEDOC and LIMOUX.

Roederer, Louis BRUT Premier NV; Rich NV; BRUT 97 99 00 02; BLANC DE BLANCS 97 99 00 02; BRUT Rosé 99 02. Top-drawer family-owned CHAMPAGNE house with enviable 143 ha estate of top v'yds. Magnificent Cristal (can be greatest of all prestige CUVÉES, viz 88' 90' 02') and Cristal Rosé (90' 95 96 99). Also owns DEUTZ, DELAS, CH DE PEZ, CH PICHON-LALANDE. See also California.

Rolland, Michel Ubiquitous and fashionable consultant winemaker and Merlot specialist working in B'x and worldwide, favouring super-ripe flavours.

Rolly Gassmann ★★ Distinguished ALSACE grower at Rorschwihr, esp for Auxerrois and MUSCAT from Moenchreben v'yds. Off-dry house style culminates in great rich Gewurz CUVÉE Yves (**00 02'**). Now biodynamic.

Romanée, La Burg r ★★★★ **96' 98** 99' **00 01** 02' 03 05' 06 07 08 GRAND CRU in VOSNE-ROMANÉE (0.8 ha). MONOPOLE of LIGER-BELAIR. Now made with flair by Vicomte Louis-Michel L-B. Older vintages distributed by BOUCHARD.

Romanée-Conti Burg r ★★★★ 54 57 59 62 64 66' 71 76 78' 80 85' 88' 89' 90' 93' 95 96' **97** 98 99' **00** 01 02' 03 04 05' 06 07 08 A 1.7-ha MONOPOLE GRAND CRU in VOSNE-ROMANÉE; 450 cases per annum. The most celebrated and expensive red wine in the world, with reserves of flavour beyond imagination.

Romanée-Conti, Domaine de la (DRC) ★★★★ Grandest estate in Burgundy. Inc the whole of ROMANÉE-CONTI and LA TÂCHE, major parts of ECHÉZEAUX, GRANDS-ECHÉZEAUX, RICHEBOURG, ROMANÉE-ST-VIVANT, and a tiny part of MONTRACHET. Crown-jewel prices (if you can buy them at all). Keep top vintages for decades.

Romanée-St-Vivant Burg r ★★★★ **88' 90' 93 95 96' 99' 00** 02' 03 05' 06 07 08 GRAND CRU in VOSNE-ROMANÉE (9.3 ha). Similar to ROMANÉE-CONTI but lighter and less sumptuous. Growers: ARLOT, CATHIARD, DRC, DROUHIN, Hudelot-Nöellat, LEROY.

Rosacker ALSACE GRAND CRU of 26 ha at Hunawihr. Produces best Ries in ALSACE (see CLOS STE-HUNE, SIPP-MACK).

Rosé d'Anjou Lo p ★→★★ DYA Pale, slightly sweet rosé enjoying a comeback in the hands of young VIGNERONS; look for Mark Angeli, Clau de Nell, Doms de la Bergerie, les Grandes Vignes, des Sablonnettes.

Rosé de Loire Lo p ★→★★ DYA The driest of ANJOU's rosés. AC technically covers SAUMUR and TOURAINE too. Best: Bablut, Ogereau, CH PIERRE-BISE, Richou.

Rosette Dordogne w s/sw ★★ DYA Pocket-sized AC for off-dry apéritif wines, eg Clos Romain, Ch Puypezat-Rosette, Doms de la Cardinolle, de Coutancie.

Rostaing, René N Rh ★★★ CÔTE-RÔTIE 8-ha estate with top-grade plots, 3 wines esp beautiful Côte Blonde (5% Viognier) and La Landonne (darker fruits, 15–20 yrs). Accomplished style, led by pure fruit, refined depth; some new oak. Also stylish CONDRIEU and LANGUEDOC DOM Puech Noble (r, w).

Roty, Joseph Burg ★★★ Small grower of classic GEVREY-CHAMBERTIN, esp CHARMES-CHAMBERTIN and MAZIS-CHAMBERTIN. Long-lived wines.

Rouget, Emmanuel Burg ★★★★ Inheritor of the legendary estate of Henri Jayer in ECHÉZEAUX, NUITS-ST-GEORGES and VOSNE-ROMANÉE. Top wine: VOSNE-ROMANÉE-Cros Parantoux.

Roulot, Domaine G Burg ★★★ Outstanding MEURSAULT producer with a fine range of v'yd sites, esp Tessons Clos de Mon Plaisir and PREMIERS CRUS, *eg* Bouchères, Perrières.

Roumier, Georges Burg ★★★★ Reference DOM for BONNES-MARES and other brilliant CHAMBOLLE wines in capable hands of Christophe R. Long-lived wines but still attractive early.

Rousseau, Domaine Armand Burg ★★★★ Grower famous for CHAMBERTIN, etc, of highest quality. Wines are intense (not deep-coloured), long-lived, mostly GRAND CRU. Brilliant CLOS ST JACQUES.

Roussette de Savoie w ★★ DYA Tastiest fresh white from south of Lake Geneva.

Roussillon Midi Top region for VDNS (eg MAURY, RIVESALTES, BANYULS). Younger vintage wines are competing with aged RANCIO wines. See CÔTES DU ROUSSILLON (and CÔTES DU ROUSSILLON-VILLAGES), COLLIOURE, for table wines and VDP Côtes Catalanes. Now included in AC LANGUEDOC.

Ruchottes-Chambertin Burg r ★★★★ **88' 90' 91 93' 95 96' 98 99' 00 01** 02' 03 05' 06 07 08 GRAND CRU neighbour of CHAMBERTIN. Similar splendid, lasting wine of great finesse. Top growers: MUGNERET, ROUMIER, ROUSSEAU.

Ruinart "R" de Ruinart BRUT NV; Ruinart Rosé NV; "R" de Ruinart BRUT (**98 99**). Oldest CHAMPAGNE house, owned by MOËT-Hennessy. Already high standards should go higher still with talented new cellar master (since 2007). Prestige Dom Ruinart is one of the 2 best vintage BLANC DE BLANCS in CHAMPAGNE (viz. **88' 95 96**). DR Rosé also v. special (88 **90'**).

Rully Burg r w (sp) ★★ (r) **05' 07** 08 (w) **06 07 08** CÔTE CHALONNAISE village. Still white and red are light but tasty. *Gd value, esp white*. Growers include Delorme, Devevey, FAIVELEY, Dom de la Folie, Jacqueson, A RODET.

Sables du Golfe du Lion Midi p r w ★ DYA VDP from Mediterranean sand-dunes: esp Gris de Gris from Carignan, Grenache, Cinsault. Small estates beginning to compete with giant Listel.

Sablet S Rh r w (p) ★★ **04' 05' 06' 07** Improving CÔTES DU RHÔNE village, often suave, cleanly fruited reds, esp DOMS de Boisson, Cabasse, Espiers, Les Goubert, Piaugier, de Verquière. Gd full whites – apéritif or food.

St-Amour Beauj r ★★ **06 07 08** Northernmost *cru* of BEAUJOLAIS: light, fruity, irresistible (esp on 14 Feb). Growers to try: Janin, Patissier, Revillon.

St-Aubin Burg w r ★★★ (w) **02' 04 05' 06 07** 08 (r) **02' 03 05' 06 07** 08 Understated neighbour of CHASSAGNE-MONTRACHET. Several Premiers Crus: light, firm, quite stylish wines; fair prices. Top growers: J C Bachelet, COLIN, JADOT, Lamy, Lamy-Pillot, H Prudhon, Ramonet.

St-Bris Burg w ★ DYA Neighbour to CHABLIS. Unique AC for Sauv Bl in Burgundy. Fresh, lively, worth keeping from J-H Goisot.

St-Chinian Midi r ★→★★★ **01 02 03 04 05** 06 07 08 Hilly area of growing reputation in COTEAUX DU LANGUEDOC. AC since 1982 for red, and for white since 2005, plus new *crus* Berlou and Roquebrun. Tasty southern reds, based on Syrah, Grenache, Carignan. Gd co-ops Berlou, Roquebrun; Ch de Viranel, Doms Canet Valette, Madura, Rimbaud, Navarre.

St-Emilion B'x r ★★→★★★★★ 89' 90' 94 95 96 98' 00' 01 03 04 05' 08 Large, Merlot-dominated district on Bordeaux's Right Bank. ST-EMILION GRAND CRU CLASSÉ AC the top designation. Warm, full, rounded style; some firm and long-lived. Top chx: ANGÉLUS, AUSONE, CANON, CHEVAL BLANC, FIGEAC, MAGDELAINE, PAVIE. Also *garagistes* LA MONDOTTE and VALANDRAUD. Gd co-op.

St-Estèphe B'x r ★★→★★★★ **88' 89' 90' 93 94 95' 96' 98 99** 00' 01 02 03 04 05' 06 08 Most northerly communal AC in the MÉDOC. Solid, structured wines. Top chx: COS D'ESTOURNEL, MONTROSE, CALON-SÉGUR. Also many gd unclassified estates, eg HAUT-MARBUZET, ORMES-DE-PEZ, DE PEZ, PHÉLAN-SÉGUR.

St-Gall BRUT NV; Extra BRUT NV; BRUT BLANC DE BLANCS NV; BRUT Rosé NV; BRUT BLANC DE BLANCS **99 00** 02; Cuvée Orpale BLANC DE BLANCS **95 96' 98**. Brand used by Union-Champagne co-op: top CHAMPAGNE growers' co-op at AVIZE. Fine value Pierre Vaudon NV and excellent BLANCS DE BLANCS Orpale (**95' 96**).

St-Georges-St-Emilion B'x r ★★ **98 00' 01 03 05'** Tiny ST-EMILION satellite. Usually gd quality. Best chx: Calon, Macquin-St-G, Tour du Pas-St-Georges, Vieux Montaiguillon.

St-Gervais S Rh r (w, p) ★ **06' 07'** west bank Rhône village. Steady co-op, local star is excellent, long-lived (10+ yrs) DOM Ste-Anne red (marked Mourvèdre flavours); white includes gd Viognier. Also DOM Clavel.

St-Jean de Minervois Min w sw ★★ Fine sweet VDN MUSCAT. Much recent improvement, esp from Dom de Barroubio, Michel Sigé, village co-op.

St-Joseph N Rh r w ★★ **90' 99' 01' 03' 05' 06' 07 03** AC running length of N Rhône (65 km). Delicious, red-fruited wines around Tournon in S; elsewhere quality mixed, more new oak used. More structure, better wines than CROZES-HERMITAGE, esp from CHAPOUTIER (Les Granits), Gonon, B Gripa, GUIGAL (Lieu-dit St-Joseph); also CHAVE, Chêne, Chèze, Courbis, Coursodon, Cuilleron, DELAS, J & E Durand, B Faurie, P Faury, Gaillard, JABOULET, Monier, Paret, A Perret, F Villard. Gd wholesome white (mainly Marsanne, drink with food), esp Barge, Chapoutier Granits, Cuilleron, Gonon, B Gripa, Faury, A Perret.

St-Julien B'x r ★★★→★★★★ 88' 89' 90' 93 94 95' 96' 98 99 00' 01 02 03 04 05' 06 07 08 Mid-MÉDOC communal AC with 11 classified (1855) estates, inc 3 LÉOVILLES, BEYCHEVELLE, DUCRU-BEAUCAILLOU, GRUAUD-LAROSE, etc. The epitome of harmonious, fragrant and savoury red wine.

St-Nicolas-de-Bourgueil Lo r p ★→★★★ 89' 90' 95 96' 97 02' 03 04 05' 06 07 08 Companion appellation to BOURGUEIL producing identical wines from Cab Fr. Ranges from easy drinking to ageworthy. More tannic and less supple than Chinon. Try: Yannick Amirault, Cognard, Lorieux, Frédéric Mabileau-Rezé, Taluau-Foltzenlogel, Gerard Vallée.

St-Péray N Rh w sp ★★ 04' 05' 06' 07' 08 White Rhône (mainly Marsanne) from granite hillside v'yds. Some MÉTHODE CHAMPENOISE – worth trying. Still white gd flinty style, can age. Top names: S Chaboud, CHAPOUTIER, CLAPE, Colombo, B Gripa (v.gd), J-L Thiers, TAIN co-op, du Tunnel, Voge.

St-Pourçain Central Fr r p w ★→★★ DYA VDQS Agreeable quaffers from the Allier. Light red and rosé from Gamay and/or Pinot N, white from Tressalier and/or CHARD (v. popular), or Sauv Bl. A strong candidate for AC status. Growers: Dom de Bellevue, Grosbot-Barbara, Pétillat, Ray, and gd co-op (Vignerons de St-Pourçain) with range of styles, inc drink-me-up CUVÉE Ficelle.

St-Romain Burg w r ★★ (w) 05' 06 07 08 *Crisp, mineral whites* and clean-cut reds from vines tucked away in the back of the CÔTE DE BEAUNE. PREMIER CRU v'yds expected soon. Alain Gras best. Also Buisson, De Chassorney.

St-Sardos SW VDQS nr Montauban r p w DYA Worthy co-op has only one competitor, its founder Dom de la Tucayne. Syrah-based wines worth trying.

St-Véran Burg w ★★ 05' 06 07 08 AC loosely surrounding POUILLY-FUISSÉ with variable results depending on soil and producer. DUBOEUF, Deux Roches, Poncetys for value, Cordier, Corsin, Merlin for top quality.

Ste-Croix-du-Mont B'x w SW ★★ 97' 98 99' 01 02 03' 05' 07 (08) Sweet white AC facing SAUTERNES across the river Garonne. Well worth trying, esp Chx Crabitan-Bellevue, Loubens, du Mont, Pavillon, la Rame.

Ste-Victoire Prov r p ★★ New sub-zone of CÔTES de PROVENCE from the southern slopes of the Montagne Ste-Victoire. Dramatic scenery as well as gd wine. Try Mas de Cadenet, Mauvan.

Salon ★★★★ The original BLANC DE BLANCS CHAMPAGNE, from LE MESNIL in the Côte des Blancs. Awesome reputation for long-lived wines – in truth sometimes inconsistent but on song recently, viz. **90 96'**.

Sancerre Lo w (r p) ★→★★★ Still benchmark for Sauv Bl, often more aromatic and vibrant than POUILLY-FUMÉ, its neighbour across the Loire. Top wines can age 8+ yrs. Top growers now making remarkable reds (Pinot N). Sancerre rosé rarely worth the money. Occasional sweet VENDANGES TARDIVES (VDT). Best include: Gérard Boulay, BOURGEOIS, Cotat, François Crochet, Lucien Crochet, André Dezat, ALPHONSE MELLOT, Mollet, *Vincent Pinard*, Pascal Reverdy, Claude Riffault, Jean-Max Roger, Vacheron, André Vatan.

Santenay Burg r (w) ★★★ 99' 02' 03 05' 06 07 08 Sturdy reds from village S of CHASSAGNE-MONTRACHET. Best v'yds: La Comme, Les Gravières, Clos de Tavannes. Top growers: GIRARDIN, Lequin-Roussot, Muzard, Vincent. Watch Dom Jessiaume

Saumur Lo r w p sp ★→★★★ 02' 03 04 05' 06 07 08 Umbrella AC for light whites plus more serious, particularly from SAUMUR-CHAMPIGNY zone; easy-drinking reds, pleasant rosés, pungent CRÉMANT and SAUMUR MOUSSEUX. Producers include: BOUVET-LADUBAY, Antoine Foucault, CLOS ROUGEARD, René-Hugues Gay, Guiberteau, Doms DES CHAMPS FLEURIS/Retiveau-Retif, Paleine, St-Just; CH DE VILLENEUVE, Cave des Vignerons de Saumur.

Saumur-Champigny Lo r ★★→★★★ 95 96' 97 02' 03 04 05' 06 07 08 Popular 9-commune AC for quality Cab Fr, ageing nicely in gd vintages. Look for Chx de

Targé, DE VILLENEUVE; Clos Cristal, CLOS ROUGEARD; Doms CHAMPS FLEURIS, de la Cune, Filliatreau, Legrand, Nerleux, Roches Neuves, St-Just, Antoine Sanzay, Val Brun; Cave des Vignerons de Saumur-St-Cyr-en-Bourg.

Saussignac Dordogne w sw ★★→★★★ 03' 04 05' 06 07 (08) Similar to but with a touch more acidity than MONBAZILLAC. Fully sweet since 2004.Best: ★★★ DOM de Richard, Lestevénie, La Maurigne, Les Miaudoux, Clos d'Yvigne, ★★ Chx Le Chabrier, Court-les-Mûts, Le Payral, Le Tap, Tourmentine.

Sauternes B'x w sw ★★→★★★★ 83' 86' 88' 89' 90' 95 96 97' 98 99' 01' 02 03' 05' 07 (08) District of 5 villages (inc BARSAC) that make France's best sweet wine, strong (14%+ alcohol), luscious and golden, demanding to be aged 10 yrs. Still underpriced compared to red equivalents. Top CHX: D'YQUEM, GUIRAUD, LAFAURIE-PEYRAGUEY, RIEUSSEC, SUDUIRAUT, LA TOUR BLANCHE, etc. Dry wines cannot be sold as Sauternes. 05s are exceptional, must have.

Sauzet, Etienne Burg ★★★ Potentially outstanding PULIGNY grower and merchant. Does not always age well. Look out for Combettes, BÂTARD-MONTRACHET.

Savennières Lo w dr sw ★★★→★★★★ 89' 90' 93 95 96' 97' 99 02' 03 04 05' 06 07 08 Small ANJOU district for pungent, extremely mineral, long-lived whites. BAUMARD, Closel, Ch de Coulaine (see CH PIERRE-BISE), Ch d'Epiré, Yves Guigniard, Dom Laureau du Clos Frémur, Eric Morgat, Vincent Ogereau, Tijou. Top sites: COULÉE DE SERRANT, ROCHE-AUX-MOINES, Clos du Papillon.

Savigny-lès-Beaune Burg r (w) ★★★ 99' 02' 03 05' 07 08 Important village next to BEAUNE; similar mid-weight wines, often deliciously lively, fruity. Top v'yds: Dominode, Guettes, Lavières, Marconnets, Vergelesses; growers include: BIZE, Camus, CHANDON DE BRIAILLES, CLAIR, Ecard, Girard, LEROY, Pavelot, TOLLOT-BEAUT.

Savoie E France r w sp ★★ DYA Alpine area with light, dry wines like some Swiss or minor Loires. APREMONT, CRÉPY, and SEYSSEL are best-known whites; ROUSSETTE is more interesting. Also gd MONDEUSE red.

Schlossberg ALSACE GRAND CRU of 80 ha at Kientzheim famed since 15th century. Glorious Ries from Faller.

Schlumberger, Domaines ★→★★★ Vast and top-quality ALSACE DOM at Guebwiller owning approx 1% of all ALSACE v'yds. Holdings in GRANDS CRUS Kitterlé, Kessler, Saering, and Spiegel. Range includes rare Ries, signature CUVÉE Ernest, and, latest addition, PINOT GR GRAND CRU Kessler.

Schlumberger, Robert de Lo SAUMUR sparkling; by Austrian method. Delicate.

Southwest growers to watch in 2010

Dom Laurent Mousset (Entraygues-et-du-Fel): working with Roussillon colleague to produce more serious wine.

Dom Peyres-Roses (Gaillac): recently installed ultra-bio growers, note esp a beautifully-balanced sweet white.

Ch Bourguet (Gaillac): improvement continues throughout the range.

Dom Boujac (Fronton): accent on typicity.

Ch Croze-de-Pys (Cahors): equally successful in traditional and more modern wines.

Ch Marnières (Bergerac): rising star of this large appellation.

Ch Jonc Blanc (Montravel): original winemaker working outside the appellation.

Dom Sédouprat (Côtes de Gascogne): good reds, unusual in this region.

Dom Barbazan (Madiran): small but the grower is talented.

Dom Ametzia (Irouléguy): a shepherd-VIGNERON whose wines are even better than the ewes' milk that goes into the local cheese.

Dom Larrédya (Jurançon): still a rising star.

Schoenenbourg V. rich successful Riquewihr GRAND CRU (ALSACE): PINOT GR, Ries, v. fine VENDANGE TARDIVE and SÉLECTION DES GRAINS NOBLES. Esp from DEISS and DOPFF AU MOULIN. Also v.gd MUSCAT.

Schoffit, Domaine ★★→★★★ Colmar ALSACE house with GRAND CRU RANGEN PINOT GR, Gewurz of top quality. Chasselas is unusual everyday delight.

Schröder & Schÿler Old Bordeaux merchant, owner of CH KIRWAN.

Sciacarello Indigenous Corsican grape variety, for red and rosé.

Sec Literally means dry, though CHAMPAGNE so called is medium-sweet (and better at breakfast, teatime, and weddings than BRUT).

Séguret S Rh r w ★★ **05' 06' 07'** Picture-postcard hillside village nr GIGONDAS. Direct, quite full reds can be peppery; clear-fruited whites. Esp Ch La Courançonne, DOMS de Cabasse, Le Camassot, J David (organic), Garancière, Mourchon (robust), Pourra, Soleil Romain.

Sélection des Grains Nobles Term coined by HUGEL for ALSACE equivalent to German Beerenauslese, and since 1984 subject to v. strict regulations. GRAINS NOBLES are individual grapes with "noble rot".

Sérafin Burg ★★★ Christian S has gained a cult following for his intense GEVREY-CHAMBERTIN VIEILLES VIGNES, CHARMES-CHAMBERTIN. Plenty of new wood here.

Seyssel Savoie w sp ★★ NV Delicate white, pleasant sparkling. eg Corbonod.

Sichel & Co One of Bordeaux's most respected merchant houses, run by 5 brothers: interests in CH D'ANGLUDET and PALMER, in CORBIÈRES, and as Bordeaux merchants (Sirius a top brand).

Signargues, Plateau de ★→★★ New CÔTES DU RHÔNE village from 2005 in 4 areas between Avignon and Nîmes (west bank). Light, fruity reds with some tannic impulse. Note: Ch Haut-Musiel, DOM Valériane.

Sipp, Jean & Louis ★★ ALSACE growers in Ribeauvillé (Louis also a NÉGOCIANT). Both make v.gd Ries GRAND CRU Kirchberg. Jean's is youthful elegance; Louis's is firmer when mature. V.gd Gewurz from Louis, esp GRAND CRU Osterberg.

Sipp-Mack ★★→★★★ Excellent ALSACE dom of 20 ha at Hunnawihr. Great Ries from GRANDS CRUS ROSACKER and Osterberg; also v.gd PINOT GR.

Sorg, Bruno ★★→★★★ First-class small ALSACE grower at Eguisheim for GRANDS CRUS Florimont (Ries) and PFERSIGBERG (MUSCAT). Also v.gd Auxerrois.

Sur Lie "On the lees". MUSCADET is often bottled straight from the vat, for maximum zest and character.

Tâche, La Burg r ★★★★ **78' 85' 88' 89' 90'** 93' 95 96' **97** 98 99' **00** 01 02' 03 05' 06 07 08 A 6-ha (1,500-case) GRAND CRU of VOSNE-ROMANÉE. One of best v'yds on earth: big perfumed, luxurious wine. See ROMANÉE-CONTI.

Taille-aux-Loups, Domaine de la Lo w sw sp ★★★ Jacky Blot, former wine broker, is now one of the Loire's leading producers – with CUVÉES of barrel-fermented MONTLOUIS and VOUVRAY, from dry to lusciously sweet; excellent Triple Zero Montlouis pétillant and fine reds from Domaine de la Butte in Bourgueil.

Tain, Cave Coopérative de 290 members in north Rhône ACS; owns one-quarter of HERMITAGE. Red Hermitage improved, esp top, oaked Gambert de Loche; modern range, esp CROZES. Sound largely Marsanne whites, also v.gd VIN DE PAILLE. Basic reds gd value.

Taittinger BRUT NV; Rosé NV; BRUT **00** 02; Collection BRUT **90 95 96**. Once-fashionable Reims CHAMPAGNE grower and merchant sold to Crédit Agricole group 2006. Distinctive silky, flowery touch, though not always consistent, often noticeably dosed. Excellent luxury brand: Comtes de Champagne BLANC DE BLANCS (**96' 98**), Comtes de Champagne Rosé (**96** 02), also gd rich Pinot Prestige Rosé NV. New CUVÉES Nocturne and Prélude. Also excellent new single v'yd, La Marquetterie. (See also California: Dom Carneros.)

Tavel Rh p ★★ DYA France's most famous, though not best, rosé: heady, strong, v. full, and dry – needs food. Best growers: DOM Corne-Loup, GUIGAL, Lafond Roc-

FRANCE

Epine, Maby, DOM de la Mordorée, Prieuré de Montézargues, Rocalière, Ch de Manissy, Trinquevedel.

Tempier, Domaine Prov r w p ★★★★ The pioneering grower of BANDOL. Wines of considerable longevity. Quality now challenged by several others.

Terrasses du Larzac Midi r w p ★★ Part of AC COTEAUX DU LANGUEDOC. Wild, hilly region inc Montpeyroux, St Saturnin, and villages nr the Lac du Salagou.

Terroirs Landais Gascony r p w ★ VDP, an extension in the *département* of Landes of the CÔTES DE GASCOGNE, a name that many growers prefer to use. Dom de Laballe is most-seen example.

Thénard, Domaine Burg Major grower of the GIVRY appellation, but best known for his substantial portion (1.6 ha) of LE MONTRACHET. Should be better.

Thevenet, Jean Burg ★★★ Mâconnais purveyor of rich, some semi-botrytized, wines eg CUVÉE Levroutée at Dom de la Bongran. Also Dom Emilian Gillet.

Thézac-Perricard SW r p ★★ 05' 06 VDP Over the boundary of LOT from CAHORS. Same grapes but lighter style. Independent ★★ DOM de Lancement even better than gd co-op.

Thiénot, Alain Broker-turned-merchant; dynamic force for gd in CHAMPAGNE. Ever-improving quality across the range. Impressive, fairly priced BRUT NV. Rosé NV BRUT **98 00** 02. Vintage Stanislas (**98 00** 02) and Voluminous Vigne aux Gamins BLANC DE BLANCS (**99 02**). Top Grande CUVÉE **96' 98** 02. Also owns Marie Stuart and CANARD-DUCHÊNE in CHAMPAGNE, Ch Ricaud in LOUPIAC.

Thomas, André & fils ★★★ V. fine ALSACE grower at Ammerschwihr attached to rigorous biological methods. An artist-craftsman in the cellar: v.gd Ries Kaefferkopf and magnificent Gewurz VIEILLES VIGNES (both **05**).

Thorin, J Beauj ★ Major BEAUJOLAIS négociant owned by BOISSET.

Thouarsais, Vin de Lo w r p ★ DYA Light Chenin Bl (with 20% CHARD permitted), Gamay, and Cab Fr from tiny (20-ha) VDQS south of SAUMUR. Esp Blet, Gigon.

Tollot-Beaut ★★★ Stylish, consistent Burgundy grower with 20 ha in CÔTE DE BEAUNE, inc v'yds at Beaune Grèves, CORTON, SAVIGNY (Les Champs Chevrey), and at its CHOREY-LÈS-BEAUNE base.

Touraine Lo r p w dr sw sp ★→★★★★ 02' 03 04 05' 06 07 08 Huge region (5,500 ha) with many ACS (eg VOUVRAY, CHINON, BOURGUEIL) as well as umbrella AC of variable quality – zesty reds (Cab Fr, Côt, Gamay, Pinot N), pungent whites (Sauv Bl, Chenin Bl), rosés, and mousseux. Many gd bistro wines, often gd value. Producers: Ch de Petit Thouars, Doms des Bois-Vaudons, Corbillières, Joël Delaunay, de la Garrelière (François Plouzeau), de la Presle; Clos Roche Blanche, Jacky Marteau, MARIONNET; Oisly & Thesée, Puzelat/Clos de Tue-Boeuf, Vincent Ricard.

Touraine-Amboise Lo r w p ★→★★ TOURAINE sub-appellation (220 ha). François Ier is tasty, food-friendly local blend (Gamay/Côt/Cab Fr). Chenin Bl for whites. Damien Delecheneau/la Grange Tiphaine, Dutertre, Xavier Frissant, de la Gabillière, .

Touraine-Azay-le-Rideau Lo ★→★★ Small TOURAINE sub-appellation (60 ha) for Chenin Bl-based dry, off-dry white and Grolleau-dominated rosé. Producers: Ch. de l'Aulée, Nicolas Paget and Pibaleau Père & Fils.

Touraine-Mesland Lo r w p ★→★★ TOURAINE sub-appellation (105 ha) best represented by its user-friendly red blends (Gamay/Côt/Cab Fr). Whites are mainly Chenin with a little CHARD. Ch Gaillard, Clos de la Briderie.

Touraine-Noble Joué Lo p ★→★★ DYA Ancient but recently revived rosé from 3 Pinots (N, Gr, Meunier) just south of Tours. Esp from ROUSSEAU and Sard. Became separate AC in 2001 and now totals 28 ha.

Trapet Burg ★★→★★★★ A long-established GEVREY-CHAMBERTIN DOM now enjoying new life and sensual wines with biodynamic farming. Ditto cousins Rossignol-Trapet – slightly more austere wines.

FRANCE

Trévallon, Domaine de Prov r w ★★★ 90' 91 92 93 94 95 96 97 **98 99 00 01** 03 04 05 06 07 In Les Baux, but VDP des Bouches du Rhône, fully deserving its huge reputation. Intense Cab Sauv/Syrah to age. White from Marsanne and Roussanne and a drop of CHARD. Well worth seeking out.

Trimbach, F E ★★★→★★★★ Growers of the greatest Ries in ALSACE (CLOS STE-HUNE) and its close contender (CUVÉE Frédéric-Emile). House style is dry but elegant with great ageing potential. Also v.gd PINOT GRIS and Gewurz. Now using term GRAND CRU for the first time, on Geisberg (rented v'yd).

Tursan SW France r p w ★★→★★★★ (Most DYA) VDQS aspiring to AC. Easy-drinking holiday-style wines. Master chef Michel Guérard keeps much of his own ★★ wine (now red as well as white) for his famous restaurants at Eugénie-les-Bains, but more traditional ★★ Dom de Perchade is just as gd in its own way. Successful co-op the only other producer.

Vacqueyras S Rh r (w, p) ★★ 90' 95' 96' 98' 99' 00' 01' 03 04' 05' 06' 07' Peppery, pretty robust Grenache-based neighbour to GIGONDAS: more sinewed, should be cheaper. Lives 10+ yrs. Note: Arnoux Vieux Clocher, JABOULET, Chx de Montmirail, des Tours, VIDAL-FLEURY; Clos des Cazaux, DOMS Armouriers, Archimbaud-Vache, Charbonnière, Couroulu, Font de Papier, Fourmone, Garrigue, Grapillon d'Or, Monardière (v.gd), Montirius (organic), Montvac, Pascal Frères, Perrin, Sang des Cailloux (v.gd).

Val de Loire Lo w r p DYA One of France's 4 regional VDPS, formerly Jardin de la France. Wide range of single varietals inc CHARD, Cab Fr, Gamay, and Sauv Bl.

Valençay Lo r p w ★ Recent AC (VDQS until 2004) in east TOURAINE 139 ha; light, easy-drinking sometimes rustic and sharp wines from similar range of grapes as TOURAINE, esp Sauv Bl. Jacky Preys, Hubert & Olivier Sinson.

Val d'Orbieu, Vignerons du ★★ Association of some 200 top growers and co-ops in CORBIÈRES, COTEAUX DU LANGUEDOC, MINERVOIS, ROUSSILLON, etc, marketing a sound range of selected MIDI AC and VDP wines. Cuvée Mythique is flagship.

Valréas S Rh r (p w) ★★ 05' 06' 07' Low-profile CÔTES DU RHÔNE village with big co-op. Sound mid-weight red (mainly Grenache, less robust than CAIRANNE, RASTEAU) and improving white. Esp Emmanuel Bouchard, Dom des Grands Devers, Ch la Décelle.

Varichon & Clerc Principal makers and shippers of SAVOIE sparkling wines.

VDQS *vins délimité de qualité supérieure*. Due to be phased out at end of 2011.

Vendange Harvest. **Vendange Tardive** Late harvest. ALSACE equivalent to German Auslese but usually higher alcohol.

Ventoux S Rh r p (w) ★★ 04' 05' 06 07' Rambling 6,000+ ha AC around Mont Ventoux between Rhône and PROVENCE for tasty red (Grenache-Syrah, café-style to much deeper flavours), rosé, and gd white (though oak use growing). Name changed from Côtes du V in 2008. Welcome cool flavours from altitude for some. Best: LA VIEILLE FERME (r) owned by BEAUCASTEL, co-op Bédoin, Goult, St-Didier, DOMS Anges, Juliette Avril, Berane, Brusset, Cascavel, Croix de Pins, Fondrèche, Font-Sane, Grand Jacquet, Martinelle, Murmurium, Pesquié, Pigeade, Terres de Solence, Valcombe, Verrière, JABOULET, VIDAL-FLEURY.

Verget Burg ★★→★★★★ The négociant business of GUFFENS-HEYNEN with mixed range from MÂCON to MONTRACHET. Intense wines, often models, from bought-in grapes. New LUBÉRON venture: Verget du Sud. Follow closely.

Veuve Clicquot Yellow Label NV; White Label DEMI-SEC NV; Vintage Réserve **98' 99 02'**; Rosé Réserve **95 96 98 99'** 02. Historic CHAMPAGNE house of highest standing, now owned by LVMH. Full-bodied, almost rich: one of CHAMPAGNE's surest things. Cellars at Reims. Luxury brands: La Grande Dame (**90' 96 98**), Rich Réserve (**96 99** 02), La Grande Dame Rosé (**96 98' 99** 02).

NB Vintages in colour are those you should choose first for drinking in 2010.

Veuve Devaux Premium CHAMPAGNE of powerful Union Auboise co-op. Excellent aged Grande Réserve NV, Oeil de Perdrix Rosé, Prestige Cuvée D.

Vézelay Burg w r Age 1-2 yrs. Up-and-coming subdistrict of generic Bourgogne. Flavoursome whites from CHARD, but gd local Bourgogne Rouge is from Pinot and rare whites from Melon, as Bourgogne Grande Ordinaire.

Vidal-Fleury, J N Rh ★→★★ Long-established GUIGAL-owned shipper of sound Rhône wines and grower of CÔTE-RÔTIE, classy, v. elegant La Chatillonne (12% Viognier). Drive to rejuvenate wines. Gd CÔTES DU RHÔNE Viognier, Côtes du VENTOUX, Muscat BEAUMES-DE-VENISE, VACQUEYRAS.

Vieille Ferme, La S Rh r w ★→★★ V.gd brand of Côtes du VENTOUX (r) and Côtes du LUBÉRON (w) made by Perrin family of CH DE BEAUCASTEL. Reliable, gd value.

Vieilles Vignes Old vines – which should make the best wine. Eg DE VOGÜÉ MUSIGNY VV. But no rules about age and can be a tourist trap.

Vieux Télégraphe, Domaine du S Rh r w ★★★ 78' 81' 85 88 89' 90 94' 95' 96' 97 98' 99' 00 01' 03' 04' 05' 06' 07' Top name, maker of well-fruited, long-lived red CHÂTEAUNEUF, and tasty white (more *gourmand* since 1990s, excellent with food, always gd in lesser yrs). Second DOM: de la Roquète, brightly fruited reds, fresh whites, both improving. Owns gd, slow-ageing, understated GIGONDAS DOM Les Pallières with US importer Kermit Lynch.

Vigne or vignoble Vineyard (v'yd), vineyards (v'yds). **Vigneron** Vine-grower.

Vin Doux Naturel (VDN) Sweet wine fortified with wine alcohol, so the sweetness is natural, not the strength. The speciality of ROUSSILLON, based on Grenache or muscat. Top wines, esp RANCIOS, can be remarkable.

Vin Gris "Grey" wine is v. pale pink, made of red grapes pressed before fermentation begins – unlike rosé, which ferments briefly before pressing. Oeil de Perdrix means much the same; so does "blush".

Vin Jaune Jura w ★★★ Speciality of ARBOIS: odd yellow wine like fino sherry. Normally ready when bottled (after at least 6 yrs). Best is CH-CHALON. See also PLAGEOLES. A halfway-house oxidized white is sold locally as *vin typé*.

Vin de Paille Wine from grapes dried on straw mats, so v. sweet, like Italian *passito*. Esp in the Jura. See also CHAVE and VIN PAILLÉ DE CORRÈZE.

Vin Paillé de Corrèze SW Revival of old-style VIN DE PAILLE nr Beaulieu-sur-Dordogne made today from Cab Fr, Cab Sauv, CHARD, Sauv Bl. 25 fanatical growers and small co-op. Drunk as aperitif, also (folklore) by breast-feeding mothers. The wine of Christian Tronche well worth looking out for.

Vin de Pays (VDP) Most dynamic category in France (with over 150 regions). The zonal VDP are best – eg CÔTES DE GASCOGNE, CÔTES DE THONGUE, Haute Vallée de l'Orb, Duché d'Uzès, among others. Enormous variety in taste and quality and some wonderful surprises.

Vinsobres S Rh r (p w) ★→★★ 05' 06' 07' Village with full AC status 04 vintage on. Best are openly fruited, helped by high v'yds, and quite substantial, plenty of Syrah. Note: Cave La Vinsobraise, DOMS les Aussellons, Bicarelle, Chaume-Arnaud, Constant-Duquesnoy, Coriançon, Deurre, Jaume, Moulin, Peysson, Puy de Maupas, Ch Rouanne, Perrin.

Vin de Table Category of standard everyday table wine, not subject to particular regulations about grapes and origin. Can be source of unexpected delights if a talented winemaker uses this category to avoid bureaucratic hassle.

Viré-Clessé Burg w ★★ 05' 06' 07 08 AC based around 2 of best white villages of MÂCON. Extrovert style, though residual sugar forbidden. Try A Bonhomme, Bret Bros, Chaland, Clos du Chapitre, JADOT, Merlin, Ch de Viré, and co-op.

Visan S Rh r p w ★★ 05' 06' 07' Improving Rhône village for steady-weight reds, some decent whites. Young growers waking it up. Look for: DOMS Coste Chaude, Florane, Fourmente, des Grands Devers, Roche-Audran.

Vogüé, Comte Georges de Burg ★★★★ Iconic CHAMBOLLE estate inc lion's share of

MUSIGNY. Heralded vintages from 1990s taking time to come round.

Volnay Burg r ★★★→★★★★ 90' 91 93 95 96' 97 98 99' 02' 03 04 05' 06 07 08 Village between POMMARD and MEURSAULT: often the best reds of the CÔTE DE BEAUNE; structured and silky. Best v'yds: Caillerets, Champans, Clos des Chênes, Santenots, Taillepieds, etc. Best growers: D'ANGERVILLE, J-M BOILLOT, HOSPICES DE BEAUNE, Lafarge, LAFON, DE MONTILLE, Rossignol.

Volnay-Santenots Burg r ★★★ Best red wine v'yds of MEURSAULT sold under this name. Indistinguishable from other PREMIER CRU VOLNAY. Perhaps more body, less delicacy. Best growers: AMPEAU, HOSPICES DE BEAUNE, LAFON, LEROY, PRIEUR.

Vosne-Romanée Burg r ★★★→★★★★ 88' 90' 91 93 95 96' 98 99' 01 02' 03 05' 06 07 08 Village with Burgundy's grandest *crus* (ROMANÉE-CONTI, LA TÂCHE, etc). There are (or should be) no common wines in Vosne. Many gd growers inc: Arnoux, CATHIARD, DRC, ENGEL, GRIVOT, GROS, Jayer, LATOUR, LEROY, LIGER-BELAIR, MÉO-CAMUZET, MUGNERET, RION.

Vougeot Burg r w ★★★ 90' 93 95' 96' 97 98 99' 00 01 03 05' 06 07 08 Village and PREMIER CRU wines. See CLOS DE VOUGEOT. Exceptional Clos Blanc de Vougeot, white since 12th century. Bertagna and VOUGERAIE best.

Vougeraie, Domaine de la Burg r ★★→★★★★ Domaine uniting all BOISSET's v'yd holdings. Gd-value BOURGOGNE rouge up to fine MUSIGNY GRAND CRU.

Vouvray Lo w dr sw sp ★★→★★★★★ For sweet Vouvray: 89' 90' 95' 96' 97' 03' 05' 08. For dry Vouvray: 89 90 96' 97 02' 03 05' 06 07 (08). Important AC east of Tours: increasingly gd and reliable. DEMI-SEC is classic style, but in gd yrs moelleux can be intensely sweet, almost immortal. Gd, dry sparkling: look out for pétillant. Best producers: Allias, Vincent Carême, *Champalou*, Clos Baudoin (CHIDAINE), Dhoye-Deruet (Dom de la Fontanerie), Foreau, Fouquet (Dom des Aubuisières), Ch Gaudrelle, Dom de la Haute Borne, HUET, DOM DE LA TAILLE-AUX-LOUPS, Vigneau-Chevreau. If you find ancient vintages – such as 21, 24, 47 or 59 – don't hesitate.

Vranken Ever more powerful CHAMPAGNE group created in 1976 by Belgian marketing man. Sound quality. Leading brand: Demoiselle. Owns HEIDSIECK MONOPOLE, POMMERY, and Bricout.

Wolfberger Al ★★ Principal label of Eguisheim co-op. Exceptional quality for such a large-scale producer. V. important for CRÉMANT.

"Y" (pronounced "ygrec") B'x 79' 80' 85 86 88 94 96 00 02 04 05 06 Intense dry white wine produced at CH D'YQUEM, lately with more regularity. Most interesting with age. Denis Dubourdieu-influenced dry style in 04, otherwise in classic off-dry mould.

Zind Humbrecht, Domaine ★★★★ ALSACE growers since 1620. Current DOM established in 1959, now vying with FALLER/DOM WEINBACH as the greatest in ALSACE: rich, powerful yet balanced wines, using v. low yields. Top wines from single v'yds *Clos St-Urbain*, Jebsal (superb PINOT GRIS 02') and Windsbuhl, and GRANDS CRUS RANGEN, HENGST, Brand, Goldert.

To decipher codes, please refer to "Key to symbols" on the front flap of jacket, or "How to use this book" on p.10.

Châteaux of Bordeaux

The following abbreviations
are used in the text:

B'x	Bordeaux
E-2-M	Entre-Deux-Mers
H-Méd	Haut-Médoc
L de P	Lalande de Pomerol
Mar	Margaux
Méd	Médoc
Pau	Pauillac
Pe-Lé	Pessac-Léognan
Pom	Pomerol
St-Em	St-Emilion
St-Est	St-Estèphe
St-Jul	St-Julien
Saut	Sauternes
ch, chx	château(x)
dom, doms	domaine(s)

More heavily shaded
areas are the wine-
growing regions

Even Bordeaux has experienced the progression of global warming but
uniformity is still a distance away. It's a marginal region for ripening
grapes, particularly Cabernet, and vintage variation remains part of the
game. Take the diversity of the last decade: the linear "classicism" of
2002, 2004 and 2006, the power and concentration of 2000 and 2005,
the atypical warmth of 2003 and the gentle reserve of 2001. Then there
are the "difficult" vintages of 2007 and 2008, years that were doomed but
for late-season sunshine and the dexterity growers showed in the v'yd.

So what should we be drinking in 2010? Well, if you've got older vintages in the cellar the choice will be broader, as the 1995s and a good number of 1996s are opening nicely, and in the Médoc the 1998s are coming round. Selecting from merchants' lists will put the accent on recent years. Vintages that offer a touch of maturity as well as the traditional Bordeaux values of balance and digestibility include 2001 (particularly Right Bank), 2002 and 2004 while for petits châteaux 2005 and 2007 are approachable today.

d'Agassac H-Méd r ★★ **98 99 00'** 02 03 04 05 **06** 07 "Sleeping Beauty" 14th-century moated fort. 42 ha nr BORDEAUX suburbs. Modern, accessible Médoc.

Andron-Blanquet St-Est r ★★ 95 96 98 00' 03 **04 05'** 06 16-ha sister CH to COS-LABORY. Smoother and riper in latter yrs.

Angélus St-Em r ★★★★ 89' 90' 92' 95 96 98' 99 00' 01 02 03' 04 05 06 07 08 Leading PREMIER GRAND CRU CLASSÉ on ST-ÉMILION CÔTES. Pioneer of the modern style; dark, rich, sumptuous. Second wine: Le Carillon de L'Angélus. Fleur de Boüard in LALANDE DE POMEROL same ownership.

d'Angludet Cantenac-Mar r ★★★ **90 94 95 96' 98'** 00 02 **03** 04 05 06 32-ha estate owned and run by négociant Sichel; classed-growth quality. Lively long-living MARGAUX of great style popular in UK. Gd value.

Archambeau Graves r w dr (sw) ★★★ (r) **98** 00 02 04 05 **06** (w) 00 **01** 02 04 05 06 07 Up-to-date 27-ha property at Illats. Gd fruity dry white; fragrant barrel-aged reds. Same ownership as improving Barsac-classed growth Ch Suau.

d'Arche Saut w sw ★★ **96** 97' 98 99 00 01' 02 **03' 05** 07 Much improved 27-ha classed growth. Top vintages are creamy. Ch d'Arche-Lafaurie is a richer selection. Also bed-and-breakfast in 17th-century *chartreuse*.

d'Armailhac Pau r ★★★ **88' 89 90' 93 94** 95' 96' **98 99** 00 01 02 **03** 04 05' 06 07 Formerly Ch Mouton Baronne Philippe. Substantial Fifth Growth under Rothschild ownership. 51 ha: top-quality PAUILLAC with more finesse than sister CLERC MILON but less punch. MOUTON ROTHSCHILD is big brother of both.

L'Arrosée St-Em r ★★★ **95 96 98'** 00 01 02 03 **04** 05' 06' 07 A 9.7-ha CÔTES estate with new owner and investment from 2002. Aromatic, structured wines with plenty of Cab Fr and Cab Sauv (60%).

Ausone St-Em r ★★★★ **85 86' 88 89'** 90 93 94 95 **96'** 97 **98'** 99 00' 01' 02 03' 04 05' 06 07 08 Illustrious First Growth with 6.8 ha (about 2,500 cases); best position on the CÔTES with famous rock-hewn cellars. On superb form since 1996, hence the astronomical price. Long-lived wines with volume, texture and finesse. Second wine: La Chapelle d'Ausone also excellent.

Balestard-la-Tonnelle St-Em r ★★ **95 96** 98' **00'** 01 03 **04** 05 06 Historic 11-ha classed growth on limestone plateau. Associate of Michel ROLLAND consults. More concentration since 2003.

Barde-Haut St-Em r ★★ **98 99** 00 01 02 **03 04** 05' 06 07 The 17-ha sister property of CLOS L'ÉGLISE and HAUT-BERGEY. Rich, modern, and opulent in style.

Bastor-Lamontagne Saut w sw ★★ **95 96'** 97' **98 99** 01' 02 **03' 05** 07 Large (56 ha) Preignac sister to BEAUREGARD. Consistent quality; excellent rich wines. Second label: Les Remparts de Bastor. Fruity Caprice (from 2004) for early drinking. Also Ch St-Robert at Pujols: red and white GRAVES.

Vintages shown in light type should be opened now only out of curiosity to gauge their future. Vintages in bold are deemed (usually by their makers) ready for drinking. Remember, though: the French tend to enjoy the vigour of young wines, and many 89s, 90s, 95s, and 96s have at least 10 more years of development before them. Vintages marked 00' are regarded as particularly successful for property in question. Vintages in colour are first choice for 2010.

Batailley Pau r ★★★ **94 95 96** 98 00 02 **03 04** 05' 06 Fifth Growth property (55 ha) bordering PAUILLAC and ST-JULIEN. Fine, firm, strong-flavoured. *Gd-value Pauillac*. Even better since 2000. Home of Castéja family of BORIE-MANOUX.

Beaumont Cussac, H-Méd r ★★ **95 96** 98 00' 02 04 **05'** 06 07 One of the largest (114 ha) estates in the MÉDOC; *easily enjoyable wines*. Second label: Ch Moulin d'Arvigny. 40,000 cases. In the same hands as BEYCHEVELLE.

Beauregard Pom r ★★★ **89' 90' 94' 95' 96'** 98' 00' 01 02 **03 04** 05' 06 A 17-ha v'yd; fine 17th-century CH nr LA CONSEILLANTE. Top-rank rich wines. Consultant Michel ROLLAND. Second label: Benjamin de Beauregard.

Beau-Séjour-Bécot St-Em r ★★★ 89' 90' **94 95' 96 98'** 99 00' 01 02 03 04 05' 06 07 18-ha estate owned by the Bécots since 1969. Controversially demoted in class in 1985 but properly re-promoted to PREMIER GRAND CRU CLASSÉ in 1996. More finesse from 2001. GRAND-PONTET and LA GOMERIE in same family hands.

Beauséjour-Duffau St-Em r ★★★ 89' 90' **93' 94 95 96** 98 99 00 01 02 03 04 05' 06 7-ha PREMIER GRAND CRU CLASSÉ estate on west slope of the CÔTES owned by Duffau-Lagarrosse family (younger generation now at helm); only 2,000+ cases of firm-structured, concentrated, even hedonistic wine.

Beau-Site St-Est r ★★ **95 96** 98 00 03 04 05 06 Property in same hands as BATAILLEY etc. Usually solid and firm, if unexceptional.

Belair-Monange St-Em r ★★★ 88' 89' 90' **94 95'** 96 98 99 00' 01 02 03 04 05' 06 08 Classed-growth neighbour of AUSONE. Name changed from 2008 – used to be plain Belair. Négociant J-P MOUEIX owner since 2008 but still under management of long-time winemaker Pascal Delbek. Fine, fragrant, elegant style; 08 much more concentration. Second wine: Ch Haut Roc Blanquant.

Belgrave St-Laurent, H-Méd r ★★ **95 96' 98'** 00' 02' 03 04' 05' 06 07 60-ha Fifth Growth well managed by CVBG-Dourthe (see LA GARDE, REYSSON). Progress and investment since 1998. Second label: Diane de Belgrave.

Bellefont-Belcier St-Em r ★★ **98 99** 00 01 02 **03 04** 04 05' 06 07 Promotion to GRAND CRU CLASSÉ in 2006 invalidated by the courts. Neighbour of LARCIS-DUCASSE on the CÔTES at St-Laurent-des-Combes. Taken in hand from 1994. Ripe, modern but minerally.

Bel-Orme-Tronquoy-de-Lalande St-Seurin-de-Cadourne, H-Méd r ★★ **95 96 98'** 00 02 03 **04** 05 24-ha estate north of ST-ESTÈPHE. Known for tannic wines; more tempting since 1997. Same owner as CROIZET-BAGES, RAUZAN-GASSIES.

Berliquet St-Em r ★★ **95 96 98' 99** 00' 01 02 03 04 05' 06 A 9.3-ha GRAND CRU CLASSÉ well located on the CÔTES. Previously made by ST-EMILION cooperative. Moved into top gear from 1997 onwards.

Bernadotte H-Méd r ★★ **98 99** 00' 01 02 03 04 05' 06 07 30-ha estate managed by PICHON-LALANDE team since 97. ROEDERER owner since 06. Structured wines.

Bertineau St-Vincent L de P r ★★ **98 99** 00' 01 03 04 05 06 Top oenologist MICHEL ROLLAND owns this 4-ha estate. Consistent quality. (See also LE BON PASTEUR.)

Beychevelle St-Jul r ★★★ **95 96** 98 99 00' 01 02 **03 04** 05 06 07 Fourth Growth (90 ha) with historic mansion. Insurance company and Suntory (LAGRANGE) owners. Wines of consistent elegance rather than power. Second wine: Amiral de Beychevelle.

Biston-Brillette Moulis r ★★ **98 00** 01 02 03 04 **05'** 06 Attractive, fruit-bound, gd-value MOULIS. 24 ha in production.

Bonalgue Pom r ★★ **95 96'98'** 99 00 01 03 04 05 06 Dark, rich, meaty POMEROL. As gd value as it gets. MICHEL ROLLAND consults.

Bonnet E-2-M r w ★★ (r) **04** 05 (w) DYA Owned by octogenarian André Lurton. Big producer (270 ha!) of some of the best E-2-M and red BORDEAUX. New CUVÉE Prestige, Divinus, from 2000. LA LOUVIERE, COUHINS-LURTON same stable.

Le Bon Pasteur Pom r ★★★ **95 96' 98' 99** 00 01 02 03 04 05' 06 Excellent property on ST-ÉMILION border, owned by MICHEL ROLLAND. Concentrated, even creamy

> **Why Bordeaux?**
> People ask whether Bordeaux still justifies its own separate section of this international guide. The answer: it remains the motor of the fine wine world, by far its biggest producer, stimulating debate, investment, and collectors worldwide.

wines virtually guaranteed. (See also BERTINEAU ST-VINCENT.)

Le Boscq St-Est r ★★ **95' 96' 98** 00 01 03 04 05' 06 Quality-driven 18-ha estate owned by CVBG-Dourthe, giving excellent value in tasty ST-ESTÈPHE.

Bourgneuf-Vayron Pom r ★★ **95' 96' 98' 99** 00 01' 03 04 05' 06 07 Rich, warm, firm-edged POMEROL from this 9-ha estate on sandy-gravel soils.

Bouscaut Pe-Lé r w ★★ (r) **89 90 94 95 98** 00 01 02 04 05' 06 07 (w) **98 00 01 02 03 04 05' 06 07** Steadily improving 46-ha classed growth owned by sister of BRANE-CANTENAC's Henri Lurton. Hitting its stride since 2004.

Boyd-Cantenac Mar r ★★★ **95 96' 98' 00** 02 03 04 05' 06 07 Little-known 18-ha Third Growth in better form since 2000. Cab Sauv-dominated with a little peppery Petit Verdot. Second wine: Jacques Boyd. See also POUGET.

Branaire-Ducru St-Jul r ★★★ **89' 90' 93' 94** 95 96 98 99 00 01 02 03 04 05' 06 Fourth Growth ST-JULIEN of 51 ha. Has set the bar of quality and consistency high. Dense, linear, cassis style. Second label: Duluc.

Brane-Cantenac Cantenac-Mar r ★★★ **95 96 98 99 00'** 01 02 03 04 05' 06 07 Big (85-ha) Second Growth. Dense, fragrant MARGAUX. Henri Lurton, brother of Gonzague (DURFORT-VIVENS), at the helm. Second label: Baron de Brane.

Brillette Moulis r ★★ **95 96 98 99** 00 02 03 04 05 06 MOULIS estate (40-ha). Wines of gd depth and fruit. Reliable and attractive. Second label: Berthault Brillette.

Cabanne, La Pom r ★★ **95 96 98'** 00 04 05 06' A regarded 10-ha property. Rustic POMEROL in style; finer and fleshier in 06. Second wine: Dom de Compostelle.

Cadet-Piola St-Em r ★★ **94' 95 98** 00 01 03 04 05 06 Distinguished small property (7 ha) on ST-ÉMILION's limestone plateau with a feminine touch (owner and label). Fresh, firm, long-lived wines.

Caillou Saut w sw ★★ **89' 90' 95** 96 97 98 99 01' 02 03' 05 Well-run second-rank 13-ha BARSAC v'yd for firm fruity wine. CUVÉE Reine (**97 99 01' 03'**) is a top selection. CUVÉE Prestige another selection.

Calon-Ségur St-Est r ★★★ **89' 90' 94** 95 96' 98 99 00' 01 02 03 04 05' 06 07 08 Big (60-ha) Third Growth with great historic reputation. Mme Capbern-Gasqueton the matriarchal owner. Greater consistency since 1995. Second label: Marquis de Calon.

Cambon La Pelouse H-Méd r ★★ **96' 98' 99** 00 01 02 03 04 05' 06 07 Big, accessible southern HAUT-MÉDOC *cru*. A sure bet for supple MÉDOC.

Camensac St-Laurent, H-Méd r ★★ **95 96' 98** 00 03 05 06 75-ha Fifth Growth. Quite lively if not exactly classic wines. New owner (2005) has CHASSE-SPLEEN connection; expect change. Second label: La Closerie de Camensac.

Canon St-Em r ★★★ **96 98' 99** 00 01 02 03 04 05' 06 07 08 Famous first-classed growth with walled-in 22 ha on plateau W of the town, bought in 96 by owners of RAUZAN-SÉGLA. Investment and restructuring of v'yd (70% replanted) has paid. Elegant, long-lived wines. Second label: Clos Canon. (Value.)

Canon-de-Brem Canon-Fronsac r ★★ **98 99** 00 01 03 04 05' RIP from 2006. Bought by Jean Halley of Carrefour supermarkets in 2000, wine now absorbed into CH DE LA DAUPHINE. Massive recent investment. Firm, pure expression.

Canon La Gaffelière St-Em r ★★★ **89' 90' 94'** 95 96 98' 99 00' 01 02 03 04 05' 06 08 Leading 19-ha GRAND CRU CLASSÉ on the lower slopes of the CÔTES. Same ownership as CLOS DE L'ORATOIRE, LA MONDOTTE, and Aiguilhe in Castillon. Derenoncourt consults. Stylish, upfront, impressive wines with 35% Cab Fr.

Cantegril Graves r Saut w sw ★★ (r) **00 02 04 05 06** (w) **02 03 04 05' 06 07** Supple red, fine BARSAC-SAUTERNES from DOISY-DAËNE and CLOS FLORIDÈNE connection.

Cantemerle Macau, H-Méd r ★★★ **89' 90 95** 96' 98 00 01 02 03 04 05' 06 07 Large 90-ha property in south MÉDOC. Now merits its Fifth Growth status. Sandy-gravel soils give finer style. Second label: Les Allées de Cantemerle.

Cantenac-Brown Cantenac-Mar r ★★→★★★ **90' 94** 95 96 98 99 00 01 02 03 04 05' 06 07 42-ha Third Growth sold in 06 to private investor; owned since late 80s by AXA Millésimes. Powerful, but more elegance since 2000. Second label: Brio du Ch Cantenac Brown.

Capbern-Gasqueton St-Est r ★★ **95 96 98** 00 02 **03 04** 05 06 34-ha property offering solid fare; same owner as CALON-SÉGUR.

Cap de Mourlin St-Em r ★★ **95 96 98' 99** 00 01 03 04 05 06 Well-known 15-ha property of the Capdemourlin family, also owners of CH BALESTARD and Ch Roudier, MONTAGNE-ST-ÉMILION. A vigorous but tasty ST-ÉMILION.

Carbonnieux Pe-Lé r w ★★★ **95 96 98 99** 00 02 04 05' 06 07 Large (90-ha), historic estate at Léognan for **sterling red and white**. Charismatic owner Antony Perrin died 2008; sons Eric and Philibert now in charge. The whites, 65% Sauv Bl (eg **98 99 00 01 02 03 04 05 06 07**), can age up to 10 yrs. Chx Le Pape and Le Sartre are also in the family. Second label: La Tour-Léognan.

de Carles Fronsac r ★★ **98 99** 00 01 02 03 04 05' 06 Haut Carles is the top selection here with its own modern, gravity-fed cellars. Iron fist in a velvet glove. de Carles now the juicy second wine.

Les Carmes Haut-Brion Pe-Lé r ★★★ **89 90' 94** 95 96 98 99 00 01 02 **03 04** 05' 06 07 Small (4.7-ha) neighbour of HAUT-BRION with classed-growth standards. 55% Merlot. Family-owned. A former head of Bordeaux's Faculté d'Oenologie consults.

Caronne-Ste-Gemme St-Laurent, H-Méd r ★★→★★★ **98 99** 00 01 02 03 **04 05** 06 40-ha MÉDOC estate. Steady, stylish quality repays patience.

Carteau Côtes-Daugay St-Em r ★★ **98' 99 00** 01 02 03 04 05 Consistent 13-ha GRAND CRU; full-flavoured wines maturing fairly early.

Certan-de-May Pom r ★★★ **95 96 98** 00' 01' **04** 05' 06 07 Tiny property (1,800 cases) on the POMEROL plateau. Has been inconsistent but 2005 shows the true potential. Opulent with firm, fine tannic frame.

Certan-Marzelle Pom Little J-P Moueix estate for **fragrant, light, juicy Pomerol**.

Chantegrive Graves r w ★★→★★★ **98' 99'** 00 01 02 03 04 05' 06 07 With 87 ha, the largest estate in the AC; modern GRAVES of v.gd quality. Reds rich and finely oaked. CUVÉE Caroline is top white (**98' 99 00 01 02 03 04 05' 06 07**).

Chasse-Spleen Moulis r (w) ★★★ **95 96 98** 99 00 01 02 **03 04** 05' 06 07 A 80-ha estate at classed-growth level. Consistently gd, often outstanding (eg **90' 00'** 05'), long-maturing wine. Second label: Ermitage de Chasse Spleen. One of the surest things in Bordeaux. Makes a little white too. See also CAMENSAC and GRESSIER-GRAND-POUJEAUX.

Chauvin St-Em r ★★ **95 96 98' 99** 00 01 03 04 05 06 Steady performer; increasingly serious stuff. New v'yds purhased in 1998.

Cheval Blanc St-Em r ★★★★ **85' 86 88** 89 90' **93 94 95 96' 97 98'** 99 00' 01' 02 03 04 05' 06 07 08 40-ha PREMIER GRAND CRU class (a) of ST-ÉMILION. High percentage of Cab Frc (60%). Rich, fragrant, vigorous wines with some of the voluptuousness of neighbouring POMEROL. Delicious young; lasts a generation. For many, the first choice in Bordeaux. Same ownership and management as YQUEM and Quinault L'Enclos (ST-ÉMILION). Second wine: Le Petit Cheval. Like all all First Growths prices are super high.

Chevalier, Domaine de Pe-Lé r w ★★★★ **89 90' 95 96' 98' 99'** 00' 01' 02 03 04' 05' 06 07 08 Superb estate of 47 ha at Léognan. Impressive since 1998, the red has gained in finesse, fruit, texture. Complex, long-ageing white has

> **Four appellations in one**
> 2008 will launch the first vintage of the new appellation of Côtes de Bordeaux. The label is set to embrace and eventually replace CÔTES DE CASTILLON, CÔTES DE FRANCS, PREMIÈRES CÔTES DE BLAYE, and PREMIÈRES CÔTES DE BORDEAUX. Cross-blending of wines from these regions will be allowed. For those wanting to maintain the identity of a single terroir, stiffer controls will permit AC Côtes de Bordeaux with the suffixes Blaye, Castillon, Francs, and Cadillac (for the Premières Côtes de Bordeaux). The CÔTES DE BOURG is not part of the new designation.

remarkable consistency and develops rich flavours (**89 90' 93 94 95 96' 97 98' 99** 00 01 02 03 04 05' 06 07 08). Second wine: Esprit de Chevalier. Look out for Dom de la Solitude, PESSAC-LÉOGNAN.

Cissac Cissac-Méd r ★★ **95 96' 98** 00 00 02 03 04 05 Pillar of the bourgeoisie. 50-ha MÉDOC *cru*. Steady record for tasty, long-lived wine. Second wine: Les Reflets du Ch Cissac.

Citran Avensan, H-Méd r ★★ **95 96 98 99** 00 00 02 03 04 05' 06 90-ha estate owned by Villars-Merlaut (patriarch Jacques Merlaut died in 2008) family since 1996 (see CHASSE-SPLEEN, GRUAUD-LAROSE). Now ripe, supple; accessible early. Second label: Moulins de Citran.

Le Clarence de Haut-Brion Pe-Lé r ★★★ **89' 90 93 94 95 96' 98 99** 00 01 02 03 04 05' 06 07 *The second wine of Ch Haut-Brion*, known as Bahans Haut-Brion until 2007. Gd value if you can find it. Blend changes considerably with each vintage.

Clarke Listrac r (p w) ★★ **98' 99** 00 01 02 03 04 05' 06 Large (54-ha) Listrac estate. Massive (Edmond) Rothschild investment. Now v.gd Merlot-based red. Also a dry white Le Merle Blanc du Ch Clarke. Ch Malmaison in MOULIS same connection.

Clerc Milon Pau r ★★★ **89' 90' 94** 95 96' **98' 99** 00 01 02 03 04 05 06 07 Once-forgotten Fifth Growth owned by (Mouton) Rothschilds. Now 30 ha and a top performer; weightier than sister ARMAILHAC.

Climens Saut w sw ★★★★ **83' 85' 86' 88' 89 90' 95** 96 97' **98 99'** 00 01' 02 03' 04 05' 06 07 A 30-ha BARSAC classed growth making some of the world's most stylish wine (but not the sweetest) for a gd 10 yrs' maturing. Second label: Les Cyprès. Owned by Berenice Lurton (sister of Henri at BRANE-CANTENAC). Pricier than in the past.

Clinet Pom r ★★★★ **95 96 98' 99** 00 01 02 03 04 05' 06 07 Made a name for intense, sumptuous wines in the 1980s. New owner (1998) continues the style. MICHEL ROLLAND consults. New winery 2004 with wooden vats. Second label: Fleur de Clinet.

Clos de l'Oratoire St-Em r ★★ **95 96 98 99** 00' 01 03 04 05' 06 07 Serious performer on the northeastern slopes of ST-ÉMILION. Same stable as CANON-LA-GAFFELIÈRE and LA MONDOTTE, but lighter than both.

Clos l'Eglise Pom r ★★★ **95 96 98 99** 00' 01 02 03 04 05' 06 07 A 6-ha v'yd on one of the best sites in POMEROL. Fine wine with more depth since 1998. Same family owns HAUT-BERGEY and BARDE-HAUT.

Clos Floridène Graves r w ★★ (r) **99** 00 01 02 03 04 05 06 (w) **98 99** 00 01' 02 03 04' 05' **06 07** *A sure thing* from one of Bordeaux's most famous white-winemakers, Denis Dubourdieu. Oak-fermented Sauv Bl/Sem to keep 5+ yrs; fruity red. See also Chx CANTEGRIL, DOISY-DAËNE and REYNON.

To decipher codes, please refer to "Key to symbols" on front flap of jacket, or "How to use this book" on p. 10.

Clos Fourtet St-Em r ★★★ 89 90 94 95 96 98 99 00 01 02 03 04 05' 06 07 08 Well-placed First Growth on the plateau, cellars almost in town. New owner and investement from 2001; on stellar form. Also owns POUJEAUX. Second label: Dom de Martialis.

Clos Haut-Peyraguey Saut w sw ★★ 86' 88' 89 90' 95' 96 97' 98 99 00 01' 02 03' 04 05' 06 07 Family DOMAINE. Tiny production (12 ha) of consistently excellent medium-rich wine. Haut-Bommes is the second label.

Clos des Jacobins St-Em r ★★ 95 96 98 00 01 02 03 04 05' 06 07 Classed growth with greater stature since 2000. New ownership from 2004; new creamy style. ANGÉLUS owner consults. Same family owns Ch La Commanderie and FLEUR CARDINALE.

Clos du Marquis St-Jul r ★★→★★★ 98 99 00 01 02 03 04 05 06 07 The outstanding second wine of LÉOVILLE-LAS-CASES, cut from the same durable and powerful cloth and regularly a match for many well-rated classed growths.

Clos Puy Arnaud Castillon r ★★ 00 01' 02 03 04 05' 06 Biodynamic estate at the top of this revived AC. 8.5 ha producing wines of depth and distinction. Owner formerly connected to PAVIE.

Clos René Pom r ★★ 95 96 98' 00' 01 04 05' 06 Merlot-dominated wine with a little spicy Malbec. Less sensuous than top POMEROL but gd value. Alias Ch Moulinet-Lasserre.

La Clotte St-Em r ★★ 95' 96 98' 99 00' 01 02 03 04 05 Tiny CÔTES GRAND CRU CLASSÉ: pungent, supple wine. Drink at owners' ST-ÉMILION restaurant, Logis de la Cadène. Second label: Clos Bergat Bosson.

Colombier-Monpelou Pau r ★★ 98 99 00' 02 03 04 05 06 24-ha PAUILLAC estate; fairly supple, early drinking style of wine.

La Conseillante Pom r ★★★★ 88 89 90' 94 95' 96' 98' 99 00' 01 02 03 04 05' 06' 07 08 Historic 12-ha property on plateau between PÉTRUS and CHEVAL BLANC. Some of the noblest and most fragrant POMEROL; drinks well young or old. New *chai* in 2009. Second wine (from 2007): Duo de Conseillante.

Corbin St-Em r ★★ 96 98 99 00' 01 02 04 05 Much improved 12-ha GRAND CRU CLASSÉ. New management and investment since 1999. Round and supple with soft red fruit.

Corbin-Michotte St-Em r ★★ 95 96 98' 99 00 01 02 04 05 06 Well-run, modernized, 7.6-ha classed growth; generous POMEROL-like wine. In same hands as Chx Calon and Cantelauze.

Cordeillan-Bages Pau r ★★ A mere 1,000 cases of savoury PAUILLAC made by the Lynch-Bages team. Rarely seen outside Bordeaux. Better known for its luxury restaurant and hotel.

Cos d'Estournel St-Est r ★★★★ 88' 89' 90' 94 95 96' 98' 00 01 02 03 04 05' 06 07 08 A 67-ha Second Growth with eccentric pagoda *chai*. Most refined ST-ESTÈPHE and regularly one of the best wines of the MÉDOC. New state-of-the-art cellars in 2008. Pricey white from 2005. Second label: Les Pagodes de Cos. Same owner as CH MARBUZET and super-modern Goulée (MÉDOC).

Cos-Labory St-Est r ★★ 89' 90' 94 95 96' 98' 99 00 02 03 04 05' 06 07 Little-known Fifth Growth neighbour of COS D'ESTOURNEL with 15 ha. Recent vintages have more depth and structure. Gd value. ANDRON-BLANQUET is sister CH.

Coufran St-Seurin-de-Cadourne, H-Méd r ★★ 95 96 98 99 00 01 02 03 04 05 06 76 ha Coufran and VERDIGNAN, in extreme north of the HAUT-MÉDOC, are co-owned. Coufran is mainly Merlot for supple wine. SOUDARS is another, smaller sister.

Couhins-Lurton Pe-Lé w r ★★→★★★ (w) 98' 99 00 01 02 03 04 05 06 07 (r) 02 03 04 05 Fine, minerally, long-lived classed-growth white made from Sauv Bl. Now a supple, Merlot-based red from 2002 (17 ha). Same family as LA LOUVIÈRE and BONNET.

La Couspaude St Em r ★★★ 95 96 98 99 00' 01 02 03 04 05 06 Classed growth well-located on the STÉMILION plateau. Modern style; rich and creamy with lashings of spicy oak.

Coutet Saut w sw ★★★ 86' 88' 89' 90' 95 96 97' 98' 99 01' 02 03' 04 05 07 Traditional rival to CLIMENS; 37 ha in BARSAC. Slightly less rich; at its best equally fine. CUVÉE Madame is a v. rich selection in certain yrs (90 95 01).

Couvent des Jacobins St-Em r ★★ 95 96 98' 99 00' 01 03 04 05 06 10.7-ha GRAND CRU CLASSÉ vinified within the walls of ST-ÉMILION. Splendid cellars. Lighter, easy style. Denis Dubourdieu consults. Second label: Le Menut des Jacobins.

Le Crock St-Est r ★★ 95 96 98 99 00' 01 02 03 04 05 06 07 V. fine property (30 ha) in the same family (Cuvelier) as LÉOVILLE-POYFERRÉ. Classic, robust ST-ESTÈPHE.

La Croix Pom r ★★ 95 96 98 99 00 01 04 05 06 07 Well-reputed 10-ha property owned by négociant Janoueix. Appealing plummy POMEROL. Also La Croix-St-Georges, La Croix-Toulifaut, Castelot, and HAUT-SARPE (ST-ÉMILION).

La Croix du Casse Pom r ★★ 95 96 98 99 00' 01' 04 05 06 A 9-ha property on sandy-gravel soils in the south of POMEROL. Usually lighter in style. Since 2005 owned by BORIE-MANOUX.

La Croix-de-Gay Pom r ★★★ 89 90 94' 95 96 98 99 00' 01' 02 04 05 06 12 ha in the best part of the commune. Recently on fine form. La Fleur-de-Gay is the best selection. Same family as Faizeau (MONTAGNE ST-ÉMILION).

Croizet-Bages Pau r ★★ 89 90' 95 96' 98 00' 03 04 05 06 07 A 26-ha Fifth Growth. Same owners as RAUZAN-GASSIES. A new regime in the cellar is producing richer, more serious wines, but could still be better.

Croque-Michotte St-Em r ★★ 95 96 98 00 01 03 04 05 A 14-ha estate on the POMEROL border. Gd steady wines but not grand enough to be *classé*.

Cru Bourgeois, Cru Bourgeois Supérieur, Cru Bourgeois Exceptionnel See Cru Bourgeois box, p 98.

de Cruzeau Pe-Lé sw r w ★★ (r) 95 96 98 00 01 02 04 05 06 (w) 00 01 02 03 04 05 06 07 Large 97-ha (two-thirds red) PESSAC-LÉOGNAN v'yd developed by André Lurton of LA LOUVIÈRE. Gd value wines. Sauv Bl-dominated white.

Dalem Fronsac r ★★ 95 96'98' 99 00 01 02 03 04 05' 06 Used to be a full-blooded FRONSAC. Now a feminine touch has added more charm. 15 ha: 85% Merlot.

Dassault St-Em r ★★ 95 96 98' 99 00 01 02 03 04 05' 06 Consistent, modern, juicy 23-ha GRAND CRU CLASSÉ. Owning family of Dassault aviation fame.

de la Dauphine Fronsac r ★★ 98' 99 00 01 03 04 05 06' Total makeover since purchased by new owner in 2000. Renovation of CH and v'yds plus new, modern winery in 2002. Stablemate CANON-DE-BREM integrated in 2006 so look out for a more structured style.

Dauzac Labarde-Mar r ★★→★★★ 89' 90' 94 95 96 98' 99 00' 01 02 04 05 07 A 49-ha Fifth Growth south of MARGAUX; underachiever for many yrs but investment and evolution since the 1990s. Owned by an insurance company; managed by André Lurton of LA LOUVIÈRE. Second wine: La Bastide Dauzac.

Desmirail Mar r ★★→★★★ 95 96 98 00' 01 02 03 04 05 06 07 Third Growth (30 ha) owned by Denis Lurton, brother of Henri BRANE-CANTENAC. Fine, delicate style.

Destieux St-Em r ★★ 98 99 00' 01 03' 04 05' 06 07 Promotion to GRAND CRU CLASSÉ in 2006 annulled. 8-ha estate to the east of ST-ÉMILION at St-Hippolyte. New *chai* and investment since 1996. ROLLAND consults. Bold, powerful style.

Doisy-Daëne Barsac w (r) sw dr ★★★ 88' 89' 90' 95 96 97' 98' 99 01' 02 03 04 05

Vintages shown in light type should be opened now only out of curiosity to gauge their future. Vintages in bold are deemed (usually by their makers) ready for drinking. Remember, though: the French tend to enjoy the vigour of young wines, and many 89s, 90s, 95s, and 96s have at least 10 more years of development before them. Vintages marked 00' are regarded as particularly successful for property in question. Vintages in colour are first choice for 2010.

BORDEAUX

06 07 (08) Forward-looking 15-ha estate producing a crisp, oaky, dry white and CH CANTEGRIL, but above all renowned for its notably fine (and long-lived) sweet BARSAC. L'Extravagant (**90 96 97 01 02 03 04** 05 06 07) is a super-CUVÉE.

Doisy-Dubroca Barsac w sw ★★ **88' 89 90' 95** 96 97' **99 01 03' 04** 05 07 Tiny (3.4-ha) BARSAC classed growth allied to CH CLIMENS.

Doisy-Vedrines Saut w sw ★★★ **88' 89' 90 95 96 97' 98 99 01' 03' 04** 05 07 A 20-ha classed growth at BARSAC, nr CLIMENS and COUTET. Delicious, sturdy, rich: for keeping almost indefinitely. A sure thing for many yrs.

Le Dôme St-Em r ★★★ Micro-wine that used to be super-oaky (200%) but is now aimed at elegance and terroir expression. Two-thirds old-vine Cab Fr. Owned by Jonathan Maltus, who has a string of other ST-ÉMILIONS (eg Ch Teyssier, Le Carré, Les Astéries) and Australia's Barossa Valley (Colonial Estate).

La Dominique St-Em r ★★★ **89' 90' 94 95 96 98 99** 00' 01 04 05' 06 Classed growth adjacent to CHEVAL BLANC. Potential for rich, aromatic wines. Managed by owner of VALANDRAUD since 2006. To watch. Second label: St Paul de Dominique.

Ducluzeau Listrac r ★★ **95 96 00 01 03 04 05** 06 Tiny sister property of DUCRU-BEAUCAILLOU. 10 ha, 50/50 Merlot/Cab Sauv.

Ducru-Beaucaillou St-Jul r ★★★★ **82' 83' 85' 94** 95' 96' **98 99** 00' 01 02 03 04 05' 06 07 08 Outstanding Second Growth, excellent form except for a patch in the late 80s; 75 ha overlooking the river. Added impetus from owner Bruno Borie from 2003. Classic cedar-scented claret suited to long ageing. See also LALANDE-BORIE. Second wine: Croix de Beaucaillou.

Duhart-Milon Rothschild Pau r ★★★ **90 94 95 96' 98 00' 01 02 03 04'** 05' 06 07 Fourth Growth neighbour of LAFITE, under same management. Greater precision from 02; increasingly fine quality. Second label: Moulin de Duhart.

Durfort-Vivens Mar r ★★★ **89' 90 94 95 96 98 99 00 02 03 04** 05' 06 Relatively small (32-ha) Second Growth owned and being improved by Gonzague Lurton, president of the Margaux winegrowers' association . Recent wines have structure (lots of Cab Sauv) and finesse.

de l'Eglise, Domaine Pom r ★★ **89 90 95 96 98 99** 00 01 02 03 04 05' 06 07 Small property on the clay-gravel plateau: stylish, resonant wine distributed by BORIE-MANOUX. Denis Dubourdieu consults.

L'Eglise-Clinet Pom r ★★★ **89 90' 93' 94 95 96 98' 99** 00' 01' 02 03 04 05' 06 07 08 6-ha estate. Top-flight POMEROL with great consistency; full, concentrated, fleshy wine. Expensive and limited quantity. Second label: La Petite Eglise.

L'Evangile Pom r ★★★★ **88' 89' 90 95 96 98' 99** 00' 01 02 03 04' 05' 06 07 08 13 ha between PÉTRUS and CHEVAL BLANC. Deep-veined elegant style in a POMEROL classic. Investment by owners (LAFITE) Rothschild has greatly improved quality. New cellars in 2004. Second wine: Blason de l'Evangile.

de Fargues Saut w sw ★★★ **85' 86 88 89 90 95 96 97 98 99' 01 02 03' 04** 05' 06 07 A 15-ha v'yd by ruined castle owned by Lur-Saluces, previous owner of YQUEM. Rich, unctuous wines, but balanced – maturing earlier than YQUEM.

Faugères St-Em r ★★ **98 99 00' 02 03 04 05** 06 07 A 49-ha property. Dark, fleshy, modern ST-ÉMILION. Cuvée Péby is the garage wine. Sister to Cap de Faugères in CÔTES DE CASTILLON and Chambrun in LALANDE DE POMEROL.

Faurie-de-Souchard St-Em r ★★ **95 96 98' 00 03 04** 05 06 07 Underperforming CH on the CÔTES. Lost classified status in 2006, then reinstated. Recent investment and greater effort from new generation. Stéphane Derenoncourt consults. To watch.

de Ferrand St-Em r ★★ **90' 94 95 96 98 00 01 03 04** 05 Big (30-ha) St-Hippolyte

To decipher codes, please refer to "Key to symbols" on front flap of jacket, or "How to use this book" on p. 10.

estate. Rich, oaky wines, with plenty of tannin to age.

Ferrande Graves r (w) ★★ 00 01 02 04 05 06 Major estate at Castres owned by négociant Castel: over 40 ha. Easy, enjoyable red and gd white wine; at their best in 1–4 yrs.

Ferrière Mar r ★★→★★★ 95 96' 98 99 00' 02 03 04 05 06 Tiny third growth with a CH in Margaux village restored by same capable hands as LA GURGUE and HAUT-BAGES-LIBÉRAL. Dark, firm, perfumed *wines need time*.

Feytit-Clinet Pom r ★★ 90' 94 95 96 98 99 00 01 03 04 05' 06 07 Tiny 6.5-ha property. Once managed by J-P MOUEIX; back with owning Chasseuil family since 2000. Improvements since. Rich, full POMEROL with ageing potential.

Fieuzal Pe-Lé r (r) ★★★ (r) 98' 00 01 06 07 (w) 98' 99 01 02 03 05 06 07 08 Classed growth at Léognan. Red form has dipped from the heights of the mid-1980s but improvements from 2006. White more consistent. New Irish owner from 2011. ANGÉLUS owner now consults for reds. So back to winning ways?

Figeac St-Em r ★★★★ 95' 96 98' 99 00' 01 02 03 04 05' 06 07 08 First growth, 40-ha gravelly v'yd with unusual 70% Cab Fr and Cab Sauv. Rich but always elegant wines; *deceptively long ageing*. Owner Thierry Manoncourt has notched up more than 60 vintages. Second wine: Grange Neuve de Figeac.

Filhot Saut w sw dr ★★ 90 95 96' 97' 98 99 01' 02 03' 04 05 07 Second-rank classed growth with splendid CH, 60-ha v'yd. Difficult young, more complex with age. Light and fine in style.

Fleur Cardinale St-Em r ★★ 98 99 00 01 02 03 04 05' 06 07 18-ha property east of ST-ÉMILION. Gd from the 1980s but into overdrive since 2001 with new owner and *chai*. Promoted then demoted in 2006 classification. Ripe, unctuous, modern style.

La Fleur-de-Gay Pom r ★★★ 1,000-case super-CUVÉE of CH LA CROIX DE GAY.

La Fleur-Pétrus Pom r ★★★★ 89' 90' 94 95 96 98' 99 00' 01 02 03 04 05' 06 A 13-ha v'yd flanking PÉTRUS; same J-P MOUEIX management. Concentration, richness, finesse. This is POMEROL at its most stylish (and expensive).

Fombrauge St-Em r ★★→★★★ 95 96 98 99 00' 01 02 03 04 05 06 A Bernard Magrez wine (see PAPE CLÉMENT), so don't expect restraint. Big estate: 52 ha east of ST-ÉMILION. Since 1999 rich, dark, chocolatey, full-bodied wines. Magrez-Fombrauge is its GARAGE wine.

Fonbadet Pau r ★★ 95 96' 98' 00' 01 02 03 04 05 06 20-ha PAUILLAC estate. Reliable, gd value and typical of AC style.

Fonplégade St-Em r ★★ 95 96 98 00' 01 02 03 04 05 06' 07 A 19-ha GRAND CRU CLASSÉ New American owner from 2004. Michel ROLLAND consults. Watch for riper, modern, more fruit-driven style.

Fonréaud Listrac r ★★ 95 96 98 00' 02 03 04 05 06 07 One of the bigger (39 ha) and better LISTRACS producing savoury, mouthfilling wines. Investment since 1998. 2 ha of white: Le Cygne, barrel-fermented. See LESTAGE. Gd value.

Fonroque St-Em r ★★★ 95 96 98 01 03 04 05 06 19 ha on the plateau north of ST-ÉMILION. Biodynamic from 2008. Big, deep, dark wine: firm, tannic edge. Managed by Alain Moueix (see MAZEYRES). MOULIN DU CADET sister estate.

Fontenil Fronsac r ★★ 95 96 98' 99' 00' 01' 02 03 04 05 06 Leading FRONSAC started by ROLLAND in 86. Dense, oaky, new-style. GARAGE: Défi de Fontenil.

Les Forts de Latour Pau r ★★★ 88 89' 90' 93 94 95' 96' 97 98 99 00' 01 02 03 04' 05' 06 07 The (worthy) second wine of CH LATOUR; the authentic flavour in slightly lighter format at Second Growth price from enlarged v'yds.

Fourcas-Dupré Listrac r ★★ 89' 90 95 96' 98' 99 00' 01 02 03 04 05 06 07 Top-class 46-ha estate making consistent wine in tight LISTRAC style. Second label: Ch Bellevue-Laffont. Complete renovation in 2000.

Fourcas-Hosten Listrac r ★★→★★★ 89' 90' 95' 96' 98' 00 01 02 03 04 05 A 48-ha estate with new owners (Hermès fashion connection) from 2006. Firm wine with a long life. Less consistent than FOURCAS-DUPRÉ.

de France Pe-Lé r w ★★ (r) **90' 95' 96' 98 99 00 02 03 04** 05 06 (w) **96 98 99 01'** 02 03 04 05 06 07 Well-known northern GRAVES neighbour of CH DE FIEUZAL making consistent wines in a ripe, modern style. MICHEL ROLLAND consults.

Franc-Mayne St-Em r ★★ **90' 94 95 96 98' 99 00' 01 03 04 05** 06 A 7.2-ha GRAND CRU CLASSÉ. New owners in 1996 and again in 2004 (sister property CH DE LUSSAC). Investment and renovation. Round but firm wines. To watch.

du Gaby Canon-Fronsac r ★★ **00' 01' 03 04 05** 06 07 The finest situation in Bordeaux? New owners in 1999 and again in 2006 (Canadian). Serious wines.

La Gaffelière St-Em r ★★★ **88' 89' 90' 94 95 96 98' 99 00' 01 03 04** 05' 06 07 08 A 22-ha First Growth at foot of the CÔTES. Elegant, long-ageing wines. More precision and purity from 2000. Derenoncourt consulting from 2004.

Galius St-Em r ★★ **00 01 03 04 05** Oak-aged selection from ST-ÉMILION co-op, to a high standard. Formerly called Haut Quercus.

La Garde Pe-Lé r w ★★ (r) **96' 98' 99 00 01' 02 04** 05 06 07 (w) **01 02 04 05 06 07** Substantial property of 58 ha owned by négociant CVBG-Dourthe; reliable red and improving. Tiny production of Sauv Bl and Sauv Gris-based white.

Le Gay Pom r ★★★ **89' 90' 95 96 98 99 00 01 03 04** 05' 06 07 Fine 5.6-ha v'yd on northern edge of POMEROL. Major investment, with MICHEL ROLLAND consulting. Now v. ripe and plummy in style. Ch Montviel same stable and AC. Owner has Cristal d'Arques glassware origins.

Gazin Pom r ★★★ **89' 90' 94' 95 96 98' 99 00' 01 02 03 04** 05' 06 07 08 Large (for POMEROL) 23 ha, family-owned (of name: de Bailliencourt dit Courcol) neighbour of PÉTRUS. Now on v.gd form. Second label: L'Hospitalet de Gazin.

Gilette Saut w sw ★★★ **49 53 55 59 61 67 70 71 75 76 78 79 81 82 83 85 86 88** Extraordinary small Preignac CH stores its sumptuous wines in concrete vats to a great age. Only about 5,000 bottles of each. Ch Les Justices is its sister (**96 97 99 01 02 03'** 05 07).

Giscours Labarde-Mar r ★★★ **88 89' 90 95 96' 98 99 00' 01 02 03 04** 05' 06 07 Splendid Third Growth south of Cantenac. V.gd vigorous wine in 70s and now 80s v. wobbly; new (Dutch) ownership from 95 and revival since 99. 2nd label: La Sirène de Giscours. Ch La Houringue is baby sister. DU TERTRE stablemate.

du Glana St-Jul r ★★ **95 96 98 99 00 02 03 04** 05 06 Large, 44-ha St-Julien estate. Expansion through the acquisition of parcels of land from CH LAGRANGE. Undemanding; undramatic; value. Same owner as Bellegrave in PAUILLAC. Second wine: Pavillon du Glana.

Gloria St-Jul r ★★→★★★ **95' 96 98 99 00' 01 02 03 04** 05' 06 07 A 45-ha ST-JULIEN estate. Same ownership as ST-PIERRE. Wines of vigour, with a recent return to long-maturing style. Second label: Peymartin.

La Gomerie St-Em r 1,000 cases, 100% Merlot, *garagiste*. See BEAUSÉJOUR-BÉCOT.

Grand-Corbin-Despagne St-Em r ★★→★★★ **90' 94 95 96 98 99 00' 01 03 04** 05 06 Victim of the 2006 classification: demoted from GRAND CRU CLASSÉ in 96 but reinstated in 06, only to have it annulled by courts. In between: investment and hard graft. Aromatic wines now with a riper, fuller edge. Also Ch Maison Blanche, MONTAGNE ST-ÉMILION. Second label: Petit Corbin-Despagne.

Grand Cru Classé See ST-ÉMILION classification box, p. 102.

Grand-Mayne St-Em r ★★★ **89' 90' 94 95 96 98 99 00' 01' 02 03 04** 05' 06 07 Leading 16-ha GRAND CRU CLASSÉ on western CÔTES. Noble old CH with wonderfully rich, tasty wines. New generation in control.

Grand-Pontet St-Em r ★★★ **95' 96 98' 99 00' 01 02 03 04** 05 06 A 14-ha estate revitalized since 1985. Quality much improved. See BEAUSÉJOUR-BÉCOT.

Grand-Puy-Ducasse Pau r ★★★ **89' 90 94 95 96' 98' 99 00 01 02 03 04** 05' 06 07 Fifth Growth enlarged to 40 ha under expert management; improvements in the 1990s, but lacks vigour of next entry. Second label: Ch Artigues-Arnaud.

Grand-Puy-Lacoste Pau r ★★★ 82 85' 86' 88' 89' 90' 94 95' 96' 98 99 00' 01 02 03 04 05' 06 07 Leading 50-ha Fifth Growth famous for full-bodied egs of PAUILLAC. Same ownership as HAUT-BATAILLEY. Second label: Lacoste-Borie.

La Grave à Pomerol Pom r ★★★ 89' 90 94 95 96 98' 00 01 02 03 04 05 06 Verdant CH with small, first-class v'yd owned by Christian MOUEIX. V. fine POMEROL of medium richness. Formerly known as La Grave Trigant de Boisset.

Gressier-Grand-Poujeaux Moulis r ★★→★★★ 89 90 94 95 96 98 00 01 03 04 05 20-ha MOULIS property. Fine firm wine with gd track record. Repays patient cellaring. Since 2003, same owners as CHASSE-SPLEEN.

Greysac Méd r ★★ 95 96 98 00' 02 03 04 05 06 Elegant 70-ha MÉDOC estate. Same management as CANTEMERLE. Fine, consistent style.

Gruaud-Larose St-Jul r ★★★★ 86' 88 89' 90' 95' 96' 98 99 00' 01 02 04 05' 06 07 One of the biggest, best-loved Second Growths. 82 ha. Smooth, rich, stylish claret; ages 20+ yrs. Second wine: Sarget de Gruaud-Larose. GRESSIER-GRAND-POUJEAUX connections.

Guadet-St-Julien St-Em r ★★ 89 90' 95 96'98 00 01 04 05 06 Firm, classic style. Poor track record resulted in contested demotion from GRAND CRU CLASSÉ in 06 – eventually reinstated. Now a Derenoncourt consultancy. Expect change.

Guiraud Saut w (r) sw (dr) ★★★ 88' 89' 90' 95 96' 97' 98 99 01' 02 03 04 05' 06 07 Top quality classed growth. Over 100 ha. New owning consortium from 2006 includes existing manager, Xavier Planty, and CANON LA GAFFELIERE and DOM DE CHEVALIER connections, as well as Peugeot car family.

La Gurgue Mar r ★★ 98 00' 01 02 03 04 05' 06 Well-placed 10-ha property, for fine MARGAUX. Same management as HAUT-BAGES-LIBÉRAL.

Hanteillan Cissac r ★★ 96 98 00' 02 03 04 05' 06 Huge 82-ha HAUT-MÉDOC v'yd: v. fair wines, conscientiously made. 50% Merlot. Second wine: Ch Laborde.

Haut-Bages Averous Pau r ★★ 95 96 98 99 00 01 02 03 04 05 The second wine of LYNCH-BAGES. Tasty drinking and fairly consistent.

Haut-Bages-Libéral Pau r ★★★ 96' 98 99 00 01 02 03 04 05' 06 Lesser-known Fifth Growth of 28 ha (next to LATOUR) in same stable as LA GURGUE. Results are excellent, *full of Pauillac vitality. Usually gd value.*

Haut-Bages-Monpelou Pau r ★★ 95 96 98 99 00 03 04 05 06 A 15-ha stablemate of CH BATAILLEY on former DUHART-MILON land. Gd minor PAUILLAC.

Haut-Bailly Graves r ★★★★ 89' 90' 95 96 98' 99 00 01 02 03 04 05' 06 07 08 Over 30 ha at Léognan. Since 79 some of the best savoury, intelligently made red GRAVES. New US ownership and investment from 98 (but same manager) have taken it to greater heights. Second label La Parde de Haut-Bailly.

Haut-Batailley Pau r ★★★ 89' 90' 95 96' 98 99 00 02 03 04 05' 06 07 Smaller part of divided Fifth Growth BATAILLEY: 20 ha. Gentler than sister CH GRAND-PUY-LACOSTE. New cellar in 2005;more precision. Second wine: La Tour-d'Aspic.

Haut-Beauséjour St-Est r ★★★ 89 98 99 00 01 03 04 05 18-ha property revitalised since 1992 by owner CHAMPAGNE house ROEDERER. See also DE PEZ.

Haut-Bergey Pessac-L r (w) ★★ (r) 98 99 00 01 02 04 05 06 07 (w) 02 03 04 05 06 07 A 29-ha estate now producing a denser, more modern GRAVES with oak overlay. Also a little dry white. Completely renovated in the 1990s. Same ownership as BARDE-HAUT and CLOS L'EGLISE. Sister Ch Branon.

Haut-Brion Pessac, Graves r ★★★★ (r) 78' 79' 81 82' 83' 85' 86' 88' 89' 90' 93 94 95' 96' 97 98' 99 00' 01 02 03 04 05' 06 08 Oldest great CH of Bordeaux and only non-MÉDOC First Growth of 1855 owned by American Dillon family since 1935. 51 ha. Deeply harmonious, never-aggressive wine with endless, honeyed, earthy complexity. Consistently great since 1975. A little dry, sumptuous white: 90 93 94 95 96 98 99 00' 01 02 03 04'05' 06 07. See LE CLARENCE DE HAUT-BRION, LA MISSION-HAUT-BRION, LAVILLE-HAUT-BRION.

Haut Condissas Méd r ★★ 99 00 01 02 03 04 05 06 New *cru* at Bégadan. Old-vine selection from Ch Rollan-de-By. Same owns as Chx La Clare, La Tour Séran.

Haut-Marbuzet St-Est r ★★→★★★ 89' 90' 95 96' 98 99 00' 01 02 03 04 05' 06 07 Leading non-classified ST-ESTÈPHE estate. Rich, unctuous wines that age well. M Duboscq has reassembled ancient Dom de Marbuzet, (in total 71 ha). Also owns Chambert-Marbuzet, MacCarthy, Tour de Marbuzet. Haut-Marbuzet is 60% Merlot, seductive and remarkably consistent. Ch Layauga-Duboscq in AC MEDOC is new venture (2005).

Haut-Pontet St-Em r ★★ 98 00 01 03 04 05 Reliable 4.8-ha Merlot v'yd of the CÔTES. New owner (Janoueix – see next entry) from 2007.

Haut-Sarpe St-Em r ★★ 89 90' 94 95 96 98 00' 01 03 04 05 06 21-ha GRAND CRU CLASSÉ with elegant CH and park, 70% Merlot. Same owner (Janoueix) as CH LA CROIX, POMEROL. Modern style.

Hortevie St-Jul r ★★ 90 95 96 98 00 02 03 04 05 06 One of the few non-classified ST-JULIENS. This tiny v'yd and its bigger sister TERREY-GROS-CAILLOU are gd value.

Hosanna Pom r ★★★★ 99 00 01 02 03 04 05' 06 07 08 Formerly Certan-Guiraud until purchased and renamed by J-P MOUEIX. Only best 4.5 ha retained. First vintages confirm class. New cellar in 07. Stablemate of PÉTRUS and TROTANOY.

d'Issan Cantenac-Mar r ★★★ 95 96' 98 99 00' 01 02 03 04' 05 06 07 Restored moated CH nr Gironde with 45-ha Third Growth v'yd. Fragrant wines; more substance since late 90s. Owner Emmanuel Cruse is the new Grand Master of the Commanderie de Bontemps Confrérie. Second label: Blason d'Issan.

Kirwan Cantenac-Mar r ★★★ 88 89' 90' 94 95 96 98 99 00' 01 02 03 04 05' 06 07 A 35-ha Third Growth; from 1997 majority owned by SCHRÖDER & SCHŸLER. Mature v'yds now giving classy wines. Rich style: MICHEL ROLLAND influenced until 2007. Second label: Les Charmes de Kirwan.

Labégorce Mar r ★★ 95 96 98 99 00 01 02 03 04 05' 07 Substantial 41-ha estate north of MARGAUX revamped since 1989; meaty, long-lived MARGAUX. See also next entry and MARQUIS D'ALESME-BECKER.

Labégorce-Zédé Mar r ★★→★★★ 89' 90' 95 96' 98 99 00' 01 02 03 04 05' 06 07 28 ha north of MARGAUX with same ownership as LABEGORCE. Typically delicate, fragrant, classic. Second label: Dom Zédé. One to watch.

Lafaurie-Peyraguey Saut w sw ★★★ 82 83' 85 86' 88' 89' 90' 95 96' 97 98 99 01' 02 03' 04 05' 06 07 (08) Fine 40-ha classed growth at Bommes; owners Groupe Banque Suez. One of best buys in SAUTERNES. Second wine: La Chapelle de Lafaurie.

Lafite-Rothschild Pau r ★★★★ 82' 83 85 86' 88' 89' 90' 93 94 95 96' 97 98' 99 00' 01' 02 03' 04' 05' 06 07 08 First Growth of famous elusive perfume and style, but never huge weight, although more density and sleeker texture from 1996. Great vintages keep for decades; recent vintages well up to form. Amazing circular cellars. Joint ventures in Chile (88), California (89), Portugal (92), Argentina (99), now the MIDI, Italy – even China. Second wine: Carruades de Lafite. 91 ha. Also owns CHX DUHART-MILON, L'ÉVANGILE, RIEUSSEC.

Lafleur Pom r ★★★★ 83 85' 86 88' 89' 90' 93 94 95 96 98' 99' 00' 01' 02 03 04' 05' 06 07 08 Superb 4.8-ha property. Elegant, intense wine of less fleshy kind for maturing and investment. 50% Cab Fr. Second wine: Pensées de Lafleur.

Lafleur-Gazin Pom r ★★ 89 90 94 95 96 98 00 01 04 05 06 Distinguished small J-P MOUEIX estate on the northeastern border of POMEROL.

Lafon-Rochet St-Est r ★★★ 88' 89' 90' 94 95 96' 98 99 00 01 02 03' 04 05' 06 Fourth Growth neighbour of COS D'ESTOURNEL, 45 ha with distinctive yellow cellars (and label). Investment, selection, and a higher percentage of Merlot have made this ST-ESTÈPHE more opulent since 1998. Second label: Les Pèlerins de Lafon-Rochet.

Lagrange Pom r ★★ 89' 90' 94 95 96 98 00 01 04 05 06 An 8-ha v'yd in the centre of POMEROL run by the ubiquitous house of J-P MOUEIX. Gd value but not in the same league as HOSANNA, LA FLEUR-PÉTRUS, LATOUR-À-POMEROL, etc.

Lagrange St-Jul r ★★ 88' 89' 90' 94 95 96 98 99 00' 01 02 03 04 05' 06 08 Formerly neglected Third Growth owned since 1983 by Suntory. 113 ha now in tip-top condition with wines to match. Marcel Ducasse oversaw the resurrection until retirement in 2007. Dry white Les Arums de Lagrange since 97. Second wine: Les Fiefs de Lagrange.

La Lagune Ludon, H-Méd r ★★ 90' 95 96' 98 00' 02 03 04 05' 80-ha Third Growth in southern MÉDOC with sandy-gravel soils. Dipped in the 90s but on form from 00. Fine-edged, now with added structure and depth. New *chai* 04. Owned by J-J Frey; recently acquired JABOULET AÎNÉ. Daughter Caroline the winemaker.

Lalande-Borie St-Jul r ★★ 96 98 00 01 02 03 04 05 06 07 A baby brother (25 ha) of the great DUCRU-BEAUCAILLOU created from part of the former v'yd of CH LAGRANGE. Gracious, easy-drinking wine.

de Lamarque Lamarque, H-Méd r ★★ 90' 94 95 96 98 99 00' 02 03 04 05 06 Splendid medieval fortress in central MÉDOC with 35-ha v'yd; competent, mid-term wines. Second wine: Donjon de L.

Lamothe Bergeron H-Méd r ★★ 89 90 95 96' 98' 00 02 03 04 05 Large 67-ha estate in Cussac Fort Médoc making reliable claret.

Lanessan Cussac, H-Méd r ★★ 89' 90' 94 95 96' 98 00' 02 03 04 05 Distinguished 44-ha property just south of ST-JULIEN. Fine rather than burly, but ages well. Horse museum and tours.

Langoa-Barton St-Jul r ★★★ 90' 94 95' 96' 98 99 00' 01 02 03 04' 05' 06 07 08 15-ha Third Growth sister CH to LÉOVILLE-BARTON. V.old (1821) Barton-family estate; impeccable standards, gd value. Second wine: Réserve de LÉOVILLE-BARTON.

Larcis-Ducasse St-Em r ★★ 88' 89' 90' 94 95 96 98' 00 02 03 04 05' 06 07 08 Top classed-growth property of St-Laurent, eastern neighbour of ST-ÉMILION, on the CÔTES. 12 ha in a gd situation; wines on an upward swing since new management in 2002 (PAVIE-MACQUIN and PUYGUERAUD).

Larmande St-Em r ★★★ 89' 95' 96 98' 00 01 03 04 05 07 Substantial 24-ha property owned by Le Mondiale insurance (as is SOUTARD). Replanted, re-equipped, and now making rich, strikingly scented wine, silky in time. All female winemaking and management team. Second label: Ch des Templiers.

Laroque St-Em r ★★→★★★ 88 89 90 94 95 96 98 99 00' 01 02 03 04 05 06 07 Important GRAND CRU CLASSÉ in St-Christophe; 58-ha v'yd on ST-ÉMILION CÔTES with 17th-century CH. Well-structured wines for ageing. Progress from 2000.

Larose-Trintaudon St-Laurent, H-Méd r ★★ 98 00 01 02 03 04 05 The biggest v'yd in the MÉDOC: 172 ha. Modern methods make reliable, fruity and charming wine to drink young. Second label: Larose St-Laurent. Special CUVÉE (from 1996): Larose Perganson; from 33-ha parcel.

Laroze St-Em r ★★ 90' 95 96' 98' 99 00 01 02 05 06 07 Large v'yd (30 ha) on western CÔTES. Lighter-framed wines from sandy soils, more depth from 1998; approachable when young. New "tribaie" grape-sorting machine (v. ingenious, sorts according to specific gravity, and thus ripeness) in use. Second label: La Fleur Laroze.

Larrivet-Haut-Brion Pe-Lé r w ★★★ (r) 90 94 95 96' 98' 00 01 02 03 04' 05' 06 07 Substantial 56-ha Léognan property with classed-growth aspirations; MICHEL ROLLAND consulting. Rich, modern red. Also 4,500 cases of fine, barrel-fermented white (96' 98' 99 00 01 02 04' 05 06 07). New barrel cellar and tasting room in 2007. Second wine: Les Demoiselles de Larrivet-Haut-Brion.

Lascombes Mar r (p) ★★★ 89' 90' 95 96' 98' 99 00 01 02 03 04 05' 06 07 A 97-ha Second Growth owned by US pension fund. Wines have been wobbly, but real improvements from 2001. MICHEL ROLLAND consults. Winemaker previously with LAFITE-ROTHSCHILD and EVANGILE. Second label: Chevalier de Lascombes.

Latour Pau r ★★★★ 78' 81 82' 85 86' 88' 89' 90' 91 93 94 95' 96' 97 98 99 00' 01

02 03' 04' 05' 06 08 First Growth considered the grandest statement of the MÉDOC. Profound, intense, almost immortal wines in great yrs; even weaker vintages have the characteristic note of terroir and run for many yrs.Recently enlarged: 80+ ha inc 48 ha "Enclos" for the *grand vin*. Latour always needs 10 yrs to show its hand. New state-of-the-art *chai* (2003) allows more precise vinification. Second wine: LES FORTS DE LATOUR; *third wine: Pauillac.*

Latour-Martillac Pe-Lé r w ★★ (r) **98 00 01 02 03 04** 05' 06 07 A 46-ha classed-growth property in Martillac. Regular quality (red and white); gd value at this level. The white can age admirably (**98' 99 00 01 02 03 04 05 06 07**).

Latour-à-Pomerol Pom r ★★★ **88' 89' 90' 94 95 96 98' 99 00' 01 02 04** 05' 06 07 Top growth of 7.6 ha under J-P MOUEIX management. POMEROL of great power and perfume, yet also ravishing finesse.

des Laurets St-Em r ★★ **98 00 01 03 04** 05 Major property in PUISSEGUIN-ST-ÉMILION and MONTAGNE-ST-ÉMILION, with 72 ha of v'yd evenly split on the CÔTES (40,000 cases). Owned by Benjamin de Rothschild of CH CLARKE (2003).

Laville-Haut-Brion Pe-Lé w ★★★★ **89' 90 92 93' 94 95' 96' 98 99 00' 01 02 03 04' 05'** 06 07 08 Only 6,000 bottles/yr of v. best white GRAVES for long, succulent maturing, made at La Mission-Haut-Brion. Great consistency. Mainly Sem.

Léoville-Barton St-Jul r ★★★★ **86' 88' 89' 90' 93' 94' 95' 96' 98 99 00' 01 02** 03' 04 05' 06 07 08 A 45-ha portion of great Second Growth LÉOVILLE v'yd in Anglo-Irish hands of the Barton family for over 180 yrs (Anthony Barton is present incumbent). Powerful, classic claret; traditional methods, v. fair prices. Investment raised v. high standards to Super Second. See LANGOA-BARTON.

Léoville-Las-Cases St-Jul r ★★★★ **82' 83' 85' 86' 88 89' 90' 93 94 95' 96' 97 98 99** 00' 01 02 03' 04' 05' 06 07 08 The largest LÉOVILLE; 97 ha with daunting reputation. Elegant, complex, powerful, austere wines, for immortality. Second label CLOS DU MARQUIS is also outstanding.

Léoville-Poyferré St-Jul r ★★★ **86' 88 89' 90' 94 95 96 98 99** 00' 01 02 03' 04 05' 06 07 08 For yrs the least outstanding of LÉOVILLES, but a renaissance in the 80s and 90s. Now at Super Second level with dark, rich, spicy, long-ageing wines. ROLLAND consults at the 80-ha estate. Second label: Ch Moulin-Riche.

Lestage Listrac r ★★ **90' 95 96 98 00 02 03 04** 05 06 A 42-ha LISTRAC estate in same hands as CH FONREAUD. Firm, slightly austere claret. Second wine: La Dame du Coeur de Ch Lestage.

Lilian Ladouys St-Est r ★★ **95 96 98 00 02 03 04** 05 06 07 Created in the 1980s, the v'yd now covers 45 ha with 100 parcels of vines. Firm, sometimes robust wines; recent vintages more finesse. New owner in 2008. Same management as Belle-Vue in HAUT-MEDOC.

Liot Barsac w sw ★★ **88 89' 90' 95 96 97' 98 99** 01' 02 03 05 07 Consistent, fairly

---

Crus Bourgeois – the second coming

First, there was the Cru Bourgeois label (since 1932), then following the official annulment of the 2003 reclassification of the Crus Bourgeois of the MÉDOC there wasn't (although the designation could be used for vintages up to and including 2007). Now, the winegrowers' association has adopted a new system to keep the Cru Bourgeois label alive. Starting with the 2008 vintage an independent body, Bureau Véritas, will oversee the assessment of wines and estates, awarding the Cru Bourgeois certificate on a yearly basis. Failure to obtain the label one year will not compromise applications for subsequent vintages. Producers throughout the MÉDOC can apply for the yearly designation providing they have obtained their AC credentials and possess a minimum 4.5 ha in a communal AC or 7 ha in the ACS MÉDOC and HAUT-MÉDOC.

light, golden wines from 20 ha. Gd to drink early, but they last.

Liversan St-Sauveur, H-Méd r ★★ **90' 95 96 98** 00 02 **03** 04 05 07 A 47-ha estate inland from PAUILLAC. Same owner – Jean-Michel Lapalu – as PATACHE D'AUX. Quality oriented. Second wine: Les Charmes de Liversan.

Loudenne St-Yzans, Méd r ★★ **90 94 95 96' 98** 00 **00 01 02 03**04 05 Beautiful riverside CH owned for a century (until 2000) by Gilbeys. ROLLAND consults, so wines are getting bigger, denser. Well-made red from 63 ha. Also an oak-scented Sauv Bl white best at 2–4 yrs (**00 01 02 04 05 06** 07).

Loupiac-Gaudiet Loupiac w sw ★★ **96 97 98 99** 01 02 03' **05** 07 A reliable source of gd-value "almost-SAUTERNES", just across river Garonne.

La Louvière Pe-Lé r w ★★★ (r) **95 96' 98 99 00' 01 02 04** 05 06 07 (w) **98' 99 00 01 02 03** 04' 05' 06 **07** A 55-ha Léognan estate with classical mansion restored by André Lurton. Excellent white and red of classed-growth standard. See also BONNET, COUHINS-LURTON, DE CRUZEAU and DE ROCHEMORIN.

de Lussac St-Em r ★★ **99 00** 03 04 **05** 06 07 One of the best estates in LUSSAC-ST-ÉMILION. New owners and technical methods since 2000. Same stable as FRANC-MAYNE and Vieux Maillet in POMEROL.

Lynch-Bages Pau r (w) ★★★★ **82' 85' 86' 88' 89' 90' 94 95' 96' 98 99 00' 01 02** 03 04' 05' 06 07 08 Always popular, now a regular star. Priced higher than its Fifth Growth status. 90 ha. Rich, robust wine: deliciously dense; aspiring to greatness. See HAUT-BAGES-AVEROUS. From 90, gd oaky white – Blanc de Lynch-Bages. Same owners (Cazes family) as LES ORMES-DE-PEZ and Villa Bel-Air.

Lynch-Moussas Pau r ★★ **90' 95' 96' 98** 00' 01 02 **03** 04 05' 07 Fifth Growth restored by director of BATAILLEY. On the up since 00 but still relatively simple.

du Lyonnat Lussac-St-Em r ★★ **98 00' 01 03** 04 05 49-ha estate; well-distributed, reliable wine. The Rhône's Jean-Luc Colombo is the consulting oenologist.

Macquin-St-Georges St-Em r ★★ **99 00 01 03** 04 05 06 Steady producer of delicious, not weighty, satellite ST-ÉMILION at ST-GEORGES.

Magdelaine St-Em r ★★★ 86 88 89'**90' 94** 95 96 98' **99 00** 01 03 04 05 06 08 Leading CÔTES First Growth: 11 ha owned by J-P MOUEIX. Top-notch, Merlot-led wine; complex, fine and deceptively long-lived.

Malartic-Lagravière Pe-Lé r (w) ★★★ (r) **90' 95 96** 98 99 00' 01 02 03 04' 05' 06 (w) **98 99 00 01'** 02 03 04' 05' 06 07 08 Léognan classed growth of 53 ha (majority red). Rich, modern red wine since late 90s; a *little long-ageing Sauv Bl white*. Belgian owner (since 97) has revolutionized the property. ROLLAND advises. Ch Gazin Rocquencourt (PESSAC-LÉOGNAN) new acquisition in 2006.

Malescasse Lamarque, H-Méd r ★★ **96 98** 00 01 02 03 04 05 06 07 Renovated property with 40 well-situated ha between MARGAUX and ST-JULIEN. Second label: La Closerie de Malescasse. Supple wines, accessible early.

Malescot-St-Exupéry Mar r ★★★ **90' 94 95 96 98 99** 00' 01 02 **03 04** 05' 06 07 Third Growth of 24 ha returned to fine form in the 1990s. Now ripe, fragrant, and finely structured. MICHEL ROLLAND advises.

de Malle Saut w r sw dr ★★★ (w sw) **89' 90' 94** 95 96' **97' 98 99** 01' 02 03' **05** 06 07 Beautiful Preignac CH of 50 ha. V. fine, medium-bodied SAUTERNES; also M de Malle dry white and GRAVES Ch du Cardaillan.

Marbuzet St-Est r ★★ **90 94** 95' **96' 98 99** 00' 01 02 03 04 05' 06 Second label of COS-D'ESTOURNEL until 1994. Same owners. Now a separate estate of 7 ha. Firm but generous ST-ESTÈPHE style.

Margaux, Château Mar r (w) ★★★★ 83' **85' 86' 88' 89' 90' 91 93 94** 95' **96' 97 98' 99** 00' **01' 02** 03' 04' 05' 06 07 08 First Growth (85 ha); the most seductive and fabulously perfumed of all in its frequent top vintages. Consistent since its purchase by André Mentzelopoulos in 1977. Now run by daughter Corinne. Pavillon Rouge (**96' 98 99 00' 01 02 03** 04' 05' 07) is second wine. Pavillon Blanc is best white (Sauv Bl) of MÉDOC, but expensive (**99 00' 01' 02 03** 04' 05 06 07).

Marojallia Mar r ★★★ 99 00' 01 02 03 04 05' 06 07 Micro-CH with 2.5 ha, looking for big prices for big, rich, beefy, un-MARGAUX-like wines. VALANDRAUD owner consults. Upmarket B&B as well. Second wine: Clos Margalaine.

Marquis-d'Alesme-Becker Mar r ★★ 89 90 95 98 00 01 04 05 06 17-ha Third Growth. Disappointing in recent yrs. Purchased by CH LABÉGORCE in 2006, so keep an eye out for change.

Marquis-de-Terme Mar r ★★→★★★ 89' 90' 95 96 98 99 00' 01 02 03 04 05' 06 07 Renovated Fourth Growth of 40 ha. Wobbled in the 1990s but looks better since 2000. Solid rather than elegant MARGAUX.

Martinens Mar r ★★ 96 98 99 00 02 03 04 05 Worthy 30-ha in Cantenac.

Maucaillou Moulis r ★★ 96 98' 00' 01 02 03 04 05 06 An 80-ha property in MOULIS with gd standards. Clean, fresh, value wines. Cap de Haut-Maucaillou is second wine.

Mazeyres Pom r ★★ 95 96' 98' 99 00 01 04 05' 06 Consistent, if not exciting lesser POMEROL. 20 ha on sandier soils. Better since 1996. Alain Moueix, cousin of Christian of J-P MOUEIX, manages here. See FONROQUE.

Meyney St-Est r ★★→★★★ 89' 89' 90' 94 95 96 96 98 00 01 02 03 04 05' 06 Big (50-ha) riverside property in a superb situation next to MONTROSE. Rich, robust, well-structured wines. Second label: Prieur de Meyney.

La Mission-Haut-Brion Pe-Lé r ★★★★ 83 85' 86 88 89' 90' 93 94 95 96' 98' 99 00' 01 02 03 04' 05' 06 07 08 Neighbour and long-time rival to HAUT-BRION; since 1983 in same hands. Consistently grand-scale, full-blooded, long-maturing wine; more flamboyant than HAUT-BRION and sometimes more impressive. 26 ha. LA TOUR HAUT-BRION v'yd integrated from 2006. Second label: La Chapelle de la Mission. White: LAVILLE-HAUT-BRION.

Monbousquet St-Em (w) ★★★ 95 96 98 99 00' 01 02 03 04 05' 06 Substantial property on ST-ÉMILION's gravel plain revolutionized by new owner Gerard Pérse. Now super-rich, concentrated and voluptuous wines. Aborted GRAND CRU CLASSÉ status in 2006. *Rare v.gd white (AC Bordeaux) from 1998*. New owners also acquired PAVIE and PAVIE-DECESSE in 1998.

Monbrison Arsac-Mar r ★★→★★★ 88' 89' 90 95 96' 98 99 00 01 02 04 05 06 MARGAUX of a v. fine, elegant, lacy style. Sometimes too light. 13 ha.

La Mondotte St-Em r ★★★→★★★★ 96' 97 98' 99 00' 01 02 03 04' 05' 06 Intense, always firm, virile *garagiste* wines from micro-property owned by Comte Stephan von Neipperg (CANON-LA-GAFFELIÈRE, CLOS DE L'ORATOIRE).

Montrose St-Est r ★★★→★★★★★ 88 89' 90' 93 94 95 96' 98 99 00' 01 02 03' 04' 05' 06 07 64-ha Second Growth famed for deep-coloured, forceful claret. Known as the LATOUR of ST-ESTÈPHE. Vintages 79–85 (except 82) were lighter. After 110 yrs in same family hands, change of ownership in 2006. Ex-HAUT-BRION director, Jean-Bernard Delmas, now managing. New investment, so watch this space. Second wine: La Dame de Montrose.

Moulin du Cadet St-Em r p ★★ 95 96 98 00 01 03 05 Little 5-ha GRAND CRU CLASSÉ v'yd on the limestone plateau, now managed by Alain Moueix (see also MAZEYRES). Biodynamics practised. Fragrant, medium-bodied wines.

Moulinet Pom r ★★ 95 96 98 00 01 04 05 06 One of POMEROL's bigger CHX; 18 ha on lightish soil. Denis Durantou of l'ÉGLISE-CLINET consults. Gd value.

Moulin Pey-Labrie Canon-Fronsac r ★★ 90 94 95 96 98' 99 00' 01 02 03 04 05' 06 Leading property in FRONSAC. Stylish wines with elegance and structure.

Moulin de la Rose St-Jul r ★★ 95 96 98 00' 01' 02 03 04 05 06 Tiny 4-ha in ST-JULIEN; high standards.

Moulin-St-Georges St-Em r ★★ 95 96 98 99 00' 01 02 03 04 05 06 Stylish and rich wine. Classed-growth level. Same ownership as AUSONE.

Moulin-à-Vent Moulis r ★★ 95 96' 98 00' 02 03 04 05' 06 A 25-ha MOULIS estate; usually regular quality. Lively, forceful wine.

Mouton Rothschild Pau r (w) ★★★★ **82' 83'** 85' **86' 88' 89'** 90' **93' 94** 95' **96** 97 **98' 99** 00' **01' 02** 03 04' 05' 06' 07 08 Officially a First Growth since 1973, though in reality far longer. 84 ha (77% Cab Sauv) can make majestic rich wine, often MÉDOC's most opulent (also, from 1991, white Aile d'Argent). Artists' labels and unique private museum of art relating to wine. New chief winemaker from 2006, previously at BRANAIRE-DUCRU. Second wine: Le Petit Mouton from 1997. See also Opus One (California) and Almaviva (Chile).

Nairac Saut w sw ★★ **86' 88 89** 90' 95' **96** 97' **98 99** 01 02 03' 04 05' 07 (08) Perfectionist BARSAC classed growth. Intense botrytized wines from 16 ha.

Nenin Pom r ★★★ **89 90 94' 95 96** 98 **99 00'** 01 02 03 04 05 06 07 LÉOVILLE-LAS-CASES ownership since 1997. Massive investment. New cellars. 4 ha of former Certan-Giraud acquired in 1999. Now a total of 34 ha. On an upward swing. Gd-value second wine: Fugue de Nenin.

Olivier Graves r w ★★★ (r) **95 96** 00 01 **02 04'** 05' 06 (w) **96 97 98'** 00 01 02 03 04' 05' 06 **07** A 55-ha classed growth (majority red), surrounding a moated castle at Léognan. A sleeper finally being turned around. New investment and greater purity, expression and quality from 2002.

Les Ormes-de-Pez St-Est r ★★→★★★ **90' 94 95 96** 98 **99 00'** 01 02 03 04 05 06 07 Outstanding 29-ha property owned by LYNCH-BAGES. Consistently one of the most delicious ST-ESTÈPHES.

Les Ormes-Sorbet Méd r ★★ **95 96 98' 99 00' 01 02 03'** 04 05 06 Long-time leader in northern MÉDOC. 21 ha at Couquèques. Elegant, gently oaked wines that age. Second label: Ch de Conques.

Palmer Cantenac Mar r ★★★★ **78' 78' 81 82 83' 85 86' 88' 89** 90 93 94 95 **96' 98' 99** 00 01' **02 03** 04' 05' 06 07 08 The star of Cantenac: a Third Growth on a par with the Super Seconds. Wine of power, delicacy, and much Merlot (47%). 55 ha with Dutch, British (the SICHEL family), and French owners. New winemaker (since 2004) formerly with ORNELLAIA. Second wine: Alter Ego de Palmer.

Pape-Clément Pe-Lé r (w) ★★★→★★★★ (r) **90' 94 95 96 98'** 99 00' 01 02 03 04 05 06 07 (w) **01** 02 03 04 **05' 07** 08 Ancient PESSAC v'yd (35 ha) owned by Bernard Magrez; record of seductive, scented, not ponderous reds. 2.5 ha of elegant, barrel-fermented white. Ambitious new-wave direction, oak and potency from 2000 (grapes hand-destemmed!). Also Ch Poumey at Gradignan.

de Parenchère r (w) ★★ 00 01 02 03 04 05 06 Useful AC Ste-Foy BORDEAUX and AC BORDEAUX SUPÉRIEUR from handsome CH with 65 ha. CUVÉE Raphael best.

Patache d'Aux Bégadan, Méd r ★★ **98 99** 00 02 03 04 05' 06 07 A 43-ha property in the northern MÉDOC. Fragrant, largely Cab Sauv wine with the earthy quality of its area. See also LIVERSAN.

Pavie St-Em r ★★★★ 90' **94 95 96 98' 99** 00' 01 02 03' 04 05' 06 07 08 Splendidly sited First Growth; 37 ha mid-slope on the CÔTES. Great track record. Bought by owners of MONBOUSQUET, along with adjacent PAVIE-DECESSE. This is new-wave ST-ÉMILION: intense, strong, mid-Atlantic, and subject of heated debate.

Pavie-Decesse St-Em r ★★ 90 95 **96** 98' **99 00' 01' 02** 03 04 05' 06 07 Small 3.6-ha classed growth. Brother to the above and on form since 1998.

Pavie-Macquin St-Em r ★★★ **89' 90' 94** 95 **96' 98' 99 00'** 01 02 03 04 05' 06 07 08 Robbed of PREMIER GRAND CRU CLASSÉ status by the annulment of 06 classification. 15-ha v'yd on the limestone plateau E of ST-EMILION. Astute

Vintages shown in light type should be opened now only out of curiosity to gauge their future. Vintages in bold are deemed (usually by their makers) ready for drinking. Remember, though: the French tend to enjoy the vigour of young wines, and many 89s, 90s, 95s, and 96s have at least 10 more years of development before them. Vintages marked 00' are regarded as particularly successful for property in question. Vintages in colour are first choice for 2010.

management and winemaking by Nicolas Thienpont of PUYGUERAUD and Derenoncourt consultant. Powerful, structured wines that need time in bottle.

Pedesclaux Pau r ★★ **98' 99 00 02 03 04** 05 06 Underachieving Fifth Growth being steadily revived and reorganized. New management and investment from 1996. Supple wines with up to 50% Merlot.

Petit-Village Pom r ★★★ **90' 94 95 96 98' 99 00' 01 03 04** 05 06 07 Top property aiming for greater heights since 2004. Derenoncourt now consulting. New cellar in 2007. 11 ha; same owner (AXA Insurance) as PICHON-LONGUEVILLE since 1989. Powerful, plummy wine. Second wine: Le Jardin de Petit-Village.

Pétrus Pom r ★★★★ **71' 75' 76 78 79' 81 82' 83 85' 86 88' 89' 90 93' 94 95' 96 97 98' 99** 00' 01 **02** 03 04' 05' 06 07 08 The (unofficial) First Growth of POMEROL: Merlot solo *in excelsis*. 11 ha of gravelly clay giving 5,000 cases of massively rich, concentrated wine, on allocation to the world's millionaires. Each vintage adds lustre. Long-time winemaker J-C Berrouet (44 vintages) retired in 07. Son Olivier now at helm.

Peyrabon St-Sauveur, H-Méd r ★★ **98 99 00' 01 02 03 04** 05 Serious 53-ha HAUT-MÉDOC estate owned by négociant (Millésima). Also La Fleur-Peyrabon PAUILLAC.

de Pez St-Est r ★★→★★★ **89 90' 94 95' 96' 98' 99 00 01 02 03** 04 05' 06 07 Outstanding ST-ESTÈPHE *cru* of 24 ha. As reliable as any of the village's classed growths, if not quite so fine. Bought in 1995 by ROEDERER.

Phélan-Ségur St-Est r ★★★ **88' 89' 90' 95 96' 98 99 00' 01 02 03** 04 05' 06 07 Big and important estate (89 ha); rivals the last as one of ST-ESTÈPHE's best. From 1988 has built up a strong reputation.

Pibran Pau r ★★ **89' 90' 94 95 96 99 00' 01 03 04** 05' 06 07 Small 17-ha property allied to PICHON-LONGUEVILLE. Classy wine with PAUILLAC drive.

Pichon-Longueville (formerly **Baron de Pichon-Longueville**) Pau r ★★★★ **83 85 86' 88' 89' 90' 93 94' 95 96 98 99** 00' **01 02** 03' 04' 05' 06 07 08 Second Growth (73 ha) with revitalized powerful PAUILLAC wine on a par with the following entry. Owners AXA Insurance. New barrel cellar (under an artificial lake) and visitor centre in 2008. Second label: Les Tourelles de Longueville.

Pichon-Longueville Comtesse de Lalande (Pichon Lalande) Pau r ★★★★ **76 78' 79' 81 82' 83 85' 86' 88' 89' 90' 94 95 96 98 99** 00 01 02 03' 04 05' 06 07 Super-Second Growth neighbour to LATOUR (75 ha). Always among the v. top performers; a long-lived, Merlot-marked wine of fabulous breed, even in lesser yrs. ROEDERER now owner; same management, but May-Eliane de Lencquesaing sorely missed. Second wine: Réserve de la Comtesse. Other property: CH BERNADOTTE.

Le Pin Pom r ★★★★ **82 83 85 86 88 89** 90' 94 95 96 97 98' 99 00 01 02 04' 05' 06 07 08 The original of the BORDEAUX cult mini-*crus* made in a cellar not much bigger than a garage. A mere 500 cases of Merlot, with same family behind it as VIEUX-CH-CERTAN (a much better buy). Almost as rich as its drinkers, but

---

St-Émilion classification – back to 1996

After a game of legal ping-pong (which still hasn't finished) the 2006 ST-ÉMILION classification was officially annulled in 2008. However, the case was referred to the French Senate, which reinstated the 1996 classification (until 2010) as a last desperate measure. So those demoted in 2006 are still in and those promoted are out or remain within their 1996 ranking. You have to feel sympathy for the latter (BELLEFONT-BELCIER, DESTIEUX, FLEUR CARDINALE, GRAND CORBIN, GRAND-CORBIN-DESPAGNE, MONBOUSQUET, PAVIE-MACQUIN and TROPLONG MONDOT). The 1996 classification comprises 13 PREMIER GRANDS CRUS CLASSÉS and 55 GRANDS CRUS CLASSÉS.

prices well beyond PÉTRUS are ridiculous.

de Pitray Castillon r ★★ **95 96' 98' 00' 03** 04 05 Large (31-ha) v'yd on CÔTES DE CASTILLON. Flavoursome wines, once the best-known of the AC.

Plince Pom r ★★ **89' 90 94 95 96** 98' **99 00' 01 04** 05 06 Reliable 8-ha property nr Libourne. Vines planted in a single parcel on sandy soil. Lightish wine.

La Pointe Pom r ★★→★★★ **89' 90' 95 96** 98' **99 00' 01 04** 05' 06 07 Prominent 25-ha estate; wines recently plumper and more pleasing. New owner.

Pontac-Monplaisir Pe-Lé r (w) ★★ **96 98 99 00 02** 04 05' **06 07** 16-ha property nearly lost to B'x sprawl. Useful white and red of surprising quality.

Pontet-Canet Pau r ★★★ **86' 88 89' 90 94'** 95 96' 98 99 00' **01 02'** 03 04' 05' 06 07 08 An 81-ha neighbour to MOUTON-ROTHSCHILD. Dragged its feet for many yrs. Old hard tannins were a turn-off. Since mid-1990s v. fine results. V. PAUILLAC in style. Biodynamic aspirations; even horse-ploughing. Second wine: Les Hauts de Pontet-Canet.

Potensac Méd r ★★ **89' 90' 94 95 96** 98 99 **00 01 02 03** 04' 05' 07 Well-known 70-ha property of northern MÉDOC. Owned and run by Delon family of LEOVILLE-LAS-CASES. Class shows, in the form of rich, silky, balanced wines for ageing. Second wine: Chapelle de Potensac.

Pouget Mar r ★★ **89 90 94** 95 96 98' **00' 02 03** 04 05' 06 07 Obscure 11-ha Fourth Growth attached to BOYD-CANTENAC. MARGAUX style. New *chai* in 2000.

Poujeaux Moulis r ★★ **89' 90' 94'** 95' 96' 98 99 00' 04 05 06 Recently purchased (2007) by CLOS FOURTET owner; 57 ha. With CHASSE-SPLEEN and MAUCAILLOU the high point of MOULIS. 20,000-odd cases of characterful, reliable, tannic wine for a long life. Second label: La Salle de Poujeaux.

Premier Grand Cru Classé See ST-ÉMILION CLASSIFICATION box below.

Prieuré-Lichine Cantenac-Mar r ★★★ **89' 90' 94'** 95 96 98' **99 00' 01 02 03** 04 05 06 07 A 70-ha Fourth Growth brought to the fore by the late Alexis Lichine. New owners 1999; now advised by Stéphane Derenoncourt (see CANON LA GAFFELIÈRE, PAVIE-MACQUIN). Fragrant MARGAUX currently on gd form. Second wine: Ch de Clairefont. A gd white Bordeaux, too.

Puygueraud Côtes de Francs r ★★ **95' 96** 98 99 00' 01' **02 03 04** 05' Leading CH of this tiny AC. Wood-aged wines of surprising class. Chx Laclaverie and Les Charmes-Godard follow the same lines. Special CUVÉE George from 2000 with Malbec in blend. Same winemaker as PAVIE-MACQUIN.

Rabaud-Promis Saut w sw ★★→★★★ **88' 89' 90 95 96** 97' **98 99 01'** 02 03' 05' 06 07 (08) A 30-ha classed growth in Bommes. Nr top rank since 86. Rich stuff.

Rahoul Graves r w ★★ (r) **95 96 98' 00' 01 02 04 05** 30-ha v'yd at Portets; still a sleeper despite long record of gd red (70% Merlot) and Sémillon-dominated white **(00 01 02 04' 05 07)**.

Ramage-la-Batisse H-Méd r ★★ **95 96' 98 99 00' 02 03 04 05'** 07 Consistent and widely distributed HAUT-MÉDOC; 65 ha at St-Sauveur, N of PAUILLAC. Ch Tourteran is second wine.

Rauzan-Gassies Mar r ★★ **90' 95 96' 98 99 00 01' 02 03** 04 05' 07 The 30-ha Second Growth neighbour of RAUZAN-SÉGLA that has long lagged behind it. New generation making strides since 2000 but still has a long way to go.

Rauzan-Ségla Mar r ★★★★ **86' 88' 89' 90' 94'** 95 96 98 99 00' **01 02** 03 04' 05 07 08 A Second Growth (51 ha) long famous for its fragrance; owned by owners of Chanel (see CANON). A great MARGAUX name right at the top, with rebuilt CH and *chais*. Second wine: Ségla.

Raymond-Lafon Saut w sw ★★★ **85 86' 88 89' 90' 95 96' 97 98 99' 01' 02 03' 04** 05 06 07 (08) SAUTERNES estate (18 ha) acquired by YQUEM ex-manager and now run by his children. Rich, complex wines that age. Classed-growth quality.

Rayne Vigneau Saut w sw ★★★ **88' 89 90' 95 96 97 98 99 01' 02 03** 05' 07 (08) Large 80-ha classed growth at Bommes. Gd but less power and intensity than the top growths. Sweet wine and dry Rayne sec.

Respide Médeville Graves r w ★★ (r) 99 00' 01 02 04 05' 06 07 (w) 96' 99 00 01 02 04' 05' 07 One of better unclassified properties for both red and white. Same owner as GILETTE. Drink reds at 4–6 yrs; longer for the better vintages.

Reynon Premières Côtes r w ★★ 40 ha for fragrant white from Sauv Bl 01' 02 03 04' 05' 06 07; also serious red (98 99 00 01 02 03 04' 05' 06 07), too. See also CLOS FLORIDÈNE. Second wine (red): Ch Reynon-Peyrat. From 1996 v.gd Ch Reynon Cadillac liquoreux, too.

Reysson Vertheuil, H-Méd r ★★ 95 96 00 02 03 04 05 06 Recently replanted 49-ha HAUT-MÉDOC estate; managed by négociant CVBG-Dourthe (see BELGRAVE, LA GARDE). Rich, modern style.

Ricaud Loupiac w sw (r dr) ★★ 96 97 99 01' 02 03' 05 07 Substantial grower of SAUTERNES-like ageworthy wine just across the river.

Rieussec Saut w sw ★★★★ 82 83' 85 86' 88' 89' 90' 95 96' 97' 98 99 01' 02 03' 04 05' 06 07 (08) Worthy neighbour of YQUEM with 90 ha in Fargues, bought in 1984 by the (LAFITE) Rothschilds. Vinified in oak since 96. Fabulously powerful, opulent wine. Also dry "R", now made in modern style – with less character. Second wine: Carmes de Rieussec.

Ripeau St-Em r ★★ 95 98 00' 01 04 05' 06 Lesser 16-ha GRAND CRU CLASSÉ on sandy soils nr CHEVAL BLANC. Lower yields and improvement from 2000.

de la Rivière Fronsac r ★★ 95 96' 98' 99 00' 01 02 03 04 05' 06 The biggest and most impressive FRONSAC property, with a Wagnerian castle and cellars. Formerly big, tannic wines are now more refined. New winery in 1999. MICHEL ROLLAND consults. Special CUVÉE: Aria.

de Rochemorin Pe-Lé r w ★★→★★★ (r) 95 96 98' 99 00' 01 02 04 05 06 (w) 00 01 02 03 04 05 06 07 An important restoration at Martillac by the Lurtons of LA LOUVIÈRE: 105 ha (three-quarters red) of maturing vines. New state-of-the-art winery in 2004. Fairly consistent quality and widely distributed.

Rol Valentin St-Em r ★★★ 95 96 98 99 00' 01' 02 03 04 05' 06 New (1994) 7.5-ha estate (mainly Merlot) going for modestly massive style (and price). Owned by former footballer. 1,900 cases. Stéphane Derenoncourt consults.

Rouget Pom r ★★ 89' 90 95 96 98' 99 00' 01' 03 04 05' 06 07 Attractive old estate on the northern edge of POMEROL. 17 ha. New Burgundian owners in 1992 and investment since (new cellars). Now excellent; rich, unctuous wines. Gd value.

Royal St-Emilion Brand name of important, dynamic growers' co-op. See GALIUS.

St-André-Corbin St-Em r ★★ 98' 99 00' 01 03 04 05 A 22-ha estate in MONTAGNE-and ST-GEORGES-ST-ÉMILION. Above-average wines.

St-Georges St-Georges-St-Em r ★★ 89' 90' 95' 96 98' 00' 01 03 04 05' Noble 18th-century CH overlooking the ST-ÉMILION plateau from the hill to the north. 51 ha (25% of St-Georges AC). Gd wine sold direct to the public.

St-Pierre St-Jul r ★★★ 82' 85 89 90' 94 95' 96' 98 99 00' 01'02 03 04 05' 06 07 08 Fourth Growth (17 ha) owned by the president of Bordeaux football club. Stylish and consistent classic ST-JULIEN. See GLORIA.

de Sales Pom r ★★ 89' 90' 95 96 98' 00' 01' 04 05 06 Biggest v'yd of POMEROL (47 ha) on sandy-gravel soils, attached to grandest CH. Lightish wine; never quite poetry. Try top vintages. Second label: Ch Chantalouette.

Sansonnet St-Em r ★★ 99 00' 01 02 03 04 05' 06 A small 6.8-ha estate ambitiously run in the new ST-ÉMILION style (rich, fat) since 1999. Derenoncourt consulting from 2006, so perhaps more elegance in future?

Saransot-Dupré Listrac r (w) ★★ 90 95 96 98' 99 00' 01 02 03 04 05 06 Small 12-ha property with delicious, appetizing wines. Lots of Merlot. Also one of LISTRAC's little band of whites (60% Sémillon).

Sénéjac H-Méd r (w) ★★ 95 96 98 99 00 01 02 03 04 05' 06 37-has in southern MÉDOC owned since 1999 by the same family as TALBOT. Tannic reds to age and unusual all-Sem white, also to age. Special CUVÉE: Karolus.

La Serre St-Em r ★★ **90 94 95 96 98' 99 00' 01 02 03** 04 05 06 Small (6.5-ha) GRAND CRU CLASSÉ, on the limestone plateau. Pleasant, stylish wines; more flesh and purity of fruit since 2000.

Sigalas-Rabaud Saut w sw ★★★ **83 85 86 88 89' 90' 95' 96' 97' 98 99 01' 02 03' 04** 05' 07 (08) The smaller part of the former Rabaud estate: 14 ha in Bommes; same winemaking team as LAFAURIE-PEYRAGUEY. V. fragrant and lovely. Top-ranking now. Second wine: Le Cadet de Sigalas Rabaud.

Siran Labarde-Mar r ★★→★★★ **88 89' 90' 95 96 98 99 00' 01 02 03** 04 05 06 07 A 40-ha property of passionate owner who resents lack of *classé* rank. The wines age well and have masses of flavour. ROLLAND consults.

Smith-Haut-Lafitte Pe-Lé r (w p) ★★★ (r) **90' 94 95 96 98 99 00' 01 02 03 04'** 05' 06 07 08 (w) **96 97 98 99' 00 01 02 03 04 05 06 07** 08 Classed growth at Martillac: 67 ha (11 ha make oak-fermented white). Ambitious owners (since 1990) continue to spend hugely to spectacular effect, inc a luxurious wine therapy (external!) spa and hotel-restaurant. White is full, ripe and sappy, red generous but with GRAVES minerality. Second label: Les Hauts de Smith. Also look out for their Ch Cantelys, PESSAC-LÉOGNAN.

Sociando-Mallet H-Méd r ★★★ **88' 89' 90' 94 95 96' 98' 99 00' 01' 02** 03 04 05' 06 07 Splendid, widely followed estate at St-Seurin. Independently minded owner. Classed-growth quality; 75 ha. Conservative big-boned wines to lay down for yrs. Second wine: Demoiselle de Sociando.

Soudars H-Méd r ★★ **94 95 96' 98 99 00' 01 03 04 05** 06 Sister to COUFRAN and VERDIGNAN; 22 ha. Relatively traditional and regular quality.

Soutard St-Em r ★★★**88' 89' 90' 94 95 96 98' 99 00' 01 02** 03 04 05 06 Potentially excellent 19-ha classed growth on the limestone plateau; 70% Merlot. Potent wines can be long-lived. Now owned by same insurance group as LARMANDE (2006). Changes in store. Second label: Clos de la Tonnelle.

Suduiraut Saut w sw ★★★★ **81 82' 83 85 86 88' 89' 90' 95 96 97' 98 99' 01' 02' 03' 04** 05' 06 07 (08) One of the best classed-growth SAUTERNES: 90 ha with renovated CH and gardens by Le Nôtre. New owner, AXA Insurance, has achieved greater consistency and luscious quality. See PICHON-LONGUEVILLE. Second wine: Castelnau de Suduiraut. New dry wine, S, v. promising.

du Tailhas Pom r ★★ **90 94 95 96' 98' 99 00** 00 01 04 05 10-ha property nr FIGEAC. POMEROL of the lighter kind.

Taillefer Pom r ★★ **89 90 94 95' 96 98' 00' 01 02 03 04 05'** 11-ha v'yd on the edge of POMEROL. Astutely managed by Catherine Moueix. Less power than top estates but gently harmonious. Gd value.

Talbot St-Jul (w) ★★★ **88' 89' 90 94 95 96' 98' 99 00' 01 02 03** 04 05' 06 07 08' Important 102-ha Fourth Growth, for many yrs younger sister to GRUAUD-LAROSE. Wine similarly attractive: rich, ***consummately charming, reliable***. Second label: Connétable de Talbot. White: Caillou Blanc matures as well as a gd Graves, but drinks well young. SÉNÉJAC in same family ownership.

Terrey-Gros-Caillou St-Jul r ★★ **94 95 96 98 99 00 02 03 04** 05 Sister CH to HORTEVIE; 15 ha; at best, equally noteworthy and stylish.

du Tertre Arsac-Mar r ★★★ **89' 90' 94 95 96' 98' 99 00' 01 03 04'** 05' 06 07 Fifth Growth (50 ha) isolated south of MARGAUX. History of undervalued fragrant (20% Cab Fr) and fruity wines. Since 1997, same owner as CH GISCOURS. New techniques and massive investment have produced a concentrated, structured wine, really humming from 2003.

Tertre Daugay St-Em r ★★★ **89' 90' 94 95 96 98 99 00' 01 03 04** 05 06 Small, well sited estate, sister to LA GAFFELIÈRE. Temporarily declassified from GRAND CRU CLASSÉ in 06 but improvement in progress. Derenoncourt consulting from 04.

Tertre-Rôteboeuf St-Em r ★★★★ **86 88' 89' 90' 93 94 95 96 97 98' 99 00' 01 02**

03' 04 05' 06 07 08 A cult star (6 ha) making concentrated, dramatic, largely Merlot wine since 1983. Frightening prices. Also CÔTES DE BOURG property, Roc de Cambes of ST-ÉMILION classed-growth quality.

Thieuley E-2-M r p w ★★ Supplier of consistent quality red and white AC Bordeaux; fruity CLAIRET; oak-aged red and white CUVÉE Francis Courselle. Also owns Clos Ste-Anne in PREMIÈRES CÔTES DE BORDEAUX.

La Tour-Blanche Saut w (r) sw ★★★ **83' 85 86 88' 89' 90' 95 96 97' 98 99 01' 02 03 04** 05' 06 07 (08) Historic leader of SAUTERNES, now a government wine college. Coasted in 1970s; since 1988 a top player again.

La Tour-de-By Bégadan, Méd r ★★ **89' 90' 94 95 96' 98 00 01 02 03 04 05'** 06 V. well-run 74-ha family estate in northern MÉDOC with a name for sturdy but reliable wines with a fruity note. A sure thing.

La Tour-Carnet St-Laurent, H-Méd r ★★ **85 86 89' 90 94' 95 96 98 99 00' 01 02 03 04'** 05' 06 Fourth Growth (65 ha) with medieval moated fortress, long neglected. New ownership (see FOMBRAUGE, PAPE-CLÉMENT) and investment from 2000 has produced richer wines in more modern style. Second wine: Les Douves de Ch La Tour Carnet. Also *garage* Servitude Volontaire du Tour Carnet.

La Tour Figeac St-Em r ★★ **89' 90' 94' 95 96' 98' 99 00' 01' 02 04** 05 06 07 A 15-ha GRAND CRU CLASSÉ between FIGEAC and POMEROL. California-style ideas since 1994. Biodynamic methods. Opulent at its best.

La Tour Haut Brion Graves r ★★★ **89 90 94 95 96' 98' 99 00' 01 02 03 04'** 05' RIP from 2005 for this classed growth. The 5.05-ha v'yd has now been integrated into that of LA MISSION-HAUT-BRION. Same owner.

Tour Haut-Caussan Méd r ★★ **96 98 00' 01 02 03 04 05'** Well-run property at Blaignan to watch for full wines. Same ownership as Ch Cascadais, CORBIÈRES.

Tour-du-Haut-Moulin Cussac, H-Méd r ★★ **88' 89' 90' 94 95 96 98 00' 02 03 04** 05' 06 Conservative grower in Cussac Fort Médoc: intense, consistent, no-nonsense wines to mature.

La Tour de Mons Soussans-Mar r ★★ **89 90' 94 95 96' 98' 99 00 01 02 04** 05' 06 Famous MARGAUX *cru* of 44 ha, in the same family for 3 centuries. A long dull patch but new (1995) TALBOT influence is returning to the old fragrant, vigorous, ageworthy style.

Tournefeuille Lalande de Pom r ★★ **95' 98' 99 00' 01' 02 03 04** 05 06 07 Well-known Néac CH. 17 ha. On the upswing since 1998 with new owners.

Tour-du-Pas-St-Georges St-Em r ★★ **95 96 98 99 00' 01 03 04 05** 06 Wine from 16 ha of ST-GEORGES-ST-ÉMILION owned by BELAIR winemaker. Recent investment.

La Tour du Pin St-Em r ★★ **89' 90' 95 96 98 00' 01 04** 05 06 8 ha, formerly La Tour du Pin Figeac-Moueix but bought and renamed by CHEVAL BLANC in 2006. Unimpressive form previously, but new team turning things around. To watch.

Tour-St-Bonnet Méd r ★★ **95 96 98 99 00' 02 03 04 05** 06 Consistently well-made potent northern MÉDOC from St-Christoly; 40 ha.

Tronquoy-Lalande St-Est r ★★ **89 90' 94 95 96 98 99 00' 02 03 04** 05 06 07 Same owners as MONTROSE from 2006. Lots of Merlot and Petit Verdot; 19 ha. High-coloured wines to age. Second wine: Tronquoy de Ste-Anne.

Troplong-Mondot St-Em r ★★★★ **88' 89' 90' 94' 95 96' 98' 99 00' 01' 02 03 04** 05' 06 07 08 Temporarily PREMIER GRAND CRU CLASSÉ (2006) and now fuming at the annulment. Well-sited 30 ha on a high point of limestone plateau. *Wines of power and depth with increasing elegance.* MICHEL ROLLAND consults. Second wine: Mondot.

Trotanoy Pom r ★★★★ **85' 88 89' 90' 93 94 95 96 98' 99 00' 01 02** 03 04' 05' 06 07 08 Home to Jean-François Moueix, owner of PÉTRUS. Only 7 ha; at best (eg **98**) a glorious, fleshy, structured, perfumed wine. Wobbled a bit in the 1980s, but back on top form since 1989.

Trottevieille St-Em r ★★★ **89' 90 94 95 96 98 99 00' 01 02** 03' 04 05' 06 07 First

Growth on the limestone plateau. Dragged its feet for yrs. Same owners as BATAILLEY and DOMAINE DE L'EGLISE have raised its game since 2000. Denis Dubourdieu consults.

Valandraud St-Em r ★★★★ 93 94 95' 96 98 99 00' 01' 02 03 04 05' 06 07 08 Leader among *garagiste* micro-wines fulfilling aspirations to glory. But silly prices for the sort of thick, vanilla-scented wine California can make. V'yds now expanded to 20 ha; better terroir and more balance. Now an average 15,000 bottles. Second and third wines: Virginie and Axelle.

Valrose St-Est r ★★ 02 03 04 05' A newcomer since 1999, co-owned with CLINET. Special cuvée: Aliénor. To watch.

Verdignan Méd r ★★ 95' 96 98 99 00' 01 02 03 04 05 06 Substantial 60-ha HAUT-MÉDOC estate; sister to COUFRAN and SOUDARS. More Cab Sauv than COUFRAN. Gd value and ageing potential.

La Vieille Cure Fronsac r ★★ 95 96 98 99 00' 01' 02 03 04 05 06 A 20-ha property, US-owned, leading the commune. Accessible from 4 yrs. Reliable value.

Vieux-Ch-Certan Pom r ★★★★ 82' 83' 85 86' 88' 89 90' 94 95' 96' 98' 99 00' 01 02 04' 05' 06 07 08 Traditionally rated close to PÉTRUS in quality, but totally different in style (30% Cab Fr and 10% Cab Sauv); almost HAUT-BRION build with plenty of finesse. 14 ha. Same (Belgian) family owns tiny LE PIN.

Vieux Ch St-André St-Em r ★★ 00' 01 02 03 04 05 06 Small 6-ha v'yd in MONTAGNE-ST-ÉMILION owned by former winemaker of PÉTRUS. Regular quality.

Villegeorge Avensan, H-Méd r ★★ 89 90 94 95 96' 98' 99 00' 02 03 04 05 06 A 15 ha HAUT-MÉDOC north of MARGAUX. Fine, traditional MÉDOC style. Sister Chx Duplessis in MOULIS and La Tour de Bessan in MARGAUX.

Vray Croix de Gay Pom r ★★ 88 89 90 95 96 98' 00' 04 05 06 V. small (4 ha); in the best part of POMEROL. Greater efforts from 04. Sister to Ch Siaurac in LALANDE DE POMEROL and Le Prieuré in ST-ÉMILION. Derenoncourt consults.

Yon-Figeac St-Em r ★★ 90 95 96 98 99 00' 02 03 04 05 06 24-ha estate. V'yd restructured between 1985 and 1995. Improvements from 2000. Declassified from GRAND CRU CLASSÉ in 2006 but then reinstated.

d'Yquem Saut w sw (dr) ★★★★ 76' 79 80' 81' 83' 85 86' 88' 89' 90' 93 94 95' 96 97' 98 99' 00 01' 02 03' 04 05' The world's most famous sweet wine estate. 101 ha; only 200 bottles per hectare of v. strong, intense, luscious wine, kept 4 yrs in barrel. Most vintages improve for 15+ yrs; some live 100+ yrs in transcendent splendour. After centuries in the Lur-Saluces family, in 1998 control was surrendered to Bernard Arnault of LVMH. The new management (same as CHEVAL BLANC) is forward-thinking, and pushing prices sky-high. Also makes dry "Y" (ygrec).

BORDEAUX

Italy

More heavily shaded areas are the wine-growing regions

The following abbreviations are used in the text:

Ab	Abruzzo	**Sar**	Sardinia	
Ap	Apulia	**Si**	Sicily	
Bas	Basilicata	**T-AA**	Trentino-	
Cal	Calabria		Alto Adige	
Cam	Campania	**Tus**	Tuscany	
E-R	Emilia-Romagna	**Umb**	Umbria	
F-VG	Friuli-Venezia	**VdA**	Valle d'Aosta	
	Giulia	**Ven**	Veneto	
Lat	Latium			
Lig	Liguria			
Lom	Lombardy	**cs**	Cantine Sociale	
Mar	Marches	**fz**	*frizzante*	
Pie	Piedmont	**pa**	*passito*	

Map labels: VALLE D'AOSTA, L Com, L Maggiore, Milan, LOMBAR, Turin, PIEDMONT, Genoa, Po, LIGURIA, Ligurian Sea

Although Italy has slipped to second place after France in terms of average annual production, she continues to offer by far the widest range of scents and flavours, derived from her extraordinary diversity of grape varieties. As anyone who has travelled in Italy will testify, she is not one nation but a commonwealth of localities united by a common language – and even that often has to take second place to the local dialect. Every locality has its own customs and cuisine – and even where grape varieties are similar, styles of wine often are not. What fun can be had in lining up a tasting of, say, indigenous grapes of the northeast: Lagrein from Alto Adige, Teroldego from Trentino, Corvina from Veneto, Refosco from Friuli; or from the northwest, with Nebbiolo and Barbera, Dolcetto and Freisa; Sangiovese, Montepulciano and Sagrantino from the centre; Aglianico, Negroamaro, Primitivo and Gaglioppo from the southern mainland; Nero d'Avola, Nerello Mascalese, Cannonau and Carignano from the islands. On the white side keep an eye out for grapes such as Arneis and Cortese from Piedmont, Pinot Bianco and Traminer (native to South Tyrol) in Alto Adige, Garganega and Prosecco in Veneto, Friulano and Ribolla in Friuli, Verdicchio in Le Marche, Vermentino in Tuscany, Grechetto in Umbria, Greco, Fiano and Falanghina in Campania and the south, Inzolia and Grecanico in Sicily and Vermentino in Sardinia. Grape varieties are the best place to start. Official DOCs are a wobbly guide. A few famous brands are prominent, but either expensive or boring. Individual growers often seem to disappear behind their loquacious labels. An open mind and a sense of fun are the only essentials on a voyage of discovery.

Recent Vintages

Tuscany

2008 A very wet spring followed by a very dry summer, punctuated by rare and occasionally violent rain and hailstorms. Heat and drought brought some problems, but on the whole results were good to excellent for a third year.

2007 A rainy May followed a mild, dry winter and summery Apr. Summer itself was very hot and arid. Late Aug rains came to the rescue. Ideal vintage conditions made for a smaller than average but high quality crop.

2006 A year of balance, no temperature extremes, measured rainfall. Cool Aug but good weather at vintage time apart from two days' downpour in late Sept. A top oenologist in Chianti Classico dubbed it "the greatest of the last 20 vintages".

2005 Most successful along the coast and for those who picked early. Sangiovese at every quality level imaginable, from first-rate to diluted.

2004 Exceptionally promising along the coast, in Montepulciano, and in Montalcino, where 5-star rating begins to be justified. Despite cool temperatures some truly elegant wines throughout.

2003 High sugar content meant uppish alcohol with green tannins for early-picked grapes, or low-acid jamminess for later-picked.

2002 Generally poor with some notable exceptions.

2001 Beginning to be seen as a great year for laying down top wines.

Older fine vintages: 99 97 95 90

Piedmont

2008 As in Tuscany, a wet spring led to a dry hot summer, but not as hot as 2003. some great Nebbiolos and Barberas are foreseen.

2007 Very short but good to excellent quality for Barolo/Barbaresco. Early and mid-term ripeners such as Dolcetto and Barbera fared well too, again at a cost in volume. Fears of unbalanced wines proved unfounded, and some classic wines are beginning to work their way through.

2006 Excellent Dolcetto, very fine Nebbiolo and Barbera; another great vintage.

2005 Pleasurable Dolcetto; spotty for Barbera, with some rot from persistent rains; Nebbiolo rather uneven with some good wines for early drinking.

2004 Very long growing season, high level of quality for all major red grapes (Dolcetto, Barbera, Nebbiolo). Classic year for Barbaresco and Barolo.

2003 Sweltering summer, but v. positive for Barbera, Dolcetto, and Moscato. Nebbiolo more irregular, difficult to find well-balanced wines.

2001 Classy and firm Nebbiolo and Barbera, developing into another classic.

Older fine vintages: 00 99 98 97 96 95 90 89 88

Amarone, Veneto

2008 A textbook year in terms of temperature and rainfall leading to a vintage carried out under ideal conditions. Quantity a bit short, but classic wines of high quality.

2007 High hopes were dashed for some by vicious hailstorms at the end of Aug. Those not wiped out made some excellent wines, but very short crop, with steeply rising prices.

2006 Outstanding, with new record established for the grape tonnage reserved for drying, 30% higher than any previous vintage.

2005 A difficult harvest due to damp weather, but grape-drying technology saved Amarone and Recioto. Less successful vintage for Soave and whites.

2004 Classic, less concentrated and rich than 2003.

2003 Very concentrated and sugar-rich grapes; some outstanding Amarone and Recioto wines.

2002 Heavy rains throughout the ripening season. Best wines were downgraded top *crus*.

2001 Classic for some, others preferred 2000.

Marches & Abruzzo reds

2008 East of the Apennines conditions were rainier and cooler than in the north and west, with a perfect end of the season. Excellent wines are expected.

2007 Spectacularly low crop due to heat and water shortage, leading to some fairly dramatic price rises. But some excellent quality.

2006 Irregular. Generally positive where hail did not fall; better than 2004 and 2005, but not as good as 2003.

2005 Wines of good ripeness and structure for those who waited to pick.

2004 Irregular. Better in Rosso Conero than Rosso Piceno in the Marches; best in Colline Teramane DOCG, Abruzzo.

2003 One of the most successful areas in Italy in 2003, as the Montepulciano grape stood up to the heat and drought, giving first-rate results.

2001 Fragrant wines with much complexity and depth.

Campania & Basilicata

2008 The south did not suffer the prolonged rains, nor the accompanying moulds, which prevailed in spring/summer in the north and centre. A dry and long summer. A classic year for Aglianico; good, too, for whites.

2007 Very low yields due to heat/drought aggravated by mildew devastation. Good quality for those who sprayed and waited for balanced grapes.

2006 Rain and problems of rot in lower-lying zones, much sun and a very long growing season in higher vineyards, with predictably superior results.

2005 Traditionally the last grapes to be picked, Aglianico had weight, complexity, and character – perhaps the finest wines of all Italy in 2005.

2004 Slow and uncertain ripening for Aglianico; has exceeded expectations.

2003 Scorching and drought-stressed growing conditions, but the altitude of the v'yds worked in late-picked Aglianico's favour. Generally a success.

2001 Intense, perfumed, and ageworthy wines.

Aglianico del Vulture Bas DOC r dr ★★★ 97' 98 00 01' 03 04 05' 06 07 (08) VECCHIO after 3 yrs, RISERVA after 5 yrs. Southern Italy's greatest grape, v. late ripener – often into Nov. Top: Alovini, d'Angelo, Basilisco, Cantina del Notaio, Elena Fucci, Di Palma, PATERNOSTER, Le Querce, Tenuta del Portale, Torre degli Svevi.

Alba Major wine city of PIEDMONT, southeast of Turin. Centre of various DOC/GS inc BAROLO, BARBARESCO, NEBBIOLO d'Alba, ROERO, BARBERA d'Alba and DOLCETTO d'Alba. Proposed as DOC in own right, but that may change with new rules.

Albana di Romagna E-R DOCG w dr s/sw sw (sp) ★→★★★ DYA Varietal white, Italy's first white DOCG, justifiably for the sweet PASSITO version, not for the undistinguished dry styles. ZERBINA, **Fattoria Paradiso** and Giovanna Madonia make excellent versions, Fattoria Paradiso and Tremonti's are v.gd.

Alcamo Si DOC w ★ Racy if somewhat one-dimensional whites from prolific Catarratto grape. Rapitala and Terre di Ginestra are best of an uninspired lot.

Aleatico Red Muscat-flavoured grape for sweet, aromatic, often fortified wines, chiefly in south Aleatico di Puglia DOC (best: Candido and Santa Lucia) is better and more famous than Aleatico di Gradoli (Latium) DOC, best example Occhipinti's Monte Maggiore. Other gd examples come from Jacopo Banti and Brancatelli in Val di Cornia and Sapereta, Acquabona on ELBA.

Alessandria, Gianfranco ★★★ Small, new-wave producer of high-level ALBA wines at Monforte d'Alba, esp BAROLO San Giovanni, BARBERA D'ALBA Vittoria.

Alezio Ap DOC p (r) ★★ One of many quasi-superfluous DOCS in Puglia's Salento peninsula all sharing similar regulations based on NEGROAMARO, making perfumed but sturdy rosés and juicy reds. Best producers Rosa del Golfo/Calo with Rosa del Golfo (p) and Michele Calò with NEGROAMARO IGT Spano (r).

Allegrini Ven ★★★ Top-quality Veronese producer; outstanding single-v'yd IGT wines (Palazzo della Torre, Grola, and Poja), AMARONE, and RECIOTO.

Altare, Elio Pie ★★★ Pioneering, influential small producer of v.gd modern BAROLO. Look for BAROLO Arborina, BAROLO Brunate, LANGHE DOC Arborina (Nebbiolo), Larigi (BARBERA), La Villa, VDT L'Insieme and DOLCETTO D'ALBA.

Alto Adige T-AA DOC r p w dr sw sp ★→★★★ Alto Adige or SÜDTIROL DOC with almost 50 types of wine, the best being white and varietal. Sub-denominations include VALLE ISARCO/Eisacktal, TERLANO/Terlaner, Val Venosta/Vinschgau, AA SANTA MADDALENA/ST-MAGDALENER, Bozner Leiten, Meranese di Collina/Meraner).

Ama, Castello di ★★★ One of the best and most consistent modern CHIANTI CLASSICO estates, near Gaiole. La Casuccia and Bellavista are top single-v'yd wines. Gd IGTS, CHARD, and MERLOT (L'Apparita).

Amabile Semi-sweet.

Amaro Bitter. Suffix "–one" means "big", so Amarone means "big bitter".

Amarone della Valpolicella (formerly Recioto della Valpolicella Amarone) Ven DOC r p ★★→★★★★ 90' 93 95 **97** 98 **00** 01 03' 05 06 07 (08) Relatively dry version of Recioto della Valipolicella from air-dried VALPOLICELLA grapes; concentrated, fairly long-lived. (For producers see Valpolicella box.) Older vintages are hard to come by but tend to dry out beyond 20 years.

Anselmi, Roberto ★★★ A leader in SOAVE with his single-v'yd Capitel Foscarino and exceptional sweet dessert RECIOTO i Capitelli. Having renounced the DOC(G), this rebel's wines are now IGT.

Antinori, Marchesi L & P ★★→★★★★ V. influential Florentine house of highest repute, owned by Piero A, sharing management with his 3 daughters and oenologist Renzo Cotarella. Famous for CHIANTI CLASSICO (*Tenute Marchese Antinori* and Badia a Passignano), Umbrian (CASTELLO DELLA SALA), and PIEDMONT (PRUNOTTO) wines. Pioneer of new IGT, eg TIGNANELLO, SOLAIA (TUS, white Cervaro della Sala (Umbria) Expanding into south Tuscan MAREMMA (Fattoria Aldobrandesca), MONTEPULCIANO (La Braccesca), MONTALCINO (Pian delle Vigne), in ASTI (for BARBERA), in FRANCIACORTA for sparkling (Montenisa), and in APULIA (Vigneti del Sud). V.gd DOC BOLGHERI Guardo al Tasso.

Apulia Puglia. Italy's heel, producing almost a sixth of Italy's wine, increasing in quality and value. Best DOC: BRINDISI, CASTEL DEL MONTE, MANDURIA (PRIMITIVO DI), SALICE SALENTINO. Producers: ANTINORI, Botromagno, Candido, Cantele, Cantine Paradiso, Casale Bevagna, Castel di Selva, Co-op Due Palme, Conti Zecca, Coppadoro, La Corte, Li Veli, D'Alfonso del Sordo, Felline, Masseria Monaci, Masseria Pepe, Michele Calò, RIVERA, Rubino, Rosa del Golfo, Sinfarosa, TAURINO, Valle dell'Asso, VALLONE.

Aquileia F-VG DOC r w ★ (r) **04 05 06** 07 (08) A group of 12 moderately interesting single-varietal wines from around the town of Aquileia. Gd REFOSCO, Sauv Bl. Ca' Bolani and Denis Montanar are not bad.

Argiano Avant-garde BRUNELLO estate where Hans Vinding-Diers also makes controversial blend Solengo and smooth 100% Sangiovese Suolo.

Argiano, Castello di, aka *Sesti*. Giuseppe Maria Sesti turns out classy biodynamic Brunello and Bordeaux-influenced Terra di Siena.

Argiolas, Antonio ★★→★★★ SARDINIAN producer. High-level CANNONAU, NURAGUS, VERMENTINO, Bovale. Red IGTS Turriga (★★★) and Korem are among the best.

Arneis Pie w ★★→★★★ DYA Fine peachy/appley white from around ALBA, revived from nr extinction in 1970s by GIACOSA and VIETTI. Fragrant, fruity, intense. ROERO Arneis DOCG, NW of ALBA, is normally better than LANGHE Arneis DOC. Try: Correggia, BRUNO GIACOSA, Malvirà, Angelo Negro, PRUNOTTO, Sorilaria, VIETTI.

Assisi Umb IGT r (w) ★ DYA IGT ROSSO and BIANCO di Assisi, a town more notable for tourism than wine. Sportoletti is acceptable.

Asti Pie DOCG w sw sp ★→★★★ NV Piedmontese zone producing some excellent BARBERAS, better known as sweet fizz from the Muscat grape, which rarely rises above the industrial except in the form of MOSCATO D'ASTI. The big Asti houses are not interested in improving quality but in holding down price. Despite unique potential, Asti is a cheap supermarket product with a massive market in Russia. A few producers care: Alasia, WALTER BERA, CASCINA FONDA,

> **The best Barbaresco to seek out**
> For top Nebbiolo look for: CERETTO, CIGLIUTI, Fratelli Giacosa, GAJA, BRUNO GIACOSA, GRESY, Cortese, Lano, Moccagatta, Montaribaldi, Ada Nada, Fiorenzo Nada, Paitin, Giorgio Pelissero, PIO CESARE, PRODUTTORI DEL BARBARESCO, PRUNOTTO, Punset, Ressia, Massimo Rivetti, Rizzi, Roagna, Albino Rocca, BRUNO ROCCA, GIORGIO RIVETTI, Varaldo.

CONTRATTO, Dogliotti-Caudrina, Vignaioli di Santo Stefano.

Avignonesi ★★★ Noble MONTEPULCIANO house, recently changed ownership. Hitherto highly experimental, with a v. fine range: VINO NOBILE, Desiderio, 50:50. Best known for long-aged, super-low-production VIN SANTO (★★★★).

Azienda agricola/agraria An estate (large or small) making wine from own grapes.

Azienda/casa vinicola A négociant making wine from bought-in and own grapes.

Badia a Coltibuono ★★→★★★ Historic CHIANTI CLASSICO producer run by Stucchi Prinetti family. Top wine is 100% BARRIQUE-aged SANGIOVESE "Sangioveto".

Banfi (Castello or Villa) ★★→★★★ MONTALCINO CANTINA of biggest US importer of Italian wine. Huge plantings at Montalcino, mostly recently developed SANGIOVESE or own experimental clones; also SYRAH, PINOT N, CAB SAUV, CHARD, SAUV BL, etc. Poggio all'Oro and *Poggio alle Mura* are ★★★ BRUNELLOS. Summus and Excelsus are top SANT'ANTIMO reds. In PIEDMONT, also gd Banfi Brut, BRACCHETO D'ACQUI, GAVI, PINOT GR.

Barbaresco Pie DOCG r ★★→★★★★ 88 89' 90' 95 96' 97 98 99' 00 01 04 06 07 (08) Classic Italian red, 100% NEBBIOLO. Like its neighbour BAROLO, combines depth of complex flavour with bright, clean tannins. At 4 yrs becomes RISERVA.

Barbatella, Cascina La ★★★ Top producer of BARBERA D'ASTI: excellent Vigna dell'Angelo and MONFERRATO Rosso Sonvico (BARBERA/CAB SAUV).

Barbera Prolific red variety, dominant in PIEDMONT, also varietally in Lombardy and (for blends) throughout Italy, indeed the world. High acidity, low tannin and distinctive cherry fruit are defining characteristics. Capable of diverse wine-styles from BARRIQUED and serious to semi-sweet and frothy.

Barbera d'Alba Pie DOC r ★★→★★★ 01 03 04 05 06 07 (08) Potentially acidic red here generally smoothed by BARRIQUE ageing, but all too often playing second fiddle to NEBBIOLO. Best age up to 7 yrs. Some excellent wines, often from producers of BAROLO, BARBARESCO and ROERO.

Barbera d'Asti Pie DOC r ★★→★★★ 01 03 04 05 06 07 (08) The real thing, some say, from lands where BARBERA comes first. Two styles, fresh, fruity and somewhat sharp, or rounded by wood ageing.

Barbera del Monferrato Pie DOC r ★→★★ DYA Easy-drinking BARBERA from ALESSANDRIA and ASTI. Can be slightly fizzy, sometimes sweetish. Delimited area is almost identical to BARBERA D'ASTI but style simpler although serious and more important wines now appearing from Accornero, Valpane, Vicara.

Barco Reale Tus DOC r ★★ 05 06 07 (08) DOC for junior wine of CARMIGNANO.

Bardolino Ven DOC r (p) ★→★★ DYA Pale, summery, slightly bitter red from Lake Garda. Bardolino CHIARETTO: paler and lighter. Best include Buglioni, Cavalchina, Guerrieri Rizzardi, Le Fraghe, MONTRESOR, Pantini, ZENATO, Zeni.

> **The best of Barbera d'Asti**
> BAVA, BERA, Bersano, Bertelli, Alfiero Boffa, BRAIDA, Cascina Castlèt, CHIARLO, Contratto, COPPO, cs Nizza, cs Vinchio e Vaglio, Dezzani, HASTAE, La Barbatella, La Morandina, La Tenaglia, Marchesi Alfieri, Marengo, Beppe Marino, Martinetti, Elio Perrone, Prunotto, GIORGIO RIVETTI, Bruno Rocca, Scrimaglio, Scagliola, Terre da Vino and VIETTI.

> **The Barolo role of honour: the traditionalists**
> Anselma, Ascheri, Barale, Borgogno, Brezza, Brovia, BURLOTTO,
> Cappellano, Cavallotto, Ciabot Berton, ALDO CONTERNO, GIACOMO
> CONTERNO, FONTANAFREDDA, BRUNO GIACOSA, Marcarini, GIUSEPPE
> MASCARELLO, Massolino, Monchiero, PIO CESARE (BAROLO), Poderi Colla,
> Francesco Rinaldi, Giuseppe Rinaldi, Schiavenza, CASTELLO DI VERDUNO.

Barolo Pie DOCG r ★★★→★★★★ **88' 89' 90' 95 96' 97' 98' 99' 00 01'** 04' 05 06' 07'
(08) World-class red wine named for village south of ALBA : tannic, alcoholic
(min 13%), dry but wonderfully complex and fragrant (roses and, with age, tar)
with a long, deceptively almost porty finish. From NEBBIOLO grapes, 100%.
Ages for up to 20–25 yrs (minimum 3 yrs, RISERVA after 5 yrs).

Barolo Chinato A dessert wine made from BAROLO DOCG, alcohol, sugar, herbs,
spices, and Peruvian bark. Producers: Cappellano, CERETTO, Giulio Cocchi.

Barrique This 225-litre French oak container has been the major weapon of the
internationalists in Italy and the *bête noire* of the traditionalists, who reject its
smoky, vanilla tones in favour of the neutrality of the Slavonian oak BOTTE.

Basciano ★★ Producer of gd DOCG CHIANTI RUFINA and IGT wines.

Bava ★★ Producer of BARBERA D'ASTI Piano Alto and Stradivarius, MONFERRATO
BIANCO, BAROLO CHINATO; the Bava family controls the old firm Giulio Cocchi in
ASTI, where it produces gd sparkling METODO CLASSICO.

Bellavista ★★★ FRANCIACORTA estate with expensive but convincing Champagne-
style wines (Gran Cuvée Franciacorta is top). Also Satèn (a crémant-style
sparkling). TERRE DI FRANCIACORTA DOC and Sebino IGT Solesine (both CAB
SAUV/MERLOT blends). Owner Vittorio Moretti also expanding into Tuscan
MAREMMA, Val di Cornia (Petra), and Monteregio.

Bera, Walter ★★→★★★ Small estate nr BARBARESCO. V.gd MOSCATO D'ASTI, ASTI,
BARBERA D'ASTI, BARBARESCO, and LANGHE NEBBIOLO.

Berlucchi, Guido ★★ Italy's biggest producer of sparkling METODO CLASSICO.

Bersano Historic wine house in Nizza Monferrato, with BARBERA D'ASTI Generala,
and BAROLO Badarina, most PIEDMONT DOC wines inc BARBARESCO, MOSCATO
D'ASTI, ASTI SPUMANTE.

Bertani ★★→★★★ Well-known quality wines from Verona, esp traditional AMARONE
and Valpolicella Valpantena Secco Bertani.

Bianco di Custoza Ven DOC w (sp) ★→★★ DYA Fresh white from Lake Garda, made
from an eclectic mix of grapes inc SOAVE'S GARGANEGA and PIEDMONT'S CORTESE.
Gd: Cavlchina, Le Tende, Le VIGNE di San Pietro, MONTRESOR, Zeni.

Bibi Graetz ★ Fine reds from hills of Fiesole nr Florence. Testamatta Rosso
(SANGIOVESE and other Tuscan reds) and Bugia Bianco (Ansonica).

Biondi-Santi ★★★★ Founding family, on Il Greppo estate, of BRUNELLO DI
MONTALCINO. Genuinely long-lasting wines capable of great finesse.

Bisol Top brand of PROSECCO.

Boca Pie DOC r ★★ 99' 00 01' **03'** 04' 05 06' 07' (08) Obscure, NEBBIOLO-based red
from northern PIEDMONT. Le Piane and Poderi ai Valloni (Vigneto Cristiana ★★)
can be good if they can be found.

Boccadigabbia ★★★ Top Marche producer of IGT wines: SANGIOVESE
(Saltapicchio), CAB SAUV (Akronte), PINOT N (Il Girone), CHARD (Montalperti).
Proprietor also owns fine Villamagna estate in ROSSO PICENO DOC.

Boglietti, Enzo ★★★ Dynamic young producer of La Morra in BAROLO zone. Top
modern-style Barolos and outstanding BARBERA d'Alba.

Bolgheri Tus DOC r p w (sw) ★★→★★★★ Ultra-modish region on the Costa degli
Etruschi, south of Livorno. Home of SASSICAIA, ORNELLAIA (FRESCOBALDI) and
other wealthy bandwagonists. CAB SAUV/MERLOT/SYRAH/SANGIOVESE blends.

Other top producers: CA' MARCANDA (GAJA), Caccia al Piano, Giorgio Meletti Cavallari, Campo alla Sughera, Campo al Mare, Casa di Terra, Collemassari/Grattamacco, Guado al Tasso (ANTINORI), Poggio al Tesoro, San Guido/SASSICAIA, Michele SATTA.

Bolla ★★ Historic Verona firm for SOAVE, VALPOLICELLA, AMARONE, RECIOTO. Owned by American giants Brown-Forman, fighting to escape from industrial image.

Bonarda Lom DOC r ★★ 05 06 07 (08) Soft, fresh FRIZZANTE and still wines from OLTREPÒ PAVESE, actually made from Croatina grapes. Not to be confused with Piedmontese Bonarda.

Borgo del Tiglio ★★★ →★★★★ FRIULI estate for one of NE Italy's top MERLOTS, ROSSO della Centa; also superior COLLIO CHARD, MALVASIA, and Bianco.

Boscarelli, Poderi ★★★ Small estate with v.gd VINO NOBILE DI MONTEPULCIANO and barrel-aged IGT Boscarelli.

Botte Large barrel, anything from 6 to 250 hectolitres, usually between 20 and 50, traditionally of Slavonian but increasingly of French oak. To traditionalists the ideal vessel for wines in which an excess of oak aromas is undesirable.

Brachetto d'Acqui Pie DOCG r sw (sp) ★★ DYA Sweet, sparkling red with enticing Muscat scent.

Braida ★★★ The late Giacomo Bologna's estate; for top BARBERA D'ASTI (BRICCO dell'Uccellone, BRICCO della Bigotta, Ai Suma).

Bramaterra Pie DOC r ★★ 99' 00 01' 03 04' 06' 07' (08) Neighbour to GATTINARA. NEBBIOLO grapes predominate in a blend. Gd producer: Sella.

Breganze Ven DOC r w ★→★★★ (r) 99 01 02 03 04 06 07 (08) Major production area for Pinot Grigio, also gd Cab. Top producer: MACULAN.

Brindisi Ap DOC r p ★★ 01 03 04 05 06 07 (08) (r) DYA (p) Smooth NEGROAMARO-based red with MONTEPULCIANO, esp from VALLONE, Due Palme, Rubino. Rosato version can be one of Italy's best. See also ROSATO DEL SALENTO.

Brolio, Castello di ★★→★★★★ Historic, once trend-setting estate now thriving in the hands, once again, of the Ricasoli family after a period of foreign-managed decline. *V.gd Chianti Classico* and IGT Casalferro.

Brunelli ★★→★★★ V.gd quality producer of AMARONE and RECIOTO.

Brunelli, Gianni ★★★ Recently deceased small-scale producer of elegant, refined BRUNELLO DI MONTALCINO and owner of Siena's excellent restaurant, Le Logge. Not to be confused with others called Brunelli.

Brunello di Montalcino Tus DOCG r ★★★→★★★★ 85' 87 88 90' 93 95' 97' 99 00 01 03 04 05 06 07 With BAROLO, Italy's most celebrated red: strong, full-bodied, high-flavoured, tannic, long-lived. Four yrs' ageing; after 5 yrs becomes RISERVA. Arguments rage on as to whether Brunello, and/or Rosso di Montalcino, should remain 100% Sangiovese.

Best Brunello di Montalcino to buy

Altesino, ARGIANO, BANFI, Barbi, Baricci, BIONDI-SANTI, GIANNI BRUNELLI, La Campana, Campogiovanni, Canalicchio di Sopra, Caparzo, CASANOVA DI NERI, Casanuova delle Cerbaie, Casato Prime Donne, Camigliano, CASE BASSE, CASTELGIOCONDO, Cerbaiona, Il Colle, Costanti, EREDI FULIGNI, La Fuga, La Gerla, Lambardi, LISINI, La Magia, La Mannella, Le Potazzine, Marroneto, Oliveto, SIRO PACENTI, Palazzo, Pertimali, Ciacci Piccolomini, Pieri Agostina, PIEVE DI SANTA RESTITUTA, La Poderina, POGGIO ANTICO, POGGIONE, Salvioni-Cerbaiola, Sesti, Uccelliera, Val di Suga, Valdicava.

Burlotto, Commendatore G B ★★★ Fabio Alessandria turns out beautifully crafted and defined PIEDMONT varietals, esp Barolo Cannubi and Monvigliero, the latter's grapes being crushed by foot.

Bussola, Tommaso ★★★★ Leading producer of AMARONE and RECIOTO in

Brunellopoli or "Brunellogate"
Unofficial nickname for scandal involving Brunello producers accused in 2008 of using grapes (mainly Merlot) other than Sangiovese in Brunello. Many were investigated, 4 major producers had their 2003 sequestrated. After some politicking ANTINORI (Pian delle Vigne), ARGIANO, BANFI and FRESCOBALDI (Castelgiocondo) were cleared to sell their wines.

VALPOLICELLA stunning AMARONE Vigneto Alto and Recioto TB.

Caberlot Mellow, flavoury red from crossing of Cab Fr and Merlot claimed to be unique to the v'yds of Bettina Rogosky at her Il Carnasciale estate in the Arezzo hills of Tuscany. Sold only in magnum.

Cabernet Franc Increasingly preferred to CAB SAUV by Italy's internationalists. Much of what was thought in NE Italy to be Cab Fr was actually Carmenère.

Cabernet Sauvignon The great B'x grape has played a key role in the renaissance of Italian red wine (eg see SASSICAIA). Particularly influential in Tuscany as a lesser partner for SANGIOVESE. Now losing ground to indigenous blenders.

Ca' del Bosco ★★★★ FRANCIACORTA estate; some of Italy's best sparklers (outstanding DOCG Annamaria Clementi ★★★★) and Dosage Zero, v.gd CHARD and CAB SAUV blend (Maurizio Zanella), PINOT N (Pinèro). Intriguing Carmenère.

Ca' dei Frati ★★★ The best producer of DOC LUGANA, also v.gd dry white blend IGT Pratto, sweet Tre Filer and red IGT Ronchedone.

Cafaggio, Villa ★★★ V. reliable CHIANTI CLASSICO estate with excellent IGTS San Martino (SANGIOVESE) and Cortaccio (CAB SAUV).

Caiarossa Tus ★★★ Riparbella in the northern MAREMMA is starting to attract serious winemakers for its combination of altitude and proximity to the sea. This international project (Dutch owner Jelgersma from B'x, French winemaker Dominique Genot with Australian background) is turning out some v. classy reds (Pergolaia, Caiarossa) plus v. tasty Caiarossa Bianco.

Calatrasi Si ★★→★★★ Gd red/white IGT producer, esp D'Istinto range.

Caldaro (Lago di Caldaro) T-AA DOC r ★ DYA German name Kalterersee. Light, soft, bitter-almond SCHIAVA. From a huge area. CLASSICO (smaller area) is better.

Ca' Marcanda BOLGHERI estate created by GAJA since 1996. Focus on international varieties: CAB SAUV, MERLOT, CAB FR, SYRAH.

Campania Historic centre of Italy's southern mainland with capital in Naples. Excellent grape varieties (AGLIANICO, Falanghina, FIANO, GRECO, Piedirosso), volcanic soils, and cool v'yds all add up to high potential. Alas, prices higher than is often justified by quality. Best DOCS are FALERNO DEL MASSICO, FIANO D'AVELLINO, GRECO DI TUFO, ISCHIA, TAURASI, but many newer areas now coming to the fore. Established producers include Caggiano, Cantina del Taburno, Caputo, Colli di Lapio, D' Ambra, De Angelis, Benito Ferrara, FEUDI DI SAN GREGORIO, GALARDI, MASTROBERARDINO, Molettieri, MONTEVETRANO, Mustilli, Terredora di Paolo, Trabucco and VILLA MATILDE.

Cannonau di Sardegna Sar DOC r (p) dr Cannonau (Grenache) is the basic red grape of SE Sardinia forms the backbone of some top blends such as Argiolas' Turriga. Best: ARGIOLAS, CONTINI, Giuseppe Gabbas, Jerzu, Loi, Sedilesu.

Cantalupo, Antichi Vigneti di ★★→★★★ Top GHEMME wines, esp single-v'yd Breclemae and Carellae.

Capannelle ★★★ V.gd producer of IGT and CHIANTI CLASSICO, plus 50:50 SANGIOVESE/MERLOT joint venture with AVIGNONESI .

Capezzana, Tenuta di (or Villa) ★★★ Tuscan estate of the Contini Bonacossi family. Gd Barco Reale, excellent CARMIGNANO (esp Villa Capezzana, Villa Trefiano). Also v.gd B'x-style red, Ghiaie Della Furba.

Capichera ★★★ Proclaimed, high-price producer of VERMENTINO DI GALLURA, esp

VENDEMMIA Tardiva. Excellent red Mantènghja from Carignano grapes.

Caprai ★★★→★★★★ Leading modernist in Umbria's Montefalco. Superb DOCG SAGRANTINO, esp 25 Anni, v.gd DOC ROSSO DI MONTEFALCO.

Capri Cam DOC r p w ★→★★ Legendary island with widely abused name. Only interesting wines are from La Caprense.

Carema Pie DOC r ★★→★★★ 99 00 01 03 04' 06' 07' (08) Elegant NEBBIOLO red from steep slopes on Aosta border. Best: Luigi Ferrando.

Carignano del Sulcis Sar DOC r p ★★→★★★ Ageworthy red. Best: TERRE BRUNE and Rocca Rubia from CS DI SANTADI.

Carmignano Tus DOCG r ★★ 90' 95 97' **99' 00 01** 03 04 05 06 07 (08) Region W of Florence. Sangiovese plus CAB FRANC, MERLOT make distinctive red. Best: Ambra, CAPEZZANA, Farnete, PIAGGIA, Le Poggiarelle, Pratesi.

Carpenè-Malvolti Historic producer of classic PROSECCO and other sparkling wines at Conegliano, Veneto. Seen everywhere in Venice.

Carso F-VG DOC r w ★★→★★★ (r) 01 04 05 06 07 (08) V. obscure DOC nr Trieste includes gd MALVASIA. Terrano del Carso is a REFOSCO red. Top growers: EDI KANTE, Zidanich.

Cartizze Famous, frequently too expensive and too sweet, DOC PROSECCO of supposedly best sub-zone of Valdobbiadene.

Casanova di Neri ★★★ BRUNELLO DI MONTALCINO, Pietradonice (SANGIOVESE/CAB SAUV) and v.gd ROSSO DI MONTALCINO from Neri family.

Cascina Fonda ★★★ Brothers Marco and Massimo Barbero have risen to the top in MOSCATO D'ASTI DOC. VENDEMMIA Tardiva and METODO CLASSICO ASTI SPUMANTE.

Case Basse ★★★★ Eco-geek Gianfranco Soldera claims to make the definitive BRUNELLO, and maddeningly he is right. V. expensive and rare.

Castelgiocondo ★★★ FRESCOBALDI estate in MONTALCINO: v.gd BRUNELLO and IGT MERLOT Lamaïone.

Castellare ★★→★★★ Small CHIANTI CLASSICO producer. First-rate SANGIOVESE IGT I Sodi di San Niccoló and old-style CHIANTI updated, esp Riserva Vigna Il Poggiale. Also Poggio ai Merli (MERLOT) and Coniale (CAB SAUV).

Castello Castle. (See under name – eg SALA, CASTELLO DELLA.)

Castell' in Villa ★★★ V. gd CHIANTI CLASSICO estate in Castelnuovo Berardenga.

Castel del Monte Ap DOC r p w ★★→★★★ (r) Dry, fresh, well-balanced wines. Rosé best known. Gd Pietrabianca and excellent *Bocca di Lupo* from Vigneti del Sud (ANTINORI). V.gd Il Falcone, Puer Apuliae, and Cappellaccio from RIVERA, Le More from Santa Lucia. Interesting new reds from Cocevola, Giancarlo Ceci.

Castelluccio ★★→★★★ Quality SANGIOVESE di Romagna. IGT RONCO dei Ciliegi and RONCO delle Ginestre. Massicone is an excellent SANGIOVESE/CAB SAUV blend.

Cataratto Sicilian white grape with as yet unrealized potential.

Caudrina-Dogliotti Romano ★★★ Top MOSCATO D'ASTI: La Galeisa and Caudrina.

Cavalleri ★★→★★★ V.gd reliable FRANCIACORTA producer, esp sparkling.

Cavicchioli E-R ★→★★ Large producer of LAMBRUSCO and other sparkling wines: Lambrusco di Sorbara VIGNA del Cristo is best. Also TERRE DI FRANCIACORTA.

Ca' Viola PIEDMONT Play-on-words name of home base of influential consultant Beppe Caviola. Classy DOLCETTO and BARBERA-based wines.

Ca' Vit (Cantina Viticoltori) Group of co-ops nr Trento. Top wines: Brune di Monte (red and white) and sparkling Graal.

Cecchi Tus ★→★★ Bottler, producer; La Gavina, Spargolo, CHIANTI CLASSICO RISERVA.

Cerasuolo Ab DOC p ★ The ROSATO version of MONTEPULCIANO D'ABRUZZO.

Cerasuolo di Vittoria Si DOCG r ★★ 01 03 04 05 06 07 Aromatic red from Frappato and NERO D'AVOLA grapes; try PLANETA, Valle dell'Acate, and Cos.

Ceretto ★★→★★★ Much hyped grower of BARBARESCO (BRICCO Asili), BAROLO (BRICCO Rocche, Brunate, Prapò), LANGHE ROSSO Monsordo, and ARNEIS. Also v.gd METODO CLASSICO SPUMANTE La Bernardina.

Chardonnay The Burgundian white variety has a vast and important presence in Italy, from ALTO ADIGE to SICILY and from PIEDMONT to FRIULI.

Chianti Tus DOCG r ★→★★★ Local wine of Florence, Siena. At best fresh, fruity, tangy. Of the sub-districts, RUFINA (★★→★★★), COLLI Fiorentini (★→★★★), CHIANTI Montespertoli can make CLASSICO-style RISERVAS. Montalbano, COLLI Senesi, Aretini, Pisani: lighter wines.

Chianti Classico Tus DOCG r ★★→★★★★ 97' 99 **01** 03 04' 06' 07' (08) The historic Tuscan red from the Chianti hills between Florence and Siena. Currently the fight is on between modernists who are allowed 20% of B'x (and other) grapes with 80% SANGIOVESE, and purists who see this as a travesty. Battle leaning toward latter. The Gallo Nero (black rooster) Consorzio now controls DOCG registration, so all producers are obliged to cooperate.

Chiaretto Rosé (the word means "claret") produced esp around Lake Garda. See BARDOLINO, RIVIERA DEL GARDA BRESCIANO.

Chiarlo, Michele ★★→★★★ Gd PIEDMONT producer (BAROLOS Cerequio and Cannubi BARBERA D'ASTI, LANGHE, and MONFERRATO ROSSO). Also BARBARESCO.

Chionetti ★★→★★★ Makes top DOLCETTO di Dogliani (look for Briccolero).

Cigliuti, Renato ★★★ Small quality estate for BARBARESCO and BARBERA D'ALBA.

Le Cinciole ★★→★★★ DOCG CHIANTI CLASSICO, the best is RISERVA Petresco.

Cinqueterre Lig DOC w dr sw ★★ Fragrant, fruity white from precipitous coast nr La Spezia. PASSITO is known as SCIACCHETRÀ (★★→★★★). Gd from Co-op Agricola di Cinqueterre and Forlini Cappellini.

Cirò Cal DOC r (p w) ★→★★★ Strong red from Gaglioppo grapes; *light, fruity white* (DYA). Best: Caparra, Ippolito, LIBRANDI (Duca San Felice ★★★), San Francesco (Donna Madda, RONCO dei Quattroventi), Santa Venere.

Classico Term for wines from a restricted area within the limits of a DOC. By implication, and often in practice, the best of the district. When applied to sparkling wines, it denotes the classic method (as for Champagne).

Clerico, Domenico ★★★ Established modernist BAROLO producer, esp *crus* Percristina and Ciabot Mentin Ginestra. Also NEBBIOLO/BARBERA blend Arte.

Coffele ★★★ Grower with some of the finest v'yds in SOAVE CLASSICO, making steely, minerally wines of classic concept.

Colle Santa Mustiola High-level SANGIOVESE from small estate just outside VINO NOBILE DI MONTEPULCIANO zone.

Colli Hills (from sing. Colle). Occurs in many wine names.

Colli Berici Ven DOC r p w ★★ **04** 05 06 07 (08) Hills south of Vicenza. Best wine is CAB SAUV. Top producer: Villa Dal Ferro.

Colli Bolognesi E-R DOC r w ★★ Southwest of Bologna, 8 wines, 5 varieties. TERRE ROSSE, the pioneer, now joined by Bonzara (★★→★★★) and others.

Who makes really good Chianti Classico?

AMA, ANTINORI, BADIA A COLTIBUONO, Bibbiano, Bossi, BROLIO, Cacchiano, CAFAGGIO, CAPANNELLE, Capraia, Carobbio, Casa Emma, Casafrassi, Casale dello Sparviero, Casaloste, Casa Sola, CASTELLARE, CASTELL'IN VILLA, Collelungo, Colombaio di Cencio, Le Corti, Mannucci Droandi, FELSINA-BERARDENGA, Le Boncie, Le Filigare, FONTERUTOLI, FONTODI, ISOLE E OLENA, LE CINCIOLE, Lilliano, Il Molino di Grace, MONSANTO, MONTE BERNARDI, NITTARDI, Nozzole, PALAZZINO, PANERETTA, Panzanello, Petroio-Lenzi, Poggerino, Poggiolino, Poggiopiano, Poggio al Sole, Poggio Bonelli, Querceto, QUERCIABELLA, RAMPOLLA, RIECINE, Rocca di Castagnoli, Rocca di Montegrossi, RUFFINO, San Fabiano Calcinaia, SAN FELICE, Savignola Paolina, Selvole, Vecchie Terre di Montefili, VERRAZZANO, VICCHIOMAGGIO, VIGNAMAGGIO, Villa Mangiacane, Villa La Rosa, Viticcio, VOLPAIA.

Colli Euganei Ven DOC r w dr s/sw (sp) ★→★★★ DYA DOC southwest of Padua for 7 wines. Adequate red; white and sparkling are pleasant. Best producers: Ca' Lustra, La Montecchia, Speaia, VIGNALTA.

Colline Novaresi Pie DOC r w ★→★★ DYA New DOC for old region in Novara province. Seven different wines: BIANCO, ROSSO, NEBBIOLO, BONARDA, Vespolina, Croatina, BARBERA. Includes declassified BOCA, FARA, GHEMME, SIZZANO.

Collio F-VG DOC r w ★★→★★★★ (r) Makes 19 wines, 17 named after their grapes. V.gd whites from: Attems, BORGO DEL TIGLIO, Il Carpino, La Castellada, CASTELLO di Spessa, Damijan, MARCO FELLUGA, Fiegl, GRAVNER, Renato Keber, LIVON, Aldo Polencic, Primosic, Princic, RONCO dei Tassi, Russiz Superiore, SCHIOPETTO, Tercic, Terpin, Toros, Venica & Venica, VILLA RUSSIZ, Zuani.

Colli Orientali del Friuli F-VG DOC r w dr sw ★★→★★★★ Hills E of Udine. 20 wines (18 named after their grapes). Both white and red can be v.gd.

Colli Piacentini E-R DOC r p w ★→★★ DYA DOC inc traditional GUTTURNIO and Monterosso Val d'Arda among 11 types grown south of Piacenza. Gd fizzy MALVASIA. Most wines FRIZZANTE. New French and local reds: Montesissa, Mossi, Romagnoli, Solenghi, La Stoppa, Torre Fornello, La Tosa.

Colli del Trasimeno Um DOC r w ★→★★★ (r) 01' 03 04 05 06' 07' (08) Lively white wines from nr Perugia, but now more important reds as well. Best: Duca della Corgna, La Fiorita, Pieve del Vescovo, Poggio Bertaio.

Colterenzio CS (or Schreckbichl) T-AA ★★→★★★ Pioneering quality leader among ALTO ADIGE co-ops. Look for: Cornell line of selections; Lafoa CAB SAUV and SAUV BL; Cornelius red and white blends.

Col d'Orcia ★★★ Third largest and top-quality MONTALCINO estate owned by Francesco Marone Cinzano. Best wine: BRUNELLO RISERVA Poggio al Vento.

Conterno, Aldo ★★★★ Legendary grower of BAROLO at Monforte d'Alba. V. gd CHARD Bussiadoro, BARBERA D'ALBA Conca Tre Pile. Best BAROLOS are made traditionally: *Gran Bussia*, Cicala, Colonello. Langhe Favot is a modern BARRIQUE-aged version of NEBBIOLO.

Conterno, Giacomo ★★★★ Iconic grower of super-traditional BAROLO at Monforte d'Alba, Giacomo's grandson Roberto now carrying on father Giovanni's work. Two Barolos: Cascina Francia and Monfortino, long-macerated to age for yrs.

Conterno-Fantino ★★★ Two families joined to produce excellent BAROLO Sori Ginestra and Vigna del Gris at Monforte d'Alba. Also NEBBIOLO/BARBERA blend.

Contini, Attilio ★→★★★ Famous SARDINIAN producer of VERNACCIA DI ORISTANO; best is vintage blend Antico Gregori. Also gd Cannonau.

Contratto ★★ At Canelli (owned by GRAPPA-producing family Bocchino); produces v.gd BARBERA D'ASTI, BAROLO, SPUMANTE, ASTI (De Miranda), MOSCATO D'ASTI.

Copertino Ap DOC r (p) ★★ 01 04 06 07 (08) Savoury, ageworthy, strong red of NEGROAMARO from the heel of Italy. Look for the CS's RISERVA and MASSERIA MONACI's Eloquenzia for bargains.

Coppo ★★→★★★ Ambitious producers of BARBERA D'ASTI (Pomorosso), CHARD.

Cordero di Montezemolo-Monfalletto ★★→★★★ Historic maker of gd BAROLO, now with fine BARBERA D'ALBA and CHARD.

Corini New house in remote area of Umbria. Produces intriguing, innovative blend of SANGIOVESE/MONTEPULCIANO/MERLOT.

Cortese di Gavi See GAVI. (Cortese is the grape.)

Cortona Tuscan DOC contiguous to Montepulciano's Vino Nobile. Various red and white grapes, best results so far from AVIGNONESI's Desiderio, a B'x blend, and first-rate SYRAH from Luigi d'Alessandro, Il Castagno, La Braccesca..

Corzano & Paterno, Fattoria di ★★★ Dynamic CHIANTI COLLI Fiorentini estate. V.gd RISERVA, red IGT Corzano, and outstanding VIN SANTO.

CS, Cantina Sociale Cooperative winery.

Dal Forno, Romano ★★★★ V. high-quality VALPOLICELLA, AMARONE, and RECIOTO grower whose perfectionism is the more remarkable for the fact that his v'yds are outside the Classico zone.

Del Cerro, Fattoria ★★★ Estate with v.gd DOCG VINO NOBILE DI MONTEPULCIANO (esp *cru* Antic Chiusina), red IGTS Manero (SANGIOVESE), and Poggio Golo (MERLOT). Also owns La Poderina (BRUNELLO DI MONTALCINO), Colpetrone (MONTEFALCO SAGRANTINO) and the 1,000 ha (!) northern MAREMMA estate of Monterufoli.

Di Majo Norante ★★ →★★★ Lone star of Molise, S of Abruzzo, with v.gd Biferno ROSSO, Ramitello, Molise Rosso Riserva Don Luigi, and Molise Aglianico Contado, white blend Falanghina-Greco Biblos and Moscato Passito Apianae.

Dolcetto ★ →★★★ PIEDMONT's earliest-ripening red grape, for v. attractive everyday wines: dry (despite the name), fruity, fresh, with deep purple colour.

Donnafugata Si w r ★★→★★★ Well-crafted Sicilian wines of Contessa Entellina DOC: top reds are Mille e Una Notte and Tancredi; top whites Chiaranda and VIGNA di Gabri. Also v. fine Moscato Passito di Pantelleria Ben Rye.

Duca di Salaparuta Si ★★ Vini Corvo. Popular SICILIAN wines. Sound dry reds; pleasant soft whites. *Duca Enrico* (★★→★★★) was one of SICILY's pioneeering ambitious reds. Valguarnera is premium oak-aged white.

Le Due Terre Small producer in COLLI ORIENTALI DEL FRIULI for choice MERLOT, PINOT N, Sacrisassi ROSSO (Refosco/Schioppettino), and white Sacrisassi BIANCO.

Elba TUS r w (sp) ★ DYA The island's white is v. drinkable with fish; look for Sapereta's Vigna Thea. In exile here, Napoleon loved the sweet red ALEATICO; try Acquabona and Sapereta, also Sapereta's Elba Moscato.

Enoteca Wine library; also wine shop or restaurant with extensive wine list. The impressive original is the state-financed Enoteca Italiana of Siena.

Eredi Fuligni ★★★ V.gd producer of BRUNELLO and ROSSO DI MONTALCINO.

Est! Est!! Est!!! Lat DOC w dr s/sw ★ DYA Unextraordinary white from Montefiascone, north of Rome. Trades on the improbable origin of its name.

Etna Si DOC r p w ★★ (r) **00 01 04** 05 06 07 (08) Wine from volcanic slopes and often considerable altitude. New investment has brought forth wines from Nerello Mascalese-based wines from Grazia and the like, not dissimilar to, fine burgundy. Other gd producers inc: Benanti, Bonaccorsi Cambria, Nicosia.

Falchini ★★ →★★★ Producer of gd DOCG VERNACCIA DI SAN GIMIGNANO esp fresh, light (12º) VIGNA a Solatio and complex, BARRIQUED Ab Vinea Doni. Giacomo Tachis is behind excellent reds: B'x blend IGT Campora and SANGIOVESE-based Paretaio.

Falerno del Massico ★★→★★★ Cam DOC r w ★★ (r) **00' 01' 03** 04 06 07 (08) Falernum was the best-known wine of ancient times, probably sweet white. Today elegant red from AGLIANICO, fruity white from Falanghina. V.gd producer: VILLA MATILDE. Other producers: Amore Perrotta, Felicia, Moio, Trabucco.

Falesco ★★→★★★ Latium estate of Cotarella brothers, v.gd MERLOT Montiano and CAB SAUV Marciliano (both ★★★). Gd red IGT Vitiano and DOC EST! EST!! EST!!!

Fara Pie DOC r ★★ **97' 99' 01' 04'** 06 07' (08) Gd NEBBIOLO from Novara, north PIEDMONT; worth ageing; esp from Dessilani.

Farnese Ap ★★ Gd quality supplier of the Abruzzi's favourites, esp Montepulciano d'Abruzzo Colline Teramane Riserva Opis.

Farnetella, Castello di ★★ Estate nr MONTEPULCIANO where Giuseppe Mazzocolin of FELSINA makes gd SAUV BL and CHIANTI COLLI Senesi. Also v.gd PINOT N Nero di Nubi and red blend Poggio Granoni.

Faro Si DOC r ★★ **00 01'** 04' 05 06' 07' (08) Full-bodied but elegant red from Nerello Mascalese and Nerello Cappuccio grown in the hills behind Sicily's Messina. Palari, the major producer, administered the kiss of life with the critic Veronelli's encouragement.

Fazi-Battaglia ★★ Well-known producer of VERDICCHIO, best selections: Massaccio, Le Moie, San Sisto. Owns Fassati (VINO NOBILE DI MONTEPULCIANO).

Felluga, Livio ★★★ Substantial estate, consistently fine COLLI ORIENTALI DEL FRIULI

> **What do the initials mean?**
> **Denominazione di Origine Controllata (DOC)**
> Means much the same as *appellation d'origine contrôlée* (see France). .
> **Denominazione di Origine Controllata e Garantita (DOCG)**
> Like DOC but with an official "guarantee" of quality.
> **DOP, Denominazione di Origine Protetta (protected)**
> The EU seems to be aiming at this qualification taking over from DOC(G).

wines, esp *Pinot Gr*, Sauv Bl, TOCAI, PICOLIT, and MERLOT/REFOSCO blend.

Felluga, Marco ★★→★★★ The brother of Livio owns a négociant house bearing his name plus Russiz Superiore in COLLIO DOC, Castello di Buttrio in COLLI ORIENTALI DOC. Marco's daughter Patrizia is now owner of Zuani estate in COLLIO.

Felsina-Berardenga ★★★ CHIANTI CLASSICO estate; famous for BARRIQUE-aged RISERVA Rancia, IGT Fontalloro, both 100% SANGIOVESE. CHIANTI CLASSICO and RISERVA also v.gd, as are IGT CHARD I Sistri and CAB SAUV Maestro Raro.

Ferrari T-AA ★★→★★★ Cellars making dry sparkling nr Trento. Giulio Ferrari RISERVA is best. New reds from TUSCANY and Umbria as well.

Feudi di San Gregorio ★★★→★★★★ Top Campania producer, with DOCG TAURASI, DOCG FIANO, *Falanghina*, Greco di Tufo. Red IGT Serpico and Patrimo (MERLOT), white IGT Campanaro. Now active in Basilicata and APULIA as well.

Fiano di Avellino Cam DOCG w ★★→★★★ DYA Fiano is rapidly becoming the best native white grape of S Italy, planted successfully in Molise, Puglia, Calabria and Sicily as well as in Campania, its birthplace. Fiano di Avellino can be intense, slightly honeyed, memorable. Best producers: Caggiano, Caputo, COLLI di Lapio, Benito Ferrara, FEUDI DI SAN GREGORIO, Grotta del Sole, MASTROBERARDINO, San Paolo, Vesevo, Villa Raiano.

Florio Historic quality producer of MARSALA. Best wine: Marsala Vergine Secco Baglio Florio. Best name: Terre Arse.

Folonari Ambrogio Folonari and son Giovanni have split off from RUFFINO to create their own house. Will continue to make Cabreo (a CHARD and a SANGIOVESE/CAB SAUV), wines of NOZZOLE (inc top CAB SAUV Pareto), BRUNELLO DI MONTALCINO La Fuga, VINO NOBILE DI MONTEPULCIANO Gracciano Svetoni, with new offerings from BOLGHERI, MONTECUCCO, and COLLI ORIENTALI DEL FRIULI.

Fontana Candida ★★ One of the biggest producers of FRASCATI. Single-v'yd Santa Teresa stands out. See also GRUPPO ITALIANO VINI.

Fontanafredda ★★→★★★ Producer of PIEDMONT wines on former royal estates, inc single-v'yd BAROLOS and ALBA DOCS. V.gd SPUMANTE Brut (esp ★★★ Gattinera).

Fonterutoli ★★★ Historic CHIANTI CLASSICO estate of the Mazzei family at Castellina with space-age new cantina. Notable are *Castello di Fonterutoli* (dark oaky CHIANTI), IGT Siepi (SANGIOVESE/MERLOT). Mazzei also owns Tenuta di Belguardo in MAREMMA, gd MORELLINO DI SCANSANO and IGT wines.

Le Fonti ★★→★★★ V.gd CHIANTI CLASSICO house in Poggibonsi; look for RISERVA and IGT Vito Arturo (SANGIOVESE).

Fontodi ★★★ Top Panzano CHIANTI CLASSICO estate for CHIANTI and RISERVA, esp RISERVA del Sorbo. Top SUPER TUSCAN 100% SANGIOVESE IGT Flaccianello, Case Via PINOT N and SYRAH are among the best of those varietals in Tuscany.

Foradori ★★★ Elizabetta F make best *Teroldego*. Also oak-aged TEROLDEGO Granato, white IGT Myrto. Wines from new Ampeleia estate in Tuscan MAREMMA already first class.

Forte, Podere Pasquale Forte's Val d'Orcia estate, just S of MONTALCINO, puts cutting-edge technology at the service of ambitious SANGIOVESE and CAB SAUV/MERLOT/Petit Verdot wines.

Forteto della Luja ★★★ Pioneer in LOAZZOLO; v.gd BARBERA/PINOT N Le Grive.

Fossi, Enrico ★★★ High-level small estate in Signa, W of Florence, v.gd SANGIOVESE, CAB SAUV, SYRAH, Malbec, Gamay, and CHARD.

Franciacorta Lom DOCG w (p) sp ★★ →★★★★ Small Champagne-style sparkling-wine centre growing in quality and renown. Wines exclusively bottle-fermented. Top producers: Barone Pizzini, BELLAVISTA, CA' DEL BOSCO, Castellino, CAVALLERI, Gatti, UBERTI, Villa; also v.gd: Contadi Gastaldi, Monte Rossa, Il Mosnel, Ricci Curbastri. For white and red, see TERRE DI FRANCIACORTA.

Frascati Lat DOC w dr s/sw sw (sp) ★ →★★ DYA Best-known wine of Roman hills: should be limpid, golden, tasting of whole grapes. Most is disappointingly neutral today: look for Castel de Paolis, Conte Zandotti, Villa Simone, or Santa Teresa from FONTANA CANDIDA. The sweet version is known as Cannellino.

Freisa Pie DOC r dr s/sw sw fz (sp) ★★ DYA fz Usually light, frivolous, often FRIZZANTE red, tasting of raspberries and roses; sometimes serious, almost Barolo-like. Either way, gd with salami. Look for Brezza, CIGLIUTI, CLERICO, ALDO CONTERNO, COPPO, Franco Martinetti, GIUSEPPE MASCARELLO, Parusso, Pecchenino, Pelissero, Sebaste, Trinchero, VAJRA, Vigneti Massa, and VOERZIO.

Frescobaldi ★★→★★★★ Ancient noble family, leading CHIANTI RUFINA pioneer at Nipozzano estate (look for Montesodi ★★★), also Brunello from Castelgiocondo estate in MONTALCINO. Sole owners of LUCE estate in MONTALCINO and ORNELLAIA in BOLGHERI. V'yds also in MAREMMA, Montespertoli and COLLIO.

Friuli-Venezia Giulia The northeast region on the Slovenian border. Many wines; the DOCS ISONZO, COLLIO, and COLLI ORIENTALI include most of the best.

Frizzante (fz) Semi-sparkling. Used to describe wines such as MOSCATO D'ASTI.

Gaja ★★★★ Old family firm at BARBARESCO under direction of Angelo Gaja. Top-quality – and price – wines. BARBARESCO is the only Piedmontese DOCG remaining after Gaja downclassed Barbaresco *crus* SORÌ Tildin, SORÌ San Lorenzo and Costa Russi as well as Barolo Sperss to LANGHE DOC so that he could blend small proportions of BARBERA in with NEBBIOLO. CHARD (Gaia e Rey), CAB SAUV Darmagi. Acquisitions elsewhere in Italy: Marengo-Marenda estate (BAROLO), commercial Gromis label; PIEVE DI SANTA RESTITUTA in MONTALCINO CA' MARCANDA in BOLGHERI.

Galardi ★★★→★★★★ Producer of Terra di Lavoro, a mind-boggling blend of AGLIANICO and Piedirosso, in north Campania nr FALERNO DEL MASSICO DOC.

Gambellara Ven DOC w dr s/sw (sp) ★ DYA Neighbour of SOAVE. Dry wine similar. Sweet (RECIOTO di Gambellara), nicely fruity. Gd producer: La Biancara.

Gancia Famous ASTI house also producing gd sparkling.

Garda Ven DOC w p r ★→★★ DYA (w p) 01 03 04 05 06 07(08) (r) Catch-all DOC for generally early-drinking wines of various colours from provinces of Verona in Veneto, Brescia and Mantua in Lombardy. Gd are Cavalchina, Zeni.

Garganega Principal white grape of SOAVE and GAMBELLARA.

Garofoli ★★→★★★ One of quality leaders in the Marches (nr Ancona). Notable style in VERDICCHIO Podium, Macrina, and Serra Fiorese. ROSSO CONERO Piancarda and v.gd Grosso Agontano.

Gattinara Pie DOCG r ★★★ 89'90' 95 96' 97' 98 99' 00 01' 03 04' 05 06 07' (08) Potentially fine NEBBIOLO-based red, considered the best from north PIEDMONT, though that's not saying a lot. Best: Travaglini (RISERVA), Antoniolo (single-v'yd wines). Others: Bianchi, Nervi, Torraccia del Piantavigna.

Gavi Pie DOCG w ★→★★★ DYA At (rare) best, subtle dry white of Cortese grapes. LA SCOLCA is best-known, gd from BANFI (esp VIGNA Regale), Castellari Bergaglio, Franco Martinetti, Toledana, Villa Sparina. Broglia, Cascina degli Ulivi, CASTELLO di Tassarolo, CHIARLO, La Giustiniana, PODERE Saulino are also fair.

Ghemme Pie DOCG r ★★ 89' 90' 95 96' 97' 98 99' 00 01' 03 04 05 06 07' (08) Neighbour of GATTINARA, not considered as gd, but sometimes better. Stars: Antichi Vigneti di Cantalupo, Ioppa, Rovellotti and Torraccia del Piantavigna.

Giacosa, Bruno ★★→★★★★ Considered Italy's greatest winemaker by some, this brooding genius recently suffered a stroke but goes on working, crafting outstanding traditional-style BARBARESCOS (Asili, Santo Stefano) and BAROLOS (Falletto, Rocche di Falletto). Plus a range of fine reds (DOLCETTO, NEBBIOLO, BARBERA), whites (ARNEIS) and an amazing Brut METODO CLASSICO.

Grappa Pungent and potent spirit made from grape pomace (skins, etc, after pressing), can be anything from disgusting to inspirational.

Grasso, Elio ★★★ V.gd BAROLO (look for Runcot, Gavarini, Casa Maté), full, barrel-aged BARBERA D'ALBA VIGNA Martina, DOLCETTO D'ALBA, and CHARD Educato.

Grave del Friuli F-VG DOC r w ★→★★ (r) **03 04** 06 07 (08) DOC covering 15 different wines, 14 named after their grapes, from central part of region. Gd REFOSCO, MERLOT, and CAB SAUV. Best producers: Borgo Magredo, Le Fredis, Di Lenardo, Le Monde, Plozner, Vicentini-Orgnani, Villa Chiopris.

Gravner, Josko ★★★ Controversial COLLIO producer, believing in maceration on skins and long wood ageing for whites. His wines are either loved for their complexity or hated for being oxidized. Expensive and hard to find.

Grechetto Umbrian white grape (Pulcinculo in Tuscany); more flavour than TREBBIANO, often used in blends or solo in ORVIETO and other parts of Umbria. Look for Barberani, Bigi, Caprai, Cardeto, Colli Amerini, FALESCO, Palazzone.

Greco Various "Grecos" (of Greek origin?) exist in southern Italy, not necessarily related, eg GRECO DI TUFO is different from Greco of CIRO.

Greco di Tufo Cam DOCG w (sp) ★★→★★★ DYA One of the best whites from the south: fruity, slightly wild in flavour, and ageworthy. V.gd examples from Caggiano, Caputo, Benito Ferrara, FEUDI DI SAN GREGORIO, Macchialupa, MASTROBERARDINO (Nova Serra and Vignadangelo), Vesevo, Villa Raiano.

Gresy, Marchesi di (Cisa Asinari) ★★★ Consistent, sometimes inspired producer of traditional-style BARBARESCO (crus Gaiun and Camp Gros). Also v.gd SAUV BL, CHARD, MOSCATO D'ASTI, BARBERA D'ASTI.

Grevepesa CHIANTI CLASSICO co-op – quality now rising.

Grignolino Pie DOC r ★ DYA lively light red of PIEDMONT. Two types: d'Asti (BRAIDA, Marchesi Incisa della Rocchetta); del Monferrato Casalese (Accornero, BRICCO Mondalino, La Tenaglia).

Gruppo Italiano Vini (GIV) Complex of co-ops and wineries, biggest v'yd holders in Italy; estates inc Bigi, Ca'Bianca, Conti Serristori, FOLONARI, FONTANA CANDIDA, LAMBERTI, Macchiavelli, MELINI, Negri, Santi, Vignaioli di San Floriano. Has also expanded into south: Sicily and Basilicata.

Guerrieri-Gonzaga ★ See SAN LEONARDO.

Gutturnio dei Colli Piacentini E-R DOC r dr ★→★★ DYA BARBERA/BONARDA blend from the hills of Piacenza. Producers: Castelli del Duca, La Stoppa, La Tosa.

Haas, Franz ★★★ ALTO ADIGE producer; v.gd PINOT N, LAGREIN, and IGT blends.

Hofstätter ★★★ ALTO ADIGE producer of top PINOT N. Look for Barthenau Vigna Sant'Urbano, LAGREIN, CAB SAUV/Petit Verdot, Gewurz.

Ischia Cam DOC w (r) ★→★★ DYA Island off Naples. Top producer D'Ambra: DOC red Dedicato a Mario D'Ambra, IGT red Tenuta Montecorvo, IGT white Tenuta Frassitelli, and Piellero. Also gd: Il Giardino Mediterraneo, Pietratorcia.

Indicazione Geografipca Tipica (ITG) 1990s category for quality wines unable to fit into DOC zones or regulations; replaced anomaly of glamorous VDTS.

Insolia Southern white grape with untapped potential; in Tuscany, Ansonica.

Isole e Olena ★★★→★★★★ Top CHIANTI CLASSICO estate run by astute Paolo de Marchi, with fine red IGT Cepparello. V.gd VIN SANTO, CAB SAUV, CHARD, and L'Eremo Syrah. See also LESSONA.

Isonzo F-VG DOC r w ★★★ (r) DOC covering 19 wines (17 varietals) in NE. Best white and MERLOT compare to COLLIO wines. Esp from Borgo Conventi, Borgo San Daniele, La Bellanotte, LIS NERIS, Masut da Rive, Pierpaolo Pecorari, RONCO del Gelso, Sant'Elena, VIE DI ROMANS, Villanova.

Jermann, Silvio ★★→★★★ Family estate with v'yds in COLLIO and ISONZO: top white VDT, inc blend Vintage Tunina, oak-aged Capo Martino, and "Were dreams, now it is just wine" (yes, really). Also excellent red Pignacoluse.

Kalterersee German (and local) name for LAGO DI CALDARO.

Kante, Edi ★★→★★★ Leading light of CARSO; fine DOC CHARD, Sauv Bl, MALVASIA; gd red Terrano.

Lacrima di Morro d'Alba DYA Curiously named Muscatty light red from a small commune in the Marches, no connection with ALBA or La Morra in PIEDMONT. Gd producers: Mancinelli, MONTE SCHIAVO.

Lacryma (or Lacrima) Christi del Vesuvio Cam r p w dr (sw fz) ★→★★ DYA Famous but disappointing wines from Vesuvius (DOC Vesuvio). Caputo, De Angelis, Grotta del Sole and MASTROBERARDINO are producers.

La Fiorita Lamborghini family property nr Lake Trasimeno in Umbria, with touchstone SANGIOVESE/MERLOT blend Campoleone.

Lageder, Alois ★★→★★★ Top ALTO ADIGE producer. Most exciting wines are single-v'yd varietals: *Sauv Bl Lehenhof*, PINOT GR Benefizium Porer, Chard Lowengang, Gewurz Am Sand, PINOT N Krafuss, LAGREIN Lindenberg, Cab Sauv Cor Römigberg. Also owns Cason Hirschprunn for v.gd IGT blends.

Lago di Corbara Umb r ★★ 03 04' 05 06' 07' (08) Relatively recently created DOC to include quality reds of the Orvieto area. Best from Barberani (Villa Monticelli) and Decugnano dei Barbi (Il).

Lagrein T-AA DOC r p ★★→★★★ 99 00' 01 03 04' 05 06' 07' (08) Highly coloured grape with a bitter twist. Good fruity wine – at best, full, minerally, and v. appealing. The rosé: Kretzer; the dark: Dunkel. Best growing zone: commune of Gries. Best producers: Colterenzio co-op, Gojer, Gries co-op, HAAS, HOFSTÄTTER, LAGEDER, Laimburg, Josephus Mayr, Thomas Mayr, Muri Gries, NIEDERMAYR, NIEDRIST, St-Magdalena, TERLANO co-op, TIEFENBRUNNER.

Lamberti ★★ Large producer of SOAVE, VALPOLICELLA, BARDOLINO, etc, at Lazise on the eastern shore of Lake Garda. Owned by GIV.

Lambrusco E-R DOC (or not) r p dr s/sw ★→★★ DYA Once extremely popular fizzy red, mainly in industrial, semi-sweet, non-DOC version. Best is secco, traditional with second fermentation in bottle (with sediment). DOCS: L Grasparossa di Castelvetro, L Salamino di Santa Croce, L di Sorbara. Best: Bellei, Caprari, Casali, CAVICCHIOLI, Graziano, Lini Oreste, Medici Ermete (esp Concerto), Rinaldo Rinaldini, Venturini Baldini.

Langhe The hills of central PIEDMONT, home of BAROLO, BARBARESCO, etc. DOC name for 6 Piedmontese varietals plus blends BIANCO and ROSSO. Those wishing to blend other grapes with their NEBBIOLO (or BAROLO or BARBARESCO), such as GAIA, can do so at up to 15% under "Langhe Nebbiolo".

Latisana F-VG DOC r w ★→★★★ (r) DOC for 13 varietal wines from 80 km NE of Venice. Best wine is 'Friulano' (ex-TOCAI). Try wines of Grandi e Gabana.

Lessona Pie DOC r ★★ 99 01' 04 06 07 (08) Dry, claret-like wine from Vercelli province. NEBBIOLO, Vespolina, BONARDA grapes. Best producer: Sella, plus new estate of Paolo de Marchi of ISOLE E OLENA, Sperino.

Librandi ★★★ Top Calabria producer pioneering research into Calabrian varieties. V.gd red CIRÒ (RISERVA Duca San Felice is ★★★), IGT Gravello (CAB SAUV/Gaglioppo blend), Magno Megonio (r) from Magliocco grape and Efeso IGT (w) from Mantonico grape. Other local varietals in experimental phase.

Liquoroso Means strong; usually sweet and always fortified.

Lisini ★★★→★★★★ Historic estate for some of the finest and longest lasting BRUNELLO, esp RISERVA Ugolaia.

Lis Neris ★★★ Top ISONZO estate for gd white wines, esp PINOT GR, CHARD (Jurosa), SAUV BL (Picol), Friulano (Fiore di Campo) plus blends Confini and Lis. Also v.gd Lis Neris Rosso (MERLOT/CAB SAUV) and sw w Tal Luc (VERDUZZO/RIES).

Livon ★★→★★★ Substantial COLLIO producer, also some COLLI ORIENTALI wines like VERDUZZO. Expanded into the CHIANTI CLASSICO and MONTEFALCO DOCGS.

Loazzolo Pie DOC w sw ★★★ 03 04 05 06 07 (08) DOC for MOSCATO dessert wine from botrytized, air-dried grapes: expensive and sweet. Gd from Borgo Isolabella, Forteto della Luja, and Pianbello.

Locorotondo Ap DOC w (sp) ★ DYA Pleasantly fresh southern white.

Luce ★★★ Joint Mondavi/FRESCOBALDI venture launched in 1998, now solely FRESCOBALDI having bought out partners Mondavi. SANGIOVESE/MERLOT blend.

Lugana Lom and Ven DOC w (sp) ★→★★ DYA whites of southern Lake Garda, main grape Trebbiano di Lugana (or T. di Soave = Verdicchio). Dry, sappy and flavourful. Best: CA' DEI FRATI, ZENATO, Zeni.

Lungarotti ★★→★★★ Leading producer of TORGIANO, with cellars, hotel, and museum nr Perugia. Star wine Rubesco RISERVA DOCG. Gd IGT Sangiorgio (SANGIOVESE/CAB SAUV), Aurente (CHARD), and Giubilante. Now operating in Montefalco as well. See TORGIANO.

Le Macchiole ★★★→★★★★ Fine Paleo ROSSO (100% CAB FR), world-class Messorio IGT (MERLOT), and v.gd Scrio IGT (Syrah). Also gd BOLGHERI DOC ROSSO (blend).

Maculan Ven ★★★ Excellent CAB SAUV (Fratta, Ferrata), CHARD (Ferrata), MERLOT (Marchesante), and Torcolato (esp RISERVA Acininobili).

Malvasia Ancient grape of Greek origin planted so widely for so long that various sub-varieties can bear little resemblance to one another: can be white or red, sparkling or still, strong or mild, sweet or dry, aromatic or neutral. Best is probably sw *Malvasia delle Lipari*, from islands off Sicily.

Mandurla (Primitivo di) Ap DOC r c/sw ★★→★★★ Dark red, naturally strong, rarely sweet from nr Taranto. Gd: Accademia dei Racemi (inc Dunico, Felline, Masseria Pepe, Pervini, Sinfarosa), also Casale Bevagna, Feudi di San Marzano, Ginafranco Fino, Pozzopalo.

Manzone, Giovanni ★★★ V.gd ALBA wines from estate nr Monforte d'Alba. Single-v'yd BAROLO, BARBERA D'ALBA, DOLCETTO.

Marchesi di Barolo ★★ Important ALBA house: BAROLO (esp Cannubi and Sarmassa), BARBARESCO, DOLCETTO D'ALBA, BARBERA, FREISA D'ASTI, and GAVI.

Maremma Southern coastal area of TUSCANY, esp province of Grosseto. Name also applies to province of Livorno. DOCS inc BOLGHERI and VAL DI CORNIA (Livorno), MONTECUCCO, MONTEREGIO, MORELLINO DI SCANSANO, PARRINA, Pitigliano, SOVANA (Grosseto). Attracting interest and investment for potential demonstrated by wines. Maremma IGT, limited to province of Grosseto, now used by many top producers, inc new investors, for major wines.

The Maremma: beside the seaside

Names to look for in the Maremma include, for IGT: Look for: Ampeleia, Belguardo, La Carletta, Casina, Col di Bacche, Fattoria di Magliano, Lhosa, Marsiliana, Monteti, MORIS FARMS, Montebelli, Podere 141, La Parrina, Poderi di Ghiaccioforte, Poggio Argentiera, Poggio Foco, Poggio al Lupo, Poggio Paoli, Poggio Verrano, Rascioni e Cecconello, Rocca di Frasinello, San Matteo, Sassotondo, La Selva, Solomaremma, Suveraia.

For Morellino di Scansano, go for: Belguardo, La Carletta, Fattoria di Magliano, Fattorie LE PUPILLE, Mantellasi, MORIS FARMS, Podere 414, Poderi di Ghiaccioforte, Poggio Argentiera, Poggio al Lupo, Poggio Paoli, San Matteo, La Selva, Cantina di Scansano, Terre di Talamo, and Villa Patrizia.

Marino Lat DOC w dr s/sw (sp) ★→★★ DYA A neighbour of FRASCATI with similar wine; often a better buy. Look for Di Mauro.

Marsala DOC w sw Sicily's once famous fortified wine (★→★★★), invented by Woodhouse Bros from Liverpool in 1773. An excellent apéritif or for dessert, but used mostly in inferior versions for zabaglione. Dry ("virgin"), sometimes made by the *solera* system, must be 5 yrs old. Top producers: FLORIO, Pellegrino, Rallo. See also VECCHIO SAMPERI. V. special old vintages ★★★★.

Martini & Rossi Vermouth and sparkling-wine house now controlled by Bacardi group. (Has a fine wine-history museum in Pessione, nr Turin.)

Marzemino Trentino T-AA DOC r ★→★★ 04 05 06 07 (08) Pleasant local red. Fruity and slightly bitter. Esp from Bossi Fedrigotti, CA' VIT, De Tarczal, Gaierhof, Letrari, Longariva, Simoncelli, E Spagnolli, Vallarom.

Mascarello The name of 2 top producers of BAROLO, etc: Bartolo M and Giuseppe M & Figli. Look for the latter's supreme BAROLO Monprivato.

Masi ★★→★★★ Exponent/researcher of VALPOLICELLA, AMARONE, RECIOTO, SOAVE, etc, inc fine Rosso Veronese Campo Fiorin and AMARONE-style wines from Friuli and Argentina. V.gd barrel-aged red IGT Toar, from CORVINA and Oseleta, also Osar (Oseleta). Top Amarones Mazzano and Campolongo di Torbe.

La Massa ★★★ Highly rated producer of top Tuscan reds La Massa and Giorgio Primo, no longer CHIANTI CLASSICO.

Masseria Monaci ★★ Estate of Severino Garofano, for decades the oenologist behind the continuing rise of quality wine in Puglia's Salento. Characterful Negroamaro (Eloquenzia, Simpotica), superb late-picked Le Braci, also Uva di Troia (Sine Pari) and Aglianico (Sine Die).

Mastroberardino ★★→★★★ Historic producer of mountainous Avellino province in Campania, quality torch-bearer for Italy's south during dark yrs of mid-20th century. Top *Taurasi* (look for Historia Naturalis and Radici), also FIANO DI AVELLINO More Maiorum and GRECO DI TUFO Nova Serra.

Melini ★★ Long-established producers of CHIANTI CLASSICO at Poggibonsi. Gd quality/price; look for single-v'yd CHIANTI CLASSICO Selvanella and RISERVAS La Selvanella and Masovecchio. See GRUPPO ITALIANO VINI.

Merlot Red grape grown today throughout Italy, used varietally and to blend with Sangiovese *et al*. Many Merlot DOCS esp in the NE, where grape is traditional.

Metodo classico or tradizionale Mandatory terms to identify classic method sparkling wines. "Metodo Champenois" banned since 1994

Mezzacorona ★★ TRENTINO co-op with gd DOC TEROLDEGO, METODO CLASSICO Rotari.

Moccagatta ★★→★★★ Modern-style BARRIQUED single-v'yd BARBARESCO specialist: Basarin, Bric Balin (★★★), VIGNA Cole. BARBERA D'ALBA is better.

Molino ★★★ Talented producer of elegant ALBA wines at La Morra; look for BAROLOS Gancia and Conca, BARBERA Gattere, and DOLCETTO.

La Monacesca ★★→★★★ Fine producer of VERDICCHIO DI MATELICA. Top wine: Mirum.

Monferrato Pie DOC r p w sw ★★ Hills between river Po and Apennines. A recent DOC; inc ROSSO, BIANCO, DOLCETTO, Casalese, FREISA, and Cortese.

Monica di Sardegna Sar DOC r ★→★★ DYA The mainstay of Sardinian light dry red.

Monsanto ★★★ Esteemed CHIANTI CLASSICO estate, esp for Il Poggio v'yd and IGTS Fabrizio Bianchi (SANGIOVESE) and Nemo (CAB SAUV).

Montalcino Small town in province of Siena (TUSCANY), famous for concentrated, expensive BRUNELLO and more approachable, better-value ROSSO DI MONTALCINO.

Montecarlo Tus DOC w r ★★ DYA (w) White, and increasingly red, wine area nr Lucca in northern TUSCANY. Whites are smooth, neutral blend of TREBBIANO with range of better grapes; basic reds are CHIANTI-style. Gd producers: Buonamico (red IGTS Cercatoja Rosso and Fortino), Carmignani (v.gd red IGT For Duke), red IGTS of La Torre, Montechiari, Fattoria del Teso.

Montecucco Recent TUSCAN DOC between MONTALCINO and MORELLINO DI SCANSANO. Look for Castello di Potentino (Sacromonte), also Begnardi, Ciacci Piccolomini, Colli Massari, Fattoria di Montecucco, Villa Patrizia. Much new investment: FOLONARI, MASI, Pertimali, RIECINE, Talenti.

Montefalco Sagrantino Umb DOCG r dr (sw) ★★★→★★★★ Super-tannic, long-

> **The best producers of Montepulciano d'Abruzzo**
> Barone Cornacchia, Cataldi-Madonna, Ciccio Zaccagnini, Contesa, Filomusi-Guelfi, Illuminati, Marammiero, Masciarelli, Monti, Montori, Nicodemi, Orlandi Contucci Ponno, Roxan, Tollo, La Valentina, VALENTINI.

lasting SECCO wines, plus sweet PASSITO red from Sagrantino grapes. Gd from Adanti, Alzatura, Antonelli San Marco, Paolo Bea, Benincasa, CAPRAI, Colpetrone, Madonna Alta, Scacciadiavoli, Tabarrini, Terre de' Trinci.

Montellori, Fattoria di ★★→★★★ TUSCAN producer making CHIANTI, all-SANGIOVESE IGT Dicatum, CAB SAUV/MERLOT blend Salamartano, white IGT Sant'Amato (SAUV BL), and METODO CLASSICO SPUMANTE.

Montepulciano An important red grape of EC Italy as well as the TUSCAN town.

Montepulciano, Vino Nobile di See VINO NOBILE DI MONTEPULCIANO.

Montepulciano d'Abruzzo Ab DOC r p ★→★★★ 03' 04' 05 06' 07' (08) Highly popular, deep-coloured, full-flavoured red and zesty, savoury pink (CERASUOLO) of generally excellent value for money from Adriatic coast.

Monteregio Emerging DOC nr Massa Marittima in MAREMMA, high-level SANGIOVESE and CAB SAUV wines from Campo Bargello, MORIS FARMS, Tenuta del Fontino. Big-name investors (ANTINORI, BELLAVISTA, Eric de Rothschild, ZONIN) have flocked in.

Monte Schiavo ★★→★★★ Medium-large producer of gd to outstanding VERDICCHIO (esp Le Giuncare) and MONTEPULCIANO-based reds in the Marches.

Montescudaio Tus DOC r w ★★ DOC between Pisa and Livorno; best are SANGIOVESE or SANGIOVESE/CAB SAUV blends. Try Merlini, Poggio Gagliardo, La Regola, Sorbaiano.

Montevertine ★★★★ Radda estate. Non-DOCG but classic Chianti-style wines. IGT Le Pergole Torte a fine pioneering example of pure, long-ageing SANGIOVESE.

Montevetrano ★★★ Small Campania producer; superb IGT Montevetrano (Cab Sauv, Merlot, Aglianico).

Montresor ★★ Verona wine house: gd LUGANA, BIANCO DI CUSTOZA, VALPOLICELLA.

La Morandina ★★★ Small family estate with top MOSCATO and BARBERA D'ASTI.

Morellino di Scansano Tus DOC r ★→★★★ 03' 04' 05 06' 07' (08) Local SANGIOVESE of the MAREMMA, the south TUSCAN coast. Cherry-red, should be lively and tasty, young or matured; many have been over-oaked. (See Maremma box.)

Moris Farms ★★★ V.gd producer in MONTEREGIO and MORELLINO DI SCANSANO, respectively to north and south of Grosseto; look for RISERVA and IGT Avvoltore, a rich SANGIOVESE/CAB SAUV/SYRAH blend.

Moscadello di Montalcino Tus DOC w sw (sp) ★★ DYA Revived traditional wine of MONTALCINO, once better known than BRUNELLO. Sweet fizz and sweet to high-octane MOSCATO PASSITO. Best: BANFI, COL D'ORCIA, La Poderina.

Moscato Family of fragrant fruity grapes which include Moscato Bianco/di Canelli (used in ASTI and MONTALCINO), Moscato Giallo (TRENTINO-ALTO-ADIGE, Ven, etc) and Moscato d'Alessandria (Sicily, Pantelleria), making a diverse range of wines: sparkling or still, light or full-bodied, but always sweet.

Moscato d'Asti Pie DOCG w sp sw ★★→★★★ DYA Similar to DOCG ASTI, but usually better grapes; lower alcohol, sweeter, fruitier, often from small producers. Best DOCG MOSCATO: L'Armangia, BERA, BRAIDA, Ca'd'Gal, CASCINA FONDA, Cascina Pian d'Oro, Caudrina, Il Falchetto, Forteto della Luja, DI GRESY, Icardi, Isolabella, Manfredi/Patrizi, Marino, LA MORANDINA, Marco Negri, Elio Perrone, Rivetti, Saracco, Scagliola, VAJRA, Vietti, Vignaioli di Sante Stefano, Viticoltori Acquese.

Müller-Thurgau Variety of some interest in T-AA and FRIULI. Top producers: LAGEDER, Lavis, POJER & SANDRI, Zeni. TIEFENBRUNNER's Feldmarschall from 1000-m high v'yd in ALTO ADIGE is possibly the best dry M-T in the world.

Murana, Salvatore Si ★★★ V.gd MOSCATO and PASSITO DI PANTELLERIA.

Muri Gries ★★ V.gd producer of ALTO ADIGE DOC, specialists in LAGREIN.

Nada, Fiorenzo ★★★ Fine producer of smooth, elegant DOCG BARBARESCO.

Nebbiolo The best red grape of PIEDMONT, possibly of Italy, used in BAROLO, BARBARESCO and other wines of the northwest (eg Lombardy's VALTELLINA), though so far unsuccessful elsewhere in the wine world.

Nebbiolo d'Alba Pie DOC r dr (s/sw sp) ★★ 99 00 01' 03 04' 06 07 (08) From Alba but 2 styles: full and complex, similar to BAROLO/BARBARESCO; and light, fruity and fragrant. Top examples of former from PIO CESARE, GIACOSA, FONTANAFREDDA. Other gd ones from Marziano Abbona, Alario, BRICCO Maiolica, Cascina Chicco, La Contea, Paolo Conterno, Correggia, Damilano, De Marie, FONTANAFREDDA, Bruna Grimaldi, Hilberg, Mario Marengo, Gianmatteo Pira, Paitin, PRUNOTTO, Rizieri, SANDRONE, Tenuta Rocca, Val di Prete. See also ROERO.

Negroamaro APULIAN "black bitter" red grape with potential for both high quality or high volume. See ALEZIO, BRINDISI, COPERTINO, and SALICE SALENTINO.

Nerello Mascalese Medium-coloured, characterful Sicilian red grape which seemed to have lost its spark till rediscovered by the excellent Palari in Messina (FARO DOC) and growers on the upper slopes of ETNA.

Nero d'Avola Dark red grape (Avola is south of Siracusa) with great promise, alone or in blends, from all over SICILY but mainly southeast.

Niedermayr ★★★ V.gd DOC ALTO ADIGE, esp LAGREIN, PINOT N, Gewurz, SAUV BL, and IGT Euforius (LAGREIN/CAB SAUV) and Aureus (sweet white blend).

Niedrist, Ignaz ★★★ Small, gifted producer of white and red ALTO ADIGE wines (esp LAGREIN, PINOT N, PINOT BL, RIES).

Nipozzano, Castello di ★★★ FRESCOBALDI estate in RUFINA east of Florence making Montesodi CHIANTI.

Nittardi ★★ →★★★ Reliable source of high-quality, modern-style CHIANTI CLASSICO.

Nosiola (Trentino) T-AA DOC w dr sw DYA Light, fruity white from Nosiola grapes. Also gd VINO SANTO. Best from Castel Noarna, POJER & SANDRI, Giovanni Poli, Pravis, Zeni. See VIN SANTO.

Nozzole ★★ →★★★ Famous estate now owned by Ambrogio FOLONARI, in heart of CHIANTI CLASSICO, north of Greve.

Nuragus di Cagliari Sar DOC w ★ DYA Lively Sardinian w from the Nuragus grape.

Oasi degli Angeli Benchmark all-MONTEPULCIANO wines from small producer in southern Marches; lush and mouth-filling.

Oberto, Andrea ★★ →★★★ La Morra producer: BARRIQUED BAROLO, BARBERA D'ALBA.

Oddero ★★ →★★★ Well-known La Morra estate for excellent BAROLO (look for Mondoca di Bussia, Rocche di Castiglione, and VIGNA Rionda).

Oltrepò Pavese Lom DOC r w dr sw sp ★ →★★★ 14 wines from Pavia province, most named after grapes. Sometimes v.gd PINOT N and SPUMANTE. Gd growers: Anteo, Barbacarlo, Casa Re, Castello di Cigognola, CS Casteggio, Le Fracce, Frecciarossa, Monsupello, Mazzolino, Ruiz de Cardenas, Travaglino, Verces del Castellazzo, La Versa co-op.

Ornellaia Tus ★★★★ 95 96 98' 99 00 01 03 04' 05 06' 07'(08) Famous estate n BOLGHERI founded by Lodovico ANTINORI who sold to Frescobaldi/Mondav consortium, now owned solely by FRESCOBALDI. Estate has many prestigious wines: excellent BOLGHERI DOC Ornellaia, superb IGT Masseto (MERLOT), v.gd BOLGHERI DOC Le Serre Nuove and IGT Le Volte.

Orvieto Umb DOC w dr s/sw sw ★ →★★★ DYA The classic Umbrian white, from the ancient spiritual centre of the Etruscans. Wines comparable to Vouvray from tufaceous soil. SECCO version is most popular today, AMABILE is more traditional. Sweet versions from noble rot (*muffa nobile*) grapes can be superb, eg BARBERANI's Calcaia. Other gd producers Co.Vi.O, Decugnano de Barbi, La Carraia, Palazzone, Vi.C.Or. See CASTELLO DELLA SALA.

Pacenti, Siro ★★★ Hand-crafted, barriqued BRUNELLO and ROSSO DI MONTALCINO.

Pagani De Marchi New face north of BOLGHERI. Impressive IGT varietal wines from CAB SAUV, SANGIOVESE and, in particular, MERLOT.

Palazzino, Podere Il ★★★ Small estate with admirable CHIANTI CLASSICO.

Pancrazi, Marchese ★★→★★★ Estate nr Florence: touted but v. untypical PINOT N.

Paneretta, Castello della ★★→★★★ To follow for v. fine CHIANTI CLASSICO, IGTS Quatrocentenario, Terrine.

Pantelleria Island off the Sicilian coast noted for MOSCATO, particularly intense brown PASSITO. Watch for Abraxas, Colosi, De Bartoli, DONNAFUGATA, MURANA.

Parrina Tus DOC r w ★★ Grand estate nr classy resorts of Argentario. Gd white Ansonica, improving reds (SANGIOVESE/CAB SAUV and MERLOT) from MAREMMA.

Pasqua, Fratelli ★→★★ Massive producer and bottler of Verona wines: VALPOLICELLA, AMARONE, SOAVE. Also BARDOLINO and RECIOTO.

Passito (pa) Strong, mostly sweet wine from grapes dried on the vine, on trays under the sun, or indoors on trays or hanging vertically.

Paternoster ★★→★★★ Top AGLIANICO DEL VULTURE, esp Don Anselmo.

Patriglione Ap IGT r ★★★ Dense red IGT (NEGROAMARO/MALVASIA Nera). See TAURINO.

Pecorino Ab IGT Colli Pescaresi w ★★→★★★ Not a cheese but alluring dry white from a recently nr-extinct variety. Gd producers Contesa, Franco Pasetti.

Petit Verdot This Bordelais vine has begun to catch on in Italy, esp among internationalists. Casale del Giglio in Latium makes an interesting varietal.

Piaggia Outstanding producer of Carmignano Riserva, IGT Il Sasso and superb new CAB FR Poggio dei Colli.

Piave Ven DOC r w ★→★★ (r) 04 05 06 07 (08) (w) DYA Flourishing DOC northwest of Venice for 4 red and 4 white wines named after their grapes. CAB SAUV, MERLOT, and RABOSO reds can all age. Gd examples from Duca di Castelanza, Loredan Gasparini, Molon, Villa Sandi.

Picolit F-VG DOC w s/sw sw ★★→★★★ 01 03 04 05 06 07 (08) Delicate sweet wine from COLLI ORIENTALI DEL FRIULI, but with an exaggerated reputation. A little like France's Jurançon. Ages up to 6 yrs, but v. overpriced. Best from LIVIO FELLUGA, Meroi, Perusini, Specogna, VILLA RUSSIZ, Vinae dell'Abbazia.

Piedmont (Piemonte) With TUSCANY, the most important Italian region for top-quality wine. Turin is the capital, ASTI and ALBA the wine centres. See BARBARESCO, BARBERA, BAROLO, DOLCETTO, GRIGNOLINO, MOSCATO, ROERO, etc.

Piemonte Pie DOC r w p (sp) ★→★★ All-PIEMONT blanket DOC inc BARBERA, BONARDA, BRACHETTO, Cortese, GRIGNOLINO, CHARD, SPUMANTE, MOSCATO. Set to disappear with new rules?

Pieropan ★★★ Outstanding SOAVE and RECIOTO: deserving its fame, esp Soave La Rocca and Calvarino, sweet PASSITO DELLA ROCCA.

Pieve di Santa Restituta ★★★ GAJA estate for admirable BRUNELLO DI MONTALCINO.

Pigato Lig DOC w ★★ Often outclasses VERMENTINO as Liguria's finest white, with rich texture and structure. Gd from Bruna, Lupi, TERRE ROSSE.

Pinot Bianco (Pinot Bl) Potentially excellent grape making many DOC wines in the northeast, esp from high sites in ALTO ADIGE ★★★. Best AA growers include Colterenzio, HOFSTÄTTER, LAGEDER, Nals Margreid, NIEDRIST, TERLANO, Termeno. Gd COLLIO ★★→★★★ producers include Renato Keber, Aldo Polencic, Russiz Superiore, SCHIOPETTO, VILLA RUSSIZ. Best from COLLI ORIENTALI ★★→★★★ La

---

The "grey" list – the best Pino Grigio DOCs

DOCS ALTO ALDIGE (SAN MICHELE APPIANO, CALDARO, LAGEDER, Nals Margreid, Termeno), COLLIO (Renato Keber, LIVON, Aldo Polencic, RUSSIZ SUPERIORE, SCHIOPETTO, Tercic, Terpin, Venica, VILLA RUSSIZ), COLLI ORIENTALI (Livio FELLUGA), and ISONZO (Borgo San Daniele, LIS NERIS, Masut da Rive, Pierpaolo Pecorari, Ronco del Gelso, VIE DI ROMANS).

Viarte, Zamò & Zamò. From ISONZO try Masut da Rive.

Pinot Grigio World-popular varietal white of medium-low acidity and broadly appealing fruit. Has given birth to countless copycats, not to say fraudulent versions. *Caveat emptor*. The real thing can be excellent, usually dry (unlike Alsace's residual-sugar Pinot Gr), full-bodied and velvety; and not cheap.

Pinot Nero (Pinot N) Planted in much of NE Italy. DOC status and some quality in LOMBARDY (Ca' del Bosco Pinero) and in ALTO ADIGE (co-ops of Caldaro, Colterenzio and Nals Margreid, HAAS, Haderburg, HOFSTÄTTER, LAGEDER, Laimburg, NIEDERMAYR, SAN MICHELE APPIANO, Termeno) and in OLTREPÒ PAVESE (Frecciarossa, Ruiz de Cardenas). Not bad in FRIULI (LE DUE TERRE, Masut da Riva); gets worse as you head south, except for on Mt Etna in SICILY.

Pio Cesare ★★ →★★★ Long-established ALBA producer, offers BAROLO and BARBARESCO in both modern (BARRIQUE) and traditional (large cask-aged) versions. Probably the best NEBBIOLO D'ALBA.

Planeta ★★ →★★★ Top SICILIAN estate: Segreta BIANCO blend, Segreta ROSSO; *outstanding Chard*, CAB SAUV, Fiano, MERLOT, NERO D'AVOLA (Santa Cecilia).

Podere Small TUSCAN farm, once part of a big estate.

Poggio Means "hill" in Tuscan dialect. "POGGIONE" means "big hill".

Poggio Antico ★★★ Admirably consistent, top-level BRUNELLO DI MONTALCINO.

Poggione, Tenuta Il ★★★ V. reliable estate for BRUNELLO considering large volume; also ROSSO DI MONTALCINO.

Pojer & Sandri ★★ →★★★ GdTRENTINO producers red and white wines, SPUMANTE.

Poliziano ★★★ MONTEPULCIANO estate. Federico Carletti makes superior VINO NOBILE (esp Asinone) and gd IGT Le Stanze (CAB SAUV/MERLOT).

Pomino Tus DOC w r ★★★ r7 **01 03 04** 06 07 (08) Fine red and white blends (esp Il Benefizio). Virtually a FRESCOBALDI exclusivity.

Pra ★★★ Excellent SOAVE CLASSICO producer, esp *cru* Monte Grande and new Staforte, 6 mths in steel tanks on lees with *bâtonnage*.

Produttori del Barbaresco ★★ →★★★ Co-op and one of DOCG's most reliable producers. Often v.gd single-v'yd wines (Asili, Montefico, Montestefano).

Prosecco di Conegliano-Valdobbiadene Ven DOC w s/sw fz sp (dr) ★★ DYA Fashionable light sparkler consumed as apéritif in all bars in Venice and throughout Italy. Off-dry is normal, truly dry (brut) is rare. Sweetest are called Superiore di Cartizze. CARPENÈ-MALVOLTI best known; also Adami, BISOL, Bortolin, Canevel, Case Bianche, Col Salice, Le Colture, Col Vetoraz, Nino Franco, Gregoletto, La Riva dei Frati, Ruggeri, Zardetto.

Prunotto, Alfredo ★★★ →★★★★ Traditional ALBA company modernized by ANTINORI in 1990s, and run by Piero's daughter, Albiera. V.gd BARBARESCO (Bric Turot), BAROLO (Bussia), NEBBIOLO (Occhetti), BARBERA D'ALBA (Pian Romauldo), BARBERA D'ASTI (Costamiole) and MONFERRATO ROSSO (Mompertone, BARBERA/SYRAH blend).

Puglia See APULIA.

Le Pupille ★★★ Top producer of MORELLINO DI SCANSANO (look for Poggio Valente), excellent IGT blend Saffredi (CAB SAUV/MERLOT/ALICANTE).

Querciabella ★★★★ Top CHIANTI CLASSICO estate with IGT *crus* Camartina (SANGIOVESE/CAB SAUV), barrel-fermented white Batàr, and Palafreno, a SANGIOVESE/MERLOT.

Quintarelli, Giuseppe ★★★★ No spitting allowed at the winery of this arch-traditionalist, artisanal producer of VALPOLICELLA, RECIOTO, and AMARONE. No wonder, considering the high prices.

Raboso del Piave (now DOC) Ven r ★ →★★ **04** 05 06 07 (08) Powerful, sharp, interesting country red; at best, needs age. Look for Molon.

Le Ragose ★★ →★★★ Family estate, one of VALPOLICELLA's best. AMARONE (Marta Galli) and RECIOTO top quality, various VALPOLICELLA Superiore *crus*.

Rampolla, Castello dei ★★★→★★★★ Fine estate in Panzano in CHIANTI CLASSICO, notable CAB SAUV-based IGT wines Sammarco and Alceo.

Recioto di Soave Ven DOCG W SW (sp) ★★★→★★★★ **01 04** 05 07 (08) SOAVE made from selected half-dried grapes: sweet, fruity, slightly almondy; sweetness is cut by high acidity. Outstanding from ANSELMI, COFFELE, Gini, PIEROPAN, Tamellini, often v.gd from Ca' Rugate, Pasqua, Pra, Suavia, Trabuchi.

Recioto della Valpolicella Ven DOC r s/sw (sp) ★★★→★★★★ Potentially stunning, rich, cherry-chocolaty red from grapes dried on trays up to 6 mths. Ages for yrs.

Refosco (dal Peduncolo Rosso) r ★★→★★★ 04 05 06 07 (08) Dark, gutsy red sometimes gd for ageing. Best from COLLI ORIENTALI DOC, Moschioni, Le Vigne di Zamo, Volpi Pasini: gd from LIVIO FELLUGA, Miani and from Dorigo, Ronchi di Manzano, Venica, Ca' Bolani, and Denis Montanara in AQUILEIA DOC.

Regaleali See TASCA D'ALMERITA.

Ribolla Colli Orientali del Friuli and Collio, F-VG DOC W ★→★★ DYA Acidic but characterful northeastern white. The best comes from COLLIO. Top estates: Il Carpino, La Castellada, Damijan, Fliegl, GRAVNER, Primosic, Radikon, Tercic.

Ricasoli Historic TUSCAN family, 19th-century proposers of CHIANTI blend, whose CHIANTI CLASSICO is named after the medieval castle of BROLIO. Related Pirasolis own Castello di Cacchiano and Rocca di Montegrossi.

Riecine Tus (★)★★ First-class v. small CHIANTI CLASSICO estate at Gaiole, created by its late English owner, John Dunkley. Also fine IGT La Gioia SANGIOVESE.

Riesling Today refers only to Rheinriesling, used mainly in blends of northeast. Best from DOC ALTO ADIGE ★★ (esp HOFSTÄTTER, Kuenhof, Laimburg, NIEDRIST, La Vis co-op, Unterortl); DOC OLTREPÒ PAVESE (Lom) ★★ (Brega, Frecciarossa, Le Fracce); DOC ISONZO RONCO del Gelso and VIE DI ROMANS. Also gd from Le Vigne di San Pietro (Ven), JERMANN, VAJRA (Pie).

Ripasso VALPOLICELLA re-fermented on RECIOTO or AMARONE grape skins to make a complex longer-lived wine. V.gd from BUSSOLA, Castellani, DAL FORNO, QUINTARELLI, ZENATO. MASI's Campo Fiorin IGT claimed to be first and entitled to exclusivity of the title. Others say it's traditional and the name is generic.

Riserva Wine aged for a statutory period, usually in casks or barrels.

Rivera ★★ Reliable winemakers at Andria in APULIA. ★★★ CASTEL DEL MONTE Il Falcone RISERVA; v.gd Cappellaccio; VIGNA al Monte; Puer Apuliae.

Rivetti, Giorgio (La Spinetta) ★★★ Fine MOSCATO d'Asti, excellent BARBERA, interesting IGT Pin, series of super-concentrated oaky BARBARESCOS. Now owner of v'yds both in the BAROLO and the CHIANTI Colli Pisane DOCGS. Early vintages of BAROLO along lines of BARBARESCO.

Riviera del Garda Bresciano Lom DOC w p r (sp) ★→★★ **04** 05 06 07(08) (r) Rarely seen DOC (post GARDA DOC) in SW corner of Lake Garda; red based on Gropello, white on Ries. Producers: Ca' dei Frati, Comincioli, Costaripa, Monte Cigogna.

Rocca, Bruno ★★★ Admirable modern-style BARBARESCO (Rabajà) and other ALBA wines, also v. fine BARBERA D'ASTI.

Rocche dei Manzoni ★★★ Modernist estate at Monforte d'Alba. Oaky BAROLO (esp VIGNA d'la Roul, Cappella di Stefano, Pianpolvere), **Bricco Manzoni** (pioneer BARBERA/NEBBIOLO blend), Quatr Nas (LANGHE).

Roero Pie DOCG r ★★' **96 97' 98' 99' 00 01'** 03 04' 05 06' 07' (08') Potentially serious, occasionally BAROLO-level NEBBIOLOS from the LANGHE hills across the Tanaro from ALBA. Best: Almondo, Buganza, Ca' Rossa, Cascina Chicco, Correggia, Funtanin, Malvirà, Monchiero-Carbone, Morra, Pace, Pioiero, Taliano, Val di Prete. See also ARNEIS.

Ronco Term for a hillside v'yd in northeast Italy, esp FRIULI-VENEZIA GIULIA.

Ronco del Gnemiz ★★★ Small estate, v. fine COLLI ORIENTALI DEL FRIULI.

Rosato Rosé; also CHIARETTO, esp around Lake Garda; and CERASUOLO, from Abruzzo; and Kretzer, from ALTO ADIGE.

Rosato del Salento Ap p ★★ DYA From near BRINDISI. Sturdy NEGROAMARO-based wine from a zone that has specialized in rosé. See COPERTINO, SALICE SALENTO.

Rosso Red.

Rosso Conero Mar DOCG r ★★→★★★ 01' 03' 04 05 06' 07' (08) Some of Italy's best MONTEPULCIANO (the grape, that is): GAROFOLI's Grosso Agontano, Moroder's Dorico, MONTE SCHIAVO's Adeodato, TERRE CORTESI MONCARO's Nerone and Vigneti del Parco, Le Terrazze's Sassi Neri and Visions of J. Also gd: Casato, FAZI-BATTAGLIA, Lanari, Leopardi Dittajuti, Malacari, Marchetti, Piantate Lunghe, Poggio Morelli, UMANI RONCHI.

Rosso di Montalcino Tus DOC r ★★→★★★ 01' 03 04' 05 06' 07' (08) DOC for younger wines from BRUNELLO grapes, from younger or lesser v'yd sites.

Rosso di Montefalco Umb DOC r ★★ ·★★★ 99' 00' 01' 03 04' 05 06' 07' (08) SANGIOVESE/Sagrantino blend, often with a splash of softening MERLOT. For producers, see MONTEFALCO SAGRANTINO.

Rosso di Montepulciano Tus DOC r ★★ 03 04 05 06 07 (08) Junior version of VINO NOBILE DI MONTEPULCIANO, growers similar. While ROSSO DI MONTALCINO is increasingly expensive, ROSSO DI MONTEPULCIANO offers value.

Rosso Piceno Mar DOC r 01' 03 04 05 06 07 (08) Gluggable MONTEPULCIANO/SANGIOVESE blend from southern half of Mar, SUPERIORE from restricted classic zone nr Ascoli, much improved in recent yrs and v. good value. Best: Aurora, BOCCADIGABBIA, Bucci, Fonte della Luna, Montecappone, MONTE SCHIAVO, Saladini Pilastri, TERRE CORTESI MONCARO, Velenosi Ercole, Villamagna.

Ruchè (also Rouchè/Rouchet) Rare PIEDMONTESE grape of French origin; fruity, fresh, rich-scented red wine (sweet/semi-sweet). Ruchè di Castagnole MONFERRATO is recent DOC. Look for Biletta, Borgognone, Dezzani, Garetto. SCARPA's Rouchet Briccorosa is dry (★★★).

Ruffino ★→★★★ Famous CHIANTI merchant at Pontassieve, east of Florence. Best are RISERVA Ducale Oro and Santedame. Oaky IGT CHARD Solatia, SANGIOVESE/CAB SAUV Modus. Owns Lodola Nuova in MONTEPULCIANO for VINO NOBILE DI MONTEPULCIANO, and Greppone Mazzi in MONTALCINO for BRUNELLO DI MONTEPULCIANO. Excellent MERLOT/Colorino blend Romitorio di Santedame. Also owns Borgo Conventi estate in FRIULI-VENEZIA GIULIA.

Rufina ★★★ Important sub-region of CHIANTI. Best wines from Basciano, CASTELLO DI NIPOZZANO (FRESCOBALDI), CASTELLO del Trebbio, Colognole, Frascole, Lavacchio, SELVAPIANA, Tenuta Bossi, Travignoli. Villa di Vetrice/Grati do old vintages, sometimes aged 20 yrs+ in oak barrels or concrete vats.

Sala, Castello della ★★→★★★ ANTINORI estate at ORVIETO. Campogrande is the regular white. Top wine is Cervaro della Sala, oak-aged CHARD/Grechetto. Muffato della Sala was a pioneering example of an Italian botrytis-influenced dessert wine. PINOT N also creditable.

Le Salette ★★→★★★ Small VALPOLICELLA producer: look for v.gd AMARONE Pergole Vece and RECIOTO Le Traversagne.

Salice Salentino Ap p ★★→★★★ 03 04 06 07 (08) Smooth red from Puglia's southern tip, made from NEGROAMARO and MALVASIA NERA grapes and redolent of plums. RISERVA after 2 yrs. Top makers: Apollonio, Candido, Castello Monaci, Due Palme, Resya, Tornavento, TAURINO, Valle dell'Asso, VALLONE.

Sandrone, Luciano ★★★ Exponent of modern-style ALBA wines with deep, concentrated BAROLO Cannubi Boschi and Le Vigne, DOLCETTO, BARBERA D'ALBA, and NEBBIOLO D'ALBA.

San Felice ★★ Large CHIANTI CLASSICO resort/estate. Fine RISERVA Poggio ROSSO. Pugnitello, made from a Tuscan grape recovered from near-extinction, a fascinating addition. Also red IGT Vigorello (the very first SUPER TUSCAN, from 1968) and BRUNELLO DI MONTALCINO Campogiovanni.

San Gimignano TUSCAN town famous for its towers and dry white VERNACCIA, often overpriced and overvalued but occasionally convinces with a serious white wine. Some gd red wines, too. Producers include Cesani, Cusona, FALCHINI, Il Palagione, Le Calcinaie, Le Tre Stelle, Mormoraia, Montenidoli, Palagetto, Palagione, Panizzi, Paradiso, Pietrafitta, La Rampa di Fugnano, Teruzzi & Puthod.

Sangiovese (Sangioveto) Principal red grape of west central Italy with a reputation of being v. difficult to get right but sublime, and long lasting, when it is. Currently the subject of enormous research and experimentation, new clones are yielding more reliable fruit. Dominant in CHIANTI, VINO NOBILE, BRUNELLO DI MONTALCINO, MORELLINO DI SCANSANO and various fine IGT offerings. Also in Umbria generally (eg MONTEFALCO ROSSO and TORGIANO RISERVA) and across the Apennines in Romagna and the Marches. Not so clever in the warmer, lower-altitude v'yds of the Tuscan coast, nor in other parts of Italy despite its near ubiquity.

Sangiovese di Romagna Mar DOC r ★★ →★★★ Often well made and v.gd value from La Berta, Berti, Calonga, Ca' Lunga, Cesari, Drei Donà, Paradiso, San Patrignano, Tre Monti, Trere (E-R DOC), Zerbina, IGT RONCO delle Ginestre, RONCO dei Ciliegi from CASTELLUCCIO.

San Giusto a Rentennano ★★★ →★★★★ V. fine CHIANTI CLASSICO producers (★★★). V.gd but v. rare VIN SANTO. Top, long-lasting SANGIOVESE IGT Percarlo (★★★★).

San Guido, Tenuta See SASSICAIA.

San Leonardo ★★★ Top estate in TRENTINO, with v. fine San Leonardo (Cab Sauv), outstanding *San Leonardo (Cab Sauv)* and promising Villa Gresti MERLOT.

San Michele Appiano Top ALTO ADIGE co-op, esp for whites. Look for PINOT BIANCO Schulthauser and Sanct Valentin (★★★) selections: CHARD, PINOT GR, SAUV BL, CAB SAUV, PINOT N, Gewurz.

Santadi ★★★ Consistently fine wines from SARDINIAN co-op, esp DOC CARIGNANO DEL SULCIS Grotta Rossa, Rocca Rubia, TERRE BRUNE and IGT Baie Rosse (Carignano), *Vermentino Villa Solais*, Villa di Chiesa (VERMENTINO/CHARD).

Santa Maddalena (or St-Magdalener) T-AA DOC r ★ →★★ DYA Superior SCHIAVA ALTO ADIGE red, usually blended with LAGREIN for added body. CS St-Magdalena (Huck am Bach), Gojer, Josephus Mayr, Georg Ramoser, Hans Rottensteiner (Premstallerhof), Heinrich Rottensteiner.

Santa Margherita Large Veneto (Portogruaro) merchants, famous for decent but overpriced PINOT GR. Also owns: Veneto (Torresella), ALTO ADIGE (Kettmeir), TUSCANY (Lamole di Lamole and Vistarenni), and Lombardy (CA' DEL BOSCO).

Sant'Antimo Tus DOC r w SW ★★ →★★★ Catch-all DOC for (almost) everything in Montalcino zone that isn't BRUNELLO DOCG or ROSSO DOC.

Santi See GRUPPO ITALIANO VINI.

Saracco, Paolo ★★★ Small estate with top MOSCATO D'ASTI.

Sardinia (Sardegna) The Med's 2nd-biggest island produces much decent and some v.gd wines, eg, Turriga from ARGIOLAS, Arbeskia and Dule from Gabbas, VERMENTINO of CAPICHERA, CANNONAU RISERVAS of Jerzu and Loi, VERMENTINO and CANNONAU from Dettori and the amazing flor-affected VERNACCIA of CONTINI. Best DOCS: VERMENTINO di Gallura (eg Canayli from Cantina Gallura) and CARIGNANO DEL SULCIS (TERRE BRUNE and Rocca Rubia from SANTADI).

Sartarelli ★★★ One of top VERDICCHIO DEI CASTELLI DI JESI producers (Tralivio); outstanding, rare Verdicchio VENDEMMIA Tardiva (Contrada Balciana).

Sassicaia Tus r ★★★★ 85' 88' 90' 95' 97 98' 99 01' 03 04' 05 06 07' (08) First Italian CAB SAUV to take on the world, considered Italy's best wine in 1970s and 1980s, no longer since indigenous varieties took centre stage. Made by Marchese Incisa della Rocchetta at Tenuta San Guido BOLGHERI. Promoted early 1990s from SUPER TUSCAN VDT to special sub-zone status in BOLGHERI DOC. Conservative style, real finesse.

Satta, Michele ★★★ Virtually the only BOLGHERI grower to succeed with 100% SANGIOVESE (Cavaliere). Also BOLGHERI DOC red blends Piastraia and

SUPERIORE | Castagni.

Sauvignon Blanc The Loire's great white grape is vinified varietally throughout the NE and elsewhere in Italy, generally for blending. V. successful in AA and F-VG. Try Voglar from Peter Dipoli (AA) and Piere from Vie de Romans (F-VG).

Scarpa ★★→★★★ Old-fashioned Piedmontese house with BARBERA D'ASTI (La Bogliona), rare Rouchet (RUCHÈ), v.gd DOLCETTO, BAROLO, BARBARESCO.

Scavino, Paolo ★★★ Successful modern-style BAROLO producer. Sought-after single-v'yd wines: Rocche dell'Annunziata, Bric del Fiasc, Cannubi, and Carobric. Also oak-aged BARBERA and LANGHE Corale.

Schiava High-yielding red grape of ALTO ADIGE, used for light reds such as LAGO DI CALDARO, SANTA MADDALENA, etc. Known locally as Vernatsch.

Schioppetto, Mario ★★★→★★★★ Legendary late COLLIO pioneer with spacious modern winery. V.gd DOC SAUV BL, *Pinot Bl*, TOCAI, IGT blend Blanc de Rosis, etc. Recent offerings include wines from COLLI ORIENTALI v'yds.

Sciacchetrà See CINQUETERRE.

La Scolca ★★ Famous GAVI estate for gd GAVI and SPUMANTE.

Secco Dry.

Sella & Mosca ★★ Major SARDINIAN grower and merchant with v. pleasant white Torbato and light, fruity VERMENTINO Cala Viola (DYA). Gd Alghero DOC Marchese di Villamarina (CAB SAUV) and Tanca Farrà (CANNONAU/CAB SAUV). Also interesting port-like Anghelu Ruju.

Selvapiana ★★★ Top CHIANTI RUFINA estate. Best wines are RISERVA Bucerchiale and IGT Fornace. Also, under the Petrognano label, some fine red DOC POMINO, the DOC's only significant producer apart from FRESCOBALDI.

Settesoli, c.s. ★→★★ Huge quality-conscious Sicilian cooperative with nearly 7,000 ha, run by PLANETA family and giving SICILY a good name with v. well-made varietals (**Nero d'Avola**, SYRAH, MERLOT, CAB SAUV, CHARD, Grecanico, Viognier and blends.) at v. modest prices. Look for brand Mandrarossa.

Sforzato See VALTELLINA.

Sicily The Med's largest island has been dubbed the "new California" for its creative approach to winemaking, using both native grapes (NERO D'AVOLA, Frappato, Inzolia, Grecanico) and international varieties. To seek out: Benanti, Ceusi, Colosi, Cos, Cusumano, De Bartoli, De Grazia, Di Giovanna, DONNAFUGATA, DUCA DI SALAPARUTA, Fazio, Firriato, Fornaci, Gulfi-Ramada, Miceli, Morgante, MURANA, Pellegrino, PLANETA, Principe di Butera (ZONIN), Rapitalà, Sallier de la Tour, Santa Anastasia, SETTESOLI, SIV, Spadafora, TASCA D'ALMERITA, Tenuta dell'Abate, VECCHIO SAMPERI.

Sizzano Pie DOC r ★★ 99 01' 03 04 06 07 (08) Elegant but hard-to-find red from Sizzano, (Novara); mostly NEBBIOLO. Ages up to 10 yrs. Esp: Bianchi, Dessilani.

Soave DOC W (sw) ★→★★★ DYA Famous, still underrated Veronese. From the CLASSICO zone can be intense, mineral, v. fine and quite long-lived. When labelled SUPERIORE is DOCG, but best CLASSICO producers shun the "honour", stick to DOC. Sweet RECIOTO can be superb. Best: Cantina del Castello, La Cappuccina, Ca' Rugate, Cecilia Beretta, COFFELE, Dama del Rovere, Fattori, Gini, Guerrieri-Rizzardi, Inama, Montedonto, PIEROPAN, Portinari, Pra, Sartori, Suavia, Tamellini, TEDESCHI.

Solaia Tus r ★★★★ 85' 90' 95' 97' 99' 01' 04 06 07' (08) V. fine B'x-style IGT of CAB SAUV and a little SANGIOVESE from ANTINORI; first made in 1978.

Sorì Term for a high south-, southeast-, or southwest-oriented site in PIEDMONT.

Sovana MAREMMA DOC; inland nr Pitigliano. Look for SANGIOVESE, Ciliegiolo from Tenuta Roccaccia, Pitigliano, Ripa, Sassotondo, Malbec from ANTINORI.

Spanna Local name for NEBBIOLO in a variety of north PIEDMONT zones (BOCA, BRAMATERRA, FARA, GATTINARA, GHEMME, LESSONA, SIZZANO).

Sportoletti ★★★ V.gd wines from Spello, nr ASSISI, esp Villa Fidelia.

Spumante Sparkling, inc both METODO CLASSICO (best from TRENTINO, ALTO ADIGE, FRANCIACORTA, PIEDMONT, OLTREPÒ PAVESE) occasionally gd from FRIULI and Veneto) and tank-made cheapos of higher pressure (as distinct from lower-pressure FRIZZANTE. What used to be called ASTI Spumante is now just ASTI.

Südtirol The local name of German-speaking ALTO ADIGE.

Superiore Wine with more ageing than normal DOC and 0.5–1% more alcohol. May indicate a restricted production zone, eg Rosso Piceno Superiore.

Super Tuscan Term coined in 1980s for innovative wines from TUSCANY, often involving pure SANGIOVESE or international varieties, BARRIQUES, heavy bottles, and elevated prices.

Syrah The Rhône's great grape has taken Italy, esp TUSCANY and SICILY, by storm, mainly as a blender. For gd varietals try TUSCANY's Il Bosco from d'Alessandro or l'Eremo from ISOLE E OLENA.

Tasca d'Almerita ★★★ Historic SICILIAN producer owned by noble family (between Palermo and Caltanissetta to the southeast). Gd IGT red, white, and ROSATO Regaleali; v. gd *Rosso del Conte*: impressive CHARD and CAB SAUV.

Taurasi Cam DOCG r ★★★ 95 97' 98 99 00 01' 03' 04' 05 06 07' (08) CAMPANIA's historic and most celebrated red, one of Italy's outstanding wines, though not easy to appreciate. RISERVA after 4 yrs. V.gd from Caggiano, Caputo, FEUDI DI SAN GREGORIO, MASTROBERARDINO, Molettieri, Vesevo, and Villa Raiano.

Taurino, Cosimo ★★★ Best-known producer of Salento-APULIA when Cosimo was alive, v.gd SALICE SALENTINO, VDT Notarpanoro, and IGT PATRIGLIONE ROSSO.

Tedeschi, Fratelli ★★→★★★ Well-known producer of VALPOLICELLA, AMARONE, RECIOTO. Gd Capitel San Rocco red IGT.

Tenuta Farm or estate. (See under name – eg SAN GUIDO, TENUTA.)

Terlano T-AA w ★★→★★★ DYA Terlano DOC incorporated into ALTO ADIGE. ALTO ADIGE Terlano DOC is applicable to one white blend and 8 white varietals, esp PINOT BIANCO and SAUV BL. Top producer CS Terlano (Pinot Bianco Vorberg, capable of remarkable ageing), also LAGEDER, NIEDERMAYR, NIEDRIST.

> ### It's all at the co-op
> For nearly 100 years they have bridled at the idea of being incorporated in such a chaotic and corrupt country as Italy, but the co-ops of the ex-Austrian SÜDTIROL are today doing very nicely, thank you, out of the deal, being master white-winemakers in a land of (mainly) reds. The roll of honour includes: COLTERENZIO, Cornaiano, Cortaccia, Gries, Nals Margreid, SAN MICHELE APPIANO, SANTA MADDALENA, TERLANO and Termeno (home of Traminer). And the list doesn't stop there.

Teroldego Rotaliano T-AA DOC r p ★★→★★★ Attractive blackberry-scented red; slightly bitter aftertaste; can age v. well. Esp FORADORI's. Also gd from CA' VIT, Dorigati, Endrizzi, MEZZACORONA's RISERVA Nos, Zeni.

Terre Brune Sard r ★★★ Splendid earthy Carignano del Sulcis DOC from SANTADI, a flag-carrier for SARDINIA.

Terre Cortesi Moncaro Mar ★★★ Marches co-op, now making wines that compete with the best of the region at remarkably low prices: gd VERDICCHIO DEI CASTELLI DI JESI Le Vele, ROSSO CONERO, Riserva Nerone and ROSSO PICENO Superiore Campo delle Mura.

Terre di Franciacorta Lom DOC r w ★★★ 01 03 04 06 07 (08) So named to distinguish table wines from sparkling Franciacorta. The red is an unusual blend of CAB SAUV, BARBERA, NEBBIOLO, MERLOT. Less adventurous whites from CHARD, PINOT GR. Best producers: see FRANCIACORTA.

Terre Rosse ★★ Pioneering small estate nr Bologna. Its CAB SAUV, CHARD, PINOT BL, RIES, even Viognier, were trail-blazing wines for the region.

Ten DOCs into one do go
More popularly thought of as Italy's stiletto, the Salento peninsula currently boasts no fewer than 10 DOCs. They're not that different from each other: negroamaro with or without MALVASIA NERA, MONTEPULCIANO and SANGIOVESE. There are just three of which normal people might conceivably have heard: SALICE SALENTINO, COPERTINO and BRINDISI, though the latter may be more familiar as a port on the way to Greece. The new EU regulations propose replacing the whole lot with DOP Salento, demonstrating that the new law is not wholly an ass.

Terre da Vino ★→★★★ Association of 27 PIEDMONT co-ops and private estates inc most local DOCs. Best: BARBARESCO La Casa in Collina, BAROLO PODERE Parussi, BARBERA D'ASTI La Luna e l Falò.

Terriccio, Castello di ★★★ Large estate south of Livorno: excellent, v. expensive IGT Lupicaia, v.gd IGT Tassinaia, both CAB SAUV/MERLOT blends. Impressive new IGT Terriccio, an unusual blend of mainly Rhône grapes.

Tiefenbrunner ★★→★★★ Medium-sized grower-négociant situated at a quaint Teutonic castle (Turmhof) in southern ALTO ADIGE village of Entiklar. Christof T has taken over from octogenarian father Herbert (winemaker since 1943 and counting) producing a wide range of mountain-fresh white and well-defined red varietals, French, Germanic and local, esp 1,000m high Feldmarschall (see MULLER-THURGAU) and Linticlarus range CHARD/Lagrein/PINOT NERO.

Tignanello Tus r ★★★ 95 97' 98 **99' 00 01'** 03 04' 06' 07' (08) SANGIOVESE/CAB SAUV blend, BARRIQUE-aged, the wine that put SUPER TUSCANS on the map (if not the first: see SAN FELICE), created by ANTINORI in the early 1970s.

Tocai ★→★★ Controversial white grape bearing no resemblance to Hungarian Tokaji but banned by the EU from using its historic name. Best is what used to be called Tocai Friulano, now 'Friulano' , from FRIULI-VENEZIA GIULIA (esp COLLIO and COLLI ORIENTALI) ★★→★★★. Best producers: Borgo San Daniele, BORGO DEL TIGLIO, Livio FELLUGA, Renato Keber, LIS NERIS, Masut da Rive, Meroi, Mirani, Pierpaolo Pecorari, Aldo Polencic, RONCO del Gelso, RONCO DEL GNEMIZ, Russiz Superiore, SCHIOPETTO, Venica & Venica, LE VIGNE DI ZAMÒ, VILLA RUSSIZ.

Torgiano Umb DOC r w p (sp) ★★ and **Torgiano, Rosso Riserva** Umb DOCG r ★★→★★★ 97 **99 00' 01'** 03 04 06 07'(08) Gd to excellent CHIANTI-style red from Umbria, denomination dominated by Lungarotti's Rubesco. Rubesco RISERVA VIGNA Monticchio outstanding in vintages such as 75, 79, 85; keeps for many yrs. Antignano's Torgiano offers interesting contrast.

Traminer Aromatico T-AA DOC w ★★→★★★ DYA (German: Gewurztraminer) Pungent white with all the aromatics of the Alsatian versions minus the residual sugar. Best from its birthplace Tramin (Italian: Termeno), notably CS Termeno and HOFSTÄTTER. Other gd producers include co-ops Caldaro, Colterenzio, Prima & Nuova, SAN MICHELE APPIANO, TERLANO plus Abbazia di Novacella, HAAS, Kuenhof, LAGEDER, Laimberg, Nals Margreid, NIEDERMAYR.

Trebbiano Principal white grape of TUSCANY, found all over Italy in many different guises. Best is as Trebbiano di SOAVE or Trebbiano di LUGANA (VERDICCHIO), or in TUSCANY'S VIN SANTO. Some gd dry whites under DOCs Romagna or ABRUZZO.

Trebbiano d'Abruzzo Ab DOC w ★→★★ DYA Gentle, neutral white grape of gd acidity from Pescara. That of VALENTINI is considered excellent, other gd versions from Contesa, Masciarelli, Nicodemi, La Valentina, and Valori.

Trentino T-AA DOC r w dr sw ★→★★★ DOC for 20 wines, most named after grapes. Best: CHARD, PINOT BL, MARZEMINO, TEROLDEGO. Provincial capital is Trento.

Triacca ★★→★★★ V.gd producer of VALTELLINA; also owns estates in TUSCANY (CHIANTI CLASSICO: La Madonnina; MONTEPULCIANO: Santavenere).

Trinoro, Tenuta di ★★★ Individualist TUSCAN red wine estate in DOC Val d'Orcia between MONTEPULCIANO and MONTALCINO. Early vintages of B'x-blend Trinoro caused great excitement, then the price shot up. Cincinnato is an unusual example of wine from Lazio's Cesanese d'Affile grape, while Le Cupole adds Cesanese and Uva di Troia (from Puglia) to Cab/Merlot. Andrea Franchetti also vinifies Nerello Mascalese on Mt Etna.

Tua Rita ★★→★★★★ The first producer to establish Suvereto as the new BOLGHERI in the 1990s. Producer of possibly Italy's greatest MERLOT in Redigaffi, also outstanding B'x blend Giusto di Notri.

Tuscany (Toscana) Italy's central wine region, includes DOCS CHIANTI, MONTALCINO, MONTEPULCIANO, etc, regional IGT TOSCANA, and – of course – SUPER TUSCAN.

Uberti ★★→★★★ Producer of DOCG FRANCIACORTA. V.gd TERRE DI FRANCIACORTA.

Umani Ronchi ★★→★★★★ Leading Marches merchant and grower, esp for VERDICCHIO (Casal di Serra, Plenio), ROSSO CONERO Cumaro white IGT Le Busche, red IGT Pelago.

Vajra, G D ★★★ V.gd consistent BAROLO producer, esp for BARBERA, BAROLO, DOLCETTO, LANGHE, etc. Also a serious still FREISA.

Valcalepio Lom DOC r w ★→★★★ From nr Bergamo. Pleasant red from B'x varieties; lightly scented fresh white from Burgundy grapes. Gd from Brugherata, CASTELLO di Grumello, Monzio.

Val di Cornia Tus DOC r p w ★★→★★★ 97 98 **99' 00 01'** 03 04' 05 06' 07'(08) DOC S of BOLGHERI, province of Livorno. SANGIOVESE, CAB SAUV, MERLOT, SYRAH and MONTEPULCIANO. Look for: Ambrosini, Jacopo Banti, Bulichella, Gualdo del Re, Incontri, Montepeloso, Petra, Russo, San Michele, Tenuta Casa Dei, Terricciola, Tua Rita.

Valdadige T-AA DOC r w dr s/sw ★ Name for the simple wines of the valley of the ALTO ADIGE – in German, Etschtaler.

Valentini, Edoardo ★★★ Recently deceased producer of long-macerating, non-filtered, non-fined, hand-bottled MONTEPULCIANO and TREBBIANO D'ABRUZZO. His son continues the tradition.

Valle d'Aosta (VdA) DOC r w p ★★ Regional DOC for some 25 Alpine wines, geographically or varietally named, inc Premetta, Fumin, Blanc de Morgex et de La Salle, Chambave, Nus Malvoisie, Arnad Montjovet, Torrette, Donnas, and Enfer d'Arvier. Tiny production, wines rarely seen abroad.

Valle Isarco Eisacktal, T-AA DOC w ★★ DYA ALTO ADIGE Valle Isarco DOC is applicable to 7 varietal wines made northeast of Bolzano. Gd Gewurz, MÜLLER-THURGAU, RIES, and Silvaner. Top producers: Abbazia di Novacella, Eisacktaler, Kuenhof.

Vallone, Agricole ★★→★★★ Large scale private v'yd-holder in APULIA's Salento peninsula, best known for its AMARONE-like semi-dried-grape wine Graticciaia.

Valpolicella Ven DOC r ★→★★★★ 00 01 **03 04** 05 06 07 (08) (SUPERIORE) Complex

Valpolicella: the list
Whether it's AMARONE, RECIOTO or plain VALPOLICELLA, these are good to superb: Accordini, Serego Alighieri, ALLEGRINI, Baltieri, Begali, BERTANI, BOLLA, Boscaini, BRUNELLI, BUSSOLA, Ca' La Bianca, Campagnola, Ca' Rugate, Castellani, Cesari, Corteforte, Corte Sant Alda, CS Negrar, CS Valpantena, CS VALPOLICELLA, Valentina Cubi, DAL FORNO, Farina, Aleardo Ferrari, Guerrieri-Rizzardi, I Saltari, MASI, Mazzi, Nicolis, PASQUA, QUINTARELLI, Roccolo Grassi, LE RAGOSE, LE SALETTE, Sant'Alda, Sant'Antonio, Sartori, Speri, Tarrelli, TEDESCHI, Tommasi, Trabucchi, Valentina Cubi, Vaona, Venturini, Villa Bellini, Villa Monteleone, VIVIANI, ZENATO, Zeni. Interesting IGTS: BUSSOLA'S L'Errante, MASI'S Toar and Osar, ALLEGRINI'S La Grola, La Poja, Palazzo della Torre, Zyme's Harlequin, Oz.

denomination inc everything from light quaffers through stronger SUPERIORES to AMARONES and RECIOTOS of ancient lineage. Bitter cherry the common flavour characteristic. Best tend to come from CLASSICO sub-zone. Explore.

Valtellina Lom DOC r ★★→★★★ DOC for tannic but elegant wines: mainly from Chiavennasca (NEBBIOLO) in northern Alpine Sondrio province. V.gd SUPERIORE DOCG from Grumello, Inferno, Sassella, Valgella v'yds. Best: Caven Camuna, Conti Sertoli-Salis, Fay, Nera, Nino Negri, Plozza, Rainoldi, TRIACCA. *Sforzato* is the most concentrated type of Valtellina; similar to AMARONE.

VDT, Vino da Tavola "Table wine": the humblest class of Italian wine. No specific geographical or other claim to fame. Occasionally some excellent wines that do not fit into official categories despite prohibition, since 1990s, of mention of place or grape name, or vintage, on label. Changes afoot in new EU rules.

Vecchio Samperi Si ★★★ Vergine-like VDT from v.gd MARSALA estate. Best is barrel-aged 30 yrs, a blend of young and v. old vintages. Owner Marco De Bartoli also makes top DOC MARSALAS and outstanding Passito di Pantelleria Bukkuram.

Vendemmia Harvest or vintage.

Venegazzu ★★→★★★ Iconic B'x blend from eastern Veneto producer Loredan Gasparini. Even more prestigious is the *cru* Capo di Stato (being originally created to be served at the table of the President of the Italian Republic).

Verdicchio dei Castelli di Jesi Mar DOC w (sp) ★★→★★★ DYA Versatile white from nr Ancona, can be light and quaffable, or sparkling, or structured, complex and long-lived (esp RISERVA, minimum 2 yrs old). Also CLASSICO. Best from: Accadia, Bonci-Vallerosa, Brunori, Bucci, Casalfarneto, Cimarelli, Colonnara, Coroncino, FAZI-BATTAGLIA, Fonte della Luna, GAROFOLI, Laila, Lucangeli Aymerich di Laconi, Mancinelli, Montecappone, MONTE SCHIAVO, Santa Barbara, SARTARELLI, TERRE CORTESI MONCARO, UMANI RONCHI.

Verdicchio di Matelica Mar DOC w (sp) ★★→★★★ DYA Similar to above, smaller, less known, longer lasting. Esp Barone Pizzini, Belisario, Bisci, La Monacesca, Pagliano Tre, San Biagio.

Verduno Pie DOC r ★★ DYA Pale red with spicy perfume, from Pelaverga grape. Gd producers: BURLOTTO, Alessandria and CASTELLO DI VERDUNO.

Verduno, Castello di Pie ★★★ Husband/wife team Franco Bianco, with v'yds in Neive, and Gabriella Burlotto, with v'yds in Verduno, turn out v.gd Barbaresco Rabaja and Barolo Monvigliero with the help of winemaker Mario Andrion.

Verduzzo Colli Orientali del Friuli, F-VG DOC w dr s/sw sw ★★→★★★ Full-bodied white from indigenous Friulian variety. Ramandolo is regarded sub-zone. Top: Dario Coos, Dorigo, Giov Dri, Meroi. Superb sweet VDT Tal Luc from LIS NERIS.

Vermentino Lig w ★★ DYA Best seafood white of Riviera, esp from Pietra Ligure and San Remo. DOC is Riviera Ligure di Ponente. See PIGATO. Esp gd: Lambruschi, Lupi. Also TUSCANY/Umbria coast: ANTINORI, Barberani, San Giusto a Rentennano, SATTA, .

Vermentino di Gallura Sar DOCG W ★★→★★★ DYA *Best dry white of Sardinia*, stronger and more intensely flavoured than DOC Vermentino di Sardegna. Esp from CAPICHERA,, CS di Gallura, CS del Vermentino, Depperu.

Vernaccia di Oristano Sar DOC w dr (sw fz) ★→★★★ **90' 93' 97'** 00 01 04 06 07 (08) Sardinian flor-affected wine, like light sherry, a touch bitter, full-bodied. SUPERIORE 15.5% alcohol, 3 yrs of age. Top: CONTINI.

Vernaccia di San Gimignano See SAN GIMIGNANO.

Verrazzano, Castello di ★★ Gd CHIANTI CLASSICO estate near Greve.

Vestini Campagnano Small producer north of Naples specializing in forgotten local grapes. Excellent results from Casavecchia, Pallagrello BIANCO, and Pallagrello Nero.

Vicchiomaggio ★★→★★★ CHIANTI CLASSICO estate nr Greve, owned by John Matta.

Vie di Romans ★★★→★★★★ Gianfranco Gallo has built up his father's ISONZO estate to top FRIULI status. Excellent ISONZO CHARD, PINOT GR Dessimis, SAUV BL Piere and Vieris (oaked), MALVASIA/RIES/TOCAI blend called Flors di Uis.

Vietti ★★★ Exemplary producer of characterful PIEDMONT wines, inc BAROLO, BARBARESCO Masseria, BARBERA D'ALBA Carati, and D'ASTI La Crena at Castiglione Falletto in BAROLO region.

Vigna (or vigneto) A single v'yd, generally indicating superior quality.

Vignalta ★★ Top producer in COLLI EUGANEI near Padova (Veneto); v.gd COLLI Euganei CAB SAUV RISERVA and MERLOT/CAB SAUV blend Gemola.

Vignamaggio ★★→★★★ Historic, beautiful, and v.gd CHIANTI CLASSICO estate nr Greve. Leonardo da Vinci is said to have painted the Mona Lisa here.

Le Vigne di Zamò ★★★ First-class FRIULI estate. PINOT BIANCO, TOCAI, Pignolo, CAB SAUV, MERLOT, and Picolit from v'yds in 3 areas of COLLI ORIENTALI DEL FRIULI DOC.

Villa ★★→★★★ Worthy producer of DOCG FRANCIACORTA.

Villa Matilde ★★★ Top Campania producer of Falerno ROSSO (Vigna Camararato) and BIANCO (Vigna Caracci), Eleusi PASSITO.

Villa Russiz ★★★ Impressive w DOC COLLIO Goriziano: v.gd SAUV BL and MERLOT (esp "de la Tour" selections), PINOT BL, PINOT GR, TOCAI, CHARD.

Vino Nobile di Montepulciano Tus DOCG r ★★→★★★ '95 '97 '98 99' 00 01' 03 04' 05 06' 07'(08) Historic SANGIOVESE (here called Prugnolo Gentile) from the town (as distinct from the grape) MONTEPULCIANO, often tough with drying tannins, but complex and long-lasting from best producers, who include AVIGNONESI, Bindella, BOSCARELLI, La Braccesca, La Calonica, Canneto, Le Casalte, Contucci, Dei, Fattoria del Cerro, Gracciano della Seta, Gracciano Svetoni, Icario, Nottola, Palazzo Vecchio, POLIZIANO, Romeo, Salcheto, Trerose, Valdipiatta, Villa Sant'Anna. RISERVA after 3 yrs. Relative to rival BRUNELLO, reasonably priced.

Vin Santo or Vinsanto, Vin(o) Santo Term for certain strong, sweet wines made from PASSITO grapes, usually TREBBIANO, MALVASIA and/or SANGIOVESE in TUSCANY ("Vin Santo"), Nosiola in TRENTINO ("Vino Santo").

Vin Santo Toscano Tus W S/SW ★→★★★ Extremely variable wine which can be anything from quasi-dry and sherry-like to sweet and incredibly rich. May spend 3–10 unracked yrs in small barrels called *caratelli*. AVIGNONESI'S is mythic. Also excellent are CAPEZZANA, CORZANO & PATERNO, Fattoria del Cerro, FELSINA, Frascole, ISOLE E OLENA, Rocca di Montegrossi, San Gervasio, San Giusto a Rentennano, SELVAPIANA, Villa Sant'Anna, Villa di Vetrice.

Vivaldi-Arunda ★★→★★★ Winemaker Josef Reiterer makes top ALTO ADIGE sparkling wines. Best: Extra Brut RISERVA, Cuvée Marianna.

Viviani ★★★ Claudio Viviani is among the best of the new-wave producers who are transforming VALPOLICELLA. Outstanding AMARONE Tulipano Nero.

Voerzio, Roberto ★★★→★★★★ BAROLO modernist. Top, v. expensive single-v'yd BAROLOS: Brunate, Cerequio, Rocche dell'Annunziata-Torriglione, Sarmassa, Serra; impressive BARBERA D'ALBA.

Volpaia, Castello di ★★→★★★. V.gd CHIANTI CLASSICO estate at Radda. SUPER TUSCANS Coltassala (SANGIOVESE/Mammolo), Balifico (SANGIOVESE/CAB SAUV).

Zenato Ven ★★ V. reliable estate for VALPOLICELLA, SOAVE, AMARONE, LUGANA.

Zerbina, Fattoria ★★★ Leader in Romagna; best sweet ALBANA DOCG (Scacco Matto), v.gd SANGIOVESE (Pietramora); BARRIQUE-aged IGT Marzieno.

Zibibbo Si ★★ Local PANTELLERIA name for Muscat of Alexandria. Best from: MURANA, De Bartoli.

Zonin ★→★★ One of Italy's biggest private estates, based at GAMBELLARA, with DOC and DOCG VALPOLICELLA. Also in ASTI, APULIA, CHIANTI CLASSICO, SAN GIMIGNANO, FRIULI, SICILY and Virginia (US). Quality rising under winemaker Franco Giacosa.

ITALY

Germany

The following abbreviations of
regional names are used in the text:

Bad Baden
Frank Franken
M-M Mittelmosel
M-S-R Mosel-Saar-Ruwer
Na Nahe
Pfz Pfalz
Rhg Rheingau
Rhh Rheinhessen
Würt Württemberg

More heavily shaded
areas are the wine-
growing regions

We should be celebrating. German wine is better than it has ever been:
an apparently endless series of good to very good vintages (is that
tempting fate?) has produced wines of raciness and balance, excitement
and skill, year after year after year. The 2007s are sensational and the
2008s will be nothing to be ashamed of.

It's also ten years since Germany introduced its new categories of
First Growth (*Erstes Gewächs*) and Great Growths (*Grosses Gewächs*).
Think Burgundy, think terroir. This was a huge change: a country that had
focused, until then, on ripeness as the be-all-and-end-all, now switched
its gaze to terroir. And quite right, too: Riesling expresses its terroir better

than any other white grape, and Germany has terroir in buckets. These categories (which are invariably dry) certainly show just what German Riesling can do – even if they do tend to err on the side of power at the expense of delicacy.

Delicacy is, at least to this non-German palate, the key to German Riesling. Structure, yes; longevity, yes; but delicacy, interwoven with all that. The fashion may be for power – the domestic market seems to admire it – but this is surely only a phase. German Riesling is the most ethereal of wines, and the most resilient; the most apparently fragile, yet able to live for decades, if not centuries.

But don't let that put you off. Yes, you can keep it; but Kabinett is a delight young, while it is fresh and juicy. Even Spätlesen and Auslesen can be drunk younger than used to be the case.

And global warming is helping. As far as German Riesling is concerned, the effects of warmer summers is beneficial so far. As I say, we should be celebrating. Well, we have to celebrate something.

Recent vintages

Mosel-Saar-Ruwer

Mosels (including Saar and Ruwer wines) are so attractive young that their keeping qualities are not often enough explored. But well-made Riesling wines of Kabinett class gain from at least five years in bottle and often much more, Spätlese from 5 to 20, and Auslese and Beerenauslese anything from 10 to 30 years. As a rule, in poor years the Saar and Ruwer make sharp, lean wines, but in good years, which are becoming increasingly common, they can surpass the whole world for elegance and thrilling, steely "breed".

2008 Early flowering, but a classic cool summer with rain and sun. Cool Sept temperatures slowed down ripeness and kept acidity high. Wet Oct made harvesting difficult; meticulous selection was necessary. Mostly average qualities – but this kind of vintage is always good for a surprise.

2007 A warm, cloudy summer and rainy Aug did not bode well, but a fine Sept ripened grapes fully for an early Oct harvest. V. early flowering: growing season exceptionally long. Gd quality with high acidity levels in beautiful Kabinetts – gd quantity, too. Some botrytis at the end of harvest.

2006 A cool, wet Aug and more poor weather during the autumn dampened expectations. The best growers achieved v. high ripeness and vibrant acidity, but ruthless selection means that quantities are low.

2005 Superb warm autumn weather from late Sept through to Nov brought grapes to very high ripeness levels, but with far better acidity than, say, 2003. Exceptional , especially in the Saar.

2004 A humid summer led growers to fear the worst, but the vintage was saved by a glorious autumn. At harvest, grapes were healthy and v. ripe. A fine year to start drinking.

2003 Hot weather brought high ripeness levels but rather low acidity. Ironically, some great sites suffered from drought, while less esteemed cooler sites often fared better. So there is considerable variation in quality, with the best, including some powerful dry wines, superb. Some sensational Trockenbeerenauslesen too.

2002 It is a small miracle how the Riesling grapes survived one of the wettest harvests on record to give ripe, succulent, lively wines (mostly Kabinett and Spätlese), attractive drunk young or mature.

2001 Golden Oct resulted in the best Mosel Riesling since 1990. Saar and Ruwer less exciting but still perfect balance. Lots of Spätlesen and Auslesen.

2000 Riesling stood up to harvest rain here better than most other places. Dominated by good QbA and Kabinett. Auslesen rarer, but exciting.

1999 Excellent in Saar and Ruwer, lots of Auslesen; generally only good in the Mosel due to high yields. Best drank well young and will age.

1998 Riesling grapes came through a rainy autumn to give astonishingly good results in the Middle Mosel; the Saar and Ruwer were less lucky, with mostly QbA. Plenty of Eiswein.

1997 A generous vintage of consistently fruity, elegant wines from the entire region. Marvellous Auslesen in the Saar and Ruwer.

1996 Variable, with fine Spätlesen and Auslesen, but only from top sites. Many excellent Eisweins.

1995 Excellent vintage, mainly of Spätlesen and Auslesen of firm structure and long ageing potential.

1994 Another good vintage, with unexceptional QbA and Kabinett, but many Auslesen and botrytis wines.

1993 Small, excellent vintage: lots of Auslesen/botrytis; near perfect harmony. Now wonderful to drink.

1990 Superb vintage, though small. Known for its powerful and still-elegant acidity – a cellar must-have for Riesling lovers.

Fine older vintages: 89 88 76 71 69 64 59 53 49 45 37 34 21.

Rheinhessen, Nahe, Pfalz, Rheingau

Even the best wines can be drunk with pleasure when young, but Kabinett, Spätlese and Auslese Riesling gain enormously in character by keeping for longer. Rheingau wines tend to be longest-lived, improving for 15 yrs or more, but best wines from the Nahe and Pfalz can last as long. Rheinhessen wines usually mature sooner, and dry Franken and Baden wines are generally best at 3 to 6 years.

2008 Difficult vintage: gd quantity, uneven quality. Wet summer favoured mildew. Rainy Sept and Oct made it difficult to choose the picking dates. Some gd late harvest wines – but only where botrytis was under control. The Rheingau seems to have done quite well.

2007 Those who waited to pick until Oct, and sunny autumn conditions allowed this, had v. ripe grapes with cool nights conserving good acidity levels. Should be excellent for Spätburgunder (Pinot N) and other reds as well as Riesling. As in the Mosel, an exceptionally long growing season resulted in wines of structure and extract. Dry wines seem to be maturing faster than expected.

2006 Warm, rainy weather in Sept and early Oct forced growers to pick early before rot took too firm a hold. Top estates in the Pfalz and Rheinhessen were obliged to leave rotting fruit unpicked. Grauburgunder (Pinot Gris) worst affected, also Pfalz Riesling. Much of what was picked turned out well, so not a disastrous vintage, though quantities low.

2005 The summer was warm, but rain kept drought at bay. A v. fine autumn led to high ripeness levels, accompanied by excellent acidity and extract. A superb year.

2004 After an indifferent summer, a fine autumn delivered ripe, healthy grapes throughout the Rhein lands. A larger than average crop, so there could be some dilution, though not at top estates.

2003 V. hot weather led to rich wines in the Rheingau; many lack acidity. The Pfalz produced superb Rieslings. Red wines fared well everywhere.

2002 Few challenge the best from 01, but v.gd for both classic-style Kabinett/Spätlese and for dry. Excellent Pinot N.

2001 Though more erratic than in the Mosel, here, too, this was often an exciting vintage for both dry and classic styles; excellent balance.

2000 The farther south, the more difficult was the harvest, the Pfalz catching worst of harvest rain. However, all regions have islands of excellence.

1999 Quality was average where yields were high, but for top growers an excellent vintage of rich, aromatic wines with lots of charm.

1998 Excellent: rich, balanced wines, many good Spätlesen and Auslesen with excellent ageing potential. Rain affected much of Baden and Franken. But a great Eiswein year.

1997 V.clean, ripe grapes gave excellent QbA, Kabinett, Spätlese in dry and classic styles. Little botrytis, so Auslesen and higher are rare.

1996 An excellent vintage, particularly in the Pfalz and the Rheingau, with many fine Spätlesen. Great Eiswein.

1995 Rather variable, but some excellent Spätlesen and Auslesen maturing well – like the 90s. Weak in the Pfalz due to harvest rain.

1994 Gd vintage, mostly QmP, with abundant fruit and firm structure. Some superb sweet wines.

1993 A small vintage of very good to excellent quality. Spätlesen and Auslesen now at their peak.

Fine older vintages: 90, 83 76 71 69 67 64 59 53 49 45 37 34 21.

Achkarren Bad w (r) ★★ Village on the KAISERSTUHL, known esp for GRAUBURGUNDER. First Class v'yd: Schlossberg. Wines generally best drunk during first 5 yrs. Gd wines: DR. HEGER, Michel, SCHWARZER ADLER, and co-op.

Adelmann, Weingut Graf ★★→★★★ Estate based at the idyllic Schaubeck castle in WÜRTTEMBERG. The specialities are subtle red blends (notably Vignette), RIES, and the rare Muskattrollinger.

Ahr ★★→★★★ 97 99 03 04 05 06 07 (08) South of Bonn. Mineral, elegant SPÄTBURGUNDER and FRÜHBURGUNDER, previously renowned for their lightness. Global warming boosts ripeness on the valley's slate soils: now the wines regularly exceed 14° – unfortunately. Best producers: Adeneuer, DEUTZERHOF, Kreuzberg, MEYER-NÄKEL, Nelles, STODDEN.

Aldinger, Weingut Gerhard ★★★ One of WÜRTTEMBERG'S leading estates: dense LEMBERGER and SPÄTBURGUNDER, complex Sauv Bl. Gd RIES too.

Amtliche Prüfungsnummer (APNr) Official test-number, showing up on every label of a quality wine. Useful for discerning different lots of AUSLESE a producer has made from the same v'yd.

Assmannshausen Rhg r ★→★★★ 93 95 96 97 98 99 01 02 03 04 05 07 (08) Craggy

---

German vintage notation

The vintage notes after entries in the German section are given in a different form from those elsewhere in the book. Two styles of vintage are indicated:

Bold type (eg **99**) indicates classic, ripe vintages with a high proportion of SPÄTLESEN and AUSLESEN; or, in the case of red wines, gd phenolic ripeness and must weights.

Normal type (eg 98) indicates a successful but not outstanding vintage.

German white wines, esp RIES, have high acidity and keep well, and they display pure fruit qualities because they are unoaked. Thus they can be drunk young for their intense fruitiness, or kept for a decade or two to develop more aromatic subtlety and finesse. This means there is no one ideal moment to drink them, so no vintages are specifically recommended for drinking now.

RHEINGAU village known specifically for its cassis-scented, ageworthy SPÄTBURGUNDERS from slate soils. First Class v'yd: Höllenberg. Growers include KESSELER, Robert König, WEINGUT KRONE, and the state domain.

Auslese Wines from selective harvest of super-ripe bunches, in many yrs affected by noble rot (*Edelfäule*) and correspondingly unctuous in flavour. Dry Auslesen are usually too alcoholic and clumsy for me.

Ayl M-S-R (Saar) w ★★★ **90 93 95** 96 **97 99** 00 **01 02 03 04 05 07** (08) All Ayl v'yds are known since 1971 by the name of its historically best site: Kupp. Growers inc BISCHÖFLICHE WEINGUTER, *Lauer*.

Bacharach w (r) ★→★★★ **96** 97 **01 02** 03 **04 05 07** Main wine town of MITTELRHEIN. Racy, austere RIES, some v. fine. First Class v'yds: Hahn, Posten, Wolfshöhle. Growers include BASTIAN, JOST, RATZENBERGER.

Baden Bad Huge southwest area of scattered v'yds best known for the Pinots, and pockets of RIES, usually dry. Best areas: KAISERSTUHL, ORTENAU.

Badische Bergstrasse Small district of north BADEN, surrounding the city of Heidelberg. Gd RIES and SPÄTBURGUNDER. Best producer: Seeger.

Badischer Winzerkeller Germany's (and Europe's) biggest co-op, absorbing the entire crop of 38 other co-ops to produce almost half of BADEN'S wine: dependably unambitious.

Bassermann-Jordan ★★★ **90 96 97 99 01** 02 **03 04 05 07** (08) MITTELHAARDT estate, under new ownership since 2003, with 45 ha of outstanding v'yds in DEIDESHEIM, FORST, RUPPERTSBERG, etc. Winemaker Ulrich Mell excels at producing *majestic dry Ries* and lavish sweet wines too.

Bastian, Weingut Friedrich ★★ 6 ha BACHARACH estate. Racy, austere RIES with MOSEL-like delicacy, esp from the First Class Posten v'yd.

Becker, J B ★★→★★★ The best estate at WALLUF specializing in old-fashioned, cask-aged (and long-lived) dry RIES and SPÄTBURGUNDER.

Beerenauslese, BA Luscious sweet wine from exceptionally ripe, individually selected berries concentrated by noble rot. Rare, expensive.

Bercher ★★★ KAISERSTUHL estate; 25 ha at Burkheim, yielding consistently excellent GRAUBURGUNDER, CHARD, and SPÄTBURGUNDER.

Bergdolt, Weingut ★★ South of Neustadt in the PFALZ, this 24-ha estate produces v. fine WEISSBURGUNDER (Pinot Bl), as well as gd RIES and SPÄTBURGUNDER.

Bernkastel M-M w ★→★★★★ **83 88 89 90 93 94 95 97 99** 01 02 03 **04 05 06 07** (08) Top wine town of the MITTELMOSEL; the epitome of RIES. Great First Class (if overpriced) v'yd: Doctor, 3.2 ha; First Class v'yds: Graben, Lay. Top growers include Kerpen, LOOSEN, PAULY-BERGWEILER, PRÜM, Studert-Prüm, THANISCH (both estates), WEGELER.

Bernkastel (Bereich) Includes all the MITTELMOSEL. Wide area of deplorably dim quality and superficial flowery character. Mostly MÜLLER-THURGAU. Avoid.

Beulwitz, Weingut von ★★→★★★ Reliable 6-ha RUWER estate with wines from Kaseler Nies'chen.

Bischöfliche Weingüter M-S-R ★★ Famous estate located at TRIER, uniting cathedral's v'yds with those of 3 other charities, the Friedrich-Wilhelm-Gymnasium, the Bischöfliches Priesterseminar and the Bischöfliches Konvikt. Owns 130 ha of top v'yds, esp in SAAR and RUWER. Middling quality but new director (since 07) promises improvements.

Bocksbeutel Inconvenient flask-shaped bottle used in FRANKEN and north BADEN.

Bodensee Idyllic district of south BADEN, on Lake Constance. Dry wines are best drunk young. RIES-like MÜLLER-T a speciality. Top village: Meersburg.

Boppard ★→★★★ **90** 97 **01 02** 03 **04 05 07** (08) Important wine town of MITTELRHEIN with best sites all in amphitheatre of vines called Bopparder Hamm. Growers: Toni Lorenz, Matthias Müller, August Perll, WEINGART. Unbeatable value for money.

Germany's quality levels

The official range of qualities and styles in ascending order is:

1 Deutscher Tafelwein: sweetish light wine of no specified character. (From certain producers, can be atypical but excellent.)

2 Landwein: dryish Tafelwein with some regional style.

3 Qualitätswein: dry or sweetish wine with sugar added before fermentation to increase its strength, but tested for quality and with distinct local and grape character. Don't despair.

4 Kabinett: dry or dryish natural (unsugared) wine of distinct personality and distinguishing lightness. Can occasionally be sublime.

5 Spätlese: stronger, often sweeter than Kabinett. Full-bodied. Today many top SPÄTLESEN are *trocken* or completely dry.

6 Auslese: sweeter, sometimes stronger than SPÄTLESE, often with honey-like flavours, intense and long-lived. Occasionally dry and weighty.

7 Beerenauslese: v. sweet, sometimes strong, intense. Can be superb.

8 Eiswein: from naturally frozen grapes of BEEREN- or TROCKEN-BEERENAUSLESE quality: concentrated, sharpish, and v. sweet. Some examples are extreme, unharmonious.

9 Trockenbeerenauslese (TBA): intensely sweet and aromatic; alcohol slight. Extraordinary and everlasting.

Brauneberg M-M w ★★★★ 88 89 90 93 94 95 96 **97** 98 **99 01 02** 03 **04 05** 06 07 Top M-S-R village nr BERNKASTEL (304 ha): excellen full-flavoured RIES – *grand cru* if anything on the MOSEL is. Great First Class v'yd: Juffer-SONNENUHR. First Class v'yd: Juffer. Growers: F HAAG, W HAAG, PAULINSHOF, RICHTER, SCHLOSS LIESER, THANISCH.

Breuer, Weingut Georg ★★★→★★★★ Family estate in RÜDESHEIM (24 ha) and RAUENTHAL (7.2 ha), giving superb dry RIES. V. fine SEKT too. Pioneering winemaker Bernhard Breuer died suddenly in 04, quality is undiminished.

Buhl, Reichsrat von ★★★ Historic PFALZ estate, 55 ha (DEIDESHEIM, FORST, RUPPERTSBERG). Bought in 2005 by businessman Achim Niederberger, who also owns BASSERMANN-JORDAN and DR.DEINHARD. 80% dry wines.

Bürgerspital zum Heiligen Geist ★★★★ Ancient charitable WÜRZBURG estate. 111 ha. Rich, dry wines, esp SILVANER, RIES. In some yrs, eg 05, great TBA.

Bürklin-Wolf, Dr. ★★★→★★★★ Dynamic PFALZ family estate. 85 ha in FORST, DEIDESHEIM, RUPPERTSBERG, and WACHENHEIM, inc many First Class sites. The full-bodied *dry wines from these are often spectacular*. Now biodynamic. Family bust-up in 2006 leaves quality unaffected.

Busch, Weingut Clemens M-S-R ★★→★★★★ Since 1985 Busch has demonstrated the excellence of steep but obscure Pündericher Marienburg in lower MOSEL. Both dry and notably sweet RIES.

Castell'sches Fürstlich Domänenamt ★→★★★ Historic 65-ha estate in FRANKEN. SILVANER, RIES, RIESLANER, dry and sweet, and a growing reputation for red wines. Superb monopoly v'yd Casteller Schlossberg.

Chardonnay Grown throughout Germany; over 1,120 ha. Only the best convince, eg BERCHER, BERGDOLT, HUBER, JOHNER, REBHOLZ, DR. WEHRHEIM, WITTMANN.

Christmann ★★★ 17-ha estate in Gimmeldingen (PFALZ) making rich, dry RIES and SPÄTBURGUNDER from First Class v'yds, notably Königsbacher Idig. Biodynamic farming. Young Stefan Christmann is new president of the VDP.

Christoffel, J J ★★★ Tiny domain in URZIG. Classic, elegant RIES. Since 01 leased to Robert Eymael of MÖNCHHOF.

Clüsserath, Ansgar ★★→★★★ 5-ha family estate with remarkably ageworthy dry

RIES from TRITTENHEIMER Apotheke: delicate and mineral without being tart.

Clüsserath-Weiler, Weingut ★★★ Classic RIES from top TRITTENHEIMER Apotheke and the rare Fährfels v'yd. Steadily improving quality.

Crusius ★★→★★★ 17-ha family estate at TRAISEN, NAHE. Vivid and ageworthy RIES *from Bastei and Rotenfels of Traisen* and SCHLOSSBÖCKELHEIM.

Dautel, Weingut Ernst ★★★ A reliable source of WÜRTTEMBERG'S red specialities, esp LEMBERGER.

Deidesheim Pfz w (r) ★★→★★★★ **90 94 96** 97 **99 01 02** 03 **04 0507** (08) Largest top-quality village of the PFALZ (405 ha). Richly flavoured, lively wines. First Class v'yds: Grainhübel, Hohenmorgen, Kalkofen, Kieselberg, Langenmorgen, Leinhöhle. Top growers: BASSERMANN-JORDAN, Biffar, BUHL, BÜRKLIN-WOLF, CHRISTMANN, DEINHARD, MOSBACHER.

Deinhard, Dr. ★★★ Fine 35-ha estate: some top sites in DEIDESHEIM and FORST. Now owned by Achim Niederberger (see BASSERMANN-JORDAN and BUHL).

Deutscher Tafelwein Officially the term for v. humble German wines. Now, confusingly, the flag of convenience for some costly novelties as well, often barrique-aged.

Deutzerhof, Weingut ★★→★★★ 9-ha AHR estate producing concentrated, barrique-aged SPÄTBURGUNDER. Fine quality, alarming prices.

Diel, Schlossgut ★★★ Fashionable 17-ha NAHE estate; pioneered ageing GRAUBURGUNDER and WEISSBURGUNDER in barriques. Its traditional RIES is often exquisite. Also serious SEKT.

Dönnhoff, Weingut Hermann ★★★★ **90 94 95 96** 97 **98** 99 00 **01 02 03 04 05** 06 **07** (08) 20-ha leading NAHE estate with magnificent RIES at all quality levels from NIEDERHAUSEN, Oberhausen, SCHLOSSBÖCKELHEIM. Dazzling EISWEIN.

Dornfelder Red grape making deep-coloured, usually rustic wines. Plantings have doubled since 2000 to an astonishing 8,200 ha.

Duijn, Jacob ★★★ Former sommelier/wine merchant, now BADEN winegrower specializing in spicy, tannic SPÄTBURGUNDER from steeply sloping granite v'yds in the Bühler valley, ORTENAU. 10 ha.

Durbach Baden w (r) ★★→★★★ **01** 02 03 **04 05** 07 Village with 314 ha of v'yds, of which Plauelrain is First Class. Top growers: LAIBLE, H. Männle, Schloss Staufenberg. KLINGELBERGER (RIES) is the outstanding variety.

Egon Müller zu Scharzhof ★★★★ **59 71 76 83** 85 **88 89** 90 **93 94 95** 96 **97** 98 **99** 00 **01 02 03 04 05** 06 **07** Top SAAR estate of 8 ha at WILTINGEN, the v'yds rising steeply behind the Müllers' manor house. Its rich and racy SCHARZHOFBERGER RIES in AUSLESEN vintages is among the world's greatest wines, sublime, honeyed, immortal; best are given gold capsules. *Kabinetts* are feather-light. Gallais is a second 4-ha estate in WILTINGER Braune Kupp; gd quality, but the site is less exceptional.

Einzellage Individual v'yd site. No to be confused with GROSSLAGE.

Eiswein Made from frozen grapes with the ice (ie water content) discarded, producing v. concentrated wine in flavour, acidity, and sugar – of BEERENAUSLESE ripeness or more. Alcohol content can be as low as 5.5%. V. expensive. Outstanding Eiswein vintages were 98, 02, and 04.

Eitelsbach M-S-R (Ruwer) w ★★→★★★★ **89 90 93** 94 **95** 96 **97 98 99** 01 02 **03 04 05** 06 **07** (08) RUWER village bordering TRIER, inc superb Great First Class KARTHAUSERHOFBERG v'yd site.

Elbling Grape introduced by the Romans, nowadays only grown on upper MOSEL. Can be sharp and tasteless, but capable of real freshness and vitality.

Ellwanger, Weingut ★★→★★★ Jürgen Ellwanger pioneered oak-aged red wines in WÜRTTEMBERG. Today aided by his sons, who continue to turn out sappy but structured LEMBERGER, SPÄTBURGUNDER and Zweigelt.

Emrich-Schönleber ★★★ Located in NAHE village of Monzingen. Since the late

1980s winemaker Werner Schönleber has produced RIES that is now among Germany's finest, esp his sumptuous EISWEIN.

Erben Word meaning "heirs", often used on old-established estate labels.

Erden M-M w ★★★ 88 89 90 93 95 96 **97 98 99 01** 02 03 **04 05** 06 **07** (08) Village adjoining ÜRZIG: noble, full-flavoured, vigorous wine (more herbal and mineral than the wines of nearby BERNKASTEL and WEHLEN but equally long-living). Great First Class v'yds: Prälat, Treppchen. Growers include J J CHRISTOFFEL, Erbes, LOOSEN, Lotz, Meulenhof, MÖNCHHOF, Peter Nicolay, Weins-Prüm.

Erstes Gewächs Translates as "first growth". Applies only to RHEINGAU v'yds.

Erzeugerabfüllung Bottled by producer. Being replaced by GUTSABFÜLLUNG, but only by estates. Co-ops will continue with *Erzeugerabfüllung*.

Escherndorf Frank w ★★→★★★ **93 97 00 01** 02 03 04 **05** 06 **07** (08) Important wine town nr WÜRZBURG. Similar tasty, dry wine from RIES and SILVANER. First Class v'yd: Lump. Growers include Michael Fröhlich, JULIUSSPITAL, H SAUER, Rainer Sauer, Egon Schäffer.

Feinherb Imprecisely defined term for wines with around 10–20 g of sugar per litre. Favoured by some as a more flexible alternative to HALBTROCKEN. Used on label by, among others, Kerpen, VON KESSELSTATT, MOLITOR.

Forst Pfz w ★★→★★★★ 90 96 **97 99** 01 02 03 04 05 07 (08) MITTELHAARDT village with over 200 ha of Germany's best v'yds. Ripe, richly fragrant, full-bodied but subtle wines. First Class v'yds: Jesuitengarten, Kirchenstück, Freundstück, Pechstein, Ungeheuer. Top growers include: Acham-Magin, BASSERMANN-JORDAN, BÜRKLIN-WOLF, DEINHARD, MOSBACHER, WOLF.

Franken Franconia region of distinctive dry wines, esp SILVANER, mostly bottled in round-bellied flasks (BOCKSBEUTEL). The centre is WÜRZBURG. Bereich names: MAINDREIECK, MAINVIERECK, STEIGERWALD. Top producers: BÜRGERSPITAL, CASTELL, FÜRST, JULIUSSPITAL, LÖWENSTEIN, RUCK, H SAUER, STAATLICHER HOFKELLER, STÖRRLEIN, WIRSCHING, etc.

Franzen, Weingut Reinhold ★→★★ From Europe's steepest v'yd, Bremmer Calmont, Franzen make reliable, sometimes exciting dry RIES and EISWEIN.

Frühburgunder An ancient mutation of Pinot N, found mostly in the AHR but also in FRANKEN and WÜRTTEMBERG, where it is confusingly known as Clevner. Lower acidity and thus more approachable than Pinot N.

Fuder Traditional RIES cask with sizes from 500 to 1,500 litres depending on the region. Unlike a barrique, a *fuder* is used for dozens of years. Traditionalists use cask for fermentation, giving individuality to each *fuder's* wine.

Fürst ★★★→★★★★ 18-ha estate in Bürgstadt making some of the best wines in FRANKEN, particularly Burgundian SPÄTBURGUNDER (arguably Germany's finest), full-flavoured RIES, and oak-aged WEISSBURGUNDER.

Gallais, Le See EGON MÜLLER ZU SCHARZHOF.

Gewürztraminer (or Traminer) Highly aromatic grape, speciality of Alsace, also impressive in Germany, esp in PFALZ, BADEN, SACHSEN.

Graach M-M w ★★★ 88 89 90 93 94 95 96 **97** 98 **99 01** 02 **03 04 05** 06 **07** (08) Small village between BERNKASTEL and WEHLEN. First Class v'yds: Domprobst, Himmelreich, Josephshof. Top growers inc: Kees-Kieren, VON KESSELSTATT, LOOSEN, M MOLITOR, J J PRÜM, S A PRÜM, SCHAEFER, SELBACH-OSTER, WEINS-PRÜM.

Grans-Fassian ★★★ Fine MOSEL estate at Leiwen. V'yds there and in TRITTENHEIM

The barter society

If you're a winegrower there is no limit to what you can swap for wine. A quick survey of German growers produces: handmade suits; dentistry; a hernia operation; an SUV. Unlike cash these days, it improves with age.

and PIESPORT. EISWEIN a speciality. Consistently high quality since 95.

Grauburgunder (or Grauer Burgunder) Both synonyms of RULÄNDER or Pinot Gr: grape giving soft full-bodied wine. Best in BADEN (esp KAISERSTUHL) and south PFALZ. 4,400 ha planted.

Grosser Ring Group of top (VDP) MOSEL-SAAR-RUWER estates, whose annual Sept auction sometimes sets world-record prices.

Grosses Gewächs Translates as "great/top growth". This is the top tier in the v'yd classification launched in 2002 by the growers' association VDP, except in the RHEINGAU, which has its own ERSTES GEWÄCHS classification. Wines released as *Grosses Gewächs* must meet strict quality criteria.

Grosslage A collection of secondary v'yds with seemingly similar character – but no indication of quality.

Beware of Bereich and Grosslage

Bereich means district within an *Anbaugebiet* (region). "Bereich" on a label should be treated as a flashing red light. The wine is a blend from arbitrary sites within that district. Do not buy. The same holds for wines with a GROSSLAGE name, though these are more difficult to identify. Who could guess if "Forster Mariengarten" is an EINZELLAGE or a GROSSLAGE?

Gunderloch ★★★ →★★★★ 93 96 97 99 01 02 03 **04 05 07** (08) At this NACKENHEIM estate Fritz Hasselbach makes some of the finest RIES on the entire Rhine, esp at AUSLESE level and above. Also owns Balbach estate in NIERSTEIN.

Gutedel German name for the ancient Chasselas grape, grown in south BADEN (MARKGRÄFLERLAND). Fresh, but neutral, white wines.

Gutsabfüllung Estate-bottled. Term for genuinely estate-bottled wines.

Haag, Weingut Fritz M-S-R ★★★★ 88 89 90 94 95 96 97 98 **99 01 02 03 04 05 06 07** (08) BRAUNEBERG'S top estate, run for decades by MITTELMOSEL veteran Wilhelm Haag and now by his son Oliver. MOSEL RIES of crystalline purity for long ageing. Haag's other son, Thomas, runs SCHLOSS LIESER estate.

Haag, Weingut Willi M-S-R ★★ 6 ha BRAUNEBERG estate. Old-style RIES, AUSLESEN.

Haart, Reinhold ★★★★ Best estate in PIESPORT and Wintrich. Refined, aromatic wines capable of long ageing. Mineral and racy copybook MOSEL RIES.

Haidle, Karl ★★ →★★★ 19-ha family estate in Stetten, WÜRTTEMBERG, specializing in graceful RIES from gd Pulvermächer v'yd. TROCKEN and sweet, inc EISWEIN.

Halbtrocken Medium-dry (literally semi-dry), with 9–18 g of unfermented sugar per litre. Popular category, often better balanced than TROCKEN. See FEINHERB.

Hattenheim Rhg w ★★ →★★★★ 90 93 95 97 99 01 02 **03 04 05 07**(08) Superlative 202-ha wine town, though not all producers achieve full potential. The First Class v'yds are Mannberg, Nussbrunnen, Pfaffenberg, Wisselbrunnen, and, most famously, STEINBERG (Ortsteil). Estates include Barth, Knyphausen, Lang, LANGWERTH VON SIMMERN, RESS, SCHLOSS SCHÖNBORN, STAATSWEINGUT.

Heger, Dr. ★★★ Leading estate of KAISERSTUHL in BADEN with v.gd dry WEISSBURGUNDER, GRAUBURGUNDER, SILVANER and *Burgundy inspired Spätburgunder* reds. Less emphasis on RIES and Muscat, which can also be v.gd. Wines from rented v'yds released under Weinhaus Joachim Heger label.

Hessen, Prinz von ★★ →★★★ Famous 42-ha estate in JOHANNISBERG, KIEDRICH, and WINKEL. Improving quality since the late 90s but yet to show full potential.

Hessische Bergstrasse w (r) ★★ →★★★ 90 93 95 96 **97 98 99** 01 02 **03 04 05 07** (08) Small wine region (436 ha), north of Heidelberg. Pleasant RIES from STAATSWEINGÜTER, Simon-Bürkle and Stadt Bensheim.

Heyl zu Herrnsheim ★★ Leading NIERSTEIN estate, 80% RIES. Inconsistent in recent vintages; bought in 06 by Detlev Meyer. Occasional dry RIES and sweet wines of exceptional quality.

Heymann-Löwenstein ★★★ Estate in Lower MOSEL nr Koblenz with most consistent dry RIES in MOSEL-SAAR-RUWER and some remarkable AUSLESEN and TROCKENBEERENAUSLESEN. Löwenstein has inspired other WINNINGEN growers to adopt his style. Spectacular wines in 05.

Hochheim Rhg w ★★→★★★★ **90 03 95 96 97 98 99** 01 02 **03 04 05** 07 (08) 242-ha wine town 24 km east of main RHEINGAU area, once thought of as best on Rhine. The region's most full-bodied wines, whether dry or sweet; can be earthy. First Class v'yds: Domdechaney, Hölle, Kirchenstück, Königin Viktoria Berg (5-ha monopoly of Hupfeld family). Growers include Himmel, Königin-Victoriaberg, KÜNSTLER, SCHLOSS SCHÖNBORN, STAATSWEINGUT, Werner.

Hock Traditional English term for Rhine wine, derived from HOCHHEIM.

Hoensbroech, Weingut Reichsgraf zu ★★ Top KRAICHGAU estate. Dry WEISSBURGUNDER from Michelfelder Himmelberg is the best wine.

Hohenlohe-Oehringen, Weingut Fürst zu ★★ Noble 17-ha estate in Oehringen, WÜRTTEMBERG. Earthy, bone-dry RIES and powerful, structured reds from LEMBERGER, Merlot, and other grapes.

Hövel, Weingut von ★★★ Fine SAAR estate at OBEREMMEL (Hütte is 4.8-ha monopoly) and in SCHARZHOFBERG. Erratic quality, but 05s best in many yrs.

Huber, Bernhard ★★★ Leading estate of Breisgau area of BADEN, with powerful long-lived SPÄTBURGUNDER, MUSKATELLER, and Burgundian-style WEISSBURGUNDER, CHARD.

Ihringen Bad r w ★→★★★ 97 **99 01 02 03 04 05** 07 (08) Justly celebrated village of the KAISERSTUHL, BADEN. SILVANER stronghold, but better known for its prestigious SPÄTBURGUNDER and GRAUBURGUNDER. The superb Winklerberg v'yd is made up of steep terraces on shallow volcanic soils. Unfortunately the law permits wines from a loess plateau to be sold under the same name. Top growers: DR. HEGER, Konstanzer, Pix, Stigler.

Iphofen Frank w ★★→★★★★ **93 97** 98 99 **00 01** 03 **04 05** 06 **07** Village nr WÜRZBURG renowned for RIES, SILVANER, RIESLANER. First Class v'yds: Julius-Echter-Berg, Kalb. V.gd v'yd: Kronsberg. Growers: JULIUSSPITAL, RUCK, WIRSCHING, Zehntkeller.

Jahrgang Year – as in "vintage".

Johannisberg Rhg w ★★→★★★★ **89 90 93 95** 96 **97** 98 **99 01** 02 03 **04 05** 07 (08) A classic RHEINGAU village with superlative long-lived RIES. First Class v'yds: Hölle, Klaus, SCHLOSS JOHANNISBERG. GROSSLAGE: Erntebringer. Top growers: JOHANNISHOF, SCHLOSS JOHANNISBERG, HESSEN.

Johannishof ★★★ JOHANNISBERG family estate RIES that are often the best from the great Johannisberg v'yds. Excellent RÜDESHEIM wines too.

Johner, Karl-Heinz ★★→★★★ 17-ha BADEN estate at Bischoffingen, long specializing in New World-style SPÄTBURGUNDER and oak-aged WEISSBURGUNDER, CHARD, GRAUBURGUNDER.

Josephshof First Class v'yd at GRAACH, the sole property of KESSELSTATT.

Jost, Toni ★★★ Leading estate of the MITTELRHEIN: 9 ha, mainly RIES, in BACHARACH (sharply mineral wines), and also at WALLUF in the RHEINGAU.

Juliusspital ★★★ Ancient WÜRZBURG religious charity with 170 ha of top FRANKEN v'yds. Consistently gd quality. Look for its dry Silvaners (they age well) and RIES and its top white blend called BT.

Kabinett See "Germany's quality levels" box on p.145.

Kaiserstuhl Outstanding BADEN district, with notably warm climate and volcanic soil. Villages inc: ACHKARREN, Burkheim, IHRINGEN, Jechtingen, Oberrotweil.

Remember that vintage information for German wines is given in a different form from the ready/not ready distinction applying to other countries. See the explanation at the bottom of p. 143.

> **Spot the interloper**
> Yes, international grapes are moving in – but with a twist. Dry, late-harvest Sauv Bl with a pinch of residual sugar – now there's a recipe – has become oddly trendy amongst young drinkers. More seriously, Viognier seems to show well in BADEN. Even more startling are trials of Syrah, Sangiovese and Nebbiolo. Brave? Misguided? Hmmm.

Renowned for Pinot varieties, w and r, and some surprising RIES and Muscat.

Kanzem M-S-R (Saar) w ★★★ 93 94 95 96 **97 99** 01 02 **03 04 05** 06 **07** (08) Small neighbour of WILTINGEN. First Class v'yd: Altenberg. Growers include BISCHÖFLICHE, OTHEGRAVEN, VEREINIGTE HOSPITIEN, Weingüter.

Karlsmühle ★★★ Small estate with two Lorenzhöfer monopoly sites making classic RUWER RIES; also wines from First Class KASEL v'yds sold under Patheiger label. Consistently excellent quality.

Karthäuserhof ★★★★ Outstanding RUWER estate of 19 ha at Eitelsbach with monopoly v'yd Karthäuserhofberg. Easily recognized by bottles with only a neck label. Admired if austere TROCKEN wines (made less austere by a run of warm yrs), but magnificent AUSLESEN.

Kasel M-S-R (Ruwer) w ★★→★★★ **90 93** 98 **99** 01 03 04 05 06 07 Stunning flowery RIES. First Class v'yds: Kehrnagel, Nies'chen. Top growers: BEULWITZ, BISCHÖFLICHE, WEINGÜTER, KARLSMÜHLE, KESSELSTATT.

Keller, Weingut ★★★★ Deep in unfashionable southern RHEINHESSEN, the Kellers show what can be achieved with scrupulous site selection. Superlative, crystalline GROSSES GEWÄCHS RIES from Dalsheimer Hubacker and 2 other v'yds. Also astonishing TBA and *Spätburgunder*.

Kellerei Winery (ie a big commercial bottler).

Kesseler, Weingut August Rhg ★★★ 21-ha estate making fine SPÄTBURGUNDER reds in ASSMANNSHAUSEN and RUDESHEIM. Also v.gd classic-style RIES.

Kesselstatt, von ★★★ The largest private MOSEL estate, 650 yrs old. Run for two decades by the quality-obsessed Annegret Reh-Gartner. Some 38 ha through MOSEL-SAAR-RUWER producing aromatic, generously fruity MOSELS. Consistently high quality wines from Josephshof monopoly v'yd, PIESPORTER Goldtröpfchen, KASEL, and SCHARZHOFBERG (NB 2007).

Kesten M-M w ★→★★★ 93 94 **97** 98 **99** 01 03 04 **05 06** 07 Neighbour of BRAUNEBERG. Best wines (from Paulinshofberg v'yd) similar. Top growers: Bastgen, Kees-Kieren, PAULINSHOF.

Kiedrich Rhg w ★★→★★★★ **93 95 97** 98 **99** 01 02 **03 04 05** 07 (08) RHEINGAU village linked inseparably to WEIL'S outstanding RIES from Gräfenberg v'yd. Other gd growers include HESSEN, KNYPHAUSEN.

Klingelberger ORTENAU (BADEN) term for RIES, esp at DURBACH.

Kloster Eberbach Rhg Glorious 12th-century Cistercian abbey in HATTENHEIM forest. Monks planted STEINBERG, Germany's Clos de Vougeot. Now the label of the STAATSWEINGÜTER with a string of great v'yds in ASSMANNSHAUSEN, RÜDESHEIM, RAUENTHAL, etc. Director Dieter Greiner has injected new life into a previously moribund organization with a spanking new winery.

Knebel, Weingut ★★★ WINNINGEN is the top wine village of the Lower MOSEL and Knebel showed how its sites could produce remarkable RIES in all styles. The founder died tragically in 04; the estate continues to maintain high quality.

Knipser, Weingut ★★★→★★★★ Leading family estate in PFALZ, and one of the most serious and reliable in all Germany, 39 ha. Brothers Werner and Volker specialize in barrique-aged SPÄTBURGUNDER and other red such as St-Laurent, Syrah, and Cuvée X (a B'x blend). Dry RIES can be exceptional. Look for the Kalkmergel label.

Koehler-Ruprecht ★★→★★★★ 93 96 **97** 98 **99 01** 02 **03** 04 **05 07** 08 Outstanding Kallstadt grower. Bernd Philippi's winemaking is entirely traditional, delivering v. long-lived dry RIES from Kallstadter Saumagen. Outstanding SPÄTBURGUNDER and gd barrique-aged Pinot varieties under the Philippi label.

Kraichgau Small BADEN district southeast of Heidelberg. Top growers: Burg Ravensburg, HOENSBROECH, Hummel.

Krone, Weingut Rhg ★★ 4-ha estate in ASSMANNSHAUSEN, with some of the best plots in the First Class Höllenberg v'yd. Famous for richly perfumed, full-bodied and ageeable SPÄTBURGUNDER. Now run by WEGELER, and considerable investments are underway.

Kröv M-M w ★→★★★ **93 98 99 01** 02 03 04 **05** 06 07 Popular tourist resort famous for its GROSSLAGE name: Nacktarsch, or "bare bottom". Be v. careful. Best growers: Martin Müllen, Staffelter Hof.

Kruger-Rumpf, Weingut ★★→★★★★ Most important estate of Münster, NAHE, with charming RIES and well-crafted SPÄTBURGUNDER.

Kühn, Weingut Peter Jakob ★★★ Excellent RHEINGAU estate in OESTRICH. Kühn's obsessive v'yd management pays dividends in a full range of classic wines.

Kuhn, Philipp ★★★ Talented and reliable producer in Laumersheim, PFALZ. Dry RIES are rich and harmonious even at QBA level. Barrel-aged SPÄTBURGUNDER combine succulence, power and complexity.

Künstler, Franz ★★★ 25-ha estate in HOCHHEIM run by the uncompromising Gunter Künstler. Produces superb dry RIES esp from First Class Domdechaney, Hölle, and Kirchenstück v'yds; also excellent AUSLESE.

Laible, Weingut Andreas ★★★ 7-ha DURBACH estate. Limpid, often crystalline dry RIES from Plauelrain v'yd as well as SCHEUREBE and GEWÜRZ. Consistently rewarding quality.

Landwein See "Germany's quality levels" box on p.145.

Langwerth von Simmern, Weingut ★★→★★★★ Famous ELTVILLE family estate. Top v'yds: Baiken, Mannberg, MARCOBRUNN. After disappointing quality during the 1990s back on form since 01.

Lauer, Weingut Peter ★★ The SAAR village of AYL lacked conscientious growers, until in the early 2000s Florian Lauer began exploring its subtleties with a range of v.gd parcel selections.

Leitz, J ★★★ Fine RÜDESHEIM family estate for rich but elegant dry and sweet RIES. Since 1999 Johannes Leitz has gone from strength to strength.

Leiwen M-M w ★★→★★★ **93 97** 98 **99** 00 **01 02** 03 **04 05 07** First Class v'yd: Laurentiuslay. Village between TRITTENHEIM and TRIER. GRANS-FASSIAN, CARL LOEWEN, Rosch, SANKT URBANS-HOF have put these once overlooked v'yds firmly on the map.

Lemberger Red grape variety imported to Germany and Austria in the 18th century, from Hungary, where it is known as Kékfrankos. Blaufränkisch in Austria. Deep-coloured, moderately tannic wines; a speciality from WÜRTTEMBERG.

Liebfrauenstift-Kirchenstück A walled-in 13.5-ha v'yd in city of Worms producing aromatic (though rarely spectacular) RIES. Producers: Gutzler, Schembs.

Lieser M-M w ★★ **97 01** 02 03 **03 04 05 07** Once neglected v'yds between BERNKASTEL and BRAUNEBERG. First Class v'yd: Niederberg-Helden. Top grower: SCHLOSS LIESER.

Loewen, Carl ★★→★★★★ Enterprising grower of LEIWEN on MOSEL making ravishing AUSLESE from town's First Class Laurentiuslay site, and from Thörnicher Ritsch, a v'yd Loewen rescued from obscurity.

Loosen, Weingut Dr. M-M ★★→★★★★ **93 94 95** 96 **97** 98 **99** 00 **01 02 03** 04 **05** 06 **07** Dynamic 18-ha estate in BERNKASTEL, ERDEN, GRAACH, ÜRZIG, WEHLEN. Deep, intense classic RIES from old vines in some of the MITTELMOSEL's greatest v'yds. **Reliable Dr. L Ries**, from bought-in grapes. Also leases WOLF in the PFALZ since 1996. Joint-venture RIES from 99 Washington State with Ch Ste Michelle.

Lorch Rhg w (r) ★→★★ **90** 97 99 **01 02** 03 **04 05 07** Extreme west of RHEINGAU. Some fine MITTELRHEIN-like RIES. Best growers: von Kanitz, Kesseler, Ottes.

Löwenstein, Fürst ★★★ Top 30-ha FRANKEN estate. Tangy, savoury SILVANER and mineral RIES from historic **Homberger Kallmuth**, v. dramatic slope with 12 km of stone walls in the v'yd. Also owns a 22 ha RHEINGAU estate in Hallgarten.

Lützkendorf, Weingut ★→★★ Leading SAALE-UNSTRUT estate, producing a wide range of varietals. Best are usually the elegant, bone-dry SILVANER and WEISSBURGUNDER.

Maindreieck District name for central FRANKEN, inc WÜRZBURG.

Mainviereck District name for western FRANKEN. Best known are the SPÄTBURGUNDER v'yds of Bürgstadt and Klingenberg.

Marcobrunn Historic RHEINGAU v'yd in ERBACH; potentially one of Germany's v. best. Contemporary wines scarcely match this v'yd's past fame.

Markgräflerland District south of Freiburg, BADEN. Typical GUTEDEL wine can be refreshing when drunk v. young.

Maximin Grünhaus M-S-R (Ruwer) w ★★★★ 88 89 90 93 96 **97** 98 99 **0103 05 07** (08) Supreme RUWER estate of 31 ha at Mertesdorf. Wines, dry and sweet, that are miracles of delicacy, subtlety and longevity. Greatest wines come from Abtsberg v'yd, but Herrenberg can be almost as fine, and if warmer summers continue, might end up as gd or better. Breathtaking 07 collection.

Meyer-Näkel, Weingut ★★★★ AHR estate; 15 ha. Fine SPÄTBURGUNDERS in Dernau, Walporzheim, and Bad Neuenahr exemplify modern oak-aged German reds.

Mittelhaardt The north central and best part of the PFALZ, inc DEIDESHEIM, FORST, RUPPERTSBERG, WACHENHEIM, largely planted with RIES.

Mittelmosel M-M The central and best part of the MOSEL, inc BERNKASTEL, PIESPORT, WEHLEN, etc. Its top sites are (or should be) entirely RIES.

Mittelrhein Northern and dramatically scenic Rhine area popular with tourists. BACHARACH and BOPPARD are the most important villages of this 465-ha region. Delicate yet steely RIES, underrated and underpriced. Many gd sites lie fallow.

Molitor, Markus M-M ★★★ With 38 ha of outstanding v'yds throughout the MOSEL and SAAR, Molitor has since 1995 become a major player in the region. Magisterial sweet RIES, and acclaimed if earthy SPÄTBURGUNDER.

Mönchhof, Weingut M-M ★★ From an exquisite manor house in ÜRZIG, Robert Eymael makes fruity, stylish RIES from ÜRZIG and ERDEN. ERDENER Prälat usually the best wine. Also leases J.J. CHRISTOFFEL estate.

Mosbacher, Weingut Pfz ★★★ Fine 15-ha estate for some of best GROSSES GEWÄCHS RIES of FORST. Going from strength to strength. Decent Sauv Bl.

Moselland, Winzergenossenschaft Huge MOSEL-SAAR-RUWER co-op, at BERNKASTEL, inc Saar-Winzerverein at WILTINGEN, and, since 2000, a major NAHE co-op too. Its 3,290 members, with a collective 2,400 ha, produce 25% of MOSEL-SAAR-RUWER wines (inc classic-method SEKT). Little is above average.

Mosel-Saar-Ruwer M-S-R 8,980-ha region between TRIER and Koblenz; inc MITTELMOSEL, RUWER, and SAAR. 58% RIES. From 07 wines from the 3 regions can be labelled only as Mosel. (We tend to use the French spelling Moselle.)

Müller-Catoir, Weingut Pfz ★★★→★★★★ **90 93 96** 97 **98** 99 **01** 02 **03 04 05** 07 Since the 70s, this outstanding Neustadt estate has bucked conventional wisdom, focusing on non-interventionist winemaking. Resulting wines are v. aromatic and powerful (GEWÜRZ, GRAUBURGUNDER, MUSKATELLER, RIES,

Remember that vintage information for German wines is given in a different form from the ready/not ready distinction applying to other countries. See the explanation at the bottom of p. 143.

RIESLANER, SCHEUREBE, WEISSBURGUNDER). Under new management since 02. Continues to produce impressive sweet wines, but the dry have lost their previous charm.

Müller-Thurgau Fruity, early ripening, usually low-acid grape; most common in PFALZ, RHEINHESSEN, NAHE, BADEN, and FRANKEN; was 21% of German v'yds in 1998, but 14% today. Easy-to-drink wines, nothing more.

Muskateller Ancient aromatic white grape with crisp acidity. A rarity in the PFALZ, BADEN, and WÜRTTEMBERG, where it is mostly made dry.

Nackenheim Rhh w ★→★★★★ 93 96 97 98 99 01 02 **03 04** 05 06 07 NIERSTEIN neighbour also with top Rhine terroir; similar best wines (esp First Class Rothenberg). Top grower: GUNDERLOCH, Kühling-Gillot.

Nahe Na Tributary of the Rhine and a high-quality wine region with 4,135 ha. Balanced, fresh, clean, but full-bodied, even minerally wines; RIES best. EISWEIN a growing speciality.

Neckar The river with many of WÜRTTEMBERG'S finest v'yds, mainly between Stuttgart and Heilbronn.

Neipperg, Graf von ★★→★★★★ Noble estate in Schwaigern, WÜRTTEMBERG: elegant dry RIES and robust LEMBERGER. MUSKATELLER up to BEERENAUSLESE quality a speciality. A scion of the family, Count Stephan von Neipperg, makes wine at Ch Canon La Gaffelière in St Emilion.

Niederhausen Nahe w ★★→★★★★ 93 95 96 97 98 99 01 02 03 04 05 07 (08) Neighbour of SCHLOSSBÖCKELHEIM. Graceful, powerful RIES. First Class v'yds include Hermannsberg, Hermannshöhle. Growers: CRUSIUS, DÖNNHOFF, Gutsverwaltung Niederhausen-Schlosshörkelheim Mathern

Nierstein Rhh w ★→★★★★ 93 96 97 98 99 01 02 03 **04 05** 07 (08) 526 ha. Famous but treacherous village name. Beware GROSSLAGE Gutes Domtal: a supermarket deception now less frequently encountered. Superb First-Class v'yds: Brüdersberg, Glöck, Hipping, Oelberg, Orbel, Pettenthal. Ripe, aromatic, elegant wines, dry and sweet. Try Gehring, **Guntrum**, HEYL ZU HERRNSHEIM, Kühling-Gillot, ST-ANTONY, Strub.

Oberemmel M-S-R (Saar) w ★★→★★★★ 90 93 94 95 96 97 98 99 01 02 03 04 05 07 Next village to WILTINGEN. V. fine from First Class v'yd Hütte, etc. Growers: von HÖVEL, Willems-Willems.

Obermosel (Bereich) District name for the upper MOSEL above TRIER. Wines from the ELBLING grape, generally uninspiring unless v. young.

Ockfen M-S-R (Saar) w ★★→★★★★ 90 93 95 96 97 98 99 01 02 03 04 05 07 Superb fragrant wines from First Class v'yd: Bockstein. Growers: Dr. Fischer, Weinhof Herrenberg, OTHEGRAVEN, SANKT URBANS-HOF, WAGNER, ZILLIKEN.

Oechsle Scale for sugar content of grape juice.

Oestrich Rhg w ★★→★★★ 90 97 99 01 02 03 04 05 07 Big village; variable, but some splendid RIES. First Class v'yds: Doosberg, Lenchen. Top growers: August Eser, Peter Jakob KÜHN, Querbach, SPREITZER, WEGELER.

Oppenheim Rhh w ★→★★★ 93 96 97 98 99 01 02 03 04 05 07 (08) Town south of NIERSTEIN; spectacular 13th-century church. First Class Kreuz and Sackträger. Growers include: Heyden, Kühling-Gillot, Manz. The younger generation is starting to realize the full potential of these sites.

Ortenau District around and south of Baden-Baden. Gd KLINGELBERGER (RIES) and SPÄTBURGUNDER, mainly from granite soils. Top villages: DURBACH, Neuweier, Waldulm.

Othegraven, Weingut von ★★→★★★★ This KANZEM, SAAR estate was mediocre until in 1999 Dr Heidi Kegel inherited the estate, with its superb Altenberg v'yds, and restored its reputation. Look esp for Altenberg old-vines Spätlese.

Palatinate English for PFALZ.

Paulinshof, Weingut M-M ★★ 8-ha estate, once monastic, in KESTEN and

BRAUNEBERG. Unusually for the MITTELMOSEL, the Jüngling family specializes in TROCKEN and HALBTROCKEN wines, as well as fine AUSLESEN.

Pauly-Bergweiler, Dr. ★★★ Fine BERNKASTEL estate. V'yds there and in WEHLEN, but wines sold under the Peter Nicolay label from ÜRZIG and ERDEN are usually best. EISWEIN and TBA can be sensational.

Perlwein Semi-sparkling wine.

Pfalz Pfz Usually balmy 23,400-ha v'yd region south of RHEINHESSEN. The MITTELHAARDT area is the source of full-bodied, often dry RIES. The more southerly SÜDLICHE WEINSTRASSE is better suited to the Pinot varieties, white and red. Biggest RIES area after MOSEL-SAAR-RUWER.

Pfeffingen Weingut ★★ Doris and Jan Eymael make v.gd RIES and sometimes remarkable SCHEUREBE at UNGSTEIN, PFALZ.

Piesport M-M w ★→★★★★ **90 93** 94 95 96 **97** 98 **99** 00 **01 02** 03 **04 05** 06 07 (08) Tiny village with famous vine amphitheatre: at best glorious rich, aromatic RIES. Great First Class v'yds: Goldtröpfchen, Domherr. Treppchen far inferior. GROSSLAGE: Michelsberg (mainly MÜLLER-THURGAU; avoid). Esp gd are GRANS-FASSIAN, Joh. Haart, R HAART, Kurt Hain, KESSELSTATT, SANKT URBANS-HOF.

Portugieser Second-rate red wine grape, mostly grown in RHEINHESSEN and PFALZ, now often used for WEISSHERBST. 4,550 ha in production.

Prädikat Special attributes or qualities. See QMP.

Prüm, JJ ★★★★ **71 76 83 88 89** 90 94 **95** 96 **97** 98 **99** 00 **01 02** 03 **04 05** 06 07 (08) Superlative and legendary 20-ha MOSEL estate in BERNKASTEL, GRAACH, WEHLEN. Delicate but long-lived wines with astonishing finesse, esp in WEHLENER SONNENUHR. Long lees ageing makes the wines hard to taste when young but they reward patience. Gd vintages keep 30 yrs.

Prüm, S A ★★→★★★ **89** 90 **95** 96 **97** 98 **99 01 02** 03 04 **05** 07 If WEHLEN neighbour JJ PRÜM is resolutely traditional, Raimond Prüm has dipped his toe into the late 20th century. Sound, if sometimes inconsistent, wines from WEHLEN and GRAACH.

QbA, Qualitätswein bestimmter Anbaugebiete The middle quality of German wine, with sugar added before fermentation (as in French *chaptalization*), but controlled as to areas, grapes, etc.

QmP, Qualitätswein mit Prädikat Top category, for all wines ripe enough not to need sugaring (KABINETT to TBA).

Randersacker Frank w ★★→★★★ **97** 99 **01** 02 03 04 **05** 06 07 (08) Leading village just south of WÜRZBURG known for distinctive dry wine. First Class v'yds include Pfülben, Sonnenstuhl. Top growers inc: BURGERSPITAL, JULIUSSPITAL, STAATLICHER HOFKELLER, Schmitt's Kinder, STÖRRLEIN, Trockene Schmitts.

Ratzenberger ★★ Estate making racy dry and off-dry RIES in BACHARACH; best from First Class Posten and Steeger St-Jost v'yds. Gd SEKT, too.

Rauenthal Rhg w ★★★→★★★★ **93 97** 98 **99 01** 02 **03 04 05** 07 Supreme village on inland slopes: spicy, complex wine. First Class v'yds: Baiken, Gehrn, Nonnenberg, Rothenberg, Wülfen. Top growers: BREUER, KLOSTER EBERBACH, LANGWERTH VON SIMMERN.

Rebholz Pfz ★★★→★★★★ Top SÜDLICHE WEINSTRASSE estate for decades, maintaining extraordinary consistency. Makes some of the best dry MUSKATELLER, GEWÜRZ, CHARD (Burgundian style), and SPÄTBURGUNDER in PFALZ. Outstanding GROSSES GEWÄCHS RIES.

Regent New dark red grape suited for organic farming and enjoying considerable success in southern wine regions. 2,180 ha are now planted. Plum-flavoured tannic wines of little complexity.

Words within entries marked like this *Alter Ego de Palmer* indicate wines especially enjoyed by Hugh Johnson over the past 12 months (mid '08–'09).

Ress, Balthasar ★★ 42-ha RHEINGAU estate based in HATTENHEIM. Gd estate Ries, and basic "Von Unserm" label, red and white, can offer gd value.

Restsüsse Unfermented grape sugar remaining in (or in cheap wines added to) wine to give it sweetness. Can range from 3 grams/litre in a TROCKEN wine to 300 in a TBA.

Rheingau Rhg Best v'yd region of Rhine, west of Wiesbaden. 3,097 ha. Classic, substantial but subtle RIES, yet on the whole recently eclipsed by brilliance elsewhere and hampered by some underperfoming if grand estates. Controversially, one-third of the region is classified since 2000 as ERSTES GEWÄCHS (First Growth), subject to regulations that differ from those created by the VDP for GROSSES GEWÄCHS.

Rheinhessen Vast region (26,330 ha) between Mainz and Worms, bordered by river NAHE to west. Much dross, but includes top RIES from NACKENHEIM, NIERSTEIN, OPPENHEIM, etc. Remarkable spurt in quality in south of region from growers such as KELLER and WITTMANN.

Rheinpfalz See PFALZ.

Richter, Weingut Max Ferd ★★→★★★ Top MITTELMOSEL estate, at Mülheim. Fine Ries made from First Class v'yds *Brauneberger Juffer-Sonnenuhr*, GRAACHER Domprobst, Mülheim (Helenenkloster), WEHLENER SONNENUHR. Produces superb EISWEIN from Helenenkloster almost every yr. Wines from purchased grapes carry a slightly different label.

Rieslaner Cross between SILVANER and RIES; known for low yields and difficult ripening. Makes fine AUSLESEN in FRANKEN, where most is grown.

Riesling The best German grape: fragrant, fruity, racy, long lived. Only CHARD can compete as the world's best white grape.

Ruck, Weingut Johann ★★ Reliable and spicy SILVANER and RIES from IPHOFEN in FRANKEN'S STEIGERWALD district.

Rüdesheim Rhg w ★★→★★★★ 89 90 93 96 97 98 99 01 02 03 04 05 07 (08) Rhine resort with First Class v'yds; the 3 best (Roseneck, Rottland and Schlossberg) are called Rüdesheimer Berg. Full-bodied wines, fine-flavoured, often remarkable in off yrs. Many of the top RHEINGAU estates own some Rüdesheim v'yds. Best growers: BREUER, JOHANNISHOF, KESSELER, LEITZ, RESS, SCHLOSS SCHÖNBORN, STAATSWEINGÜTER.

Ruländer (Pinot Gris) Now more commonly known as GRAUBURGUNDER.

Ruppertsberg Pfz w ★★→★★★ 97 99 01 02 03 04 05 07 Southern village of MITTELHAARDT. Patchy quality but First Class v'yds inc Gaisböhl, Linsenbusch, Nussbein, Reiterpfad. Growers include: BASSERMANN-JORDAN, Biffar, BUHL, BÜRKLIN-WOLF, CHRISTMANN, DR. DEINHARD.

Ruwer 89 90 93 97 99 01 02 03 04 05 07 Tributary of MOSEL nr TRIER. V. fine, delicate but highly aromatic and remarkably long-lived RIES both sweet and dry. A string of warm summers has helped ripeness. Best growers: BEULWITZ, KARLSMÜHLE, KARTHÄUSERHOF, KESSELSTATT, MAXIMIN GRÜNHAUS.

Saale-Unstrut 03 05 07 (08) Climatically challenging region of 660 ha around confluence of these two rivers at Naumburg, nr Leipzig. The terraced v'yds of WEISSBURGUNDER, SILVANER, GEWÜRZ, RIES, and SPÄTBURGUNDER have Cistercian origins. Quality leaders: Böhme, Bom, Gussek, Kloster Pforta, LÜTZKENDORF, Pawis.

Saar 89 90 93 94 95 96 97 98 99 01 02 03 04 05 07 Hill-lined tributary of the MOSEL south of RUWER. Climate differs considerably from MITTELMOSEL: v'yds are 50–100m higher in altitude. The most brilliant, austere, steely RIES of all. Villages include AYL, KANZEM, OCKFEN, Saarburg, Serrig, WILTINGEN (SCHARZHOFBERG). Many fine estates here, often at the top of their game.

Saarburg Small town in the SAAR valley, Rausch v'yd is one of the best of the area. Best growers: ZILLIKEN, WAGNER.

Alternative stoppers – the German way

Riesling is, of all grapes, one of the most easily affected by even the tiniest of cork taints. Maybe it's to do with the way that it reflects its terroir so expressively: just a whiff of corkiness will glare through.

You'd think Germans would have fled to screwcaps in their dozens. But not a bit of it. They're trying all sorts of other complicated alternative closures, and you can't help wondering why they don't just bite the bullet. The State Wine Domaine in Hessen, however, will be switching to screwcaps, even for reds. The first of a tidal wave?

Sachsen 03 04 05 07 (08) A region of 441 ha in the Elbe Valley around Dresden and Meissen. MÜLLER-THURGAU still dominates, but WEISSBURGUNDER, GRAUBURGUNDER, TRAMINER, and RIES give dry wines with real character. Best growers: Vincenz Richter, SCHLOSS PROSCHWITZ, Schloss Wackerbarth, Martin Schwarz, Zimmerling.

St-Antony, Weingut ★★ Once excellent Rheinhessen estate, now faltering. But new owner (same as HEYL ZU HERRNSHEIM) seems to be turning things around.

Salm, Prinz zu Owner of Schloss Wallhausen in NAHE and Villa Sachsen in RHEINHESSEN. Until 2006 president of VDP, which implemented the v'yd classification system against some stern opposition.

Salwey, Weingut ★★★ Leading BADEN estate at Oberrotweil, esp for RIES, WEISSBURGUNDER, and RULÄNDER. SPÄTBURGUNDER can be v.gd too, and fruit schnapps are an intriguing sideline.

Samtrot Red WÜRTTEMBERG grape, a mutation of Pinot Meunier. Light yet complex red with subtle fruit and little tannin. Gd examples from ALDINGER, DAUTEL and NEIPPERG.

Sankt Urbans-Hof ★★★ New star based in LEIWEN, PIESPORT, and OCKFEN. Limpid RIES of impeccable purity and raciness from 30 ha.

Sauer, Horst ★★★ ESCHERNDORFER Lump is one of FRANKEN'S top sites, and Sauer is the finest exponent of its SILVANER and RIES. Notable dry wines, and sensational TROCKENBEERENAUSLESEN.

Schaefer, Willi ★★★ The finest grower of GRAACH (but only 4 ha). Classic pure MOSEL RIES.

Schäfer-Fröhlich, Weingut ★★★ Increasingly brilliant RIES, dry and nobly sweet, from this 12-ha estate in Bockenau, NAHE.

Scharzhofberg M-S-R (Saar) w ★★★★ 71 83 88 89 90 93 94 95 96 97 98 99 01 02 03 04 05 06 07 (08) Superlative SAAR v'yd: austerely beautiful wines, the perfection of RIES, best in AUSLESEN. Top estates: BISCHÖFLICHE WEINGÜTER, EGON MÜLLER, VON HÖVEL, *von Kesselstatt*, van Volxem.

Scheurebe Grapefruit-scented grape of high quality (and RIES parentage), esp used in PFALZ. Excellent for botrytis wine (BEERENAUSLESEN, TROCKENBEERENAUSLESEN). Try Lingenfelder and PFEFFINGEN.

Schlossböckelheim Nahe w ★★→★★★ 90 96 97 98 99 01 02 03 04 05 07 Village with top NAHE v'yds, inc First Class Felsenberg, In den Felsen, Königsfels, Kupfergrube. Firm yet delicate wine that ages well. Top growers: *Crusius*, DÖNNHOFF, Gutsverwaltung NIEDERHAUSEN-SCHLOSSBÖCKELHEIM, SCHÄFER-FRÖHLICH.

Schloss Johannisberg Rhg w ★★→★★★ 90 94 95 96 97 98 99 01 02 03 04 05 07 Famous RHEINGAU estate of 35 ha, 100% RIES, owned by Henkell. Deservedly popular tourist destination, but more importantly the original Rhine "first growth". Until recently, high prices reflected reputation more than quality. Since 05, improved v'yd managemen under new director Christian Witte. The 07 wines are promising.

Schloss Lieser ★★★ 9-ha estate owned by Thomas Haag, from *Fritz Haag estate*, making pure racy RIES from underrated Niederberg Helden v'yd in LIESER.

Schloss Neuweier ★★★ Leading producer of dry RIES in BADEN, from the volcanic soils of Mauerberg and Schlossberg v'yds nr Baden-Baden.

Schloss Proschwitz ★★ A resurrected princely estate at Meissen in SACHSEN, which leads former East Germany in quality, esp with dry WEISSBURGUNDER and GRAUBURGUNDER.

Schloss Reinhartshausen Rhg ★★★ Fine estate, 75 ha in Erbach, HATTENHEIM, KIEDRICH, etc. Originally property of Prussian royal family, now in private hands. Model RHEINGAU RIES. The mansion beside the Rhine is now a luxury hotel. Under new management since 2003, the estate is back on form with excellent 05s and respectable 07s.

Schloss Saarstein, Weingut ★–★★★★ 90 93 97 99 01 02 03 04 05 07 Steep but chilly v'yds in Serrig need warm yrs to succeed but can deliver steely minerally, and long-lived AUSLESE and EISWEIN.

Schloss Schönborn ★★★ Widespread 50-ha RHEINGAU estate with superb sites, based at HATTENHEIM. Full-flavoured wines, variable, but excellent when at their best. The Schönborn family also own a large wine estate in FRANKEN.

Schloss Vaux ★★–★★★ Superior SEKT manufacturer, specalizing in bottle-fermented RIES and SPÄTBURGUNDER from top RHEINGAU sites (eg STEINBERG or ASSMANNSHAUSER Höllenberg). The company does not own v'yds itself, but purchases wine from leading estates (mainly from VDP members).

Schloss Vollrads Rhg w ★★90 98 **99 01** 02 **03 04 05** 07 One of the greatest historic RHEINGAU estates, owned by a bank since the sudden death of owner Erwein Count Matuschka in 1997. Since 1998, quality, under Rowald Hepp, is much improved, but the estate's full potential has yet to be defined.

Schmitt's Kinder ★★–★★★ Uncompromising TROCKEN wines from RANDERSACKER's best v'yds. 18 ha. Textbook FRANKEN SILVANER and RIES. Gd barrel-aged SPÄTBURGUNDER and sweet SCHEUREBE too.

Schnaitmann, Weingut ★★–★★★ Although this new WÜRTTEMBERG star makes gd RIES and Sauv Bl, its reputation rests on a complex range of full-bodied red wines from a range of varieties.

Schneider, Cornelia and Reinhold ★★–★★★ 7-ha family estate in Endingen, KAISERSTUHL. Ageworthy SPÄTBURGUNDER and old-fashioned, opulent RULÄNDER.

Schoppenwein Café (or bar) wine, ie wine by the glass.

Schwarzer Adler, Weingut ★★–★★★ Fritz Keller makes top BADEN GRAU-, WEISS-, and SPÄTBURGUNDER on 55 ha at Oberbergen, KAISERSTUHL. A firm opponent of residual sugar in Pinot. Selection "A" signifies the top barrique wines.

Schwarzriesling This grape, with 2390 ha, is none other than the Pinot Meunier of northern France. In WÜRTTEMBERG a light-bodied red.

Schwegler, Albrecht ★★★ Small WÜRTTEMBERG estate known for unusual yet tasteful red blends such as Granat (Merlot, Zweigelt, LEMBERGER and other varieties). 2 ha only, but worth looking for.

Schweigen Pfz w r ★★ **97 99** 01 02 **03 04 05** 07 (08) Southern PFALZ village. Best growers: Friedrich Becker, esp for SPÄTBURGUNDER, Bernhart, Jülg.

Sekt German sparkling wine v. variable in quality. Bottle-fermentation is not mandatory; cheap examples may be produced in a pressure tank. Reputable wine-growers' labels are certainly a gd choice, but even at this level, sekt is sometimes only a by-product. Estates that are sekt specialists include

Remember that vintage information for German wines is given in a different form from the ready/not ready distinction applying to other countries. See the explanation at the bottom of p. 143.

GERMANY

Raumland, SCHLOSS VAUX, Wilhelmshof.

Selbach-Oster ★★★ Scrupulous 17-ha ZELTINGEN estate among MITTELMOSEL leaders. Also makes wine from purchased grapes: estate bottlings are best.

Silvaner Third-most-planted German white grape variety with 5,260 ha and thus 5% of the surface. Best examples in FRANKEN, where Silvaner's lovely floral flavours and its bone-dry mineral taste reach perfection. Worth looking for as well in RHEINHESSEN and KAISERSTUHL (esp IHRINGEN).

Sonnenuhr Sundial. Name of several v'yds, esp First Class sites at WEHLEN and ZELTINGEN.

Spätburgunder (Pinot Noir) The best red wine grape in Germany – esp in AHR, BADEN and WÜRTTEMBERG, and increasingly PFALZ – steadily improving quality, but most still underflavoured or over-oaked. The best are convincing (eg FÜRST, HUBER, KNIPSER, Näkel etc). Allegedly, Charles the Fat first brought Pinot N from Burgundy to the shores of Lake Constance (BODENSEE) in 884.

Spätlese Late harvest. One better (riper, with more alcohol, more substance and usually more sweetness) than KABINETT. Gd examples age at least 7 yrs, often longer. TROCKEN Spätlesen, often similar in style to GROSSES GEWÄCHS, can be v. fine with food.

Spreitzer, Weingut ★★★ Since 1997, brothers Andreas and Bernd Spreitzer in OESTRICH, RHEINGAU, have been making deliciously racy and consistent RIES.

Staatlicher Hofkeller ★★ The Bavarian state domain. 120 ha of the finest FRANKEN v'yds with spectacular cellars under the great baroque Residenz at WÜRZBURG. Quality sound but rarely exciting.

Staatsweingut (or Staatliche Weinbaudomäne) The state wine estates or domains. Some have been privatized in recent yrs.

Steigerwald District in eastern FRANKEN. V'yds lie at considerable altitude but bring powerful SILVANER and RIES. Look for: CASTELL, RUCK, Weltner, WIRSCHING.

Steinberg Rhg w ★★→★★★ **90 95 96** 97 **99 01** 02 **03 04 05 07** Famous 32-ha HATTENHEIM walled v'yd, planted by Cistercian monks 700 yrs ago. A monopoly of KLOSTER EBERBACH. Disappointing for years but now one to watch.

Steinwein Wine from WÜRZBURG's best v'yd, Stein. Goethe's favourite.

Stodden, Weingut Jean ★★★ A new star in the AHR. Burgundy enthusiast Gerhard Stodden crafts richly oaky SPÄTBURGUNDER. First rate since 1999, but v. pricey.

Störrlein, Weingut ★★→★★★ Sterling dry, expressive SILVANER and RIES from RANDERSACKER in FRANKEN; fine GROSSES GEWÄCHS from Sonnenstuhl v'yd.

Südliche Weinstrasse (Bereich) District name for south PFALZ. Quality has improved tremendously in past 25 yrs. See BERGDOLT, REBHOLZ, SCHWEIGEN, DR. WEHRHEIM.

Tafelwein See "Germany's quality levels" box on p. 145.

Tauberfranken Underrated district of northeast BADEN: FRANKEN-style wines from shell limestone soils, bone-dry and distinctly cool-climate in style.

TBA See TROCKENBEERENAUSLESE.

Thanisch, Weingut Dr. ★★→★★★ BERNKASTEL estate, inc part of the Doctor v'yd. This famous estate was divided in the 80s, but the two confusingly share the same name: Erben Müller-Burggraef identifies one; Erben Thanisch the other. Similar in quality but the latter sometimes has the edge.

Traisen Nahe w ★★★ **90 93 95 96** 97 **98** 99 **01** 02 03 04 05 **07** Small village inc First Class Bastei and Rotenfels v'yds, capable of making RIES of concentration and class. Top grower: CRUSIUS.

Traminer See GEWÜRZTRAMINER.

Trier M-S-R w ★★→★★★ Great wine city of Roman origin, on MOSEL, between RUWER and SAAR. Big charitable estates have cellars here among Roman ruins.

Trittenheim M-M w ★★★ **90 93 95** 96 97 98 **99 01** 02 **03 04 05** 06 **07** Attractive south MITTELMOSEL light wines. Top v'yds are Altärchen, Apotheke (apart from the second-rate flat land included since 1971); First Class v'yds are Felsenkopf, Leiterchen. Growers include ANSGAR CLÜSSERATH, Ernst Clüsserath, CLÜSSERATH-WEILER, GRANS-FASSIAN, Milz.

rocken Dry. *Trocken* wines have a maximum 9 g of unfermented sugar per litre. Some wines are austere, others (better) have more body and alcohol. Quality has increased dramatically since the 1980s, when most were tart, even sour. Most dependable in PFALZ and all points south.

rockenbeerenauslese (TBA) Sweetest, most expensive category of German wine, extremely rare, with concentrated honey flavour. Made from selected shrivelled grapes affected by noble rot (botrytis).

ollinger Pale red grape variety of WÜRTTEMBERG; identical with South Tyrol's Vernatsch; mostly over-cropped but locally v. popular.

rzig M-M w ★★★★ 90 93 94 95 96 97 98 99 01 02 03 04 05 06 07 Village on red sandstone and red slate, famous for firm, full, spicy wine unlike other MOSELS. First Class v'yd: Würzgarten. Growers include Berres, CHRISTOFFEL, LOOSEN, MÖNCHHOF, PAULY-BERGWEILER (Peter Nicolay), WEINS-PRÜM.

an Volxem, Weingut ★★→★★★ Lacklustre SAAR estate revived by brewery heir Roman Niewodniczanski since 1999. V. low yields from top sites result in ultra-ripe dry (or slightly off-dry) RIES. Atypical but impressive.

dP, Verband Deutscher Prädikats und Qualitätsweingüter The pace-making association of premium growers. Look for its eagle insignia on wine labels. President: Steffen CHRISTMANN.

ereinigte Hospitien ★★ "United Hospices". Ancient charity at TRIER with large holdings in PIESPORT, Serrig, TRIER, WILTINGEN, etc. Wines below their wonderful potential.

ollenweider, Weingut ★★★ Daniel Vollenweider from Switzerland has since 2000 revived the Wolfer Goldgrube v'yd nr Traben-Trarbach. Excellent RIES, but v. small quantities.

achenheim Pfz w ★★★→★★★★ 90 96 97 98 99 01 02 03 04 05 07 340 ha, inc exceptional RIES. First Class v'yds: Belz, Gerümpel, Goldbächel, Rechbächel, etc. Top growers: Biffar, BÜRKLIN-WOLF, Karl Schäfer, WOLF.

agner, Dr. ★★ 9-ha estate with v'yds in Saarburg and OCKFEN. Traditional methods: all wines ferment and age in FUDER casks. Many fine wines, inc TROCKEN.

agner-Stempel, Weingut ★★★ 13-ha estate, 50% RIES, in RHEINHESSEN nr NAHE border in obscure Siefersheim. Recent yrs have provided excellent wines, great in 2005 and 2007, both GROSSES GEWÄCHS and nobly sweet.

alluf Rhg w ★★★ 90 96 97 98 99 01 02 03 04 05 07 Neighbour of Eltville. Underrated wines. First Class v'yd: Walkenberg. Growers include BECKER, JOST.

egeler ★★→★★★ Important family estates in OESTRICH, MITTELHARDT, and BERNKASTEL. The Wegelers owned the merchant house of DEINHARD until 1997. Estate wines remain of high quality.

ehlen M-M w ★★★→★★★★ 89 90 93 94 95 96 97 98 99 01 02 03 04 05 06 07 (08) BERNKASTEL neighbour with equally fine, somewhat richer wine. Location of First Class v'yd: SONNENUHR. Top growers are: Kerpen, LOOSEN, M MOLITOR, J J PRÜM, S A PRÜM, RICHTER, Studert-Prüm, SELBACH-OSTER, WEGELER, WEINS-PRÜM.

ehrheim, Weingut Dr. ★★★ In warm SÜDLICHE WEINSTRASSE Pinot varieties and CHAR as well as RIES ripen fully. Both whites and reds are v. successful here.

eil, Weingut Robert ★★★★ 90 94 96 97 98 99 00 01 02 03 04 05 06 07 Outstanding estate in KIEDRICH; owned since 88 by Suntory of Japan. Superb EISWEIN, TROCKENBEERENAUSLESEN, BEERENAUSLESEN; standard wines also v.gd.

Words within entries marked like this *Alter Ego de Palmer* indicate wines specially enjoyed by Hugh Johnson over the past 12 months (mid '08–'09).

GERMANY

> **Who drinks it all?**
> An average German vintage yields 8 to 10 m hl. A good 80 per cent is
> drunk at home. Abroad, in terms of quantity, no one can beat the UK. In
> terms of price, however, it's the Swiss who take the lead. Their importers
> paid an average of €6.37 per litre – compared to €1.52 for an average litre
> destined for the UK. The USA takes some 300,000 hl at an average price
> of €3.43 – probably the best value of all.

Accepted to be RHEINGAU's No 1 in sweet wines, with prices to match.

Weingart, Weingut ★★→★★★ Outstanding MITTELRHEIN estate, with 11 ha in BOPPARD. Superb value.

Weingut Wine estate.

Weins-Prüm, Dr. ★★★ Small estate; based at WEHLEN. 4 ha of superb v'yds in MITTELMOSEL. Scrupulous winemaking from owner Bert Selbach, who favours a taut, minerally style.

Weissburgunder (Pinot Blanc) Increasingly popular for culinary TROCKEN wines that exhibit more burgundian raciness than German CHARD. Best from southern PFALZ and from BADEN. Some leading producers are now turning back to traditional larger oak casks instead of barriques. Also much used for SEKT.

Weissherbst Usually a pale pink wine, QBA or above, sometimes botrytis affected and occasionally even BEERENAUSLESE, made from a single variety often SPÄTBURGUNDER.

Wiltingen M-S-R (Saar) w ★★→★★★★ 90 93 95 96 **97** 98 **99** 01 02 **03 04 05** 06 **07** Heartland of the SAAR. 320 ha. Beautifully subtle, austere wine. Great First Class v'yd is SCHARZHOFBERG (ORTSTEIL); and First Class are Braune Kupp Gottesfuss, Hölle. Top growers: BISCHÖFLICHE WEINGÜTER, EGON MÜLLER KESSELSTATT, VAN VOLXEM, etc.

Winningen M-S-R w ★★→★★★★ Lower MOSEL town nr Koblenz: excellent dry RIES and TBA. First Class v'yds: Röttgen, Uhlen. Top growers: HEYMANN-LÖWENSTEIN KNEBEL, Richard Richter.

Winzergenossenschaft (WG) A wine-growers' cooperative, often making sound and reasonably priced wine. Referred to in this text as "co-op". V. important in BADEN and WÜRTTEMBERG.

Winzerverein The same as above.

Wirsching, Hans ★★★ Estate in IPHOFEN, FRANKEN. Dry RIES and *Silvaner*, powerful and long-lived. 72 ha in First Class v'yds: Julius-Echter-Berg, Kalb and Kronsberg.

Wittmann, Weingut ★★★ Since 1999 Philipp Wittmann has propelled this 25-ha organic estate to the top ranks in RHEINHESSEN. Crystal-clear, mineral dry RIES from QBA to GROSSES GEWÄCHS RIES and magnificent TROCKENBEERENAUSLESEN.

Wöhrwag, Weingut ★★→★★★ Just outside Stuttgart, this 20-ha WÜRTTEMBERG estate produces succulent reds and often brilliant RIES, esp EISWEIN.

Wolf J L ★★→★★★★ Estate in WACHENHEIM leased long-term by Ernst LOOSEN of BERNKASTEL. Dry PFALZ RIES with a MOSEL-like finesse. Sound and consistent rather than dazzling.

Wonnegau District name for south RHEINHESSEN.

Württemberg Wurt Vast area in the south, 11,520 ha, little known outside Germany Local consumption absorbs most of the production, maybe that's

Remember that vintage information for German wines is given in a different form from the ready/not ready distinction applying to other countries. See the explanation at the bottom of p. 143.

why the region has been distinctly underperforming for a long time. But ambitions now rising, esp with concentrated, fruit-driven reds (esp LEMBERGER, SAMTROT, SPÄTBURGUNDER). Further experiments inc SAUV BL or dark new crossings bred by the Weinsberg research station. RIES (mostly TROCKEN) tends to be rustic, although the Remstal area close to Stuttgart can have refinement.

Würzburg Frank ★★→★★★★ 93 97 98 99 **01** 02 03 **04 05** 06 **07** (08) Great baroque city on the Main, centre of FRANKEN wine: fine, full-bodied, dry RIES and esp SILVANER. First Class v'yds: Abtsleite, Innere Leiste, Stein, Stein-Harfe. See MAINDREIECK. Growers: BÜRGERSPITAL, JULIUSSPITAL, STAATLICHER HOFKELLER, Weingut am Stein.

Zehnthof, Weingut ★★ Wide-ranging wines, notably SILVANER and Pinot varieties, from Luckert family's 12-ha estate in Sulzfeld, FRANKEN.

Zell M-S-R w ★★→★★★★ 93 97 99 **01** 02 **03 04 05** 07 Best-known lower MOSEL village, esp for awful GROSSLAGE: Schwarze Katz (Black Cat). RIES on steep slate gives aromatic wines. Top growers: S. Fischer, Kallfelz.

Zeltingen M-M w ★★→★★★★ 90 93 95 96 **97 98** 99 01 02 **03 04 05** 06 07 Top but sometimes underrated MOSEL village nr WEHLEN. Lively crisp RIES. First Class v'yd: SONNENUHR. Top growers: Markus MOLITOR, J J PRÜM, Schömann, SELBACH-OSTER.

Ziereisen, Weingut ★★ Carpenter and ex-co-op member Hans-Peter Ziereisen turned winemaker some yrs ago, with stunning success. A full palette from BADEN: dry Pinot whites, mineral Gutedel Steingrüble, and Syrah. But best are the SPÄTBURGUNDERS from various small v'yd plots with dialect names: Schulen, Tschuppen, Rhini.

Zilliken, Forstmeister Geltz ★★★→★★★★ Former estate of Prussian royal forester with 11 ha at Saarburg and OCKFEN, SAAR. Produces intensely minerally Ries from Saarburger Rausch, inc superb AUSLESE and EISWEIN with excellent ageing potential.

Luxembourg

Luxembourg has 1,250 ha of v'yds on limestone soils on the Moselle's left bank. High-yielding Elbling and Rivaner (Müller-Thurgau) have been the dominant varieties, but are in gradual decline; Chard is growing, though primarily for sparkling wine. There are also Ries, Gewürz, and (usually best) Auxerrois, Pinot Bl, and Pinot Gris. These give light to medium-bodied (10.5–11.5% alcohol), dry, Alsace-like wines. Perhaps as a result of climatic change, there has been a growth in more full-bodied, richer wines, including some late-harvested Vendanges Tardives and *vins de paille*. Pinot N now accounts for 7% of plantings. The most important producer by far is Les Doms des Vinsmoselle, a grouping of six co-ops. The Domaine et Tradition association, founded in 1988, groups seven estates that impose stricter rules on themselves than the regulations demand. The following vintages were all **gd**: 89 90 92 95 97; **outstanding** 97; **average** 98; similar but **softer** 99; **poor** 00 and 06; much **better** 01 and 02; while 03 and 05 are gd for red as well as white wines. Best from: Bastian, Bentz, Cep d'Or, Abi Duhr, Gales, Alice Hartmann, Krier Frères, Krier-Welbes, *Bernard Massard* (gd classic method sparkling), Château Pauqué, Schumacher-Knepper, and Sunnen-Hoffmann.

Spain & Portugal

**More heavily shaded areas are the
wine-growing regions**

The following abbreviations are used in the text:

Alen	Alentejo
Bair	Bairrada
Bul	Bullas
Cos del S	Costers del Segre
El B	El Bierzo
Emp	Empordà-Costa Brava/Ampurdán
Est	Estremadura
La M	La Mancha
Mont-M	Montilla-Moriles
Nav	Navarra
Pen	Penedès
Pri	Priorato/Priorat
Rib del D	Ribera del Duero
Rib del G	Ribera del Guadiana
R Ala	Rioja Alavesa
R Alt	Rioja Alta
RB	Rioja Baja
Set	Setúbal
Som	Somontano
U-R	Utiel-Requena
res	*reserva*

Remember when Spain was Europe's poor relation in the wine world? No longer. The second decade of the third millennium ushers in a profoundly different country. Confident, independent, with its own favoured varieties (Tempranillo, Mencía, Monastrell in the reds; Verdejo, Albariño, Godello in the whites; and many more besides). In addition, there is a remarkable group of creative, independent-minded winemakers. Spain's wines today benefit from as much know-how as the world's most advanced regions, adding the originality of indigenous grapes and culture.

Next door in Portugal, the Douro Valley has, within a short dozen years, established a world-class reputation for red, and now white wines. While we absorb the possibilities of port country for table wines other regions are polishing their acts. Dão has become interesting, Barrida fascinating and the Alentejo experimental; all, happily, profiting from local varieties and updating local traditions. Vinho verde, once an export hit, may well have a big future. Wathc Terras do Sado, too. Watch Portugal

Port, sherry and madeira have a separate chapter on page 184.

Spain

Recent vintages of the Spanish classics

Rioja

2008 The wettest May on record and a cool summer promises wines in the classic style. The best will be fresh and aromatic, a little lower in alcohol.

2007 A long harvest following spring hail and summer mildew. Considered very satisfactory and of good ageing potential.

2006 Biggish harvest of lowest yields since 2001 with a generally favourable weather cycle. Results considered generally positive and expectations good. Wines are lightish but fragrant.

2005 A large, healthy, and plentiful harvest, with exceptionally favourable weather. Rated as exceptional and unprecedented. Wines are full, immediate, and without much complexity.

2004 A large harvest with magnificent quality expectations for those who were selective enough given the tricky weather. Wines are dark, structured and tannic, and many now ready to drink.

2003 Biggish harvest of fair quality. The top *cuvées* are sublime; but most have proved short-lived and are already past their prime.

2002 Small harvest of doubtful quality, like a cross between 1999 and 2000. The best are still delicious; the run-of-the-mill have already peaked.

2001 Medium-sized harvest of excellent quality; the best are at their peak or just over.

2000 Huge harvest; wines distinctly bland, with little real flavour or definition.

1999 A difficult harvest; its light but very graceful wines have mainly peaked.

1998 A huge vintage of high quality; its wines are now largely over-mature.

Ribera del Duero

2008 Rot was a major risk with spring rainfall. This was followed by a cool summer, and frosts in Sept, in a continuation of the pattern of cooler summers since 2005. Selection was essential for quality.

2007 While yields improved (up 20% on 06) quality producers consider it the most disastrous vintage since 97. All appeared fine until a very damp spring followed by a summer lacking in both heat and sunshine.

2006 A dry, mild winter followed by a hot spring; midsummer storms with flash downpours caused widespread oidium; then intense heat in early Sept followed by copious rain and the threat of botrytis. Some picked a whole month early, but the true professionals picked super-selectively and finished a month later. As polarized as 05.

2005 A bitterly cold winter, followed by sparse rainfall yet high temperatures in May, June, and the run-up to an early harvest (with one major frost in mid-Sept). Those who picked too early have green, unbalanced wines. Very good only for the true professionals.

2004 A better year than in most regions. Despite extremes of temperature in Sept, good-quality wines and a plentiful harvest.

2003 A cold winter, mild spring, scorching summer, and Oct rains resulted in a tricky harvest. The best wines are of good colour, glycerine, and alcohol, but low in acidity.

2002 Hot weather followed by heavy rain in late summer led to a large harvest. Quality generally very good.

2001 Medium-sized harvest of excellent quality; wines fulfilling their promise.

2000 Very large harvest but ripening was uneven. Some bodegas made spectacular wines; but in general good.

1999 Almost perfect weather and bumper harvest, but rainfall around harvest time resulted in lack of acidity. Very good, but fading.

Navarra

2008 As elsewhere a wet spring and a very late harvest. The slow ripening, however, will give elegance, where selection was careful.

2007 Following a damp spring, mild summer of lowish temperatures and little sunshine, but a dry autumn. Exceptional for the best sites. At best fantastically aromatic, impeccably balanced fruit which will produce exceptional wines that will age well.

2006 Complicated, given a wet spring, hot summer, mild, damp autumn. Young wines good. Only true professionals will produce wines of ageing potential.

2005 Possibly best-ever vintage, with perfect climatic conditions, resulting in wines of immense colour, full flavours, and sweet, powerful tannins.

2004 Low spring and summer temperatures with much rain. Good, intense wines for those who picked late and selectively.

2003 The hot, dry summer was followed by extended torrential rain and outbreaks of botrytis and mildew. As in 02, only the best and most professional producers obtained decent results, so quality is patchy and the best are already mature.

2002 Torrential Aug rains affected the quality of wines from the south of the region; others are excellent but drinking now.

2001 An excellent year, with big, ripe, balanced wines that are still developing.

2000 Very dry year of prolific yields, calling for rigorous selection. Best wines are big and fleshy, and drinking nicely.

1999 Most frost-afflicted vintage of the decade, with soaring grape prices. Wines are well structured and long-ageing. Excellent but now hard to find.

Penedès

2008 Heavy spring rains presaged rot for many producers, and uneven fruit set. A good vintage for the better producers.

2007 A textbook year of optimum weather has led to the vintage being qualified as excellent and considered one of the best in the last 50 years.

2006 An average-sized vintage. Gd climatic conditions, despite a burst of heavy mid-Sept rain, healthy and properly developed fruit resulted in very good acidity and alcohol levels. The vintage is officially excellent on all levels.

2005 The hardest drought of the last 50 years reduced yields by 30–40%, but thanks to cold summer nights quality was excellent for reds and whites.

2004 A cold spring and late summer rains delayed the harvest, but sunny days and cold nights in autumn resulted in a memorable year for red wines.

2003 A very dry and long summer, refreshed with rains in Aug, then cool nights and sunny days in Sept, resulted in a great vintage.

2002 A splendid Sept gave wines of good quality.

2001 Apr frosts reduced the yield but warm summer produced very good wines.

2000 Perfect ripening of the grapes gave well-balanced wines. Very good.

1999 Dry summer but abundant harvest. Very good.

Aalto, Bodegas y Viñedos Rib del D r ★★→★★★ 00 01 02 03 04' Newish estate with two lavishly concentrated reds with dense, plummy black fruit, big tannins, liquorice and oak. Top *cuvée* PS is more than twice the price.

Abadía Retuerta Castilla y León r ★★★ 04 05 06 One of the classic non-DO/VDT wineries. Next door to RIBERA DEL DUERO; making a range of pricey, savoury reds from Tempranillo, Cab Sauv, Merlot, and Syrah. Round, fruity Rivola; spicier, more austere Selección Especial; loftier, chocolatey pure Tempranillo PAGO Negralada; and elegant, mineral Syrah PAGO la Garduña.

Albariño High-quality aromatic white grape of GALICIA and the best-regarded Spanish white variety. See PALACIO DE FEFIÑANES, PAZÓ DE BARRANTES, PAZO DE SEÑORANS, RÍAS BAIXAS.

Albet i Noya Pen r w p ★★→★★★ 01 03 04 05 06 07 Spain's most famous organic producer. Best is Cab/Syrah/Tempranillo/Merlot La Milana (**05**).

Alella r w (p) dr sw ★★ DYA Small demarcated region N of Barcelona; best for fresh, lively whites made from indigenous Pansa Blanca. Best producers PARXET, Alta Alella, Marfil Alella.

Alicante r w sw ★→★★★★ 04 05 06 07 Alicante is looking up, building a reputation for Monastrell reds plus sweet wines. Quality is still variable; reds better than whites (Monastrell, Syrah, Cab, Garnacha and Merlot; also Petit Verdot and Pinot N). Some outstanding sweet Moscatels; historic FONDILLON. Best producers: GUTIÉRREZ DE LA VEGA Enrique Mendoza, Bernabé Navarro, El Sequé, Sierra Salinas.

Alión Rib del D r ★★★ 01 02 03 04 05 VEGA SICILIA's second BODEGA makes rich, elegant, damson/blackberry 100% Tinto Fino (Tempranillo) aged in Nevers.

Allende, Finca R Ala r ★★★→★★★★ 04 Discreet recent (1995) bodega in Briones. Wild, exuberantly fruity Calvario and more traditional Allende show Duero influence. Aurus is showy and expensive. Single v'yd to come.

Artadi Bodegas y Viñedos R Ala r (w p) ★★★→★★★★ 04 05 06 Outstanding, serious RIOJA: complex, toasty, Viñas del Gaín; taut, powerful VIÑA El Pisón; spicy, elegant PAGOS Viejos.

Astrales, Bodegas Los Rib del D r ★★★ 03 04 05 Small estate in Anguix with old-vine Tempranillo vinified 18 mths in new oak; first vintage 01. Came into its own with lush, vibrant 03, with 04 promising, but significantly lighter.

Baigorri, Bodegas R Ala r (w p) ★★★ 04 05 Spectacular winery producing pricey new-wave RIOJA with primary black fruits, bold tannins, and upbeat oak. Best: buzzy CRIANZA, lush RESERVA, more expressive Garage.

Bascula, La Wine brand started by South African winemaker Bruce Jack and UK MW Ed Adams to identify interesting wines from all over Spain. Typical eg of the interest in Spain shown by external investors.

Berberana, Bodegas See BODEGAS UNIDAS.

Bierzo r w ★→★★★ 03 04 05 06 V. fashionable DO N of Léon showing potential of the indigenous black Mencía (aromatic with steely tannin) plus white Godello. Top wineries: Bodegas Peique, Bodegas Pittacum, DOMINIO DE TARES. Descendientes de J Palacios, biodynamic producer, led by nephew of ALVARO PALACIOS, impresses with French-oaked Mencías – Moncerbal, *Pétalos del Bierzo* and Villa de Corullón.

Binissalem r w ★★ 05 06 Tiny but best-known MALLORCA DO NE of Palma. Two-thirds red production, mainly Mantonegro. Best: Macía Batle.

Bodega Spanish term for (i) a wineshop; (ii) a concern occupied in the making, blending, and/or shipping of wine; and (iii) a cellar.

Briones Small Riojan hilltop town nr Haro, peppered with underground cellars. Home to FINCA ALLENDE and one of the most comprehensive wine museums in the world, El Museo de la Cultura de Vino.

Bullas ★→★★ 04 05 06 Small, high (400–800 m), dry Murcia DO trying hard in an excessively Mediterranean climate. Best: Bodega Monastrell Chaveo.

Calatayud ★→★★★ 05 06 07 08 Improving, mountainous Aragón DO specializing in brooding Garnacha often from old vines, sometimes blended with Syrah. Best producers: Bodegas Ateca (see ORDONEZ), Bodegas y Viñedos el Jalón.

Campo de Borja ★→★★★ 06 07 08 Aragón DO making excellent, great value DYA modern, juicy Garnachas and Tempranillos, eg Bodegas Aragonesas. For more complexity, try Tres Picos Garnacha (05) from Bodegas Borsao. Top wine Alto Moncayo's Aquilón.

Canary Islands (Islas Canarias) r w p ★→★★ Has an astonishing 9 DOS. Quality is mixed; occasionally stunning dessert Malvasías and Moscatels. Many native varieties (white Listán and Marmajuelo, black Negramoll and Vijariego); given climate and shallow volcanic soils it has potential with exploration.

Cariñena ★→★★ 03 04 05 06 07 Solid, workmanlike Aragón DO The 2 leading producers are Bodegas Añadas and Bodegas Victoria.

Casta Diva See GUTIÉRREZ DE LA VEGA.

Castell del Remei Cos del S r w p ★★→★★★ 03 05 06 07 Picturesque restored 18th-century estate. Gd white blends; v.gd vanilla-tinged, sour-red-cherry-flavoured Gotim Bru (05) and the marvellous, minerally 1780.

Castilla-La Mancha, Vino de la Tierra In 1999, 600,000 ha of this vast region were granted VDT status by the EU. Since then dozens of large firms have moved into the area to make wine. A catch-all grouping of great inconsistency.

Castilla de Perelada, Vinos y Caves del Emp r w p res sp ★★→★★★ 04 05 06 07

Large range of still wines and CAVA, inc fresh DYA Sauv Bl and 3 opulent, old-style, top reds: lush Gran Claustro, fine mineral Finca Garbet, the Ex Ex (Experiencias Excepcionales) series .

Castillo de Ygay R Alt r w ★★★★ (r) **54 64 70 89 91 94 96 97 98 99 01** Legendary, long-lived top wines from MARQUÉS DE MURRIETA.

Catalunya 04 05 06 07 Vast new (2004) DO covering the whole Catalan area. Confusion arises as this now includes wines from more than 200 well-known producers using grapes from outside their own strictly local DO. Top names include some of the biggest: ALBET I NOYA, FREIXENET, JEAN LÉON, and TORRES. PENEDÈS DO claims that 20% of its production "escapes" into this alternative.

Cava Contrary to popular assumption the DO (since 1986) covers traditional-method fizz from more than 270 producers up and down Spain, although most is produced in or around San Sadurní de Noya in PENEDÈS. Dominated by FREIXENET and CODORNÍU. Quality is often higher, with a price tag to match, from smaller producers such as Castell Sant Antoni, CASTILLA DE PERELADA, GRAMONA, JUVÉ & CAMPS, MARQUÉS DE MONISTROL, Mestres, PARXET, Raimat, Recaredo, Signat, and Sumarroca. Cava is best drunk young, though local taste often favours those with major bottle age.

> **Cava's fizz grows**
> Cava is improving. Producers are working on all fronts, from selection of grape varieties to ageing. A lot of the best are niche wines you may not find outside Spain. Recaredo even makes one that costs €95 (3,000 bottles only, vines planted in 1940): ambitious or what?

Cérvoles, Celler Cos del S r w ★★★★ **03 04 05** High mountainous estate just N of PRIORATO making concentrated reds from Cab Sauv/Tempranillo/Garnacha and powerful, creamy, lemon-tinged barrel-fermented Blanc.

Chacolí País Vasco w (r) ★★ DYA Split into 3 separate DOs: Alava, Guetaria and Vizcaya. All produce fragrant DYA but often quirkily sharp, *pétillant* whites, locally poured into tumblers from a height. The historic Chueca-family-owned Txomin Etxaniz rounds off the aggression of the primary Hondarribi Zuri (white) with 15% of low-alcohol Hondarribi Beltza.

Chivite, Bodegas Julián Nav r w (p) dr sw res ★★→★★★ **03 04 05** 06 07 Biggest, most historic and best-known NAVARRA BODEGA. Popular range Gran Feudo esp Rosado and new Rosado *sobre lias* (sur lie). High spots of pricier Colección 125 range are serious Burgundian Chard in modern style; elegant botrytis Moscatel and top of range Pago de Arinzano, still finding its feet. Promising Verdejo Baluarate, from RUEDA, first vintage 2008.

Cigales r p (w) ★→★★★★ Small, high DO N of Valladolid. Produces both commercial, DYA reds, and more complex old-vine Tempranillo. Two outstanding producers each make a single wine: the lush, voluptuous César Príncipe; and more restrained, old-vine Traslanzas (**02 03**).

Clos d'Agón See MAS GIL.

Clos Mogador Pri r ★★★→★★★★★ **01 02 03 04 05** 06 07 René Barbier continues to rank as one of PRIORATO'S pioneers, a godfather to the younger generations of winemakers. Simpler, second wine Manyetes is gd but Clos Mogador is breathtaking and usually gd for a decade. Also exceptionally interesting is the spicy, fragrant, honeyed and complex Garnacha Blanca/Viognier/Marsanne/ Macabeo/Pinot N Clos Nelin white (**05**).

Codorníu Pen w sp ★★→★★★★ One of the two largest CAVA firms, owned by the Raventós family. Has always been at odds with arch-rival FREIXENET favouring non-indigenous varieties, esp Chard. Best offerings: Jaume de Codorníu, Anna de Codorníu, the v. dry Non Plus Ultra, and pale, smoky Pinot N. Also owns the gradually improving Raímat in COSTERS DEL SEGRE, as well as the once great but now slumbering Bilbainas in RIOJA.

Compañía Vinícola del Norte de España (CVNE) R Alt r w dr (p) ★→★★ Famous RIOJA BODEGA; benchmark 20 yrs ago. Seek out its pre-1970 GRS of light, elegant, high-acid Imperial or fleshier VIÑA Real. See also CONTINO.

Conca de Barberà w (r p) **04 05 06** Small Catalan DO once purely a feeder of quality fruit to large enterprises now has some excellent wineries, inc the biodynamic ESCODA-SANAHUJA. Top TORRES wines Grans Muralles and Milmanda both produced in this DO.

Condado de Haza Rib del D r ★★→★★★ **03 04 05** Pure, oak-aged Tinto Fino from PESQUERA, Alejandro Fernández's 1988-founded second winery.

Consejo Regulador Organization for the control, promotion, and defence of a DO.

Contino, Viñedos del R Ala r res ★★★★ **04 05** First single-v'yd of RIOJA (1973) and a subsidiary of CVNE, makes exceptional long-lasting reds with scrupulous attention. Gd balsamic Graciano, a fine example of the variety for the curious, RESERVA and impressive VIÑA del Olivo (**04 05**)

Costers del Segre S r w p sp ★★→★★★ **03 04 05** 06 Smallish area around city of Lleida (Lérida) of which little is heard though it has some excellent producers. Initially known purely for the modern, fruity wines and vivacious CAVA of CODORNÍU-owned Raimat. Top producers: CASTELL DEL REMEI, CÉRVOLES, TOMÁS CUSINÉ and VINYA L'HEREU DE SERÓ.

Criado y embotellado por... Spanish for "Grown and bottled by..."

Crianza Literally "nursing"; the ageing of wine. New or unaged wine is *sin crianza* or JOVEN. Reds labelled *crianza* must be at least 2 yrs old (with 1 yr in oak, in some areas 6 mths) and must not be released before the third yr. See RESERVA.

Cusiné, Tomás Cos del S r ★★★ **04 05** 06 The former motor of CASTELL DEL REMEI and CELLER CÉRVOLES on his own since 2003. Two wines: modern, upbeat Vilosell (Tempranillo/Cab/ Merlot/Grenache/Syrah) and oakier, intense Geol.

DO, Denominación de Origen Official wine region.

DOCa, Denominación de Origen Calificada Classification for wines of the highest quality; so far only RIOJA (since 1991) and PRIORATO (DOQ – the Catalan equivalent – since 2002) benefit.

Empordà-Ampurdán r w p ★→★★ **04 05 06** Small, fashionable DO nr French border, not far from the celebrated El Bulli restaurant. Best wineries are CASTILLO DE PERELADA, Oliver Conti and Pere Guardiola; the curious will be tempted by the playful and experimental Espelt, growing any number of varieties though with variable results. Stick to the reds.

Enate Somontano r w p res ★★★ **04 05 06** 07 Best producer in SOMONTANO with gd DYA Gewurz and barrel-fermented Chard, gd if somewhat overpowering Syrah, but round, satisfyingly balanced, mature Cab/Merlot reserva Especial.

Escoda-Sanahuja Conca de Barbera r ★★★ **04 05** 06 Passionate producers of biodynamic wines. Coll de Sabater is hillside Merlot and Cab Fr; La Llopetera is pure Pinot; and Les Paradetes is Sumoll with a little Garnacha and Cariñena.

Espumoso Sparkling (but see CAVA).

Finca Farm (See under name – eg ALLENDE, FINCA.)

Fondillon Traditional Alicante wine, made from ripe Monastrell grapes matured in oak for long periods. Made in small quantities by GUTIERREZ DE LA VEGA.

Freixenet, Cavas Pen w sp ★★→★★★ Huge CAVA firm owned by the Ferrer family. Arch-rival of similarly enormous CODORNÍU; much more dynamic albeit less interesting. Best known for frosted black-bottled Cordón Negro and standard Carta Nevada. Strongly supported by advertising. Dull still wines – Ash Tree Estate. Also controls Castellblanch, Conde de Caralt, and Segura Viudas.

Galicia Rainy, northwestern corner of Spain producing some of Spain's best whites (see RÍAS BAIXAS, MONTERREI, RIBEIRO and VALDEORRAS). Reds, often made of the Mencía grape are best drunk locally and chilled, or avoided.

Generoso Apéritif or dessert wine rich in alcohol.

Gramona Pen r w dr sw res ★★→★★★ Sizeable family firm making wide range of wines. Gd DYA Gewurz, CAVA, esp spicy Xarel-lo dominated Celler Batlle. Sw wines inc icewines and impressive Chard/Sauv Gra a Gra Blanco Dulce.

Gran Reserva, GR See RESERVA.

Guelbenzu, Bodegas r res ★★→★★★ 04 05 06 Historic, ex-NAVARRA DO family enterprise now VDT Ribera del Queiles with estates in Navarra (Cascante) and Aragón (La Lombana) specializing in stylish reds: upfront fruits-of-the-forest Garnacha multiblend Vierlas, Tempranillo/Cab/Merlot French-oaked Azul, intense Graciano-predominant La Lombana, deep cedary Cab/Merlot Evo, and fine elegant super-*cuvée* Lautus. Also in Chile.

Gutiérrez de la Vega, Bodegas Alicante r w res ★★→★★★ 02 05 06 Small estate founded by opera-loving former general in 1978. Expanding range all branded CASTA DIVA with excellent, fragrant sweet whites made from Moscatel. Best is Cosecha Miel and Monte Diva. Historic Monastrell sweet red, FONDILLON.

Hacienda Monasterio, Bodegas Rib del D r res ★★→★★★ 06 Peter Sisseck's involvement since 1990 has resulted in excellent Tinto Fino/Cab/Merlot blends. Currently a delicious, expressively fruity Tinto, approachable CRIANZA, and elegantly round, complex RESERVA.

Haro Spiritual and historic centre of the RIOJA Alta. Though growing, still infinitely more charming and intimate than commercial capital Logroño; and home to LÓPEZ DE HEREDIA, MUGA, BODEGAS LA RIOJA ALTA, among others.

Huerta de Albalá V de T Cadiz r ★★→★★★ 06 Ambitious new (2006) estate in foothills of Sierra de Grazalema, blending Syrah, Merlot, Cab Sauv and local Tintilla de Rota. V. promising, small-production Taberner No 1 with dense fruit and expressive French oak; gd Taberner. Barba Azul is introductory label.

Inurrieta, Bodega Nav r p w res ★★→★★★ 04 05 06 Hi-tech estate nr Falces. Gd French-oaked Norte Cab/Merlot and lively DYA Mediodía Rosado. Top wine: Altos de Inurrieta. Promising production of Graciano and experiments with other varieties not yet permitted by DO.

Jaro, Bodegas y Viñedos del Rib del D r res ★→★★★ 04 05 06 Founded in 2000 by a member of the Osborne (sherry) family. Best: intense, mineral Chafandín (**05**), seriously expensive, opulent, black-fruit-scented Sed de Caná (**04**).

Joven (vino) Young unoaked wine. Also see CRIANZA.

Jumilla r (w p) ★→★★★ 04 05 06 Arid, apparently unpromising DO in mountains N of Murcia, now discovered by ambitious modern winemakers. Best known for dark, fragrant Monastrell. Also gd Tempranillo, Merlot, Cab, Syrah and now Petit Verdot. Wines do not generally age gracefully so drink within 2 or 3 yrs. Many gd producers: Agapito Rico, CASA CASTILLO, Casa de la Ermita, Juan Gil, Luzón, and Valle del Carche.

Juvé & Camps Pen w sp ★★★ 04 05 Family firm making top-quality CAVA from free-run juice. RESERVA de la Familia is the stalwart, with top-end GR (**03**) and Milesimé Chard GR (**02**).

León, Jean Pen r w res ★★★ 99 03 04 05 Small firm; TORRES-owned since 1995. Gd oaky Chards; expressive Merlot (04); and high-priced super-*cuvée* Zemis (**03**).

López de Heredia R Alt r w (p) dr sw res ★★→★★★★ 81 85 87 88 89 95 96 98 99 01 02 Picturesque, old-established family BODEGA in HARO that still ferments everything in wood and oak-ages in old casks. Graceful, plummy Cubillo, medium-intense Bosconia, and lighter, ripe *Tondonia*. Fascinating Rosado is always released with 10 yrs of age. Don't miss the whites.

Málaga Once-famous DO now all but vanished in the face of rocketing real-estate values. One large, super-commercial firm remains – with wide range of styles: Málaga Virgen. Winemaking has been revived here by former young Turk

TELMO RODRÍGUEZ with a clear, subtle, sweet white ***Molino Real Moscatel***.

Mallorca Small, pricey producers continue to flourish; maybe it's the influence of the film stars who spend summers here. Best: Anima Negra, tiny Sa Vinya de Can Servera, Hereus de Ribas and Son Bordils. Stick to reds, usually a blend of traditional varieties (Mantonegro, Callet, Fogoneu) plus Cab, Syrah and Merlot. Whites (usually native Prensal plus Chard or Malvasía) less gd.

La Mancha r w ★→★★ 01 02 03 04 05 06 07 Vast demarcated region N and NE of VALDEPEÑAS. The area has long been striving to improve its reds, which are mainly Cencibel-based (Tempranillo). Best producers are the relatively small Centro Españolas (with an excellent Tempranillo/Merlot), giant Vinícola de CASTILLA and Vinícola de Tomelloso.

Marqués de Cáceres, Bodegas R Alt r p w res ★★★ 01 04 05 06 Gd, reliable, commercial RIOJAS made by modern French methods.

Marqués de Griñón Dominio de Valdepusa r w ★★★ 04 05 Enterprising nobleman Carlos Falcó, a graduate of UC Davis, has been one of Spain's pioneering wine personalities. The first Spaniard to cultivate Syrah and Petit Verdot, introduce drip irrigation and a scientific approach to v'yd management on his estate nr Toledo. His varietals, which also include Cab, are savoury, worthwhile and v. concentrated – try the v. approachable Summa blend first. Top *cuvée* Emeritus is excellent but v. pricey. Confusingly, the Griñón name also appears on a cheap Rioja from BERBERANA – a leftover from an old distribution deal.

Marqués de Monistrol, Bodegas Pen p r sp d r sw res ★→★★ Old BODEGA now owned by BODEGAS UNIDAS. Gd reliable CAVA; but once lively modern PENEDÈS reds no longer so lively.

Marqués de Murrieta R Alt r p w res ★★★→★★★★ 98 02 03 04 05 Historic BODEGA at Ygay nr Logroño, growing all its own grapes and making intense RESERVA reds. Most famous for its magnificent CASTILLO DE YGAY. Best value is the dense, flavoursome RESERVA with excellent acid balance; most striking is the intense, modern premium red Dalmau. See also PAZO DE BARRANTES.

Marqués de Riscal R Ala & Rueda r (p) w dr ★★★ 01 02 03 04 05 Don't be put off by the exhibitionist hotel by Frank Gehry of Guggenheim Bilbao fame. Serious, historic and always experimental winery. Gd light reds and a powerful black Barón de Chirel RESERVA made with some Cab Sauv. Also mature, ripe, pure Tempranillo Selección Gehry. A pioneer in RUEDA (since 1972) making gd fragrant DYA Sauv Bl and lively Verdejo/Viura blend.

Marqués de Vargas, Bodegas R Ala ★★★ 01 02 Relative newcomer (1989) making v.gd well-balanced old-style wines: a RESERVA (**02**), RESERVA Privada (**01**), and limited-production Hacienda Pradolagar RESERVA Especial.

Mas d'en Gil Pri r ★★★→★★★★ 04 05 06 Small estate in Calonge, Gerona, making fresh, spicy, herbal Viognier/Roussanne/Marsanne Clos d'Agón Blanc and delicious modern, deeply flavoured Cab/Syrah/Merlot/Cab Fr Clos d'Agón Negre as well as lesser seen Clos Valmaña duo.

Mas Martinet Pri r ★★★→★★★★ 01 02 03 04 05 Boutique PRIORATO pioneer, producer of excellent Clos Martinet. Second wine Martinet Bru.

Mauro, Bodegas r 01 03 04 05 06 Young BODEGA in Tudela del Duero making gd, reliable non-DO/VDT reds. Mauro now with a touch of Syrah; best is pricey Old-World-meets-New, complex VENDIMIA Seleccionada (**03**) though "top *cuvée*" is

---

It's the grapes, stupid

Spanish consumers have always confused oak with quality, and wine makers have obliged. Newcomer regions routinely start by overdoing oak and extraction. Wait until they calm down and let their grapes shine through.

actually the powerful Terreus (03). Sister winery Maurodos, in TORO.

Miguel Merino, Bodegas R Alt r ★★ Enthusiast's tiny BRIONES BODEGA with flavoursome traditional wines, eg GR 2000.

Monterrei w ★→★★★ DYA Small but growing DO in Ourense, SC GALICIA, making interesting, full-flavoured aromatic whites from Treixadura, Godello, and Doña Blanca, showing there is more to Galicia than Albariño. Best is Gargalo.

Montilla-Moriles w sw ★→★★★ Medium sized DO in S Córdoba once best known for unfortified fino styles but now concentrating on dark, unctuous, often bittersweet dessert wines made from PX (Pedro Ximénez). Until recently TORO ALBALÁ was virtually the only player, but Alvear and Pérez Barquero are now also serious.

Montsant r ★→★★★ 04 05 06 Small newish DO (since 2001) encircled by PRIORATO. Its best wines are big, dense, minerally, and made from the same varieties – but often have an astringent edge, hold their alcohol and age less gracefully because of quite different soils. Pioneering Celler de Capçanes makes the most approachable wines; also try Agrícola Falset-Marçà, Cellers Capafons-Ossó, Celler Masroig and Joan D'Aguera.

Muga, Bodegas R Alt r (w sp) res ★★★→★★★★★ 98 00 01 03 04 05 Family firm in HARO, known for some of RIOJA's most spectacular and balanced reds. Gd barrel-fermented DYA Viura reminiscent of burgundy; reds finely crafted and highly aromatic. Best are wonderfully fragrant GR Prado Enea (98 00); warm, full and long-lasting Torre Muga; expressive and complex Aro; and dense, rich, structured, full-flavoured Seleccíon Especial.

Navajas, Bodegas R Alt r w res ★★→★★★ 01 03 04 05 06 Unpretentious family firm in picturesque Navarrete making young, fruity reds and fine CRIANZAS.

Navarra r p (w) ★★→★★★ 01 02 03 04 05 06 07 Extensive DO east of RIOJA. Once known for rosé, most of its BODEGAS now produce v.gd mid-priced Tempranillo/Cab Sauv blends that are often livelier than those of its more illustrious neighbour RIOJA – despite often higher yields. Unlike RIOJA, no outstanding estates; up-and-coming names include Tandem, Garcia Burgos, Asension. Navarra has been trying to improve its rosés and regain lost ground. Best producers: Alzaña, Artazu, CHIVITE, INURRIETA, Nekeas, the much improved Ochoa, Otazu, PAGO de Cirsus, Sarría.

Ordoñez, Grupo US-based Spaniard, importing top Spanish wines. Investor in Spanish v'yds, specializing in reinvigorating forgotten regions. See CALATAYUD.

Pago A v'yd or area of limited size. The term now has legal status, eg, DO Dominio de Valdepusa (see MARQUÉS DE GRIÑÓN). Should be a guarantee of the highest quality, but so far inconsistent.

Pago de Carraovejas Rib del D r res ★★★ 01 03 04 05 06 Founded in 1988, quality still excellent and still unable to satisfy demand. Top *cuvée* v.gd Cuesta de las Liebres (03).

Pago, Vinos de Category, introduced in 2002, that confers DO status to 6 individual high-quality estates. The first 4 were in CASTILLA-LA MANCHA: Dehesa del Carrizal, Dominio de Valdepusa (see MARQUÉS DE GRIÑÓN), Manuel Manzeneque's Finca Elez, and the Sánchez Militerno family's Pago Guijoso. A further 2 were declared in NAVARRA: Prado Irache and PAGO de Arinzano. PAGO status can deliver eye-watering prices, but quality is inconsistent.

Palacio de Fefiñanes Rías Baixas w dr ★★★★ DYA Oldest BODEGA of RÍAS BAIXAS – first bottled wines in 1927. Standard *cuvée* remains one of the finest, most delicate pure ALBARIÑOS. Two superior styles: creamy but light-of-touch barrel-fermented version 1583 (the year the winery was founded); and a super-fragrant, pricey, lees-aged, mandarin-orange scented III.

Palacios, Alvaro Pri r ★★→★★★★ 02 03 04 05 06 Best known for excessively priced and short-lived L'Ermita, the outstanding Finca Dofí is the one to cellar and Les Terrasses the one to drink. See also PALACIOS REMONDO.

Palacios, Rafael Vald w ★★★ Small estate producing exceptional wine from old Godello vines in the Bibei Valley. Rafael – ALVARO PALACIOS' younger brother – is devoted to white wines. Two distinct styles, both DYA: As Sortes is intense, toasty, with striking citric and white peach elements as well as high acidity, a v. fine expression of Godello; Louro do Bolo is easier and fresher.

Palacios Remondo, Bodegas RB w r ★★→★★★ 04 05 06 Following phenomenal success in PRIORATO, ÁLVARO PALACIOS has revved up his family winery (founded 1945). Interesting DYA oaked white Plácet with citric, peach and fennel characters; and in red, super-fruity, unoaked La Vendimia; organic, smoky, red-fruit-flavoured La Montesa; and big, mulberry-flavoured, Garnacha-dominated Propiedad.

Parxet Alella w p sp ★★→★★★ DYA Small CAVA producer valiantly competing with real-estate agents from Barcelona. Zesty CAVA styles include *cuvée* 21, excellent Brut Nature, fragrant Titiana Pinot N and expensive dessert version *Cuvée* Dessert; best known for refreshing, off-dry Pansa Blanca and still white Marqués de Alella. Concentrated Tionio is from outpost in RIBERA DEL DUERO.

Pazo de Barrantes Rías Baixas w ★★★ DYA ALBARIÑO RÍAS BAIXAS; estate owned by MARQUÉS DE MURRIETA. Firm, delicate, exotic, but vintages variable.

Pazo de Señorans Rías Baixas w dr ★★★ DYA Exceptionally fragrant wines from a BODEGA considered a benchmark of the DO by virtue of its finesse.

Penedès r w sp ★→★★★ 98 99 00 01 02 03 04 05 06 Demarcated region W of Barcelona best known for CAVA and TORRES, has had trouble establishing an identity. Styles range from light citric whites to highly oaked reds. Other gd producers inc: ALBET I NOYA, Can Ràfols dels Caus, GRAMONA, JEAN LEÓN.

Pérez Pascuas Hermanos Rib del D r res ★★★ 00 01 05 Family BODEGA founded 1980 and run by 3 brothers. Opulent, approachable Viña Pedrosa CRIANZA, tighter, more intense Cepa Gavilán and mature but balanced VIÑA Pedrosa GR.

Pesquera Rib del D r ★★★ 94 95 04 05 Alejandro Fernández was the creative force behind modern RIBERA DEL DUERO and is still a benchmark. Satisfying CRIANZA and excellent, mature, well-seasoned Janus for those who can afford the price tag. See also CONDADO DE HAZA.

Pingus, Dominio de Rib del D r ★★★★ 01 03 04 05 Danish Peter Sisseck's 5-ha estate has since 1995 wowed the v. few who can afford its tiny productions. Pingus is intense, fresh and opulent with minerally black fruits, fresh herbal overtones, subtle interlaced oak and tannins; second label *Flor de Pingus* is more floral fruit.

Plá i Llevant de Mallorca r w dr ★→★★★ 04 05 06 07 11 wineries comprise this tiny DO in MALLORCA. Aromatic but not particularly modern whites and intense, spicy reds. Best: Toni Gelabert, Jaime Mesquida, and Vins Can Majoral.

Priorato/Priorat br r ★★★→★★★★ 01 04 05 06 DO enclave of Tarragona, once known for rancio and the co-op's tarry Garnacha/Cariñena reds. The early new wave – CLOS MOGADOR, MAS MARTINET and ÁLVARO PALACIOS – are still best, producing balanced, minerally reds; with over 70 wineries now, results are uneven and prices stellar. Other gd producers: Celler Val-Llach, Cims de Porrera, Clos Erasmus, Clos de l'Obac, Mas Perinet, *Torres*, Viñedos de Íthaca.

Remírez de Ganuza, Bodegas Fernando R Ala w dr r res ★★→★★★ 02 03 04 Boutique winery making somewhat austere Tempranillo-based wines.

Remelluri, La Granja R Ala w dr r res ★★★ 99 03 Small mountainous estate making pedigree RIOJA reds from its own 105 ha. Best is the *delicate, graceful Reserva* (03), other wines increasingly old-fashioned; though DYA white made from 6 different varieties remains as intriguing as it was originally.

Reserva Gd-quality wine matured for long periods. Red *reservas* must spend at least 1 yr in cask and 2 yrs in bottle; *gran reservas*, 2 yrs in cask and 3 yrs in bottle. Thereafter, many continue to mature for years. Many producers now eschew *reserva*/CRIANZA regulations, preferring clear vintage declaration.

Rías Baixas w ★★→★★★★ DYA GALICIAN DO increasing in global reputation and production. Founded on the ALBARIÑO variety, in 5 sub-zones: – Val do Salnés, O Rosal, Condado do Tea, Soutomaior and Ribera do Ulla. Quality and style inconsistent, but the best are outstanding: Adegas Galegas, As Laxas, Castro Baroña, Fillaboa, Coto de Xiabre, GERARDO MÉNDEZ, new kid on the block Viña Nora, PALACIO DE FEFIÑANES, PAZO DE BARRANTES, QUINTA do Lobelle, Santiago Ruiz, Terras Gauda, La Val and Valdamor.

Ribeiro w r ★→★★★ DYA GALICIAN DO in western Ourense. Spain's favourite wine, after Rioja. Whites are low in alcohol and acidity, made from Treixadura, Torrontés, Godello, Loureiro, Lado. Top producers VIÑA MEIN, Lagar do Merens. Also speciality sweet wine style, Tostado.

Ribera del Duero Rib del D ★★→★★★★ 01 02 03 04 05 06 07 Fashionable, still-expanding DO east of Valladolid with almost 250 wineries. Tinto Fino (Tempranillo) holds sway. Some Cab and Merlot. A handful of outstanding wineries; but there is much confusion of styles and quality is inconsistent. The big worry is the plan for new motorway right across the middle. Best producers: AALTO, ALIÓN, ASTRALES, CONDADO DE HAZA, HACIENDA MONASTERIO, Jaro, Pago de los Capellanes, PAGO DE CARRAOVEJAS, PÉREZ PASCUAS HERMANOS, PESQUERA, PINGUS, VALBUENA, VEGA SICILIA. See also VDT ABADÍA RETUERTA and MAURO. Others to look for: Balbás, Bohórquez, Dehesa de los Canónigos, O. Fournier, Hermanos Sastre, Tinio (see PARXET), and Vallebueno.

Rioja r p w sp ★→★★★★ 64 70 75 78 81 82 85 89 91 92 94 95 96 98 99 00 01 02 03 04 05 Situated in the Ebro Valley, Spain's best-known wine region now consists of 1,200 wineries. Once known for its graceful, long-lived reds, today it is hard to say what is typical. A few, notably LA RIOJA ALTA and LÓPEZ DE HEREDIA, continue to make exceptional, old-fashioned styles; there are the pedigree traditionalists such as CONTINO, MARQUÉS DE MURRIETA, MARQUÉS DE RISCAL, MARQUÉS DE VARGAS, PALACIOS REMONDO, REMELLURI, RODA, and San Vicente; others, such as FINCA ALLENDE, ARTADI, BAI GORRI and MUGA, are producing more energetic styles. There are also many brands: the vigorous but basic VIÑA Pomal of formerly revered Bilbaínas; dark, often jarring Campo Viejo, the once spectacular CVNE, the smooth reds of Faustino, the eminently quaffable Bordón from Franco Españolas, the ever-reliable MARQUÉS DE CÁCERES; and VALDEMAR. There are lots of small, workmanlike producers who simply make gd wine, such as the very drinkable, sometimes modern Luis Cañas, NAVAJAS, Sierra Cantabria, and Tobía. With sales of Rioja whites decreasing, in 2007 the DO authorized Chard, Sauv Bl and Verdejo.

Rioja Alta, Bodegas La R Alt r w (p) dr (sw) res ★★★ 98 99 00 01 Discover traditional RIOJA. Delicate, mature, in a range of styles. Alberdi is light and cedary with overtones of tobacco and redcurrants; Arana is similar but with rather more body and depth; *Ardanza* riper, a touch spicier but still v. elegant; the excellent, tangy, vanilla-edged GR 904 and the fine, multilayered GR 890.

Roda, Bodegas R Alt r ★★★★ 00 01' 03 04' 05' Ambitious young (1994) BODEGA with impressive cellar making serious modern RESERVA reds from low-yield

---

Rioja reborn?

Could Rioja be coming into its own again? Having looked a bit, well, dowdy for a few years the best producers there seem to be steering a middle course between aggressive modernity (which we're sick of) and faded frailty (which still looks too faded). Soft, silky tannins go well with modern foods: try them when you would normally choose a white wine.

Tempranillo, backed by strong R&D. Roda, Roda I and Cirsión.

Rueda br w ★★→★★★ DYA Small but ever-growing DO S of Valladolid with Spain's most modern, crisp DYA whites, made from indigenous Verdejo, Sauv Bl, Viura and blends thereof. Barrel-fermented versions remain fashionable. Best Alvarez y Diez, **Belondrade**, MARQUÉS DE RISCAL, Naia, Ossian, José Pariente Palacio de Bornos, Javier Sanz, SITIOS DE BODEGA, Veracruz and Vinos Sanz.

Sandoval, Finca Manchuela ★★★ 02 03 05 Victor de la Serna is back on form: his Finca Sandoval (Syrah/Monastrell/Bobal) a wine of impressive balance, dark fruits, soft tannins, herbal notes and gd acid; second wine Salia (Syrah/Garnacha/Bobal) altogether simpler and half the price.

Sitios de Bodega ★★→★★★ Fifth-generation winemaker Ricardo Sanz and siblings left father Antonio Sanz's Palacio de Bornos to set up their own winery in 2005. Excellent DYA RUEDA whites (Con Class and Palacio de Menade). Associated Bodegas Terna, from its base in La Seca, produces interesting, high-quality reds from other regions, inc Spain's first sweet Tempranillo – La Dolce Tita VDT.

Somontano ★★→★★★ 04 05 06 07 Cool-climate DO in Pyrenean foothills E of Zaragoza that has failed to fulfil expectations. Whites should be more expressive and reds are often over-extracted, over-oaked, without sufficient maturity of fruit or any binding regional character. Much use of international varietals also reduces regionality. Opt for Merlot, Gewurz or Chard. Best producers: ENATE, VIÑAS DEL VERO, recently acquired by Gonzalez Byass; interesting newcomers inc the space-age Bodegas Irius and Bodegas Laus.

Tares, Dominio de El B r w ★★★ 04 05 06 Up-and-coming producer whose dark, spicy purple-scented Bembibre and Cepas Viejas prove what can be done with Mencía. Sister winery VDT Dominio dos Tares makes a range of wines from the interesting black Prieto Picudo variety: the simple Estay, more muscular Leione and big, spicy Cumal.

Telmo Rodríguez, Compañía de Vinos r w ★★→★★★ Gifted oenologist Telmo Rodríguez, formerly of REMELLURI, makes and sources a wide range of excellent DO wines from all over Spain inc MÁLAGA (Molina Real Moscatels), RIOJA (Lanzaga and Matallana), RUEDA (Basa), TORO (Dehesa Gago, Gago, and PAGO la Jara), and **Valdeorras** (DYA Gaba do Xil Godello).

Toro r ★★→★★★ 03 04 05 06 Unstoppably fashionable DO in Zamora province, W of Valladolid. Forty wineries now do their best with the local Tinta de Toro (acclimatized Tempranillo). Some continue to be clumsy, rustic, and over-alcoholic. But others are boldly expressive; try Maurodos – with fresh, black-fruit-scented Prima and glorious old-vine San Román as well as VEGA SICILIA-owned Pintia. Also recommended: Dom Magrez Espagne, PAGO la Jara from TELMO RODRÍGUEZ, QUINTA de la Quietud, and Sobreño.

Toro Albalá Mont-M ★★→★★★ Antonio Sánchez is known for his eccentric wine museum and his remarkable old PXs. Labelled Don PX and made from sun

---

Tempranillo: moving on, moving out
Across Spain this grape variety masquerades under a number of aliases, from Tinto Fino to Cencibel. Tempranillo *is* Spain, and yet it's increasingly Australia as well: lots of Australian winemakers see climatic parallels between the two countries, and are busy planting it, aided and abetted by advisers such as Dr Richard Smart, the flying vine doctor. That's perhaps one explanation for the rise in interest in Spain itself for Mencía and Monastrell – both of which are troublesome, with the risk of brisk tannins and chewy fruit. But the reward is that they are individual wines, the goal of the independent winemaker today.

dried grapes, barrique-aged for a minimum of 25 yrs. Black, replete with flavours of molasses, treacle, figs, they age indefinitely. Current vintage is 1979, yet the 1910 was only recently released. Look out for young, unaged amber-coloured DYA Dulce de Pasas, tasting of liquid raisins and apricots.

Torres, Miguel Pen r w p dr s/sw res ★★→★★★★ 01 02 03 04 05 06 07 Spain's best-known family wine firm with properties in Chile and California, continues to make some of the best: ever-reliable DYA CATALUNYA VIÑA Sol and grapey VIÑA Esmeralda and PENEDÈS Sauv/Parellada *Fransola*. Best reds include: rich CATALUNYA GranSangre de Toro, fine PENEDÈS Cabernet Mas la Plana balanced, old-style RESERVA Real (**02**). Its CONCA DE BARBERÀ duo (*Milmanda* – one of Spain's finest Chards – and Grans Muralles multiblend) are stunning, and JEAN LEÓN has v.gd offerings, too. The range continues to expand with a workmanlike offering from RIBERA DEL DUERO (Celeste), gd PRIORATO (Salmos) and wines now on horizon from RIOJA. Impressive new BODEGA opened 2008. Miguel Torres (father) speaks of retirement, and both son and daughter work in the business. But will the indefatigable Miguel ever really retire?

Unidas, Bodegas Umbrella organization controlling MARQUÉS DE MONISTROL, and the BERBERANA brand, as well as workmanlike RIOJA Marqués de la Concordia and Durius from RIBERA DEL DUERO. Controls MARQUÉS DE GRIÑÓN Rioja brand.

Utiel-Requena U-R r p (w) ★→★★ Satellite region of VALENCIA attempting to forge its own identity by virtue of excellent Bobal variety but hampered by its size (more than 40,000 ha), which has made it primarily a feeder for the industrial requirements of nearby VALENCIA. To watch.

Valbuena Rib del D r ★★★★ 99 00 01 02 04 Made with the same grapes (Tinto Fino, Cab, Merlot, Malbec and a touch of Albillo) as VEGA SICILIA but sold when just 5 yrs old. Best at about 10 yrs; some prefer it to its elder brother. For a more modern take see ALIÓN.

Valdemar, Bodegas R Ala r p w res ★→★★★ 01 02 03 06 The Martínez-Bujanda family, from their base in Oyón, have been making wines since 1890 and continue to offer a wide choice of *reliable Rioja* styles on all levels.

Valdeorras w r ★→★★★ DYA GALICIAN DO in NW Ourense fighting off its co-op-inspired image by virtue of its DYA Godello: a highly aromatic and nationally fashionable variety, also grown in nearby BIERZO. Best producers: Adegas A Coroa, RAFAEL PALACIOS, A Tapada and TELMO RODRÍGUEZ.

Valdepeñas La M r (w) ★→★★ 01 02 04 05 06 07 Big DO nr Andalucían border. V.gd-value lookalike RIOJA reds, made primarily from Cencibel grape. Young reds often over-extracted and its old RESERVAS just old. One producer shines, Félix Solís: VIÑA Albali brand offers full-flavoured reds at bargain prices.

Valencia r w ★ 00 01 03 04 05 06 07 Big DO of some 18,000 ha exporting vast quantities (71% of production) of clean and drinkable table wine. Also primary source of sweet, budget, Spanish Moscatel.

Vega Sicilia Rib del D r res ★★★★ 60 62 68 70 81 87 89 90 91 94 95 96 Spain's most famous and historic BODEGA, whose costly, sought-after wines are still matured v. slowly in oak and best at 12–15 yrs. Wines are deep in colour, with aromatic cedarwood nose, intense and complex in flavour, finishing long. Dense, un-vintaged RESERVA Especial can be spectacular but commands mega prices. See also VALBUENA, ALIÓN, Pintia in TORO, and Oremus Tokaji (Hungary).

Vendimia Vintage.

Viña Literally, a v'yd. But wines such as Tondonia (LÓPEZ DE HEREDIA) are not necessarily made only with grapes from the v'yd named.

Viña Meín Ribeiro ★★★ Small estate, in a gradually emerging DO, making two DYA exceptional whites of same name: one in steel and one barrel-fermented; both from some 7 local varieties.

Viñas del Vero Som w p r res ★★→★★★ 03 04 05 06 07 SOMONTANO estate. Gd commercial varietals. Mature, toasty Cab/Merlot/Gran Vos Reserva is worth a look, as is Secastilla. Now owned by Gonzalez Byass

Vino común/corriente Ordinary wine.

Vino de la Tierra, VDT Table wine of superior quality made in a demarcated region without DO. Covering immense geographical possibilities, this category inc many prestigious producers who are non-DO by choice in order to be freer from often inflexible regulation and produce the varieties they want.

Vinya L'Hereu de Seró Cos del S r ★★★ **03 05** 14-ha estate since 2002 making 2 intensely flavoured wines from Syrah, Cab and Merlot. Richest and most complex with extra maturity is Flor de Grealó (**03 04**) whereas younger brother Petit Grealó (03 04 05) is considerably tighter.

Vivanco, Dinasti ★ R Alt Major family-run commercial BODEGA in BRIONES with simple juicy wines and an astonishing wine museum.

Portugal

Recent vintages

2008 Almost uniformly excellent; BAIRRADA and ALENTEJO particularly promising. Low yields, a long ripening period and ideal harvest conditions produced great fruit intensity, balance and aroma.

2007 Low yields, a cool summer and dry autumn produced aromatic whites and well-balanced reds with round tannins.

2006 Another very warm, dry summer. Expect forward reds with soft, ripe fruit and whites with less acidity than usual.

2005 An extraordinarily dry summer, especially in the south, produced powerful reds; the DOURO's finely balanced reds shine.

2004 A cool, wet summer but a glorious Sept and Oct. Well-balanced reds.

2003 Hot summer produced soft, ripe, early-maturing wines, especially in the south. Best BAIRRADA for a decade.

2002 Challenging vintage with heavy rain during picking. Better in the south.

Adega A cellar or winery.

Alenquer Est r w ★★→★★★ **02 03'** 04 05 06 07 08 Sheltered DOC making gd reds just N of Lisbon. Estate wines from Pancas, QUINTA da Setencostas (see CASA SANTOS LIMA) and MONTE D'OIRO.

Alentejo r (w) ★→★★★★ **00' 01 02** 03 04' 05 06 07 08' Huge, southerly DOC divided into sub-regions with own DOCS: BORBA, REDONDO, REGUENGOS, PORTALEGRE, Evora, Granja-Amareleja, Vidigueira, and Moura. A reliably dry climate makes rich, ripe reds: key international varieties include Syrah and Alicante Bouschet. Gd whites from Antâo Vaz, blended with ARINTO and Roupeiro. Established players CARMO, CARTUXA, CORTES DE CIMA, ESPORÃO, Herdade de MOUCHÃO, MOURO, JOÃO RAMOS and Zambujeiro have potency and style. Of the new guard, HERDADES DA MALHADINHA NOVA, dos Grous and Dona Maria impress. Names to watch inc Herdades São Miguel and Paco de Camoes and QUINTA do Centro. Best co-ops are at BORBA, REDONDO, and REGUENGOS.

Algarve r w ★→★★ Southern coast DOCS include Lagos, Tavira, Lagoa, and Portimão. Mostly quaffers. Crooner Cliff Richard's Vida Nova and new Onda Nova Syrah, also QUINTA do Morgado are more serious.

Aliança, Caves Bair r w sp res ★★→★★★ Large firm with 4 estates in BAIRRADA, inc QUINTA das Bacelada making gd reds and classic-method sparkling. Also interests in BEIRAS (Figueira de Castelo Rodrigo), ALENTEJO (QUINTA da Terrugem), DÃO (QUINTA da Garrida), and the DOURO (QUATRO VENTOS).

Alorna, Quinta de Ribatejo r w ★→★★ DYA Appealingly zippy, ARINTO-driven whites, creamy rosé and gd reds from indigenous and international varieties.

Altano Douro r w DYA Well-made range from Symington. Look out for Reserva and organic red Altano Biologica (07).

Alvarinho With LOUREIRO, best white grape in VINHO VERDE, making fragrant, attractive wines. Known as Albariño in neighbouring Galicia.

Ameal, Quinta do w ★★★ DYA One of best VINHOS VERDES. 100% LOUREIRO; Escolha is oaked.

Aragonez Successful red grape (Spain's Tempranillo) in ALENTEJO for varietal wines. See TINTA RORIZ.

Arinto White grape. Best from C and S Portugal have Ries-like citrus acidity – adds zip to blends and produces fragrant, crisp, dry white wines.

Arruda r w ★ DOC in ESTREMADURA with large co-op.

Aveleda, Quinta da w ★→★★ DYA Reliable estate-grown VINHO VERDE made by the Guedes family whose portfolio inc acclaimed brands CASAL GARCÍA (VINHO VERDE), Charamba (DOURO) and Follies (VINHO VERDE and BAIRRADA) with national and international varieties.

Azevedo, Quinta do w ★★ DYA Superior LOUREIRO-led VINHO VERDE from SOGRAPE.

Bacalhoa, Quinta da Set r res ★★★ 01 02 03 04 05 Estate nr SETÚBAL. Elegant, midweight Cab Sauv/Merlot blend made by BACALHOA VINHOS. Fleshier Palácio de Bacalhoa has more Merlot. Gd new white B'x blend with ALVARINHO.

Bacalhoa Vinhos Set Est Alen w r sp sw ★★→★★★ Formerly JP Vinhos. Broad but accomplished range inc BACALHOA, JP, Serras de Azeitão, Só, Catarina, Cova da Ursa and traditional SETÚBAL Moscatel (SETÚBAL/Terras do Sado), Loridos (ESTREMADURA), TINTO DA ANFORA and now QUINTA DO CARMO (ALENTEJO).

Bairrada r w p sp ★→★★★ 97' 98 99 00 01 03 04 05' 06 07 08' DOC in C Portugal. Reputation for astringent reds from challenging Baga grape being laid to rest since law permits different grape varieties, though DOC Bairrada Classico stipulates min 50% Baga. Best wines reward keeping: eg CASA DE SAIMA, LUÍS PATO, Caves SÃO JOÃO will keep for yrs. Most white sparkling but see LUIS PATO.

Barca Velha Douro r res ★★★★ 52 54 58 64 65 66' 78 81 82 85 91' 95' 99 00 Portugal's most famous red, made by FERREIRA in v. limited quantities. Intense, complex with a deep bouquet, it forged the DOURO's reputation for stellar wines. Distinguished, traditional style (aged several yrs before release). Second wine known as Reserva Ferreirinha.

Beira Interior ★ Isolated DOC nr Spain's border. Huge potential from old and elevated v'yds; QUINTA do Cardo impresses.

Beiras ★→★★ VINHO REGIONAL covering DÃO, BAIRRADA, and granite ranges of central Portugal. Used by innovative producers such as Luis and Filipa PATO.

Borba Alen r ★→★★ ALENTEJO sub-region small DOC with limestone and schist soils; also well-managed go-ahead co-op.

Branco White.

Brejoeira, Palácio de w ★★ DYA Prestigious ALVARINHO VINHO VERDE; increasing competition from estates around Monção and Melgaço.

Bright Brothers ★★ DYA Well-made everyday wines from Portugal-based Australian flying-winemaker inc Hearty Red and aluminium-bottled Bright Pink, White and Red range. See also FIUZA & BRIGHT.

Buçaco Beiras r w (p) res ★★★★ (r) 53 59 62 63 70 78 82 85 89 92 Legendary speciality of the Palace Hotel at Buçaco, north of Coimbra, not seen elsewhere. An experience worth the journey.

Bucelas Est w ★★ DYA Tiny DOC north of Lisbon focused on whites from the ARINTO grape (known as "Lisbon Hock" in 19th-century England). QUINTAS da Romeira and da Murta make tangy, racy wines.

Cabriz, Quinta de r w ★★→★★★ 03 04 05 Owned by DÃO SUL; fruity and fresh well-priced wines.

Cadaval, Casa Ribatejo r w ★★ **02 03 05'** 06 Gd varietal reds esp TRINCADEIRA, Pinot N, Cab Sauv, and Merlot. Great-value Padre Pedro and stunning red Reserva, Marquês de Cadaval.

Campolargo Bair r w **04 05 06** 07 Large estate, until 2004 sold grapes to ALIANÇA. Interesting reds from Baga, Cab Sauv, Petit Verdot, and Pinot N. Early days but B'x varietals promising, esp Diga Petit Verdot.

Carcavelos Est br sw ★★★ NV Minute DOC west of Lisbon. Rare sweet apéritif or dessert wines average 19% alcohol and resemble honeyed MADEIRA.

Carmo, Quinta do Alen r w res ★★→★★★ 01 03 04 05 50-ha once co-owned by Rothschilds (Lafite), now 100% owned by BACALHÔA VINHOS. Fresh white and polished reds with Cab Sauv have B'x restraint. Second wine: Dom Martinho.

Cartuxa, Herdade de Alen r w ★★→★★★ (r) 200-ha estate nr Evora. Famous flagship Pera Manca red (**94 95 97 98 01** 03) is big but pricey; white impressive too. Also Foral de Evora, Cerca Nova, EA.

Carvalhais, Quinta dos Dão r w p sp ★★★ (r) **01 03 04** 05 06 (w) DYA SOGRAPE's principal DÃO brand: eponymous single-estate wines inc flagship Unico, also volume Duque de Viseu marque from estate and bought-in grapes.

Casal Branco, Quinta de Ribatejo r w ★★ Large family estate. Gd entry-level Cork Grove blends local CASTELÃO and FERNÃO PIRES with others. Old-vine, local fruit struts pedigree in Falcoaria range, esp Reserva red (**01 03** 04' 05').

Casal García w ★★ DYA Big-selling off-dry VINHO VERDE, made at AVELEDA.

Casal Mendes w p ★ DYA The VINHO VERDE from ALIANÇA.

Castelão Planted throughout S Portugal, esp in TERRAS DO SADO. Nicknamed PERIQUITA. Firm-flavoured, raspberryish reds develop a figgish, tar-like quality.

Chocapalha, Quinta de Est r w p ★★→★★★ (r) **03 04** 05 06 Fine modern estate. TOURIGA NACIONAL and TINTA RORIZ underpin rich reds, Cab Sauv is sinewy. New ARINTO-driven unoaked white joins fine oaked Chard/native white blend.

Chryseia Douro r ★★★→★★★★ **01' 03'** 04 05' 06 V. successful partnership of Bordeaux's Bruno Prats and the Symington family; dense yet elegant wine from port varieties now sourced from dedicated v'yd, QUINTA de Perdiz. V.gd second wine *Post Scriptum* (04 05' 06).

Churchill Estates Douro r p Gd reds from port shipper Churchill, esp single-estate QUINTA da Gricha (**03 04** 05 06). New super-floral rosé is 100% TOURIGA NACIONAL.

Colares r w ★★ Small DOC on the sandy coast W of Lisbon. Unique heritage of ungrafted Ramisco vines saved from developers by Fundação Oriente and Stanley Ho charities. Traditional, tannic reds; decent Malvaseía-based whites.

Consumo (vinho) Ordinary (wine).

Cortes de Cima Alen r w ★★★ (r) **02 03 04** 05 06 (w) DYA Southerly estate nr Vidigueira owned by Danish family. produces heady, fruit-driven reds from ARAGONEZ, TRINCADEIRA, TOURIGA NACIONAL, Syrah (inc flagship Incognito) and PERIQUITA. Second label: Chaminé.

Côtto, Quinta do Douro r res ★★→★★★ r **99 01** 03 05 06 Pioneer of Douro table wines and screwcaps. Flagship is *Grande Escolha* (**95 00 01** 07).

Crasto, Quinta do Douro r w ★★→★★★★ **00 01 02 03'** 04 05' 06 w DYA Excellent lush varietal wines (TOURIGA NACIONAL, TINTA RORIZ) and blends; res and 2 superb single-v'yd wines made only in top vintages from low-yielding old vines: Vinha da Ponte (98 00' 01 03 04) and María Theresa (**00' 03' 05'** 06) Also Port. Xisto is joint-venture red with Jean-Michel Cazes from Bordeaux.

Dão r w ★★→★★★ **00' 01 02 03'** 04 05 06 Established DOC in central Portugal. Once dominated by co-ops, investment by quality-focused producers large and small has improved consistency and calibre. Established names: SOGRAPE (CARVALHAIS) and QUINTAS MAIAS, PELLADA, ROQUES and SAES. Rising stars: DÃO SUL, Casa da Insua, QUINTA da Vegia and Casa da Mouraz (organic).

Structured, elegant reds and substantial, dry whites come into own with food.

Dão Sul Dão r w ★★→★★★★ Dynamic DÃO-based venture. Impressive range with international appeal inc QUINTAS CABRIZ, SANTAR and dos Grilos (DÃO), Sá de Baixo and das Tecedeiras (DOURO), do Encontro (BAIRRADA), do Gradil (ESTREMADURA) and Herdade Monte da Cal (ALENTEJO). Innovative multi-regional Portuguese and cross-border blends: Homenagen (with LUÍS PATO); Four Cs; Dourat (DOURO TOURIGA NACIONAL/Spanish Garnacha) and Pião (DÃO TOURIGA NACIONAL/Italian Nebbiolo).

DFJ Vinhos r w ★→★★★ DYA Huge range, mostly from RIBATEJO and ESTREMADURA. Premium label Grand'Arte also sourced from the DOURO, DÃO and ALENTEJO. Volume fruity, entry-level brands inc Pink Elephant rosé, Segada (r w) Manta Preta (r) and Bela Fonte.

DOC, Denominacão de Origem Controlada Demarcated wine region controlled by a Regional Commission. See also IPR, VINHO REGIONAL.

Doce (vinho) Sweet (wine).

Douro r w ★★→★★★★ 97 00' 01 02 03' 04' 05' 06 Famous for port and now world-class wines inc sumptuous powerful red wines, the best with sinewy, mineral core and surprisingly fine whites of Burgundian depth and complexity. Look for BARCA VELHA, CHRYSEIA, CRASTO, NIEPOORT, POIERA, VALE DONA MARIA, VALE MEÃO and WINE & SOUL. Names to watch: Conceito, QUINTA da Romaneira, QUINTA do Noval.

Duas Quintas Douro ★★★ r 01 02 03' 04 05 06 w DYA Gd red from port shipper Ramos Pinto. V.gd Reserva and outstanding but expensive Reserva Especial.

Esporão, Herdade do Alen w r ★★→★★★★ 02 03 04 05 06 Quality-driven big estate (600 ha). Monte Velho, Alandra and Vinha da Defesa brands showcase ALENTEJO's ripe fruit. Quatro Castas, single-varietal range, Esporão Reservas, Private Selection (r w), GARRAFEIRA and flagship Torre do Esporão offer depth and complexity. Recently acquired QUINTA das Murças in the Douro – 2008 is its maiden vintage.

Espumante Sparkling.

Estremadura ★→★★★★ VINHO REGIONAL on west coast. Gd, inexpensive wines from local estates and co-ops; handful of ambitious premium wines: CHOCAPALHA, MONTE D'OIRO. DOCS: ALENQUER, ARRUDA, BUCELAS, CARCAVELOS, COLARES, Encostas d'Aire, Obidos, TORRES VEDRAS.

Falua Rib r w p DYA JOÃO PORTUGAL RAMOS' state-of-the-art venture. Gd entry-level Tagus Creek range of indigenous and international blends, plus more upmarket Tâmara and Conde de Vimioso.

Fernão Pires White grape making aromatic, ripe-flavoured, slightly spicy whites in RIBATEJO. (Known as María Gomes in BAIRRADA.)

Ferreira Douro r ★→★★★★ SOGRAPE-owned port shipper making gd to v.gd DOURO wines under Casa Ferreirinha labels: Esteva, Vinha Grande, QUINTA de Leda, Reserva Especial Ferreirinha, and BARCA VELHA.

Fiuza & Bright Ribatejo r w ★★ DYA Joint venture between Peter Bright (BRIGHT BROTHERS) and the Fiuza family. Gd inexpensive Chard, Merlot, Cab Sauv and Portuguese varietals.

Fonseca, José María da Est r w p dr sw sp res ★★→★★★ Historic family-owned estate. Oldest producer of SETÚBAL fortified Moscatel, but also go-ahead brands LANCERS and PERIQUITA. Dynamic sixth generation remains at vanguard: no-expense-spared winery, Colecção Privada label for experimentation, revamped Periquita range inc white, rosé and reserva. Other brands: Montado, Terras Altas (DÃO), QUINTA de Camarate, Pasmados, Privada Domingos Soares Franco and flagships: FSF, Domini/Domini Plus (DOURO) and Hexagon.

Gaivosa, Quinta de Douro r w ★★★→★★★★ 01 03 04 05' 06 Leading estate nr

Régua. Characterful, concentrated old-vine red varietals and blends from different terroir inc Abandonado, QUINTA das Caldas, Vinha de Lordelo, Reserva Pessoal and Vale da Raposa. Gd white: Branco da Gaivosa.

Garrafeira Label term: merchant's "private reserve", aged for minimum of 2 yrs in cask and one in bottle, often much longer.

Gazela w ★★ DYA Reliable VINHO VERDE made at Barcelos by SOGRAPE.

Generoso Apéritif or dessert wine rich in alcohol.

IPR, Indicação de Proveniência Regulamentada Portugal's second tier of wine regions: Lafões, Biscoitos, Pico, Graciosa. See also DOC.

Lagoalva, Quinta da Ribatejo r w ★★ 02 03 05' Go-ahead RIBATEJO estate; judicious use of Portuguese and international varieties. Second label: Monte da Casta.

Lancers p w sp ★ Semi-sweet (semi-sparkling) rosé, widely shipped to the US by JOSÉ MARÍA DA FONSECA; new low-alcohol version. Also Lancers ESPUMANTE Brut.

Lavadores de Feitoria Douro r w 18 small quality-conscious estates blending fruit from across the 3 Douro regions. Principal labels: Meruge, Três Bagos.

Loureiro Best VINHO VERDE grape variety after ALVARINHO: crisp, fragrant whites.

Madeira br dr sw ★★→★★★★★ Portugal's Atlantic island: makes unfortified reds and whites (Terras Madeirenses VINHO REGIONAL and Madeirense DOC), mostly for the local market; whites from Verdelho on the up. See Madeira section for famous fortified dessert and apéritif wines.

Maias, Quinta das Dão ★★ r 01 03 04 05' 06 w DYA Sister of QUINTA ROQUES. Benchmark Jaen and DÃO's only Verdelho; Flor das Maias 2005 is showy maiden TOURIGA NACIONAL-dominated blend.

Malhadinha Nova, Herdade da Alen r w p ★★★ 03' 04 05 06 Young vines but mature, quality-focused approach: v.gd big spicy reds and rich, oak-aged white from ALENTEJO's deep south.

Mateus Rosé p sp (w) ★ World's best-selling, medium-dry, lightly carbonated rosé table wine, from SOGRAPE. Original is Portuguese but international versions hail from France (Shiraz) and Spain (Tempranillo).

Messias r w ★→★★★ Large BAIRRADA-based firm; interests in DOURO (inc port). Old-school reds best.

Minho River between N Portugal and Spain and VINHO REGIONAL; QUINTA do Covela (organic) impresses.

Monte d'Oiro, Quinta do Est r w ★★★→★★★★ 01 03 04' 05 José Bento dos Santos' flagships are outstanding Rhône-style Syrah/Viognier reds and Madrigal, Viognier. Gd second wine: Vinha da Nora. Chapoutier (see France) consults on winemaking and biodynamics and is new joint-venture partner for exciting Bento & Chapoutier Ex Aequo Syrah/TOURIGA NACIONAL (06 07).

Mouchão, Herdade de Alen r res ★★★ 99 00 01 03' Leading traditional estate. Intense, fragrant wines realize full potential of the Alicante Bouschet grape. Flagship Tonel 3–4, exceptional yrs only, has complexity and persistence. Ponte das Canas (05, 06), new premium release, blends Alicante Bouschet with TOURIGAS NACIONAL and Franca and Shiraz; Dom Rafael gd value.

Mouro, Quinta do Alen r ★★★→★★★★ 98 99 00 04' Fabulous old-style reds, mostly ALENTEJO grapes. Dry farmed, low yields, concentrated, supple wines. O Mouro made with NIEPOORT.

Murganheira, Caves ★ Largest producer of ESPUMANTE. Now owns RAPOSEIRA.

Niepoort Douro r w ★★★→★★★★ Family port shipper making exceptional, exciting DOURO wines. Core range is aromatic Tiara (w), Vertente (r), Redoma (r w p, inc w reserve, p) 01 03 04 05' 06'; Robustus (r) 04 05, sinewy Batuta (r) 01' 03 04 05' and sumptuous Charme (r) 02 04 05' 06. Drink Me is approachable red, Projectos is experimental range, and also collaborates with PELLADA (Dado), SOALHEIRO (Girasol and Primeiras Vinhas) and MOURO (O Mouro).

Palmela Terras do Sado r w ★→★★★ CASTELÃO-focused DOC (see PEGOS CLAROS) can be long-lived.

Pancas, Quinta de Est r w res ★★→★★★ (r) **01 03** 05' (w) DYA Prestigious estate nr ALENQUER. Owner since 2006, Companhia das Quintas has overhauled range. Flagship is Grande Escolha followed by Reserva range: TOURIGA NACIONAL and Cabernet Sauvignon and Selecção do Enólogo.

Passadouro, Quinta do Douro r w Superb Reserva comes from single parcel of older vines (**03** 04' 05' 06). Recently acquired v'yds to boost wine and port; new white and entry label "Passa" red.

Pato, Filipa r w sp sw LUÍS PATO's dynamic daughter producing exciting wines under eponymous and new Vinhos Doidos labels from BAIRRADA and DÃO inc Ensaios, FLP (dessert wine made with father), "3b" fizz, "Lokal" (r) and Bossa and Nossa (w).

Pato, Luís Bair r w sp sw ★★→★★★ **95' 97 99 00 01'** 03' 04 05' 06 *Exquisite single-v'yd Baga*: Vinhas Barrio, Pan, Barrosa and flagship QUINTA do Ribeirinho Pé Franco (ungrafted vines). QUINTA do Ribeirinho 1st Choice is a Baga/TOURIGA NACIONAL blend. João Pato, early-drinking TOURIGA NACIONAL, now joined by single v'yd TOURIGA from Vinha Formal. Shows equal flair with whites (Vinhas Formal and Velhas) and sparkling wines. Uses BEIRAS classification.

Pegos Claros r **01 03** 04 05' Benchmark PALMELA CASTELÃO, foot-trodden and aged minimum 3 yrs before release.

Pellada, Quinta de Dão r w 04 05' 06 Owned with SAES by leading DÃO light Alvaro de Castro. Intense not dense reds inc flagship Pape (TOURIGA NACIONAL from Passarela v'yd with Pellada Baga) and Carrocel, 100% TOURIGA. Primus is old-vine, textured white.

Periquita The nickname for the CASTELÃO grape and successful brand name for JOSÉ MARÍA DA FONSECA CASTELÃO.

Poeira, Quinta do Douro r w ★★★★ (02 **03'** 04' 05' 06) Elegant flagship red from north-facing slopes from Jorge Moreira, QUINTA de la ROSA'S winemaker. Second wine J re-named Pó de Poeira and joined by Pó ALVARINHO.

Ponte de Lima, Cooperativa de r w sp ★ Impressive top tier "Seleccionado" VINHO VERDE inc bone-dry red.

Portal, Quinta do Douro r w p ★★★ **01 03** 04 05' 06 New plantings and winery reaping dividends at former Sandeman estate; satisfying red wines inc Grande Reserva and port.

Portalegre Alen r w ★→★★★ Northernmost, elevated ALENTEJO DOC with granite soils producing ageworthy, balanced reds at MOUCHAO, Monte de Penha and go-ahead local co-op.

Quatro Ventos, Quinta dos Douro r **03 04 05** 06 Well-made reds from estate belonging to Caves ALIANÇA; Bordeaux oenologist Pascal Chatonnet consults.

Quinta Estate (see under name, eg PORTAL, QUINTA DO).

Ramos, João Portugal Alen r w DYA Well-made ALENTEJO range from Loios and Vila Santa to premium single-varietal range and blends: QUINTA da Viçosa and v.gd Marquês de Borba. Reserva (**03 05**). Duorum is new DOURO joint venture.

Raposeira Douro w sp ★★ Well-known fizz with native varieties and Chard made by classic method at Lamego.

Real Companhia Velha Douro r w p sw ★★→★★★ r **00' 01'** 02 **03** 04 05 Historic port company with extensive premium table wine v'yds across the DOURO inc Chard, Sauv Bl, Semillon. Brands: flagship Evel Grande Reserva, Porca de Murça, QUINTA dos Aciprestes, QUINTA de Cidro, Grantom, sw Granjó from Sem.

Redondo Alen r w ★ DOC in heart of ALENTEJO with well-managed co-op.

Reguengos Alen r (w) res ★→★★★ Important DOC nr Spanish border with granite and schist outcrops. Includes JOSÉ DE SOUSA and ESPORÃO estates, plus large co-op for gd reds.

PORTUGAL

Ribatejo Rib r w Engine room of gd-value wines from CASTELÃO, TRINCADEIRA and FERNÃO PIRES raising its game with switch to poorer soils and introduction of Portugal's best red varieties, TOURIGA NACIONAL, TINTA RORIZ and international grapes: Cab Sauv, Syrah, Pinot N, Chard, and Sauv Bl. Gd results already at, eg Pinhal da Torre and FALUA. Sub-regions: Almeirim, Cartaxo, Coruche, Chamusca, Tomar, Santarem. Also VINHO REGIONAL Ribatejano.

Roques, Quinta dos Dão r w ★★→★★★ (r) **01 03' 04** 05 06 V.gd estate for ageworthy reds, esp flagship GARRAFEIRA blend and white Encruzado. Varietal wines from TOURIGA NACIONAL, TINTA RORIZ, Tinta Cão, and Alfrocheiro Preto. Gd value entry-level Correio label.

Roriz, Quinta de Douro r ★★★ **02 03'** 04 05' 06 One of the great QUINTAS of the DOURO. Fine reds (and vintage port) now made at QUINTA DO VALE DONA MARIA. Second wine: Prazo de Roriz.

Rosa, Quinta de la Douro r w p ★★★ **04** 05' 06 Firm, rich estate reds, esp Reserva, also QUINTA das Bandeiras and Passagem (in partnership with winemaker, Jorge Moreira) from warmer DOURO Superior.

Rosado Rosé.

Saes, Quinta de Dão r w ★★★→★★★★ **01** 02 03 Alvaro Castro's other v'yd (see PELLADA), producing equally characterful wines inc Dado – see NIEPOORT.

Saima, Casa de Bair r (w DYA) sp p ★★★ **01 02 03'** 04 05' 06 Small, traditional estate; big tannic reds (esp GARRAFEIRAS **90' 91 95' 97' 01**) and *fresh whites*.

Santar, Casa de Dão r ★★★ **00** 01 02 03 04 Well-established estate now linked to DÃO SUL making welcome comeback. Structured reds; Burgundian approach paying dividends with Reserva and Condessa whites.

Santos Lima, Casa Est r w p ★★ DYA New-wave family-owned ALENQUER company. Diverse, well-made range reflects extensive v'yds at QUINTAS da Boavista/das Setencostas, de Bons-Ventos, da Espiga, das Amoras, do Vale Perdido, do Espírito Santo and do Figo.

São João, Caves Bair ★★→★★★ sp r **95 97 00 01** 03 w DYA Small, traditional firm for v.gd old-fashioned wines. Reds can age for decades. BAIRRADA: *Frei João*. DÃO: Porta dos Cavaleiros. Poço do Lobo: well-structured Cab Sauv.

Seco Dry.

Setúbal Set br (r w) sw (dr) ★★★ Tiny DOC south of the River Tagus. Fortified dessert wines made predominantly from the Moscatel (Muscat) grape inc rare red Moscatel Roxo. Main producers: JOSÉ MARIA DA FONSECA and BACALHOA VINHOS.

Sezim, Casa de w ★★ DYA Beautiful estate making v.gd VINHO VERDE.

Soalheiro, Quinta de w ALVARINHO specialist making revelatory VINHO VERDE inc old-vine Primeiras Vinhas (with NIEPOORT), barrel-fermented Reserva and ESPUMANTE. Warm, 50km inland Melgaço location brings structure, concentration and texture.

Sogrape ★→★★★★ Portugal's largest wine concern, making VINHO VERDE (AZEVEDO, GAZELA, Morgadio da Torre), DÃO (CARVALHAIS), ALENTEJO (Herdade do Peso), MATEUS ROSÉ, and owner of FERREIRA, Sandeman, Offley port and BARCA VELHA in the DOURO. Approachable multi-regional brands Grão Vasco, Pena de Pato and Callabriga from VINHO VERDE, DOURO, DÃO, ALENTEJO. Also making wine in Spain, Argentina, New Zealand and Chile.

Sousa, José de Alen r res ★★→★★★ **03 04** 05 Small ALENTEJO firm acquired by JOSÉ MARÍA DA FONSECA; wines now slightly lighter in style but flagship Mayor is solid, foot-trodden red fermented in clay amphoras and aged in oak.

Teodósio, Caves Dom Ribatejo r w ★→★★ Large RIBATEJO producer. Brands include Serradayres and Casaleiro; top wines from QUINTA de São João Batista. Also making wine in DÃO and Palmela.

Terras do Sado up-and-coming VINHO REGIONAL covering sandy plains around

Sado Estuary. Best producers: BACALHOA VINHOS, Cooperativa de Pegões, Casa Ermelinda Freitas (QUINTA da Mimosa and Leo d'Honor). Names to watch: Soberanas, Herdade da Comporta, QUINTAS de Catralvos and Alcube.

Tinta Roriz Major port grape (alias Tempranillo) making v.gd DOURO wines. Known as ARAGONEZ in ALENTEJO.

Tinto Red.

Tinto da Anfora Alen r ★★→★★★ **03 04 05'** 06 Reliable red from BACALHOA VINHOS. Impressively rich Grande Escolha.

Touriga Nacional Top red grape used for port and DOURO table wines; now increasingly elsewhere, esp DÃO, ALENTEJO, and ESTREMADURA.

Trás-os-Montes DOC with sub-regions Chaves, Valpaços and Planalto Mirandês. Reds and whites from international grape varieties grown in the DOURO. VINHO REGIONAL Transmontano.

Trincadeira V.gd red grape in ALENTEJO for spicy wines. Known as Tinta Amarela in the DOURO.

Vale Dona Maria, Quinta do Douro ★★★ r w **01 02 03'** 04' 05' 06 Cristiano van Zeller's highly regarded QUINTA. *V.gd plush yet elegant reds* inc CV, Casa Casal de Loivos and new VZ. Also gd port.

Vale Meão, Quinta do Douro r ★★★★ **01' 03** 04 05' 06 Once the source of BARCA VELHA. Impressively structured wines typified by high percentage of TOURIGA NACIONAL and warm easterly location. V.gd second wine: Meandro.

Vallado ★★★ r w (r) **02 03'** 04 05' 06 (w) DYA Family-owned DOURO estate; v.gd-value sweet fruited varietals and blends, esp Reserve; new, old-vine red raises bar.

Vidigueira Alen w r ★→★★★ Hot ALENTEJO DOC. Best producer: *Cortes de Cima*. On the up, respected consultant Paulo Laureano's eponymous wines.

Vinho Regional Larger provincial wine regions, with same status as French Vin de Pays: Acores, ALENTEJANO, ALGARVE, BEIRAS, Duriense, ESTREMADURA, MINHO, RIBATEJANO, Terras Madeirenses, TERRAS DO SADO, Transmontano. More leeway for experimentation than DOC. See also DOC, IPR.

Vinho Verde w r ★→★★★ (w) p ★ (r) DOC between river DOURO and north frontier, for "green wines": made from high-acidity grapes. Large brands such as Gazela, Gatão and Casal Garcia usually varietal blend with added carbon dioxide – DYA. Best have natural spritz and are single QUINTA, single-varietal ageworthy wines. Look out for ALVARINHO from Monçâo and Melgaço (eg ADEGA de Monção and QUINTA SOALHEIRO) and LOUREIRO (eg AMEAL) from Lima.

Wine & Soul Douro r w (r Pintas) **02 03'** 04' 05' 06 (w Guru) **05** 06' 07 Rich, imposing wines (and port) from renowned winemaking couple Sandra Tavares and Jorge Serôdio Borges. Second wine: Pintas Character (r).

Port, Sherry & Madeira

These great fortified wines – all the product of centuries of ingenious problem-solving in the winery and all of them wines of startling originality – are still managing to startle us. A pink port has met with, shall we say, mixed reactions; age-dated white ports are less controversial but just as innovative. Madeira, a more placid place altogether than the Douro, is concentrating on new plantings and putting Colheita in 50cl bottles. No, don't faint. And sherry? Well, it's still attracting investors; or was, until the credit crunch. In the past decade, Alvaro Domecq, Tradicion, Rey Fernando de Castilla, Valdivia, and Equipa Navazos have all hit the headlines with exceptional sherries, and there are more openings promised. Of course, being wines from a solera system, none of these businesses has started with completely new wine, but rather from an expert selection of butts from pre-existing bodegas. Like the fairy story, there is great wine sleeping in the cathedral bodegas of Jerez ready to be awakened.

Anybody too old to want to admit their age will remember Rumasa, and its expropriation by the Spanish government 25 years ago. Well, Rumasa is back, in the guise of Nueva Rumasa, and is steadily acquiring brands again under the Garvey name, and is also buying wineries across Spain. What goes around comes around.

Recent port vintages

2007 Classic year, widely declared. Late but mild, dry vintage produced deep coloured, rich but well-balanced wines.

2006 A difficult year, yielding only a handful of single-quinta wines. Stars: Vesuvio, Roriz, Barros Quinta Galeira.

2005 Single-quinta year. Stars: Niepoort, Taylor de Vargellas, Dow da Senhora da Ribeira – iron fist in velvet glove.

2004 Also a single-quinta year. Stars: Pintas, Taylor de Vargellas Vinha Velha, Quinta de la Rosa – balanced, elegant wines.

2003 Classic vintage year. Hot, dry summer. Powerfully ripe, concentrated wines, universally declared. Drink from 2015/2020.

2001 Another single-quinta year. Stars: Noval Nacional, Fonseca do Panascal, do Vale Meão – wet year; relatively forward wines.

2000 Classic year. A very fine vintage, universally declared. Rich, well-balanced wines for the long term. Drink from 2015.

1999 Single-quinta year. Stars: Vesuvio, Taylor de Terra Feita, do Infantado – smallest vintage for decades; powerful.

1998 Single-quinta year. Stars: Dow da Senhora da Ribeira, Graham dos Malvedos, Cockburn dos Canais – bullish, firm wines.

1997 Classic year. Fine, potentially long-lasting wines with tannic backbone. Most shippers declared. Drink 2012 onward.

1996 Single-quinta year. Stars: Graham dos Malvedos, Warre da Cavadinha, Taylor de Vargellas – power and finesse.

1994 Classic year. Outstanding vintage with ripe, fleshy fruit disguising underlying structure at the outset. Universal declaration. Drink 2010–2030.

1992 Classic year. Favoured by a few (especially Taylor and Fonseca) over 91. Richer, more concentrated, a better year than 91. Drink 2008–2025.

1991 Classic year. Favoured by most shippers (especially Symingtons with Dow,

Graham, and Warre) over 92; classic, firm but a little lean in style. Drink now–2020.

1987 Classic year. Dense wines for drinking over the medium term, but only a handful of shippers declared. Drink now–2015.

1985 Classic year. Universal declaration, which looked good at the outset but has thrown up some disappointments in bottle. Now–2020 for the best wines.

1983 Classic year. Powerful wines with sinewy tannins. Most shippers declared. Now–2020.

1982 Classic year. Rather simple, early-maturing wines declared by a few shippers. Drink up.

1980 Classic year. Lovely fruit-driven wines, perfect to drink now and over the next 15 years. Most shippers declared.

1977 Classic year. Big, ripe wines declared by all the major shippers except Cockburn, Martinez, and Noval. Many evolved wines, drink soon.

Almacenista Sherry stockholder; owner of smallish bodega who sells sherries to shippers rather than on the open market. A number were acquired in 1990s and 2000s by non-Jerez investors. A few remain in JEREZ and EL PUERTO; still important to MANZANILLA production. Wines can be superb quality. LUSTAU offers wide Almacenista range in 80s. Almacenista suppliers named on label.

Alvaro Domecq ★★→★★★ One of the newer sherry bodegas. Created by DOMECQ family members to re-establish Domecq name in Jerez. Based on SOLERAS of Pilar Aranda, said to be the oldest bodega in JEREZ . Fine FINO La Janda. V.gd 1730 label wines, inc PALO CORTADO, OLOROSO. Best sherry vinegar to be found.

Alvear Largest producer of v.gd sherry-like apéritif and sweet wines in MONTILLA.

Andresen Family-owned port house making gd 20-yr-old TAWNY and COLHEITA (**1900' , 68, 82, 91**); first to register a white port with age indication (10-yr-old).

Barbadillo, Antonio ★★→★★★★ Largest of the SANLÚCAR sherry producers. Wide portfolio, inc Solear Manzanilla, Muy Fina FINO, austere Príncipe AMONTILLADO, Obispo Gascon PALO CORTADO, Cuco dry OLOROSO, Eva Cream. Notable for its MANZANILLA EN RAMA, with seasonal sacas. Superb Reliquía line of AMONTILLADO, v.gd PALO CORTADO, OLOROSO seco, and v.gd PX. Dominant producer of table wines with popular, lightweight (w) Castillo de San Diego.

Barbeito Dynamic producer of finely honed madeiras with no added caramel. Pioneers of robotic LAGARE for madeira, single-cask COLHEITAS, 20-yr-old and 30-yr-old MALVASIA and VERDELHO/BUAL blend ("vb"). Bright, citrus COLHEITAS (MALVASIA 2000) and stylish FRASQUEIRA (BOAL 82, VERDELHO 81) .

Barros Almeida Large port house with several brands (inc Feist, Feuerheerd, KOPKE) owned by Sogevinus: excellent 20-yr-old TAWNY and COLHEITAS (**78' 96'**); vintage ports on the up.

Barros e Sousa Traditional madeira producer. Tiny output of 100% CANTEIRO-aged wines inc rare vintages, gd 10-yr-old and unusual 5-yr-old Listrao blend.

Blandy Best-known name of the MADEIRA WINE COMPANY thanks to popular 3-yr-old "Duke" range; Duke of Clarence sports sharp new livery. Impressive inventory of aged wines yielding fine old vintages (eg BUAL 1964, VERDELHO 1977 and SERCIAL 1966). Recent innovations include COLHEITAS (MALMSEY 1990, 2001, BUAL 1993) Alvada, a moreish blend of BUAL and MALVASIA.

Borges, H M Family company. V.gd 10-yr-olds, stylish COLHEITAS (VERDELHO, BOAL and SERCIAL 1995, MALMSEY 1998) and vintages, esp SERCIAL 1979, BOAL 1977.

Bual (or Boal) Traditional Madeira grapes, making tangy, smoky, sweet wines; not as rich as MALMSEY.

Burmester Small port house owned by Sogevinus and behind innovative fruity and forward Gilbert's label. Best known for fine, soft, sweet 20- and 40-yr-old

TAWNY and COLHEITAS (1955', 1989); vintage improving.

Cálem Established Sogevinus-owned port house. Velhotes is the main brand; gd LBV. Fine reputation for COLHEITAS (94) and v.gd VINTAGE PORTS in 66' and 70'; returning to form (03' 05).

Canteiro Method of naturally cask-ageing the finest madeira in warehouses known as lodges. Creates subtler, more complex wines than ESTUFAGEM.

Churchill 82 85 91 94 97 00 03 Independent, family-owned port shipper founded in 1981. V.gd traditional LBV. Quinta da Gricha is the single-QUINTA port (01 04 05' 06). Benchmark aged white port and new 10-yr-old white.

Sherry styles

Manzanilla A pale, light dry sherry ; usually more delicate than a FINO. Matured in the humid, maritime conditions of SANLÚCAR DE BARRAMEDA (as opposed to the other towns of the "Sherry Triangle" (EL PUERTO DE SANTA MARÍA and JEREZ). Should be drunk cold and fresh. Deteriorates rapidly once opened (always refrigerate and buy half bottles where possible). Eg HEREDEROS DE ARGÜESO San León.

Manzanilla Pasada MANZANILLA aged longer than most; v. dry, complex. Eg HIDALGO-LA GITANA'S single v'yd MANZANILLA Pasada Pastrana.

Fino The lightest and driest of sherries; as with MANZANILLA has a minimum age of 3 yrs. Eg GONZÁLEZ-BYASS Tío Pepe. Drink cold and fresh.

Amontillado A FINO in which the layer of protective yeast, FLOR, which grows on top of the wine in barrel, has died, allowing the wine to oxidize and create a more powerful complexity, still with an echo of the original FLOR. Naturally dry. Eg VALDESPINO'S Tío Diego.

Oloroso Not aged under FLOR. Heavier and less brilliant when young, but matures to an intense richness and pungency. Naturally dry. Also sweetened with PEDRO XIMÉNEZ and sold as an oloroso dulce/sweet oloroso. Eg DOMECQ Río Viejo (dry), LUSTAU Old East India (sweet).

Palo Cortado V. fashionable among sherry fans. Traditionally, a wine that had lost its FLOR and become in style between AMONTILLADO and OLOROSO. Today, often blended to create the style, which has a "lactic" or "bitter butter" note. Dry, rich, complex – worth looking for. Eg BARBADILLO Reliquía and GUTIÉRREZ COLOSÍA.

Cream A blended sherry sweetened with grape must, PX, and/or MOSCATEL for an inexpensive, medium-sweet style. Unashamedly commercial. Eg HARVEY'S Bristol Cream, CROFT Pale Cream.

Pedro Ximénez, PX Raisined sweet, dark sherry from partly sun-dried Pedro Ximénez grapes (the grapes are mainly sourced from MONTILLA; the wine is made in the JEREZ DO). Concentrated, unctuous, decadent, and a bargain. The perfect thing to drink with ice cream. Overall, the world's sweetest wine. Eg REY FERNANDO DE CASTILLA Antique, EMILIO HIDALGO Santa Ana 1861.

Moscatel As with Pedro Ximénez grape, though it rarely reaches PX's level of concentration or richness. Eg LUSTAU Emilín.

Age-dated sherries Vintage-dated (in contrast to SOLERA-aged) sherries, verified by carbon dating. Applies only to AMONTILLADO, OLOROSO, PALO CORTADO, and PX. Exceptional quality at relatively low prices makes these among the fine-wine world's best bargains. 20-yr-old is called VOS (Very Old Sherry/Vinum Optimum Signatum); 30-yr-old is VORS (Very Old Rare Sherry/Vinum Optimum Rare Signatum). Also 12-yr-old and 15-yr old. Eg VOS WILLIAMS & HUMBERT Don Guido Solera Especial Oloroso (sweet); VORS GONZÁLEZ-BYASS AMONTILLADO del Duque.

Cockburn Owned by the US Fortune Brands, though SYMINGTON bought its assets in 2006. Popular Special Reserve RUBY. New-look 50cl bottles for white and age-dated TAWNY encourage experimentation. Dry house style for VINTAGE PORTS: **63 70 75 83' 91 94** 97 00 03' 07. Gd single-QUINTA wines from Quinta dos Canais (98 01' 05' 06 07).

Colheita Vintage-dated port or madeira of a single yr, cask-aged at least 7 yrs for port and 5 yrs for madeira. Bottling date shown on the label.

Cossart Gordon Top-quality label of the MADEIRA WINE COMPANY; drier style than BLANDY. Best known for the Good Company brand. Also 5-yr-old reserves, COLHEITAS (SERCIAL 1988, *Bual 1995*, MALVASIA 1995), old vintages (1977 Terrantez, 1908, 1958 BUAL).

Croft One of the oldest firms, estb 1588. Now part of FLADGATE, who reintroduced foot-treading for the much-improved 03 VINTAGE PORT. Vintages: **60' 63' 66 67 70 75 77 82 85 91 94** 00 03'. Lighter QUINTA da Roêda. Indulgence, Triple Crown and Distinction: most popular brands. "Pink" is pioneering rosé port served chilled or on ice; reactions have been varied.

Croft Jerez Sherries with strong British appeal; sweet Original Pale CREAM and drier Particular. Owned by GONZÁLEZ-BYASS.

Crusted Style of port usually blended from several vintages, bottled young and aged so it throws a deposit, or "crust", and needs decanting.

Delaforce Port shipper. Brand recently acquired by Real Companhia Velha from FLADGATE, which is still producing the ports. Curious and Ancient 20-yr-old TAWNY and COLHEITAS (**64 79 88**) are jewels; VINTAGE PORTS are improving: **63 66 70' 75 77 82 85 92' 94** 00 03. Single-QUINTA wines from Quinta da Corte.

Delgado, Zuleta ★★→★★★ Old (1774) SANLÚCAR firm, known for marvellous aged La Goya MANZANILLA PASADA.

Dios Baco ★→★★ Family-owned JEREZ bodega. V.gd Imperial VORS PALO CORTADO.

Domecq ★★→★★★★ Formerly great name in sherry, latterly tossed about in the corporate brand sales that penetrated even the cathedral-like silence of the bodegas of JEREZ. Now owned by OSBORNE. An exceptional range: the excellent La Ina FINO, Rio Viejo OLOROSO. Outstanding collection of VORS: AMONTILLADO 51-1A, *Sibarita Oloroso*, Capuchino PALO CORTADO, Venerable PX.

Douro Rising in Spain as the Duero, the river Douro flows through port country, lending its name to the region, which is divided into the Cima (Upper) Corgo and Douro Superior, home of the best ports, and the Baixo Corgo.

Dow Brand name of port house Silva & Cosens. Belongs to the SYMINGTON family; drier style than other producers in group (GOULD CAMPBELL, GRAHAM, QUARLES HARRIS, RORIZ, SMITH WOODHOUSE, VESÚVIO, WARRE). V.gd range, inc CRUSTED, 20- and 30-yr-old TAWNIES, single-QUINTAS Bomfim and, since 1998, v.g da Senhora da Ribeira; vintage: **63 66 70 72 75 77 80 83 85' 91 94** 97 00' 03 07.

Emilio Hildago ★★→★★★★ Small JEREZ bodega making exquisite Privilegio 1860 PALO CORTADO and v.gd Santa Ana PX. FINO Panesa is gd value.

En rama Sherry bottled from the butt without filtration or cold stabilization. Prized for its purity. Needs to be sold and drunk young, so it is not popular with many wine shops. BARBADILLO has bottlings labelled by the season: "*Saca de Primavera*" (Spring Extraction), and so on.

Equipo Navazos ★★★★ Impressive new sherry project started by a group of aficionados, originally seeking out butts to bottle privately. Has rapidly built reputation for the highest quality, as well as for its accuracy in giving the origin and bottling date.

Estufagem Bulk process of slowly heating, then cooling, cheaper madeiras to attain characteristic scorched-earth tang; less subtle than CANTEIRO process.

Ferreira Leading Portuguese-owned shipper belonging to Sogrape. Bestselling brand in Portugal. Well-structured, rich, spicy Reserve (Don Antónia), 10- and

20-yr-old TAWNIES, Quinta do Porto and *Duque de Bragança*. Early-maturing vintages : **66 70 75 77 78 80 82 83 85 87 90 91 94** 95' 97 00 03 07.

Fladgate See TAYLOR'S.

Flor Spanish word for "flower": refers to the layer of *saccharomyces* yeasts that grow atop FINO/MANZANILLA sherry in barrel, keeping oxidation at bay and changing the wine's flavour, making it aromatic and pungent. When the *flor* dies, the wines that are aged further without it, become AMONTILLADO.

Fonseca Guimaraens Port shipper; belongs to FLADGATE. Bin 27 and organic Terra Prima reserve RUBIES and sumptuous yet structured vintages (the latter now only estate grapes) among best: Fonseca **63' 66' 70 75 77' 80 83 85'** 92 94' 97 00' 03'. Impressive, earlier-maturing Fonseca Guimaraens and single-QUINTA Panascal made when no classic declaration.

Forrester See OFFLEY.

Frasqueira The official name for "vintage" madeira from a single yr. Exceptionally intense wines bottled after at least 20 yrs in wood. Date of bottling compulsory; the longer in cask, the more concentrated and complex .

Garvey ★→★★★ Famous old sherry shipper in JEREZ. Classic San Patricio FINO, Tío Guillermo AMONTILLADO, and Ochavico OLOROSO. Also age-dated 1780 line. Owned by Nueva Rumasa, the holding company of the Ruiz-Mateos family. The first Rumasa had extensive holdings in JEREZ until expropriated by the government in 1983. The Garvey Group also owns SANDEMAN, VALDIVIA.

González-Byass ★→★★★★ Large family bodega with the most famous and one of the best FINOS: *Tío Pepe*. Other brands include La Concha AMONTILLADO, Elegante FINO, 1847 sweet OLOROSO. Age-dated line includes Del Duque AMONTILLADO, Matúsalem OLOROSO, Apóstoles PALO CORTADO and the outstanding, ultra-rich Noé PX. Extensive collection of vintages, and one of the few bodegas to sell vintage sherries. Growing business in quality table wines from JEREZ region, as well as large interests in brandy.

Gould Campbell Port shipper belonging to SYMINGTON. Gd-value, full-bodied VINTAGE PORTS 70 **77' 80 83 85' 91 94** 97 00 03' 07.

Gracia Hermanos Mont-M Firm within the same group as PÉREZ BARQUERO and Compañia Vinícola del Sur making good-quality MONTILLAS. Labels include María del Valle FINO and Dulce Viejo PX.

Graham One of port's greatest names, belonging to SYMINGTON. V.gd range from Six Grapes RESERVE RUBY, LBV and TAWNY (RESERVE) to excellent yr-aged TAWNIES and some of richest, sweetest VINTAGE PORTS **63 66 70' 75 77' 80 83' 85' 91'** 94 97 00' 03' 07. V.gd single-QUINTA vintage: dos Malvedos.

Gran Cruz The single biggest port brand. Mostly light, inexpensive TAWNIES.

Guita, La ★→★★★ *Especially fine manzanilla pasada* made by Pérez Marín in SANLÚCAR. Also owns Gil Luque label for other sherries. Both acquired by Grupo Estevez, owner of VALDESPINO.

Gutiérrez Colosía ★★★ Family-owned and run former ALMACENISTA on the Guadalete R. in EL PUERTO with a consistent range. Excellent old PALO CORTADO.

Hartley & Gibson See VALDESPINO.

Harvey's ★→★★ Major sherry producer, famed for Bristol CREAM (medium-sweet) the icon of creams, and Club AMONTILLADO. Owned by Beam Global.

Henriques, Justino The largest madeira shipper belonging, along with GRAN CRUZ ports, to Martiniquaise. Gd 10-yr-old, fruity, forward COLHEITA (1995, 1996) and vintage – eg 1934 VERDELHO, 1978 Terrantez.

Henriques & Henriques Independent madeira shipper. Rich, well-structured wines. Outstanding 10- and 15-yr-olds; v. fine RESERVES, vintage and SOLERA wines, inc SERCIAL 1964, Terrantez 1976, MALVASIA 1954, BUAL 1954 and 1980, Century MALMSEY-SOLERA 1900. Innovative extra-dry apéritif Monte Seco and Tinta Negra Mole COLHEITA Single Harvest Medium Rich Madeira 1998. John

> **We want it fresh**
> Why don't all sherry producers allow us to know when the stuff was
> bottled? The key to MANZANILLA and FINO is drinking it fresh, and that
> means being able to read the bottling code on the label. Come on, guys:
> make it clear.

Cossart, chairman and industry spokesman, died in 2008.

Herederos de Argüeso ★★ →★★★ MANZANILLA specialist in SANLÚCAR with v.gd *San Leon* and Las Medallas; and the desirable VOS AMONTILLADO Viejo. .

Hidalgo, La Gitana ★★★→★★★★ Old (1792) family sherry firm in SANLÚCAR fronted by the indefatigable Javier Hidalgo. Flagship is the excellent pale *manzanilla La Gitana*; also fine OLOROSO, lovely PALO CORTADOS, and single vyd, v. fine Pastrana MANZANILLA PASADA .

Jerez de la Frontera Centre of sherry industry, between Cádiz and Seville. "Sherry" is a corruption of the name, pronounced "hereth". In French, Xérès.

Jordões, Casal dos Organic port producers: decent LBV and vintage wines.

Kopke The oldest port house, founded in 1638. Now belongs to BARROS ALMEIDA. Mostly early-maturing, fair-quality vintage wines, but some v.gd (**83 85** 87 89 91 94 97 00 03 04 05' 07); v.fine 40-yr-old TAWNY and COLHEITAS (**66 80' 87 89**).

Krohn Port shipper; gd 20 & 30-yr-old TAWNY and excellent COLHEITAS (**61' 64 82 83'**), some dating back to 1800s.

Lagare Shallow granite "paddling pool" in which port is trodden by foot – or, these days, increasingly by robot.

LBV (Late Bottled Vintage) Port from a single yr kept in wood for twice as long as VINTAGE PORT (about 5 yrs) so ready to drink on release; much larger volumes, robustly fruity but much less powerful and complex than vintage. No need to decant unless unfiltered wine that can age for 10 yrs or more (CHURCHILL, FERREIRA, NIEPOORT, NOVAL, SMITH WOODHOUSE, WARRE).

Leacock Volume label of the MADEIRA WINE COMPANY. Main brand is St John, popular in Scandinavia. Older vintages include 1927, 1963 SERCIAL, 1914 BUAL, and SOLERA 1808 and 1860.

Lustau ★★→★★★★ Sherry house based in JEREZ. *Extensive range of wines*. Pioneering shipper of excellent ALMACENISTA sherries inc MANZANILLA AMONTILLADO Jurado, PALO CORTADO Vides. Other v.gd sherries include East India SOLERA, Emilín MOSCATEL. Owned by the Caballero group.

Madeira Wine Company Formed in 1913 by 2 firms as the Madeira Wine Association, subsequently to include all 26 British madeira firms though today focused on BLANDY, COSSART GORDON, LEACOCK and MILES. Now run by a partnership of the BLANDY and SYMINGTON families, increased investment has improved production facilities. Though cellared together, wines preserve individual house styles; BLANDY and COSSART GORDON lead the pack. All except basic wines CANTEIRO-aged.

Malmsey (or Malvasia) The sweetest and richest of traditional madeira grape varieties; dark amber and honeyed, yet with madeira's unique sharp tang.

Martinez Gassiot Port firm now owned by SYMINGTON, known esp for excellent rich, and pungent Directors 20-yr-old TAWNY. Gd-value, ageworthy vintages in drier, traditional style: **63 67 70 75 82 85 87 91** 94 97 00 03 07.

Miles Madeira shipper, part of the MADEIRA WINE COMPANY. Mostly basic wines for export; niche premium range for home market.

Montecristo Mont-M Brand of popular MONTILLAS by Compañía Vinícola del Sur.

Montilla-Moriles Mont-M DO nr Córdoba. Not sherry, but close, with soft FINO and AMONTILLADO, and luscious PX. At best, singularly toothsome apéritifs. Important source for PX for use in DO JEREZ, to make up for shortfall.

Niepoort Small family-run port house; sensational table wines. Consistently fine vintages inc. classic Garrafeira, aged in demijohn (**63 66 70' 75 77 78 80 82 83 87** 91 92 94 97 00' 03 05' 07) and Secundum, designed for earlier drinking. Exceptional TAWNIES and COLHEITAS. Benchmark Dry White joined by new 10-yr-old white.

Noval, Quinta do French(AXA)-owned historic port house. Intensely fruity, structured, elegant VINTAGE PORT; around 2.5 ha of ungrafted vines make small quantity of Nacional – extraordinarily dark, full, velvety, slow-maturing. Also v.gd age-dated TAWNY and gd COLHEITAS. Vintages: **62 63 66 67 70 75 78 82 85 87** 91 **94' 95** 97' 00' 03' 04. Second vintage label: Silval. Also v.gd LBV.

Offley Brand name belonging to Sogrape. Gd accessible, fruity range inc Duke of Oporto volume label, Baron de Forrester for age-dated TAWNY and Boa Vista for vintage: **63 66 67 70 72 75 77 80 82 83 85 87 89** 94 95 97 00' 03.

Osborne ★→★★★★ Huge Spanish firm producing sherry, a wide range of Spanish wines, and quality port. Its instantly recognizable bull logo dots the Spanish countryside. Sherries include FINO QUINTA, Coquinero, FINO AMONTILLADO. Declared VINTAGE PORTS in 95 97 00' 03' 07. (FLADGATE making ports since 2005). Owned by the Caballero Group, which now also owns DOMECQ .

Paternina, Federico ★★→★★★★ Marcos Eguizabal from Rioja acquired the sherry firm Diez-Merito, retaining 3 VORS wines for his Paternina label, the excellent and unique *fino Imperial*, OLOROSO Victoria Regina, and PX Vieja SOLERA.

Pedro Romero ★→★★★ Expanding SANLÚCAR family operation in an array of bodegas, recently acquired Gaspar Florido. V. wide range; inconsistent.

Pereira d'Oliveira Vinhos Family-owned madeira company. Gd basic range, COLHEITAS (1989 SERCIAL & MALMSEY) and substantial stock of fine old vintages (labelled reserva) held in cask dating back to 1850 (1937, 1971 SERCIAL, 1966 VERDELHO, 1958 BUAL).

Pérez Barquero Mont-M Excellent MONTILLAS include Gran Barquero FINO, AMONTILLADO, and OLOROSO.

Pilar Plá/El Maestro Sierra ★→★★★ Owned by JEREZ'S grandest dame Pilar Plá. Wines inconsistent, but gd FINO and some gd value at medium ages esp AMONTILLADO.

Poças Family-run Portuguese port firm; v.gd tawnies and COLHEITAS (67' 94). Gd LBV and recent vintages (97 00' 03 04 05' 07). Single-QUINTA from Quinta de Sta Barbera. Gd table wines, too.

Puerto de Santa María, El The former port of sherry, one of the 3 towns forming the "Sherry Triangle". Production now in serious decline; remaining bodegas include former ALMACENISTA GUTIÉRREZ COLOSÍA.

Quarles Harris One of the oldest port houses, since 1680, now owned by SYMINGTON. Mellow, well-balanced vintages, often v.gd value: **63 66 70 75 77 80 83 85 91** 94 97 00' 03 07.

Quinta Portuguese for "estate", traditionally denotes VINTAGE PORTS from shipper's single v'yds; declared in gd but not exceptional yrs. An increasing number of independent *quintas* (growers) make port from top vintages. Rising stars inc Passadouro, Portal, Romaneira, Whytingham's Vale Meão (07), Wine

---

Top frasqueira/colheita madeira selection for 2010Tinta Negra Mole:
HENRIQUES & HENRIQUES Fine Rich Single Harvest 1995 & Medium Rich Single Harvest 1998

Sercial (Dry): PEREIRA D'OLIVEIRA Harvest 1989, HM BORGES 1995

Verdelho (Medium Dry): BLANDY 1977, BARBEITO 1981

Bual (Medium Rich): HM BORGES 1977, BLANDY 1948

Malmsey (Rich): BARBEITO 2000, PEREIRA D'OLIVEIRA Harvest 1989

& Soul's Pintas (07).

Ramos Pinto Dynamic port house owned by Champagne house Louis Roederer; gd wines too. Outstanding single-QUINTA de Ervamoira and TAWNIES (de Ervamoira and do Bom Retiro). Rich, sweet, generally early maturing vintages.

Reserve/Reserva Premium ports, mostly RESERVE RUBY but some RESERVE TAWNY, bottled without a vintage date or age indication but better than basic style.

Rey Fernando de Castilla ★★→★★★★ JEREZ veteran Norwegian Jan Pettersen has made a small sherry revolution with his excellent wines, which, although he chooses not to label them AGE-DATED, could qualify. Top Antique line of AMONTILLADO, OLOROSO, and PX; FINO less impressive.

Roriz, Quinta de Historic estate now working with Cristiano van Zeller. V.gd single-QUINTA DOURO wines and ports: 99 00' 01 02 03' 04 05 06 07.

Rosa, Quinta de la V.gd single-QUINTA port from the Bergqvist family also making gd wines using traditional methods. Look for **94 95** 00 03' 04 05' 07 vintages.

Royal Oporto Real Companhia Velha's main port brand. Decanter-style bottles. Gd TAWNIES, COLHEITAS (53' 77) and recent vintages, foot-trodden since 1997.

Rozès Port shipper owned by Champagne house Vranken alongside São Pedro das Aguias. V. popular in France. Douro Superior Single Quinta do Grifo, acquired 2004, shows promise.

Ruby Youngest, cheapest port style: simple, sweet, red; best labelled RESERVE.

Sanchez Romate ★★→★★★ Family firm in JEREZ since 1781. Best known in Spanish-speaking world, esp for brandy Cardenal Mendoza. Gd sherry: OLOROSO La Sacristía de Romate, PX Duquesa, AMONTILLADO NPU.

Sandeman Jerez ★→★★★ Large firm owned by Sogrape. Founder George Sandeman set up twin establishments in Oporto and JEREZ in 1790. Gd sherries include an aged Don FINO, dry and sweet Imperial Corregidor and *Royal Ambrosante* OLOROSOS. The sherry and port companies are now separate, hence separate entries here.

Sandeman Port: lightest of Sogrape brands with gd aged TAWNIES, esp 20-yr-old. Vintage elegant but until recently patchy; new winery at Quinta do Seixo bodes well (**63 66** 70 75 **77 94** 97 00 03 07). Second label: seductive Vau Vintage (**97' 99** 00).

Sanlúcar de Barrameda One of the 3 towns of the "Sherry Triangle" at the mouth of the Guadalquivir. Strong maritime influence affects the MANZANILLA.

Santa Eufemia, Quinta de Family port estate with v.gd old TAWNIES. Stunning 10-, 20- & 30-yr-old aged white ports dressed to impress in 50cl bottles with contemporary packaging.

Sercial Madeira grape for the driest of the island's wines – supreme apéritif.

Silva, C da Port shipper. Mostly inexpensive RUBIES and TAWNIES, but gd aged TAWNIES and COLHEITAS under Dalva label.

Smith Woodhouse Port firm founded in 1784. Now firmly focused on limited production, high-quality port: v.gd unfiltered LBV and some v. fine vintages: **63 66 70 75 77' 80 83 85 91** 94 97 00' 03 07. Occasional single-estate wines from Quinta da Madelena.

Solera System used in ageing sherry. Consists of topping up progressively more mature barrels with slightly younger wine of same sort from next stage or *criadera*. The object is continuity in final wine, maintaining vigour of FLOR in FINO and MANZANILLA soleras. Old solera wines in bottle fetch high prices.

Symington See DOW and MADEIRA WINE COMPANY.

Tawny Style of port that implies ageing in wood (hence tawny in colour), though many basic tawnies are little more than attenuated RUBIES. Look for wines with an indication of age: 10-, 20-, 30-, 40-yr-old or RESERVE.

Taylor, Fladgate & Yeatman (Taylor's) One of the best known port shippers, highly rated for rich, long-lived VINTAGE PORTS (**63 66 70 75 77' 80 83** 85 92' 94

PORT, SHERRY & MADEIRA

97 00' 03'). Member of the Fladgate Partnership alongside CROFT and FONSECA GUIMARAENS. V.gd range inc RESERVE, LBV and aged TAWNIES. QUINTAS Vargellas and Terra Feita produce impressive single-QUINTA vintage, esp rare Vargellas "Vinha Velha" (95, 97, 00, 04) from 70 +-yr-old vines. Recently acquired A-rated QUINTA da Eira Velha.

Terry, S A ★→★★ Sherry bodega at EL PUERTO; part of Beam Brands.

Tío Pepe The most famous of FINO sherries (see GONZÁLEZ-BYASS).

Toro Albalá, Bodegas Mont-M Family firm making Eléctrico FINOS, AMONTILLADOS, and a PX that is among the best in MONTILLA and Spain.

Tradición ★★★ One of the new wave of sherry bodegas focusing exclusively upon small quantities of VOS and VORS. Gd AMONTILLADO, PALO CORTADO, and OLOROSO, from an art-filled cellar in back streets of JEREZ.

Valdespino ★→★★★★ Famous JEREZ bodega producing *Inocente fino* from the esteemed Macharnudo v'yd area. Notably Inocente is fermented in American oak not stainless steel, and SOLERA has 10 stages or *criaderas*. Fine Manzanilla Deliciosa; Tío Diego is terrific dry AMONTILLADO; also vibrant, youthful SOLERA 1842 OLOROSO VOS; remarkable, aged Toneles MOSCATEL.

Valdivia ★★→★★★★ One of newer sherry bodegas, part of JEREZ revival. V.gd 15-yr-old Sacromonte AMONTILLADO and OLOROSO. Acquired by Grupo GARVEY.

Vale D Maria, Quinta do Gd value, beautifully elegant, forward single-QUINTA VINTAGE PORT (00 01 02 03 05 07).

Ventozelo, Quinta de Huge, beautifully situated estate recently acquired by Real Companhia Velha. Gd value single-QUINTA VINTAGE PORTS.

Verdelho Traditional madeira grape for medium-dry wines; pungent but without the searing austerity of SERCIAL. Increasing in popularity for table wines.

Vesúvio, Quinta do 19th-century estate restored to former glory by SYMINGTON, who have doubled v'yd area. VINTAGE PORT: **91 92 94 95' 96'** 97 00' 01 03' 04 05' 06 07. Exceptional 2007 vintage sees first table wine.

Vila Nova de Gaia City on the south side of the river DOURO from Oporto, where major port shippers traditionally mature their wines in lodges.

Vintage port Classic vintages are the best wines declared in exceptional yrs by shippers between 1 Jan and 30 Sept in the 2nd yr after vintage. Bottled without filtration after 2 yrs in wood, the wine matures v. slowly in bottle throwing a CRUST or deposit – always decant. Modern vintages broachable earlier but best will last over 50 yrs. Single-QUINTA vintage ports also drinking earlier.

Warre Oldest of British port shippers (since 1670); owned by the SYMINGTON family (see DOW) since 1905. Fine, elegant, long-maturing vintage wines, gd RESERVE, vintage character (Warrior), excellent unfiltered, bottle-matured LBV; 10- and 20-yr-old Otima TAWNY. Single-QUINTA vintage from Quinta da Cavadinha. Vintages: **63 66 70' 75 77' 80 83 85 91** 94 97 00' 03 07.

White port Port made with white grapes, occasionally sweet (*lagrima*) but mostly off-dry apéritif styles (driest labelled "Dry"), perfect with tonic and fresh mint. Since 2006, exciting, age-designated 10-, 20-, 30-, or 40-yr-old styles are raising the bar.

Williams & Humbert ★→★★★★ Famous sherry bodega with v.gd old wines. Dry Sack (medium AMONTILLADO) is bestseller; SOLERA Especial is its PALO CORTADO.

Age-dated whites

If you thought white port was just a cocktail ingredient, think again. New age-dated 10-, 20- and 30-yr-old white ports from the likes of Andresen, Churchill, Niepoort and Quinta de Santa Eufémia treat white port as a serious wine rather than just a way of cheering up tonic water.

Switzerland

More heavily shaded areas are the wine-growing regions

There's a lot going on in this small wine country. Experiments with new vine varieties (or ones just new to Switzerland) such as Vidal, Johanitter, Blaufränkisch or Cabernet Dorsat are to be found everywhere, and consumers seem to like the results. Warmer weather also help. Reds are getting richer and fruitier, and thin wines are getting fewer.

Wines are becoming more terroir-driven: the focus is on structure, elegance and complexity, and ancient grape varieties such as Heida, Petite Arvine and Cornalin are in fashion. The influence of the New World is increasing. The reason is simple: today Swiss winemakers travel. Just two generations ago 99 per cent of them never left Switzerland and seldom tasted anything that wasn't Swiss.

"Swissness" is the fashionable term now. Many restaurants have opened serving only Swiss products; and traditional wines such as Chasselas and Müller-Thurgau are part of this. Swiss winemakers are certainly flying the flag.

Recent vintages

2008 Difficult year with lots of rain. Quality okay but not tops.

2007 Reds are less opulent than 2006. Whites are superb.

2006 Very promising and being compared to 2005.

2005 Low in quantity but high in quality.

2004 Less complex than 2003 but very promising. Drink now.

Aargau 06 07 08 Swiss German canton (393 ha) for fragrant Müller-THURGAU, fruity BLAUBURGUNDER. Best producer: Weingut zum Sternen.

Aigle Vaud r w ★★→★★★ Well known for elegant whites and supple reds.

Aligoté White grape becoming more popular in the Geneva area.

Amigne Traditional VALAIS white grape, esp of VÉTROZ. Total planted surface: 39 ha. Full-bodied, tasty, often sweet. Best producer: André Fontannaz ★★ 06 **07'** 08 or JEAN-RENÉ GERMANIER. Quality rating based on residual sugar: one bee – yes, as in the insect – means 0–8 grams per litre RS, 2 bees mean 9–25g/l RS, 3 bees mean over 25 g/l RS.

AOC Compulsory since Jan 1, 2008 for all regions; each region has different rules.

Arvine Old VALAIS white grape (also Petite Arvine): dry and sweet, elegant, long-lasting wines with salty finish. 138 ha planted. Producers: MARIE-THÉRÈSE CHAPPAZ, Benoît Dorsaz, Simon Maye & Fils, Rouvinez, Provins.

Auvernier Neuchâtel r p w ★★→★★★ Old wine village on Lake NEUCHÂTEL and biggest wine-growing commune of the canton.

Bachtobel, Schlossgut ★★★→★★★★ 04 05 06' 07' V. fine estate in Weinfelden run by Hans-Ulrich Kellring until his death in 08. V.gd PINOT N, RIES and Sauv Bl.

Basel Second-largest Swiss town and canton. Best producers: Jauslin Weine, Weingut Fibl, Domaine Nussbaumer und Buess Weinbau.

Bern Capital and canton. V'yds in west (BIELERSEE: CHASSELAS, PINOT N, white SPÉCIALITÉS) and east (Thunersee: BLAUBURGUNDER, Müller-THURGAU); 262 ha.

Bielersee r p w ★→★★ 06 07 08 Wine region on northern shore of the Bielersee lake (dry, light CHASSELAS, PINOT N and specialities such as Viognier, Sauv Bl and Malbec). Best producers: Charles Steiner, Hans Perrot, Lukas Hasler.

Blauburgunder German name for PINOT N; aka Clevner. Wide range of wines, from rosé to heavily oaked reds. Switzerland's main red variety. Limited editions are the trend at the top end: Pure from Salgesch, Pinot R(h)ein from Maienfeld or Tête de Cru Staatskellerei from Zurich.

Blauburgunderland Successful promotion body for the wines of SCHAFFHAUSEN.

Bündner Herrschaft Grisons r p w ★★→★★★ Best German-Swiss region includes top villages: Fläsch, Jenins, Maienfeld, Malans. BLAUBURGUNDER ripens esp well due to warm Föhn wind, cask-aged v.gd. Also Chard, Müller-THURGAU, COMPLETER. Best: Gantenbein ★★★, Davaz ★★, FROMM ★★★ 05' 06 07' 08. Switzerland's best BLAUBURGUNDER is from here.

Chablais Vaud r w ★★→★★★ Wine region on right bank of Rhône and upper end of Lake GENEVA, includes villages AIGLE, Bex, Ollon, Villeneuve, YVORNE.

Champagne The Swiss village continues to fight against the French wine-growing area that forbids everybody to use the name "Champagne" on the label. Since 2004 the Swiss wine-growers have been forbidden to use their village name.

Chanton, Josef-Marie and Mario ★★★ *Terrific Valais specialities*: HEIDA, Lafnetscha, Himbertscha, Hibou, Resi, Gwäss.

Chappaz ★★★ Marie-Thérèse Chappaz of FULLY is the queen of sweet wine. Outstanding Petite Arvine Grain Noble.

Chasselas (Gutedel in Germany) Main white variety. Neutral flavour, takes on

---

Top 10 Swiss bottles for 2010

Marsanne Blanche 2004, Grain Noble, Marie-Thérèse CHAPPAZ
Grains de Malice 2006, Maître de Chais, PROVINS
Domaine Tourbillon 2004, PROVINS
Pinot Noir 2006, DANIEL & MARTHA GANTENBEIN
Pinot Noir 2006, Nr.3, Der Andere, SCHLOSSGUT BACHTOBEL
Pinot Noir 2006, Uris, Davaz
Bianco del Ticino 2006, Castello Luigi, Luigi ZANINI
Heida 2005, Spätlese, MARIO CHANTON
Cayas 2006, JEAN-RENÉ GERMANIER
Cornalin 2006, Anne-Catherine & Denis MERCIER

local character: elegant (GENEVA); refined, full (VAUD); exotic, racy (VALAIS); pétillant (lakes Bienne, NEUCHÂTEL, Murtensee). Only east of BASEL. Called FENDANT in VALAIS. Accounts for almost a third of Swiss wines but increasingly replaced. Best: Dom Blaise Duboux, Philippe Gex, Raymont PACCOT, PROVINS. More and more producers avoid the malolactic fermentation thus conserving acidity, and have started to use oak barrels.

Completer Native white grape, mostly used in GRISONS, making aromatic wines with high acidity. ("Complet" was a monk's final daily prayer, or "nightcap".) Best: Adolf Boner, Malans ★★, Volg Weinkellereien.

Cornalin ★★→★★★ 05' 06 07 08 Local VALAIS speciality that has become more popular since production increased; dark, spicy, v. strong red. Best: JEAN-RENÉ GERMANIER (★★), Denis MERCIER, PROVINS. Oldest living vine in Switzerland is a Cornalin plant in Leuk, Valais, from 1798 (www.vitisantiqua1798.ch).

La Côte Vaud r p w ★→★★★ Largest VAUD wine area between LAUSANNE and GENEVA. Traditional whites with elegant finesse; fruity, harmonious reds. Esp from MONT-SUR-ROLLE, Vinzel, Luins, FÉCHY, MORGES, etc.

Dézaley Vaud w (r) ★★→★★★ Celebrated LAVAUX v'yd on slopes above Lake GENEVA, once tended by Cistercian monks. Potent CHASSELAS, develops esp after ageing.

Dôle Valais r ★★→★★★ Appellation for PINOT N, often blended with GAMAY and other reds from the VALAIS: full, supple, often v.gd. Lightly pink Dôle Blanche is pressed straight after harvest. Try Simone Maye et Fils.

Epesses Vaud w (r) ★→★★★ 06 07' 08 LAVAUX AOC: supple, full-bodied whites.

Ermitage Alias Marsanne; a VALAIS SPÉCIALITÉ. Concentrated, full-bodied dry white, sometimes with residual sugar. Best: Dom Cornulus, Philippoz Frères.

Féchy Vaud ★→★★ Famous appellation of LA CÔTE, esp elegant whites. DYA

Federweisser German-Swiss name for white wine from BLAUBURGUNDER.

Fendant Valais w ★→★★★ VALAIS appellation for CHASSELAS. The ideal wine for Swiss cheese dishes such as fondue or raclette. *Provins*, Les Fils de Charles Favre, Antoine & Christophe Bétrisey, Maurice Zufferey.

Flétri/Mi-flétri Late-harvested grapes for sweet/slightly sweet wine .

Fribourg Smallest French-Swiss wine canton (115 ha, nr Jura).

Fromm ★★★ 04 05' 06 07' Malans grower. Sold his 2nd estate in New Zealand and focuses on outstanding BLAUBURGUNDER and Chardonnay wines in GRISONS.

Fully Valais r w ★★→★★★ Village nr Martigny: excellent ERMITAGE and GAMAY. Best producer: Marie-Thérèse CHAPPAZ SW ★★→★★★ 06 07' 08.

Gamaret Red Resistant variety created 1970 from the crossing of GAMAY and Reichensteiner.

Gamay Beaujolais grape; abounds in French cantons. Mainly thin wine used in blends (Salvagnin, DÔLE) and also more and more as a single variety. Try: Le Satyre Gamay from Noémie & Noé Graff.

Gantenbein, Daniel & Martha 05' 06 07 08 Most famous growers in Grisons. Top Pinot N from Dom de la Romanée-Conti clones, and RIES with clones from Loosen in Mosel.

Garanoir Grape: twin of GAMARET. Found all over Switzerland, except in the TICINO.

Geneva Capital, and French-Swiss wine canton; third largest (1,297 ha). Key areas: Mandement, Entre Arve et Rhône, Entre Arve et Lac. Mostly CHASSELAS, GAMAY. Also GAMARET, Chard, PINOT N, Muscat, and gd ALIGOTÉ. Best: Jean-Michel Novelle ★★★; interesting: Jacques Tatasciere, Dom de la Rochette ★★.

Germanier, Jean-René VÉTROZ winemaker; Cayas (100% Syrah) ★★★ 01 02 03' 04 05' 06; Mitis (sweet) ★★★ 01' 02 03 04 05' 06. Also a pure Cornalin 05' 06 and the PINOT N Clos du Four ★★★. Look out for new GAMAY Grand Cru.

Glacier, Vin du (Gletscherwein) Fabled oxidized, wooded white from rare Rèze grape of Val d'Anniviers. Almost impossible to find on sale. Keep looking.

SWITZERLAND

Grain Noble ConfidenCiel Quality label for top Swiss Sweet wines.

Grisons (Graubünden) Mountain canton, mainly in German Switzerland (BÜNDNER HERRSCHAFT, Churer Rheintal; esp BLAUBURGUNDER) and partly south of Alps (Misox, esp MERLOT). PINOT N is king. Best producers: DAVAZ, FROMM, Gantenbein, Peter Wegelin, von Tscharner.

Heida (Païen) Old VALAIS white grape (Jura's Savagnin) for country wine of upper Valais (VISPERTERMINEN v'yds at 1,000+ m). Full-bodied wine with high acidity. Best: Josef-Marie Chanton ★★ **06** 07' 08. Try Heida from PROVINS, Imesch Vins, St. Jodernkellerei, Rouvinez Vins.

Huber ★★★ **05' 06** 07' Ticino. Merlot Montagna Magica is superb and inspiring for other growers in Ticino.

Humagne Strong native white grape (VALAIS SPÉCIALITÉ), older than CHASSELAS. Humagne rouge is not related to it but also common in the VALAIS. Esp from Chamoson, Leytron, Martigny.

Johannisberg Synonym for Sylvaner in the VALAIS.

Lafnetscha Indigenous grape variety, apparently the result of an alliance between COMPLETER and HUMAGNE Blanche.

Lausanne Capital of VAUD. No longer with v'yds in town area, but long-time owner of classics: Abbaye de Mont, Ch Rochefort (LA CÔTE); Clos des Moines, Clos des Abbayes, Dom de Burignon (LAVAUX).

Lavaux Vaud w (r) ★→★★★ Now a UNESCO world heritage site: v'yd terraces stretching for 30 km along the south-facing N shore of Lake Geneva from the Ch de Chillon to the eastern outskirts of LAUSANNE. Main grape: CHASSELAS. Wines named for the villages: Lutry, ST SAPHORIN, Ollon, EPESSES and more.

Mauler ★★→★★★ V.gd name for sparkling in NEUCHÂTEL, esp Cuvée Exellence.

Merlot Brought to the TICINO in 1907 by the scientist Alderige Fantuzzi (after phylloxera destroyed local varieties): soft to v. powerful wines. Also used with Cab Sauv. Best: Castello Luigi, Conte di Luna, Stucky Zanini, Tenimento dell'Ör.

Mercier ★★★ **01 02 03' 04** 05' 06 07 Growers in Sierre with outstanding CORNALIN.

Mont-sur-Rolle Vaud w (r) ★★ DYA Important appellation within LA CÔTE.

Morges Vaud r p w ★→★★ DYA Largest LA CÔTE/VAUD AC: CHASSELAS, fruity reds.

Neuchâtel City and canton; 600 ha from Lake Neuchâtel to BIELERSEE. CHASSELAS: fragrant, lively (sur lie, sparkling). Gd OEIL DE PERDRIX, PINOT GRIS, Chard. Try: Ch Souaillon.

Non Filtré Speciality available in springtime from NEUCHÂTEL, produced from CHASSELAS grapes.

Nostrano Word meaning "ours", applied to red wine of TICINO, made from native and Italian grapes (Bondola, Freisa, Bonarda, etc).

Novelle ★★★→★★★★ **05' 06** 07 Geneva-based producer with v.gd Sauv Bl, Petit Manseng and GAMAY.

Oeil de Perdrix PINOT N rosé. DYA esp NEUCHÂTEL'S; name can be used anywhere.

Paccot ★★★ **06 07'** 08 Féchy. Look here for excellent CHASSELAS, esp. Le Brez.

Petite Arvine See Arvine.

Pinot Blanc (Weissburgunder) Booming variety producing full-bodied, elegant wines. Best: Bad Osterfingen **07' 08**.

Pinot Gris (Malvoisie) Widely planted white grape for dry and residually sweet wines. Makes v. fine late-harvest wines in VALAIS.

Pinot Noir (Blauburgunder) See BLAUBURGUNDER Try: Gantenbein; Davaz (Fläsch); Kesselring (Ottoberg); Pircher (Eglisau); Baumann (Oberhallau); Meier (Kloster Sion); Christian Obrecht (Jenins) ★★★ **05' 06** 07' 08.

Provins Biggest co-op in the VALAIS with a large range. Outstanding for Maître de Chais and Crus des Domaines labels, and interesting Les Titans range.

Räuschling Old white ZÜRICH grape; discreet fruit and elegant acidity. Try: Hermann Schwarzenbach, Meilen.

Riesling Petit Rhin Mainly in the VALAIS. Try Kesseling (Ottoberg) **07 08**.

Riesling-Sylvaner Old name for Müller-THURGAU. Typically elegant wines with flowery aroma and some acidity. Best producers: Daniel Marugg, Andrea Davaz, Baumann (Oberhallau) ★★' 08.

St-Gallen Eastern wine canton (218 ha). Esp for BLAUBURGUNDER, Müller-THURGAU, SPÉCIALITÉS. Try: Weingut Schmidheiny, Weingut Gonzen.

St-Saphorin Vaud w (r) ★★→★★★ **07' 08** Famous LAVAUX AOC for fine, light whites.

Salgesch Important wine village in the upper VALAIS. Try Adrian Mathier, Cave du Rhodan or Caves Fernand Cina.

Salvagnin Vaud r ★→★★ **07'** 08 GAMAY and/or PINOT N appellation.

Schaffhausen German-Swiss canton/wine town on the Rhine. BLAUBURGUNDER; also Müller-THURGAU and SPÉCIALITÉS. Best: Baumann, Bad Osterfingen ★★. The latest trend is reds and whites with plenty of residual sugar.

Schenk Europe-wide wine giant, founded and based in Rolle (VAUD). Owns firms in France (Burgundy and Bordeaux), Germany, Italy, and Spain.

Sierre Valais r w ★★→★★★ Sunny resort and famous wine town. Known for FENDANT, PINOT N, ERMITAGE, Malvoisie. V.gd DÔLE. Visit Ch de Villa – wine museum and vinotheque with largest Valais wine collection.

Sion Valais r w ★★→★★★ Capital/wine centre of VALAIS. Esp FENDANT de Sion.

Spécialités (Spezialitäten) Wines of unusual grapes: vanishing local Gwäss, Himbertscha, Roter Eyholzer, Bondola, etc, ARVINE and AMIGNE, or modish Chenin Bl, Sauv Bl, Cab Sauv, Syrah. Of 47 VALAIS varieties, 43 are SPÉCIALITÉS. New varieties such as Solaris, Vidal, Johanitter or Cabernet Dorsat are found in the north of the country.

Thurgau German-Swiss canton beside Bodensee Lake (265 ha). Wines from Thur Valley: south shore of the Untersee. Typical: BLAUBURGUNDER, also gd Müller-Thurgau. SPÉCIALITÉS include Kerner, PINOT GR, Regent. Best producer: Hans Ulrich Kesselring, died in 2008.

Ticino Italian-speaking southern Switzerland (with Misox), growing mainly MERLOT (gd from mountainous Sopraceneri region) and SPÉCIALITÉS. Try Cab Sauv (oaked B'x style), Sauv Bl, Sem, Chard, Merlot white, and rosé (1,065 ha). Best producers: Guido Brivio, Daniel Huber, Adriano Kaufmann, Werner Stucky, Luigi Zanini, Christian Zündel. All ★★★ **05' 06** 07' 08.

Valais (Wallis) Rhône Valley from German-speaking upper-Valais to French lower-Valais. Largest and most varied and exciting wine canton in Switzerland (source 30% of Swiss wine). Wide range: 47 grape varieties, plus many SPÉCIALITÉS; FLÉTRI/MI-FLÉTRI wines.

Vaud (Waadt) French Switzerland's second largest wine canton; stronghold of CHABLAIS, LA CÔTE, LAVAUX, Bonvillars, Côtes de l'Orbe, VULLY. CHASSELAS.

Vétroz Valais w r ★★→★★★ Top village nr SION, esp famous for AMIGNE.

Vevey-Montreux Vaud r w ★★ Up-and-coming appellation of LAVAUX. Famous wine festival held about every 30 yrs.

Visperterminen Valais w (r) ★→★★ Upper VALAIS v'yds, esp for SPÉCIALITÉS. The highest v'yds in Europe (at 1,000+ m). Try Stoffel Weine.

Vully Vaud w (r) ★→★★ Refreshing white from Lake Murten/FRIBOURG area.

Yvorne Vaud w (r) ★★ **04 05** Top CHABLAIS AOC for strong, fragrant wines.

Zanini ★★★→★★★★ **05' 06** 07' Top Ticino name with focus on MERLOT. Tops are Castello Luigi and Vinattieri.

Zundel ★★★ **05' 06** 07' A grower to remember for top Ticino MERLOT.

Zürich Capital of largest canton. BLAUBURGUNDER mostly; esp Müller-THURGAU, RAUSCHLING, Kerner (613 ha). Try Ladolt, Schwarzenbach, Zweifel Weine.

To decipher codes, please refer to "Key to symbols" on the front flap of jacket, or "How to use this book" on p. 10.

SWITZERLAND

Austria

More heavily shaded areas are the wine-growing regions

There's aëë definite buzz in Austria's vineyards, as growers are debating and defining the difference between a wine made in Austria and an Austrian wine with all the distinctive hallmarks of terroir, varieties, and local traditions that the term implies. Some of the world's most seductive white wines are to be found here, particularly mineral Riesling and dazzling Grüner Veltliner, as well as Sauvignon Blanc, Chardonnay, and fragrant Gelber Muskateller, and monumental sweet wines. The real changes, however, are taking place among the reds. Blaufränkisch is the most exciting, with a range of styles and expressions, and Sankt Laurent is yielding results to watch, although many growers see great Pinot Noir as the ultimate goal. They may well get there.

Recent vintages

2008 A nerve-racking vintage that could produce outstanding results in the hands of the most careful producers. Protracted cool and rainy spells in Oct and Nov made harvesting very difficult in Lower Austria and in the Burgenland, and in the southern regions, the autumn was more clement.

2007 In Styria, the cool autumn brought gd quality. Overall the Burgenland shows fine fruit with good results for Blaufränkisch, Zweigelt and Pinot Noir. Excellent yields in Vienna, better for Grüner Veltliner than for Ries.

2006 A great year. A cold winter was followed by a wet spring and one of the hottest late summers on record. Healthy and perfectly ripe grapes produced wonderfully well-rounded and complex wines with great ageing potential. Very good for reds and outstanding for whites.

2005 A cool year yielding exceptionally elegant wines to those practising rigorous grape selection, particularly in Lower Austria, but with great discrepancies in quality. Not outstanding for reds. Sensational botrytis conditions for Burgenland dessert wines.

2004 A cooler year. Grüner Veltliner and Ries fared well after meticulous vineyard care, especially in Wachau. A mild Oct in Burgenland helped reds ripen nicely, while bringing plentiful botrytis for dessert wines.

2003 A hot dry summer, a powerful year. Very good for Grüner Veltliner whites and Burgenland reds, esp Blaufränkisch and Zweigelt. Little botrytis.

2002 Much maligned, but the best producers created wonderfully elegant and balanced wines. Difficult for reds but excellent dessert wines. Drink now.

2001 Great for dry whites; very good late-harvest wines. Reds more erratic.

Achs, Paul r (w) ★★★ Exceptional GOLS estate, esp reds: Pannobile blends, Ungerberg, BLAUFRÄNKISCH and Pinot N. BIODYNAMIC producer (see below).

Allram w ★ Increasingly good KAMPTAL estate, esp for RIES and GRÜNER VELTLINER.

Alzinger w ★★★ 95 97 98 99 00 01 02 03 04 05 06 07 Outstanding WACHAU estate: deep, mineral RIES and GRÜNER VELTLINER.

Angerer, Kurt ★ Maverick KAMPTAL winemaker producing highly original and powerful GRÜNER VELTLINER and RIES.

Ausbruch PRÄDIKAT wine with sweetness levels between Beerenauslese and Trockenbeerenauslese. Traditionally produced in RUST.

Ausg'steckt ("hung out") HEURIGEN are not open all yr; when they are, a green bush is hung above their doors, also to show wine is being served.

Bayer r w ★★★ Well-made reds from bought-in grapes, often v. elegant.

Beck, Judith r w ★★ Rising BIODYNAMIC NEUSIEDLERSEE winemaker. Well-crafted reds, esp gd Pinot N.

Biodynamism For biodynamic Austrians, look out for P ACHS, J BECK, Fritsch, Geyerhof, GRAF HARDEGG, HIRSCH, LOIMER, Sepp Muster, NIKOLAIHOF, OTT, J NITTNAUS, Pittnauer, WENINGER.

Blauburger Austrian red grape variety. A cross between BLAUER PORTUGIESER and BLAUFRÄNKISCH. Dark-coloured but produces light-bodied, simple wines.

Blauer Burgunder (Pinot N) Undergoing a renaissance and stylistic evolution among top winemakers. Best in BURGENLAND, KAMPTAL, THERMENREGION (from growers ACHS, BECK, BRÜNDLMAYER, LOIMER, PÖCKL, Preisinger, PRIELER, SCHLOSS GOBELSBURG, SCHLOSS HALBTURN, WENINGER, WIENINGER).

Blauer Portugieser Light, fruity wines to drink slightly chilled when young. Also a gd blending variety. Not for high quality wines.

Blauer Zweigelt BLAUFRÄNKISCH/ST LAURENT cross. High-yielding grape, rich in colour. Lower yields and improved methods can produce appealing, velvety reds. Top producers: Grassl, HEINRICH, J NITTNAUS, Pitnauer, PÖCKL, Scheibelhofer, Schwarz, WINKLER-HERMADEN.

Blaufränkisch Lemberger in Germany, Kékfrankos in Hungary. Probably Austria's top potential red grape variety, widely planted in MITTELBURGENLAND: gd body and structure, peppery acidity, a characteristic salty note, berry aromas and eucalyptus. Often blended with Cab Sauv or ZWEIGELT. Best from P ACHS, Gesellmann, HEINRICH, Igler, KOLLWENZ, KRUTZLER, MORIC, J NITTNAUS, PRIELER, Schiefer, ERNST TRIEBAUMER, WENINGER.

Bouvier Indigenous aromatic grape, generally producing light, low-acidity wines, esp gd for Beeren- and Trockenbeerenauslesen.

Brandl, Günter w ★★ Small but consistently *fine Kamptal estate* known esp for RIES and GRÜNER VELTLINER Novemberlese.

Bründlmayer, Willi r w sw sp ★★★★ 98 99 00 01 02 03 04 05 06 07 Fine Langenlois-KAMPTAL estate. Innovator making world-class RIES, GRÜNER VELTLINER. Also Austria's best sparkling *méthode champenoise*.

Burgenland Province and wine region (14,564 ha) in the east bordering Hungary. Warm climate. Ideal conditions for red wines and esp botrytis wines nr NEUSIEDLERSEE. Four areas: MITTELBURGENLAND, NEUSIEDLERSEE, NEUSIEDLERSEE-

HÜGELLAND, SÜDBURGENLAND.

Buschenschank A wine tavern, often a HEURIGE country cousin.

Carnuntum r w Up-and-coming region SE of VIENNA now showing gd reds. Best: Glatzer, Grassl, G Markowitsch, Netzl, Pitnauer, Weingut Marko.

Chardonnay Both oaked and unoaked, often international in style, particularly in STYRIA and BURGENLAND. Known in STYRIA as MORILLON: strong fruit, lively acidity. Esp BRÜNDLMAYER, GROSS, KOLLWENTZ, LOIMER, Malat, POLZ, SATTLER, STIEGELMAR, TEMENT, VELICH, WIENINGER.

Christ w r Reliable VIENNA producer, particularly for GEMISCHTER SATZ.

Deutschkreutz r (w) MITTELBURGENLAND red wine area, esp for BLAUFRÄNKISCH.

Districtus Austriae Controllatus, DAC Austria's first appellation system, introduced in 2003. Similar to France's AC and Italy's DOC. Kamptal joins WEINVIERTEL, CARNUNTUM, MITTELBURGENLAND, KREMSTAL and TRAISENTAL.

Domäne Wachau w (r) ★ 98 99 00 01 02 06 07 08 Important growers' co-op in Dürnstein. Back from the wilderness and on song once more. V.gd GRÜNER VELTLINER and RIES.

Donabaum, Johann w ★★ Young and v. talented WACHAU grower with fine RIES and GRÜNER VELTLINER.

Ehmoser w Small individualist Wagram producer, gd GRÜNER VELTLINER Aurum.

Eichinger Consistent KAMPTAL producer, GRÜNER VELTLINER, RIES. Heiligenstein.

Federspiel Medium quality level of the VINEA WACHAU categories, roughly corresponding to Kabinett. Fruity, elegant, dry wines.

Feiler-Artinger Burgenland r w sw ★★★ 95 96 97 98 99 00 01 02 03 04 05 06 07 08 Outstanding RUST estate with top AUSBRUCH dessert wines. Also gd dry whites and exciting red blends. Beautiful baroque house, too.

Forstreiter w ★ Consistent KREMSTAL producer, particularly good RIES.

Furmint Rare white variety cultivated in and around RUST. Fine sweet and increasingly gd dry wines.

Gemischter Satz A blend of grapes varietals (mostly white) planted in one v'yd and vinified together. Traditional wine, currently undergoing a renaissance with v. interesting results.

Gesellmann r w ★★. Consistent and often fine MITTELBURGENLAND producer focusing on BLAUFRÄNKISCH and red cuvées: Opus Eximium.

Gols r w dr sw Wine commune on N shore of NEUSIEDLERSEE in BURGENLAND. Top producers: P ACHS, J BECK, GESELLMANN & HANS, G HEINRICH, A & H Nittnaus, Pitnauer, Preisinger, Renner, STIEGELMAR.

Graf Hardegg r w ★Well-regarded WEINVIERTEL estate, unusually for the area. V.gd Viognier, Syrah, Pinot N, and RIES.

Gross w ★★★ 97 98 99 00 01 02 03 04 05 06 07 Outstanding and perfectionist south STYRIAN producer. Esp CHARD, Sauv Bl, and Pinot Bl.

Grüner Veltliner Austria's flagship white grape covering 37% of v'yds. Remarkably diverse: from lively spiced fruitiness in youth, to concentrated elegance with age. Best: ALZINGER, BRÜNDLMAYER, HIRTZBERGER, Högl, M Huber, KNOLL, Laurenz V, LOIMER, MANTLERHOF, NEUMAYER, NIGL, NIKOLAIHOF, OTT, PFAFFL, FX PICHLER, PRAGER, Schmelz, Sommer.

Gsellmann & Hans r w sw ★ Formerly Gsellmann & Gsellmann, in GOLS.

Gumpoldskirchen w r dr sw Famous HEURIGE village S of VIENNA, centre of THERMENREGION. Distinctive, tasty, often sweet wines from ZIERFANDLER and ROTGIPFLER grapes. Best producers: Biegler, Spaetrot, Zierer.

Harkamp, Hannes w Reliable S STYRIA producer, esp. Morillon and Sauv Blanc.

Heinrich, Gernot r w dr sw ★★★ 99 01 02 03 04 05 06 07 08 Leading GOLS estate, member of the PANNOBILE group. Now moving towards BIODYNAMIC viticulture.

Heinrich, Johann r w dr sw ★★★ 97 98 99 00 01 02 03 04 05 06 08 Leading MITTELBURGENLAND producer. V.gd BLAUFRÄNKISCH Goldberg Reserve. Ever more balanced and stylish wines, esp excellent *cuvée* Cupido.

Heurige Wine of the most recent harvest, called "new wine" for one yr. **Heurigen** are wine taverns in which growers-cum-patrons serve their own wine with simple local food – a Viennese institution.

Hiedler w sw ★★★ Leading KAMPTAL producer. V.gd RIES Maximum.

Hirsch w ★★★ Innovative KAMPTAL producer. Esp Heiligenstein, Lamm, and Gaisberg v'yds. Also Austria's screwcap pioneer.

Hirtzberger, Franz w ★★★★ 99 00 01 02 03 04 05 06 07 08 Top WACHAU producer with 20 ha at SPITZ AN DER DONAU. *Great dry Ries* and GRÜNER VELTLINER, esp from the Honivogl and Singerriedel v'yds.

Högl w sw Small WACHAU producer with often fine RIES and GRÜNER VELTLINER.

Horitschon MITTELBURGENLAND region for reds: Anton Iby, WENINGER.

Igler r Consistent grower of red wines in MITTELBURGENLAND: Ab Ericio, Vulcano.

Illmitz w (r) dr sw SEEWINKEL region famous for Beeren- and Trockenbeerenauslesen. Best from Angerhof, Martin Haider, KRACHER, Helmut Lang, Opitz.

Jamek, Josef w 97 98 99 00 01 02 03 04 05 06 07 Well-known WACHAU estate with restaurant. Not typical WACHAU style: often some residual sugar.

Jurtschitsch/Sonnhof w (r) dr (sw) ★★ 97 98 99 00 01 02 03 04 05 06 07 Large KAMPTAL estate: v. reliable whites (RIES, GRÜNER VELTLINER, CHARD).

Kamptal r w Wine region, along river Kamp N of WACHAU. Top v'yds: Langenlois, Strass, Zöbing. Best growers: Angerer, Brandl, BRÜNDLMAYER, Ehn, EICHINGER, Hiedler, Hirsch, JURTSCHITSCH, LOIMER, Rabl, STEININGER, SCHLOSS GOBELSBURG. Kamptal is now DAC (from 2008 vintage) for GRÜNER VELTLINER and RIES.

Kattus Producer of traditional Sekt in VIENNA.

Kerschbaum r ★★★ MITTELBURGENLAND BLAUFRÄNKISCH specialist, individualist and often fascinating.

Klosterneuburg r w Main wine town of Donauland. Rich in tradition, with a wine college founded in 1860. Best producers: Stift Klosterneuburg, Zimmermann.

KMW Abbreviation for Klosterneuburger Mostwaage ("must level"), the unit used in Austria to measure the sugar content in grape juice.

Knoll, Emmerich w ★★★★ 97 98 99 00 01 02 03 04 05 06 07 08 Traditional outstanding estate in Loiben, WACHAU. *Showpiece Grüner Veltliner and Ries*.

Kollwentz-Römerhof w r dr (sw) ★★★★ 99 01 02 03 04 05 06 07 08 Pioneering producer nr Eisenstadt: Sauv Bl, CHARD, Eiswein, v.gd reds.

Kracher w (r) dr (sw) ★★★★ 95 96 97 98 99 00 01 02 03 04 05 06 07 Top-class ILLMITZ producer specializing in botrytized PRÄDIKATS (dessert); barrique-aged (Nouvelle Vague), others in steel (Zwischen den Seen); gd reds since 97. After Alois Kracher's death in 2007 the estate is now led by his son Gerhard.

Kremstal w (r) Wine region esp for GRÜNER VELTLINER and RIES. Top growers: Malat, S MOSER, NIGL, SALOMON, WEINGUT STADT KREMS.

Krutzler r ★★★ South BURGENLAND producer of v.gd BLAUFRÄNKISCH, esp Perwolff.

Leithaberg V'yd hill on the northern shore of Lake Neusiedl, also a lively group of producers seeking to refine regional styles.

Leitner r w sw Rising NEUSIEDLERSEE growers belonging to the PANNOBILE group. Gd Ungerberg and PANNOBILE *cuvées*.

Loimer, Fred w ★★★ Innovative KAMPTAL producer with 31-ha estate, 50% GRÜNER VELTLINER; also RIES, CHARD, Pinot Gr, v.gd Pinot N. Leading exponent of BIODYNAMIC winemaking.

Mantlerhof w ★★ Fine KREMSTAL producer with a well-considered, traditional approach. Gd Roter Veltliner.

Mayer am Pfarrplatz w Viennese producer and Heurigen now in new ownership, with marked improvement in the wines.

NB Vintages in colour are those you should choose first for drinking in 2010.

Minkowitsch w Traditional WEINVIERTEL producer, interesting Gewürztraminer.

Mittelburgenland r (w) dr (sw) Wine region on Hungarian border protected by 3 hill ranges. Makes large quantities of red (esp BLAUFRÄNKISCH). Producers: GSELLMANN & HANS, J HEINRICH, Iby, Igler, P Kerschbaum, WENINGER.

Moric ★★★Outstanding red, terroir-oriented BLAUFRÄNKISCH wine made by Roland Velich from old vines in the MITTELBURGENLAND. Stylistically a beacon.

Morillon Name given in STYRIA to CHARD.

Moser, Lenz Austria's largest producer, based in Krems. Perfectly all right, but could be a lot better.

Moser, Sepp w r sw KREMSTAL grower of elegant, aromatic RIES, GRÜNER VELTLINER.

Müller, Domaine Individualist West STYRIAN producer with international outlook, esp Sauv Bl and CHARD.

Müller-Thurgau See RIES-SYLVANER.

Muskateller Rare, aromatic grape for dry whites. Best from STYRIA and WACHAU. Top growers: Gross, HIRTZBERGER, Lackner-Tinnacher, FX PICHLER, POLZ, SATTLER.

Muskat-Ottonel Grape for fragrant, often dry whites, interesting PRÄDIKATS.

Neuburger Indigenous white grape that has long been neglected but has its stubborn advocates: mainly in the WACHAU (elegant, flowery), THERMENREGION (mellow, ample-bodied), and North BURGENLAND (strong, full). Best from BECK, DOMÄNE WACHAU , HIRTZBERGER.

Neumayer w ★★★ 00 01 02 03 04 05 06 07 08 Top TRAISENTAL estate making powerful, focused, dry GRÜNER VELTLINER and RIES.

Neumeister w ★★★ V.gd innovative SE STYRIAN producer, esp Sauv Bl and CHARD.

Neusiedlersee (Lake Neusiedl) V. shallow BURGENLAND lake on Hungarian border. Warmth and autumn mists encourage botrytis. See next entry.

Neusiedlersee r w dr sw Wine region N and E of Lake Neusiedl. Best: ACHS, BECK, HEINRICH, KRACHER, J NITTNAUS, PÖCKL, STIEGELMAR, UMATHUM, VELICH.

Neusiedlersee-Hügelland r w dr sw Wine region west of Neusiedlersee based around Oggau, RUST, and Mörbisch on the lake shores, and Eisenstadt in the Leitha Mts foothills. Best producers: FEILER-ARTINGER, KOLLWENTZ, Prieler, Schandl, SCHRÖCK, Sommer, ERNST TRIEBAUMER, WENZEL.

Niederösterreich (Lower Austria) Northern region with 58 per cent of Austria's v'yds: CARNUNTUM, Donauland, KAMPTAL, KREMSTAL, THERMENREGION, TRAISENTAL, WACHAU, WEINVIERTEL.

Nigl w ★★★★ 98 99 00 01 02 03 04 05 06 07 08 The best in KREMSTAL, making sophisticated dry *ageworthy Ries and Grüner Veltliner* with remarkable mineral character from Senftenberg v'yd.

Nikolaihof w ★★★★ 95 97 98 99 00 01 02 03 04 05 06 07 08 Built on Roman foundations, this impeccable WACHAU estate has pioneered BIODYNAMISM in Austria and produces focused RIES from the Steiner Hund site.

Nittnaus, John w r sw ★★★ Searching, organic NEUSIEDLERSEE winemaker. Esp elegant and ageworthy reds: Comondor.

Ott, Bernhard w ★★→★★★ GRÜNER VELTLINER specialist from Donauland. Fass 4; also Der Ott and Rosenberg. Part of BIODYNAMIC movement.

Pannobile Association of youngish and highly ambitious NEUSIEDLERSEE growers centered in GOLS and aiming to create great wine with regional character. Current members are: PAUL ACHS, BECK, GSELLMANN, GERNOT HEINRICH, LEITNER, JOHN NITTNAUS, Pittnauer, PREISINGER, Renner.

Pfaffl w r ★★★ 99 00 01 02 03 04 05 06 07 08 WEINVIERTEL estate nr VIENNA, in Stetten. Known for wonderful dry GRÜNER VELTLINER (Goldjoch) and RIES (Terrassen Sonnleiten), he also makes surprisingly gd reds. Also runs nearby Schlossweingut Bockfliess estate.

Pichler, Franz Xavier w ★★★★ 95 96 97 98 99 00 01 02 03 04 05 06 07 08 Top WACHAU producer and one of Austria's best. Intense and *concentrated Ries* and GRÜNER VELTLINER (esp Kellerberg).

Pichler, Rudi w ★★→★★★ Fine WACHAU producer of powerful, expressive RIES and GRÜNER VELTLINER.

Pöckl, Josef & René r (sw) ★★ Father-and-son team in NEUSIEDLERSEE (Mönchhof). Well-made reds, esp Admiral, Rêve de Jeunesse, and Rosso e Nero. Also gd Pinot N and ZWEIGELT.

Polz, Erich & Walter w ★★ 99 00 01 02 03 04 05 06 07 V.gd large south STYRIAN (Weinstrasse) growers; esp Hochgrassnitzberg: Sauv Bl, CHARD, Grauburgunder, WEISSBURGUNDER.

Prädikat, Prädikatswein Quality-graded wines from Spätlese upwards (Spätlese, Auslese, Eiswein, Strohwein, Beerenauslese, AUSBRUCH, and Trockenbeerenauslese). See Germany.

Prager, Franz w ★★★★ 95 96 97 98 99 00 01 02 03 04 05 06 07 08 Pioneer, together with JOSEF JAMEK, of top-quality WACHAU dry whites. RIES and GRÜNER VELTLINER of impeccable elegance and mineral structure: Wachstum Bodenstein.

Claus Preisinger Ambitous young winemaker with stylish reds, esp. Pinot N.

Prieler w r ★★★ V.gd NEUSIEDLERSEE-HÜGELLAND producer. Esp gd: BLAUFRÄNKISCH Goldberg.

Proidl, Erwin ★★ Fine and highly individual KREMSTAL grower making interesting, ageworthy RIES and GRÜNER VELTLINER.

Rabl, Günter ★ Fine KAMPTAL grower long overshadowed by more famous colleagues. V.gd GRÜNER VELTLINER.

Riesling On its own, this always means Rhine RIES. WELSCHRIESLING is unrelated. In Austria this is one of the greatest varieties, particularly in KAMPTAL, KREMSTAL, and WACHAU. Top growers: ALZINGER, BRÜNDLMAYER, HIRTZBERGER, Högl, KNOLL, NIGL, NIKOLAIHOF, PFAFFL, FX PICHLER, PRAGER, SALOMON.

Rotgipfler Fragrant, indigenous grape of THERMENREGION. With ZIERFANDLER, makes lively interesting wine. Esp Biegler, Spaetrot, Stadlmann, Zierer.

Rust w r dr sw BURGENLAND region, famous since 17th century for dessert AUSBRUCH; now also for red and dry white. Esp from FEILER-ARTINGER, Schandl, HEIDI SCHRÖCK, ERNST TRIEBAUMER, Paul Triebaumer, WENZEL.

> **Back to the roots**
>
> Authenticity is the new buzzword. Ten years ago, everybody wanted to create international wines, but now the pendulum has swung and it's all about terroir, regional character, and indigenous grapes such as GRÜNER VELTLINER and BLAUFRÄNKISCH. In an attempt to work with nature instead of against it, many Austrian wineries are also switching to organic or even BIODYNAMIC production methods.

St Laurent Indigenous red variety with brambly aromas and gd tannic structure. Esp from BECK, Fischer, Johanneshof, Pitnauer, Hannes Schuster, UMATHUM.

Salomon-Undhof w ★★★ V.gd Krems producer: RIES, WEISSBURGUNDER, Traminer. V.gd quality for more than a decade. Since Erich Salomon's death his brother Berthold, who produces wine in Australia, is in charge of v'yds and cellar.

Sattler, Willi w ★★★ 97 98 99 00 01 02 03 04 05 06 07 Top south STYRIA grower. Esp for Sauv Bl, MORILLON, often grown on v. steep v'yds. Recently his style has become more classical.

Schilcher Rosé wine from indigenous Blauer Wildbacher grapes (sharp, dry, high acidity). A local taste, or at least an acquired one. Speciality of west STYRIA. Try: Klug, Lukas, Reiterer, Strohmeier.

Schloss Gobelsburg ★★★→★★★★ 01 02 03 04 05 06 07 Renowned KAMPTAL estate run by Michael Moosbrugger. Excellent dry RIES and GRÜNER VELTLINER of discreet opulence. Also outstanding RIES and GRÜNER VELTLINER Tradition, vinified as it would have been 100 yrs ago, and fine Pinot N.

Schloss Halbturn w r sw ★★ Recently revitalized estate creating ever-better wines with German and French winemakers. Esp *cuvée* Imperial, also outstanding Pinot N. With new v'yds coming into production a lot may be expected here.

Schlumberger Largest sparkling winemaker in Austria (VIENNA). Also on the Loire.

Schmelz w ★★→★★★ Fine, often underestimated WACHAU producer, esp outstanding RIES.

Schröck, Heidi w sw r ★★★ Wines of great purity and focus from a thoughtful grower. V.gd AUSBRUCH. Also v.gd Furmint. See Hungary.

Schuster w r Solid NEUSIEDLERSEE-HÜGELLAND producer; ST LAURENT by son Hannes particularly fine.

Schwarz r sw Small but classy NEUSIEDLERSEE producer specializing in ZWEIGELT and Strohwein.

Seewinkel ("lake corner") Name given to the part of NEUSIEDLERSEE inc Apetlon, ILLMITZ, and Podersdorf. Ideal conditions for botrytis.

Smaragd Highest-quality category of VINEA WACHAU, similar to dry Spätlese.

Spätrot-Rotgipfler Typical, 2-grape blend of THERMENREGION. Aromatic and weighty wines.

Spitz an der Donau w Cool WACHAU microclimate, esp from Singerriedel v'yd. Top growers are: DONAUBAUM, HIRTZBERGER, Högl, Lagler.

Stadlmann w r sw Good THERMENREGION producer specializing in opulent ZIERFANDLER-ROTGIPFLER wines.

Steinfeder VINEA WACHAU quality category for light fragrant dry wines.

Steininger sp w r ★★ KAMPTAL grower with a range of v. fine single-varietal sparkling wines, as well as still ones.

Stiegelmar (Juris-Stiegelmar) w r dr sw ★★Well-regarded GOLS grower. CHARD, Sauv Bl. Reds: ST LAURENT.

Strohwein Sweet wine made from grapes air-dried on straw matting.

Styria (Steiermark) Southernmost wine region of Austria. Some gd dry whites, esp Sauv Bl and CHARD, called MORILLON in Styria. Also cool fragrant MUSKATELLER. Inc SÜDSTEIERMARK, SÜD-OSTSTEIERMARK, WESTSTEIERMARK (South, Southeast, West STYRIA).

Südburgenland r w Small south BURGENLAND wine region. V.gd BLAUFRÄNKISCH wines. Best producers: Krutzler, Wachter-Wiesler, Schiefer.

Süd-Oststeiermark SE Styria w (r) STYRIAN region with islands of excellent v'yds. Best producers: Neumeister, Winkler-Hermaden.

Südsteiermark S Styria w Best STYRIA region; popular whites (MORILLON, MUSKATELLER, WELSCHRIESLING, and Sauv Bl). Best: Gross, Jaunegg, Lackner-Tinnacher, POLZ, Potzinger Sabathi, SATTLER, Skoff, TEMENT, Wohlmuth.

Tegernseerhof w Traditional WACHAU producer, newly invigorated by a young incumbent and producing v. interesting RIES and GRÜNER VELTLINER.

Tement, Manfred w ★★★★ 00 01 02 03 04 05 06 07 08 Renowned south STYRIA estate with well-made Steirische Klassik and gently oaked Sauv Bl and MORILLON from Zieregg site. International-style wines, modern reds.

Thermenregion r w dr sw Wine/hot-springs region, south of VIENNA. Indigenous grapes (eg ZIERFANDLER, ROTGIPFLER), historically one of the most important regions for reds (esp ST LAURENT) from Baden, GUMPOLDSKIRCHEN, Tattendorf, Traiskirchen areas. Producers: Alphart, Biegler, Fischer, Johanneshof, Schafler, Spätrot-Gebelshuber, Stadelmann, Zierer.

Traisental 700 ha just south of Krems on Danube. Dry whites can be similar to WACHAU in style, not usually in quality. Top producers: Huber, NEUMAYER.

Triebaumer, Ernst r (w) dr sw ★★★★ 95 97 98 99 00 01 02 03 04 05 06 07 08 Important RUST producer; *some of Austria's best reds*: BLAUFRÄNKISCH (inc the legendary Mariental), Cab Sauv/Merlot blend. v.gd AUSBRUCH.

Uhudler Local South BURGENLAND speciality. Wine made directly from American rootstocks, with a foxy, strawberry taste. Not for export.

Umathum, Josef w r dr sw ★★★ V.gd and thoughtful NEUSIEDLERSEE producer. v.gd reds inc Pinot N, ST LAURENT; gd whites.

Velich Neusiedlersee w sw ★★★★ A searching, intellectual producer. Excellent Burgundian-style Tiglat CHARD (**99 00 01** 02 03 06) with fine barrel-ageing. Some of top PRÄDIKATS in the SEEWINKEL.

Vienna w (r) Wine region in suburbs. Simple, lively wines, served to tourists in HEURIGEN. Quality producers on the rise: CHRIST, WIENINGER, Zahel.

Vinea Wachau WACHAU appellation started by winemakers in 1983 with 3 categories of dry wine: STEINFEDER, FEDERSPIEL, and the powerful SMARAGD.

Wachau w World-renowned Danube region, home to some of Austria's best wines. Top producers: Alzinger, J DONABAUM, FREIE WEINGÄRTNER WACHAU, HIRTZBERGER, Högl, JAMEK, KNOLL, Lagler, NIKOLAIHOF, FX PICHLER, R Pichler, PRAGER, Schmelz, Wess.

Wagram w (r) Wine region just west of VIENNA, inc KLOSTERNEUBURG. Mainly whites, esp GRÜNER VELTLINER. Best producers include: Ehmoser, Fritsch, Stift Klosterneuburg, Leth, BERNHARD OTT, Wimmer-Czerny, R Zimmermann.

Weingut Stadt Krems ★★ Co-op steered by Fritz Miesbauer, reliable and increasingly fine. Miesbauer also vinifies for Stift Göttweig.

Weinrieder w sw WEINVIERTEL grower with expressive GRÜNER VELTLINER and RIES.

Weinviertel ("Wine Quarter") w (r) largest Austrian wine region, between Danube and Czech border. First to adopt DAC appellation system. Striving for quality and regional character. Refreshing whites, esp from Poysdorf, Retz. Best: Bauer, J Diem, GRAF HARDEGG, Gruber, PFAFFL, Schwarzböck, Weinrieder, Zull.

Weissburgunder (Pinot Blanc) Ubiquitous: gd dry wines and PRÄDIKATS. Esp BECK, Fischer, Gross, HEINRICH, HIRTZBERGER, Lackner-Tinnacher, POLZ, TEMENT.

Welschriesling White grape, not related to RIES, grown in all wine regions: simple, fragrant dry wines for everyday drinking.

Weninger, Franz r (w) ★★★ Top MITTELBURGENLAND (Horitschon) estate, with fine reds, esp BLAUFRÄNKISCH, Dürrau, and Merlot. Son runs Hungarian estate.

Wenzel w r sw ★★★ V.gd AUSBRUCH. Junior Michael makes ambitous and increasingly fine reds. Father Robert pioneered the Furmint revival in RUST.

Wess w ★ Good new WACHAU winemaker, vinifying bought-in grapes, some from famous v'yds.

Weststeiermark W Styria p Small wine region specializing in SCHILCHER. Best: Klug, Lukas, DOM MÜLLER, Reiterer, Strohmeier.

Wien See VIENNA.

Wieninger, Fritz w r ★★ **97 98 99 00 01 02 03** 04 05 06 07 08 V.gd VIENNA-Stammersdorf grower with HEURIGE: CHARD, BLAUER BURGUNDER, esp gd GRÜNER VELTLINER and *Ries*. Wines of great balance and depth.

Winkler-Hermaden r w sw ★★★ Outstanding and individual southeast STYRIAN producer, excellent Traminer and MORILLON, also one of the region's few v.gd reds, the ZWEIGELT-based Olivin.

Winzer Krems Important KREMSTAL co-op with 1,300 growers. Esp GRÜNER VELTLINER.

Zierer w r THERMENREGION producer, especially fine ROTGIPFLER.

Zierfandler (Spätrot) White variety almost exclusive to THERMENREGION. Often blended with ROTGIPFLER. Best: Biegler, Spaetrot, Stadelmann, Zierer.

Zweigelt See BLAUER ZWEIGELT.

To decipher codes, please refer to "Key to symbols" on the front flap of jacket, or "How to use this book" on page 10.

AUSTRIA

Central & Southeast Europe

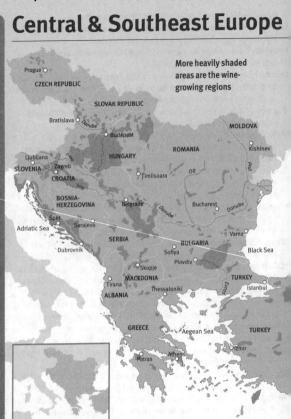

More heavily shaded
areas are the wine-
growing regions

Hungary

Hungary is a country transformed. Two decades after the fall of
communism, the wine industry has shaken off the chains of its
collectivized legacy and seen the emergence of a new wave of passionate,
quality-focused private winemakers. Hungary has long had a claim to
global fame through its luscious Tokaji, famously dubbed the "wine of
kings and king of wines". Today, not only have Tokaji producers continued
to improve so that their sweet wines really are world-class, but Hungary
has shown that it has many more strengths. The emergence of terroir-
driven dry whites and impressive reds, especially from Cab Franc, as well
as local Kékfrankos, suggest a future worthy of attention.

Alföld Hungary's Great Plain makes mostly everyday wine from 3 districts: Hajós-
Baja (Brillant Holding, Sümegi), Csongrád (Somodi), Kunság (Frittmann).

Árvay & Co w dr sw ★★★ **00', 03'**, (05'), (06'), (07) TOKAJ cellar established in 2000
by former DISZNÓKŐ winemaker János Árvay. Hétfürtös is the brand name. V.gd
ASZÚ (5/6 PUTTONYOS) and superb *cuvée* Edés Élet (**01, 03'**). Increasingly
impressive Dry FURMINT (06', 07').

Ászár-Neszmély w dr ★→★★★ Region in NW Hungary nr the Danube. International and native grapes; mainly white. Hilltop is leading winery (Kamocsay).

Aszú Botrytis-shrivelled grapes and the sweet wine made from them in TOKAJ. The wine is graded in sweetness, from 3 PUTTONYOS up.

Aszú Essencia Tokaj sw ★★★★ 93 96' 99' 00' 02 03' (05') (06') (07') Second sweetest TOKAJI quality. 7 PUTTONYOS-+; should be superb amber elixir.

Badacsony w dr sw ★★→★★★ Wine district on north shore of Lake BALATON, on slopes of extinct volcano, home to native variety KÉKNYELÜ. The basalt soil can give rich, highly flavoured white wines; esp well-made Ries and SZÜRKEBARÁT; Pinot N also promising. Look for SZEREMLEY and Villa Tolnay.

Balaton Europe's largest freshwater lake. Wines from BADASCONY and BALATONFURED-CSOPAK on north shore. Wines from BALATONBOGLÁR on south.

Balatonboglár r w dr ★★→★★★ Name of wine district and also a progressive winery owned by Henkell & Söhnlein on south shore of Lake BALATON. Decent whites (Chard, Sem, Muscat). Top producers: GARAMVÁRI, KONYÁRI, Légli.

Balatonfured-Csopak r w dr ★★ District on north shore of Lake BALATON. Mainly whites, esp OLASZRIZLING, Chard. Best producers Feind, Jasdi, Figula.

Balaton-Melleke (S Pannonia) w dr Small region in Zala Hills. Mainly whites, esp Tramini, Pinot Gr, OLASZRIZLING. Wines of Dr Bussay impress.

Béres w dr sw ★★→★★★ New and immaculate TOKAJ producer.

Bikavér r ★→★★★ 03 05 06 (07) Literally "Bull's Blood" with past reputation for ordinary quality. Now being revived as flagship blended red. Can be produced by law only in SZEKSZÁRD and EGER. Egri Bikavér gained protected origin status from 04. Szekszárdi Bikavér will be protected from 09. Must be blend of at least 3 varieties; best producers include a local grape, usually KÉKFRANKOS, and in SZEKSZÁRD sometimes KADARKA. Reserve level requires minimum of 4 varieties, obligatory tasting, and restricted yield. Best producers for Egri Bikavér: Grof Buttler, TIBOR GÁL, St Andrea, Thummerer.

Bock, József r dr ★→★★★ Leading family winemaker in VILLÁNY. Hearty reds, varietal and blends. Best wines are Cab Fr-based Capella Cuvée 00 03' 06' and Syrah 03' 05' 06' and juicy Portugieser 07 08.

Bodrogkeresztúr Village in TOKAJ region with several up-and-coming estates inc DERESZLA, Füleky, Tokajbor Bene, Timon.

Bor "Wine": *vörös* is red; *fehér* is white; Edes is sweet, Száraz is dry.

Csányi r ★→★★★ Major investment in VILLÁNY. Ch Teleki range is best.

DHC Districtus Hungaricus Controllatus. New quality and controlled origin designation in VILLÁNY from 2006, symbolized by local crocus on label.

Dégenfeld, Grof w dr sw ★★→★★★ 99 00 03 (05) (06) Large TOKAJ estate. Produces dry FURMINT, semi-dry Muscat and HÁRSLEVELÜ, classic ASZÚ, late-harvest Fortissimo and EDES SZAMORODNI Also a luxury hotel at TARCAL.

Dereszla w dr sw ★★★ 50-ha TOKAJ estate owned by D'Aulan family from Champagne. V.gd ASZÚ, inc ASZÚ ESSENCIA and flor-matured dry SZAMORODNI.

Demeter, Zoltan Winemaker at KIRÁLYUDVAR; v.gd ASZÚ wines under own name.

Disznókő w dr sw ★★→★★★★ 96' 97 99' 00' 03' (05) (06) (07) Important TOKAJ estate, owned by French company AXA. Sauternes-style wines of the early yrs have given way to more typically Hungarian note, imparted by a Hungarian winemaker. Single-v'yd Kapi 6 PUTTONYOS ASZÚ 99' is notable.

Dobogó ★★★ 99' 00' 03' (05) (06) (07) Fine small TOKAJ estate. V gd ASZÚ. Also excellent late-harvest Mylitta, superb Mylitta Alma (modern take on ASZÚ ESSENCIA) 05' 06' and increasingly gd dry FURMINT 05 06' 07'.

Eger r w dr sw ★→★★★ Best-known red wine centre of N Hungary with attractive baroque city of cellars. BIKAVÉR most famous wine, but increasingly recognized for Cab Fr, Pinot N and Syrah. Whites include LEÁNYKA, OLASZRIZLING, Chard, Pinot Bl. Top producers: Grof Buttler, Demeter, Tibor Gál,

CENTRAL & SOUTHEAST EUROPE

Gundel, Kaló, Pók-Polonyi, St Andrea, Thummerer, Vincze.

Essencia ★★★★93 96 99 (03) The fabulous quintessence of TOKAJI: intensely sweet and aromatic from grapes wizened by botrytis. Properly grape juice of v. low, if any, alcoholic strength, reputed to have miraculous properties: inc raising the dead. Its sugar content can be over 850g per litre.

Etyek-Buda Wine region nr Budapest. Some gd crisp varietal whites, esp Chard and Sauv Bl, Pinot Gr, and IRSAI OLIVÉR. Leading producers: Etyeki Kúria, Nyakas (Budai label), György Villa (owned by TÖRLEY).

Ezerjó Literally "thousand blessings". Widespread traditional grape variety: usually one-dimensional wines with sharp acids. Try Frittmann Maurus.

Furmint The classic grape of TOKAJ, with great flavour, acidity, and potential for both great dry and sweet wines. Also grown in SOMLÓ.

Gál, Tibor r w dr ★★→★★★ Winery in EGER founded by charismatic Tibor Gál, who made his name as winemaker at Ornellaia. Tragically died in 2005; his family continues his work, esp single-v'yd bottlings of Pinot N and v.gd dry Viognier.

Garamvári r w dr sp ★→★★ Family-owned v'yd and St Donatus winery at Balatonlelle. Also owns *Ch Vincent*, Hungary's top bottle-fermented sparkling wine, plus négociant Vinarium.

Gere, Attila r ★★→★★★★ Highly-reputed family winemaker in VILLÁNY with gd, forward-looking reds, esp rich Solus Merlot **02** 03' 06', intense Kopar Cuvée **00 03'** 04 06'. New top wine Grand Vin de Villány 03'.

Gundel TOKAJ venture at MÁD, making wines for famous Gundel's restaurant in Budapest. Also v'yds and cellar at EGER.

Hárslevelü "Linden-leaved" grape variety widely grown. Gd in SOMLÓ and important as second grape of TOKAJ. Gentle, mellow wine; peach aroma.

Hétszölö w dr sw ★★→★★★ Noble first-growth 55-ha TOKAJ estate owned by French group Grands Millésimes de France. Wines have been disappointing.

Hilltop Neszmély w r dr sw ★ Winery in ÁSZÁR-NESZMÉLY makes international-style wines, inc Riverview and Woodcutters White from Cserszegi Füszeres. Premier Vintage range best.

Irsai Olivér Local white cross of 2 table varieties making aromatic Muscat-like wine for drinking young.

Kadarka Traditional red grape with light colour and distinct spicy character, largely fallen out of production, but being revived esp in SZEKSZÁRD where regarded as essential element of BIKAVÉR. Known as Gamza in Bulgaria.

Kékfrankos Hungarian for Blaufränkisch. Most widely planted red variety. Gd light or full-bodied reds.

Kéknyelü "Blue stalk". High-flavoured, low-yielding white grape needing a cross pollinator and making the best and most structured wine of BADACSONY. Best is complex with mineral undertones from SZEREMLEY.

Királyudvar w dr sw ★★★ **99' 00' 01 02** 03' 05 06' (07) .Fine TOKAJ winery in old royal cellars at TARCAL, owned by Anthony Hwang. Wines inc dry and late-harvest FURMINT 05 06 07, Cuvée Ilona (early-bottled ASZÚ), **03'** 07', stunning Cuvée Patricia 06 and 6 PUTTONYOS Lapis ASZÚ **99' 00' 02' 03'** (05) (06) (07).

Konyári r w dr ★★→★★★ Father-and-son team making high-quality red and white from own estate at BALATONBOGLÁR, esp Loliense and Sessio Merlot.

Leányka "Little girl". White grape from Transylvania known as Fetească Albă in Romania. Attractive, aromatic, light dry wine. Királyleányka or Fetească Regală is a cross of Fetească Albă with Grasă of Cotnari.

Mád Old commercial centre of the TOKAJ region with top v'yds. Growers inc Alana-Tokaj, GUNDEL, József Monyok, PENDITS, ROYAL TOKAJI, SZEPSY, Tokaj Classic.

Malatinszky r w dr ★★★ Owner/winemaker was previously sommelier at GUNDEL. Immaculate winery making top-quality unfiltered Kúria Cab Fr) **03'** 04 06' (07) Cab Sauv **03'** 04 06' (07). Gd KÉKFRANKOS rosé 07 08, Pinot Bleu 06, Siklosi

Chard **05** 06 07. New single v'yd blended red Kövesföld 06.

Mátra w (r) ★→★★ District in foothills of Mátra range. Promising dry SZÜRKEBARÁT (Pinot Gr), Chard, MUSKOTÁLY, Sauv Bl. Producers worth a mention include Karner, Szöke Mátyás and former state farm turned co-operative Szölöskert (Nagyrede and Spice Trail labels).

Megyer, Château w dr sw ★★→★★★★ TOKAJ estate bought by Jean-Louis Laborde of Ch Clinet in Pomerol. Also owns CH PAJZOS. Megyer is lighter wine from cooler N of region. Quality improving, esp FURMINT 06 07, ASZÚ 6 PUTTONYOS **93 99 00** 03' 05 06' (07) . Appealing dry Muscat.

Mézes Mály IN TARCAL. This and SZARVAS are historically the best v'yds of TOKAJ.

Minöségi Bor Quality wine. Hungary's appellation contrôlée (see France).

Mór N Hungary w ★→★★ Region famous for fresh, dry EZERJÓ. Now also Ries and Sauv Bl.

Muskotály Muscat; usually Ottonel, except TOKAJ where Sárga Muskotály is yellow Muscat or Muscat Lunel. A little goes into the TOKAJI blend. V. occasionally makes a v.gd ASZÚ wine solo; try KIRÁLYUDVAR'S Cuvée Patricia.

Olaszrizling Hungarian name for the Italian Ries or Welschriesling.

Oremus w dr sw ★★→★★★★★ **99' 00'** 02 03' 05 06' (07) Ancient TOKAJ v'yd of founding Rakóczi family, owned by Spain's Vega Sicilia with HQ at Tolcsva. First-rate ASZÚ and recently v.gd dry FURMINT Mandolás. Also a lesser TOKAJ grape, renamed Zéta.

Pajzos, Château w dr sw ★★→★★★ **93 99 00** 02 03' 05 06' (07) Bordeaux-owned TOKAJ estate with some fine ASZÚ. See MEGYER.

Pannonhalma w r dr ★★ Region in north. Recent joint venture has revived historic Pannonhalma Abbey winery and y'yds dating back to AD 996. Soil and climate Alsace-like; TRAMINI Ries do well and v.gd value. Also attractive white blend Tricollis Cuvée and young Pinot N.

Patricius w dr sw ★★★ **00'** 02 03' 05 06' (07) New quality TOKAJ estate, first vintage in 2000. V.gd dry FURMINT and ASZÚ wines. 4 PUTTONYOS is unusual but has lovely balance.

Pécs (S Pannonia) formerly Mecsek w (r) ★→★★ Newly renamed wine district in southern Hungary, around the city of Pécs. Known for whites, inc OLASZRIZLING, local Cirfandl, and Sauv Bl. Pinot N reported to be promising. Ebner Borhaz most respected producer.

Pendits Winery w SW ★★★ TOKAJ estate certified organic from 08 and working on biodynamic lines run by Márta Wille-Baumkauff. Luscious ASZÚ ESSZENCIA 00 03, Botrytis Selection 01. Attractive Szello Cuvée 06 07 and Dry Muscat 07.

Puttonyos Measure of sweetness in TOKAJI ASZÚ. A "puttony" is a 25-kg measure, traditionally a hod of grapes. The number of "putts" per barrel (136 litres) of dry base wine or must determines the final richness of the wine, from 3 putts to 6 (3 putts = 60g of sugar per litre, 4 = 90g, 5 = 120g, 6 =150g, 7 = 180g). See also ASZÚ ESSZENCIA and ESSZENCIA.

Royal Tokaji Wine Co Pioneer foreign joint venture at MÁD in 1989. 81 ha, mainly first- or second-growth. First wines 90 91 and (esp) 93 led renaissance of TOKAJ. **96 99 00** (03) (06) to follow. (I am a co-founder.) Also well-made dry FURMINT and v.gd value Late harvest Áts cuvee 06 07. New winery built 2009.

Sauska ★★→★★★ 06 07 New immaculate winery in VILLÁNY, owned by co-owner of ÁRVAY. Finely crafted examples of KADARKA, KÉKFRANKOS, Cab Fr and red blends.

Siklós City of southern Hungary; part of VILLÁNY-SIKLÓS Best known for whites esp HÁRSLEVELÜ and ripe, fruity Chard. Plantings of promising reds esp Cab Fr.

Somló w ★★ Isolated small district N of BALATON: whites (formerly of high repute) from FURMINT, HÁRSLEVELÜ, and Juhfark ("sheep's tail") in both traditional barrel-fermented and fresh, fruity styles. Top producers include Fekete, Györgykovács, Hollóvár, Kreinbacher, Tornai.

Sopron W Hungary r ★★→★★★ Historic enclave south of Neusiedlersee (see Austria). Traditionally known for lighter reds from KÉKFRANKOS but showing promise for more full-bodied reds, plus Cab Sauv, Syrah, Pinot N. Top producer WENINGER, promising Jandl, Lövér, Luka, Pfneiszl, Ráspi, Taschner.

Szamorodni Literally "as it was born"; describes TOKAJI not sorted in the v'yd. Dry or (fairly) sweet, depending on proportion of ASZÚ grapes present. In vintage TOKAJ ASZÚ yrs, sweet style can offer ASZÚ character at less cost. Recent trend for late-harvest wines that are similar but bottled younger in more fruity style.

Szarvas TOKAJ v'yd at Tarcal; a top site. Solely owned by TOKAJ TRADING HOUSE and state-run Research Institute for Vine and Wine.

Szekszárd r ★★→★★★ District in S Hungary; some of country's top reds from KÉKFRANKOS, Cab Sauv, Cab Fr, and Merlot. Also KADARKA being revived. Look for: Dúzsi, Heimann, Sebestyén, Szent Gaál, Takler, Vesztergombi, Vida.

Szepsy, István w dr sw ★★★★ 99' 00' 02 03' (05) (06) (07) Impeccable small production of long-ageing TOKAJI ASZÚ from own winery in MÁD. Recent releases of *excellent single-v'yd dry wines from Furmint* and HÁRSLEVELŰ 05 06' (07), and new sweet Szamorodni from 03. Same family name as the man who created the ASZÚ method in 17th century, though not related.

Szeremley, Huba r w dr sw ★★→★★★ Leader in BADACSONY. Ries, SZÜRKEBARÁT, KÉKNYELŰ, sweet Zeus are modern wines. Promising Pinot N since 03.

Szürkebarát Literally "Grey Monk": Pinot Gr. Widely planted and produces high-quality dry wines and inexpensive Italian lookalikes, esp around BALATON.

Tarcal TOKAJ commune with 2 great first growths and several gd producers: GRÓF DEGENFELD, KIRÁLYUDVAR, Andrássy Kúria.

Tiffán, Ede ★★ VILLÁNY grower: full-bodied, oaked reds.

Tinon, Samuel Tokaji ★★→★★★ French ASZÚ specialist at BODROGKERESZTÚR. Also fine SZAMORODNI.

Tokaj/Tokaji w dr sw ★★→★★★★ Tokaj is the town; Tokaji is the wine, Tokay the old French and English name. Appellation covers 5,967 ha. See ESSZENCIA, FURMINT, PUTTONYOS, SZAMORODNI. Also dry table wine of character.

Tokaj Trading House State-owned TOKAJ company, buying grapes from over 2,000 small growers plus 55 ha own vines inc the fine SZARVAS v'yd. Also called Kereskedőház or Crown Estates.

Tolna Declared separate region from SZEKSZÁRD in 1997. Largest single estate is Antinori-owned Bátaapáti with 155ha. Good TRAMINI, Chard, blended reds. German-owned Danubiana based here though most of its v'yds are at MÁTRA.

Törley r w dr ★→★★★ Large company (was Hungarovin): international varietals (Chard, Cab Sauv, Merlot), also *cuve close*, transfer, and classic sparkling (the one to try). Owned by German Sekt specialist Henkell & Söhnlein. Chapel Hill is commercial brand, Gyorgy-Villa and Kemendy for better selections.

Tramini Gewurz, esp in SIKLÓS.

Villány-Siklós (S Pannonia) Southern wine region with 2 main towns. Villány makes mostly red, often good-quality B'x styles. Siklós makes mostly white. High-quality producers: BOCK, CSÁNYI, ATTILA GERE, Gere Tamas, Heumann, MALATINSZKY, Polgár, SAUSKA, TIFFÁN, Wunderlich, VYLYAN.

Vylyan r w dr ★★→★★★ 00 03' 04 06' (07) Investment from the late Pal Debreczeni, now run by his wife Monika. 130 ha with local and international varieties. Burgundian consultant's influence shows in stylish Pinot N. *Duennium Cuvée* (Cab Fr, Cab Sauv, Merlot, and Zweigelt) is flagship red.

Weninger r ★★★ Standard-setting winery in Balf, SOPRON, run by Austrian Franz Weninger Jr. Biodynamic since 2006. Single-v'yd *Spern Steiner Kékfrankos* 04' (06) one of best in country. Syrah, Pinot N, and red blends also impressive.

Weninger & Gere r ★★★ Austro-Hungarian joint venture since 1992 between

Franz Weninger Sr and ATTILA GERE. Cab Fr Selection excellent **00' 02 03' 04'** (06), gd value Cuvée Phoenix **04 06'**.

Zéta A cross of Bouvier and FURMINT used by some in ASZÚ production.

Bulgaria

Visitors to Bulgaria are invariably impressed by its wines, but with domestic demand high, very few of the better quality wines are exported. The 08 vintage was divided into two parts by heavy rain; the early period produced almost the high quality of 07, but the remainder was poorer.

Assenovgrad r ★→★★ Ageworthy MAVRUD and RUBIN specialists. MAVRUD **04** 07.

Belvedere Group Owns Menada, Katarzyna, Oriachovitza, and Vinimpex brands.

Bessa Valley r ★★★ B'x specialist Stephan von Neipperg and K-H Hauptmann's exciting winery nr Pazardjik. Enira and Enira Reserve **06**. Promising new Syrah.

Blueridge r w ★→★★ Large DOM BOYAR winery, label. Gd Chard and Cab Sauv.

Chateau de Val r ★★ Small producer of distinctive top-end wines. Grand Claret **03**. Award-winning new white, Cuvée Trophy **07**.

Damianitsa r ★★→★★★ Winery specializing in MELNIK grape. V.gd Redark Merlot **04**; Uniqato and No Man's Land labels consistent quality.

DGO "Quality wines with declared geographical origin".

Dimiat Native white grape. Gd examples from BLUERIDGE and POMORIE.

Domaine Boyar Main exporter to UK, own v'yds and wineries. Best-known producer in Bulgaria, recently launched premium quality Vinoteka Vin du Garage. Award winning Solitaire Merlot Vintage **06**.

Gamza Red grape (Kadarka of Hungary) with potential, mainly from Danube region. NOVO SELO is specialist.

Katarzyna ★★ Promising quality from new cellar. Look for Question Mark **07**.

Khan Krum ★→★★ Gd whites, esp Chard and TRAMINER.

Korten ★★ Boutique cellar of DOMAINE BOYAR. Traditional styles.

Leventa ★★ Small new winery in Russe with particularly gd whites, esp TRAMINER. 06 Chard and Merlot Grand Selections also recommended.

Logodaj ★→★★ Winery at Blagoevgrad. Soetto Cab Fr **05**. Nobile Rubin **06**. Value.

Mavrud Considered the best indigenous red variety, v. popular at home. Can make highly ageworthy, dark, plummy wines only grown in the Plovdiv area.

Maxxima r (w) Full-bodied reds esp Cab Sauv, Merlot, and MAVRUD. First producer of Premium Reserve oak-aged reds. Private Reserve **03** is recommended.

Melnik Southwest village and highly prized grape variety grown throughout Struma Valley. Dense reds that can age up to 20 yrs.

Menada Stara Zagora r ★★ Thracian Plain winery, owned by Belvedere group. Menada Trinity Mavrud **04**.

Eduardo Miroglio r w ★★ Italian investor with own v'yds. Improving quality, still pricey. Sauv Bl and Pinot N recommended. Producer of Bulgaria's best sparkling wine: Miroglio Brut Metodo Classico **05**.

Misket Indigenous grape, mildly aromatic. The basis for most country whites. Sungurlare and Karlovo in the Valley of the Roses are specialists.

Novo Selo Gd red GAMZA from the northwest.

Oriachovitza r ★★ Winery owned by Belvedere. Gd Reserve Cab Sauv **04**. Richly fruity reds at their best after 4–5 yrs.

Pamid Light, soft, everyday red in southeast and northwest.

Pomorie w (r) ★ Black Sea winery. Esp gd Chard, Sauv Bl and MISKET.

Rubin Bulgarian cross (Nebbiolo x Syrah); gd in blends, but gaining favour in single-varietal niche wines.

Sakar Southeast area with some of Bulgaria's best Merlot.

Santa Sarah r w ★★ Premium wine brand for fine Cab Sauv, Merlot. Privat, a blend of Cab Sauv and MAVRUD, **06** is outstanding. Voted Bulgaria's best wine of 2008. Also gd whites.

Shumen w r ★ New World-style reds and esp whites from Black Sea-region winery. Good TRAMINER, popular on home market.

Slaviantsi ★ Gd varietal whites.

Sliven, Vini r (w) ★→★★ Thracian Valley winery for Merlot, MISKET, and Chard. Tuida Merlot Cab Sauv **07**.

Targovishte w ★ Winery in east. Quality Chard, Sauv Bl, and TRAMINER.

Telish r ★★ Innovative winery in north. Quality Cab Sauv and Merlot. Gd value.

Terra Tangra r w ★★→★★★ Winery in SE nr Harmanli fulfilling early promise, own v'yds in a gd area. Impressive wines, widely recommended. Try the Cab Sauv and Merlot Grand Reserves **06**, Roto **06** and Cuvée **06**.

Todoroff r (w) ★→★★ Thracian-region high-profile winery (25 ha): Cab Sauv, MAVRUD, Merlot.

Traminer Fine whites with hints of spice. Most popular white in Bulgaria.

Valley Vintners ★★ Bulgaria's first terroir wine Sensum **03** is excellent. Dux 03 recommended.

Villa Lyubimets ★→★★ V'yds in southeast nr Greek-Turkish borders. Mainly reds. Villa Hissar is sister white label. Syrah **06** is worth a try.

Vinimpex A major exporter of Bulgarian wines.

Yambol r w ★ Winery in Thracian Plain, specializing in Cab Sauv and Merlot.

Slovenia

Long-time star of the Balkans with v'yds that border both Italy and Austria, and are in effect extensions of both, Slovenia has some excellent terroir. Whites, often the best wines, and becoming more robust in style. There's still not much exported, but if you happen to be there, take the opportunity to experiment.

Batič ★★ Organic-oriented winegrower in VIPAVA. Try Bonissimus, Zarija **06'** 07 and Rosso.

Bjana ★★ Gd BRDA producer. Aged sparklers are much respected locally.

Blažič ★★★ BRDA producer with a sense of place. Top whites and gd reds.

Brda (Goriška) District in PRIMORJE. Centre of quality with many gd producers inc BJANA, Blažič, Četrtič, EDI SIMČIČ, Erzetič, JAKONČIČ, Kabaj, Klinec, KRISTANČIČ, MOVIA, Prinčič, SIMČIČ, ŠČUREK, VINSKA KLET GORIŠKA BRDA.

Edi Simčič ★★★ Gd BRDA producer. Best: w blend Triton Lex, Kozana (single v'yd Chard); r blend Duet Lex **02** 03' and 04' and v. expensive Kolos 03.

Čotar ★★ Leading producer from KRAS. Hazy white blend Dražna and Vitovska are made with long skin contact. Also Teran and Terra Rossa.

Čurin-Prapotnik ★★ Legendary pioneer of private wine-growing from early 1970s onward. PREDIKATES are world-class ★★★★. Also brand PRA-Vino.

Cviček Locally popular traditional pink blend of POSAVJE. Low alcohol, high acid.

Dveri-Pax ★★★Excellent winery nr Maribor. Basic DYA line offers crisp, gd value whites. Premium line, inc renowned RENSKI RIZLING "M" , 04' 06' 07, is mostly from single v'yds. V.gd MODRI PINOT **06'** 07 08 and Modra Frankinja MODRA FRANKINJA **06'** 07' 08'.

Istenič ★★→★★★ NV Barbara and Miha are gd value, while Gourmet vintage range is often Slovenia's best. Brut Nature Prestige **03'** is brut zero fizz.

Jakončič ★★★ V.gd BRDA producer with elegant whites and reds. Top wines: w 04' **05'** 06' and r 04' 05' blend Carolina. Also lighter varietals, sparkling Carolina and Carolina Noir 05.

Jeruzalem Ormož ★★ Well-known co-op producing crisp whites, esp ŠIPON

(Furmint), Sauv Bl, RENSKI RIZLING (Ries), and great value blend Terase.

Joannes ★★ Winery nr Maribor, esp Ries **04'** 05' 06' and Chard.

Kogl ★★★ Hilltop winery nr Ormož, dating back to 16th century. Whites among Slovenia's best, either varietal (Mea Culpa) or Duo, Trio, Quartet blends. Premium blends (r/w) Magna Domenica. Delicate PREDIKATS. Repays ageing.

Kras Small, famous district in PRIMORJE. Best known for TERAN but trend is toward whites, esp MALVAZIJA. Look for ČOTAR, Jazbec, Lisjak Boris, RENČEL.

Kristančič (Dušan) ★★ Important quality producer from BRDA. Consistent varietal line and oak-aged Pavo ("peacock") line.

Kupljen ★★→★★★ Dry wine pioneer nr JERUZALEM known for RENSKI RIZLING, Sauv Bl, SIVI PINOT, Chard, Pinot N. Great for ageing, consistent.

Laški Rizling Welschriesling. Most-planted variety, but rarely made as a varietal.

Ledeno vino Icewine. Getting rare but made almost every year. Can be sublime.

Ljutomer Ormož ★→★★★ Famous wine sub-district in PODRAVJE, known for crisp, delicate white varieties and top botrytis, has still more to deliver. See ČURIN, JERUZALEM ORMOŽ, KOGL, Krainz, Krajnc, KUPLJEN, VERUS.

Macerated whites Recently v. popular. Whites produced with long maceration for several days at higher temperatures. There is hardly an important producer in Primorska not using this technique at least in part.

Malvazija Slightly bitter yet generous flavour, which goes v. well with seafood. M by VINAKOPER is gd value. Also v.gd from Pucer z Vrha, Montemoro, SANTOMAS, Rojac. In recent yrs successfully grown in BRDA and KRAS.

Marof ★★ New winery in Prekmurje raising the potential of the district. DYA w, oak-aged line Breg and single-v'yd line Cru.

Mlečnik ★★★ Disciple of Italy's Joško Gravner from VIPAVA. The closest anyone in Slovenia comes to organics.

Modra Frankinja ★→★★ Austria's Blaufränkisch. Traditionally best in POSAVJE, but DVERI-PAX and PTUJSKA KLET are overtaking.

Modri Pinot (Pinot N) Slovenia's best red? Some are fine and ageworthy.

Movia ★★★★ Best-known Slovenian winery. Top wines: Veliko Belo (w) **96' 99' 00' 01'** 03' 04' 05 and Veliko Rdeče **93 96' 97' 00'** 01' (r) and released mature. V. gd varietals esp MODRI PINTO **02'** 03'. Lunar (REBULA) **05'** 06' 07 08 and sparkling Puro are out of the ordinary style. Ages well.

Penina Quality sparkling wine made by either charmat or traditional method. Lots of styles available. Look for RADGONSKE GORICE (biggest), ISTENIČ (biggest private), BJANA (most fashionable), Medot, MOVIA.

Podravje Region in the northeast. Recent comeback with aromatic whites and increasingly fine reds, mostly PINOT N and MODRA FRANKINJA.

Posavje Conservative wine region in the SE. Producers: ISTENIČ, PRUS, ŠTURM.

Predikat Wines made from botrytis-affected grapes. Expensive. Pozna Trgatev is Spätlese, Izbor is Auslese, Jagodni Izbor is Beerenauslese, Suhi Jagodni Izbor is Trockenbeerenauslese, while LEDENO VINO is Icewine. Try to find some!

Primorje Region in the southwest from the Adriatic to BRDA. Currently most forward-looking Slovenian wine region for both reds and whites.

Prus Small producer from the Bela Krajina district in POSAVJE. His delicate and complex PREDIKATS are ★★★★.

Ptujska Klet ★★→★★★ Winery in Ptuj producing gd international style white. Much improved since 2003. Brand Pullus since 07. Sauv Bl is regularly v.gd.

Radgonske Gorice ★ Well-known co-op producing best-selling Slovenian sparkler Srebrna ("silver") PENINA, classic-method Zlata ("golden") PENINA, and legendary demi-sec Traminec with black label.

Rebula Traditional white variety of BRDA. Can be exceptional. Varietal or with Chard for top blends.

Refošk ★ Refosco. Ruby, light, and unripe version is popular in local bars and restaurants. SANTOMAS and VINAKOPER show the results can be different.

Renčel ★★★ Remarkable producer from KRAS (tiny quantities, experiments).

Renski Rizling Ries. Floral and fruity, or mineral with gd ageing potential. Best: Ducal, DVERI-PAX, JERUZALEM ORMOŽ, JOANNES, Krajnc, KUPLJEN, MAROF, VALDHUBER, VERUS.

Santomas ★★★ SLOVENSKA ISTRA. Flying winemaker is helping to produce some of the country's best REFOŠK and REFOŠK-Cab Sauv blends.

Sauvignonasse Aka Tocai Friulano, mostly in BRDA. Popular locally and in Italy.

Ščurek ★★→★★★ V. reliable BRDA producer. DYA varieties Chard, REBULA, Tokaji, Sauv Bl, Cab Fr. V. particular red and white blends, Stara Brajda and classy white Dugo. Since 02 excellent premium red blend Up.

Simčič, Marjan ★★★ Excellent BRDA producer. DYA Chard, SIVI PINOT. REBULA-based blend Teodor is outstanding, while muscular MODRI PINOT gets more and more elegant. In selected yrs great sweet Leonardo.

Sipon Aka Furmint. Up-and-coming dry, crisp and delicate w. See VERUS, KUPLJEN, Ducal, Püklaver, Miro, Krainz, JERUZALEM-ORMOZ. Excellent for botrytis.

Sivi Pinot Pinot Grigio. Increasingly fine, fruity, with much more character and body than in neighbouring Fruili Venezia-Giulia. Fine aromatics in PODRAVJE.

Slovenska Istra Coastal district in PRIMORJE, known for REFORSK and constantly improving MALVAZIJA. SANTOMAS and VINAKOPER lead.

Štajerska Slovenija New and important wine district since 2006 that encompasses practically whole PODRAVJE region.

Steyer ★★ Top name from RADGONSKE GORICE. Best known for Traminec in all possible forms and styles.

Šturm ★★ Long-established, yet lone star of the Bela Krajina district in POSAVJE. Many PREDIKATS are outstanding.

Sutor ★★★ Excellent producers from VIPAVA. Look for MODRI PINOT and Chard 04 05' 06', w blend Burja 06' 07' and Merlot.

Teran ★ REFOŠK from KRAS. Dark, high-acidity red, v. popular locally.

Tilia ★★ Young couple from VIPAVA produce international style white and red. MODRI PINOT 06' is usually great.

Valdhuber ★★★ Dry wine pioneers in PODRAVJE. Top wine is (dry) Traminec.

Verus Vinogradi ★★★ 07' 08' Young team with distinctive white varietals in JERUZALEM; worldwide acclaim for maiden vintage 2007, esp with SIPON.

Vinakoper ★★ Large company with own v'yds in SLOVENKSA ISTRA Gd-value brand Capris line and premium Capo d'Istria Cab Sauv 99' 02 03'.

Vinska Klet Goriška Brda ★→★★★ Immensely improved big winery from BRDA. Big range, mostly varietals, often excellent value, esp Quercus line.

Vipava District in PRIMORJE. Fine producers: BATIČ, Guerila, Štokelj, MLEČNIK, SUTOR, TILIA. Vipava co-op ★ has premium brand Lanthieri ★★.

Croatia

The Dalmatian and Istrian coasts offer highly original wines from indigenous vines and steep limestone slopes. The only catch is the cost: they don't undervalue their excellent whites or reds.

Agrolaguna ★→★★ Co-op at Poreč, ISTRIA. Solidly gd value, esp reds.

Babič Dark, native red from Primošten (north DALMATIA), grown in stony seaside v'yds. Exceptional quality potential. Try Gracin, VINOPLOD.

Badel 1862 ★→★★★ Biggest wine producer, surprisingly gd. Best: IVAN DOLAC (PZ Svirče), DINGAČ (PZ i Vinarija Dingač).

Bibich ★★ Export-oriented winery nr Šibenik. Gives back hope to native white Debit as DYA and oak aged Lučica. Native Plavina, Babič, Lasina and Rhône grapes used for elegant reds.

Bura ★★★ 04' 05' Considered best DINGAČ producer. Tiny quantities.

Coronica, Moreno ★★★ Top MALVAZIJA (DYA) Gran Malvazija 02 03' 04' 05' and gd Gran Teran from ISTRIA. Also Cab Sauv Grabar. Classic.

Cult wines Highly regarded reds produced in minute quantities. Controversial pioneer Stagnum 03' 04 05, excellent DINGAČ BURA 04' 05', powerful POSTUP Mare 04' 05' (16 degrees!), new Merlotina 04' (Merlot), love-or-hate Mendek Selekcija 03' 04' and outrageously expensive Medvid 03' 04 05.

Dalmacija-vino ★ Giant co-op at Split: v.gd Faros.

Dalmatia Dalmacija. The coast of Croatia is a grower's paradise. Traditionally high in alcohol. Whites (Debit, Maraština) improving, reds improving faster.

Dingač 03' 04' 05' V'yd designation on PELJEŠAC's steep southern slopes. "Grand cru" for PLAVAC MALI. Made from partially dried grapes: full-bodied robust, dry (over)expensive red. Look for: BURA, Kiridžija, Radovič, and Skaramuča.

Enjingi, Ivan ★★ Producer of v.gd sweet botrytis and dry whites, esp Venje blend from Požega. GRAŠEVINA, Sivi Pinot, and superb white blend Venje.

Graševina Welschriesling. Best in SLAVONIJA. Look for Adžić, Djakovačka vina, ENJINGI, KRAUTHAKER, KUTJEVO, Vinarija Daruvar. From dry to top botrytis.

Grgić ★★→★★★ "Paris tasting" winner (see Grgich Hills, California); produces PLAVAC and oaky POŠIP on PELJEŠAC peninsula. Daughter Violet is taking over.

Hvar Beautiful island in mid-Dalmatia. Gd reds from PLAVAC MALI from steep southern slopes. Interesting native wines from plateau. Look for: IVAN DOLAC, Carić Faros, Plančić, Zlatan Plavac, PZ Svirče, Tomić .

Istria N Adriatic peninsula. MALVAZIJA is the name here. Gd for Cab Sauv and Teran. Look for Benvenuti, Clai (Ottocento r/w), CORONICA, KOZLOVIĆ, MAIOŠEVIĆ, Pilato, Radovič.

Ivan Dolac Area on south slopes of HVAR. "Grand cru" for PLAVAC MALI.

Korak Excellent gd whites and Pinot N from PLEŠIVICA. Full-bodied Chard (esp sur lie 06') and Ries, Sauv Bl.

Kozlović ★★★ V.gd white producer from ISTRIA. Esp MALVAZIJA. Also reds.

Krauthaker, Vlado ★★★ Top Croatian producer of dry whites from KUTJEVO, esp Chard (Rosenberg) and GRAŠEVINA Mitrovac. Reds are ★★.

Kutjevo Name shared by a town in SLAVONIJA, centre of GRAŠEVINA and ★★→★★★ co-op. Gewurz, GRAŠEVINA and top botrytis.

Malvazija Malvasia White queen of ISTRIA shows here its full potential and diversity. Several styles are available, mostly to be drunk young with seafood.

Matošević, Ivica ★★→★★★ Pioneer and leader from ISTRIA. MALVAZIJA Alba.

Pelješac Beautiful peninsula and region in south DALMATIA. Some v.gd PLAVAC MALI. Home of POSTUP, DINGAČ. See also CULT WINES, GRGIĆ.

Pjenušac Sparkling. Look for Tomac, Persūrić, also Šenpjen. Legendary and once barely drinkable Bakarska Vodica has improved.

Plavac Mali The best DALMATIAN red grape: wine of body, strength, and even ageability. See PELJEŠAC, HVAR. Promising on island of Brač (Baković).

Plešivica Quality sub-region nr Zagreb, known for whites, esp Chard and sparkling. Look for: KORAK, Režek, Šember Tomac.

Pošip Best DALMATIAN white, mostly on island of Korčula. Korta Katarina is new.

Postup Famous v'yd designation northwest of DINGAČ. Medium to full-bodied red. Mare, Miličić, Radovič are a gd call.

Prošek *Passito*-style dessert wine from DALMATIA.

Slavonija Sub-region in north for white. Look out for ENJINGI, Jakobović, KRAUTHAKER, KUTJEVO.

Stolno vino Table wine. Not many v.gd wines are labelled "stolno".

Suho Dry. *Polusuho* is semi-dry; *poluslatko* is semi-sweet, *sladko* is sweet.

Vinoplod ★ Co-op from Šibenik. Best is BABIĆ 06'.

Vrhunsko vino A fairly rigorous designation for high-quality wines.
Vugava Rare white from island of Vis. Linked to Viognier. Try Lipanović.
Zdjelarević ★★ White wines from SLAVONIJA, esp Chard **05' 06'**.
Žlahtina Native white from island of Krk. Look for Katunar, Toljanić.
Zlatan Otok ★★★ HVAR-based winery of Zlatan Plenković, uncrowned king of
   PLAVAC MALI. His Zlatan Plavac Grand Cru **03'** 04' 05' is constantly among top
   Croatian reds. New, big project nr Šibenik.

Bosnia & Herzegovina

Since the civil war ended in 1995, wine production in Bosnia & Herzegovina has
been dominated by small independent family operations.

Blatina Native red grape and wine.
Kameno Vino White of unique, irrigated desert v'yd in Neretva Valley.
Mostar The area around Mostar, the unofficial capital city of Herzegovina, has
   been the heartland of Herzegovinian wine production since World War II.
   Cellars such as Ljubuski (the oldest in the country) and Citluk are producing
   gd-quality ZILAVKA white and slightly less impressive BLATINA red.
Samotok Light red (rosé/*ruzica*) wine from run-off juice (and no pressing).
Zilavka White grape. Potentially dry and pungent. Fruity; faint apricot flavour.

Serbia

In the last two decades winemaking traditions have revived, with replanted
v'yds and many new private wineries. International varieties prevail but local
ones like Prokupac, Vranac (red), Smederevka and Tamjanika (white) thrive.

Aleksandrović Topola winery known for white Trijumf and pink Varijanta.
Bermet Legendary fortified wine (w or r) flavoured with herbs and spices.
Fruška Gora Region in Vojvodina mostly planted with Welschriesling.
Kovačević Winery from Fruška gora. Mostly Chard.
Negotinska Krajina Region with many private winemakers growing Gamay, Pinot
   N and TAMJANIKA.
Prokupac Native variety giving lighter, fruity reds. Often blended with Cab Sauv**.**
Radovanović Winery from central Serbia known for Cab Sauv and Chard.
Smederevka A native variety from around Smederevo giving authentic whites.
Tamjanika Local name for Muscat Blanc à Petits Grains. Grown mostly in Zupa
   and NEGOTINSKA KRAJINA.
Župa Region in South Serbia dominated by PROKUPAC.

Montenegro

Montenegro is known mostly for reds from the indigenous Vranac grape.
Biotehnički institut Podgorica Wine producer and vine research institute.
Crmnica Region near Lake Skadar, mostly planted with VRANAC.
Cemovsko polje One of the biggest v'yds in Europe, with 2,000 ha planted.
Duklja Late-harvested, semi-sweet version of VRANAC.
Krstački Native fruity white grape with crisp acidity. Most important white.
Plantaze 13 Jul Winery famous for VRANAC. Mostly state-owned.
Sjekloća Private winery from CRMNICA. Excellent VRANAC.
Vranac Indigenous variety responsible for full-bodied reds with firm tannins and
   great ageing potential. Grown also in Macedonia and Serbia.

Macedonia

There may not be a great deal of wine produced here, but it's still the country's second biggest export after tobacco. Most of it goes in bulk, especially to Germany, where they like it sweetened up, and no doubt cheap, but efforts are being made at home to improve quality. Macedonia's secret weapons are its native vines, particularly dark, rustic Vranec and light, bright Stanushina.

Bovin ★ First winery to be privatized. Focusing on quality with deep VRANEC from relatively low-yielding vines.

Cekorov ★★ Tiny 3-ha family estate. VRANEC is one of the best.

Fonko ★ Young winery, best known for Chard and Bucephall VRANEC.

Kratosija Local red grape also found in Montenegro; sound wines.

Pivka ★ Private winery in TIKVEŠ region. Gd VRANEC.

Popova Kula ★ Tikveš winery growing local grape Stanushina: light red, refreshing, distinctive. Big expansion plans, too.

Povardarie (Vardar Valley) Main wine region with 85% of production. Other two are Pcinja-Osogovo and Pelagonija-Polog. Look out for tannic, acidic VRANEC.

Skovin ★→★★ Large producer with 450 ha v'yds. Decent reds.

Smederevka Widely planted native white grape, noted for high acidity and nutty characters, also found in Serbia and Hungary.

Stanušina Indigenous light-coloured red grape making pale, fruity wines. Nearly disappeared; now making a comeback.

Temjanika Local name for Muscat Frontignan.

Tikveš ★ Macedonia's largest winery (500 ha) in region of same name.

Vranec Local name for Montenegro's red Vranac (qv); with SMEDEREVKA, accounts for half the country's red wine. Lots of tannin and acidity and quality potential.

Zilavka Well-regarded local white variety.

The Czech Republic & Slovakia

Czech Republic

Czechs are checking out their new appellation system, called *Vína Originální Certifikace*, or VOC, which is modelled on the Austrian DAC system. Prices for any wine with special attributes are reaching the stratosphere, especially in the case of wines boasting competition medals; money still seems to be available, and new wineries are springing up in both Bohemia and Moravia, the two regions of the Czech Republic where vines are grown. Things are not all rosy, though, with imports accounting for 70 per cent of all wine on the market.

Bohemia

720 ha in two demarcated wine sub-regions: Mělnická (Mělník) and Litoměrická (Litoměřice). Same latitude and similar wines to east Germany. Best in the Elbe Valley (north of Prague), notably at Mělník , Roudnice and Žernoseky. V'yd renewal, esp in Prague (Gröbovka, Salabka and Svatá Klára), inc several small boutique wineries E of the capital: Kutná Hora, Konárovice and Ch Kuks. Kosher wine production in Chrámce. Sparkling wine is mostly tank-fermented using grapes from Austria. The Bohemia Sekt group (Henkell-Söhnlein) and Soare Sekt (Sektkellerei Schloss Wachenheim) dominate the market.

Moravia

18,000 ha in four demarcated wine sub-regions: Znojemská (Znojmo), Mikulovská (Mikulov), Velkopavlovická (Velké Pavlovice) and Slovácko. V'yds situated in SE along Austrian and Slovak borders: similar grapes. Look for:

Stapleton & Springer (Bořetice), Metroflora (Milotice), S, Spielberg (Archlebov), Víno Dalibor (Zaječí), Čebav (Tvrdonice), Sedláček (Valtice), Šebesta (Březí), all young and dynamic. The established giants get stronger, as do groupings such as Collegium Vinitorum, Bonus Eventus and newcomer V8. Icing on the cake is icewine and straw wine. Beware outrageously priced 20-cl bottles. Moravia also has sparkling wine,esp the renewed Sekt Domaine label of the late Jan Petrák.

Slovak Republic

There are roughly 17,000 ha of v'yds in six wine regions along the western and southern borders: Malokarpatská (Little Carpathians), Juhoslovenská (Southern Slovakia), Nitrianska (Nitra), Stredoslovenská (Central Slovakia), Východoslovenská (Eastern Slovakia), and the smallest Tokajská (Tokaj) region, neighbouring Hungary's Tokaj. Classic central European and international varieties. Nearly all consumed locally with some sold in bulk to the Czech Republic. Leading producers: Ch Belá (Mužla) with Egon Müller's involvement, Masaryk (Skalica), Matyšák (Pezinok), Mrva & Stanko (Trnava), and J J Ostrožovič (V Tŕňa, Tokaj). For sparkling wine: J E Hubert and Pálffy Sekt.

Romania

Romania is one of Europe's largest wine-producing nations with around 195,000 ha under vine in 2008 and a wine history dating back around 4,000 years. EU membership in 2007 brought large subsidies invested into new equipment and vineyards, and the wines have improved as a result. The buoyant local market consumes most of the country's wine, though tastes are changing towards red and dry whites. This, with increasing wealth, has allowed the development of exciting premium wines from quality-orientated producers, and the revival of historic grapes. The best blends are local varieties such as Fetească Neagră with international grapes, giving wines with a growing sense of place.

Băbească Neagră Traditional "black grandmother grape" of the MOLDOVAN Hills, esp Nicoresti area; light body and ruby-red colour.

Banat Small wine region on western border, with 2 DOCS: Banat itself and Recas, ITALIAN RIES, Sauv Bl, MUSCAT OTTONEL, local Ries de Banat; light red Cadarca, Cab Sauv, MERLOT.

Blaj Wine region in TÂRNAVE (TRANSYLVANIA), dry or off-dry whites.

Bohotin East Moldavia region known for aromatic rosé Busuioacă de Bohotin.

Burgund Mare Romanian name for Blaufränkisch (Kékfrankos in Hungary).

Carl Reh ★★ German-owned winery with 190-ha v'yd in Oprisor. V.gd reds, esp La Cetate (**03 05 06'** 07 08). Val Duna is export label for gd varietal w, esp Pinot Gr.

Cotnari Region in northeast with v.gd botrytis conditions. Famous for over 500 yrs for medium to sweet GRASĂ, FETEASCĂ ALBĂ, TĂMÂIOASĂ, and dry Frâncuşă. The Tokaj of Romania.

Cotnari Winery 1,200 ha in COTNARI region. Wines range from dry to v. sweet, inc v.gd collection wines.

Cramele Recaş ★★ British/Romanian firm in BANAT region. PINOT N with potential. Best: Sole Chard, La Putere r. Gd Pinot Gr, promising new Syrah from 06 07 08.

Crişana & Maramures Western region inc DOCS of Crişana and historical Miniş (since 15th century): esp red Cadarca; crisp, white Mustoasă.

Davino Winery ★★→★★★ Premium producer with 68 ha in DEALU MARE. V.gd Dom Ceptura white **06 07** and red **04 05** (06). Alba Valahica and Purpura Valahica Fetească Neagră 06. Flagship blend is Flamboyant 03'.

Dealu Mare (Dealul Mare) "The Big Hill". Important well-situated area in southeastern Carpathian foothills. Excellent reds, esp FETEASCĂ NEAGRĂ, Cab

Sauv, MERLOT, PINOT N. Whites from TĂMÂIOASĂ.

Dobrogea Black Sea region. Inc DOC regions of MURFATLAR, Badabag, and Sarica Niculitel. Famous for sweet late-harvest Chard and now for full-bodied reds.

DOC, Denumire de Origine Controlata Denomination of origin. DOC-CMD means fully ripe; DOC-CT is late harvest; DOC-CÎB is noble late harvest, or botrytized.

Domeniile Tohani Winery ★ Major holding in DEALU MARE specializing in red wines (inc FETEASCĂ NEAGRĂ, Cab Sauv, PINOT N, MERLOT) and sweet Dollette.

Domeniul Coroanei Segarcea ★ Former crown dom in southwest with 320 ha. Gd lively whites, inc FETEASCĂ REGALĂ, Sauv Bl, Muscat Frontignan Rosé.

Drăgășani Region on river Olt south of Carpathians. Traditional (white: Crâmposie Selectionată; reds: Novac, Negru de Drăgășani) and international varieties.

Fetească Albă Romania's third-most-planted white grape with faintly Muscat aroma. Same as Hungary's Leányka, with gd potential for sparkling.

Fetească Neagră "Black maiden grape" with potential as showpiece variety. Difficult to handle, but can give deep, full-bodied wines with character.

Fetească Regală A cross of FETEASCĂ ALBĂ with GRASĂ (gd for sparkling and recently some successful barrel-fermented versions). Most-planted white.

Fontana da Vini New winery since 2006 with 80 ha of v'yds. Aurelia Visinescu is winemaker. Promising FETEASCĂ NEAGRĂ and white blends. Also Divin brand.

Grasă Local Romanian grape whose name means "fat". Prone to botrytis and v. important grape in COTNARI. Grown as Kövérszölö in Hungary's Tokaj region.

Halewood Winery ★→★★ British venture producing gd wines, esp reds. V'yds in DEALU MARE: fine FETEASCĂ NEAGRĂ, PINOT N. Also TRANSYLVANIA and MURFATLAR.

Huși Wine region in Moldova, whites, inc local Zghihara and sweet aromatic pink Busuioacă de Bohotin.

Iași Region for fresh acidic whites (FETEASCĂ ALBĂ, also RIES ITALIAN, Aligoté, sparkling MUSCAT OTTONEL). Reds: FETEASCĂ NEAGRĂ, MERLOT, Cab Sauv.

Iordana High acid, low alcohol local white grown in Apold for sparkling wines.

Jidvei ★ Requipped winery in sub-region of the same name in TRANSYLVANIA (TÂRNAVE). Whites: FETEASCĂ, ITALIAN RIES, Sauv Bl, Traminer Roz, and sparkling.

Lacrima lui Ovidiu "Ovid's Tear": sweet fortified wine aged for many yrs in oak barrels until amber coloured, from MURFATLAR.

Merlot Romania's most widely planted, red variety.

Moldova (Moldovia) Western part of former Romanian province (eastern part became Republic of Moldova). Largest wine region, lying NE of Carpathians. DOC areas inc BOHOTIN, COTNARI, Dealu Bujorului, HUȘI, IAȘI, ODOBEȘTI, Cotești, Nicorești.

Muntenia and Oltenia Hills Major wine region covering the DOC areas of DEALU MARE, Dealurile Olteniei, DRĂGĂȘANI, PIETROASA, Sâmburești, Stefanești.

Murfatlar Area with v'yds in DOBROGEA nr Black Sea; v.gd Chard, Pinot Gr, and Cab Sauv. Sub-regions are Cernavoda and Megidia.

Murfatlar Winery ★→★★ Largest bottled-wine producer. V.gd labels Trei Hectare (FETEASCĂ NEAGRĂ, Cab Sauv, Chard) and Ferma Nouă (MERLOT, Sauv Bl).

Muscat Ottonel Muscat of Eastern Europe; a Romanian speciality, esp in cool TRANSYLVANIA and in Moldava dry to sweet wines.

Nachbil Label for new small aspirational producer Weingut Brutler and Dr Vicol in CRISANA. Rhine Ries has character.

Odobești Ancient wine region in Vrancea. Local Galbenă de Odobești variety makes everyday whites.

Pietroasa in DEALU MARE for sweet whites, esp TĂMÂIOASĂ ROMÂNEASCĂ.

Pinot Noir Grown for over 100 yrs, originally as sparkling base. Newer plantings of French clones show promise.

Prince Stirbey ★★ 05 06 07 20-ha estate in DRĂGĂȘANI returned to Austrian-Romanian noble family (Kripp-Costinescu). V.gd dry from local Crâmposie

CZECH REPUBLIC/ROMANIA

Selectionată, FETEASCĂ REGALĂ, and TĂMÂIOASĂ ROMÂNEASCĂ and rosé. Has successfully revived local red varieties esp Novac and Negru de DRĂGĂŞANI.

Riesling, Italian Widely planted Welschriesling, sold locally as Riesling.

SERVE ★★→★★★ Corsican-founded DEALU MARE winery and v'yds. Excellent Terra Romana label, esp Cuvée Charlotte **03'** 04 05 (06) (blend of FETEASCĂ NEAGRĂ, Cab Sauv, MERLOT) and Cuvée Amaury **06 07**.

Tămâioasă Românească White "frankincense" grape, with exotic aroma and taste belonging to Muscat family. Often makes fine botrytis wines in COTNARI and PIETROASA.

Târnave (also Tîrnave) Cool region in TRANSYLVANIA, known for Sauv Bl and FETEASCĂ REGALĂ. Dry aromatic wines (esp Pinot Gr, Gewurz) and sparkling. See JIDVEI, BLAJ.

Transylvania Cool mountain plateau in centre of Romania. V'yds often steep and mostly producing white wines with gd acidity from FETEASCĂ ALBA, FETEASCĂ REGALĂ, MUSCAT, Traminer, ITALIAN RIES. Sub-regions include TÂRNAVE, Alba-Iulia, Lechinta, Aiud, and Apold.

Valea Călugărească "Valley of the Monks", part of DEALU MARE and site of research winery.

Vanju Mare Warm region in southwest noted for full-bodied reds.

Vinarte Winery ★★→★★★ **01 03** 05 06 (07) Italian investment covering 3 doms: Villa Zorilor in DEALU MARE, Castel Bolovanu in DRĂGĂŞANI Terase Danubiane in VANJU MARE. Best are Soare Cabernet **00 01**, Prince Matei MERLOT **02 03 04**.

Vincon Vrancea Winery One of Romania's largest producers with 2150 ha in VRANCEA plus DOBROGEA and DEALU MARE.

Vinia One of Romania's largest wineries at IAŞI. Major producer of COTNARI wines. Also whites and light reds.

Vin cu Indicatie Geografica Equivalent to VDP. Also known as Vin de Regiune.

Vin de masă Table wine.

Vinterra Dutch/Romanian venture reviving FETEASCĂ NEAGRĂ; also makes gd PINOT N, MERLOT. Black Peak is brand name.

Vrancea Important county in MOLDOVA covering Panciu, ODOBEŞTI, and Coteşti.

Greece

Greek wine has become seriously newsworthy. Top-end sommeliers, wine writers and wine traders now know that the term "world-class Greek wine" is not a contradiction in terms. How has this been achieved? The usual ways: by a lot of hard work in the vineyard, in the cellar and, for many winemakers, by spreading the word. The next part will be trickier: persuading the consumers.

Aghiorghitiko NEMEA's red grape, now planted almost everywhere, even in the north. Extemely versatile, from soft and charming to dense and ageworthy.

Aivalis ★★★ Boutique NEMEA producer: extracted style. Top (and pricey) wine is "4", from 120+-yr-old vines. Newly released Merlot.

Alpha Estate ★★★ Impressive estate in cool-climate Amindeo. Excellent Merlot/Syrah/XINOMAVRO blend, pungent Sauv Bl, unfiltered XINOMAVRO from ungrafted vines. Top wine: Alpha 1 that demands ageing. ★★★★ soon?

Antonopoulos ★★★ PATRAS-based winery, with top-class MANTINIA, crisp Adoli Ghis, Lafon-(Burgundy)-like Chard, and Cab-based Nea Dris (**97 98 00 01 02** 03 04). Top wine: violet-scented Vertzami/Cab Fr.

Argatia ★★→★★★ Small KTIMA, just outside NAOUSSA, crafting tiny quantities of excellent XINOMAVRO.

Arghyros ★★→★★★ Top SANTORINI producer with exemplary but expensive VINSANTO aged 20 yrs in cask, recently ★★★★. Exciting KTIMA white, a critically acclaimed oak-aged Vareli white, and new fragrant (dry) Aidani.

Assyrtiko One of the v. best white grapes of the Mediterranean, balancing power, minerality, extract, and high acid.

Avantis ★★★ Boutique winery in Evia with (red) v'yds in Boetia. Dense Syrah, Aghios Chronos Syrah/Viognier, pungent Sauv Bl and rich MALAGOUSIA. Top wine: elegant single-v'yd Avantis Collection Syrah **02** 03 04 05.

Biblia Chora ★★★ Polished New World-style wines. Highly sought-after Sauv Bl/ASSYRTIKO. Floral Syrah Rosé. Ovilos range is noteworthy as well as Areti AGHIORGHITIKO and ASSYRTIKO.

Boutari, J & Son ★→★★ Producers in NAOUSSA. Excellent-value wines, esp *Grande Reserve Naoussa*, popular MOSCHOFILERO. Top Santorini Kalisti Reserve, single-v'yd Skalani from CRETE. Try the sweet red Liatiko.

Cambas, Andrew ★ Large-volume brand owned by BOUTARI.

Carras, Domaine ★→★★ Estate at Sithonia, Halkidiki, with its own OPAP(Côtes de Meliton). Ch Carras **01** 03 04. Underperforming.

Cava Legal term for cask-aged still white and red table wines, eg Cava Amethystos Kosta Lazaridi, Cava Hatzimihali.

Cephalonia (Kephalonia) Ionian island: excellent, floral white Robola, emerging styles of sweet Muscat, MAVRODAPHNE.

Crete Quality improves led by Ekonomou, LYRARAKIS, Douloufakis, MANOUSSAKIS.

Dougos ★★→★★★ From the Olympus area, producing interesting Rhône blends, top Methymon range, esp opulent, dry late harvest red Opsimo.

Driopi ★★★ New venture of TSELEPOS in high NEMEA. Initial vintages are serious (esp single-v'yd KTIMA) and of the high-octane style. Tavel-like Driopi rosé.

Emery ★→★★ Historic RHODES producer, specializing in local varieties. Brands Villaré, Grand Rosé. V.gd-value Rhodos Athiri. Sweet Efreni Muscat.

Gaia ★★★ Top-quality NEMEA-based producer and winery on SANTORINI. Fun Notios label. New World-like AGHIORGHITIKO. Thought-provoking but top-class dry white Thalassitis Santorini. Top wine Gaia Estate (**97 98 99 00 01** 03 04 05). New Anatolikos dessert (sun-dried) NEMEA and dazzling Gaia S red (AGHIORGHITIKO with a touch of Syrah).

Gentilini Cephalonia ★★→★★★ Exciting whites inc *v.gd Robola*. New Unique Red Blend and serious Syrah.

Georgakopoulos Central Greece ★★→★★★ Full-throttle, New World-style reds Blanc de Noir Cab Sauv and rich unoaked Chard. Producer to watch.

Gerovassiliou ★★★ Perfectionist miniature estate nr Salonika. Benchmark ASSYRTIKO/MALAGOUSIA, smooth Syrah/Merlot blend, ageworthy, Burgundian in style Chard. Herby, red Avaton **03** from rare indigenous varieties. Top wine: Syrah (01 **02** 03 04). For many, the trend-setter for Greek wines.

Greek Wine Cellars New company name for KOURTAKIS.

Goumenissa (OPAP) ★→★★★ XINOMAVRO and Negoska oaked red from Macedonia. Esp Aidarinis, BOUTARI, Ligas and Tatsis Bros.

Hatzidakis ★★★ Low-tech but high-class producer, redefining SANTORINI appellation, esp with Cuvées No. 15 and 17. Stunning range across the board. Try the excellent Nihteri.

Hatzimichalis, Domaine ★→★★★ Large v'yds and merchant in Atalanti. Huge range. Greek and French varieties, many bottlings labelled after their v'yd names, illustrating terroir differences. Top red Rahes Galanou Merlot/Cab Fr.

Katoghi-Strofilia ★★→★★★ V'yds and wineries in Attica, Peloponnese, and N Epirus. Greek varieties but also Chard, Cab Sauv, Traminer, and even Pinot N. Katogi was the first-ever premium Greek wine. Top wine: KTIMA Averoff.

Katsaros ★★★ Small organic winery of v.gd standard on Mt Olympus. KTIMA red, a Cab Sauv/Merlot has staying power. Chard gets better with each vintage.

Kir-Yanni ★★→★★★ V'yds in NAOUSSA and at Amindeo. Vibrant w Samaropetra;

complex and ageworthy Dyo Elies r; NAOUSSA Ramnista turning towards more supple approach, making way for XINOMAVRO/Syrah blend Diaporos.

Kouros ★ Reliable, well-marketed white PATRAS and red NEMEA from KOURTAKIS.

Kourtakis, D ★★ Merchant: *mild Retsina* and gd NEMEA. See GREEK WINE CELLARS.

Ktima Estate, farm. Term not exclusive to wine.

Lazaridis, Domaine Kostas ★★★ V'yds and wineries in Drama and Kapandriti (nr Athens and sold under the Oenotria Land label). Quality Amethystos label (white, red, rosé). Top wine: unfiltered red CAVA Amethystos (**97 98 99 00** 01 02 03). First Greek consultancy of Bordeaux's Michel Rolland.

Lazaridis, Nico ★★→★★★ Spectacular post-modernist winery and v'yds in Drama, Kavala and Mykonos. Gd Ch N Lazaridis (white, rosé, and red). Top wine: Magiko Vouno white, red. Ultra-premium range under Perpetuus brand.

Lemnos (OPAP) Aegean island: mainly co-op fortified dessert wines, delicious, lemony Muscat of Alexandria. Try the dry Muscats by Kyathos-Honas winery.

Lyrarakis ★★→★★★ V.gd producer from CRETE. Whites from the rare Plyto and Dafni varieties, as well as a deep, complex blend of Syrah and Kotsifali. Top red: Grande Cuvée.

Malagousia Rediscovered perfumed white grape, stunning in the hands of AVANTIS, GEROVASSILOU and MATSA.

Manoussakis ★★★ Impressive newcomer from CRETE, with Rhône-inspired blends. Delectable range under Nostos brand, led by Roussanne and Syrah.

Mantinia (OPAP) w High central Peloponnese region. Fresh, crisp, utterly charming *Moschofilero*.

Matsa, Château ★★→★★★ Historic and prestigious small estate in Attica, owned now by BOUTARIS. Top wine: Ktima ASSYRTIKO/Sauv Bl. Excellent MALAGOUSIA.

Mavrodaphne (OPE) r sw "Black laurel", and red grape. Cask-aged port/*recioto*-like, concentrated red; fortified. Speciality of PATRAS, north Peloponnese. Dry versions (eg ANTONOPOULOS) are increasing, with much promise.

Mediterra (ex-Creta-Olympias) ★★ V.gd Cretan producer. Value Nea Ghi range, spicy white Xerolithia, red Mirabelo. New Pirorago 04 Syrah/Cab Sauv/Kotsifali blend. Fantastic and v.gd-value Silenius range.

Mercouri ★★★ Peloponnese family estate. V.gd Refosco, delicious RODITIS. Ageworthy CAVA. Classy Refosco dal Penducolo r, fine sw Belvedere Malvasia.

Mezzo Sweet wine produced in SANTORINI from sun-dried grapes, lighter and less sweet than VINSANTO. Some dispute over style – some producers (eg SIGALAS) use the term for wine made from the red Mandilaria variety, while others (eg ARGHYROS) use the same white varieties as VINSANTO.

Mitravelas ★★→★★★ Outstanding new entry in NEMEA, promising great things.

Moraitis ★★ Small quality producer on the island of Paros. V.gd smoky (white) Monemvasia, (red) tannic Moraitis Reserve .

Moschofilero Pink-skinned, rose-scented, high-quality, high-acid grape.

Naoussa (OPAP) r High-quality region for XINOMAVRO. One of two Greek regions where a *cru* notion may soon develop.

Nemea (OPAP) r Region in E Peloponnese producing dark, spicy AGHIORGHITIKO wines. Recent investment has moved it into higher gear. High Nemea merits its own appellation. Koutsi is front-runner for *cru* status (see GAIA, Oreinos Helios and DRIOPI).

Nemeion A new KTIMA in NEMEA, setting new pricing standards (esp Igemon) for the appellation, with wines to match.

Oenoforos ★★ Gd Peloponnese producer with high v'yds. Extremely elegant. RODITIS Asprolithi. Also delicate white Lagorthi, nutty Chard (Burgundian, limited release, magnum only), crisp Ries, and stylish Syrah.

OPAP "Appellation of Origin of Higher Quality". In theory equivalent to French VDQS, but in practice where many gd appellations and wines belong.

OPE "Appellation of Origin Controlled". In theory equivalent to French *apppelation contrôlée* but mainly reserved for Muscat and MAVRODAPHNE.

Papaïoannou ★★→★★★★ If NEMEA was Burgundy, Papaïoannou would be Jayer. Classy reds (inc Pinot N and Petit Verdot); flavourful whites. A wonderful flight of NEMEAS: KTIMA Papaïoannou, Palea Klimata (old vines) Microklima (a micro-single v'yd) and top-end Terroir (a super-strict, 200%-new-oaked selection).

Patras (OPAP) w White wine (based on RODITIS) and wine town facing the Ionian Sea. Home of MAVRODAPHNE. Rio-Patras (OPE) sw Muscat.

Pavlidis ★★★ Ambitious new v'yds and winery at Kokkinogia nr Drama. Gd ASSYRTIKO/Sauv Bl, v.gd ASSYRTIKO. Excellent Syrah and Tempranillo. KTIMA red recently switched from B'x blend to AGHIORGHITIKO/Syrah in a masterful move.

Pyrgakis ★★→★★★★ Highly experimental KTIMA, fully capitalizing on the highest parts of NEMEA OPAP. Try the semi-dry, late harvest, rosé AGHIOGHITIKO.

Rapsani Interesting oaked red from Mt Olympus. Rasping until rescued by TSANTALIS, but new producers, like Liappis, are moving in.

Retsina Attica speciality white with Aleppo pine resin added. Domestic consumption waning.

Rhodes Easternmost island and OPAP for red and white. Home to creamy (dry) Athiri w grape. Top wines include Caïr (co-op) Rodos 2400 and Emery's Villare. Also some sparkling.

Roditis White grape grown all over Greece. Gd when yields are low.

Samos (OPE) w sw Island nr Turkey famed for sweet, golden Muscat. Esp (fortified) Anthemis, (sun-dried) Nectar. Rare old bottlings can be ★★★★ such as the newly released 75.

Santorini Volcanic island north of CRETE and OPAP for w, dry and sw. Luscious VINSANTO and MEZZO, mineral-laden, bone-dry white from fine Assyrtiko. Oaked examples can also be v.gd. Top producers include GAIA, HATZIDAKIS, SIGALAS. Try ageing everything.

Semeli ★★→★★★ Estates nr Athens and NEMEA and a new winery in MANTINIA under the Nassiakos name. Value Orinos Helios (white and red) and convincing, top-end Grande Reserve, released after 4 yrs.

Sigalas ★★★ Top SANTORINI estate producing leading oaked SANTORINI Bareli. Stylish VINSANTO. Also rare red, Mourvèdre-like Mavrotragano.

Skouras ★★→★★★★ Innovative Peloponnese wines. First to use screwcaps on Chard Dum Vinum Sperum with most of white range following suit. New wine: Synoro (Cab Fr dominated). Top wine: Grande Cuvée Nemea 01 03 04 '05.

Spiropoulos, Domaine ★★ Organic producer in MANTINIA. Oaky, red Porfyros (AGHIORGHITIKO, Cab Sauv, Merlot). Sparkling Odi Panos has potential. New, single v'yd Astala MANTINIA.

Tetramythos ★★ Exploring the possibilities of cool-climate parts of Peloponnese, a new and promising venture. The winery was burnt in the great summer fires of 2007, but slowly returns to top form.

TO "Regional Wine", French VDP equivalent. Most exciting Greek wine category.

Tsantalis ★→★★★★ Merchant and v'yds at Agios Pavlos. Gd red Metoxi, Rapsani Res, and Grande Res, and gd-value Organic Cab Sauv and excellent Avaton.

Tselepos ★★★ Top-quality Mantinia producer and Greece's best Gewurz. Other wines: fresh, oaky Chard, v.gd Cab Sauv/Merlot, single-v'yd Avlotopi Cab Sauv. Top wine: single-v'yd Kokinomylos Merlot.

Vinsanto Sweet wine style produced in SANTORINI, from sun-dried ASSYRTIKO and Aidani. Require long ageing, both in oak and bottle. The best and oldest Vinsantos are ★★★★ and practically indestructible. See also MEZZO.

Voyatzi Ktima ★★ Small estate nr Kozani. Aromatic white, classy elegant red.

Xinomavro The tastiest of indigenous red grapes (name means "acidic-black"). Grown in the cooler north, it is the basis for NAOUSSA, GOUMENISSA, and

Amineo. High ageing and quality potential: Greece's answer to Nebbiolo.

Zafeirakis ★★→★★★★ Small κτιμα in Tyrnavos, Central Greece, uncharted territory for quality winegrowing. Fastidious winemaker and a much anticipated Limniona red, the first bottling of a v. promising and rare variety.

Zitsa Mountainous Epirus AC. Delicate Debina white, still or sparkling.

Cyprus

Why does Cyprus not have a higher international profile, possessing as it does the natural advantages of a Mediterranean climate, an ability to grow vines up to 1,500 m above sea level and interesting indigenous grapes? Put simply it's because for most of the 20th century the principal exports were wines lacking any unique Cypriot identity: they were mostly inexpensive "sherry-style" wines for the lower end of the British market and, later, very basic wines for Eastern Europe. Both those markets have now collapsed. The good news is that more progressive producers are at last starting to make the wines the island deserves.

Commandaria A sweet, deliberately oxidized wine. The greatest Cypriot wine, almost certainly the wine with the longest heritage in the world. (The poet Hesiod wrote of its ancestor in 800 BCE.) Produced in hills north of Limassol. From sun-dried XYNISTERI and MAVRO grapes.

ETKO One of largest producers. Range includes Salera from MAVRO and XYNISTERI (r and w), also Shiraz, Merlot, Chard, and a Shiraz/Mourvèdre/Grenache blend. Best: Ino Cab Sauv and Centurion Commandaria.

KEO Large, go-ahead firm. Range includes Ktima Keo red (Cab Sauv + LEFKADA) and white (Chard); also Heritage (red), oak-aged MARATHEFTIKO and COMMANDARIA St John

Lefkada Rediscovered indigenous black grape variety. Higher quality than Mavro. Used for varietal wines as well as blends with Cab Sauv.

Loel One of major producers. Reds: (indigenous) LEFKADA and MARATHEFTICO, also w Chard, and r and w blends of international and indigenous varieties.

Maratheftico Vines of superior quality making concentrated red wine; not easy to cultivate but possibly, with LEFKADA, the future grape of Cyprus.

Mavro The black grape of Cyprus. Sound, acceptable wines. Produces moderate quality if planted at high altitude. Easier to cultivate than MARATHEFTICO.

SODAP A co-op winery and one of 4 largest producers. Now using Australian consultancy: Island Vines (r, p and w) modern, fresh and value made from native and international grapes; the white considered one of best expressions of XYNISTERI. Also regional wines (r and w) including a MARATHEFTICO; and wines from international varieties.

Xynisteri Native white grape of Cyprus. Easily oxidizes if handled badly but modern techniques give delicate, fruity wines.

Malta

The introduction of new Demoninazzjoni ta' Origini Kontrollata, or DOK, regulations, enforceable from the 08 vintage, bans chaptalization and brings vy'd, winemaking and labelling practices into line with the EU. Antinori-backed Meridiana remains the driving force of the region, producing excellent Maltese Isis and Mistral Chardonnays, Astarte Vermentino, Melquart Cabernet Sauvignon/Merlot, Nexus Merlot, **outstanding Bel Syrah**, and premium Celsius Cabernet Sauvignon Res from island vines. Volume producers of note are Delicata, Marsovin, and Camilleri.

England & Wales

There's an optimism for the future of UK wines, in spite of low yields in 2007 and 2008. And it's because of fizz. Sales of bottle-fermented sparkling wines are buoyant, and plantings of Champagne varieties continue to increase; they should take over from still wine varieties by 2010. New wineries are being built or planned and as the quality of the wines improves, so too does the UK's reputation for serious winegrowing.

Astley, Worcestershire ★★ Wines continue to win awards. Late Harvest 07 v.gd.

Breaky Bottom E Sussex ★★ Sparkling wines well worth trying. Balanced, crisp Cuvée Alex Mercier 03 and refreshing Cuvée Donna Elvira 04. Kir Royal v.gd.

Camel Valley Cornwall ★★★ Lindo père et fils (Bob and Sam) improve every year. 05 06 07 quality v.gd, esp Rosé 05, Pinot 05 sparkling and zesty Bacchus 07.

Chapel Down Kent ★★★ Still UK's largest producer and, with additional 40 ha planted with Champagne varieties, should stay on top. 05 06 07 all v.gd, esp Pinot Reserve Sparkling 02, Rosé 07 and Sancerre-like Bacchus Reserve 06. New winery planned for 2010. V.gd visitor facilities inc major new restaurant.

Denbies Surrey ★★ UK's largest v'yd with 107.3 ha now produces a gd range of interesting wines. Excellent fruit-filled Rose Hill 07 is v.gd. Also Bacchus 07, Greenfields 02 sparkling and Hillside Chardonnay 06.

Nyetimber West Sussex ★★★ Recent plantings have brought total up to 107 ha, making this (just) the second-largest UK v'yd. Quality slipped slightly with change of owner and winemaker, but getting back on track. Crisp, dry Blanc de Blanc 01 and Classic Cuvée 01 still youthful.

RidgeView East Sussex ★★★ Great quality, consistency and gd value keep this winery at the top of UK producers. Cavendish 05 and Bloomsbury 05 both v. gd; also Bloomsbury 06. 25 per cent of company sold to another grower with large v'yds in 2007 which will see output rise to 325,000 bottles by 2014.

Sharpham Devon ★★ Great range of wines (and also great cheeses). Dart Valley Reserve 06 and spicy Bacchus 07 best wines.

Stanlake Park Berkshire ★★ Large range of wines of above-average quality. Lightly oaked Fumé 06, Hinton Grove 06, Pinot Blush 07 worth trying.

Three Choirs Gloucs ★★ 07 UK's second-largest producer by volume. Large range of gd value wines. Estate Reserve Siegerrebe 06 highly regarded. Cellar Door range, Bacchus 07, Siegerrebe 07 and sweet Noble Rot 07 all worth trying.

Other noteworthy producers

A'Becketts Wiltshire Estate Rosé 06 and Estate Red 06 both worth trying.
Beeches Herefordshire 06 lightly oaked, crisp Dry White.
Biddenden Kent Spicy white Ortega 06 and 07.
Bothy Oxon Refreshing white Oxford Dry 07 and flavourful Paradox 07.
Brightwell Oxon Up-and-coming producer. Try: Bacchus 07
Eglantine, Nottinghamshire North Star 04 notable sweet 'Icewine'.
Hush Heath Estate Kent Balfour Brut Rosé 05 sleek and strawberryish.
Meopham Valley Kent Well-balanced sparkling Rosé 05.
Warden Abbey Bedfordshire V.gd Sauv Bl-like Bacchus 06.
Wickham Hampshire Toasty Special Release Fumé 07.
Yearlstone Devon Lightly spiced dry white "No 5" 07 and fuller bodied, barrel-aged white "No 6" 07.

Asia, North Africa, Israel & Lebanon

Algeria Winemaking collapsed at independence in 1960 due to political and religious pressure; aggressive replanting (region naturally protected from phylloxera) is now underway to raise annual production from 50 to 150m litres. Important regions: Tlemcen (powerful reds, whites, rosé – Dom de Sebra), Mascara (Ch Beni Chougrane), Dahra (reds, rosés – Dom de Khadra), Zaccar (Ch Romain), Médéa (Ch Tellagh), Tessala, Aïn-Bessem-Bouira.

China The 6th-largest wine producer in the world. (Blending with imports is not regulated.) Extreme NW climate necessitates burying vines against the cold. Frequent hailstorms, monsoon rains and poor soils haven't stopped 500+ wineries being founded. Some 83% of production sold domestically and four-fifths is red. Recent tax changes have energized the industry esp in the market for imported wines: fine European wine poured into Hong Kong after duty there was abolished. Getting it to the mainland proved more difficult. The Napa model of wine tourism is being copied, with spas (Bodegas Langes) and tourist facilities. New orientation towards premium wine production. Twenty-six provinces produce wine, the most productive being Xinjiang, Tianjin, Shandong, Jinlin, Hebei, and Henan, and high-altitude areas of Yunnan. Production dominated by Dynasty, Changyu, and Great Wall. Some premium producers now emerging: Huadong (Chard, Ries) in Shandong, Shanxi Grace in Shanxi (Merlot, Rosé, Chairman's Reserve, B'x blend, Chard), Lou Lan, Turpan (Merlot), Suntime Manas from Xinjiang and Dragon Seal (Reserve Cab Sauv) . Others to watch: Ch Bolongbao (organic) in Hebei, Yunnan Red Wine Co, Helen Mountain, Chang Baishan (Ice wine) in Jinlin.

India The world's fastest developing wine region, with 50 wineries making over 6m litres of wine, increasing by 25% pa. Production is centred at Maharashtra, with 40+ wineries; region is home to Ch Indage (Chard, Cab Sauv, Shiraz, and Omar Khayyam sparkling) and Sula, producing Chenin Bl, Sauv Bl, Zin, and Merlot. Grover V'yds is the other well-known producer, located in Bangalore, where Michel Rolland makes La Reserve Cab Sauv/Shiraz, Viognier. The Krishna and Nandi valleys here have applied for separate AC status. Gd producers: Dajeeba, Vintage (Reveilo), Flemingo Ch D'Ori, McDowell, Mountain View, ND, Rajdheer, Sankalp, Renaissance, Mandala, and Sailo.

Japan Wine became fashionable in Japan in 2008 due to the "Wine Manga" (a cartoon). Now home to more than 200 wineries, just 3% of Japanese wines are made locally; the rest are made with imported concentrate and bulk wine. Two main wine regions: Yamanashi (nr Mount Fuji), the most important; and Nagano. Both beset with summer rain and high humidity and coupled with excessive soil fertility, this has led to producers researching new regions and indigenous varieties. Smaller regions inc Yamagata prefectures (N of Tokyo) and Hokkaido, the coldest wine region in the world.

Japan has no appellation system but efforts are being made regionally. The wine sector is also attracting foreign investment (Bernard Magrez with Katsunuma and Denis Dubourdieu with Shizen). Production is dominated by Mercian, Suntory, Sapporo (Polaire), Mann, Kyowa Hakko Kogyo (Ste Neige).

Of indigenous varieties, Koshu (disc 1186) is the most prominent, making gd crisp dry whites (gd producers: Katsunuma, Mercian, Shizen Cuvee Denis Dubourdieu). Others include Shokoshi (Coco Farm, Katsunuma), the lighter red Yama Sauvignon (Mars) and Kai Noir – a hybrid (Grace).

Red production is now moving toward lighter styles. The most interesting and expensive wines are from international varieties, such as Mann's Chard and Merlot from Nagano, Mercian's Kikyogahara Merlot and Hokushin Char, Asahi Yoshu's Kainoir, and Jyonohira Cab Sauv. Smaller wineries to watch include Alps, Obuse, Marufuji, Takeda, Shizen, Tsuno and Yamazaki.

Morocco Foreign investment could be reviving Morocco as a wine country. Bordeaux producer Bernard Magrez makes a boutique wine at Kahina in Meknèz; and Rhône producer Alain Graillot has a joint venture, called Tandem, that takes advantage of the country's stock of old Syrah vines. The slopes of the Atlas Mts (Meknes and Fez) provide best conditions for viticulture; Coastal v'yds source notable light, fruity wines. Chard, Syrah, Cab Sauv, and Merlot produce gd wine, while Cinsault, Carignan, and Grenache produce traditional reds and "Gris". Celliers de Meknes, makes 90% of Morocco's wine, of which 75% is red and 20% rosé. Cépages de Boulaouane, Cépages de Meknes and Société Thalvin also figure. Best labels include L'Excellence de Bonassia (aged Cab Sauv/Merlot), Ch Roslane's Les Coteaux de l'Atlas, Les Trois Domaines, Dom Riad Jamil, Ksar.

Tunisia Foreign investment here, too. UCCV (Vieux Magon, Reine Elissa) still dominates. Smaller wineries, Domaine's Atlas (gd Punique, Ifrikia), Ceptunes, Kelibia, Kurbis, Lansarine, Neferis, Ch St Augustin produce gd wine. French-style winemaking using international varieties is giving way to New World taste. AOCs: Mornag, Kélibia, Thibar, Côteaux d'Utique, Tébourba, Sidi Salem.

Turkey State producer Tekel was disbanded in 04. Kavaklidere (fair Altin Kopuk sparkling, white Cankaya, red Yakut and white/red Angora) and Doluca (gd Kav/V Doluca reds, a v gd Karma Sauvignon) now dominate the table market. Older makers eg Diren, Kocabag, Kutman, and Melen have been joined by a gd younger generation of producers, with Büyülübag, Cankara, Corvus, Kayra, Serafin (owned by Doluca) and Sevilen (gd Chard and gd Sauv Bl) of note. The main area of production is Thrace/Marmara (40%); other districts are central/ east/ southeast Anatolia and the Black Sea coast. Indigenous Emir and Narince make gd whites; Bogazkere, Kalecik Karasi and Okuzgozu make full, powerful reds. International varieties show promise. But the economic crisis is hitting hard, and many wineries are under threat of closure.

The Old Russian Empire

Ex-Soviet wine-producing countries are increasingly going their own way. Russia is a rapidly developing market, but quality winemaking is still in its infancy. Ukraine and Moldova rely for export on Russia. There has been some investment and help from international consultants in all countries – basic quality has improved, but there are no outstanding wines yet. Georgian winemaking is in crisis, due to the loss of distribution in Russia and v. limited export possibilities.

Ukraine The Odessa region dominates in grape growing and in wine production, but Crimea has better quality potential, yet to be realized in full. Traditionally the best wines were modelled on sherry, port and madeira – historic producers such as Massandra and Magarach have kept great cellars. Gd examples of fortified styles are made by Massandra, Koktebel, Dionis. Novy Svet, and Artyomovsk Winery produce traditional-method sparkling wines. Inkerman is known for dry wines. New names to watch: Veles, Gouliev Wines.

Georgia Possibly the oldest wine region: antique methods such as fermentation in clay vats (*kwevris*) still exist. Around 500 indigenous grape varieties, the most popular being red Saperavi (gd wines are intense and structured) and white Rkatsiteli (lively, refreshing). Wine is made in 5 defined areas, 70% is produced in Kakheti (SE). Big producers inc Tbilvino, Telavi Wine Cellar, Teliani Veli, Shumi, Askaneli. Pernod Ricard's GWS is an important ambassador for

Georgian wines internationally. First small premium producers emerging: Glakhuna (Rkatsiteli, Mtsvane, Saperavi), Khetsuriani.

Moldova Winemaking is the main agricultural activity, but gd natural and climatic conditions haven't been used to full advantage. European grapes are widely used, with gd results for Chard, Sauv Bl, Pinot Gr, Merlot, Cab Sauv. Quality leaders: Acorex Wine Holding (Sauv Bl, Traminer, Pinot N, Merlot, Cab Sauv), Vinaria Bostavan (Negru and Rosu de Purcari), Ch Vartely (Traminer, Merlot), Dionysos Mereni (Carlevana Res range, late harvest and icewine Ries) DK Intertrade (Chard, Pinot Gr, Pinot Bl, Sauv Bl), Vinaria Purcari (Negru de Purcari), Lion Gri (sp, Sauv Bl, Merlot), Cricova (sp).

Russia There are 72,000 ha of v'yds in the SW of the country. The Krasnodar, Dagestan and Stavropol regions lead in production. European and local cold-resistant varieties are grown. Most wine is still of basic quality, made in off-dry or semi-sweet styles and often anonymously blended with cheap imported bulk. There are signs of a new quality movement. Along with the pioneering Ch Le Grand Vostock (red and white Chêne Royal), premium wines are now made, with listings in Russian restaurants, by Fanagoria, esp Cru Lermont range (Merlot, Cab Sauv and Chard), Russkaya Loza (Cab Sauv, Merlot, Chard, Sauv Bl, Muscat), Myskhako, Vina Vedernikoff, Abrau-Durso (sp).

Israel & Lebanon

Israel and Lebanon share similar terroir, but their winemaking philosophies are different. Israel is more New World while Lebanon is more influenced by France. Once it was thought that quality wines could only be made in Israel's Golan Heights and Lebanon's Bekaa Valley, but now the Upper Galilee and Judean Hills are rivalling the Golan and there are new vineyard initiatives outside the Bekaa. Both Israel and Lebanon are making increasingly good wines, particularly reds, mainly using either Bordeaux or Mediterranean varieties.

Israel

Agur r ★→★★ Characterful boutique. Well integrated Kessem B'x blend.

Barkan-Segal r w ★★ Israel's second largest winery. Barkan Altitude Cabs are high quality. Good reds at every price point. Also the first single-v'yd version of Israeli grape Argaman.

Bazelet ha Golan Golan r ★ Gd Cab Sauv – ripe, rounded, approachable.

Binyamina r w ★ New owners. Spicy Gewurz best. Syrah promising.

Carmel r w sp ★★→★★★ Founded in 1882 by a Rothschild. Strong v'yd presence in Upper Galilee. Elegant Limited Edition (**03'** 04 05). Smoky, tarry Kayoumi Cab Sauv. Excellent Old-vine Carignan. Luscious, lingering late-harvest Gewurz. Appellation and new Private Collection labels gd value. New Brut sparkling.

Ch Golan Golan r (w) ★★→★★★ Extravagant winery experimenting with Mediterranean varieties. Intense, jammy Eliad. New Grenache/Syrah blend.

Chillag r ★→★★ Israel's most prominent female winemaker. Elegant Merlot.

What's Argaman?

An Israeli crossing of Carignan and the Portuguese grape Souzão, and the one you need if you want deep colour and high yields. Argaman has them in buckets and its name even means "deep purple" in Hebrew. First planted first in the 1990s as a blending variety – it was intended to replace Carignan – it never had any great quality pretensions. Ironically, though, Carignan has made a comeback in Israel, particularly from old vines giving tiny yields.

Clos de Gat Judean Hills r w ★★→★★★ Classy estate with big, blowsy wines. The spicy, powerful Sycra Syrah (04) and buttery Chard are superb.

Dalton Upper Galilee r w ★→★★★ Full bodied, oaky wines. Huge, ripe Zin.

Domaine du Castel Judean Hills r w ★★★★ Family estate in Jerusalem mountains. Consistently top performer with critics. Characterful, supple Grand Vin (**02** 03' 04' 05). Petit Castel great value. Outstanding "C" Blanc du Castel.

Ella Valley Judean Hills r w ★→★★ V.gd Chard. Cab Fr showing finesse.

Flam r (w) ★★→★★★ Family winery. Fine Cab Sauv, tight Merlot, earthy, herbal Syrah Cab. Classico gd value. Crisp, refreshing unoaked white.

Galil Mountain Upper Galilee r w ★★ Concentrated Yiron B'x blend; fruity Pinot N. Unoaked Cab Sauv and Merlot v.gd value. Fresh whites. Owned by YARDEN.

Kosher Means "pure". Workers must be religious Jews, and nothing un-kosher must be added. Otherwise standard winemaking. Some are v.gd (CASTEL, YARDEN, YATIR). Not all Israeli wines are kosher.

Margalit r ★★★ Father-and-son boutique winery. Rich succulent B'x blend, Enigma. Enigma (**03** 04' 05' 06). V. rare *Special Reserve*. Raisiny Cab Fr.

Pelter r w (sp) ★★ Flavourful, chewy Shiraz and promising Cab Fr.

Recanati r w ★★ Aromatic Sauv Bl. Quality, new world Special Reserve.

Saslove r (w) ★★ Aviv reds flavourful; "Reserved" ageworthy. .

Sea Horse r (w) ★→★★★ Idiosyncratic *garagiste*. Superb, rare old-vine Chenin Bl.

Tabor Galilee r w ★→★★ Growing fast. Lively wines. Aromatic Sauv Bl.

Teperberg r w ★ Efrat reborn. Meritage has sweet fruit, medium body.

Tishbi r w ★ Deep B'x blend from Sde Boker in desert, best yet.

Tulip r (w) ★★ Excellent Shiraz blend and Syrah Reserve. Great value.

Tzora r w ★→★★★ Kibbutz. Reds have mouthfilling flavour. Silky dessert.

Vitkin r w ★★ Steely, floral Ries and almost black, plummy Petite Sirah.

Yarden Golan Heights r w sp ★★★ Pioneering winery. *El Rom Cab Sauv* always gd structure with ageing potential. Rare B'x blend Katzrin (**96 00**' 03 04) – Israel's most expensive wine. Superb HeightsWine dessert and Blanc de Blancs sparkling. Chard and Viognier in oaky style. Gamla fruit-forward second label.

Yatir Judean Hills r (w) ★★★→★★★★ Rich, velvety, concentrated reds. Yatir Forest (01 03' 04 05') Merlot/Shiraz/Cabernet blend and new Cab great value. Minerally Sauv Bl. Fragrant Viognier. Owned by CARMEL.

Lebanon

Bell-Vue r ★→★★★ New *garagiste*. La Renaissance is top-notch red.

Château Musar r (w) ★★★ Unique, long-lasting Cab Sauv/Cinsault/ Carignan red (**95' 96' 98 99** 00' 01). Legendary to some; past its best to others. Hochar red is fruitier. Oaky white from indigenous Obaideh and Merwah.

Clos St Thomas r w ★★ Deep but silky red wines. Les Emirs great value.

Domaine des Tourelles r w ★→★★ Old winery reborn. Elegant Marquis des Beys.

Heritage r w ★ Easy-drinking, fruity wines like Le Fleuron and Nouveau.

Ka r w ★ Basic range promising, esp the white from Chard, Sauv and Sémillon.

Karam ★→★★★ Promising boutique from Jezzine, south Lebanon. Cloud 9 gd value.

Kefraya r w ★★→★★★ Spicy, minerally *Comte de M* (**00**' 01 02) from Cab, Syrah and Mourvèdre. Fruity, easy-drinking Les Bretèches. Quality dessert wine.

Kouroum r w ★ Sept Cépages is an interesting blend of 7 varieties.

Ksara r w ★★→★★★★ 150 yrs old but still progressive. Excellent value wines from Reserve du Couvent to top-range Troisième Millénaire (02 03' 04).

Nakad r w ★ Ch des Coteaux is spicy and oaky from this traditional winery.

Massaya r w ★★ Gold Reserve and Silver Selection examples of New Lebanon.

Wardy r w ★→★★ New-World-style Private Selection. Crisp, fresh whites.

North America

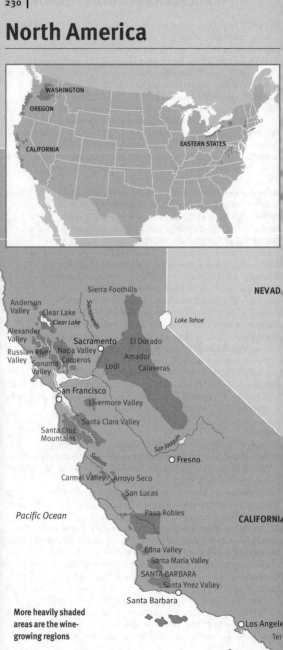

WASHINGTON

OREGON

CALIFORNIA

EASTERN STATES

Sierra Foothills

Anderson Valley

Clear Lake
Clear Lake

Alexander Valley

NEVADA

Sacramento

Lake Tahoe

Russian River Valley

Napa Valley

Sonoma Valley

Carneros

Sacramento

El Dorado

Amador

Lodi

Calaveras

San Francisco

Livermore Valley

Santa Clara Valley

Santa Cruz Mountains

San Joaquin

O Fresno

Salinas

Carmel Valley

Arroyo Seco

San Lucas

Pacific Ocean

Paso Robles

CALIFORNIA

Edna Valley

Santa Maria Valley

SANTA BARBARA

Santa Ynez Valley

Santa Barbara

More heavily shaded areas are the wine-growing regions

O Los Angeles

Ter

NB AVA: American Victicultural Area

California

A fter France, Italy and Spain, California is the world's fourth-largest wine producing region. The state produces some 95 per cent of all US wine. Two of every three bottles of wine sold in the US come from California. There are 2,687 wineries in California, up from 807 in 1990. That means there is one winery for every 13,604 men, women and children in California, give or take the odd person. The good news for the rest of the world is that there is plenty of wine left over. And most of it is pretty good. It is true that one of the great untold stories of California wine is just how good the bargain bottles do taste. Large producers such as Gallo, Constellation, The Wine Group and Bronco are offering perfectly drinkable wines at under $5 a bottle. Modern winemaking and viticultural technology plays a key role in those wines but at the high end, the Napa Cab Sauv, the North Coast Pinot N, the Central Coast Chard, the Zin and Rhône varietals from Lodi, it is a passion for excellence that drives California wine. One great strength of California is that winemakers there sit down together on a regular basis to taste wine, to talk about the wine, to share ideas and experience. This drives them all to achieve ever-higher goals in a spirit of (usually) friendly competition. Sometimes they try too hard and pack so much flavour in the bottle that food gets swpet aside.

The principal Californian vineyard areas

Central Coast
An umbrella region stretching from San Francisco Bay south almost to Los Angeles. Important sub-AVAs include:

Arroyo Seco Monterey County. Excellent Ries both dry and late harvest, citrus Chard and Cab Sauv.

Edna Valley San Luis Obispo County. Cool winds whip through a gap in the coastal range off Morro Bay. Excellent minerally Chard.

Paso Robles San Luis Obispo County. Known for Zin. Promising plantings of Syrah and Rhône varieties.

Santa Lucia Highlands Monterey County. AVA above the Salinas Valley. Excellent Syrah and Ries; outstanding Pinot N.

Santa Maria Valley Santa Barbara County. Outstanding Pinot N, gd Chard, Viognier, and Syrah.

Santa Rita Hills New AVA in Santa Barbara County offering v. gd Pinot N.

Santa Ynez Valley Santa Barbara County. Like Santa Maria but warmer inland regions. Rhône grapes, Pinot N, Chard in cool areas. Sauv Bl a gd bet.

North Coast
Lake, Mendocino, Napa, Sonoma counties, all north of San Francisco. Ranges from v. cool climate nr San Francisco Bay and the coast to very warm interior regions. Soils vary from volcanic to sandy loam. Includes following:

Alexander Valley Sonoma County. Fairly warm AVA bordering Russian River. Excellent Cab Sauv in a ripe, juicy style. Gd Sauv Bl nr the river.

Anderson Valley Mendocino County. Cool valley opening to the Pacific. Outstanding sparkling wine, v. gd Gewurz and Pinot N.

Carneros Napa and Sonoma counties. Cool and foggy region bordering San Francisco Bay. Top site for Pinot N and Chard. V. gd sparkling wine.

Dry Creek Valley Sonoma County. Relatively warm region offering distinctive Zin and Sauv Bl, with Cab Sauv a winner on rocky hillsides.

Lake County Warm to hot mountainous region centred around Clear Lake. Gd Zin, Sauv Bl nr the lake, and lush, fruity Cab Sauv on cooler hillsides.

Mendocino County Large region north of Sonoma County with a wide range of growing regions from hot interior valleys to cooler regions nr the coast.

Mount Veeder Napa County. High-altitude AVA (v'yds planted up to 730 m) best known for concentrated Cab Sauv and rich Chard.

Napa Valley Napa's v'yd land has become the most expensive outside of Europe. Great diversity of soil, climate, and topography in such a small area can produce a wide range of wines, esp the red Bordeaux varieties. Wines have achieved international acclaim, and are priced to match.

Oakville Napa County. Located in mid-valley, the heart of Cab Sauv County.

Redwood Valley Mendocino County. Warm interior region. Gd basic Cab Sauv, excellent Zin, everyday Chard, and Sauv Bl.

Russian River Valley Sonoma County. V. cool, often fog-bound until noon. Outstanding Pinot N, Zin and Cab Sauv on hillside v'yds. Green Valley is a small super-cool AVA located within the Russian River AVA.

Rutherford Napa County. Rivals Oakville as Cab Sauv heartland. Long-lived reds from hillside v'yds.

St Helena V.gd Cab Sauv with elegant fruit and a silky mouthfeel; gd Sauv Bl.

Sonoma Coast Sonoma. V. cool climate, v. poor soils. New plantings of Pinot N show great promise.

Sonoma Valley Varied growing regions produce everything from Chard to Zin. Sub-AVA Sonoma Mountain gd for powerful Cab Sauv.

Spring Mountain Napa County. V.gd Cab Sauv with pockets of delicious Sauv Bl at lower elevations, plus gd Ries.

Stags Leap Napa County. East of Napa River, distinctive Cab Sauv and Merlot.

Bay Area

Urban sprawl has wiped out most of the v'yds that once surrounded San Francisco bay, although there is still good Cab Sauv and Sauv Bl in the Livermore AVA, east of the bay, and small amounts of outstanding Cab Sauv and Pinot N from Santa Cruz County, south of the Bay.

Central Valley

About 60 per cent of California's v'yds are in this huge region that runs north to south for several hundred miles. Now shedding its image as a low-quality producer, as Valley growers realize they must go for quality to keep up. Lodi region in particular turning up v.gd Zin, Sauv Bl and Rhône, Spanish varieties.

Sierra Foothills

Vines were first planted here during Gold Rush in the 1850s. Best regions inc:

Amador County Warm region famous for old Zin v'yds producing jammy, intense wines, as well as crisp Sauv Bl.

Fiddletown Amador County. High-elevation v'yds produce a more understated, elegant Zin than much of Amador.

Shenandoah Valley Amador County. Source of powerful Zins and increasingly well-regarded Syrah.

Recent vintages

Its size and wide range of microclimates make it impossible to produce a one-size-fits-all vintage report for California. Its climate is not as consistent as its "land of sunshine" reputation suggests. Although grapes ripen regularly, they are often subject to spring frosts, sometimes a wet harvest time, and (too often) drought. The following vintage assessment relies most heavily on evaluation of Cab Sauv from N Coast regions. For Chard, the best vintages are: 04 05 07.

2008 Sept heat led to an early harvest, with most grapes picked two to three weeks earlier than normal. There is also concern that acid levels are low and in some areas the grapes may not have reached physiological ripeness. Mixed quality likely.

2007 Early bud-break and a fairly mild summer growing season with a burst of heat in Aug followed by a cool Sept seemed to set the stage for a textbook-perfect harvest; then came rains in late Sept and Oct so results were mixed, esp for Cab Sauv on the North Coast. Hang on to the Cab .

2006 Wines, esp Pinot N and Chard, looking gd. Cab Sauv better than expected. Overall, average to above average.

2004 After sorting out this vintage some of the early promise has faded. Wines likely to be for short-term consumption.

2004 Grapes ripened quickly with uneven quality. At best average.

2003 A difficult yr all around. Overall, spotty.

2002 The growing season was cool, leading to an average-sized crop with superior quality and showing well with age.

2001 Excellent quality with Cab Sauv. Drink in the next year or two.

2000 Biggest harvest on record. OK quality.

1999 Intensely flavoured and coloured wines. Outstanding quality, which is looking even better with age.

Abreu Vineyards Napa ★★★ 03 05 Massive Cab Sauv that's worth waiting for.

Acacia Carneros ★★★ (Pinot N) **04** 05 06 CARNEROS pioneer in Chard and Pinot N, always reliable, recently emphasizing single-v'yd wines. Luscious Viognier.

Acorn Russian River Valley ★★→★★★ Outstanding Zin from Heritage vines. Also v.gd Sangiovese and Syrah.

Alban Edna Valley ★★→★★★ Emphasis on Rhônes, inc excellent Viognier. Grenache, Roussanne and Marsanne also top-rated.

Alexander Valley Vineyards Sonoma ★★→★★★ Fruit-forward, drink-me-now Cab Sauv and Zin, reliable Chard.

Alma Rosa Santa Rita Hills ★★★ Richard Sanford, a master Pinot N wine whizz at Sanford and Benedict Winery, is making lovely Pinot N and Chard from organic v'yds at his new winery. Also v.gd Pinot Gr and Vin Gris from Pinot N.

Altamura Vineyards Napa ★★★ 97 99 00 01 02 03 04 05 Cab Sauv is one of NAPA's best, with a firm structure and deep flavours; also a gd Sangiovese.

Amador Foothills Winery Amador ★★→★★★ Top Zin and a bright, zingy Sauv Bl; Syrah also gd.

Andrew Murray Sta Barbara ★★★ It's Rhônes around the clock here. Outstanding Viognier and Roussanne among the whites and a solid Syrah.

Araujo Napa ★★★ 96 97 99 00 02 03 04 05 Powerful but never over-the-top cult Cab Sauv made from historic Eisele v'yd.

Armida Sonoma ★★→★★★ RUSSIAN RIVER VALLEY winery with solid Merlot, gd Pinot N, and a zippy Zin made from DRY CREEK VALLEY grapes.

Arthur Earl Sta Barbara ★★★ Artisan bottlings of mostly Rhône varietals, splashing out with an occasional Italian. Quality steadily improving.

Au Bon Climat Sta Barbara ★★★→★★★★ Owner Jim Clendenen listens to his private drummer: ultra-toasty Chard, flavourful Pinot N, light-hearted Pinot Bl. Vita Nova label for B'x varieties, Podere Olivos for Italianates. See QUPÉ.

Babcock Vineyards Sta Barbara ★★★ V.gd Pinot N, Chard and Sauv Bl from cool climate v. nr the Pacific in SANTA YNEZ VALLEY. New Grand Cuvée Pinot N has moved quality up a notch.

Barra Vineyards Mendocino ★★→★★★ Wines made from estate-grown organic grapes represent gd value as well as first-rate sipping. The Zin is a treat; Chard also gd and a robust but balanced Petite Sirah is worth a look.

Beaulieu Vineyard Napa ★★→★★★ **99** 00 03 05 Not the jewel it was when André

CALIFORNIA

Tchelistcheff was setting the style for NAPA Cab Sauv half a century ago but still worth looking out for, esp the Georges de Latour Private Reserve Cab Sauv. Decent budget wines under the Beaulieu Coastal label.

Benessere Napa ★★★ Sangiovese and Syrah worth a try. New Super Tuscan-style blend called Phenomenon is outstanding.

Benziger Family Winery Sonoma ★★★ Move towards top quality continues at this family winery. Look for new Signature line of wine made from biodynamic grapes, esp gd Sauv Bl.

Beringer Blass (Foster's Wine Estates) Napa ★→★★★ (Cab) 99 00 01 03 A NAPA classic. Single-v'yd Cab Sauv Reserves can sometimes be over the top, but otherwise worthy of ageing. Velvety, powerful Howell Mountain Merlot one of the best. Look for Founder's Estate bargain line from NORTH COAST and CENTRAL COAST grapes. Also owns CH ST JEAN ★★→★★★, ETUDE, Meridian ★, ST CLEMENT ★★★, STAGS' LEAP WINERY ★, and Taz, a brawny ★★ Pinot from Santa Barbara.

Biale Napa ★★→★★★ Small Zin specialist using mostly NAPA fruit.

Boeger El Dorado ★★→★★★ First El Dorado winery after Prohibition. Mostly estate wines. Attractive Merlot, Barbera, Zin, and Meritage. More understated than many in SIERRA FOOTHILLS and always reliable.

Bogle Vineyards Yolo ★→★★ Major growers in the Sacramento Delta, Bogle family makes an attractive line of consistently gd and affordable wines.

Bokisch Lodi ★★→★★★ The focus is on Spanish varieties at this family estate. Garnacha, Albariño and Tempranillo show gd varietal character. Tempranillo esp impressive.

Bonny Doon Sta Cruz Mtns ★★★ Original Rhône Ranger Randall Grahm has slashed production, selling off his budget brands to concentrate on single-v'yd biodynamic wines. Grahm has built a new winery in Washington State for brilliant Pacific Rim Ries and other cool-climate varietals, inc an excellent Chenin Bl and Gewurz.

Bonterra See Fetzer.

Bouchaine Vineyards Napa, Carneros ★★→★★★ Winery has had some ups and downs since its founding in 1980. Now on an up-swing with *classic, sleek Chard* and juicy but serious single-v'yd Pinot N.

Bradford Mountain Sonoma Dry Creek ★★★ Long-time grower George Hambrecht now makes wine from hillside v'yds above Dry Creek. Grist V'yd Zin is typical of Zin from that AVA. Also v. gd Syrah from the same v'yd, made in Rhône style.

Bronco Wine Company San Joaquin Founded by Fred Franzia, the nephew of Ernest Gallo. Franzia sources inexpensive Central Valley grapes for his well-known Charles Shaw Two Buck Chuck brand. Franzia also fields several other labels, inc NAPA Creek and NAPA Ridge. Quality is not the point: Franzia is selling wine as a popular beverage.

Buena Vista Napa, Carneros ★★★ Historic winery now focuses on wines from CARNEROS estate. New EVS wines from Ramal v'yd showing v. well, esp Pinot N and Chard.

Burgess Cellars Napa ★★★ (Cab) 97 99 00 01 02 03 05 Cab Sauv from Howell Mountain grapes is splendid, sleek and powerful while remaining balanced.

Cain Cellars Napa ★★★ 97 99 00 01 03 05 One of NAPA's jewels with consistent bottlings of Cain Five, a supple and elegant red wine based on Cab Sauv and its 4 B'x cousins, from Spring Mountain grapes.

Cakebread Napa ★★→★★★★ (Cab) 97 99 00 01 02 03 05 Quality improving with each vintage, esp the Cab Sauv, which shows great balance and harmony.

Calcareous Paso Robles ★★ New winery specializing in Rhône varietals. Gd Viognier and outstanding Tres Violet red (mostly Syrah) blend. One to watch.

Calera San Benito ★★★★ Josh Jensen fell in love with Pinot N while at Oxford, and still is. He makes 3 supple and fine Pinot Ns named after v'yd blocks in the dry hills of San Benito, inland from Monterey: Reed, Seleck, and Jensen; also intense, flowery Viognier.

Campion Winery Napa, Carneros ★★→★★★ Pinot N guru Larry Brooks is making only single-v'yd Pinot N from several sites. Worth seeking out.

Caymus Napa ★★★→★★★★ **91 97 99** 00 01 The Special Selection Cab Sauv is consistently one of California's most formidable: rich, intense, slow to mature. Also a regular bottling, balanced and a little lighter. Gd Chard from Mer Soleil in Monterey, inc an unoaked Chard called Silver.

Ceago Vinegarden Lake ★★→★★★ Jim Fetzer well settled into his biodynamic ranch on Clear Lake in LAKE COUNTY, produces v.gd Sauv Bl and Cab Sauv.

Ceja Vineyards Napa ★★→★★★ Estb 1999, one of few California wineries owned by former Mexican v'yd workers. Cab Sauv, CARNEROS Chard top the list.

Chalk Hill Sonoma ★★→★★★ Cab Sauv with ageing potential; buttery Chard.

Chalone Monterey ★★★ Historic mountain estate above the Salinas Valley in Monterey. Marvellous flinty Chard and rich, intense Pinot N.

Chappellet Napa ★★★ An ageworthy Cab Sauv, *esp Signature label*. Pleasing Chard; gd Cab Fr, Merlot. Chenin Bl has brisk minerality.

Château Montelena Napa ★★★→★★★★ (Chard) 01 03 05 (Cab) **96 97** 99 00 01 03 05 Historic Napa winery offers that rare thing in California, an ageworthy Chard. The estate Cab Sauv is also capable of extended ageing.

Château St Jean Sonoma ★★→★★★ Pioneered single-v'yd Chard in California under Richard Arrowood in the 1970s, still outstanding; gd Sauv Bl. Cinq Cepage, made from the 5 B'x varieties, can be ★★★★ quality. Sonoma County Cab Sauv and Chard are gd budget buys.

Chimney Rock Napa ★★★→★★★★ (Cab) **97 99** STAGS LEAP AVA producer of elegant, sometimes understated Cab Sauv capable of long ageing.

Claiborne & Churchill Santa Barbara ★★★ The accent here is Alsace with a consistently top rated Ries, v.gd Pinot Gr and Gewurz.

Clark-Claudon Napa ★★★ Balanced, silky hillside Cab Sauv from estate v'yd on the eastern slope of Howell Mountain. V.gd unoaked Sauv Bl from Pope Valley.

Cline Cellars Carneros ★→★★ Sonoma/CARNEROS winery focused on rustic Rhône blends made from old vines, and sturdy Zin.

Clos du Bois Sonoma ★★→★★★ Large-scale SONOMA producer of quaffable everyday wines, with the exception of a single-v'yd Cab Sauv (Briarcrest) and Calcaire Chard, which can be v.gd.

Clos du Val Napa ★★★→★★★★ **95 97** 99 00 01 03 05 Consistently elegant Cab Sauvs that are among the best ageing candidates in the state. *Chard is a delight* and a Sem/Sauv Bl blend called Ariadne is a charmer.

Clos Pegase Napa ★★→★★★ Is it a winery or museum? Sometimes hard to tell, but at best a sleek Cab Sauv from v'yds nr Calistoga, and a minerally Chard from CARNEROS grapes.

Cohn, B R Sonoma ★★→★★★ Ex-rock'n'roller Bruce Cohn makes powerful estate Cab Sauv in SONOMA VALLEY with gd ageing potential.

CALIFORNIA

Climate change, California-style

California grape growers and winemakers are taking the prospect of global warming seriously. One response has been to look more closely at grapes from warmer climates. Gallo has been planting Tannat, most often found in southern France and Uruguay, in Paso Robles. Other grapes being tried are Nero d'Avola, the chief red wine grape of Sicily, Touriga Nacional from Portugal, and Greco di Tufo, the white wine grape from southern Italy. Don't expect these in your local wine shop any time soon, but some of them may well play a larger role in future California vintages.

Conn Creek Napa ★★★ V.gd Cab Sauv sourced from several NAPA v'yds; elegant wines with gd structure and long ageing potential.

Constellation ★→★★★★ Owns wineries in California, NY, Washington State, Canada, Chile, Australia and NZ. Produces 90 million cases annually, selling more than any other wine company in the world. Once a bottom feeder, now going for the top. Bought Mondavi at end of 2004 and also owns FRANCISCAN, Estancia, Mount Veeder, Simi, RAVENSWOOD, among others.

Corison Napa ★★★★ 95 96 97 99 00 01 02 05 Cathy Corison is a treasure of a winemaker. While many in NAPA follow the $iren call of over-extracted powerhouse wines delivering big numbers from critics but no satisfaction in the glass, Corison continues to make flavoursome, ageworthy Cab Sauv.

Cornerstone Cellars Napa Howell Mountain ★★★ 00 01 02 03 05 Consulting winemaker Celia Mayzczek makes impressive Cab Sauv from mountain v'yds with a focus on harmony and balance. Also look for Stepping Stone label featuring small lots of wine from select NAPA v'yds.

Cosentino Napa ★★→★★★ Irrepressible winemaker-owner Mitch Cosentino always full tilt. Results sometimes odd, sometimes brilliant, never dull. Cab Sauv always worth a look; Chard can be v.gd.

Cuvaison Napa ★★★ (Cab) 00 01 02 05 Gd to sometimes v.gd Chard, Merlot, Syrah from CARNEROS. Impressive Cab Sauv from MOUNT VEEDER.

Dalla Valle Napa ★★★→★★★★ 97 99 00 01 Hillside estate with a cult following for Maya, a Cab Sauv-based deeply extracted wine that is slow to develop.

Daniel Gehrs Sta Barbara ★★→★★★ Veteran winemaker producing small lots of wines from CENTRAL COAST v'yds, inc a terrific Tempranillo and a balanced and luscious Zin from SANTA YNEZ VALLEY. Unoaked Chard is charming.

David Bruce Sta Cruz Mtns ★★★ Legendary mountain estate is still on top of the game with powerful, long-lasting Chard and superb Pinot N.

Davis Bynum Sonoma ★★★ Bynum pioneered often superb single-v'yd Pinot N in the RUSSIAN RIVER VALLEY. Chard is lean and minerally with silky mouthfeel. Winery now owned by Rodney Strong Vineyards.

Dehlinger Sonoma ★★★★ (Pinot) 04 05 06 Outstanding Pinot N from estate RUSSIAN RIVER VALLEY v'yd. Also gd Chard and Syrah.

Delicato Vineyards San Joaquin ★→★★ One-time CENTRAL VALLEY jug producer has moved up-scale with purchase of Monterey v'yds and several new bottlings from Lodi. Watch this brand for gd quality at everyday price.

Diamond Creek Napa ★★★★ 91 94 95 99 00 01 03 Austere, stunning cult Cabs from hilly v'yd nr Calistoga go by names of v'yd blocks: Gravelly Meadow, Volcanic Hill, Red Block Terrace. Wines age beautifully. One of NAPA's jewels.

Domaine Carneros Carneros ★★★ Showy US outpost of Taittinger in NAPA, CARNEROS echoes austere style of its parent in Champagne (see France) but with a delicious dollop of California fruit. Vintage Blanc de Blancs v.gd. La Rêve the luxury *cuvée*. Still Pinot N and Chard also impressive.

Domaine Chandon Napa ★★→★★★ Napa branch of Champagne house. Look for the NV Reserve, Etoile, esp the rosé.

Dominus Napa ★★★★ 95 97 99 01 02 05 Christian Moueix of Pomerol produces red B'x blend that is slow to open but ages beautifully.

C. Donatiello Russian River Valley Sonoma ★★→★★★ Newcomer producing gd Chard and Pinot N from selected v'yds. Floodgate Pinot N esp attractive.

Dry Creek Vineyard Sonoma ★★ Sauv (Fumé) Bl set standard for California for decades. Still impressive. Pleasing Chenin Bl; gd Zin.

Duckhorn Vineyards Napa ★★★→★★★★ Known for dark, tannic, almost plummy-ripe, single-v'yd Merlots (esp Three Palms) and Cab Sauv-based blend Howell Mountain. New winery in ANDERSON VALLEY for Golden Eye Pinot N in a robust style more akin to Cab Sauv than Pinot. Makes a Zin/Cab Sauv blend in

Paraduxx, a second NAPA winery.

Dunn Vineyards Napa ★★★★ 91 95 97 99 01 03 Owner-winemaker Randy Dunn makes superb and *intense Cab Sauv* from Howell Mountain, which ages magnificently; milder bottling from valley floor. One of a few NAPA winemakers to resist the stampede to jammy, lush wines to curry wine critics' favour.

Dutton-Goldfield Western Sonoma County ★★★ Winemaker-grower duo crafting outstanding Pinot N and Chard from top cool-climate sites; rapidly being recognized as modern California classics.

Duxoup Sonoma ★★★ Quirky DRY CREEK producer of excellent Rhône-style Syrah and inky, old-vine Charbono. A promising Sangiovese under Gennaio label. Limited production but worth seeking out.

Eberle Winery San Luis Obispo ★★→★★★ Powerful Cab Sauv and Zin with gd balance and a supple concentration. Viognier is a treat.

Edna Valley Vineyard San Luis Obispo ★★★ Much improved in past few vintages; v.gd Chard, crisp and fruity, *lovely Sauv Bl*, impressive Syrah.

Ehlers Estate Napa St. Helena ★★★ This 19th-century winery has been revived by Jean Leducq, a French entrepreneur and philanthropist. The v'yds are certified organic and biodynamic. The new wines are outstanding, esp an elegant Cab Sauv and a delicious Sauv Bl.

Etude Napa See BERINGER BLASS.

Failla Vineyards Napa ★★→★★★ Winery on the Silverado Trail in NAPA gaining a reputation for SONOMA COAST and RUSSIAN RIVER VALLEY Pinot N and Chard.

Far Niente Napa ★★★ (Cab) 00 01 03 05 Opulence is the goal in both Cab Sauv and Chard from luxury NAPA estate. Can go over the top.

Farella Vineyards Napa ★★★ The Farella family are growers who reserve a few key v'yd blocks for their own brand with outstanding results. Alta Cab Sauv is powerful, silky, elegant that should age v. well. Also look for Farella Park Cab Sauv, a budget version of the Alta and Farella Park Syrah.

Ferrari-Carano Sonoma ★★→★★★ Wines from this showcase estate in DRY CREEK VALLEY have been erratic in recent yrs. Cab Sauv is slow to open. Merlot is reliable and sometimes v.gd. The owners recently bought Lazy Creek winery in MENDOCINO, offering a promising old-vine Pinot N and a gd Gewurz.

Fetzer Mendocino ★★→★★★ A leader in the organic/sustainable-viticulture movement, Fetzer has produced consistent-value wines from least expensive range (Sundial, Valley Oaks) to brilliant Reserve wines. Also owns Bonterra Vineyards (all organic grapes) where *Roussanne and Marsanne are stars*. Jekel and Five Rivers brands are now made at Fetzer.

Ficklin Vineyards Madera, Central Valley ★★★ Lush and delicious port-style dessert wines made from the classic Portuguese varieties.

Fiddlehead San Luis Obispo ★★★ Winemaker Kathy Joseph makes terroir-driven balanced and elegant Pinot N and Sauv Bl from the Santa Rita Hills and Santa Ynez AVAs, and a silky Pinot N from Willamette Valley in Oregon. Also look for a zippy Sauv Bl in a minerally B'x style.

Fisher Sonoma ★★→★★★ Underrated but solid producer of gd Chard from SONOMA hillside grapes and a restrained Cab Sauv from NAPA grapes.

Flora Springs Wine Co Napa ★★★ Best are the 2 Meritage wines, red Trilogy and white Soliloquy, made from v'yds above valley floor. Juicy Merlot worth a look.

Flowers Vineyard & Winery Sonoma ★★★ Intense, terroir-driven Pinot N and Chard from v. cool-climate vines only a few miles from the Pacific. Flowers has won early critical acclaim and is clearly a winery to watch.

Foley Estates Vineyard Sta Barbara ★★→★★★ Young winery has a solid reputation for balanced, delicious Chard and Pinot N, now owns Firestone, Merus (NAPA) and Three Rivers.

Foppiano Sonoma ★★→★★★ One of the grand old families in California wine. You can count on the Zin every time but look esp for Petite Sirah, better known as "petty sir" among the California rearguard.

Forman Napa ★★★★ 99 00 01 03 05 Winemaker who found fame at STERLING in the 1970s now makes his own v.gd Cab Sauv and Chard from mountain v'yds.

Foxen Sta Barbara ★★★ An impressive range of wines from this consistently gd producer. Wines range from Rhône style to Cab Fr to brilliant Pinot N.

Franciscan Vineyard Napa ★★★ Quality has been maintained under CONSTELLATION ownership, esp the top-of-the-line wines like the graceful red Magnificant and the Cuvée Sauvage Chard, one of the first California Chards using wild-yeast fermentation. Gd budget wines under Estancia label.

Freeman Russian River Valley ★★★ Barely a decade old, Freeman has developed a cult following with outstanding cool-climate Pinot N (Akiko's Cuvée from SONOMA COAST AVA) and RUSSIAN RIVER Pinot N.

Freemark Abbey Napa ★★★→★★★★ Historic and currently underrated but consistent producer of stylish Cab Sauv to age. Single v'yd Sycamore and Bosché bottlings often reach ★★★★.

Frog's Leap Napa ★★★→★★★★ 99 00 01 02 03 Small winery, as charming as its name (and T-shirts) suggest. Lean, *minerally Sauv Bl*, toasty Chard, spicy Zin. Supple and delicious Merlot, Cab Sauv. Converting to organic and biodynamic with recent wines showing more depth and intensity. Not a coincidence.

Gallo, E & J San Joaquin ★→★★ With a history of cheap jug wines, California's biggest winery is an easy target for wine snobs. In the long view, Gallo has done more to open up the American palate to wine than any other winery. Gallo's 1960s Hearty Burgundy was a groundbreaking popular wine. It still does the basic commodity wines, but it has also created an imposing line of regional varieties, such as Anapauma, Marcellina, Turning Leaf and more, all wines of modest quality perhaps but predictable and affordable.

Gallo Sonoma Sonoma ★★→★★★ DRY CREEK VALLEY winery bottles several wines from Sonoma, NORTH COAST. Cab Sauv can be v.gd, esp the single-v'yd. Chard also better than average. Other wines made in Sonoma worth a try include Frei Brothers and McMurray, esp Pinot Gr.

Gary Farrell Sonoma ★★★→★★★★ Well established with some of the best Pinot N and Chard from the RUSSIAN RIVER VALLEY over the yrs. Also look for Zin, Chard and a v.gd Sauv Bl. Encounter, a new red B'x blend, is v.gd.

Geyser Peak Sonoma ★★→★★★ A sometimes underrated producer of toasty Chard, powerful Cab Sauv, juicy Shiraz. A recent focus on Sauv Bl is welcome.

Gloria Ferrer Sonoma, Carneros ★★★ Built by Spain's Freixenet for sparkling wine, now producing spicy Chard and bright, silky Pinot N and other varietals, all from CARNEROS fruit. Bubbly quality remains high, esp the Brut Rosé and the Royal Cuvée, inspired by a visit from King Juan Carlos of Spain.

Grace Family Vineyard Napa ★★★★ 99 00 Stunning Cab Sauv. Shaped for long ageing. One of the few cult wines that may actually be worth the price.

Greenwood Ridge Mendocino ★★→★★★ Winery well above the floor of ANDERSON VALLEY offers engaging off-dry perfumed Ries. Reds, esp Cab Sauv and Pinot N, also v.gd. Zin from Sonoma grapes.

Grgich Hills Cellars Napa ★★★→★★★★ Solid NAPA producer of supple Chard (which can age); balanced, elegant Cab Sauv; jammy, ripe Zin from Sonoma grapes and gd Sauv Bl in minerally style.

Groth Vineyards Napa ★★★★ 97 99 00 01 OAKVILLE estate Cab Sauv has been 4-star for a decade, with big, wrap-around flavours made for ageing.

Gundlach-Bundschu Sonoma ★★→★★★ Historic SONOMA VALLEY winery offers, memorable Gewurz, Merlot, Zin. Much improved Cab Sauv.

Hagafen Napa ★★ One of the first serious California kosher producers. Gd Chard and Sauv Bl and palate-friendly Zin.

> **Is it finally Riesling time?**
> After languishing for years, Riesling sales have exploded in the US. There
> is no single reason for this, although the success of fusion cuisine with its
> Asian-influenced flavours is certainly one reason. Probably even more
> important is that Ries from California (and the Pacific Northwest) simply
> tastes better than a decade ago. There have always been a few reliable
> Ries producers in California – eg SMITH-MADRONE and TREFETHEN – but
> lately relative newcomers such as CLAIBORNE & CHURCHILL have stepped
> up the quality level. Yes, there is a North American Ries in your future.

Handley Cellars Mendocino ★★★ Winemaker Mila Handley makes excellent ANDERSON VALLEY Chard, Gewurz, Pinot N. Also v.gd DRY CREEK VALLEY Sauv Bl and Chard from her family's vines in Sonoma County; also a small amount of intense sparkling wine.

Hanna Winery Sonoma ★★★ Has been reaching for 4-star status for yrs. Recent vintages of Cab Sauv and well-made Sauv Bl are excellent.

Hanzell Sonoma ★★★★ (Chard) 03 05 06 (Pinot N) 01 02 03 05 Pioneer (1950) small producer of outstanding terroir-driven Chard and Pinot N from estate vines. Always gd; quality level has risen sharply in the past few yrs. Deserves to be ranked with the best of California.

Harlan Estate Napa ★★★★ 97 99 00 01 03 Concentrated, sleek, cult Cab Sauv from small estate commanding luxury prices.

Harrison Clarke Santa Ynez ★★ All about Syrah and Grenache. Estate Syrah is worth seeking out and the Grenache has rich flavour profile and mouthfeel.

Hartford Court Sonoma ★★★ Part of KENDALL-JACKSON'S Artisans & Estates group showing v.gd single-v'yd Pinot Ns, tight coastal-grown Chard, and wonderful old-vine RUSSIAN RIVER Zins.

HDV Carneros ★★★ *Complex and layered Chard* with a minerally edge from grower Larry Hyde's v'yd in conjunction with Aubert de Villaine of Dom de la Romanée-Conti (see France).

Heitz Napa ★★★→★★★★ 99 00 01 03 05 History-making deeply flavoured, minty Cab Sauv from Martha's V'yd. Bella Oaks and newer Trailside V'yd rival but can't match Martha. Some feel quality has slipped in recent vintages.

The Hess Collection Napa ★★→★★★ Owner and art collector Donald Hess uses winery visiting area as a museum. Cab Sauv from MOUNT VEEDER AVA v'yds step up to new quality level; Chard crisp and bright; Hess Select label v.gd value.

Honig Napa ★★★ Big jump in quality after switching to organic farming. V.gd Cab Sauv in classic NAPA style and seriously delicious Sauv Bl lead the parade.

Hooper Creek Napa ★★★ This small estate has burst on the scene with an excellent trio of wines, a Chard (Sangiacomo V'yds), Zin (Los Chamisal V'yds) and an estate-bottled Merlot. A newcomer well worth seeking out.

Hop Kiln Sonoma ★★★ A new direction for this well-regarded winery with a brand called HK Generations. Chard is superb, Pinot N excellent, both made from RUSSIAN RIVER VALLEY grapes. Also gd Zin.

Iron Horse Vineyards Sonoma ★★★→★★★★ RUSSIAN RIVER family estate producing gd bubbly. Chard from RUSSIAN RIVER VALLEY is v.gd and an above-average Cab Sauv from ALEXANDER VALLEY v'yds.

Ironstone Lodi & Calaveras County ★→★★ Long-time growers with a destination winery in SIERRA FOOTHILLS making honestly priced and easy-drinking wines from mostly CENTRAL VALLEY grapes. Verdelho from Lodi is superb.

Jade Mountain Napa ★★→★★★ V.gd Rhône-style wines, esp Syrah, Mourvèdre.

Jessie's Grove Lodi ★★ Old Zin vines work well for farming family's venture.

Jordan Sonoma ★★★★ (Cab) 98 99 00 01 02 05 Winemaker Rob Davis makes consistently balanced and elegant wines from ALEXANDER VALLEY estate. The Cab Sauv tastes like a homage to B'x. And it lasts. Minerally Chard is made in a Burgundian style.

Joseph Phelps Napa ★★★★ (Insignia) **97 99** 00 01 03 05 A true Napa "first growth"; Phelps Cab Sauv, esp the Insignia and Backus bottlings, are always nr the top. Early releases of FogDog Chard and Pinot N from Freestone Vineyard on the SONOMA COAST show great promise.

Joseph Swan Sonoma ★★★ Long-time RUSSIAN RIVER producer of intense Zin and classy Pinot N capable of ageing in the 10-yr range.

JVineyards Sonoma ★★★ A creamy, rich Brut sparkling wine is one of state's best. Also look look for v.gd Pinot N and Pinot Gr from RUSSIAN RIVER VALLEY v'yds.

Kathryn Hall Vineyards Napa ★★★→★★★★ Kathryn Hall's family have been wine-grape growers in MENDOCINO for almost 4 decades. Hall purchased historic Bergfeld winery in Napa in 05. The new Hall winery was designed by architect Frank Gehry. There is a stunning Diamond Mountain Cab Sauv (★★★★) and a v.gd ST HELENA Cab Sauv. The Sauv Bl is a delicious and minerally wine.

Kendall-Jackson Sonoma ★★→★★★★ Staggeringly successful style aimed at widest market, esp broadly sourced off-dry toasty Chard. Even more noteworthy for the development of a diversity of wineries under the umbrella of Kendall-Jackson's Artisans & Estates (SEE HARTFORD COURT, STONESTREET).

Kenwood Vineyards Sonoma ★★→★★★ (Jack London Cab) 00 01 03 05 Single-v'yd Jack London Cab Sauv, Zin (several) the high points of a consistent line. Sauv Bl is reliable value.

Kistler Vineyards Sonoma ★★★ Still chasing the Burgundian model of single-v'yd Pinot N, most from RUSSIAN RIVER, with mixed success. Chards can be v. toasty, buttery, and over-the-top, though they have a loyal following.

Korbel Sonoma ★★ Largest US producer of *méthode champenoise* with focus on fruit flavours. Gd picnic wines.

Charles Krug Napa ★★→★★★ Historically important winery; wines on an upward trend under third generation of (the other) Mondavi family. New focus on red B'x styles showing gd results.

Kuleto Estate Napa ★★→★★★ Designer and restaurateur Pat Kuleto has planted hillside v'yds on the eastern edge of NAPA VALLEY. The wines are concentrated and big, but show good balance. Best of the lot is a fruit-forward Zin with intense, rounded flavours. Sangiovese also gd.

Kunde Estate Sonoma ★★★ Solid SONOMA VALLEY producer and noted grower with an elegant, understated Chard, flavourful Sauv Bl, peachy Viognier, and silky Merlot. All estate-bottled.

Lafond Santa Rita Hills ★★→★★★ Veteran grower in this exciting new appellation now making wine – and what took them so long? The Syrah is reminiscent of a southern Rhône, with bright minerality and long finish. Pinot N is also gd.

Lambert Bridge Dry Creek, Sonoma ★★★ Seductive Merlot, zesty Zin, and brilliant Sauv Bl in a "B'x meets New Zealand" style.

Lamborn Howell Mountain, Napa ★★★ V'yd planted on historic 19th-century site. Big juicy Zin, Cab Sauv coming along for this cult winery.

Landmark Sonoma ★★→★★★ Early promise of elegant Burgundian-style Chard blunted by oaky-toasty flavours in late 1990s. Now back on track.

Lane Tanner Sta Barbara ★★★ Owner-winemaker makes v. personal and superb single-v'yd Pinot N (Bien Nacido, Sierra Madre Plateau) reflecting terroir with a quiet, understated elegance.

Lang & Reed Napa ★★★ Specialist focusing on delicious Loire-style Cab Fr.

Laurel Glen Sonoma ★★★★ **95 97** 99 00 01 03 05 Floral and long-lived Cab Sauv from steep v'yd on Sonoma mountain. Mid-priced Counterpoint label is gd quality at a reasonable price; budget Reds label offers exceptional value.

Livingston Moffett St Helena, Napa ★★★ Noteworthy Cab Sauv from RUTHERFORD Ranch v'yds. Syrah also v.gd.

Lockwood Monterey ★→★★ South Salinas Valley v'yd. Gd value in Chard, Sauv Bl.

Lohr, J Central Coast ★★→★★★ Large winery with extensive v'yds; v.gd PASO ROBLES Cab Sauv Seven Oaks. Recent series of Meritage-style reds best yet. Commodity line is Cypress.

Long Meadow Napa ★★★ Elegant, silky Cab Sauv better with each vintage. Lively *Graves-style Sauv Bl* a winner as well. V'yd is organically farmed.

Longoria Winery Sta Barbara (★★→★★★) Rick Longoria makes brilliant Pinot N from top v'yds in the area. Also a charming Albariño.

Louis M Martini Napa ★★→★★★ Long history-making, ageworthy Cab Sauv, Zin. On downslide for several yrs. Now on the way back after purchase by GALLO in 2002. Recent bottlings of Cab Sauv showing v. well, esp Monte Rosso and ALEXANDER VALLEY bottlings.

L'Uvaggio Napa ★★→★★★ Former Mondavi winemaker Jim Moore specializes in Italian varieties. An outstanding Barbera leads the way; also look for Vermentino from Lodi and a rosé made from Barbera. Can't go wrong here.

MacPhail Sonoma ★★★ Pinot N specialist, not yet a decade old, offering intense wines from select v'yds on the SONOMA COAST and ANDERSON VALLEY. Wines are silky and luscious with wraparound flavours.

MacRostie Sonoma, Carneros ★★★ Toasty, ripe Chard with some complexity is flagship. Also Merlot, Pinot N from single v'yds. New Syrah is v.gd.

Mahoney Vineyards Napa, Carneros ★★→★★★ Founder of Carneros Creek, one of the CARNEROS pioneers and an early Pinot N enthusiast, now producing under own label. V.gd Vermentino and Tempranillo, excellent single-v'yd Pinot N.

Marcassin Sonoma Coast Cult queen Helen Turley's own tiny label. Worth so much at auction that few ever drink it. Concentrated Chard and dense Pinot N. Chard so densely concentrated those who do taste it never forget.

Marimar Torres Estate Sonoma ★★★★ (Chard) **03 04** 05 06 (Pinot N) **01 02** 03 05 Several bottlings of Chard and Pinot N from Don Miguel estate v'yd in Green Valley. The Chard is complex and sometimes rather edgy, with gd ageing potential. Acero Don Miguel Chard is unoaked and *a lovely expression of Chard fruit*. Pinot N from the Doña Margarita v'yd, only a few miles from the ocean, is intense and surprisingly rich for young vines. V'yds now farmed organically and moving toward biodynamics.

Markham Napa ★★★ Underrated producer of elegant Merlot and solid Cab Sauv.

Martinelli Russian River ★★★ Family growers from fog-shrouded western hills of Sonoma, famous for old-vine Jackass Hill Vineyard Zin.

Mayacamas Napa ★★★ Pioneer boutique v'yd with rich Chard and firm (but no longer steel hard) *Cab Sauv, capable of long ageing.* Also a gd Sauv Bl.

McFadden Mendocino ★★→★★★ Wines made from organically farmed v'yds in Potter Valley AVA. First rate Alsace-style Pinot Gr and a lovely unoaked Chard.

Merry Edwards Russian River ★★★★ Superstar consultant has planted her own Pinot N v'yd in RUSSIAN RIVER district and buys in grapes. Her Pinot N is "must drink". Also lovely, true-to-varietal Sauv Bl.

Merryvale Napa ★★★ Best at Cab Sauv and Merlot, which have elegant balance and supple finish. Sauv Bl can be v.gd.

Mettler Family Vineyards Lodi ★★ Long-time growers now producing a sleek and tangy Cab Sauv and a powerful Petite Sirah.

Peter Michael Sonoma ★★★→★★★★ Stunning, complex Chard from Howell Mountain in a powerful style, and a more supple ALEXANDER VALLEY bottling. Cab Sauv on the tight side.

Milano Mendocino ★★ Small producer of Zin, Cab Sauv, worth seeking out. New Hopland Cuvée, a blend of Cab Sauv and Pinot N is ★★★★ all the way.

Miner Family Wines Napa ★★★ Powerful and potentially long ageing reds based on Cab Sauv are the star turn here. Look esp for the Icon bottling, a blend of B'x varieties. The family also own Oakville Cellars.

Mitchell Katz Livermore Valley ★★→★★★ An upcoming winery in Livermore winery. Makes v.gd Cab Sauv and a blockbuster Petite Sirah. Watch for more.

Monticello Cellars Napa ★★★ **99** 01 03 05 *Top Cab Sauv* and Chard under Corley label, basic line under Monticello.

Morgan Monterey ★★★★ Top-end, single-v'yd Pinot Ns and Chards from SANTA LUCIA HIGHLANDS v'yds. Esp fine unoaked Chard Metallico. Estate Double L v'yd farmed organically. New Rhônish entry Côtes du Crows is charming.

Mount Eden Sta Cruz Mts ★★★ Founded by Californian wine guru Martin Ray in the 1940s, Produces ageworthy Chard (rare in California) and intense Pinot N.

Mount Veeder ★★★ Powerful mountain Cab Sauv repays cellar time. Owned by CONSTELLATION.

Mumm Napa Valley Napa ★★→★★★ Stylish bubbly, esp delicious Blanc de Noirs and a rich, complex DVX single-v'yd fizz to age a few yrs in the bottle.

Murphy-Goode Sonoma ★★ Large ALEXANDER VALLEY estate. Sauv Bl, Zin are tops. Tin Roof (screwcap) line offers refreshing Sauv Bl and Chard *sans* oak, in contrast to lavishly oaked Reserve line.

Nalle Sonoma ★★★ Doug Nalle makes lovely Zins from DRY CREEK fruit, juicy and delicious young will also mature gracefully. Try new bottlings of Pinot N.

Napa Wine Company Napa ★★★ Largest organic grape-grower in NAPA sells most of the fruit and operates a custom crush facility for several small premium producers. Offers v.gd Cab Sauv under own label.

Navarro Vineyards Mendocino ★★★→★★★★ Modern ANDERSON VALLEY pioneer producing Ries and Gewurz ranking with the best of the New World. Also Pinot N in 2 styles, homage to Burgundy from ANDERSON VALLEY grapes, plus a brisk and juicy bottling from bought-in grapes.

Newton Vineyards Napa ★★★→★★★★★ (Icon) 99 00 01 03 05 SPRING MOUNTAIN estate produces 3 tiers of wines, Icon, a B'x blend; The Puzzle, site-specific bottlings of Cab Sauv, Merlot and Chard, and the fruit-forward Red Label. Supple and elegant expressions of mountain v'yds. Gd ageing potential.

Nickel & Nickel Napa Specialist in exceptional terroir-driven single-v'yd Cab Sauv from NAPA and Sonoma.

Niebaum-Coppola Estate Napa ★★★ (Rubicon) **99 00** 01 "Godfather" Francis Ford Coppola has proven he is as serious about making wine as making movies. Rubicon, a B'x blend, is best on the list, although it can be too jammy in some vintages, Edizione Pennino concentrates on delightfuly old-fashioned Zin. Budget Diamond series made at Ch Souverain in Sonoma.

Oakville Ranch Napa ★★★ This estate on the Silverado trail (owned by the MINER FAMILY) produces consistently gd wines, esp a creamy Chard.

Ojai Sta Barbara ★★★ Former AU BON CLIMAT partner Adam Tolmach makes range of v.gd wines, esp Syrah and a few other Rhônes from CENTRAL COAST v'yds.

Opus One Napa ★★★★ With a lot of in-and-out yrs at Opus, the wines rarely lived up to the hype for this red B'x blend. The past few vintages, beginning with 04, are showing well with the wines harmonious and balanced.

Pahlmeyer Napa ★★★ Producer of tannic Cab Sauv and more supple Merlot.

Paradigm Napa ★★★ Westside OAKVILLE v'yd with a fine Merlot and a bright, supple Cab Sauv.

Patianna Vineyards Russian River ★★★ Biodynamic v'yds farmed by Patty FETZER. Also sources grapes from organic v'yds in MENDOCINO. Lovely Sauv Bl and v.gd Syrah are main strengths.

Patz & Hall Napa ★★★ The focus is on single v'yd Chard and Pinot N from mostly cool-climate regions of the NORTH COAST. Look esp for Hyde V'yd Chard from

CARNEROS, a balanced and lively wine, the Pisconi V'yd Pinot N from SANTA LUCIA HIGHLANDS in Monterey, a *rounded and delicious Pinot N* and the Chenoweth Ranch Pinot N from RUSSIAN RIVER VALLEY.

Paul Dolan Mendocino ★★★ Pioneer of organic and biodynamic farming when he was winemaker at Fetzer, Dolan's own brand offers outstanding Zin, Syrah, Cab Sauv, Chard and Sauv Bl from organic, biodynamic NORTH COAST v'yds.

Pedroncelli Sonoma ★★ Old hand in DRY CREEK producing bright, elbow-bending Zin, Cab Sauv, and a solid Chard.

Peltier Station Lodi ★★→★★★ The Schatz family has been growing wine grapes in the Lodi AVA for over 50 yrs. Now making their own wines, and the results are gd to outstanding. Look esp for the refreshing Viognier and a yummy Zin.

Periano Lodi ★★ Gd example of the new look of Lodi wines. Outstanding Barbera, brilliant Viognier, and v.gd Chard.

Perry Creek El Dorado ★★→★★★ An extraordinary Syrah and above-average Cab Sauv from high-elevation vines .

Philips, R H Yolo, Dunnigan Hills ★→★★ The only winery in the Dunnigan Hills AVA makes a wide range of wines. Excellent job with Rhône varieties under the EXP label and gd-value Toasted Head Chard.

Philip Togni Vineyards Napa ★★★→★★★★ 00 01 03 05 Veteran NAPA winemaker makes v. *fine long-lasting Cab Sauv* from SPRING MOUNTAIN.

Pietra Santa Monterey ★★→★★★ Family estate in the Cienga Valley AVA producing a zingy Pinot Grigio, a soft, gulpable Dolcetto and a gd Zin.

Pine Ridge Napa ★★★ Tannic and concentrated Cab Sauvs from several NAPA AVAs. The just off-dry Chenin Bl is a treat.

Preston Dry Creek Valley, Sonoma ★★★ Lou Preston is a demanding terroirist, making outstanding DRY CREEK VALLEY icons such as Zin and fruity, marvellous Barbera. His Sauv Bl is delicious as well as several gd Rhône varietals.

Provenance Napa ★★★ Lovely, elegant, and supple Cab Sauv from heart of NAPA estate. Winemaker Tom Rinaldi also makes superb Hewitt V'yd Cab Sauv. Don't overlook the crisp RUTHERFORD Sauv Bl.

Quady Winery San Joaquin ★★→★★★ Imaginative Madera Muscat dessert wines include famed orangey Essencia, rose-petal-flavoured Elysium, and Moscato d'Asti-like Electra. A recent addition, Vya Vermouth is an excellent aperitif.

Quintessa Napa ★★★ Homage to B'x blend from a biodynamic estate on the Silverado Trail developed by the Huneeus family of Chile. The wines show great finesse and balance.

Quivira Sonoma ★★★ Focus on classic and v. drinkable Dry Creek Zin; also a range of delicious Rhône varietals. V'yds farmed biodynamically.

Qupé Sta Barbara ★★★ Never-a-dull-moment cellar-mate of AU BON CLIMAT. *Marsanne*, Pinot Bl, Syrah are all well worth trying.

Rafanelli, A Sonoma ★★★→★★★★ Extraordinary DRY CREEK Zin from this family estate. The Zin will age, but it's so delightful when young, why bother?

Ramey Wine Cellars Russian River ★★★→★★★★ V.gd single-v'yd Cab Sauv from NAPA, and rich and complex Chard from cooler v'yds, esp the Hudson V'yd NAPA-Carneros. Don't pass on the intense and complex SONOMA COAST Syrah.

Kent Rasmussen Carneros ★★★ Crisp, lingering Chard and delicious Pinot N. Ramsay is an alternative label for small production lots.

Ravenswood Sonoma ★★★ Joel Peterson pioneered single-v'yd Zin. Later added a budget line of SONOMA and Vintners Reserve Zin and Merlot. Now owned by CONSTELLATION, but quality appears to be holding.

Raymond Vineyards and Cellar Napa ★★★ 99 00 01 03 05 Balanced and understated Cab Sauv from family v'yds with potential for long-term ageing.

Ridge Sta Cruz Mts ★★★★ (Cab) **95** 99 00 01 03 05 Founder and wine master Paul Draper continues to work his magic here. Supple and harmonious *Monticello*

Cab Sauv from estate is superb. Also outstanding single-v'yd Zin from SONOMA, NAPA, SIERRA FOOTHILLS, and PASO ROBLES. Most Zin has gd ageing potential. ***Outstanding Chard*** from wild-yeast fermentation often overlooked.

Robert Keenan Winery Napa ★★★ Winery on SPRING MOUNTAIN: supple, restrained Cab Sauv, Merlot; also Chard.

Robert Mondavi Napa ★→★★★★ Brilliant innovator bought in 2004 by CONSTELLATION, has wine at all price/quality ranges. At the top are the NAPA VALLEY Reserves, NAPA VALLEY appellation series (eg CARNEROS Chard, OAKVILLE Cab Sauv, etc), NAPA VALLEY (basic production). At the low end are various CENTRAL COAST wines and Robert Mondavi-Woodbridge from Lodi. While the v. top wines may be holding their quality level, mid-ranges seem to be slipping.

Rochioli, J Sonoma ★★★→★★★★ Long-time RUSSIAN RIVER grower sells most fruit to other top Pinot N producers, but holds back enough to make lovely complex Pinot N under his own label, esp the Special Cuvée Pinot N. Also v.gd Sauv Bl.

Roederer Estate Mendocino ★★★★ ANDERSON VALLEY branch of Champagne house. Supple, elegant house style. Easily one of the top 3 sparklers in California and hands-down the best rosé. Luxury *cuvée* L'Ermitage is superb.

Rosenblum Cellars San Francisco Bay ★★→★★★★ Makes a wide range of Zins and Rhône varietals from v'yds up and down the state. Quality varies, but always well above average.

Saddleback Cellars Napa ★★★→★★★★ 97 99 00 01 05 Owner-winemaker Nils Venge is a legend in NAPA. Lush Zin and long-lived Cab Sauv. In some vintages he makes a super Sauv Bl.

St Clement Napa ★★★→★★★★ 99 00 01 03 05 Long-time NAPA producer has a new life under BERINGER BLASS ownership, with a turn towards terroir-based wines. Supple, long-lived Oroppas, a Cab Sauv-based blend, is the go-to wine here. Merlot and Chard also outstanding.

St Francis Sonoma ★★★ 00 01 03 05 Deep and concentrated Cab Sauv from single v'yds. Look for the Wild Oak V'yd Chard finished with a nod to Burgundy. The old-vine Zin is super.

Saintsbury Carneros ★★★→★★★★ Outstanding Pinot N, denser than most from CARNEROS and can take a few years of bottle age. Chard full-flavoured, nicely balanced. Garnet Pinot N, made from younger vines, is a light-hearted quaff.

St-Supéry Napa ★★→★★★ Sleek and graceful Merlot; Cab Sauv can be outstanding, as is red Meritage. ***Sauv Bl one of best in state.*** Sources some grapes from warmer Pope Valley east of NAPA VALLEY. French-owned (Skalli).

Sanford Sta Barbara ★★→★★★★ Founder Richard Sanford was one of the first to plant Pinot N in Santa Barbara, but wines have hit a rough patch under new owners. The Pinot N and Sauv Bl are still worth a look.

Santa Cruz Mountain Vineyard Sta Cruz ★★→★★★ (Cab Sauv) 99 00 01 03 05 Produces wines of strong varietal character from estate grapes, inc v.gd Pinot N and an exceptional Cab Sauv – big, concentrated, ageworthy.

Sattui, V Napa ★★ King of direct-only sales (ie winery door or mail order). Wines made in a rustic, drink-now style. Reds are best, esp Cab Sauv, Zin.

Sausal Sonoma ★★→★★★ ALEXANDER VALLEY estate noted for its Zin and Cab Sauv. Century Vine Zin is a stunning example of old-vine Zin.

Sbragia Sonoma ★★★ Ed Sbragia, long-time winemaker at BERINGER BLASS, has established his own family winery in DRY CREEK VALLEY AVA. A splendid selection of single v'yd Cab Sauv and Merlot shows him at top form. Wines show classic California character, concentrated but not over-the-top. Also a v.gd Sauv Bl from estate vines.

Schramsberg Napa ★★★★ Sparkling wine that stands the test of time. The first to make a true *méthode champenoise* in the state in commercial quantity. Reserve is splendid; Blanc de Noirs outstanding. Luxury *cuvée* J Schram is

America's Krug. Mirabelle is second label for palate-pleasing bubbly. Now making a v.gd Cab Sauv, J. Davies from mountain estate vines.

Schug Cellars Carneros ★★★★ German-born and -trained owner/winemaker dabbles in other wines but outstanding CARNEROS Chard and Pinot N are his main interests.

Screaming Eagle ★★★★ Napa Small lots of cult Cab Sauv at luxury prices for those who like that kind of thing.

Sebastiani Sonoma ★ Former jug-wine king has tried to go upscale with v'yd wines with limited critical success.

Seghesio Sonoma ★★★ Respected family winery has a double focus: Italian varietals and Zin. *The Zins are superb*, drinkable when young, taking on new depth with age. The Italians are a cut above most California efforts in that line, esp Barbera and Sangiovese.

Selene Napa ★★★→★★★★ Ace winemaker Mia Klein makes rich concentrated B'x varietal wines. Hyde V'yd Sauv Bl is super; Chester V'yd red blend a must.

Sequoia Grove Napa ★★★ Estate Cab Sauvs are intense and long-lived with the trend clearly upwards. Chard is balanced and has ageing potential most yrs.

Shafer Vineyards Napa ★★★★ (Cab Sauv) **97 99** 00 01 02 03 05 (Merlot) **03** 05 Top marks for deep yet supple Cab Sauv, esp the Hillside Select and Merlot, which is capable of several years of bottle ageing. The CARNEROS Chard (Red Shoulder Ranch) has improved dramatically to reach ★★★★ status.

Signorello Napa ★★★ Concentrated and rich Cab Sauv, complex full-bodied Chard with sometimes unresolved oak tannins. Syrah is always worth a look as are single v'yd Pinots N from CARNEROS. Looking better with each vintage.

Silverado Vineyards Napa ★★★→★★★★ 99 00 01 03 05 Showy hilltop STAGS LEAP district winery offering supple Cab Sauv, lean and minerally Chard, and distinctive Sangiovese.

Silver Oak Napa/Sonoma ★★★→★★★★ Separate wineries in NAPA and ALEXANDER VALLEYS make Cab Sauv only. NAPA wines can be super-concentrated but they have a loyal following. ALEXANDER VALLEY a bit more supple.

Sinskey Vineyards Napa ★★★ Chard with gd acidic bite and luscious Pinot N are the highlights of this reliable Carneros estate.

Smith-Madrone Napa ★★ High up on SPRING MOUNTAIN, the Smith brothers make one of the state's best Ries in an aromatic off-dry style. V'yds are dry-farmed.

Sonoma-Cutrer Vineyards Sonoma ★★→★★★ Big step up for this Chard specialist with the 04 and 05 vintages, esp the SONOMA COAST bottling, flinty and hard-edge Chard with real bite, and the Les Pierres v'yd.

Spottswoode Napa St Helena ★★★★ **97 99** 00 01 03 05 *Outstanding Cab Sauv* from estate v'yd is long-lasting, balanced, and harmonious. Another California "first growth". Brilliant Sauv Bl is a bonus.

Spring Mountain Napa ★★★→★★★★ Historic mountain estate on a winning path; excellent Cab Sauv with gd structure and depth and outstanding Sauv Bl.

Staglin Napa ★★★ **99 00** 01 03 05 Elegant Cab Sauv from RUTHERFORD Bench.

Stag's Leap Wine Cellars Napa ★★★★ **97 99** 00 01 03 05 Celebrated for silky, seductive Cab Sauvs (SLV, Fay, top-of-line Cask 23) and Merlots. Gd Chard is often overlooked. Holding the line for balance and harmony against the onslaught of over-the-top, super-concentrated NAPA Cabs. Now owned by partnership of Piero Antinori and Ch Ste Michelle.

Stags' Leap Winery Napa SEE BERINGER BLASS.

Steele Wines Lake ★★→★★★★ Jed Steele is a genius at sourcing v'yds for a series of single-v'yd wines under main label and a second label called Shooting Star. Chard can get a little oaky, but Pinot N and some speciality wines such as Washington State Aligoté are outstanding. New budget line is Writer's Block, featuring an earthy and powerful Grenache, among others.

Sterling Napa ★★→★★★ NAPA estate producing Chard and understated single-v'yd Cab Sauv. Has never seemed to fulfil potential, despite gd v'yd sources.

Stonestreet Sonoma ★★★ One of the stars of Jess Jackson's Artisans & Estates stable. The ALEXANDER VALLEY Cab Sauv is a brawny but balanced wine with layers of flavours; Chard can get too buttery but worth a look.

Stony Hill Napa ★★★★ (Chard) **91 95 97** 99 00 01 03 Amazing hillside Chard for past 50 yrs, made in an elegant "homage to Chablis" style. Most wine sold from mailing list. Wines are v. long-lived.

Sutter Home Napa ★→★★ Famous for white Zin and rustic AMADOR red Zin. New upscale Signature Series and Trinchero Family Estates a step up, esp Cab Sauv. See TERRA D'ORO.

Swanson Napa ★★→★★★ Outstanding Merlot and balanced and bright Alexis Cab Sauv get top marks. Also v.gd Pinot Grigio.

Tablas Creek Paso Robles ★★★ Joint venture between owners of Ch Beaucastel and importer Robert Hass. V'yd based on cuttings from Châteauneuf v'yds. Côtes de Tablas bottlings in both red and white are amazingly gd, as is the Tablas Creek Esprit. These are *must-drink wines for Rhônistas*.

Talbott, R Monterey ★★★ Chard from single v'yds in Monterey is the name of the game, with the famed Sleepy Hollow v'yd in the SANTA LUCIA HIGHLANDS AVA at the heart. Approach is Burgundian.

Terra d'Oro Amador ★★→★★★ New line of single v'yd Zin is v.gd, esp the Deaver V'yd (100-year-old vines) and Home V'yd. Also a solid Sangiovese/Cab Sauv blend. Winery, owned by Trinchero Family Estates, formerly called Montevina.

The Terraces Napa ★★★ Supple and elegant Cab Sauv and Zin from several small v'yd plots in the eastern foothills of NAPA.

Thomas Fogarty Sta Cruz Mts ★★→★★★ Go here for a rich, complex Chard that ages fairly well. Also gd Pinot N from estate v'yds and a delightful Gewurz from Monterey grapes.

Titus Vineyards Napa ★★★ Family estate on the Silverado Trail making v.gd Cab Sauv, an outstanding spicy Zin and Cab Franc.

Trefethen Napa ★★★ Historic family winery with record for consistency and durability. Gd off-dry Ries, balanced Chard for ageing. Cab Sauv shows increasing complexity, esp top-of-the-line Halo.

Tres Sabores Rutherford ★★★ Newcomer making 3 different Zins all from the same RUTHERFORD organically farmed hillside v'yds. Wines are consistently balanced and elegant, emphasizing different elements of the v'yd.

Truchard Carneros ★★★→★★★★ Merlot in CARNEROS? For sure. From the warmer north end of CARNEROS comes one of the flavoury, firmly built Merlots that give the AVA identity. Cab Sauv and Syrah even better, and the tangy lemony Chard is a must-drink. New bottlings of Tempranillo outstanding as is a Roussanne.

Turley Alexander Valley ★★★ Former partner in FROG'S LEAP, now specializing in hefty, heady, single-v'yd Zin and Petite Sirah from old vines.

Viader Estate Napa ★★★★ **97 99** 00 01 03 05 A blend of Cab Sauv and Cab Fr from Howell Mountain hillside estate. Powerful wines, yet balanced and elegant in best yrs. This is a classic NAPA mountain red. Ages well. Also look for new series of small-lot bottlings, inc Syrah, Tempranillo.

Volker Eisele Family Estate Napa ★★★→★★★★ **97 99** 00 01 03 05 Sleek, luscious blend of Cab Sauv and Cab Fr from the little-known Chiles Valley AVA. Also look for a spicy Sauv Bl.

Wente Vineyards Livermore and Monterey ★★→★★★ Historic specialist in whites, *esp Livermore Sauv Bl* and Sem. New range of single v'yd Chard has moved the quality bar higher. Livermore estate Cab Sauv is also v.gd. Monterey sweet Ries can be exceptional. A little classic sparkling.

Whitehall Lane Napa ★★→★★★ New releases have revived this ST HELENA winery, esp the elegant and balanced Cab Sauv and a zippy Sauv Bl.

Williams Selyem ★★★ Sonoma Intense smoky RUSSIAN RIVER Pinot N, esp Rochioli and Allen v'yds. Now reaching to SONOMA COAST, MENDOCINO for grapes. Cultish favourite can sometimes lose its balance and fall.

Willowbrook Sonoma ★★★ Newcomer makes impressive entrance with three single-v'yd Pinot Ns; wines are stylish and elegant with bright opening fruit and deep flavours in the middle and finish. Keep an eye on this producer.

Wilson Vineyards Sonoma ★★→★★★ Newcomer with an eye for Zin. The estate old-vine Ellie's V'yd is outstanding – classic DRY CREEK Zin. The impressive Reserve Zin has a rich, brambly mouthfeel.

The Wine Group Central Valley The third-largest producer of wine in the world, by volume, after E & J GALLO and CONSTELLATION, offers mostly bargain wines, such as Glen Ellen, Almaden and Inglenook as well as bag-in-box bargains such as Franzia. The wine is drinkable, for the most part, and certainly helps balance out grape supply and demand in California and around the world.

York Creek Spring Mtn, Napa ★★★ Exceptional v'yd owned by Fritz Maytag, father of micro-brew revolution in US with his Anchor Steam beer. Sells to RIDGE and others. Now has own label. Mostly gd, always interesting.

Zaca Mesa Sta Barbara ★★→★★★ Now turning away from Chard and Pinot N to concentrate on estate Rhône grapes (esp Viognier) and blends (Cuvée Z).

Zahtila Vineyards Napa ★★★ Newcomer in north NAPA specializes in elegant and inviting Cab Sauv and intense Zin (one from Oat Hill estate v'yd nr Calistoga). Also makes DRY CREEK and RUSSIAN RIVER Zins from SONOMA COUNTY. To watch.

ZD Napa ★★ Overdose of oak can spoil the Chard; Cab Sauv more restrained.

The Pacific Northwest

It seems that with each new vintage, the wines of the Pacific Northwest hit a new quality standard. One blessing is that even though there are a few fairly large producers, the emphasis has always been on premium wines, even in the budget category. The explosive growth of artisan wines over the past decade has fuelled that commitment, as winemakers and growers work together to match vines, clones and rootstock to particular sites. One notable thing is that as new varieties have taken root in the Pacific Northwest, esp Rhône varieties, the wines that were the traditional strength of the area continue to shine: Pinot N and Pinot Gr in Oregon, Riesling and B'x vines in Washington, Cab Sauv and Chard in Idaho. The future looks bright for this region.

Recent vintages

Any general discussion of vintages is difficult because of the wide variation in climate over the area and the jumble of microclimates in small regions.

2008 A cool spring led to a late harvest. The typical autumn rain pattern was late to develop and wine-growers are optimistic about the future of the young wines, some calling it the best vintage of the decade. In Oregon the Pinot N looked esp promising. In Washington and Idaho the harvest was up from 2007 and grapes were in near-perfect condition.

2007 Not an easy vintage across the Northwest; rain and even some hail during harvest caused problems but, as always, those growers and wineries that paid attention will get it right.

2006 The century is young, but when talk turns to vintage of the century, this is it so far for Oregon. Incredible quality across the board. Washington and Idaho reporting similar quality.

2005 This is turning out to be an amazing vintage, if the winery paid attention.

Oregon Pinot N, Washington Cab Sauv, Merlot, could be exceptional.
2004 Wines range from below average to above average, depending on site.

Oregon

Abacela Vineyards Umpqua Valley ★★★ New producer is gaining a following in unfashionable area of Oregon. Tempranillo, Dolcetto, Cab Fr, Syrah stand out.

Adelsheim Vineyard Yamhill County ★★★→★★★★ 04 05 06 Oregon Pinot N veteran remains on top of the game with elegant Pinot N. New Dijon clone Chard, Ries, top Pinots Gr and Bl: clean, bracing.

Amalie Robert Estate Willamette ★★★ Promising new estate winery with a minerally, terroir-driven Pinot N and luscious Chard.

Amity Willamette ★★→★★★ Pioneer in Oregon with exceptional Ries and Pinot Bl. The Pinot often rises to ★★★.

Anam Cara Cellars Willamette ★★★ Newcomer with an extraordinary Chehalm Mountains Reserve Pinot N, rich and deeply concentrated, as well as an elegant estate Pinot N and a delicious estate Ries.

Andrew Rich (Tabula Rasa) Willamette ★★→★★★ Ex-California winemaker. Small lots of artisan wines, inc a supple Pinot N and exceptional Syrah.

Anne Amie Willamette ★★★ Outstanding Winemaker's Selection Pinot N, balanced and harmonious; v.gd Pinot Gr as well.

Antica Terra Willamette ★★→★★★ Now owned by 4 partners, inc ex-California winemaker Maggie Harrison (Sin Qua Non). The Pinot N, made from Amity Hills fruit, is California-meets-Oregon, with rich, deep flavours.

Archery Summit Williamette ★★★ Powerful Pinot N bottlings from several v'yds in the Red Hills AVA; made in a bold style that has won a loyal following.

Argyle Yamhill County ★★→★★★ V.gd Ries and v. fine Pinot N lead the way; also *bargain bubbly*. Winery founded by Aussie superstar winemaker Brian Croser.

Beaux Frères Yamhill County ★★★ Pinot N has more concentration than most Oregon offerings. Part-owned by critic Robert Parker.

Benton Lane Willamette ★★ A delicious Pinot N, balanced and harmonious. Also v.gd Pinot Gr. If you are lucky enough to find the rosé of Pinot N, grab it.

Bethel Heights Willamette ★★→★★★ 04 05 Deftly made estate Pinot N. Chard one of best in state; gd Pinot Bl, Pinot Gr.

Brick House Yamhill County ★★★ 01 02 Huge estate Pinot N. Dark and brooding; Estate Select a leaner, more balanced version.

Carabella Willamette ★★ Dijon Clone 76 Chard is outstanding, with a silky mouthfeel and just a touch of oak.

Chehalem Yamhill County ★★→★★★ Outstanding Chard with ageing potential, as well as a new, drink-me-now, no-oak Chard. V.gd Ries, Pinot Gr.

Coehlo Winery Willamette ★★ Pinot N-only producer is off to a good start with an aromatic, lively wine that shows promise for the future.

Cooper Mountain Willamette ★★★→★★★★ Complex Pinot N and a rich, intense Chard capable of some bottle age. Certified biodynamic v'yds.

Domaine Drouhin Willamette ★★★→★★★★ 03 04 05 06 *Outstanding Pinot N* silky and elegant, improving with each vintage. Chard also a winner.

Domaine Serene Willamette ★★★★ 02 04 05 06 Burgundian approach to single-v'yd Pinot N is usually well ahead of the pack. Bottled unfiltered.

Elk Cove Vineyards Willamette ★★→★★★ V.g Ries inc late-harvest. Top Pinot N.

Erath Vineyards Yamhill County ★★→★★★ Oregon pioneer, founded 1968. V.gd Chard, Pinot Gr, Gewurz, Pinot Bl. Pinots and Ries age well.

Evesham Wood Willamette ★★★ Small family winery with fine Pinot N, Pinot Gr, and dry Gewurz. Pinot N leaping ahead in recent vintages. Organic.

Eyrie Vineyards Willamette ★★★ Chard and Pinot Gr: rich yet crisp. All wines age.

Foris Vineyards Rouge Valley ★★ A lovely Pinot Bl and a classic red-cherry Pinot N top the list. One of the best in the south of the state.

Four Graces Willamette ★★→★★★ The great strength of this fairly new winery is an exceptional estate Pinot N offering bright, lively fruit and gd mouthfeel; also check out the Pinot Bl and Pinot Gr. A winery to watch.

Freja Willamette ★★★ Only estate-grown Pinot N. Wines are silky on the palate but with an underlying power, clearly in homage to Burgundy.

Henry Estate Rouge Valley ★★ In this warmer section of Oregon, Henry Estate makes a solid Cab Sauv and a gd Merlot. Also look for a v.gd dry Gewurz.

Ken Wright Cellars Yamhill County ★★★ 02 05 06 Highly regarded Pinot N and a v.gd Chard from single v'yds.

King Estate South Willamette ★★★→★★★★ 03 04 05 06 One of Oregon's largest wineries, is now certified organic. Lovely and constantly improving Pinot N, outstanding Chard.

Lachini Vineyards ★★★ Upcoming producer of outstanding Pinot N and v.gd Pinot Gr. V'yds farmed biodynamically. Also, new wines from v'yds in the Red Mountain AVA of Washington, a B'x blend and a bold Cab Sauv. Has recently planted Ries and Albariño on the estate.

Lange Winery Yamhill County ★★→★★★ Rich and silky Pinot N, backed by a v.gd Pinot Gr and excellent Chard.

Monk's Gate Willamette ★★★ Small-production Pinot N is complex and rich while maintaining balance and harmony. Worth looking for.

Oak Knoll Willamette ★★ Pinot is the big story at this popular winery, with intense but balanced bottlings. Also a v.gd off-dry Ries.

Panther Creek Willamette ★★ Pinot N from several v'yds is concentrated, built to age; new is a delicious unoaked Chard.

Patricia Green Cellars Yamhill County ★★→★★★ Exciting, single-v'yd Pinot N is the heart of the story here. Wines vary in style from light, racy Pinot to bolder, concentrated, but all worth a look.

Penner-Ash Yamhill County ★★★ REX HILL winemaker Lynn Penner-Ash and her husband are making intense, rich Pinot N from up to half-dozen v'yds in a bolder style than many in Oregon. Also a v.gd Viognier.

Ponzi Vineyards Willamette ★★→★★★ 03 05 06 Long-established with consistently *outstanding Pinot N* and v.gd Pinot Gr and Chard.

Resonance Yamhill Carlton ★★ Kevin and Carla Chambers now out with their own complex and delicious Pinot N made from organic and biodynamic grapes.

Retour Wines Willamette ★★★ Terroir-driven old-vine Pinot N is stunning, with touches of earthy spice and anise. Keep an eye on Retour.

Rex Hill Willamette ★★★→★★★★ Excellent Pinot N, Pinot Gr, and Chard from several north Willamette v'yds. Reserve wines can hit ★★★★.

RoxyAnn Rouge River ★★ Southern Oregon producer of an esp gd Viognier and excellent Pinot Gr. Claret red blend is a pleasing quaff.

Siduri ★★→★★★ Dedicated to single-v'yd Pinot N, Siduri makes wine from several Oregon and California v'yds. The Arbre Vert Willamette Pinot N is outstanding, with supple, balanced fruit and good acidity.

Sokol Blosser Willamette ★★★→★★★★ Superb wines throughout with an esp v.gd Pinot N, Chard, and Gewurz, balanced and harmonious. Syrah is a treat.

Soter Yamhill Carlton ★★★ Tony Soter has moved his winemaking skills from California to Oregon and he got it right with first release, *Mineral Springs V'yd Pinot N*, a superb wine, balanced and harmonious with a long, lyrical finish. He recently followed up with a North County Pinot N, elegant and sleek.

Stoller Estate Dundee Hills ★★★ The SV Estate Pinot N is a balanced, elegant wine with supple fruit, the JV Estate Pinot N is riper with softer tannins. Also a gd Chard from estate grapes.

Torii Mor Yamhill Co ★★★ V.gd single-v'yd Pinot N bottlings and superior Pinot Gr.

Tyee Wine Cellars Willamette ★★ Artisan producer of v.gd Pinot N, Pinot Gr and tasty Gewurz.

Van Duzer Winery Willamette ★★→★★★ Bright, fruity Pinot N, delicious Pinot Gr, from hillside v'yds in a v. cool part of Willamette Valley. Steadily improving.

Willakenzie Estate Yamhill County ★★★ Specialist in small lots of Pinot N, Pinot Gr, Pinot Bl and Pinot Meunier with a minuscule amount of Gamay Noir. Wines can be outstanding and are always worth a look.

Willamette Valley Vineyards Willamette ★★→★★★ Gd Ries, Chard and v.gd Pinot N. New clonal selection Chard raises the quality bar.

Washington & Idaho

Abeja Walla Walla ★★→★★★ Abeja first made a name for Cab Sauv and Chard, but the Syrah has been attracting attention recently. It shows the same balance and harmony as the Cab Sauv, with a spicy edge and lingering finish.

Alexandria Nicole Cellars Columbia Valley Washington ★★→★★★ Newish artisan estate in the Horse Heaven Hills AVA produces a number of wines, inc B'x varietals, but once more it is the Syrah that draws rave reviews, esp the Block 17 Estate Syrah. Also a delicious and minerally Grenache..

Andrew Will Puget Sound, Washington ★★★★ **97** 00 01 02 05 Owner Chris Camarda sources B'x varietals from Red Mountain, making outstanding single-v'yd reds: balanced, elegant, tremendous ageing potential.

Arbor Crest Spokane, Washington ★★ The top draw here is the Chard, followed closely by a floral Sauv Bl.

Badger Mountain Columbia Valley, Washington ★★→★★★ Washington's first organic v'yd, producing gd Cab Sauv and Chard. Also a new line of "no sulfites" organic wines.

Barnard Griffin Columbia Valley, Washington ★★→★★★ Small producer: well-made Merlot, Chard (esp barrel-fermented), Sem, Sauv Bl. Top Syrah. Viognier is a recent and welcome addition to the list.

Basel Cellars Walla Walla Valley, Washington ★★★ Newcomer sweeps the board with gd B'x varieties and a fine Syrah. Look esp for Merriment, a B'x blend.

Bergevin Lane Walla Walla ★★ Gd beginning for another new Washington winery with Syrah out in front.

Brian Carter Cellars Woodinville, Washington ★★→★★★ Limited production of gd to v.gd blends, inc a white blend of aromatic varietals, a Sangiovese-based Super Tuscan, two Bordeaux blends and Byzance, a ★★★ Rhône blend.

Bunnell Cellars Columbia Valley ★★★ Rhône rules at this estate winery. Top marks for a series of single v'yd Syrahs, a v.gd Viognier and a new Grenache.

Buty Walla Walla Valley, Washington ★★★ Winery founded in 2001 with emphasis on B'x blends and Syrah with pleasing results. Cab Sauv/Syrah blend called Reviviva of the Stones is popular favourite.

Cadaretta Walla Walla ★★★ This newcomer opened with a terrific pair of wines, SDS, a blend of Sauv Bl and Sem and a silky Syrah that will have you reaching for a second glass. Expect even better things as the estate v'yds mature.

Cayuse Walla Walla Valley, Washington ★★→★★★ Several bottlings of gd to v.gd Syrah and an outstanding B'x blend have buyers calling. Biodynamic grapes.

Château Ste-Michelle Woodinville, Washington ★★→★★★★ Washington's largest winery; also owns COLUMBIA CREST, Northstar (top Merlot), Dom Ste-Michelle, and Snoqualmie, among others. Major v'yd holdings, first-rate equipment, and skilled winemakers keep wide range of varieties in front ranks. V.gd v'yd-designated Cab Sauv, Merlot, and Chard. Links with Loosen and Antinori.

Chinook Wines Yakima Valley, Washington ★★★ **01** 02 03 Elegant Merlot and Cab Sauv; outstanding Cab Fr and a delicious Cab Fr rosé.

Columbia Crest Columbia Valley, Washington ★★→★★★ Separately run CHÂTEAU

STE-MICHELLE label for gd value wines. Cab Sauv, Merlot, Syrah, and Sauv Bl best. Also v.gd reserve wines, esp Grand Estates Shiraz.

Columbia Winery Woodinville, Washington ★★★ Pioneer and still a leader, with balanced, stylish, understated single-v'yd wines. Marvellous Syrah.

DeLille Cellars Woodinville, Washington ★★★→★★★★ 00 01 02 03 05 A B'x specialist producing v.gd to excellent wines under 4 labels: Chaleur Estate Red, D2, Harrison Hill, Chaleur Estate Blanc. New addition is Syrah, Doyenne.

Di Stefano Woodinville, Washington ★★→★★★ Best bet is B'x red, inc a v.gd, elegant Cab Sauv and an elegant Cab Franc; also a bright and juicy Syrah.

Dunham Cellars Walla Walla, Washington ★★→★★★ Artisan producer focusing on long-lived Cab Sauv and superb Syrah and a v.gd Chard.

Forgeron Walla Walla ★★ New producer making small lots of single-v'yd wines; v.gd Syrah in a juicy style and notable Roussanne and Pinot Gr.

Glen Fiona Walla Walla, Washington ★★→★★★ Syrah/Syrah blends from Rhône specialist, esp Syrah/Cinsault/Counoise *cuvée*. Can be v.gd and built to last.

Hedges Cellars Yakima Valley, Washington ★★→★★★★ V. fine B'x reds from Red Mountain AVA. Fumé is a delicious and popular blend of Chard and Sauv Bl.

The Hogue Cellars Yakima Valley, Washington ★→★★★ Large, reliable producer known for excellent, gd-value wines, esp Ries, Chard, Merlot, Cab Sauv. Produces *quintessential Washington Sauv Bl*.

Hyatt Vineyards Yakima Valley, Washington ★★→★★★ Stylish Merlot is among the state's best. Seek Black Muscat Icewine when conditions are right.

Indian Creek Idaho ★→★★ Top wine is Pinot N plus a v.gd Ries and gd Cab Sauv.

K Vintners ★★→★★★ Walla Walla Syrah specialist with a little Viognier on the side. Look for the intense Milbrandt Wahluke Slope Syrah, and don't forget the balanced and delicious Columbia Valley Viognier.

Kiona Vineyards Yakima Valley, Washington ★★ Solid wines from Red Mountain AVA, esp Cab Sauv; gd value and quality.

Lake Chelan Winery Columbia Valley, Washington ★★ A promising new winery with range of wines inc gd Cab Sauv, an attractive Syrah and a floral Ries.

L'Ecole No 41 Walla Walla ★★★→★★★★ (Merlot) 02 04 05 06 Blockbuster but balanced reds (Merlot, Cab Sauv, and super Meritage blend) with forward, ageworthy fruit. Gd barrel-fermented Sem.

Leonetti Walla Walla ★★★→★★★★ One of Washington's cult wineries, Leonetti's bold Cab Sauv is a gd match for the v. fine Merlot, one of Washington's stars.

Long Shadows Columbia Valley ★★★→★★★★ Former Ch Ste-Michelle CEO Allen Shoup brought together leading international winemakers to make wines from Washington grapes. Can't go wrong with any of them but look for *Poet's Leap Ries* by Armin Diel (Germany), Feather, a Cab Sauv made by Randy Dunn (California) and Sequel, a glorious Syrah made by John Duval (Australia).

McCrea Puget Sound ★★★ A Rhône pioneer making small lots of gd to v. fine Viognier, Syrah, and Grenache even a rare varietal bottling of Counoise.

Milbrandt Vineyards ★★→★★★ Long-time growers with more than 650 ha of vines in eastern Washington, the Milbrandt brothers are now producing their own wine. The Legacy Evergreen Chard is a winner, with crisp minerality; also look for Traditions bottlings, esp the Syrah.

Syrah Comes of Age in Washington

Syrah is rapidly becoming the go-to wine of Washington. The warmer harvest weather of the last few vintages, except for 07, has helped nudge Syrah quality higher, but behind this is the zeal of the winegrowers from large producers like CH STE. MICHELE and COLUMBIA CREST to dedicated Rhône specialists like CADARETTA. Washington is getting Syrah right.

Drinking local in Washington DC

Although the state of Virginia boasts many wineries within a 30-minute drive from Washington DC, until recently it was virtually impossible to find local wines when dining out in the capital. Change is coming as Virginia's best wines begin to gain visibility. In the heart of Washington go to Charlie Palmer Steak (across the street from the Capitol Building), the Old Ebbitt Grill (on 15th Street, steps from the White House) and Panache (across the street from the Mayflower Hotel). In Georgetown try the Peacock Café, or 1789. Restaurants in some of the capital's most elegant hotels also feature Virginia wines on their lists, including the Hay-Adams (16th Street), the Willard (Pennsylvania Avenue), and the Monaco (near the Capital Mall).

Nicolas Cole Cellars Columbia Valley, Washington ★★→★★★ Limited bottlings of balanced and elegant B'x-style reds and Rhônes that show promise of ageing.

Nota Bene Cellars Puget Sound, Washington ★★→★★★ Amazing red wines from B'x varietals sourced in Red Mountain AVA and other top Washington v'yds. Wines are built to last. Worth seeking out.

Owen Roe Washington ★★→★★★ Look for the Yakima Valley Chard and Ries; reds, esp B'x varieties, from Columbia Valley are v.gd. Gd value wines under the O'Reilly label with a v. gd Pinot Gr.

Quilceda Creek Puget Sound, Wahinton ★★★→★★★★ 01 03 04 05 Expertly crafted *Columbia Valley Cab Sauv*. Wines are beautifully balanced to age.

Reininger Walla Walla, Washington ★★→★★★ Small producer of gd Merlot and v. fine Syrah. Helix label features wines from throughout the state; esp gd Syrah.

Robert Karl Columbia Valley, Washington ★★→★★★ Spokane-based winery making small lots of single-v'yd wines from the Horse Heaven Hills AVA in the Columbia Valley. Both the Merlot and Cab Sauv can hit ★★★.

Ste Chapelle Snake River Valley, Idaho ★★ Pleasant, forward Chard, Cab Sauv, Merlot, and Syrah. Also v.gd Ries and Gewurz in dry Alsace style. Attractive sparkling wine. Chateau Series label features gd value wines.

Sandhill Winery Columbia Valley, Washington ★★★ Estate-only wines from the Red Mountain AVA. Outstanding Cab Sauv and Merlot and a v.gd Pinot Gr. Cinnamon Teal Red Table Wine is a local favourite.

Saviah Cellars Walla Walla Valley, Washington ★★→★★★ V.gd B'x blends from small family winery; outstanding Syrah.

Sawtooth Cellars Idaho ★★ Gd Cab Sauv with latest Syrah and Viognier v.gd. Recently added an excellent Roussanne.

Seven Hills Walla Walla Valley, Washington ★★→★★★ Known for balanced and elegant Cab Sauv and Merlot. Ciel du Cheval B'x blend v.gd. Pinot Gr from Oregon grapes well received.

Snoqualmie Vineyards Columbia Valley ★★→★★★ Always a reliable producer of Cab Sauv and Merlot, among others, quality has gone up with the introduction of the Naked bottlings, made from organically grown grapes. The luscious Naked Ries is an instant classic.

Three Rivers Winery Walla Walla ★★→★★★ A "destination" winery producing a wide range of wines. Look esp for the bold Syrah and v. drinkable Grenache.

Woodward Canyon Walla Walla, Washington ★★★→★★★★ (Cab) 01 02 03 04 05 The winery has set the standard for *Washington Cab Sauv* and Merlot for almost 30 years. Often overlooked, the Chard is also excellent.

East of the Rockies

Winemaking and grape-growing in the eastern United States continues its forward momentum despite a slight slow-down in the pace of start-up wineries due to the sagging global economy. New York State now has 250 wineries (up from 150 in 2002). Ohio has increased from 60 to 121, and the number of Virginia wineries has grown from 65 to 141. Quality continues to ascend as experience leads to greater understanding of which grape varieties are best suited to individual terroirs. In New York State, top Ries from the Finger Lakes are now competitive with the world's best, while Long Island's Merlot, Syrah and Cabs Sauv and Franc are gaining recognition. Virginia is turning out some notable Viognier as well as impressive Cab Franc and Petit Verdot, along with Syrah and other Rhône grapes. New York is the nation's third largest grape-growing state (after California and Washington).

Recent vintages

While it's difficult to generalize about such a vast region, 2006 was by and large a good year everywhere, from Massachusetts in the north all the way down to North Carolina. 2007 was generally outstanding overall, while 2008 was above average in some areas, average in others.

Anthony Road Finger Lakes, NY ★★★★ Fine Ries; Pinot Gr, Cab Franc-Lemberger, late-harvest Vignoles.

Barboursville Virginia ★★★★ 06' 07' 08 Oldest of the state's modern-era wineries (founded 1976), owned by the Zonin family (see Italy). Excellent Chard, Cab Fr, Barbera, Nebbiolo, Pinot Gr and Malvasia. Elegant inn and restaurant.

Bedell Long Island, NY ★★★ 06 07 08 Now owned by former CEO of New Line Cinema (and producer of *Lord of the Rings* trilogy), makes outstanding small-batch series of varietally labelled wines inc Chard, Gewurz and Cab Fr.

Breaux Virginia ★★★ 07 08' V'yd an hour from Washington DC. Gd Chard, Merlot.

Chamard ★★ 07 08 Connecticut's best winery. AVA is Southeastern New England.

Channing Daughters ★★★ 07 08 LONG ISLAND's innovative South Fork estate, with excellent and eclectic white blends (ie Tocai Friulano) inspired by Italy.

Château LaFayette Reneau Finger Lakes, NY ★★★★ 06 07 08 Stylish Chard, Ries, and top-notch Cab Sauv. Stunning lakeside setting.

Chrysalis Virginia ★★★★ Top Viognier, v.gd Petit Manseng, and native Norton.

Clinton Vineyards Hudson River, NY ★★ 08 Clean, gd dry Seyval. Exceptional sparkling, also fine cassis, wild black raspberry and peach wines.

Debonné Vineyards Lake Erie, Ohio ★★ 07 08 Largest OHIO estate winery. Chard, Ries, Pinot Gr, and some hybrids: Chambourcin and Vidal.

Ferrante Winery Harpersfield, Ohio Venerable estate (since 1937) with fine Chard, Cab Sauv, Ries, and superb Icewine.

Finger Lakes Beautiful cool upstate NY region, with over 100 wineries source of most of state's wines. Top wineries: ANTHONY ROAD, CH LAFAYETTE RENEAU, DR. FRANK, FOX RUN, HERON HILL, KING FERRY, Lakewood, LAMOREAUX LANDING, RED NEWT, STANDING STONE, Swedish Hill, and Wiemer.

Firelands Lake Erie, Ohio ★★ OHIO estate making Cab Sauv, Gewurz, Pinot Gr. Notable Icewine.

Fox Run Finger Lakes, NY ★★★ 07' 08 Some of region's best Chard, Gewurz, Ries, and Pinot N. Plus a good café for lunch or light refreshment.

Frank, Dr Konstantin (Vinifera Wine Cellars) Finger Lakes, NY ★★★★ 06 07 08 Continues to set the pace for serious winemaking. The late Dr F was a pioneer in growing European vines in the FINGER LAKES. *Excellent Ries*, Gewurz; gd Chard, Cab Sauv, and Pinot N. Also v.gd Ch Frank sparkling.

EAST OF THE ROCKIES

The Hamptons (aka **South Fork**) LONG ISLAND AVA. The top winery is moneyed WÖLFFER ESTATE. Showcase Duck Walk owns 52 ha of vines, CHANNING DAUGHTERS produces masterful blends.

Hermann J Wiemer Finger Lakes, NY ★★→★★★ 07 08 Established by creative, German-born owner/winemaker. Outstanding Ries; v.gd Chard. Winemaker Fred Merwarth recently took over operations from eponymous founder.

Heron Hill Finger Lakes ★★★ Great Ries and dessert wines by Thomas Laszlo.

Horton Virginia ★★★ 06 07 08 Established early 1990s. Gd Viognier, Mourvèdre, Cab Fr, Norton.

Hudson River Region America's oldest wine-growing district (35 producers) and NY's first AVA. Straddles the river, 2 hours' drive north of Manhattan.

Jefferson Virginia ★★★ 07 08 Nr Thomas Jefferson's Monticello estate. Fine Pinot Gr, Viognier, Chard, Petit Verdot, Merlot, B'x blend.

Keswick Virginia ★★★ 07 08 Elegant Chard, v.gd Viognier, Touriga, and Cab-based blend.

King Ferry Finger Lakes, NY ★★★ 07 08 Label is Treleaven. Gd Ries, stylish Chards.

Kluge Virginia ★★★ 07 08 Showplace moneyed estate, ambitious wines include Viognier, good brut sparkling, and B'x blend.

Lake Erie Largest grape-growing district in the eastern US; 10,117 ha along shore of Lake Erie, includes portions of NY, PENNSYLVANIA, and OHIO. Also name of a tri-state AVA: NY's sector has 16 wineries, PENNSYLVANIA's 7 and OHIO's 32. OHIO's Harpersfield sets standards for quality.

Lamoureaux Landing Finger Lakes, NY ★★★ 07 08 Among **NY's best Chard**, Ries, and Cab Fr from striking Greek-revival winery.

Lenz Long Island NY ★★★ 07 08 Classy winery of NORTH FORK AVA. Fine **austere Chard in the Chablis mode** as well as rich barrel-fermented one, also notable Gewurz, Merlot, and sparkling wine.

Linden Virginia ★★★★ 07 08 Impressive VIRGINIA producer in mts 100 km west of Washington DC. Notable Sauv Bl, Cab Fr, Petit Verdot, B'x-style "claret".

Long Island, New York Exciting wine region and a hothouse of experimentation. Currently 1,200 ha, all vinifera (35% Merlot) and 3 AVAs (Long Island, NORTH FORK, THE HAMPTONS). Most of its 49 wineries are on the NORTH FORK. Best varieties: Chard, Cab Sauv, Merlot. A long growing season; mostly frost-free but hurricane-prone. Autumnal migrations of voracious birds a serious threat to grapes. The young generation of wineries inc: Bridge, Comtesse Thérèse, Diliberto (gd reds), Martha Clara, Old Fields Shinn Estate (owned by former owners of Manhattan restaurant Home), Sherwood House (Chard and Merlot).

Maryland Has more than 35 wineries in 4 distinct growing regions. Boordy V'yds with v.gd Chard and Cab Sauv. Basignani for gd Cab Sauv, and Seyval. Fiore: Chambourcin, Merlot, and Cab Sauv. Sugarloaf: Cab Fr and Pinot Gr. Elk Run for Pinot Gr and Gewurz and Black Ankle for gd Cab blends and Albariño.

Michael Shaps/Virginia Wineworks ★★★★ 07 08 Burgundy-trained vintner turns out fine Viognier, Chardonnay, Petit Verdot under Michael Shaps label.

Michigan Impressive Ries and Gewurz, gd Pinot N, and Cab Fr are emerging; 63 wineries using Michigan grapes and 4 AVAs (730 ha grapes, two-thirds of them vinifera). Best include Black Star, Bowers Harbor, Brys, Château Grand Traverse, Peninsula Cellars (esp dry Gewurz), Tabor Hill, Willow, and Mauby for outstanding sparkling. Fenn Valley, St. Julian and Lemon Creek have large following. Up-and-coming: Dom Berrien, Ch. Fontaine, Cherry Creek, 45 North, Left Foot Charley, Longview. Great reds in 07.

Millbrook Hudson River, NY ★★★ 07 08 Chards modelled on Burgundy; Cab Fr can be delicious.

Naked Mountain Virginia 07 08 Est 1981; known for big, buttery Chard.

North Carolina Look for Chard, Viognier, Cab Fr. 80 wineries, inc Childress, Duplin (for Muscadine), Hanover Park, Iron Gate, Laurel Gray, McRitchie, Old North State, RagApple, RayLen, Raffaldini, Rockhouse, Shelton. Biltmore is most visited winery in the US.

North Fork LONG ISLAND AVA. New York AVA (2 hrs drive from Manhattan) with 49 wineries. Top producers include: Bedell, Jamesport, Lieb, LENZ, PALMER, PAUMANOK, PELLEGRINI, PINDAR, Raphael.

Ohio 121 wineries, 5 AVAs, notably LAKE ERIE and Ohio Valley. Some exceptional Pinot Gr, Ries, Pinot N, Cab Fr, Icewine.

Palmer Long Island, NY ★★★ 07 08 Superior NORTH FORK producer; byword in Darwinian metropolitan market. Tasty Chard, Sauv Bl, Chinon-like Cab Fr.

Paumanok Long Island, NY ★★★★ 07 08 NORTH FORK winery; impressive Ries, Chard, Merlot, Cab Sauv; v.gd Chenin Bl; late-harvest botrytized Sauv Bl.

Pellegrini Long Island, NY ★★★★ 07 08 An enchantingly designed winery on NORTH FORK. Opulent Merlot, stylish Chard, B'x-like Cab Sauv.

Pennsylvania 110 wineries, with quality rapidly rising. Leading estates include pioneering Chaddsford (esp Chambourcin, a Barbera/Sangiovese blend and a Cab/Sangiovese blend), Allegro (worthy Chard, Cab Sauv, Merlot), Pinnacle Ridge (v.gd sparkling and Chambourcin), Manatawny Creek (noteworthy Cabs Fr and Sauv, and B'x-style blend) and Lake Erie's Mazza for Vidal Icewine.

Pindar Vineyards Long Island, NY ★★★ 07 08 116-ha operation at NORTH FORK. Range of blends and popular varietals, inc Chard, Merlot, sparkling, v.gd B'x-style red blend, Mythology. Visits.

Pollack Virginia One of the state's most promising young wineries, Chard, Cab Fr, B'x blend, Viognier.

Red Newt Finger Lakes, NY ★★★ 07 08 Turns out top Chard, Ries, and some of the best reds in NY, esp Cab Fr, Merlot, and B'x-inspired red blend.

Sakonnet Little Compton, Rhode Island ★★ 07 08 Largest New England winery. V. drinkable wines; gd sparkling brut *cuvée*.

Standing Stone Finger Lakes, NY ★★★ 06 07 08 One of the region's finest wineries with v.gd Ries, Gewurz, and B'x-type blend.

Tomasello New Jersey ★★ Gd Chambourcin, Pinot N, Cab Sauv, and Petit Verdot.

Unionville Vineyards New Jersey ★★ Nice Chard and gd B'x-style red.

Valhalla Virginia ★★★ 07 08 V'yd at 600 m atop a granite mountain yields spicy Sangiovese, and gd red blend of all 5 B'x grapes.

Veritas Virginia ★★★ 07 08 Gd Chard, Cab Fr, Viognier, gutsy Petit Verdot and Petit Manseng.

Villa Appalaccia Virginia ★★★ 07 08 Italian-inspired winery in the Blue Ridge Mountains making limited amounts (3,000 cases total) of Primitivo, Sangiovese, Malvasia, Pinot Gr.

Virginia With 141 bonded wineries and 6 AVAs, Virginia is turning out some of the best wines in the east, with an emphasis on vinifera. The modern winemaking era now encompasses virtually every part of the state, some less than an hour's drive from Washington DC.

Wagner Vineyards Finger Lakes, NY ★★ 07 08 Chard, dry and sweet Ries, B'x blend, and Icewine. Also has micro-brewery and restaurant.

Westport Rivers Southeast New England ★★ 07 08 Massachusetts house established in 1989. Gd Chard and elegant sparkling.

Whitehall Virginia ★★★★ 07 08 A handsome estate nr historic Charlottesville. Outstanding Viognier, noteworthy Pinot Gr, lush Petit Manseng, top Chard, Cab Fr, Touriga Nacional, and Cab Sauv blend.

Wölffer Estate Long Island, NY ★★★★ 07 08 Fine Chard, vibrant rosé and gd Merlot from talented German-born winemaker.

Southeast & central states

Missouri Continues to expand, with over 50 producers in 3 AVAs: **Augusta**, **Hermann**, and **Ozark Highlands**. Best wines are Seyval Blanc Vidal, Vignoles (sweet and dry versions), and Chambourcin. **Stone Hill** in Hermann produces v.gd Chardonel (a frost-hardy hybrid of Seyval Blanc and Chard), Norton, and gd Seyval Blanc and Vidal Blanc. **Hermannhof** is also drawing notice for Vignoles, Chardonel, and Norton. Also notable: **St James** for Vignoles, Seyval, Norton; **Mount Pleasant** in Augusta for rich "port" and Norton; **Adam Puchta** for gd port-style wines and Norton, Vignoles, Vidal Blanc; **Augusta Winery** for Chambourcin, Chardonel, Icewine; **Les Bourgeois**, gd Syrah, Norton, Chardonel, Montelle, v.gd Cynthiana and Chambourcin.

Georgia There are now over a dozen wineries here. Look for: **Three Sisters** (Dahlonega), **Habersham Vineyards**, and **Ch Elan** (Braselton), which features southern splendour with v'yds, wine, and a resort.

Wisconsin Best is Wollersheim, specializing in variations of Maréchel Foch. Prairie Fumé (Seyval Bl) is a commercial success.

The Southwest

Although Southwest wineries tend to be modest, consumer interest and the number of wineries has grown. In the 1970s, Texas boasted one winery; it now ranks fifth in the United States in grape and wine production. New Mexico has 30 wineries, Colorado has over 70. Arizona has 20 and Oklahoma has over 25.

All wineries are researching a greater range of grape varieties. Southwest wineries offer a wide range of styles and varieties. Colorado and Arizona have a full-bodied, rich fruit approach, while Oklahoma and Texas tend more to a leaner style, esp with white varieties such as citrus Pinot Gris, and Viognier that captures tropical fruit flavours. Nebbiolo, rich Syrah, and fruity Sangiovese have found a home in the Southwest, along with hybrids such as Vignoles, Chardonel, and Seyval Blanc.

Texas

Becker Vineyards Stonewall ★★★ V.gd Cab Sauv, Viognier, Cab Fr, Malbec. **Brennan** Comanche: excellent Viognier, Cab Sauv, v.gd Syrah.

Cap Rock Lubbock V.gd Amarone-style; gd Merlot and blends, esp Bush Royal.

Delaney Vineyards Nr Dallas ★ Gd Cynthiana, Sauv Bl, and Chard, esp Chard Res.

Driftwood Vineyards Texas Hill ★ V.gd Muscat Canelli, Viognier, Merlot Rosé.

Fall Creek Texas Hill Country V.gd Meritus (red blend), gd Viognier, Cab Sauv.

Grape Creek Stonewall V.gd Muscat Canelli and blends, esp Bellissimo.

Haak Winery Galveston County ★ V.gd Malbec, Blanc du Bois and Madeira.

Kiepersol Estates Vineyards Tyler Excellent Sangiovese, Syrah, Cab Sauv.

Light Catcher Lake Worth V.gd Cab Sauv, Orange Muscat, Merlot Rosé.

Llano Estacado Nr Lubbock ★★★ The pioneer with v.gd Chard, Cab Sauv, Merlot and Viviano, a Tuscan-style red blend.

McPherson Cellars Lubbock Created to honour Dr Clinton McPherson, a Texas wine pioneer, with excellent Cab Sauv, Sangiovese, Viognier and Syrah.

Messina Hof Wine Cellars Bryan ★★★ Expanded wine selections with excellent Ries, Cab Sauv, Meritage (red), Shiraz and port-style wines.

Sister Creek Boerne Boutique winery with gd Pinot N, Chard, Muscat Canelli, Cab Sauv.

Val Verde Del Rio. A fourth-generation tradition. V.gd Chard, Pinot Grigio, Merlot.

Wichita Falls Iowa Park New, with promising Moscato, Sangiovese and Wichita Red (blend).

Zin Valle Anthony. V.gd Rising Star Brut (sparkling); gd Pinot N, Gewurz.

Colorado, etc.

Colorado Focus on vinifera grapes, grown between 1,200 to 1,800 m elevation and ranging from the Grand Valley on the Western Slope, to the Front Range on the east. Boulder Creek: V.gd Chard. **Carlson Cellars:** ★★★ Excellent Ries; v.gd Orange Muscat, Lemberger, fruit wines. **Canyon Wind:** V.gd Chard, Petit Verdot. **Creekside Cellars:** Gd Chard, Merlot. **Garfield Estates:** V.gd Sauv Bl and Cab Fr. **Grande River:** V.gd Syrah, Meritage (white). **Plum Creek:** ★★★ V.gd Cab Sauv, Ries Sauv Bl. **Guy Drew:** Excellent Syrah, gd Chard, Cab Sauv. **Sutcliff:** V.gd Cab Sauv. **Turquoise Mesa:** V.gd Cab Sauv; gd Cinsault. **Two Rivers:** V.gd Cab Sauv, Ries, Ruby "Port". **Debeque Canyon:** V.gd Malbec. **Winery at Holy Cross:** V.gd Ries, Merlot, Cab Fr. **Whitewater Hill:** Gd. Cab Fr.

New Mexico Emphasis on vinifera, though some French hybrids still used. **Black Mesa:** ★★ V.gd Cab Sauv, Seyval Blanc, Chard, Dolcetto. **Casa Rondeña:** ★★ V.gd Viognier, Meritage (red). **Corrales:** ★★ V.gd Merlot, Sangiovese. **Gruet:** ★★★ Excellent sparkling; v.gd Chard. **La Chiripada:** ★★ V.gd Ries, Chard, port-style wine. **Ponderosa Valley:** ★ V.gd Late Harvest Ries and blends. **La Viña:** ★★ V.gd Chard, Zin. Matheson Wine Co. V.gd Chard. New Mexico Wineries under winemaker Florent Lescombes gd variety of wines, esp Muscat Canelli and Shiraz. **Luna Rossa:** ★★ V.gd Italian-style wines, esp Nebbiolo, Sangiovese; Nini (red blend). **Tularosa:** Gd Sangiovese, Dolcetto, Gewurz.

Arizona Callaghan Vineyards: ★★ Excellent Syrah, Cab Sauv, blends. **Dos Cabezas:** ★ V.gd Cab Sauv, Sangiovese. **Colibri:** Gd Viognier, Roussanne, Syrah. **Granite Creek:** V.gd late harvest Zin. **Echo Canyon:** Gd Syrah, Triad. **Su Vino:** Excellent Zin, v.gd Malbec. **Sonoita:** Gd Sirah, Colombard Cab Sauv.

Oklahoma Vinifera emphasis but hybrids and native American grapes also grown. **Deer Creek** Edmond: Gd Muscat Canelli. **Greenfield Vineyard** Chandler: Gd Merlot, Sauv Bl. **Stone Bluff Cellars** Haskell: Gd Vignoles, Cynthiana, Chardonel. **Oak Hills Winery** Chelsea: V.gd Seyval Blanc, Traminette. **Nuyaka Creek** Bristow: Gd grape, fruit wines and cordial-style selections, esp Petite Pecan. **Tres Suenos** Luther: Gd Merlot, Cynthiana. **Stable Ridge** Stroud: V.gd Chenin Blanc, Jeremiah Red (blend).

Utah Spanish Valley (Moab): V.gd Ries, Gewurz and Cab Sauv.

Nevada Pahrump Valley Nr Las Vegas: Gd Symphony, Zin. **Tahoe Ridge** (North Nevada): Continues wine/grape research; gd white blends.

Canada

Recent vintages

05 and 06 reds, and 06 and 07 whites are drinking well right now. The best Merlot blends are definitely worth cellaring for up to five years.

British Columbia

Wineries are concentrated around a series of glacial lakes 400 km (245 miles) east of Vancouver. Characterized by low rainfall, intense sunshine and the moderating effects of the lakes, the Okanagan region now boasts 3,640 ha winegrowing hectares. Up-and-coming wineries are Dunham & Froese (Pinot Gr), Joie (Chard), Prospect (Sauv Bl, Icewine), Road 13 (Chard, Syrah), eighth generation (Ries), Herder (Chard, Merlot blend).

Cedar Creek ★→★★★ Outstanding Chard, Pinot N, Meritage, Syrah and Ries.
Inniskillin Okanagan ★★★ 05 06 07 08 Excellent Viognier Icewine.
Jackson-Triggs Okanagan ★★★ 05 06 07 08 V.gd Cab Sauv, Meritage, Shiraz, Icewine.

Lake Breeze Gd Chard, Gewurz.

Mission Hill ★→★★★★ 05 06 07 08 Acclaimed Chard, Sauv Bl, Ries, Icewine, Syrah, Merlot, and flagship Oculus. Al fresco dining, high culinary standards.

Nk'Mip ★★ Look out for Chard, Merlot. **Osoyoos Larose** Remarkably fine B'x blend red.

Quails' Gate ★★ Ries, Late Harvest Optima, Pinot N and Old Vines Foch.

Sumac Ridge ★★ **02 04** 05 06 07 Gewurz, sparkling Stellar's Jay among region's best.

Tantalus ★★★ Excellent Ries.

Wild Goose ★★ Noteworthy Ries, Gewurz.

Ontario

Comprised of four VQA (see below) wine growing regions, including the Niagara Peninsula, Canada's largest viticultural area. Diverse, ancient soils create a range of distinctive terroirs, and the region benefits from moderating air currents off Lakes Ontario and Erie. Long, warm summers and cold winters create ideal conditions for the region's emblematic super-sweet Icewine. Promising young wineries include Southbrook, Hidden Bench, Megalomaniac, Charles Baker, and Norman Hardie.

13th Street Winery ★★★ Small producer of 100% hand-picked, old-vine Gamay, Chard. Excellent range of high quality sparkling wines.

Cave Spring Cellars ★★★ Benchmark Ries, sophisticated Chard from old vines, exceptional Late Harvest and Icewines.

Château des Charmes ★★★ Showplace ch-style winery. Fine Chard, B'x-style blend, Icewines, sparkling.

Henry of Pelham ★★★ Respected family-owned winery with elegant Chard and Ries; B'x-style reds, distinctive Baco Noir, Icewine.

Hillebrand Estates ★→★★★ Large producer of gd sparkling, excellent Ries under Thirty Bench label.

Inniskillin ★★★ Important producer that spearheaded birth of modern Ontario wine industry. Skilful Burgundy-style Chards, Pinot N, Bx-style red; Icewine specialist.

Jackson-Triggs ★★★ State-of-art winery, Ries, Chard, and B'x-style reds.

Le Clos Jordanne ★★★★ Best-of-class Pinot N and Chard from organic v'yds.

Malivoire ★★→★★★ Small, innovative gravity-flow winery with v.gd Pinot N, Chard, and Gamay. Some organic.

Peninsula Ridge ★★★ Gd Chard, Sauv Bl, and B'x varieties.

Pillitteri Large family-owned winery with gd Cab Fr and Merlot. Prolific Icewine producer.

Stratus ★★★ Hi-tech winery, flagship white and red multi-varietal blends; excellent Icewine.

Tawse ★★★ Opened 2005, much admired Chard, Pinot N and Cab Fr.

Vincor International ★→★★ Now owned by CONSTELLATION. Wineries include JACKSON-TRIGGS, INNISKILLIN, Nk'Mip, LE CLOS JORDANNE, Osoyoos Larose.

Vineland Estates ★★★ Dry and semi-dry Ries; Vidal Icewine gd. Chard, Cab Sauv, Sauv Bl, and B'x-style red.

Vintners Quality Alliance (VQA) Provincially controlled appellation body guaranteeing 100% regional grapes with strict rules concerning grape production/winemaking.

Central & South America

More heavily shaded areas are the wine-growing regions

Chile

Chile is a nation on a roll, and with its best still to come. Argentina may have a more favourable image – think tango, football and plate-sized steaks – but Chile's wine producers are currently more inquisitive, informed and impassioned than their counterparts over the Andes. And they're tearing up the map of Chilean vineyard regions as we know it. Exploration continues into new parts of the country that have never been planted (especially in the foothills of the coastal mountain range), or that previously had been deemed suitable only for table grape or pisco production. Meanwhile in established regions such as Maipo and Maule, there are moves to go beyond the current appellation system, which is based on political boundaries, and to define sub-regions according to the differences in the terroir. And that greater understanding of those terroirs, combined with an expanded palette of grape varieties means that Chile can offer a diversity of styles and flavours that would have been unthinkable a decade ago.

Cabernet Sauv remains the most important grape, both as a solo performer and in Bordeaux-inspired blends, but there's renewed interest in Merlot and Cab Fr, as well as a continuing evolution of Chile's trademark grape from intense but overtly herbal to more subtle and drinkable. Syrah, in styles varying from fragrant and Rhône-like in Elqui to powerful and beefy from Colchagua, is also impressive. Pinot N is finding a home in the cooler climes of Bío-Bío, Casablanca and San Antonio, all of which also do well with white varieties. Sauv Bl and Chard lead the white pack, but there's growing interest in aromatic grapes such as Ries, Gewurz and Viognier.

South American vintages

Vintages do differ but not to the same extent as in Europe. Whites are almost without exception at their best within two years of vintage, reds within three years. The most ambitious reds (Chilean Cabernet-based wines and Syrah, Argentine Cabernets and Malbecs) can confidently be kept for a decade or more but it is debatable whether they improve beyond their fifth year. Also, the scale of improvements in recent years means that wines from a lesser vintage today outperform those from earlier good vintages.

Aconcagua Northernmost quality region. Inc CASABLANCA, Panquehue, SAN ANTONIO.

Almaviva ★★★ Expensive but classy, claret-style MAIPO red – a joint venture between CONCHA Y TORO and BARON PHILIPPE DE ROTHSCHILD.

Altaïr ★★→★★★ Ambitious joint venture between Ch Dassault (St-Emilion) and SAN PEDRO. Pascal Chatonnet of B'x is consultant; *grand vin* (mostly Cab Sauv, Carmenère) complex and earthy, second wine Sideral for earlier drinking.

Anakena Cachapoal ★→★★ Solid range. Flagship wines under ONA label include punchy Syrah; Single V'yd bottlings and Reserve Chard also gd. Look out for Viognier and ONA Pinot N.

Antiyal ★★→★★★ Alvaro Espinoza's own estate, making fine, complex red from biodynamically grown Cab Sauv, Syrah, Carmenère. Second wine Kuyen.

Apaltagua ★★→★★★ Carmenère specialist drawing on old-vine fruit from Apalta (Colchagua). Grial is rich, herbal flagship wine.

Aquitania, Viña ★★→★★★ Chilean/French joint venture involving Paul Pontallier and Bruno Prats from B'x (Paul Bruno was old label) making v.gd Lazuli Cab Sauv (MAIPO) and Sol de Sol Chard from Malleco.

Arboleda, Viña ★★→★★★ Part of the ERRÁZURIZ/CALITERRA stable, with whites from Leyda and CASABLANCA and reds from ACONCAGUA, inc polished Cab Sauv/ Merlot/Carmenère blend Seña and excellent varietal Carmenère.

Baron Philippe de Rothschild ★→★★ B'x company making simple varietal range, better Escudo Rojo red blend. Also see ALMAVIVA.

Bío-Bío Promising southern region. Potential for gd whites and Pinot N.

Botalcura ★★→★★★ Curicó venture with French winemaker Philippe Debrus. Grand Res Cab Fr and red blend Cayao are the stars, promising Nebbiolo, too.

Calina, Viña ★→★★ Kendall-Jackson (California) venture. Better reds than whites, with Cab Sauv/Merlot blend Bravura the pick.

Caliterra ★→★★ Sister winery of ERRÁZURIZ. Chard and Sauv Bl improving (more CASABLANCA grapes), reds becoming less one-dimensional, esp Tributo range and new flagship red Cenit.

Cánepa, Viña ★★ Historic winery, now controlled by CONCHA Y TORO, best for Magnificum and Finisimo MAIPO Cab Sauvs, also Genovino Curicó Carignan.

Carmen, Viña ★★→★★★ MAIPO winery; same ownership as SANTA RITA. Ripe, fresh Special Res CASABLANCA Chard and late-harvest MAIPO Sem top whites. Reds even better; esp RAPEL Merlot, MAIPO Petite Sirah, Gold Res Cab Sauv.

Carta Vieja ★→★★ MAULE winery owned by one family for 6 generations. Reds better than whites; but Gran Reserva Chard is gd.

Casablanca Cool-climate region between Santiago and coast. Little water: drip irrigation essential. Top-class Chard, Sauv Bl; promising Merlot, Pinot N.

Casablanca, Viña ★→★★ RAPEL and MAIPO fruit used for some reds; but better wines – Merlot, Sauv Bl, Chard, Gewurz – from CASABLANCA. Also look for super-*cuvée* Neblus and new Nimbus Estate varietals.

Casa Lapostolle ★★→★★★★ Impressive French-owned, Michel Rolland-inspired winery. Gd across the board, with new Sem highlight of the whites and Borobo red blend, Cuvée Alexandre Merlot and Syrah, and Carmenère-based Clos Apalta pick of the reds. Classic range now renamed Casa, and look out for lower-alcohol, more elegant whites from 08.

Casa Marín ★★★ Dynamic San Antonio white specialist, v.gd Gewurz and superb Sauv Bl. Syrah and Pinot N promising.

Casa Rivas Maipo ★★ Part of group that inc TARAPACA, Viña Mar, Missiones de Rengo. Best: Sappy Sauv Bl; gentle, citrus Chard Res; blackcurrant-pastille-y Cab Sauv; generously fruity Maria Pinto Syrah/Cab Sauv Res.

Casas del Bosque ★→★★ CASABLANCA winery, also using Cab Sauv from Cachapoal for elegant range inc juicy underrated Sauv Bl, svelte Pinot N and peppery Syrah Res.

Casa Silva ★★ Colchagua estate with solid range topped by silky, complex Altura red and Quinta Generación Red and White. Also commendable Doña Dominga range; Carmenère is v.gd.

Casas del Toqui ★→★★★ RAPEL venture by Médoc Ch Larose-Trintaudon under the Las Casas del Toqui and Viña Alamosa labels. Silky top-end Leyenda red blend and Prestige Cab Sauv.

Concha y Toro ★→★★★★ Mammoth, quality-minded operation. Best: subtle Amelia Chard (CASABLANCA); **grippy Don Melchor Cab Sauv**; Terrunyo; Winemaker Lot single-v'yd range; and complex Carmin de Peumo (Carmenère). Marqués de Casa Concha, Trio, Explorer, Casillero del Diablo offer v.gd value. Maycas del Limarí is new winery in the N (gd Chard); also recently acquired Fairtrade producer Viña Los Robles. See also BARON PHILIPPE DE ROTHSCHILD, CONO SUR, TRIVENTO (Argentina).

Cono Sur Chimbarongo, Colchagua ★★→★★★ V.gd Pinot N, headed by Ocio. Other top releases appear as 20 Barrels selection; new innovations under Visión label (BÍO-BÍO Ries is superb). Also **dense, fruity Cab Sauv**, delicious Viognier, rose-petal Gewurz, impressive new Syrah. Style is aimed at drinkability, not muscle. Second label Isla Negra; owned by CONCHA Y TORO.

Córpora ★→★★★ Major company with v'yds in various regions, inc over 700 ha in BÍO BÍO, and brands Gracia de Chile, Porta, Augustinos (good peppery Grand Reserve Malbec) and Veranda, formerly a joint venture with Boisset of Burgundy, and now making v'gd Pinot N – Millerandage is top *cuvée*.

Cousiño Macul ★★→★★★ MAIPO producer now relocated to Buin. Now more modern in style, but better? Reliable Antiguas Res Cab Sauv; zesty Sauvignon Gris; new top-of-the-range blend Lota. Cab Sauv rosé v. refreshing.

Cremaschi Furlotti ★→★★★ MAULE red specialist with herby Syrah and heady Limited Edition (Cab Sauv-based) and Venere (Carmenère-based) blends.

de Martino Maipo ★★→★★★★ Ambitious Carmenère pioneer; one of west MAIPO'S best wineries, esp for Gran Familia Cab Sauv, Single V'yd (inc 2 Bush Vin *cuvées* and Legado range.

Domus Maipo ★★→★★★ Ambitious winery making gd Chard and v.gd Domus Aurea Cab Sauv; sister Cabs Stella Aurea and Peñalolen also tasty.

Echeverría ★★ Boutique Curicó (MAULE) winery. Reliable Res Cab Sauv; gd oaked and unoaked Chard; improving Sauv Bl; elegant, fragrant Carmenère.

Edwards, Luís Felipe ★★ Colchagua winery, now with v'yds in Leyda. Citrus Chard, silky Res Cab Sauv. Shiraz and plump Doña Bernarda are specialities.

Emiliana ★→★★★ Organic/biodynamic specialist involving Alvaro Espinoza (see ANTIYAL, GEO WINES). Complex, Syrah-heavy "G" and Coyam show almost

Mediterranean-style wildness; cheaper Adobe and Novas ranges v.gd for affordable complexity.

Errázuriz ★→★★★ Main winery in ACONCAGUA, v'yds mostly in warm Panquehue district, but also new cooler coastal site, plus another property in CASABLANCA. Complex Wild Ferment Chard; brooding La Cumbre Syrah; complex Don Maximiano Cab Sauv; new KAI Carmenère. See also ARBOLEDA, CALITERRA, VIÑEDO CHADWICK.

Estampa, Viña ★★ Colchagua blend specialists for reds and whites. Savoury Syrah-based Gold Assemblage pick of solid range.

Falernia, Viña ★★ Winery in far N Elqui Valley, v'yds cooled by sea breezes range from 350 to 2,000 m in altitude, suitable for several varieties; Rhône-like Syrah, fragrant Carmenère and tangy Sauv Bl most successful so far. Labels include Alta Tierra and Mayu.

Fortuna, Viña La Lontué Valley ★★ Established winery with attractive range.

Fournier, Bodegas O ★★ Promising new venture for one of Argentina's top producers, already v'gd Leyda Sauv Bl and Centauri Red blend (MAULE).

Garcés Silva Leyda ★★→★★★ Exciting SAN ANTONIO bodega making excellent, full-bodied Sauv Bl and commendable Pinot N and Chard under the Amayna label.

Geo Wines Umbrella under which Alvaro Espinoza makes wines for several new wineries. Look for earthy Chono San Lorenzo MAIPO red blend and tangy Quintay BÍO-BÍO Ries.

Hacienda Araucano ★★→★★★ François Lurton's Chilean enterprise. Complex Gran Araucano Sauv Bl (CASABLANCA), refined Carmenère/Cab Sauv blend Clos de Lolol, and heady Alka Carmenère. But the new Humo Blanco Pinot N could be better.

Haras de Pirque ★★→★★★ Pirque (MAIPO) estate. Smoky Sauv Bl, stylish Chard, dense Cab Sauv/Merlot. Top wine Albis (Cab Sauv/Carmenère) is solid, smoky red made in joint venture with Antinori (see Italy).

Leyda, Viña ★★→★★★ SAN ANTONIO pioneers producing elegant Chard (Lot 5 Wild Yeasts is the pick), lush Pinot N (esp Lot 21 *cuvée* and lively rosé), tangy Garuma Sauv Bl. Now owned by SAN PEDRO.

Limarí Northerly, high-altitude region, so quite chilly (for Chile); already impressing with Syrah and Chard.

Loma Larga ★★→★★★ New CASABLANCA venture impressing with Sauv Bl, Pinot N, Cab Fr and Syrah. V. classy wines.

Maipo Famous wine region close to Santiago. Chile's best Cab Sauvs often come from higher, eastern sub-regions such as Pirque and Puente Alto.

Matetic San Antonio ★★★ Decent Pinot N and Chard from exciting winery. Stars are fragrant, zesty Sauv Bl and spicy, berry EQ Syrah. Second label Corralillo.

Maule Southernmost region in Central Valley. Claro, Loncomilla, Tutuven valleys.

Montes ★★→★★★★ Highlights of a first-class range are Alpha Cab Sauv, B'x-blend Montes Alpha M, *Folly Syrah from Apalta* and Purple Angel, Carmenère at its most intense. Also promising new Leyda Sauv Bl and Pinot N.

MontGras ★★→★★★ State-of-the-art Colchagua winery with fine limited-edition wines, inc Syrah and Zin. High-class flagships Ninquén Cab Sauv and Antu Ninquén Syrah. Gd value organic Soleus, gentle but fine Intriga (MAIPO) Cab Sauv and excellent Amaral (Leyda) whites.

Morandé ★★ Gd value range inc César, Cinsault, Bouschet, Carignan. Limited Edition range inc a spicy Syrah/Cab Sauv, inky Malbec; top wine is Cab Sauv-based House of Morandé.

Neyen ★★★ New project in Apalta for Patrick Valette of St Emilion, making intense old-vine Carmenère/Cab Sauv blend.

Odfjell ★→★★★ MAIPO-based, Norwegian-owned red specialist. Top wine: Aliara Cab Sauv. Orzada range, inc v.gd entry-level Armador. Wines of character.

Pérez Cruz ★★★ MAIPO winery with Alvaro Espinoza (see ANTIYAL) in charge of winemaking. Fresh, spicy Syrah, aromatic Cot, and stylish Quelen and Liguai red blends.

Rapel Central quality region divided into Colchagua and Cachapoal valleys. Great "Merlot" (much is actually Carmenère). Watch for sub-region Marchihue.

La Rosa, Viña ★★ Reliable RAPEL Chard, Merlot, and Cab Sauv under La Palma, La Capitana and Cornellana labels. Don Reca reds are the stars, plus Ossa Sixth Generation red blend.

San Antonio Coastal region west of Santiago benefiting from sea breezes; v. promising for whites, Syrah, and Pinot N. Leyda is a sub-zone.

San Pedro ★→★★★ Massive Curicó-based producer. 35 South (35 Sur) for affordable varietals; Castello di Molina a step up. Best are 1865 reds and elegant Cabo de Hornos. See also ALTAÏR, TABALÍ, VIÑA LEYDA.

Santa Alicia ★→★★★ MAIPO red specialist. Best wines: firm but juicy Millantu Cab-Sauv-based flagship wine, and lithe but structured Anke Blend 1 (Cab Fr/Petit Verdot).

Santa Carolina, Viña ★★→★★★ Historic bodega. Quality ladder goes varietal, Reserva, Barrica Selection, Reserva de Familia, and new VSC Cab Sauv/Syrah/Petit Verdot blends. Syrah and Carmenère gd at all levels.

Santa Mónica ★→★★ Rancagua (RAPEL) winery; the best label is Tierra del Sol. Ries, Sem, and Merlot under Santa Mónica label also gd.

Santa Rita ★★→★★★ Quality-conscious MAIPO bodega. Best: Casa Real MAIPO Cab Sauv; but Pehuén (Carmenère), Triple C (Cab Sauv/Cab Fr/Carmenère) and Floresta range nearly as gd.

Selentia ★★ New Chilean/Spanish venture. Res Special Cab Sauv is fine.

Seña See VIÑA ARBOLEDA.

Tabalí Limarí ★★ Winery partly owned by SAN PEDRO, making refined Chard and earthy, peppery Syrah. Look out for fine newcomers Viognier and Pinot N.

Tamaya, Viña Casa ★★ New LIMARÍ winery already on the ball with Graves-like Winemaker's Sel'n Sauv Bl, and gd Reserve Carmenère and Syrah.

Tarapacá, Viña ★★ MAIPO winery improved after investment, but inconsistent. Now owned by SAN PEDRO.

Terramater ★→★★ Wines from all over Central Valley, inc v.gd Altum Cab Sauv.

Terranoble ★→★★ Talca winery specializing in grassy Sauv Bl and light, peppery Merlot. Range now includes v.gd spicy Carmenère Gran Res.

Torreón de Paredes ★→★★ Attractive, crisp Chard, ageworthy Res Cab Sauv from this RAPEL bodega. Flagship Don Amedo Cab Sauv could be better.

Torres, Miguel ★★→★★★ Fresh whites and gd reds, esp sturdy **Manso del Velasco** single-v'yd Cab Sauv and Cariñena-based Cordillera. Conde de Superunda is rare top *cuvée*, also new organic range Tormenta. See also Spain.

Undurraga ★→★★ Historic MAIPO estate, still making gd peachy Late Harvest Sem but now also impressing with LIMARÍ Syrah and the Sauv Bls from LEYDA and CASABLANCA under the TH (Terroir Hunter) label, and lively Brut Royal Chard/Pinot N sparkler.

Valdivieso ★→★★★★ Major producer impressing in recent yrs with Reserve and Single-V'yd range from top terroirs around Chile (LEYDA Chard esp gd), NV red blend Caballo Loco, and wonderfully spicy new Carignan-based Eclat.

Vascos, Los ★→★★★ Lafite-Rothschild venture moving from B'x wannabe to more successful yet still elegant style. Top Le Dix and Grande Réserve.

Ventisquero, Viña ★→★★★ Thrusting young winery whose labels include Chilano (formerly Chileno) and Yali; top wines are two Apalta reds – rich but fragrant Pangea, a Syrah made with help from Australian John Duval, and Carmenère/Syrah blend Vertice.

Veramonte ★★ Whites from CASABLANCA fruit, red from Central Valley grapes –

all gd. Top wine: Primus red blend.

Villard ★★ Sophisticated wines made by French-born Thierry Villard. Gd MAIPO reds, esp heady Merlot, Equis Cab Sauv, and CASABLANCA whites.

Mar, Viña Casablanca ★→★★ B'x-style reds are a little scrawny, but Pinot N, Sauv Bl, and Chard all show CASABLANCA at its best. See CASA RIVAS.

Viñedo Chadwick Maipo ★★★ Stylish Cab Sauv improving with each vintage from v'yd owned by Eduardo Chadwick, chairman of ERRÁZURIZ.

Viu Manent ★→★★ Emerging Colchagua winery. Dense, fragrant Viu 1 tops range; Secreto Malbec and Viognier also v.gd. Late Harvest Sem top notch.

Von Siebenthal ★★★ Small (in Chilean terms) Swiss-owned ACONCAGUA winery. V.gd Carabantes Syrah, elegant Cab Sauv/Petit Verdot/Carmenère blend Montelig and fine-boned Petit Verdot Toknar.

Argentina

As Argentina grows in understanding of its vineyards, there's an increased maturity in the winemaking. There are still some overpowering reds to be found, but the best wines (which are not always the most expensive in the producers' portfolios) now offer power with fragrance and a sense of place. Mendoza remains the largest and most important province. With vineyards rising from 500m up to 1,500m, there's a site suited to every grape variety, and while old-vine Malbec is the real treasure, Cab Sauv is gaining ground. Sparkling wines are increasing in quality and popularity too. Further south, Rio Negro and Neuquén are making an impact with lighter, more aromatic wines (inc some fine Pinot N), and there are developments even further south at Chubut. To the north, San Juan is developing a reputation for Shiraz, while Salta is producing some excellent reds and delightfully aromatic Torrontés in some of the highest vineyards in the world.

Achaval Ferrer ★★★→★★★★ MENDOZA. Super-concentrated Altamira, Bella Vista, and Mirador single-v'yd Malbecs and Quimera Malbec/Cab/Merlot blends.

Alta Vista ★→★★★ French-owned MENDOZA venture specializing in Malbec. Dense, spicy **Alto** among best wines in the country. Also fresh, zesty Torrontés. Sister winery Navarrita makes fine Winemakers Selection Malbec.

Altos las Hormigas ★★★ Italian-owned Malbec specialist, wines made by consultant Alberto Antonini (ex-Italy's Antinori). Best: Viña las Hormigas Res.

La Anita, Finca ★★→★★★ MENDOZA estate making high-class reds, esp Syrah and Malbec, and intriguing whites, inc Sem and Tocai Friulano.

Antucura ★★★ Valle de Uco bodega with beautifully balanced, spicy Cab Sauv/Merlot blend. Calvulcura is second label.

Argento ★→★★ CATENA offshoot making gd commercial wine under the Libertad, Malambo and Argento labels.

Bianchi, Valentin ★ San Rafael red specialist. Enzo Bianchi (Cab Sauv/Merlot/ Malbec) is excellent flagship. Gd-value Elsa's V'yd inc meaty Barbera. Pithy Sauv Bl; also decent sparkling.

Bressia ★★→★★★ Tiny new winery already on form with classy Malbec-dominated Profundo from Agrelo and Conjuro Malbec from Tupungato.

Cabernet de los Andes ★★ Promising organic (and partly biodynamic) Catamarca estate with big, fragrant, balanced reds under Vicien and Tizac labels.

Canale, Bodegas Humberto ★★ Premier Río Negro winery known for its Sauv Bl and Pinot N, but Merlot and Malbec (esp Black River label) are the stars.

Cassone, Bodega ★★ MENDOZA enterprise benefiting from Alberto Antonini's winemaking expertise (ALTOS LAS HORMIGAS, Renacer, Melipal). Watch out for

Obra Prima Malbec.

Catena Zapata, Bodega ★★→★★★★ Consistently gd range rises from Alamos through Catena, Catena Alta, to flagship Nicolas Catena Zapata and Malbec Argentino, plus occasional single-v'yd Malbecs. Also joint venture with the Rothschilds of Lafite: seriously classy *Caro* and younger Amancaya; see ARGENTO; LUCA/TIKAL.

Chakana ★★ Agrelo winery to watch for joyful Malbec, Cab Sauv, Syrah, Bonarda.

Chandon, Bodegas ★→★★★ Makers of Baron B and M Chandon sparkling under Moët & Chandon supervision; promising Pinot N/Chard blend. See TERRAZAS.

Clos de los Siete ★★ Reliable, plump Vistaflores (Valle de Uco) blend of Merlot, Malbec, Syrah and Cab Sauv, with Michel Rolland overseeing winemaking (see MONTEVIEJO, VAL DE FLORES).

Cobos, Viña ★★★ Stunning Marchiori V'yd old-vine Malbec and Unico Cab/Malbec from Paul Hobbs; Bramare label for v.gd younger vine *cuvées*.

Colomé, Bodega ★★→★★★ SALTA bodega owned by California's Hess Collection. Pure, intense, biodynamic Malbec-based reds, lively Torrontés.

Dominio del Plata ★→★★★ Two ex-CATENA winemakers produce superior wines under the Crios, Susana Balbo, BenMarco, Anubis and Budini labels. Nosotros is bold Malbec/Cab Sauv flagship.

Doña Paula ★ Luján de Cuyo estate owned by Santa Rita (see Chile). Elegant, structured Malbec; modern fleshy Cab Sauv; tangy Los Cardos Sauv Bl; exotic new Naked Grape Viognier.

El Porvenir de los Andes ★★ Cafayate estate with classy Laborum reds inc fine, smoky Tannat. Amauta blends also gd.

Etchart ★★→★★★ Reds gd, topped by plummy Cafayate Cab Sauv. Torrontés also one of the best, with intriguing late-harvest Tardio.

Fabré Montmayou ★★ French-owned Luján de Cuyo bodega; fine reds and advice from Michel Rolland (see France). Also decent Chard. Infinitus is sister bodega in Río Negro making supple Gran Res Merlot.

Familia Schroeder ★★ NEUQUÉN estate impressing with reds and whites. V.gd Saurus Select range inc sappy Sauv Bl, earthy Merlot and fragrant Malbec.

Familia Zuccardi ★→★★★ Dynamic MENDOZA estate producing gd-value Santa Julia range, led by new blend Magna, better Q label (impressive Malbec, Merlot, Tempranillo), and deep yet elegant Zeta (Malbec/Tempranillo).

Fin del Mundo, Bodega del ★★ First winery in the province of NEUQUÉN; Malbec a speciality; top wine Special Blend is Merlot/Malbec/Cab Sauv.

Flichman, Finca ★★ Owned by Sogrape (see Portugal), impressing with Syrah. Best: Dedicado blend (mostly Cab Sauv/Syrah). Paisaje de Tupungato (B'x blend), Paisaje de Barrancas (Syrah-based) v.gd.

Foster, Enrique ★★ MENDOZA Malbec specialist, all excellent from young, fragrant lque to powerful Edición Limitada and single-v'yd wines.

Kaikén ★★→★★★ MENDOZA venture for Aurelio Montes (see Chile) making user-friendly range topped by Ultra Cab Sauv and Malbec.

Luca/Tikal ★★★ Classy boutique wineries owned by Nicolas CATENA's children. Winemaker Luis Reginato also makes excellent La Posta del Vinatero range.

Luigi Bosca ★★→★★★ Small MENDOZA bodega with 3 tiers of quality – Finca La Linda, Luigi Bosca Res, and a top level that includes esp gd Finca Los Nobles Malbec/Verdot and Cab Sauv/Bouchet, plus impressive Gala blends.

Lurton, François, Bodegas ★→★★★ Juicy, concentrated Piedra Negra Malbec and complex, earthy Chacayes (Malbec) head range; Flor de Torrontés more serious than most, also sweet but fresh Pasitea Torrontés/Pinot Grigio.

Marguery, Familia Top-class Malbec from old vines in the Tupungato district.

Masi Tupungato ★★→★★★ MENDOZA enterprise for the well-known Valpolicella producer (see Italy). Passo Doble is fine *ripasso*-style Malbec/Corvina/

Merlot blend; Corbec is even better Amarone lookalike (Corvina/Malbec).

Mendel ★★★ Former TERRAZAS winemaker Roberta de la Mota makes plummy Malbec and graceful Unus blend from old Luján de Cuyo vines.

Mendoza Most important province for wine (over 70% of plantings). Best sub-regions: Agrelo, Valle de Uco (includes Tupungato), Luján de Cuyo, Maipú.

Monteviejo ★★→★★★★ One of the v'yds of CLOS DE LOS SIETE, now with top-class range of reds headed by wonderfully textured Monteviejo blend (Malbec/Merlot/Cab Sauv/Syrah); Lindaflor Malbec also v.gd.

Las Moras, Finca ★★ San Juan bodega with chunky Tannat, chewy Malbec Res, and plump, fragrant Malbec/Bonarda blend Mora Negra.

Navarro Correas ★★ Gd if sometimes over-oaked reds, esp Col Privada Cab Sauv. Also reasonable whites, inc v. oaky Chard and Deutz-inspired fizz.

Neuquén Patagonian region to watch: huge developments since 2000.

Nieto Senetiner, Bodegas ★★ Luján de Cuyo-based bodega. Quality rises from *tasty entry-level Santa Isabel* through Reserva to top-of-range Cadus reds.

Noemia ★★★ Old-vine RÍO NEGRO Malbec from Hans Vinding-Diers and Noemi Cinzano. J Alberto and A Lisa new second labels. (Chacra Pinot N from nearby is another promising Vinding-Diers project.)

Norton, Bodega ★→★★★ Austrian-owned old bodega. Gd whites; v.gd reds, esp Malbec, v.gd value Privada (Merlot/Cab Sauv/Malbec), lush, complex Perdriel (Malbec/Merlot/Cab Sauv) and new Malbec-based Gernot Langes icon.

O Fournier ★→★★★ Spanish-owned Valle de Uco bodega. Urban v.gd entry-level range; then come B Crux and Alfa Crux, both fine Tempranillo/Merlot/Malbec blends. Also fragrant but rare Syrah. Now producing Chilean wines, too.

Peñaflor ★→★★★ Argentina's biggest wine company. Labels include Andean Vineyards and, finer, TRAPICHE, FINCA LAS MORAS, Santa Ana and MICHEL TORINO.

Poesia ★★→★★★★ Exciting Luján de Cuyo producer under same ownership as Clos l'Eglise of B'x; stylish Poesia (Cab Sauv/Malbec), chunkier but fine Clos des Andes (Malbec), and juicy Pasodoble Malbec/Syrah/Cab Sauv blend.

Pulenta, Carlos ★★ Vistalba bodega, basic range is Tomero, upper tier has fine trio of Malbec-based reds, Vistalba Corte A, B and C.

Pulenta Estate ★★→★★★ Luján de Cuyo winery. Gd Sauv Bl and v.gd reds. Best: Gran Corte (Cab Sauv/Malbec/Merlot/Petit Verdot), Cab Fr and Malbec.

El Retiro, Finca ★→★★ MENDOZA bodega for gd Malbec, Bonarda, Tempranillo.

La Riojana ★→★★ Dynamic La Rioja company, currently the world's largest Fairtrade wine producer. *Raza Ltd Edition Malbec* is top wine, but quality and value at all levels.

Río Negro Patagonia's oldest wine region, gd for Pinot N and Malbec.

Ruca Malen ★★→★★★★ Promising red wine specialist with v'yds in Luján de Cuyo and the Uco Valley. Kinien is top range.

Salentein, Bodegas ★★ MENDOZA bodega, impressing with Cab Sauv, Malbec, Merlot, Primus Pinot N. Finca El Portillo (a separate estate) gd for cheaper wines; also Bodegas Callia in San Juan, where Shiraz is the focus.

Salta Northerly province with some of the world's highest v'yds. Sub-region Cafayate renowned for Torrontés.

San Juan Second largest wine region, home to promising Shiraz and Tannat.

San Pedro de Yacochuya ★★★ SALTA collaboration between Michel Rolland (see France) and the ETCHART family. Ripe but fragrant Torrontés; dense, earthy Malbec; and powerful, stunning Yacochuya Malbec from oldest vines.

Soluna ★★ Ambitious new Fairtrade project making Malbec in Luján de Cuyo; top wine fleshy Primus.

Sophenia, Finca Tupungato bodega. Advice from Michel Rolland (see France). Malbec and Cab Sauv shine; gd Altosur entry-level range; top Synthesis.

Tacuil, Bodegas ★★→★★★★ 33 de Davalos is spicy Cab Sauv/Malbec blend.

Tapiz ★★ Lujan de Cuyo-based bodegas, punchy Sauv Bl, v'gd red range topped by serious Reserva Selección de Barricas (Cab Sauv/Malbec/Merlot).

Terrazas de los Andes ★★→★★★ CHANDON enterprise for still wines made from Malbec, Cab Sauv, Chard, Syrah. Three ranges: entry-level Terrazas (juicy Cab Sauv is the star), mid-price Res, and top-of-the-tree Afincado. Joint venture with Ch Cheval Blanc of B'x making superb Cheval des Andes blend.

Torino, Michel ★★ Rapidly improving organic Cafayate enterprise; Don David Malbec and Cab Sauv v.gd. Altimus is rather oaky flagship.

Toso, Pascual ★★→★★★ Californian Paul Hobbs heads a team making gd value, tasty range inc ripe but finely structured Magdalena Toso (mostly Malbec) and Malbec/Cab Sauv single v'yd Finca Pedregal.

Trapiche ★★→★★★ PEÑAFLOR premium label increasingly potent under head winemaker Daniel Pi. Trio of single-v'yd Malbecs shine out, red blend Iscay is gd but pricey; better value under the Oak Cask, Fond de Cave, Briquel and Medalla labels.

Trivento ★→★★ Owned by Concha y Toro of Chile, making gd-value range, with Viognier standing out; also under Otra Vida label.

Val de Flores ★★★★ Another Michel Rolland-driven enterprise close to CLOS DE LOS SIETE for compelling yet elegant (and biodynamic) old-vine Malbec.

Weinert, Bodegas ★→★★ Potentially fine reds, esp Cavas de Weinert blend (Cab Sauv/Merlot/Malbec), are occasionally spoiled by extended ageing in old oak. MENDOZA-based, but with Argentina's most southerly v'yd in Chubut.

Other Central & South American wines

Bolivia With just a handful of wineries, this hot, humid country is not a major wine producer. Even so, wines such as Cepas de Altura Cab Sauv from **Viños y Viñedos La Concepción** wines show what is possible. The v'yds, 1,000 km south of La Paz, are the highest in the world.

Brazil Rapid development in the last 10 years means that Brazil now has a raft of wines to interest the outside world. Most are made in the southern province of Rio Grande do Sul, with many of the best coming from the Vale dos Vinhedos near the town of Bento Gonçalves. With improved viticulture, the wineries are overcoming issues with humidity, and already there are several impressive reds (look out for Merlot and, surprisingly, Teroldego and Nebbiolo) and some decent sparklers. Further north, continuous harvesting is possible in some equatorial v'yds. Producers to watch: **Salton, Lidio Carraro, Casa Valduga** and the pioneering **Miolo**, with **Aurora** and **Rio Sol** providing gd value.

Peru Viña Tacama exports some pleasant wines, esp the Gran Vino Blanco white; also Cab Sauv and classic-method sparkling. Chincha, Moquegua, and Tacha regions are making progress, but phylloxera is a serious problem.

Uruguay With decent Tannat now emerging from other parts of South America, Uruguay needs to expand its portfolio beyond the sturdy, plummy grape (which here is often best blended with Merlot and Cab Sauv). **Carrau/Castel Pujol** is among the most impressive wineries: Amat Gran Tradición 1752 and *Las Violetas Reserva* show Tannat at its most fragrant. Juanicó is equally impressive, with flagship red blend Preludio and joint venture with Bernard Magrez of Ch Pape Clément to produce Gran Casa Magrez de Uruguay. Others: Bouza (do Albariño), Bruzzone & Sciutto, Casa Filguera, Castillo Viejo, De Lucca, Los Cerros de San Juan, Dante Irurtia, Pisano (working with Boisset of Burgundy under the Viña Progreso label), Carlos Pizzorno, and Stagnari.

CENTRAL & SOUTH AMERICA

Australia

More heavily shaded areas are the wine-growing regions

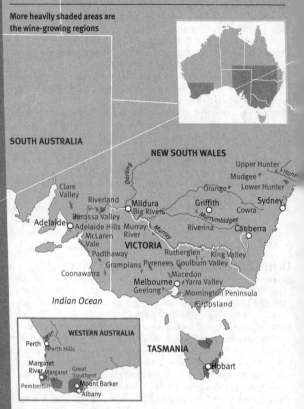

Australia's wine producers, having conquered the world, have serious troubles at home. The climate seems to have turned against them. Growers in Australia have had to contend with seemingly endless drought, floods, short bursts of extreme heat and high winds, appalling bushfires, and ensuing taint by smoke. Only frost has been missing.

Drought has been the most widespread problem. It has ruthlessly weeded out the weak, and rewarded the efficient – efficient at saving water, that is. There's a new and lucrative business now: trading in water rights. Not all regions of Australia are equally affected by lack of rain, and some farmers (dairy farmers, perhaps, or fruit growers) are simply giving up their livestock, chopping down their trees and living on the sale of the water they would otherwise have had.

Bushfires have affected only a few regions, it's true, but those affected are not going to forget them in a hurry. Apart from the loss of life, vineyards have been destroyed, and even the surviving vines may give grapes that reek of smoke, and will be unusable.

On top of this, grape prices have fallen: growers are now getting 40 per cent less than they were able to charge in 2008. And quantities are down, as well: most guesses (at the time of writing they can only be guesses) are that the 2009 vintage seems to be about 40 per cent less than in 2008, and pretty variable in quality, too. Might this be the year we finally see Australia's wine glut drain away? Yes, I know we say this every year, and somehow it keeps not happening. But there has to be some good news, doesn't there?

Recent vintages

New South Wales (NSW)

2008 Another record early start with good whites. then torrential rain destroying virtually all Hunter reds.

2007 The earliest vintage ever recorded for all regions; full flavour across white and red wines.

2006 A burst of extreme heat around Christmas in some regions did not leave a lasting mark on a vintage of overall high quality.

2005 A very good to exceptional year across almost all districts, especially the Hunter, Mudgee, and Orange.

2004 Hunter Valley suffered; other regions good to very good outcomes.

2003 Continued drought broken by heavy rain in Jan/Feb; variable outcomes.

2002 Heavy Feb rain caused problems in all but two areas. Riverina outstanding.

2001 Extreme summer heat and ill-timed rain set the tone; remarkably, Hunter Valley Semillon shone.

Victoria (Vic)

2008 Started one day later than 2007 but finished one week earlier in a hectic and compressed vintage.

2007 Broke the record for the earliest vintage; frost and bushfire smoke taint hit some regions hard.

2006 One of the earliest and most compressed vintages on record; paradoxically fruit flavour came even earlier. A charmed year.

2005 Rain up to end of Feb was followed by a freakish three-month Indian summer giving superb fruit.

2004 Near perfect weather throughout ripened generous yields.

2003 Overall, fared better than other states, except for bushfire-ravaged Alpine Valleys.

2002 Extremely cool weather led to tiny yields, but wines of high quality.

2001 Did not escape the heat; a fair to good red vintage, whites more variable.

South Australia (SA)

2008 The very early start in February turned out to create a curate's egg: excellent wines picked prior to March 6th, non-fortified ports for those picked after the record heat wave.

2007 Devastating frosts hit the Limestone Coast repeatedly. A dry, warm vintage favoured red wines across the board.

2006 A great Cabernet year; for other reds those picked before Easter rains did best. Here, too, flavour ripeness came early.

2005 Clare Valley, Coonawarra, Wrattonbully, and Langhorne Creek did best in what was a large but high-quality vintage with reds to the fore.

2004 Excellent summer and autumn weather helped offset large crops (big bunches/berries); heavy crop-thinning needed.

2003 A curate's egg. The good: Limestone Coast and Clare Riesling (yet again); the bad: rain-split Shiraz.

2002 Very cool weather led to much reduced yields in the south and to a great Riverland vintage in both yield and quality. Fine Riesling again.

2001 Far better than 2000; Clare Valley Riesling an improbable success.

Western Australia (WA)

2008 The best vintage for many years across all regions and all varieties; normal harvest dates.

2007 A v. warm quickfire vintage made white quality variable, reds better.

2006 Complete opposite to Eastern Australia; a cool, wet and late vintage – gave good whites, dubious reds.

2005 Heavy rain in late March and April spoiled what would have been the vintage of a generation for Cabernet and Shiraz in the south; whites uniformly excellent.

2004 More of the same; mild weather, long autumn. Good flavours, some lacking intensity.

2003 An in-between year, with ill-timed rainfall nipping greatness in the bud.

2002 Best since 84 in Swan District. In the south, quality is variable.

2001 Great Southern, the best vintage since 95; good elsewhere.

Adelaide Hills SA Best SAUV BL region: cool, 450-m sites in Mt Lofty ranges.

Alkoomi Mount Barker, WA r w ★★→★★★(RIES)**01 02' 04 05'** 07' **08** (CAB SAUV) **01'** 02' 04 05' 07 A veteran of 35 yrs making fine RIES and long-lived reds.

All Saints Rutherglen, Vic r w br ★★ Historic producer making creditable table wines; great fortifieds.

Alpine Valleys Vic Geographically similar to KING VALLEY. Similar use of grapes.

Angove's SA r w (br) ★→★★ Large, long-established MURRAY VALLEY family business. Gd-value range of white and red varietals.

Annie's Lane Clare V, SA r w ★★→★★★ Part of FWE. Consistently gd, boldly flavoured wines; flagship Copper Trail excellent, esp RIES.

Ashbrook Estate Margaret R, WA r w ★★★ Minimum of fuss; consistently makes 8,000 cases of exemplary SEM, CHARD, SAUV BL, VERDELHO, and CAB SAUV.

Ashton Hills Adelaide Hills, SA r w (sp) ★★★ Fine, racy, long-lived RIES and compelling PINOT N crafted by Stephen George from 25-yr-old v'yds.

Bailey's NE Vic r w br ★★ Rich SHIRAZ, and magnificent dessert Muscat (★★★★) and "Tokay". Part of FWE but on the market for sale.

Balgownie Estate Bendigo and Yarra V, Vic r w ★ Rejuvenated producer of v. well-balanced wines, now with separate YARRA VALLEY arm.

Balnaves of Coonawarra SA r w ★★★ Grape-grower since 1975; winery since 1996. V.gd CHARD; excellent supple, medium-bodied SHIRAZ, MERLOT, CAB SAUV.

Bannockburn Geelong r w ★★★ (CHARD) **00 02'** 03 04 05' 06 (PINOT N) **02' 03' 04 05'** 06 Intense, complex CHARD and PINOT N produced using Burgundian techniques. New winemaker Michael Glover is a whizz.

Banrock Station Riverland, SA r w ★→★★ Almost 1,600-ha property on Murray River, 243-ha v'yd, owned by HARDYS. Impressive budget wines.

Barossa Valley SA Australia's most important winery (but not v'yd) area; grapes from diverse sources make diverse wines. Local specialities: v. old-vine SHIRAZ, Mourvèdre, and GRENACHE.

Bass Phillip Gippsland, Vic r ★★★→★★★★ (PINOT N) **99' 02'** 03 04 05' 06' 07' Tiny amounts of stylish, eagerly sought-after PINOT N in 3 quality grades; v.

Burgundian in style, though quality can be erratic.

Bay of Fires N Tas r w sp ★★★ Pipers River outpost of CONSTELLATION empire. Produces stylish table wines and Arras super-*cuvée* sparkler.

Beechworth Vic Trendy region; Castagna and GIACONDA are best-known wineries.

Bellarmine Wines Pemberton WA w (r) ★★★ German Schumacher family is long-distance owner of this 20-ha v'yd: (*inter alia*) startling Mosel-like RIES at various sweetness/alcohol levels, at ridiculously low prices.

Bendigo Vic Widespread region with 34 small v'yds, some v.gd quality. Notable: BALGOWNIE, PONDALOWIE, Passing Clouds, Turner's Crossing, and Water Wheel.

Best's Grampians, Vic r w ★★→★★★ (SHIRAZ) 97' 01' 03' 04' 05' 06 Conservative old family winery; *v.gd mid-weight reds*. Thomson Family Shiraz from 120-yr-old vines is superb.

Big Rivers Zone NSW and Vic The continuation of South Australia's Riverland, inc the MURRAY Darling, Perricoota and Swan Hill regions.

Bindi Macedon, Vic r w ★★★→★★★★ Ultra-fastidious, terroir-driven maker of outstanding, long-lived PINOT N and CHARD.

Bloodwood, Orange, NSW r w ★★★ Old dog (1983) in up-and-coming cool, high-altitude, and picturesque region. CHARD, RIES, and Big Men in Tights Rosé gd.

Blue Pyrenees Pyrenees, Vic r w sp ★★ 180 ha of mature v'yds are being better utilized across a broad range of wines.

Boireann Granite Belt Qld r ★★→★★★ Consistently the best producer of red wines in Queensland (in tiny quantities).

Botobolar Mudgee, NSW r w ★★ Marvellously eccentric little organic winery.

Brand's of Coonawarra Coonawarra, SA r w ★★★ 91' 94 96 98' 02' 03 05' 07 Owned by MCWILLIAM'S. Super-premium Stentiford's SHIRAZ (100-yr-old vines) and Patron's CAB SAUV are tops.

Bremerton Langhorne Creek, SA r w ★★→★★★ Regularly produces attractively priced red wines with silky soft mouthfeel and stacks of flavour.

Brokenwood Hunter V, NSW r w ★★★ (ILR Res SEM) 03' 05' (07') (Graveyard SHIRAZ) 93' 97' 98' 00' 02' (03') (05') (07') and Cricket Pitch SEM/SAUV BL fuel sales.

Brookland Valley Margaret R, WA r w ★★★ Superbly sited winery (with a restaurant) doing great things, esp with SAUV BL. Owned by CWA.

Brown Brothers King V, Vic r w dr br sp sw ★→★★★ (Noble RIES) 99' 00 02' 04 05 Old family firm with new ideas. Wide range of delicate, varietal wines, many from cool mountain districts, inc CHARD and RIES. *Dry white Muscat is outstanding.* CAB SAUV blend is best red.

Buller Rutherglen, Vic br ★★★★ Rated for superb Rare Liqueur Muscat and the newly-minted name Topaque (replacing "Tokay").

Leo Buring Barossa, SA w ★★★ 79' 84' 91' 94 98 02' 04 05' 06' Part of FWE. Now exclusively RIES producer; Leonay top label, ages superbly. Screwcapped.

By Farr/Farr Rising Geelong, Vic r w ★★★ Father Gary and son Nick's own, after departure from BANNOCKBURN. CHARD and PINOT N are minor masterpieces.

Cabernet Sauvignon 27,553 ha;258,066 tonnes. Grown in all wine regions, best in COONAWARRA. From herbaceous green pepper in coolest regions, through blackcurrant and mulberry, to dark chocolate and redcurrant in warmer areas.

Campbells' Rutherglen, Vic r br (w) ★★ Smooth ripe reds and unusually elegant; Merchant Prince Rare Muscat and Isabella Rare Topaque (★★★★).

Canberra District NSW Both quality and quantity on the increase; altitude-dependent, site selection important.

Capel Vale Geographe, WA r w ★★→★★★ 165 ha estate. V'yds across 4 regions and 13 varieties make every post a winner.

Cape Mentelle Margaret R, WA r w ★★★ Robust CAB SAUV gd, CHARD even better; also ZIN and v. popular SAUV BL/SEM. Owned by LVMH Veuve Clicquot owner.

Capercaillie Hunter V, NSW r w ★★→★★★ Sudden death of owner Alasdair

Sutherland hasn't changed winning formula of supplementing local grapes with purchases from elsewhere, inc MCLAREN VALE, ORANGE etc.

Carlei Estate Yarra V, Vic r w ★★ Mercurial winemaker Sergio Carlei sources PINOT N and CHARD from cool regions to make wines with abundant character.

Casella Riverina, NSW r w ★The (Yellow Tail) phenomenon has swept all before it with multimillion-case sales in US. Like Fanta: soft and sweet.

Centennial Vineyards Southern Highlands, NSW r w ★★ Sources its best grapes from ORANGE, but winemaking skills and a large chequebook are there.

Central Ranges Zone NSW Encompasses MUDGEE, ORANGE, and Cowra regions, expanding in high-altitude, moderately cool to warm climates.

Chalkers Crossing Hilltops, NSW r w ★★→★★★ Beautifully balanced cool-climate wines made by French-trained Celine Rousseau; esp SHIRAZ.

Chambers Rosewood NE Vic br (r w) ★★→★★★ Viewed with MORRIS as the greatest maker of sticky Topaque and Muscat.

Chardonnay 366,976; tonnes 32151 ha. Familiarity breeds contempt, but commercial versions are now less obese and oaky, and cooler regions produce more elegant, tightly structured, ageworthy examples.

Charles Melton Barossa, SA r w (sp) ★★★ Tiny winery with bold, luscious reds, esp Nine Popes, an old-vine GRENACHE/SHIRAZ blend.

Clarendon Hills McLaren Vale, SA r ★★★ Deeply structured reds from small parcels of contract grapes around hills above Mclaren Vale.

Clare Valley (Clare V), SA Small high-quality area 145 km north of Adelaide. Best for RIES; also SHIRAZ and CAB SAUV.

Clonakilla Canberra District, NSW r w ★★★ Deserved leader of the SHIRAZ/Viognier brigade. RIES and other wines also v.gd.

Coldstream Hills Yarra V, Vic r w (sp) ★★★ (CHARD) **02' 03 04' 05' 06'** 07 (PINOT N) **92' 96' 02' 04' 06'** Established in 1985 by wine critic James Halliday. Delicious PINOT N to drink young, and *Reserve to age* leads Australia. V.gd CHARD (esp Res), fruity CAB SAUV, MERLOT. Part of FWE.

Constellation Wines Australia (CWA) Name for all wines/wineries previously under HARDYS brand. Like FWE seeking to shed regional wineries and v'yds.

Coonawarra SA Southernmost v'yds of state: home to most of Australia's best CAB SAUV; successful CHARD, RIES, and SHIRAZ.

Coriole McLaren Vale, SA r w ★★→★★★ (Lloyd Reserve SHIRAZ) **91' 96' 98' 02' 04' 06'** To watch, esp for old-vine SHIRAZ lloyd Reserve.

Craiglee Macedon, Vic r w ★★★ (SHIRAZ) **96' 98'** 02' 04' 05 06' Re-creation of famous 19th-century estate. Fragrant, peppery SHIRAZ, CHARD.

Crawford River Henty, Vic w r ★★★ John Thomson consistently produces some of Australia's best RIES from this ultra-cool region.

Cullen Wines Margaret R, WA r w ★★★★ (CHARD) **00' 02' 04' 05'** 07 (08') (CAB SAUV/MERLOT) **94' 95' 98'** 04' 05' (07') Vanya Cullen makes strongly structured *substantial but subtle Sem/Sauv Bl*, bold CHARD and outstanding CAB/MERLOT.

Cumulus Orange, NSW r w ★★ By far the largest v'yd owner and producer in the region but continues to have unsettled management.

Cuttaway Hill Southern Highlands, NSW ★★ r w Leads the region in the production of estate-grown wines, esp CHARD, SAUV BL, Pinot Gr.

Dalwhinnie Pyrenees, Vic r w ★★★ (CHARD) **04'** 05' 06' (SHIRAZ) **99' 00 02** 04' 05' 06' Rich CHARD and SHIRAZ. CAB SAUV best in PYRENEES.

d'Arenberg McLaren Vale, SA r w (sw br sp) ★★→★★★ Old firm with new lease of life; sumptuous SHIRAZ and GRENACHE, lots of varieties and wacky labels.

Deakin Estate Murray Darling r w ★ Part of KATNOOK group, producing large volumes of v. decent varietal table wines.

De Bortoli Griffith, NSW r w dr sw (br) ★→★★★ (Noble SEM) Irrigation-area winery. Standard red and white but v.gd sweet botrytized Sauternes-style Noble SEM.

De Bortoli Yarra V, Vic r w ★★→★★★ (CHARD) 02' 04 05' 06' 07 (SHIRAZ) 02' 04' 05' 06' (07) YARRA VALLEY's largest producer. Main label is v.gd; second label Gulf Station and third label Windy Peak v.gd value.

Delatite Upper Goldburn (r) w (sp) ★★ (RIES) 02' 04 06' 08 RIES, Gewurz, and SAUV BL are specialities of this cool mountainside v'yd.

Devil's Lair Margaret R, WA r w ★★★ Opulently concentrated CHARD and CAB SAUV/MERLOT. Fifth Leg is fast-growing trendy second label. Part of FWE.

Diamond Valley Yarra V, Vic r w ★★→★★★ (PINOT N) 02' 04' 05' 06' Outstanding PINOT N in significant quantities; others gd, esp CHARD.

Domaine A S Tas r w ★★★ Swiss owners/winemakers Peter and Ruth Althaus are ultimate perfectionists; SAUV BL (Fumé Blanc) and CAB SAUV are picks.

Domaine Chandon Yarra V, Vic sp (r w) ★★★ Classic sparkling wine from grapes grown in cooler wine regions, supported by owner Moët & Chandon. Well known in UK as Green Point.

Dominique Portet Yarra V, Vic r w ★★→★★★ After 25-yr career at TALTARNI, now in his own winery for the first time, going from strength to strength.

Eden Hall Eden V, SA r w ★★ Substantial v'yd planted in 1996 on historic property making excellent SHIRAZ/Viognier, CAB SAUV and RIES.

Eden Valley Eden V, SA Hilly region home to HENSCHKE and PEWSEY VALE; RIES and SHIRAZ of v. high quality.

Elderton Barossa, SA r w (sp br) ★★ Old vines; rich, oaked CAB SAUV and SHIRAZ.

Evans & Tate Margaret R, WA r w ★★→★★★ In October 2007 the brand was finally acquired (from receivers) by a syndicate headed by MCWILLIAMS. Wine quality has remained remarkably stable during its extended financial woes.

Ferngrove Vineyards Great Southern, WA r w ★★★ Cattle farmer Murray Burton's syndicate has established 223 ha since 1997; great RIES, Malbec.

Freycinet Tas r w (sp) ★★★ (PINOT N) 96' 00' 02' 05' 06' 07 East coast winery producing voluptuous, rich PINOT N and gd CHARD.

FWE (Fosters Wine Estates) Official name of the merged Beringer Blass and Southcorp wine groups. Has 41 brands in Australia (which use contract grapes, contract wineries, contract staff) that come and go like mushrooms after rain, but has embarked on a brand weight-loss programme.

Gapsted Wines Alpine V, Vic r w ★★ Brand of large winery that crushes grapes for 50 growers; own label commendable.

Geelong Vic Once-famous area destroyed by phylloxera, re-established in the mid-1960s. V. cool, dry climate: firm table wines from gd-quality grapes. Names inc BANNOCKBURN, BY FARR, Curlewis, SCOTCHMANS HILL.

Gemtree Vineyards McLaren Vale, SA r (w) ★★→★★★ Top-class SHIRAZ alongside Tempranillo, B'x blends and other exotica, linked by quality.

Geoff Merrill McLaren Vale, SA r w ★★ Ebullient maker of Geoff Merrill and Mt Hurtle. A questing enthusiast; his best are excellent, others unashamedly mass-market oriented. TAHBILK OWNS 50%.

Geoff Weaver Adelaide Hills, SA r w ★★★ An 8-ha estate at Lenswood. V. fine SAUV BL, CHARD, RIES, and CAB SAUV/MERLOT blend. Marvellous label design.

Giaconda Beechworth, Vic r w ★★★ (CHARD) Australia's answer to Kistler (see California). CHARD is considered by some to be the best in Australia. PINOT N is v. variable; newly introduced SHIRAZ better.

Glaetzer Wines Barossa, SA r ★★★ Hyper-rich, unfiltered, v. ripe old-vine SHIRAZ led by iconic Amon-Ra. V.gd egs of high-octane style admired by US critics.

Goulburn Valley (Goulburn V), Vic V. old (TAHBILK) and relatively new (MITCHELTON) wineries in temperate mid-Victoria region. Full-bodied table wines.

Grampians Vic Region previously known as Great Western. Temperate region in central west of state. High quality, especially SHIRAZ.

Granite Belt Qld High-altitude, (relatively) cool region just north of Queensland

/NSW border. Esp spicy SHIRAZ and rich SEM.

Granite Hills Macedon, Vic r w ★★ 30-yr-old family v'yd and winery has regained original class with fine elegant RIES and spicy SHIRAZ.

Grant Burge Barossa, SA r w (sp sw br) ★★ 400,000 cases of silky-smooth reds and whites from the best grapes of Burge's large v'yd holdings.

Great Southern WA Remote cool area; FERNGROVE and Goundrey are the largest wineries. Albany, Denmark, Frankland River, Mount Barker, and Porongurup are official sub-regions. First class RIES and SHIRAZ.

Greenstone Vineyard Heathcote, Vic r ★★ A partnership between David Gleave MW (London), Alberto Antonini (Italy) and Australian viticulturist Mark Walpole; great SHIRAZ, nascent Sangiovese.

Grenache 2,097 ha; 25,418 tonnes. Produces thin wine if overcropped, but can do much better. Growing interest in old BAROSSA and MCLAREN VALE plantings.

Grosset Clare, SA r w ★★★→★★★★ (RIES) 00' 02' 03 06' 07' (Gaia) 90' 91' 96' 98' 99 02' 04' 05' 06 Fastidious winemaker. Foremost Australian RIES, lovely CHARD, PINOT N, and exceptional Gaia CAB SAUV/MERLOT from dry v'yd in Watervale and Polish Hill subregions.

Haan Wines Barossa, SA r w ★★★ Low yields and meticulous winemaking ensure top results for Viognier, MERLOT, SHIRAZ, and B'x blend (Wilhelmus).

Hanging Rock Macedon, Vic r w sp ★→★★★ (Heathcote SHIRAZ) 00' 01' 02' 04' 06' Has successfully moved upmarket with sparkling Macedon and HEATHCOTE SHIRAZ; bread and butter comes from contract winemaking.

Hardys r w sp (sw) ★★→★★★★ (Eileen CHARD) 01' 02' 04' 05 06' (Eileen Shiraz) 70' 96' 98' 02' 04' 06' Historic company blending wines from several areas. Best are Eileen Hardy and recent Heritage Reserve Blend (HRB) series seeking synergy from classy components. Part of CWA.

Heathcote Vic The 500-million-yr-old, blood-red Cambrian soil has seemingly unlimited potential to produce reds, esp SHIRAZ, of the highest quality.

Heathcote Estate Heathcote, Vic r ★★★ SHIRAZ specialist brimming with potential for owners Kirby family; whizz Tom Carson newly installed chief winemaker; overlaps with YABBY LAKE.

Heggies Eden V, SA r w dr (sw w) ★★ V'yd at 500 m owned by S SMITH & SONS, like PEWSEY VALE with v.gd RIES, but adds Viognier esp and CHARD to its portfolio.

Henschke Eden Valley, SA r w ★★★★ (SHIRAZ) 58' 84' 86' 90' 91' 96' 98' 01 02' 04' 06' (CAB SAUV) 86' 88 90' 96' 98 99' 02' 04' 06' A 120-yr-old family business, perhaps Australia's best, known for delectable Hill of Grace (SHIRAZ), v.gd CAB SAUV and red blends, and value whites, *incl long-ageing Ries*. Lenswood v'yds in ADELAIDE HILLS add excitement. Fervent opponent of corks for reds, too.

Hewitson SE Aus r (w) ★★★ Much travelled winemaker Dean Hewitson's virtual winery sourcing parcels of v. old vines, making the wines in rented space.

Hollick Coonawarra, SA r w (sp) ★★→★★★ Has expanded estate v'yds, most recently in WRATTONBULLY. CAB SAUV, SHIRAZ and MERLOT. Top-class restaurant.

Hope Estate Lower Hunter V, NSW ★★ Snapped up Rothbury Estate Winery from FWE; also owns Virgin Hills and Western Austalia v'yds.

Houghton Swan V, WA r w ★→★★★ The most famous old winery of W Australia. Soft, ripe Supreme is top-selling, ageworthy white; *a national classic*. Also excellent CAB SAUV, VERDELHO, SHIRAZ, etc sourced from MARGARET RIVER and GREAT SOUTHERN. Part of CWA.

Howard Park Mount Barker and Margaret R, WA r w ★★★ (RIES) 97' 99' 02' 04 05' 07' 08 (CAB SAUV) 88' 94' 96' 99' 01' 05' 07' (CHARD) 01' 02' 04 05' 07' Scented RIES, CHARD; spicy CAB SAUV. Second label: MadFish Bay is excellent value.

Hunter Valley Hunter Valley, NSW Great name in NSW. Broad, soft, earthy SHIRAZ and gentle SEM that live for 30 yrs. CAB SAUV not important; CHARD is.

Jacob's Creek (Orlando), Barossa, SA r w sp (br sw) ★→★★★ Great pioneering company, now owned by Pernod Ricard. Almost totally focused on 3 tiers of Jacob's Creek wines, covering all varieties and prices, all tied historically to Jacob Gramp and his eponymous creek.

Jasper Hill Heathcote, Vic r w ★★→★★★ (SHIRAZ) **85' 96' 97' 98' 99'** 02' 04' 06' Emily's Paddock SHIRAZ/Cab Fr blend and Georgia's Paddock SHIRAZ from dry-land estate are intense, long-lived, and much admired.

Jim Barry Clare V, SA r w ★★→★★★ Some great v'yds provide gd RIES, McCrae Wood SHIRAZ, and richly robed and oaked The Armagh. SHIRAZ.

John Duval Wines Barossa, SA r ★★★ The eponymous business of former chief red-winemaker for PENFOLDS (and Grange), making delicious reds that are supple and smooth, yet amply structured.

Kaesler Barossa, SA r (w) ★★→★★★ Old Bastard SHIRAZ outranks Old Vine SHIRAZ. Wine in the glass gd, too (in heroic style).

Katnook Estate Coonawarra, SA r w (sp sw w) ★★★ (Odyssey CAB SAUV) **91' 92' 94' 96'** 97' 98' 00 01' 02' Excellent pricey icons Odyssey and Prodigy SHIRAZ.

Keith Tulloch Hunter V, NSW r w ★★★ Ex-Rothbury winemaker fastidiously crafting elegant yet complex SEM, SHIRAZ, etc.

Killkanoon Clare V, SA ★★→★★★ r W RIES and SHIRAZ have been awesome performers in shows over past yrs. In Sept 2007 acquired National Trust ranked SEPPELTSFIELD.

Kingston Estate SE Aus ★→★★★ Kaleidoscopic array of varietal wines from all over the place, consistency and value providing the glue.

King Valley Vic Altitude between 155 m and 860 m has massive impact on varieties and styles, and prolonged legal wrangling over GI boundaries. 29 wineries headed by BROWN BROS, and important supplier to many others.

Knappstein Wines Clare V, SA r w ★★→★★★ Reliable RIES, CAB SAUV/MERLOT, SHIRAZ, and CAB SAUV. Owned by LION NATHAN.

Lake Breeze Langhorne Ck, SA r (w) ★★ Long-term grape-growers turned winemakers, producing succulently smooth SHIRAZ and CAB SAUV.

Lake's Folly Hunter V, NSW r w ★★★★ (CHARD) **97' 99' 00' 01' 04' 05' 07'** (CAB SAUV) **69' 89' 93 97' 98' 03'** 05' 07' Founded by Max Lake, the pioneer of HUNTER CAB SAUV. New owners since 2000. CHARD usually better than CAB SAUV these days.

Lamont's Swan V, WA r w ★★ Winery and superb restaurant owned by Corin Lamont (daughter of legendary Jack Mann) and husband. Delicious wines.

Langmeil Barossa, SA r w ★★★ Owns oldest block of SHIRAZ (planted in 1843) in world plus other old v'yds making opulent SHIRAZ without excessive alcohol.

Leasingham Clare V, SA r w ★★→★★★ Important brand with v.gd RIES, SHIRAZ, CAB SAUV and CAB SAUV/Malbec blend. Various labels inc individual v'yds.

Leeuwin Estate Margaret R, WA r w ★★★★ (CHARD) **85' 87' 92' 97' 99' 01' 02'** 04' **05'** 06 Leading Western Australia estate Superb, ageworthy Art Series Chard. SAUV BL, RIES, and CAB SAUV also gd.

Limestone Coast Zone SA Important zone inc Bordertown, COONAWARRA, Mount Benson, Mount Gambier, PADTHAWAY, Robe, and WRATTONBULLY.

Lindemans r w ★→★★ One of the oldest firms, now owned by FWE. Low-price Bin range (esp Bin 65 CHARD) now its main focus, a far cry from former glory.

Lion Nathan New Zealand brewery; OWNS KNAPPSTEIN, MITCHELTON, PETALUMA, ST HALLET, Smithbrook, STONIER and TATACHILLA.

Macedon and **Sunbury** Vic Adjacent regions, Macedon higher elevation, Sunbury nr Melbourne airport. CRAIGLEE, GRANITE HILLS, HANGING ROCK, Virgin Hills.

Majella Coonawarra, SA r (w) ★★★→★★★★ Rising to the top of COONAWARRA cream. The Malleea is outstanding CAB SAUV/SHIRAZ super-premium red. SHIRAZ and CAB SAUV also v.gd.

Margaret River WA Temperate coastal area south of Perth, with superbly elegant wines. Australia's most vibrant tourist wine (and surfing) region.

McLaren Vale SA Historic region on southern outskirts of Adelaide. Big, alcoholic, flavoursome reds have great appeal to US, but CORIOLE, HARDYS, WIRRA WIRRA and others show flavour can be gained without sacrificing elegance.

McWilliam's Yarra V, Vic; Coonawarra SA; Margaret River, WA r w (sw br) ★★→★★★ Still family-owned (Gallo lurking with 10% of shares) but has reinvented itself with great flair, always over-delivering. *Elizabeth Sem* the darling of Sydney, cheaper Hanwood blends in many parts of the world. Elizabeth and Lovedale SEMS so consistent and ageworthy that vintages irrelevant.

Merlot Was the star of the new millennium; from 9,000 tonnes in 1996 to 125,000 tonnes in 2008. Grown everywhere, but shouldn't be.

Mitchell Clare V, SA r w ★★→★★★ (RIES) 00' 01' 04 05' 06' 07 Small family winery for excellent CAB SAUV and firmly structured dry RIES, under screwcap since 00.

Mitchelton Goulburn V, Vic r w (sw w) ★★ Reliable producer of RIES, SHIRAZ, CAB at several price points, plus speciality of Marsanne and Roussanne.

Mitolo McLaren Vale; Barossa, SA r ★★★ One of the best "virtual wineries" (ie contract v'yds, wineries, winemaker), paying top dollar for top-quality SHIRAZ and CAB; winemaking by BEN GLAETZER. Heroic but (virtually) irresistible wines.

Moorilla Estate Tas r w (sp) ★★★ Nr H Hobart on Derwent River: v.gd RIES and CHARD; PINOT N gd. Superb restaurant and world-class art gallery.

Moorooduc Estate Mornington Pen, Vic r w ★★★ Stylish and sophisticated (wild yeast, etc) producer of top-flight CHARD and PINOT N.

Mornington Peninsula Vic Exciting wines in cool coastal area 40km south of Melbourne; 1,000 ha. Many high-quality boutique wineries.

Morris NE Vic br (r w) ★★→★★★★ Old winery at RUTHERGLEN for some of Australia's greatest dessert Muscats and "Tokays".

Moss Wood Margaret R, WA r w ★★★★ (CAB SAUV) 80' 85 90' 91' 04' 05' 07' To many, the best MARGARET RIVER winery (11.7 ha). SEM, CAB SAUV, CHARD, all with rich fruit flavours.

Mount Horrocks Clare V, SA w r ★★★→★★★★ Finest dry RIES and sweet Cordon Cut RIES; *Chard best in region*. Related to GROSSET.

Mount Langi Ghiran Grampians, Vic r w ★★★ (SHIRAZ) 89' 93' 96' 03' 05' 06' Esp for superb, rich, peppery, Rhône-like SHIRAZ, one of Australia's best cool-climate versions. Sister of YERING STATION.

Mount Mary Yarra V, Vic r w ★★★★ (PINOT N) 97' 99 00' 02' 05' 06' (Quintet) 84' 86' 88' 90' 92' 96' 98' 02' 04' 06 The late Dr John Middleton made tiny amounts of suave CHARD, vivid PINOT N, and (best of all) CAB SAUV blend: Australia's most Bordeaux-like "claret". All age impeccably. His family go on.

Mudgee NSW Long-established region northwest of Sydney. Big reds, surprisingly fine SEM, and full CHARD.

Murdock Coonawarra, SA r ★★★ Long-term grower now making classic CAB SAUV.

Murray Valley SA, Vic, NSW Vast irrigated v'yds. Now at the epicentre of the drought/climate-change firestorm.

Neagles Rock Clare V, SA r w ★★★ Husband/wife industry veterans who took the plunge into winery ownership, making every post a winner. RIES, SHIRAZ and Sangiovese all v.gd. Sadly on the market for sale April 2009.

Ninth Island See PIPERS BROOK.

O'Leary Walker Wines Clare V, SA r w ★★★ Two whizz-kids have mid-life crisis and leave Beringer Blass to do their own thing – v. well.

Orange NSW Cool-climate, high-elevation region: lively CHARD, MERLOT, SHIRAZ.

Padthaway SA Large area developed as overspill of COONAWARRA. Cool climate; gd CHARD and excellent SHIRAZ (Orlando).

Pannell, SC Mclaren Vale, SA r ★★★ EX-HARDY wunderkind turned flying winemaker, Steve Pannell has produced a dazzling array of SHIRAZ- and GRENACHE-based wines for his own label.

Paringa Estate Mornington Pen, Vic r w ★★★★ Maker of quite spectacular CHARD, PINOT N, and SHIRAZ, winning innumerable trophies.

Parker Estate Coonawarra, SA r ★★★★ Small estate making v.gd CAB SAUV, esp Terra Rossa First Growth. Sister of YERING STATION since 2004.

Pemberton WA Region between MARGARET RIVER and GREAT SOUTHERN; initial enthusiasm for PINOT N replaced by RIES, CHARD, MERLOT, SHIRAZ.

Penfolds Originally Adelaide, now everywhere r w (sp br) ★★→★★★★ (Grange) 52' 53' 55' 60' 62' 63' 66' 71' 76' 78' 83' 86' 90' 94' 96' 98' 99' 02' 04' (05', 06') (Cab S Bin 707) 64' 66' 76' 86' 90' 91' 96' 98' 02' 04' (06') Consistently Australia's best red wine company, if you can decode its labels. Its Grange (was called Hermitage) is deservedly ★★★★. Yattarna CHARD was released in 98. Bin 707 CAB SAUV not far behind. Has hugely impressive 04, 05, and 06 reds coming up for release over the next 3 yrs.

Penley Estate Coonawarra, SA r w ★★★ High-profile, no-expense-spared winery. Rich, textured, fruit-and-oak CAB SAUV; SHIRAZ/CAB SAUV blend; CHARD.

Perth Hills WA Fledgling area 30 km east of Perth with a larger number of growers on mild hillside sites. Millbrook and Western Range best.

Petaluma Adelaide Hills, SA r w sp ★★★★ (WFS) 04' 05' 06' (CHARD) 01' 03' 04' 05' 06' 07 (CAB SAUV COONAWARRA) 79' 90' 91' 94' 98' 03' 05' 06' Created by the fearsome intellect and energy of (now retired) Brian Croser. Red wines richer from 1988 on. Fell prey to LION NATHAN in 2002.

Peter Lehmann Wines Barossa, SA r w (sp br sw w) ★★→★★★ Defender of BAROSSA faith; fought off Allied-Domecq by marriage with Swiss Hess group. Consistently well-priced wines in substantial quantities. Try Stonewell SHIRAZ and outstanding Reserve Bin SEM and RIES with 5 yrs age.

Pewsey Vale Adelaide Hills, SA w ★★★→★★★★ Glorious RIES, esp The Contours, released with screwcap, 5 yrs bottle-age and multiple trophies.

Pierro Margaret R, WA r w ★★★ (CHARD) 96' 99' 00' 01' 02' 03 05' (06) Highly rated producer of expensive, tangy SEM/SAUV BL and v.gd barrel-fermented CHARD.

Pinot Noir 4,490 ha; 43,923 tonnes. Mostly used in sparkling. Exciting wines from south Victoria, TASMANIA, and ADELAIDE HILLS; plantings are increasing.

Pipers Brook Tas r w sp ★★★ (RIES) 99' 00' 01' 02' 04' 06' 07 (CHARD) 00' 02' 05' 06 07' Cool-area pioneer; v.gd RIES, PINOT N, restrained CHARD, and sparkling from Tamar Valley. Second label: Ninth Island. Owned by Belgian Kreglinger family, owners of Vieux-Ch-Certan (see Châteaux of Bordeaux).

Pirramimma McLaren Vale, SA r w ★★ Century-old family business with large v'yds moving with the times; snappy new packaging, the wines not forgotten.

Pirie Estate N Tas r w sp ★★→★★★ A phoenix arisen, with its own brand and responsibility for TAMAR RIDGE and Rosevears Estate.

Plantagenet Mount Barker, WA r w (sp) ★★★ (r) 95 98' 01' 03 04' 05' 07' The region's elder statesman: wide range of varieties, esp rich CHARD, SHIRAZ, and vibrant, potent CAB SAUV.

Pondalowie Bendigo, Vic r ★★★ Flying winemakers with exciting SHIRAZ/Viognier/Tempranillo in various combinations.

Primo Estate SA r w dr (w sw) ★★★ Joe Grilli's many successes include v.gd MCLAREN VALE cherry, spicy SHIRAZ/Sangiovese, tangy Colombard, and potent Joseph CAB SAUV/MERLOT.

Pyrenees Vic Central Victoria region producing rich, often slightly minty reds.

Red Hill Estate Mornington Pen, Vic r w sp ★★→★★★ One of the larger and more important wineries; notably elegant wines.

Redman Coonawarra, SA r ★ Famous old name in COONAWARRA; red specialist: SHIRAZ, CAB SAUV, CAB SAUV/MERLOT. Wine fails to do justice to v'yd quality.

Redheads MacLaren V, SA r ★★ Tiny "studio" for super-concentrated reds.

Richmond Grove Barossa r w ★→★★★ Offers v.gd RIES at bargain prices; other wines are OK. Owned by Orlando Wyndham.

Riesling 4,400 ha; 39,305 tonnes. Clare and Eden Valleys are the womb, GREAT SOUTHERN and TASMANIA the offspring. Long-lived dry styles lead, with Mosel Kabinett-styles gaining traction all screwcapped.

Riverina NSW Large-volume irrigated zone centred around Griffith. Its water supply will be better than the MURRAY Darling over next few years, sustaining YELLOW TAIL *et al*.

Robert Channon Wines Granite Belt, Qld r w ★→★★ has 6.8 ha of permanently netted, immaculately trained v'yd producing v.gd VERDELHO.

Rockford Barossa, SA r w sp ★★→★★★★ Small producer from old, low-yielding v'yds; reds best, also iconic sparkling Black SHIRAZ.

Rosemount Estate Upper Hunter, V, McLaren Vale, Coonawarra, SA r w (sp) ★★ Rich Roxburgh CHARD, MCLAREN VALE Balmoral Syrah, MUDGEE Mountain Blue CAB SAUV/SHIRAZ, and COONAWARRA CAB SAUV lead the wide range. Part of FWE.

Rutherglen and **Glenrowan** Vic Two of 4 regions in the northeast Victoria Zone, justly famous for weighty reds and magnificent, fortified dessert wines.

St Hallett Barossa, SA r w ★★★ (Old Block)**86' 90' 91' 98 99'** 01 02' 04 05' (06') Old Block SHIRAZ the star; rest of range is smooth, stylish. LION NATHAN-owned.

St Sheila's SA p sw sp **36 22 38** Full-bodied fizzer. Ripper grog, too.

Saltram Barossa, SA r w ★★→★★★ Mamre Brook (SHIRAZ, CAB SAUV, CHARD) and No 1 SHIRAZ are leaders. An FWE brand.

Sandalford Swan V, WA r w (br) ★→★★ Fine old winery with contrasting styles of red and white single-grape wines from SWAN and MARGARET RIVER areas.

Sauvignon Blanc 6,404ha; 62,420 tonnes. Usually not as distinctive as in New Zealand, but amazingly popular. Many styles, from bland to pungent.

Scotchmans Hill Geelong, Vic r w ★★ Makes significant quantities of stylish PINOT N, gd CHARD, and spicy SHIRAZ.

Semillon 6,716 ha; 100,031 tonnes. Before the arrival of CHARD, Sem was the HUNTER VALLEY's answer to South Australia's RIES. Traditionally made without oak and extremely long-lived. Brief affair with oak terminated.

Seppelt Bendigo, Grampians, Henty, Vic r w sp br (sw w) ★★★ (St Peter's SHIRAZ) **71' 85 86' 91' 96 97' 99'** 04' 05' 06 Now a specialist table wine producer for FWE with a v. impressive array of region specific RIES, CHARD, SHIRAZ, and CABS.

Seppeltsfield Barossa SA National Trust Heritage Winery purchased by Kilikanoon shareholders in 2007 and being restored to full working order. Priceless stocks of fortified wines in barrels dating back to 1878 still under the vigilant care of long-term winemaker, James Godfrey.

Setanta Wines Adelaide Hills, SA r w ★★★ The Sullivan family, first-generation Australians from Ireland, produce wonderful RIES, CHARD, SAUV BL, SHIRAZ and CAB SAUV with Irish mythology labels of striking design.

Sevenhill Clare V, SA r w (br) ★★ Owned by the Jesuitical Manresa Society since 1851. Consistently gd wine; SHIRAZ and RIES can be outstanding.

Seville Estate Yarra V, Vic r w ★★★ (SHIRAZ) **94 97' 99' 02'** 04' 05' 06' Ownership changes have not affected quality of CHARD, SHIRAZ, PINOT N.

Shadowfax Geelong, Vic r w ★★→★★★ Stylish new winery, part of Werribee Park; also hotel based on 1880s mansion. V.gd CHARD, PINOT N, SHIRAZ.

Shaw & Smith Adelaide Hills, SA w (r) ★★★ Founded by Martin Shaw and Australia's first MW, Michael Hill Smith. Crisp SAUV BL, complex, barrel-fermented M3 CHARD, and, of course, SHIRAZ.

Shelmerdine Vineyards Heathcote, Yarra V, Vic r w ★★→★★★ Well-known family with v. elegant wines from estate in the YARRA VALLEY and HEATHCOTE.

Shiraz 43,977 ha;441,950 tonnes. Hugely flexible: velvety/earthy in the HUNTER; spicy, peppery, and Rhône-like in central and south Vic; or brambly, rum-sweet, and luscious in BAROSSA and environs (eg PENFOLDS' Grange).

2007 Notably dry autumn yielded excellent wines in Hawke's Bay and Gisborne, and punchy, ripe, slightly lower-alcohol Marlborough Sauvignon Blanc.

2006 In the North Island some reds were caught by autumn rains. Average to good Marlborough Sauvignon; some lack pungency.

2005 Exceptionally cold, wet, early summer. Late summer and autumn variable but often good. Excellent Marlborough Sauv Bl and Pinot N.

Akarua Central Otago ★★ Respected producer with powerful, concentrated Cadence Pinot N, creamy, buttery Chard, and full-bodied, dry, spicy Pinot Gr. Supple, charming, second-tier Pinot N, labelled Gullies.

Allan Scott Marlborough ★★ V.gd Ries (from vines up to 30 yrs old), elegant, fruit-focused Chard, tropical fruit-flavoured Sauv Bl; sturdy spicy Pinot N.

Alpha Domus Hawke's Bay ★★ Gd Chard and concentrated reds, esp savoury Merlot-based The Navigator, and notably dark rich Cab Sauv-based The Aviator. Top wines labelled AD.

Amisfield Central Otago ★★ Impressive fleshy, smooth Pinot Gr and floral, complex Pinot N. Lake Hayes is lower-tier label.

Astrolabe Marlborough ★★ Label part-owned by WHITEHAVEN winemaker Simon Waghorn. Strikingly intense harmonious Sauv Bl. New AWATERE Sauv Bl is more herbaceous.

Ata Rangi Martinborough ★★★ Small but highly respected winery. *Outstanding Pinot N* (03 **05** 06' 07 08) is one of NZ's greatest and v.gd young-vine Crimson Pinot N. Rich, concentrated Craighall Chard and Lismore Pinot Gr.

Auckland Largest city in NZ. Henderson, Huapai, Kumeu, Matakana, Clevedon, Waiheke Island districts – pricey, variable B'x-style reds, rich, earthy Syrah and ripe, rounded Chard – nearby.

Awatere Valley Marlborough Important sub-region, slightly cooler than the larger WAIRAU VALLEY, with racy herbaceous, minerally Sauv Bl and scented, slightly leafy Pinot N.

Babich Henderson (Auckland) ★★→★★★ Mid-size family firm, estb 1916; quality, value. AUCKLAND, HAWKE'S BAY, MARLBOROUGH v'yds. Refined, slow-maturing Irongate Chard (**04**) and elegant Irongate Cab/Merlot/ Franc (single v'yd). Ripe, dry MARLBOROUGH Sauv Bl is a big seller. Winemaker's Res is mid-tier.

Bald Hills Central Otago ★★ Bannockburn v'yd with crisp, dryish Pinot G; floral, slightly sw Ries; and generous, savoury Pinot N.

Benfield & Delamare Martinborough ★★ Tiny winery, surrounded by Pinot N, producers of elegant, long-lived B'x-style reds.

Bilancia Hawke's Bay ★★ Small producer of classy Syrah (inc brilliant, hill-grown La Collina) and rich Viognier, Pinot Gr.

Blackenbrook Nelson ★★ Small winery with perfumed, rich Gewurz, Pinot Gr, Ries; punchy Sauv Bl; sturdy, generous Pinot N. St Jacques is 2nd label.

Borthwick Wairarapa ★★ Lively, tropical-fruit-flavoured Sauv Bl; peachy, toasty Chard; and *gd Pinot N*.

Brancott Vineyards ★→★★★ Brand used by PERNOD RICARD NEW ZEALAND in US.

Brightwater Nelson ★★ Impressive whites, especially crisp, flavour-packed Ries and Sauv Bl. Top wines labelled Lord Rutherford.

Brookfields Hawke's Bay ★★ Excellent "gold label" Cab Sauv/Merlot; gd Chard, Pinot Gr, Gewurz and Syrah.

Cable Bay Waiheke Island ★★ Mid-sized producer with tight, refined Waiheke Chard and spicy, savoury, Five Hills red; subtle, finely textured MARLBOROUGH Sauv Bl. 2nd label is Culley.

Canterbury NZ's 5th largest wine region; most of its top v'yds are in warm, sheltered Waipara district. Long, dry summers favour Pinot N, Ries.

Carrick Central Otago ★★ Bannockburn winery with flinty, flavourful whites (Pinot

Gr, Sauv Bl, Chard, Ries) and densely packed Pinot N, built to last. 2nd-tier, Unravelled Pinot N is also sturdy and rich.

Central Otago (r) **07** (w) **08** Fast-expanding, cool mountainous region (now NZ's 4th largest) in southern South Island. Scented, crisp Ries and Pinot Gr; Pinot N perfumed and silky, with intense character.

Chard Farm Central Otago ★★ Fresh, *vibrant Ries*, Pinot Gr, and perfumed, graceful, supple Pinot N.

Church Road Hawke's Bay ★★→★★★ PERNOD RICARD NEW ZEALAND winery. Rich, refined Chard and elegant, *distinctly B'x-like Merlot/Cab Sauv*. Top Reserve wines; prestige, claret-style red, Tom (02'). New mid-priced Cuve range is superb quality and value.

Churton Marlborough ★★ Subtle, complex, finely textured Sauv Bl; fragrant, spicy, v. harmonious Pinot N.

Clayridge Marlborough ★★ Distinctive wines from Mike Just, ex-Lawson's Dry Hills. Excalibur range (top, more oak-influence) inc refined, rich, silky Pinot N.

Clearview Hawke's Bay ★★→★★★ Burly, lush, supercharged Reserve Chard; dark, rich Reserve Cab Fr, Enigma (Merlot-based), Old Olive Block (Cab Sauv blend).

Clifford Bay Marlborough ★★ Single-v'yd, AWATERE VALLEY producer. Scented, intense Sauv Bl is best. Now linked to Vavasour.

Clos Henri Marlborough ★★→★★★ Estb by Henri Bourgeois (see France). First vintage 03. Deliciously weighty, rounded Sauv Bl and vibrant, supple Pinot N.

Cloudy Bay Marlborough ★★★ Large-volume Sauv Bl (dry, finely textured), Chard (robust, complex, crisp), and Pinot N (floral, supple) are v.gd. Pelorus vintage-dated sparkling toasty, rich. Rarer Gewurz, Late Harvest Ries, and Te Koko (oak-aged Sauv Bl) now the finest wines. Pinot Gr is in the wings.

Constellation New Zealand Auckland ★→★★ NZ's 2nd largest wine company, previously Nobilo Wine Group, now owned by Constellation Brands. Nobilo MARLBOROUGH Sauv Bl is solid, sharply priced. Superior varietals labelled Nobilo Icon; v.gd Drylands Sauv Bl. See KIM CRAWFORD, MONKEY BAY, SELAKS.

Cooper's Creek Auckland ★★ Excellent Swamp Reserve Chard; v.gd Sauv Bl, Ries; Merlot, top-value Viognier; floral slightly spicy Arneis (NZ's first). SV (Select Vineyard) range is mid-tier.

Corbans Auckland ★→★★★ PERNOD RICARD NZ brand. Best: Cottage Block; Private Bin. Quality from basic to outstanding (esp Cottage Block Hawke's Bay Chard).

Craggy Range Hawke's Bay ★★→★★★ Mid-sized winery with v'yds in MARTINBOROUGH and HAWKE'S BAY. Restrained Sauv Bl, *stylish Chard*, Pinot N; strikingly dense, ripe firm Merlot and Syrah (esp majestic Le Sol) from GIMBLETT GRAVELS.

Daniel Le Brun Marlborough ★★ Best known for citrus, yeasty Brut NV. Now a brand of Lion Nathan.

Daniel Schuster Waipara ★★ CANTERBURY wine stalwart with light, floral Waipara Ries and classy (in top vintages) Omihi Hills Omihi Selection Pinot N.

Delegat's Auckland ★★ Large, fast-expanding company, still mostly family-owned. V'yds and other big wineries in HAWKE'S BAY and MARLBOROUGH. Reserve Chard and Cab Sauv/Merlot offer v.gd quality and value. Hugely successful Oyster Bay brand.

Delta Marlborough ★★ Promising young producer with substantial, graceful Pinot N. Top label: Hatter's Hill.

Deutz Auckland ★★★ Champagne company gives name to fine sparkling from MARLBOROUGH by PERNOD RICARD NEW ZEALAND. NV: lively, yeasty, intense. Vintage Blanc de Blancs: finely focused, citrus, piercing.

Dog Point Marlborough ★★ Grape-grower Ivan Sutherland and winemaker James Healy (both ex-CLOUDY BAY) produce unusually complex, finely textured, oak-aged Sauv Bl (Section 94), Chard, and Pinot N.

Dry River Martinborough ★★★ Tiny winery, now American-owned. Penetrating, long-lived Chard, Ries, Pinot Gr, Gewurz, and notably ripe, powerful, slowly evolving Pinot N (03' **04 05** 06').

Escarpment Martinborough ★★ Sturdy, Alsace-like Pinot Gr and complex, sometimes leafy Pinot N from Larry McKenna, ex-MARTINBOROUGH VINEYARD. Top label: Kupe. Single-v'yd reds launched from 2006.

Esk Valley Hawke's Bay ★★→★★★ Owned by VILLA MARIA. Some of NZ's most voluptuous Merlot-based reds (especially Reserve label 02' **04** 06'), excellent Merlot/Malbec rosé (NZ's best), satisfying Chards, Chenin Bl and Sauv Bl.

Fairhall Downs Marlborough ★★ Single-v'yd wines from elevated site. Weighty, dry Pinot Gr, intense, racy Sauv Bl and perfumed, smooth Pinot N.

Felton Road Central Otago ★★★ Star winery in warm Bannockburn area. Bold, supple, graceful Pinot N Block 3 and 5 and light, intense Ries outstanding; excellent Chard and *regular Pinot N*.

Fiddler's Green Waipara ★★ Flavourful, crisp, cool-climate Chard, Ries and Sauv Bl; vibrant, Pinot N. New Glasnevin brand includes scented, rich Pinot Gr.

Forrest Marlborough ★★ Mid-size winery; easy-drinking Chard, excellent Sauv Bl and Ries; gorgeous botrytized Ries; flavour-crammed HAWKE'S BAY Newton/Forrest Cornerstone (B'x red blend). Distinguished flagship range, labelled John Forrest Collection.

Foxes Island Marlborough ★★ Small producer of rich, smooth Chard, finely textured Sauv Bl, and elegant, supple Pinot N. Gd, large-volume Sauv Bl and Pinot N under Seven Terraces brand.

Framingham Marlborough ★★ Owned by Sogrape. Superb aromatic whites, notably intense zesty Ries, and lush slightly sweet Pinot Gr, Gewurz. Subtle, dry Sauv Bl. Scented, silky Pinot N.

Fromm Marlborough ★★★ Swiss-founded, focusing initially on powerful, tannic, but now more charming red wines. Sturdy, long-lived Pinot N, esp under Fromm Vineyard and Clayvin Vineyard labels. Also unusually stylish Clayvin Chard. Earlier-drinking La Strada range also v.gd.

Gibbston Valley Central Otago ★★ Pioneer winery with popular restaurant. Greatest strength is Pinot N, esp rich, complex Central Otago regional blend and robust, exuberantly fruity Reserve (06). Racy local whites, esp zingy, flavour-packed, medium-dry Ries.

Giesen Canterbury ★ German family winery. Gd, slightly honeyed Ries; bulk of production is average-quality MARLBOROUGH Sauv Bl.

Gimblett Gravels Hawke's Bay Defined area with v. free-draining soils, noted for rich, ripe, B'x-style reds and Syrah.

Gisborne (r) 07' (w) 07' NZ's 3rd-largest region. Abundant sunshine and rain, with fertile soils. Key strength is Chard (typically deliciously fragrant, ripe, and soft in its youth). Gd Gewurz and Viognier; Merlot more variable.

Gladstone Wairarapa ★→★★ Tropical-fruit-flavoured Sauv Bl and dry, weighty Pinot Gr under top label, Gladstone; 12,000 Miles is lower-priced brand.

Goldwater Waiheke Island ★★→★★★ Region's pioneer Cab Sauv/Merlot Goldie (02 **04**) has Médoc-like finesse. Also full-flavoured, finely balanced Chard and ripe non-herbaceous Sauv Bl, from MARLBOROUGH. Sold in 06 to NZ Wine Fund.

Gravitas Marlborough ★★ Solid Chard (Reserve and Unoaked), subtle, sustained Sauv Bl and graceful, flowing Pinot N. 2nd label: Wandering Piano.

Greenhough Nelson ★★→★★★ One of region's top producers, with immaculate and deep-flavoured Ries, Sauv, Chard, Pinot N. Top label: Hope Vineyard.

Greystone Waipara ★★ Impressive new producer with stylish aromatic whites – Riesl, Gewurz, Pinot Gr – and promising Pinot N.

Grove Mill Marlborough ★★→★★★ Attractive whites, inc vibrant Chard; excellent Ries, Sauv, and slightly sweet Pinot Gr. Reds less enjoyable. Gd, lower-tier

Sanctuary brand. First winery to earn CarboNZero certification.

Hans Herzog Marlborough ★★★ Estb by Swiss immigrants. Power-packed, pricey, but classy Merlot/Cab Sauv, Montepulciano, Pinot N, Chard, Viognier and Pinot Gr. Sold under Hans brand in Europe and US.

Hawke's Bay (r) 05' **06** 07 (w) 06' **07** NZ's second-largest region. Long history of winemaking in sunny climate; shingly and heavier soils. Full, rich Merlot and Cab Sauv-based reds in gd vintages; Syrah a fast-rising star; powerful Chard; rounded Sauv Bl; NZ's best Viognier.

Highfield Marlborough ★★ Japanese owned with quality Ries, Chard, Sauv Bl, and Pinot N. Elstree sparkling variable lately; can be almost Champagne-like.

Huia Marlborough ★★ Mouth-filling, subtle wines that age well, inc savoury, rounded Chard and perfumed, well-spiced Gewurz.

Hunter's Marlborough ★★→★★★ Pioneering winery (since 1982) with intense, immaculate, dry Sauv Bl. Fine, delicate Chard. Excellent sparkling (Miru Miru), Ries, Gewurz; light, elegant Pinot N.

Isabel Estate Marlborough ★→★★ Family estate with formerly outstanding Pinot N, Sauv Bl, and Chard, but lately less exciting.

Jackson Estate Marlborough ★★ Rich, ripe, full-flavoured Sauv Bl, attractive, fruit-driven Chard, and sweet-fruited and supple Pinot N (much improved since 05, esp top-tier Gum Emperor Pinot N).

Johanneshof Marlborough ★→★★ Small, low-profile winery with outstandingly perfumed, lush Gewurz. Other wines more variable.

Kaituna Valley Canterbury ★★ Small producer with v'yds nr Christchurch and in MARLBOROUGH. V. powerful, multi-award-winning Pinot N from both regions.

Karikari Northland ★★ NZ's northernmost v'yd and winery, American owned, with rich, ripe B'x-style reds, Pinotage, and Syrah. Robust, creamy-smooth Chard.

Kemblefield Hawke's Bay ★→★★ US-owned winery. Mid-tier, The Distinction range includes ripely herbal, oak-aged Sauv Bl; soft, peppery Gewurz, and fleshy, lush Chard.

Kim Crawford Hawke's Bay ★★ Now part of US-based CONSTELLATION empire. Numerous labels, inc rich, oaky GISBORNE Chard and scented, strong-flavoured MARLBOROUGH Sauv Bl. Top range labelled SP (Small Parcel).

Kumeu River Auckland ★★→★★★ Rich, refined Kumeu Estate Chard (07 08) single-v'yd Mate's Vineyard Chard even more opulent. Two new, single-v'yd Chards in 06. Weighty, floral Pinot Gr and punchy, dry MARLBOROUGH Sauv Bl. Second label: Kumeu River Village.

Lake Chalice Marlborough ★★ Small producer with vibrant, creamy Chard and incisive, slightly sweet Ries; v.gd quality Sauv Bl. Platinum premium label.

Lawson's Dry Hills Marlborough ★★→★★★ Weighty wines with intense flavours. Unusually complex Sauv Bl and *opulent Gewurz*; gd Pinot Gr and Ries.

Lincoln Auckland ★→★★ Long-established family winery. Gd-value varietals: peachy, complex HAWKE'S BAY Chard (top label Reserve). New export brand: Distant Land (includes high-flavoured MARLBOROUGH Sauv Bl).

Lindauer See PERNOD RICARD NEW ZEALAND.

Longridge ★ Now owned by PERNOD RICARD NZ. Reliable wines (inc citrus, lightly

---

The Kiwi invasion

The most popular white wine in Australia is from NZ. Oyster Bay MARLBOROUGH Sauv Bl recently became the biggest-selling white wine in Australia, in volume and dollar terms. Wines like this are tailor-made for Australia's hot, dry climate. Not content to dominate the burgeoning market for Sauv Bl, NZ is also pushing ahead with red-wine sales into Australia, where Oyster Bay is also the second most popular Pinot N.

oaked Chard) typically from HAWKE'S BAY.

Mahi ★★ Marlborough Stylish, complex, mostly single-v'yd wines from Brian Bicknell, ex-Seresin winemaker. Finely textured Sauv Bl, Chard and Pinot N.

Margrain Martinborough ★★ Small winery with firm, concentrated Chard, Ries, Pinot Gr, Gewurz, and Pinot N, all of which reward bottle-age.

Marlborough (r) **07'** (w) **07'** NZ's largest region (nearly half of all plantings). Warm days and cold nights give aromatic, crisp whites. Intense Sauv Bl, from sharp, green capsicum to ripe tropical fruit. Fresh, limey Ries (incl recent wave of low-alcohol wines); v. promising Pinot Gr and Gewurz; Chard leaner, more appley than HAWKE'S BAY. High-quality sparkling and botrytized Ries. Pinot N underrated, top examples among NZ's finest.

Martinborough (r) 06' **07** 08' (w) 07 08' Small, high-quality area in south WAIRARAPA (foot of North Island). Warm summers, dry autumns, gravelly soils. Success with white grapes, but renowned for sturdy, rich, long-lived Pinot N.

Martinborough Vineyard Martinborough ★★★ Distinguished small winery; one of NZ's top Pinot Noirs (06' **07**). Rich, biscuity Chard and intense Ries. Also single v'yd Burnt Spur and drink-young Te Tera ranges (top value Pinot N).

Matakana Estate Auckland ★→★★ Largest producer in Matakana district. Powerful, complex Chard, rich, dry Pinot Gr and spicy, earthy Syrah. Plain, lower-tier Goldridge range.

Matariki Hawke's Bay ★★ Stylish white and red, large v'yds in stony Gimblett Road. Rich Sauv Bl; tight, concentrated Chard; robust Quintology red blend. Res is top range; Aspire is everyday-drinking.

Matua Valley Auckland ★★ Producer of NZ's first Sauv Bl in 1974. Now owned by Foster's Group, with v'yds in 4 regions. Top range Ararimu inc fat, savoury Chard and dark, rich Merlot. Many attractive GISBORNE (esp Judd Chard), HAWKE'S BAY, and MARLBOROUGH wines. Shingle Peak Sauv Bl top value.

Maven Marlborough ★★ Young, quality-focused producer with eye-catching labels – several different for each vintage of each wine. Ripe, tropical fruit Sauv Bl (Reserve is partly barrel-fermented).

Mills Reef Bay of Plenty ★★→★★★ The Preston family produces impressive wines from HAWKE'S BAY grapes. Top Elspeth range include dense, rich B'x-style reds and Syrah. Reserve range reds also impressive and outstanding value.

Millton Gisborne ★★→★★★★ Region's top small winery: wines certified organic. Hill-grown, single-v'yd Clos de Ste Anne range (Chard, Viognier, Syrah, Pinot N) is v. concentrated and full of personality. *Rich, long-lived Chenin Bl* is NZ's finest (honeyed in wetter vintages; tight, pure and long-lived in drier yrs).

Mission Hawke's Bay ★→★★ NZ's oldest wine producer, established 1851, still run by Catholic Society of Mary. Solid varietals: creamy-smooth Chard is esp gd value. Reserve range includes gd B'x-style reds, Syrah and Chard. Top label: Jewelstone (v. classy, concentrated Chard).

Monkey Bay ★ CONSTELLATION NEW ZEALAND brand, modestly priced and v. popular in US. Easy-drinking, dryish Chard; gently sweet Sauv Bl; leafy, slightly sweet Cab/Merlot; fresh, fruity Merlot.

Montana Auckland ★→★★★ A key brand of PERNOD RICARD NEW ZEALAND. Top wines are Letter Series (eg "B" Brancott Sauv Bl). Terroir Series is 2nd tier, followed by Res. Big-selling varietals include peachy, lightly oaked GISBORNE Chard, crisp, grassy MARLBOROUGH Sauv Bl and floral, smooth South Island Pinot N.

Morton Estate Bay of Plenty ★→★★ Mid-size producer with v'yds in HAWKE'S BAY and MARLBOROUGH. Refined Black Label Chard is one of NZ's best (**04** 06). White Label Chard and Premium Brut v.gd and top value. Reds less exciting.

Mount Riley Marlborough ★→★★ Fast-growing company. Easy-drinking Chard; punchy Sauv Bl; dark, flavoursome Merlot/Malbec. Top wines labelled Seventeen Valley. All gd value.

Mt Difficulty Central Otago ★★ Quality producer in relatively hot Bannockburn area. Best known for v. refined, intense Pinot N (Roaring Meg is for early consumption; Single V'yd Pipeclay Terrace is dense, lasting). Classy whites (Ries, Pinot Gr).

Muddy Water Waipara ★★ Small, high-quality producer with beautifully intense Ries, minerally Chard, and savoury, subtle Pinot N (esp Slowhand).

Mud House Canterbury ★★ Large, fast-expanding, WAIPARA-based winery. Brands include Mud House (top range is Swan), Hay Maker (lower-tier) and WAIPARA HILLS. Punchy, vibrant MARLBOROUGH Sauv Bl; intense, racy WAIPARA Ries.

Nautilus Marlborough ★★ Small range of distributors Négociants (NZ), owned by S Smith & Sons (see Australia). Top wines include stylish, finely balanced Sauv Bl, savoury Pinot N, and fragrant sparkler. Lower-tier: Twin Islands. New mid-tier Opawa Pinot N – floral, supple, charming.

Nelson (r) 06 07 (w) 07 Small, steadily expanding region west of MARLBOROUGH; climate wetter but equally sunny. Clay soils of Upper Moutere hills and silty Waimea Plains. Strengths in aromatic whites, esp Ries, Sauv Bl, Pinot Gr, Gewurz; also gd Chard and Pinot N.

Neudorf Nelson ★★★ A top smallish winery. Powerful yet elegant Moutere Chard (05 06 07) is one of NZ's greatest; superb, v. savoury Moutere Pinot N. Sauv Bl and Ries also gd.

Ngatarawa Hawke's Bay ★★→★★★ Mid-sized. Top Alwyn range, inc powerful Chard and dark, generous Merlot/Cab. Mid-range Glazebrook also excellent.

Nga Waka Martinborough ★★ Steely whites of high quality. Outstanding bone-dry Sauv Bl; piercingly flavoured Ries; robust, savoury Chard. Pinot N scented and supple. Three Paddles is 2nd-tier; gd value.

Nobilo See CONSTELLATION NEW ZEALAND.

Obsidian Waiheke Island ★★ V. stylish B'x blend, Viognier and Chard under top brand, Obsidian. Gd value Waiheke reds under 2nd-tier Weeping Sands label.

Olssens Central Otago ★★ Consistently attractive Pinot N, from first Bannockburn v'yd. Softly seductive, rich Jackson Barry Pinot N is middle-tier; top wine is bold Slapjack Creek Reserve Pinot N.

Omaka Springs Marlborough ★→★★ Punchy, herbaceous Sauv Bl (esp Falveys), solid Ries, Chard, and leafy reds.

Oyster Bay Marlborough ★→★★ From DELEGAT'S, this huge-selling brand now exceeds 1.25 million cases. Vibrant, elegant, fruit-driven wines, mostly from Sauv Bl, Chard and Pinot N.

Palliser Martinborough ★★→★★★ One of the area's largest and best wineries. Superb tropical-fruit Sauv Bl in favourable seasons, excellent Chard, Ries, Pinot N. Top wines: Palliser Estate. Lower tier: Pencarrow.

Paritua Hawke's Bay ★→★★ Fast-expanding, American-owned producer, first vintage 05. Stone Paddock brand for regional blends; estate-grown wines, labelled Paritua, include refined, creamy, nutty Chard.

Pask, C J Hawke's Bay ★★ Mid-size winery, extensive v'yds in GIMBLETT GRAVELS. Gd Chard. Cab Sauv, Syrah and Merlot-based reds now consistently impressive and fine value. Top wines labelled Declaration.

Pegasus Bay Waipara ★★★ Small but distinguished range: notably taut, cool-climate Chard; complex, oaked Sauv Bl/Sem; rich, zingy, medium Ries. Merlot-based reds are region's finest. Pinot N lush and silky (especially old-vine Prima Donna). Second label: Main Divide.

Peregrine Central Otago ★★ Crisp, cool-climate Ries, Pinot Gr, Gewurz, and beautifully rich, silky Pinot N. Saddleback Pinot N esp gd value.

Pernod Ricard New Zealand Auckland ★→★★★ NZ wine giant, formerly called MONTANA. Wineries in AUCKLAND, GISBORNE, HAWKE'S BAY, and MARLBOROUGH. Extensive co-owned v'yds for MARLBOROUGH whites, inc top-value MONTANA

Sauv Bl (Reserve range esp gd). Strength in sparkling, inc DEUTZ, and huge volume, moderately yeasty, fine-value Lindauer. Elegant CHURCH ROAD reds and quality Chard. Other key brands: CORBANS, LONGRIDGE, Saints. STONELEIGH, Triplebank offers intense, racy AWATERE VALLEY wines, Camshorn is gd Waipara Ries and Pinot N.

Providence Auckland ★★★ Rare, Merlot and Cabernet Fr-based red from Matakana district. Perfumed, lush, and silky; v. high-priced.

Puriri Hills Auckland ★★ Silky, seductive, Merlot-based reds from Clevedon. Res is esp rich and plump, with more new oak.

Quartz Reef Central Otago ★★ Quality producer with weighty, flinty Pinot Gr; rich Pinot N; yeasty, lingering, Champagne-like sparkler (vintage esp gd.) Chauvet.

Richardson Marlborough ★★ Michelle Richardson, ex-VILLA MARIA chief winemaker. Stylish, rare wines from MARLBOROUGH, Waipara and CENTRAL Otago, notably a very subtle, creamy MARLBOROUGH Chard.

Rimu Grove Nelson ★★ Small, American-owned, coastal v'yd. Concentrated, minerally Chard and Pinot Gr; rich, spicy Pinot N. Bronte range has drink-young charm.

Rippon Vineyard Central Otago ★★ Stunning v'yd on shores of Lake Wanaka. Fine-scented, fruity Pinot N (Jeunesse from younger vines) and slowly evolving whites, inc steely, appley Ries.

Rockburn Central Otago ★★ Crisp, racy Chard, Pinot Gr, Gewurz, Ries, Sauv Bl. Fragrant, supple, rich Pinot N is best and an emerging star.

Sacred Hill Hawke's Bay ★★→★★★ Mid-size producer, partly Chinese-owned. Distinguished Riflemans Chard (powerful but refined, from cool, elevated site) and dark, rich Brokenstone Merlot. Punchy MARLBOROUGH Sauv Bl. Other brands: Gunn Estate (lush Skeetfield Chard), Wild South (Marlborough range).

Saint Clair Marlborough ★★→★★★ Fast-growing, export-led producer with substantial v'yds. Punchy Sauv Bl, fragrant Ries, easy Chard, and plummy, early-drinking Merlot. Rich Reserve Chard, Merlot, Pinot N. Exceedingly intense Wairau Reserve Sauv Blanc. Bewildering array of 2nd-tier Pioneer Block wines (inc 9 Sauv Bls). Vicar's Choice is lower tier, gd value.

St Helena Canterbury ★ The region's oldest winery, founded near Christchurch in 1978. Low profile in NZ, but exports crisp, MARLBOROUGH Sauv Bl in bulk.

Seifried Estate Nelson ★★ Region's biggest winery. Known initially for well-priced Ries and Gewurz; now also producing gd-value, often excellent Sauv Bl and Chard. Best wines: Winemakers Collection. Old Coach Road is 3rd tier.

Selaks Marlborough ★→★★ Now a brand of CONSTELLATION NZ. Moderately priced, fruit-driven MARLBOROUGH Sauv Bl, Ries, and Chard under Premium Selection label are its traditional strengths; reds are mostly plain but improving. Top: Founders Reserve. Emerging mid-tier, The Favourite, offers gd quality/value.

Seresin Marlborough ★★→★★★ Established by NZ film producer Michael Seresin. V. stylish, concentrated Sauv Bl, Chard, Pinots N and Gr, Ries. Second tier: Momo (gd quality/value).

Sherwood Waipara ★→★★ Family-owned firm with 3 brands – Clearwater (WAIPARA), Sherwood (Waipara or MARLBOROUGH) and Stratum (cheap).

Sileni Hawke's Bay ★★ Architecturally striking winery with extensive v'yds and classy Chard, Merlot and MARLBOROUGH Sauv Bl. Top wines: rare EV (Exceptional Vintage), then Estate Selection, and Cellar Selection. Rich, smooth MARLBOROUGH Sauv Bl (esp The Straits).

Southbank Hawke's Bay ★→★★★ Creamy, rich HAWKE'S BAY Chard and penetrating MARLBOROUGH Sauv Bl are best. Other brands: Crossroads (HAWKE'S BAY) and The Crossings (MARLBOROUGH).

Spy Valley Marlborough ★★→★★★ High-achieving company with extensive vinyards. Sauv Bl, Chard, Ries, Gewurz, Pinot Gr, and Pinot N are all v.gd and

NEW ZEALAND

priced right. Superb new top selection: Envoy.

Staete Landt Marlborough ★★ Dutch immigrants, producing v. refined Chard, Sauv Bl, and Pinot Gr; and graceful, supple Pinot N.

Stonecroft Hawke's Bay ★★→★★★ Small winery. NZ's first serious Syrah (since 1989), more Rhône than Oz. Outstanding Chard, v. rich Old Vine Gewurz.

Stoneleigh Now owned by PERNOD RICARD NEW ZEALAND. Impressive MARLBOROUGH whites (inc punchy, tropical fruit Sauv Bl, refined, medium-dry Ries and creamy-smooth Chard) and Pinot N, esp Rapaura Series.

Stonyridge Waiheke Island ★★★ Boutique winery. Famous for exceptional B'x-style red, Larose (00' **04**' 05' 06 07 08'). Also powerful, dense Rhône-style blend Pilgrim and supercharged Luna Negra Malbec. 2nd label: Fallen Angel.

Tasman Bay Nelson ★→★★ Best known for creamy-smooth Chard. Top, single-v'yd wines sold as Spencer Hill.

Te Awa Hawke's Bay ★★ US-owned estate v'yd. Classy Chard and nutty, leathery Boundary (Merlot-based blend); gd value Longlands of Te Awa labels. Now linked to Dry River.

Te Kairanga Martinborough ★→★★ One of district's largest wineries; chequered history. Now headed by new part-owner Peter Hubscher (former boss at MONTANA). Strategy is to focus on MARTINBOROUGH for only Pinot N, with other varieties drawn from elsewhere.

Te Mata Hawke's Bay ★★★→★★★★ Prestigious, long-estb winery. Fine, powerful Elston Chard; super-stylish Coleraine (Merlot/Cab Sauv/Cab Fr blend) (98' **00' 02**' 04' 05' 06'). Syrah among NZ's finest. Woodthorpe range for early drinking (v.gd Chard, Sauv Bl, Viognier, Gamay Noir, *Merlot/Cab*, Syrah/Viognier).

Te Motu Waiheke Island ★★ Top wine of Waiheke Vineyards. Concentrated mellow Cabernet/Merlot, sold when well-matured. Dunleavy 2nd label.

TerraVin Marlborough ★★ Weighty, dry, tropical-fruit-flavoured Sauv Bl, but real focus is rich, firmly structured, complex Pinot N, esp Hillside Reserve.

Te Whau ★★→★★★ Tiny Waiheke Island winery/restaurant. *Beautifully ripe, long Chard* and savoury, earthy, complex red, The Point (B'x blend).

Tohu ★→★★ Maori-owned venture with extensive v'yds. Punchy, racy Sauv Bl (Mugwi is esp powerful) and moderately complex Pinot N, both from MARLBOROUGH; full-flavoured GISBORNE Chard.

Torlesse Waipara ★→★★ Small, gd-value CANTERBURY producer of fresh, flinty Ries and firm, toasty, citrus Chard. Mid-weight Pinot N. Top range: Omihi Road.

Trinity Hill Hawke's Bay ★★→★★★★ Innovative winery with firm, concentrated reds and top-flight GIMBLETT GRAVELS Chard. Exceptional Homage Syrah – scented, muscular, dense. V. promising Tempranillo. Scented, soft, rich Pinot Gr and Viognier among NZ's best.

Two Paddocks Central Otago ★★ Actor Sam Neill produces several Pinot Ns, inc Picnic (drink-young style), First Paddock (leafy), Last Chance (warm, savoury).

Unison Hawke's Bay ★★→★★★★ Red specialist with dark, spicy, flavour-crammed blends of Merlot, Cab Sauv, Syrah. Selection label is oak-aged the longest. Also fragrant, fleshy, flavour-rich Syrah. New owners since 08.

Vavasour Marlborough ★★ Based in AWATERE VALLEY. Immaculate, intense Chard and Sauv Bl; promising Pinot N and Pinot Gr. Vavasour AWATERE VALLEY is top label; Vavasour Redwood Pass and Dashwood are regional blends (aromatic, vibrant *Sauv Bl is top value*). Linked to GOLDWATER and CLIFFORD BAY.

Vidal Hawke's Bay ★★→★★★★ Part of VILLA MARIA. Distinguished Res Chard and Res Merlot/Cab Sauv. Mid-priced Merlot/Cab Sauv is gd value. Top Syrahs (Res and Soler) outstanding. Excellent Marlborough Sauv Bl, Ries and Pinot N.

Villa Maria Auckland ★★→★★★★ NZ's largest family-owned wine company, VIDAL and ESK VALLEY. Top ranges: Reserve (express regional character) and Single Vineyard (reflect individual sites); Cellar Selection: mid tier (less oak) is often v.gd; 3rd-tier ***Private Bin wines can be excellent and gd value*** (esp Ries, Sauv Bl, Gewurz, Pinot Gr, Pinot N). Brilliant track record in competitions. Other brands: Thornbury, Northrow.

Vinoptima Gisborne ★★→★★★ Small Gewurz specialist, owned by Nick Nobilo (ex-NOBILO wines). Top vintages (04' **06'**) are full of power and personality. Also gorgeous Noble Late Harvest (04').

Voss Martinborough ★★ Small, respected producer of Pinot N (perfumed, weighty, silky); Chard (lush, creamy smooth).

Waimea Nelson ★★ One of region's top and best-value producers. Punchy, ripe, dry Sauv Bl, rich, softly textured Pinot Gr, gd Ries (Classic is honeyed, medium style). Top range: Bolitho SV. Spinyback range: DYA.

Waipara Hills Canterbury ★★ Now a brand of MUD HOUSE. Intense, ripe, racy MARLBOROUGH Sauv Bl, top-flight Waipara Ries. Equinox: top range.

Waipara Springs Canterbury ★★ Small producer of lively, cool-climate Ries, Sauv Bl, and Chard; impressive top range: Premo (inc arrestingly rich 06 Pinot N).

Wairarapa NZ's 6th largest wine region. Includes East Taratahi and Gladstone. See MARTINBOROUGH. Coolest in North Island: strength in whites and Pinot N.

Wairau River Marlborough ★★ Intense, racy Sauv Bl; full-bodied, well-rounded Pinot Gr; perfumed, softly mouth-filling Gewurz. Home Block is top label.

Wairau Valley MARLBOROUGH's largest sub-region, with most of the region's v'yds and the vast majority of its wineries. Slightly warmer than AWATERE VALLEY.

Waitaki Valley New region in N Otago. Promising Pinot N, Pinot Gr and Ries.

Wellington Capital city and official name of region; includes WAIRARAPA, Te Horo, MARTINBOROUGH.

Whitehaven Marlborough ★→★★★ Scented, v. pure and harmonious Sauv Bl is best; other whites and Pinot N: sound, easy drinking. Gallo is part-owner. Whites Bay is 2nd label.

Winegrowers of Ara Marlborough ★★ Huge vineyard, devoted to Sauv Bl and Pinot N. Top wines labelled Resolute; Composite also v.gd. Dry, minerally wines, full of interest.

Wither Hills Marlborough ★★→★★★ Large producer, owned since 2002 by Lion Nathan. Popular, crisp, gooseberry/lime Sauv Bl. Rich Chard and Pinot N; latest vintages less oak-influenced. Outstandingly intense Single V'yd Rarangi Sauv Bl since 07. Other brands: Shepherds Ridge, Two Tracks.

Wooing Tree Central Otago ★★ Young producer at Bannockburn. Rich Pinot N (Beetle Juice Pinot N less new oak).

Woollaston Nelson ★→★★★ Fast-growing producer of Pinot N, Sauv Bl, Pinot Gr and Ries, under Woollaston and Tussock brands. Ries and Pinot Gr best.

Yealands Marlborough ★→★★ Privately owned v'yd, one of NZ's biggest, in AWATERE VALLEY. First vintage 08. Top wines labelled Estate; others are regional blends. Estate Sauv Blanc: punchy, herbaceous.

South Africa

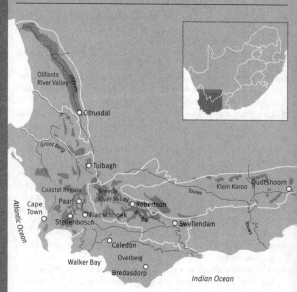

The world comes to South Africa in 2010 for one of the biggest spectacles in sport, the FIFA World Cup. The goalfest gives local wine-growers an unparalleled opportunity to show off an industry in bloom, with quality at an all-time high, exports bounding ahead, and even long-stagnant domestic demand showing signs of an upturn. Good value and variety are among the country's strongest suits. But that's not all: South Africans are also among the world leaders in sustainable wine-growing.

Leading up to kick-off, producers have been working all the angles to promote their wares. There will be an official World Cup wine range. In VIP suites, clubs and restaurants fashionable Shiraz, rosé, Sauv Bl and blended reds and whites will flow, plus stalwarts such as Cab Sauv, Merlot, Chenin Bl and Chard. The vinously intrepid may seek out rarer pleasures like Petite Sirah, Nebbiolo, Barbera and Sylvaner. And the Cinderella Pinotage will hope to attract a thousand Prince Charmings. Tables will be set, glasses polished, and an army of specially trained wine waiters will be on hand to advise the thirsty throngs. No doubt there will be many toasts to the beautiful game; and hopefully to the beautiful local wines and to arguably the world's most beautiful winelands.

Recent vintages

2009 Late, long and dry but potentially outstanding. Crisp, zingy whites and intense reds.

2008 One of the more challenging harvests in recent years but also one of the coolest, yielding ripe but elegant wines with lower than usual alcohol.

2007 Dry, largely disease-free summer. A general heatwave – soaring above 40ºC – just before picking rushed the ripening and pushed up alcohol.

2006 The fourth sound vintage in a row.

2005 Small, thick-skinned berries, concentrated reds for keeping.
2004 Above-average quality. Intense reds, esp Shiraz, Pinotage.

Vineyard practices and cellar techniques are improving each vintage: a producer's reputation is usually a better guide to wine quality than the vintage. South Africa generally experiences warm to hot summers. Most dry whites are best drunk within 2–3 years.

Adoro Wines St'bosch r w ★★★ South African stablemate of Scotch single-malts BenRiach and Glendronach. Light-textured food wines inc new Naudé Red, from far-flung coastal sites.

Alto Estate St'bosch r ★★ Historic DISTELL co-owned property on Helderberg Mountain slopes. Ageworthy CAB SAUV (00 01' 02 03 04 05).

Anthonij Rupert Wines Franschhoek r w ★★→★★★ Formerly L'Ormarins, total revamp under billionaire Johann Rupert. Impressive new 3-tier portfolio: flagship Anthonij Rupert line, mainly B'x varietal reds, CHARD Res Serruria, and white blend Nemesia. L'Ormarins range features vastly improved Optima B'x red; Italian-themed Terra del Capo line-up inc soft Sangiovese/MERLOT.

Anwilka St'bosch r ★★→★★★ New cellar and second wine, Ugaba, for partnership between KLEIN CONSTANTIA and B'x's Bruno Prats and Hubert de Boüard. Flagship Anwilka (SHIRAZ/CAB SAUV 05 06 07) sold mainly through B'x trade.

Asara Estate St'bosch r w sw ★★→★★★ 5-star hotel and winery; off-beat range includes Amarone-style PINOTAGE and new white CAB SAUV,

Ashbourne See HAMILTON RUSSELL.

Ataraxia Mountain Vineyards Walker Bay r w ★★★ Kevin Grant, ex-HAMILTON RUSSELL, flying solo to rave reviews. Penetrating, minerally CHARD among South Africa's best.

Avondale Bio-LOGIC & Organic Wines Paarl r w (sp) sw ★★→★★★ Eco-aware producer with large portfolio. Best ranges: Les Pleurs, Reserve, Green Duck.

Axe Hill Calitzdorp sw ★★★→★★★★ Outstanding tiny port-style specialist. Restrainedly opulent Cape Vintage (Touriga Nacional/Tinta Barroca/Souzão **00' 01 02'** 03' 04 05' 06); solera-aged Dry White Port from CHENIN BL.

Backsberg Estate Cellars Paarl r w (sp sw) ★★→★★★ Resurgent family enterprise with 20+ labels in 6 ranges, inc kosher and ORGANIC. New kosher MCC one of South Africa's first.

Bamboes Bay Diminutive maritime WARD in OLIFANTS RIVER region. Fryer's Cove first and still only winery, known for pyrotechnic SAUV BL.

Beaumont Wines Walker Bay r w (sw) ★★★ Rustic family home to characterful CHENIN BL, PINOTAGE, Mourvèdre, and new red "terroir blend" Vitruvian.

Bellingham r w ★→★★★ Remodelled DGB brand (estb 1947), led by flamboyant Bernard Series; above-average Legends Collection; easy-drinkers in Fusion and Blends ranges. PINOTAGE blush under construction.

Beyerskloof St'bosch r (w sp sw) ★★→★★★ Top grower/producer of PINOTAGE in Cape: 9 versions of grape on offer, inc new super-premium CAPE BLEND Faith, and CHENIN BL/PINOTAGE blush. Only B'x-style Field Blend 00 01 **02'** 03' 04 and recently added SAUV BL are PINOTAGE-free.

Biodynamic Anthroposophic mode of winegrowing practised by a small handful of local producers. Best are Reyneke and The Observatory. See also ORGANIC.

Boekenhoutskloof Winery Franschhoek r w (sw) ★★→★★★★ Consistently excellent grower/producer specializing in unfiltered, native-yeast ferments. Rich, ripe reds: spicy Syrah 01' 02' **03** 04' 05 06'; intense, minerally CAB SAUV 01' 02' 03 04' 05 06'; new B'x blend Journeyman. Also fine SEMS dry and botrytis, and gd-value second label Porcupine Ridge.

Boland Kelder Paarl r w (sw) ★→★★★ Large (21,500 tonnes), enterprising winery with two dozen labels in 5 ranges. Single V'yd SHIRAZ, No 1 RES CAB and SHIRAZ, Winemaker's Selection MERLOT are standouts.

Bon Courage Estate Robertson r w sp sw ★★→★★★ Extensive range led by improving Inkará reds, stylish MCCs, and pair of outstanding desserts (botrytis RIES and White Muscadel).

Boplaas Family Vineyards Calitzdorp r w (sp) sw ★★→★★★ Pro-environment winery best known for port-styles (esp Vintage Res 99' 01 03 04' 05' 06' and Cape Tawny). Also Family Res (unfortified) range, from cooler areas.

Boschendal Wines Paarl r w sp ★★→★★★ Famous estate (estb 1685) showing new elan under DGB ownership. Calling cards: SHIRAZ, CAB SAUV, SAUV BL and B'x/SHIRAZ blend Grand Res. Revived emphasis on bubbly seen in rosé MCC.

Bot River See WALKER BAY.

Bouchard Finlayson Hemel-en-Aarde r w ★★★ V. fine PINOT N grower. Estb labels Galpin Peak (01 02' 03 04 05 07) and barrel selection Tête de Cuvée (99 01' 03' 05' 07) now joined by Unfiltered Limited Edition 07 showing similar stellar quality. Impressive CHARDS (oaked and unwooded), and red blend Hannibal.

Breedekloof Large (12,305 ha) inland district in Breede River Valley region producing mainly bulk wine for distilling and the merchant trade. Exceptions are Bergsig, Deetlefs, Mountain Oaks, Du Preez and Merwida, with ever-improving PINOTAGE, CHARD, SEM and MCC.

Buitenverwachting Constantia r w sp ★★→★★★ Cape *grande dame*, reclining imposingly on Constantia Mountain slopes since 1796; standout SAUV BL, Husseys Vlei CHARD, restrained B'x blend Christine (**99 00 01'** 02 03), and, returning after a hiatus, botrytis dessert Noblesse.

Cabernet Sauvignon Ubiquitous grape, but truly at home on the slopes around STELLENBOSCH. Top names: DE TRAFFORD, EDGEBASTON, KANONKOP, LE RICHE, NEIL ELLIS, RUSTENBERG, Stark-Condé, THELEMA, VERGELEGEN, WATERFORD, Blue Creek; elsewhere: BOEKENHOUTSKLOOF, CEDERBERG.

Cabrière Franschhoek (r) sp ★★ Reliable NV MCC sparkling under Pierre Jourdan label (Brut Sauvage; Belle Rose). Fine PINOT N in some yrs.

Calitzdorp District in KLEIN KAROO region, climatically similar to the Douro and known for port-styles. Best: AXE HILL, BOPLAAS, DE KRANS, Peter Bayly.

Camberley Wines St'bosch r (sp) ★★→★★★ Family-run red specialist: fine SHIRAZ; impressive B'x blend Philosopher's Stone; massive, plummy PINOTAGE.

Capaia Wines Philadelphia r w ★★→★★★ German-owned hilltop winery N of DURBANVILLE employing top French and Austrian advisers for trio of B'x blends (inc new limited-release Reserve), and SAUV BL.

Cape Agulhas See ELIM.

Cape blend Somewhat nebulous category; usually a red blend with proportion of PINOTAGE. Top exponents: BEYERSKLOOF, GRAHAM BECK, GRANGEHURST, KAAPZICHT, MEINERT, RAKA, REMHOOGTE.

Cape Chamonix Wine Farm Franschhoek r w sp ★★→★★★ Rising star. V.gd PINOT N, CHARD and SAUV BL; CHARD MCC; new CAPE BLEND Armosyn van de Kaap.

Cape Point Tiny (25 ha) Atlantic-cooled district on southern tip of Cape Town's Peninsula. Mainly white varieties. Viticulturally challenging but rising to great heights in the cellars of CAPE POINT V'YDS, area's first and only winery.

Cape Point Vineyards Cape Point (r) w ★★★→★★★★ One of South Africa's most exciting producers. Complex SAUV BL/SEM blend Isliedh; outstanding minerally SEM; thrilling SAUV BLS. Trials with locally crafted amphorae, replacing imported oak casks, are promising.

Cape Winemakers Guild (CWG) Stages a benchmarking annual auction of limited, premium bottlings by 36 of South Africa's top growers.

Cederberg WARD in craggy Cederberg Mountain range. 61 ha, mainly red varieties, the highest in South Africa. Sole producer is CEDERBERG PRIVATE CELLAR.

Cederberg Private Cellar Cederberg r w ★★→★★★ Combines high-altitude minerality with intense flavour, as epitomized by SHIRAZ, CAB SAUV, SAUV BL and SEM, and Cape Atlantic SAUV BL and CHENIN BL. New Ghost Corner range (SEM and SAUV BL), from ELIM fruit, is a different take on the cool-climate genre.

Chardonnay Styles from cool and lean to warm and fleshy, with a more sensitive use of oak. ATARAXIA, BOUCHARD FINLAYSON, HAMILTON RUSSELL, CAPE CHAMONIX, GLEN CARLOU, HARTENBERG, NEWTON JOHNSON, PAUL CLUVER, RUSTENBERG, THELEMA, UVA MIRA, VERGELEGEN, WATERFORD, THE WINERY OF GOOD HOPE, JORDAN, SPRINGFIELD, DE WETSHOF, the last three also offering v.gd unwooded versions.

Chenin Blanc Rescued from long-time unfashionability, South Africa's most-planted variety in the right hands now rivals the top Loire examples. Many styles, from unwooded to heavily oaked off-dry. Brands worth trying: BEAUMONT, CEDERBERG, de Morgenzon, JEAN DANEEL, KEN FORRESTER, Old Vines, Post House, RAATS, RIJK'S, RUDERA, SPICE ROUTE, SPIER, Springfontein.

Coastal Large (32,200 ha) region inc sea-influenced districts of CAPE POINT, DARLING, Tygerberg, ST'BOSCH, Swartland and landlocked PAARL and TULBAGH.

The Company of Wine People r w (sp sw) ★→★★★ 2.5-million-case-a-yr ST'BOSCH operation with 50+ labels in a dozen tiers. Best is Kumkani, with powerful single-v'yd SAUV BL Lanner Hill and dry white VVS (Viognier/Verdelho/SAUV BL). Also well-priced easy-drinkers in expanded Arniston Bay; revamped Versus; THANDI, and Welmoed lines.

Constantia South Africa's original fine-wine growing area; home of the famous sweet Muscat-based wines of the 18th and 19th centuries, revived in recent yrs by GROOT and KLEIN CONSTANTIA. Other leading names: BUITENVERWACHTING, Constantia Glen, CONSTANTIA UITSIG, Eagles' Nest, STEENBERG.

Constantia Uitsig Constantia (r) w (sp) ★★★ Premium v'yds and tourist destination, partly black-owned. Mainly white wines, all excellent; also all-CHARD MCC sparkling, and B'x-style Constantia Red.

Dalla Cia Wine & Spirit Company St'bosch r w ★★→★★★ Italian-owned and toned wine cellar, grappa-style distillery and restaurant. New varietal CAB SAUV joins B'x blend Giorgio; lightly oaked CHARD; SAUV BL.

Danie de Wet See DE WETSHOF.

Darling Coastal district (2,700 ha) around eponymous W Coast town; best v'yds in hilly Groenekloof WARD. Top producers: Cloof, GROOTE POST and Ormonde. Much of fruit transported out of appellation to appear under variety of labels.

David Frost Estate Paarl r (w) ★→★★★ South African golfing legend's increasingly respected small range of reds now partnered by gd-value Signature Series, made in conjunction with nearby Perdeberg Winery.

De Grendel Wines Durbanville r w ★★★ Cool sites facing Table Bay on Sir David Graaff's hillside property yield brisk, layered SAUV BL, fine-grained MERLOT, and perfumed PINOT N.

De Krans Calitzdorp r w sw ★★→★★★ Old family-run Karoo v'yds make rich, impressive port-styles (esp Vintage Res 99 01 02 03' 04' 05' 06'). Tasty, value SHIRAZ and SAUV BL under new cool-climate-sourced Garden Route label.

Delaire Winery St'bosch r w ★★★ Makeover nearing completion at spectacular eyrie on Helshoogte Pass, owned by international jeweller Laurence Graff. New-look line-up comprises B'x/SHIRAZ blend, CHARD and SAUV BL.

Delheim St'bosch r w sw ★★→★★★ Eco-minded family winery. Acclaimed Vera Cruz SHIRAZ; plummy Grand Res Cab (00 01 03 04' 05). Also CHARD Sur Lie and botrytis Edelspatz, from single-v'yd RIES.

De Toren Private Cellar St'bosch r ★★★ Consistently fine, flavourful B'x blend Fusion V 01 02 03' 04 05' 06' and earlier-maturing MERLOT-based blend "Z".

Mixing it up: top red and white blends
Red: AA Badenhorst Family Wines, ANWILKA, BUITENVERWACHTING, DE TOREN, DE TRAFFORD, ERNIE ELS, JORDAN, KANONKOP, MEERLUST, MORGENSTER, RAKA, RUSTENBERG, SADIE FAMILY/SEQUILLO, SARONSBERG, TOKARA, VERGELEGEN, VILAFONTÉ, WATERFORD.
White: ANTHONIJ RUPERT, Black Oystercatcher, CAPE POINT VINEYARDS, CONSTANTIA UITSIG, DE GRENDEL, DORNIER, FLAGSTONE, Hermanuspietersfontein, KLEIN CONSTANTIA, Kumkani/THE COMPANY OF WINE PEOPLE, Lammershoek, Miles Mossop, NEDERBURG, Oak Valley, QUOIN ROCK, SADIE FAMILY/Sequillo, SOLMS-DELTA, STEENBERG, Sterhuis, TOKARA, VERGELEGEN.

De Trafford Wines St'bosch r w sw ★★★★ Exceptional boutique grower David Trafford has international reputation, and knack, for bold but elegant wines. Brilliant B'x/SHIRAZ blend Elevation 393 (00 01 03' 04 05 06); CAB SAUV (00 01 03' 04 05 06). Also cellar-worthy SHIRAZ, PINOT N, MERLOT, CHENIN BL, and Vin de Paille-style CHENIN BL. B'x blend "Plan B" is new 2nd label.

DeWaal Wines r w ★★→★★★ HQ at Uiterwyk, stately family residence nr STELLENBOSCH. PINOTAGE a forte: Top of the Hill among South Africa's best, from 60+-yr-old vines. New B'x red has replaced CAPE BLEND.

De Wetshof Estate Robertson (r) w (sw) ★★ Famed CHARD pioneer, still exponent; toasty Bateleur, Bon Vallon (South Africa's first unwooded version) and Limestone Hill (newly repackaged Danie de Wet label). Promising PINOT N.

DGB Well-established Wellington-based producer/wholesaler; brands include BOSCHENDAL, BELLINGHAM, and Douglas Green.

Diemersdal Estate Durbanville r w (sw) ★★→★★★ Family firm with dynamic younger generation. V.gd B'x red and SAUV BL in M M Louw range; single-v'yd SAUV BL; CHARD Res. Exciting West Coast joint venture, Sir Lambert SAUV BL.

Diemersfontein Wines Wellington r (w) ★★ Flagship Carpe Diem range noted for full-throttle PINOTAGE; also equally unretiring CHENIN BL.

Distell South Africa's biggest drinks company, headquartered in STELLENBOSCH. Owns many brands, spanning quality scales. Also interests in various top STELLENBOSCH wineries, inc ALTO, NEETHLINGSHOF, and STELLENZICHT.

Dornier Wines St'bosch r w ★★→★★★ Architectural showpiece in a sylvan setting. Stylish flagships under Donatus label; gd-value Cocoa Hill range; new ripe-style CHENIN BL in mid-tier Dornier line-up.

Durbanville Cool, hilly WARD extending over 1,500 ha and known for pungent, characteristically "dusty" SAUV BL, and for MERLOT. Bloemendal, DE GRENDEL, DIEMERSDAL, DURBANVILLE HILLS, Hillcrest and NITIDA worth seeking out.

Durbanville Hills Durbanville r w ★★→★★★ Maritime-cooled v'yds co-owned by DISTELL. Best is eponymous range (esp Caapmans CAB SAUV/MERLOT, SAUV BL); Rhinofields Res range with gd CHARD, also Inner and Outer Valley SAUV BLS.

Edgebaston St'bosch r w ★★→★★★ Finlayson family (of GLEN CARLOU fame). V.gd GS CAB SAUV; CHARD; lightly oaked SAUV BL; spicy Pepper Pot red.

Elgin Cool upland WARD east of Cape Town; burgeoning corps of vintners; winemaker Ross Gower and viticulturist Paul Wallace with eponymous labels; PAUL CLUVER, Oak Valley, Iona, Catherine Marshall, and Elgin Vintners.

Elim Sea-breezy WARD (142 ha) in southernmost district, Cape Agulhas. Mainly SAUV BL and SHIRAZ. Aromatic, elegant wines from Black Oystercatcher, Lomond, The Berrio, Strandveld and Zoetendal.

Ernie Els Wines St'bosch r ★★★→★★★★ South African golfer's joint venture with Jean Engelbrecht (RUST EN VREDE). Rich, aromatic B'x blend Ernie Els (01 02' 03 04' 05 06) among Cape's priciest wines. Also gd Engelbrecht-Els Proprietor's

Blend. V.gd Guardian Peak range inc SMG (Syrah/Mourvèdre/Grenache), and new Tannat/Malbec.

Estate Wine Official term for wines grown, made, and bottled on "units registered for the production of estate wine". Not a quality designation.

Fairview Paarl r w sw ★★→★★★★ Dynamic, export-savvy, innovative proprietor Charles Back. South Africa's first varietal bottling of Petite Sirah. Also under Fairview label, a top range of singe-v'yd and "terroir-specific" wines, led by flagship Cyril Back (SHIRAZ). Plus kaleidoscope of blends and varietals, all open, generous, ready-to-drink. Also successful with Goats do Roam – taunting, gimmicky labels that usually over-deliver. See also SPICE ROUTE.

FirstCape Vineyards r w ★★ A South African export success. Joint venture of NEWTON JOHNSON, Brand Phoenix in UK, and 5 local co-ops; HQ at Simondium nr PAARL. V.gd price/quality in 5 ranges, inc new Millstone collection.

Flagstone Winery Somerset West r w ★★→★★★★ Hotbed of innovation, owned by Constellation. Founder and prime mover Bruce Jack retains winemaking control. Two dozen cheerfully idiosyncratic labels. Grapes sourced from many v'yds. Best: Mary Le Bow B'x/SHIRAZ. Dark Horse SHIRAZ; Longitude red blend: Free Run SAUV BL. Collaboration with Riebeek Cellars, The Springtree Wine Co, aims to catapult Fish Hoek brand into international big leagues.

Franschhoek Well-heeled French Huguenot-founded WARD in Paarl district. 1,200 ha, mainly SAUV BL, CAB SAUV and CHARD. Many wineries (and restaurants) notable are ANTHONIJ RUPERT, BOEKENHOUTSKLOOF, CABRIÈRE, CAPE CHAMONIX, GRAHAM BECK, LA MOTTE, Mõrīsōn, SOLMS-DELTA and Stony Brook.

Fleur du Cap r w sw ★★→★★★★ DISTELL premium label; includes v.gd Unfiltered Collection (CAB SAUV, CHARD, SAUV BL and Viognier limited releases). Also plush new B'x blend Laszlo, racy botrytis RIES and new ORGANIC range.

The Foundry St'bosch r w ★★★ MEERLUST winemaker Chris Williams' small-scale production, buying in site-specific parcels for outstanding Syrah and Viognier.

Gilga Wines St'bosch r ★★→★★★★ Boutique label; intense Syrah; floral SHIRAZ-based blend Amurabi.

Glen Carlou Paarl r w ★★→★★★★ First-rate winery, v'yds, fine art gallery and restaurant, owned by Donald Hess. Standout, spicy Syrah 02 03 04' 05 06; *fine B'x blend Grand Classique* (00 01 02 03 04 05) and full-bodied PINOT N. The Welder, a Natural Sweet from CHENIN BL, debuted recently.

Graham Beck Wines Robertson/Franschhoek r w sp (sw) ★★→★★★★ Avant-garde properties of mining tycoon Graham Beck, making classy MCC sparkling inc new prestige *cuvée* from PINOT N/CHARD, named in memory of oldest Beck son Clive. Also outstanding The Ridge Syrah; Coffeestone CAB SAUV; The William CAPE BLEND; Pheasants' Run SAUV BL.

Grangehurst Winery St'bosch r ★★→★★★ Small, top red specialist, mostly buying in grapes. Cape blend Nikela (98 99 00 01 02); v.gd PINOTAGE (97 98 **99** 01 02); concentrated CAB SAUV/MERLOT; SHIRAZ/CAB SAUV.

Groot Constantia Constantia r w (sp sw) ★→★★ Historic estate nr Cape Town. Legendary red and white Muscat desserts in early 19th century; Grand Constance revives tradition. V.gd PINOTAGE in standard range B'x blend Reserve, new SEM, and CHARD under Gouverneurs label.

Groote Post Vineyards Darling r w (sp sw) ★★→★★★★ Ocean-facing property of the Pentz family. V.gd CHARDS and SAUV BL Res, juicy PINOT N. Blush MCC from MERLOT (NV), and botrytis CHARD are recent additions.

Guardian Peak See ERNIE ELS.

Hamilton Russell Vineyards (HRV) Walker Bay r w ★★★★ Cape's Burgundian-style specialist estate at Hermanus. Fine PINOT N **01' 03' 04** 05 06 07; classy CHARD 03 04 05' **06 07**. Small yields, French-inspired vinification, careful barrelling. Also gd SAUV BLS, PINOTAGES under Southern Right and Ashbourne labels.

Hartenberg Estate St'bosch r w ★★★★ Cape front-ranker. Trio of outstanding SHIRAZES: always serious SHIRAZ 01 02 03 04' 05 flagship single-site The Stork 03 04' 05 and Gravel Hill, now available commercially; fine MERLOTS inc new Snuffbox; The McKenzie B'x blend; award-winning CHARDS; top is The Eleanor.

Havana Hills Philadelphia r w ★★→★★★ Hilltop winery north of DURBANVILLE. Flagship is B'x blend Kobus. Well-structured, fruity reds in Du Plessis range.

Hemel-en-Aarde Valley Celebrated cool-climate WARD (82 ha) in Walker Bay district. Produces some of South Africa's finest PINOT N, CHARD and SAUV BL. BOUCHARD FINLAYSON and HAMILTON RUSSELL are top names. Sister appellation is Upper Hemel-en-Aarde.

Ingwe St'bosch r w ★→★★★★ Alain Moueix (see France) among early 90s French investors; elegant MERLOT-based blend Ingwe.

J C le Roux St'bosch sp ★★ South Africa's largest sparkling-wine house, DISTELL owned. Best are PINOT N, Scintilla (CHARD/PINOT N), and PINOT N Rosé, all MCC.

Jean Daneel Wines Napier r w (sp) ★★★ Outstanding Signature Series, esp *Chenin Bls*, CAB SAUV/MERLOT/SHIRAZ, CHARD MCC sparkling.

Jordan Estate St'bosch r w ★★→★★★ Consistency, quality and value, from entry-level Bradgate and Chameleon lines to immaculate CWG Auction bottlings. Flagship CHARD Nine Yards; B'x blend Cobblers Hill (00 01 03 04' 05); CAB SAUV; MERLOT; SAUV BL; and RIES botrytis dessert.

J P Bredell Wines St'bosch r (w) sw ★★→★★★ Best known for port-styles, esp plushy Cape Vintage Res 97 98 00 01 03; excellent Late Bottled Vintage, and new Cape Tawny.

Kaapzicht Estate St'bosch r w (sw) ★★★ Family-run red wine specialist. Concentrated Vision CAPE BLEND 00 01' 02' 03' 04 05 06' and PINOTAGE under Steytler banner.

Kanonkop Estate St'bosch r ★★→★★★★ Grand local status past 3 decades, mainly with oak-polished PINOTAGE 01 02 03' 04 05 06 and, with a fanatical following, B'x blend Paul Sauer 00 01 02 03 04' 05, plus CAB SAUV. Second label is CAPE BLEND Kadette. New art gallery a hit with visitors.

Kanu Wines St'bosch r w sw ★★→★★★ Reputation for barrel-aged CHENIN BL; also v. gd B'x red Keystone, SHIRAZ, and botrytis CHENIN BL Kia-Ora.

Ken Forrester Wines St'bosch r w sw ★★→★★★ Vintner/restaurateur Ken Forrester and wine-grower Martin MEINERT collaboration. Benchmark CHENIN BL in Ken Forrester range; also outstanding, luscious off-dry FMC version, from old bush vines. Hearty but fine Grenache/SHIRAZ/Mourvèdre Gypsy. Sumptuous botrytis CHENIN BL named "T".

Klein Constantia Estate Constantia r w (sp) sw ★★→★★★ From 1986, with luscious (non-botrytis) Vin de Constance 99 00' 01 02' 04 05, re-created legendary 18th-century Muscat dessert. Current line-up inc elegant SEM/SAUV Mme Marlbrook, ageworthy RIES, classy new Brut MCC. Estate increasingly focusing on VdC and SAUV BL. See also ANWILKA.

Kleine Zalze Wines St'bosch r w ★★→★★★ CAB SAUV and SHIRAZ head v.gd Family Res and V'yd Selection reds; oaked and unwooded CHENIN BL and CHARD.

Klein Karoo Inland semi-arid region with 2,800 ha under vine. Best quality in CALITZDORP district and Tradouw WARD (Joubert-Tradauw Private Cellar). Cool, high-altitude WARDS of Outeniqua (Herold Wines) and Upper Langkloof (The Goose Wines) show potential.

Kosher Growing category. BACKSBERG, Kleine Draken, Rose Garden, Tempel.

Krone sp ★★★ Fine, elegant brut MCCS, inc Borealis, Rosé, and new prestige *cuvée* Nicolas Charles Krone, from CHARD/PINOT N, by Twee Jonge Gezellen Estate.

Kumala r w Hugely successful Constellation-owned export label undergoing quality boost under aegis of Bruce Jack, of sister brand FLAGSTONE.

KWV Paarl r w (sp) sw ★→★★★ Formerly the national wine co-op and controlling

---

Ten wineries to visit

Anthonij Rupert Wines, Franschhoek. Superb collection of automobiles.

Constantia Uitsig, Constantia. Luxury hotel, spa and restaurants.

Delheim, Stellenbosch. Garden restaurant, picnic area, Simonsberg Mountain conservancy.

Fairview, Paarl. Restaurant, wine and cheese tastings in winelands' buzziest visitor centre.

Groot Constantia, Constantia. Historic estate (1685) museum, guided tours, themed tastings.

Hazendal, Stellenbosch. Museum of Russian art and culture, restaurant.

Rust en Vrede/Guardian Peak, Stellenbosch. Fine dining, exceptional mountain views.

Solms-Delta, Franschhoek. Cultural museum, archaeological sites, restaurant and picnics.

Spier, Stellenbosch. Accommodation, restaurants, picnics, cheetah conservation project, and much more.

Vergelegen, Stellenbosch. Homestead tour, restaurant, camphor forest picnics. Trenchant winemaker a tourist attraction in own right.

---

body, today a listed, partly black-owned group. Top ranges are Cathedral Cellar, Laborie, KWV Res, and new KWV Mentors. B'x/SHIRAZ blend Roodeberg, a Cape institution, now has white namesake; also vast range of reds, whites, sparkling, port-styles, and fortified desserts.

Lamberts Bay Recent standalone West Coast WARD (20 ha) closeby Atlantic. Mostly SAUV BL; Sir Lambert, local joint venture with DIEMERSDAL, a cracker.

La Motte Franschhoek r w ★★→★★★★ Increasingly ORGANIC venture by the Ruperts, a leading Cape wine family. Fine, distinctive SHIRAZ/Viognier. Organically grown SAUV BL and new SHIRAZ/Grenache. Also excellent B'x-style red Millennium, stylish SHIRAZ.

Lanzerac Wines St'bosch r w ★★ Venerable property (inc luxury hotel) owned by banking/retailing magnate Christo Wiese. PINOTAGE remains speciality, esp Pioneer (previously "Reserve") bottling. Sister farm to LOURENSFORD.

L'Avenir Vineyards St'bosch r w (sp sw) ★★→★★★ Historic focus on PINOTAGE and CHENIN BL continues under owner Michel Laroche of Chablis. Portfolio now features lightly wooded Grand Vin CHENIN BL and MCC Brut Rosé in Icon range.

Le Riche Wines St'bosch r (w) ★★★ Fine CAB SAUV-based boutique wines, hand-crafted by respected Etienne le Riche and family. Recently a Sangiovese/CAB SAUV blend Pensiero.

L'Ormarins Private Cellar See ANTHONIJ RUPERT.

Lourensford St'bosch r w ★★ Vast v'yds, winery/tourism project owned by Christo Wiese (LANZERAC). Best bottlings: Viognier, SEM botrytis dessert, flagship CAB SAUV/SHIRAZ blend Seventeen Hundred, new Syrah. Eden Crest and Five Heirs are entry-level labels.

Lower Orange Standalone inland "super WARD" (12,700 ha) following contours of the Gariep (Orange) River; hot, dry, dependent on irrigation; overwhelmingly white-wine territory; major winery is Oranjerivier Wine Cellars.

Meerlust Estate St'bosch r w ★★★ Prestigious v'yds and cellar, probably South Africa's best-known quality red label, still in the control of the Myburgh family after 250 yrs. Hallmark elegance and restraint in flagship Rubicon 97 98 99 00 01' 03' 04, one of Cape's first B'x blends; also excellent MERLOT and occasional CAB SAUV; individual CHARD and PINOT N.

Meinert Wines St'bosch r ★★★ Small-scale producer/consultant Martin Meinert makes 2 fine blends, Devon Crest (B'x) and Synchronicity (B'x/PINOTAGE), and

MERLOT from Devon Valley v'yds. New SAUV BL from ELGIN and DARLING fruit.

Merlot Temperamental and site-specific, thus seldom rises to great heights. Amani, Bein, DE GRENDEL, HARTENBERG, Hillcrest, JORDAN, Laibach, QUOIN ROCK, RAKA, STEENBERG, THELEMA and VEENWOUDEN are consistent performers.

Méthode Cap Classique (MCC) South African term for classic-method sparkling wine. Ambeloui, BON COURAGE, BOSCHENDAL, CABRIÈRE, Colmant, CONSTANTIA UITSIG, GRAHAM BECK, JC LE ROUX, KLEIN CONSTANTIA, KRONE, Silverthorn, SIMONSIG, *Tanzanite*, VILLIERA and WELTEVREDE have real style.

Morgenhof Estate St'bosch r w (sp) sw ★→★★★ Old property (1692) revitalized by Anne Cointreau (of Cognac/liqueur family). Reputation for MERLOT, B'x red The Morgenhof Estate (previously "Première Sélection") and CHENIN BL. Gd everyday Fantail range.

Morgenster Estate St'bosch r ★★★ Immaculate Italian-owned wine and olive farm, Pierre Lurton of Cheval Blanc consulting. Classically styled B'x blend Morgenster 00 01 03 04 05', similarly restrained 2nd label Lourens River Valley. Nabucco (Nebbiolo) and Tosca (mainly Sangiovese/CAB SAUV) in new Italian Collection have style and character.

Mulderbosch Vineyards St'bosch r w (sw) ★★★ Mike Dobrovic's individualistic offerings inc SAUV BLS, just-dry and botrytis; wood-fermented CHARDS; oak-brushed CHENIN BL, Steen op Hout; and affable B'x-style blend Faithful Hound.

Mvemve Raats St'bosch r ★★★ Partnership between Mzokhona Mvemve, first university-qualified black winemaker, and Bruwer Raats. Complex B'x blend De Compostella. Promising Sagila range, by Mvemve working solo.

Nederburg Wines Paarl r w sw sp s/sw ★→★★★ Among South Africa's biggest (1 million+ cases per annum) and best-known brands, owned by DISTELL, restored to form. Stages annual wine event, the Nederburg Auction. Superb new Ingenuity Red and White 07'; excellent Manor House label (esp CAB and new CHARD); reliable Winemaster's Reserves (previously "Classic Range") inc Edelrood and Baronne reds. Also inexpensive quaffers in Foundation (previously "Lifestyle") segment. Small quantities of v.gd Private Bins for auction, inc reputed CHENIN BL botrytis Edelkeur 02 03' **04' 05** 06 07'.

Neethlingshof Estate St'bosch r w sw ★★ Tourist magnet CO-owned by DISTELL. Best in flagship Lord Neethling range (esp botrytis RIES); v.gd floral Gewurz.

Neil Ellis Wines St'bosch r w ★★★ Veteran winemaker Neil Ellis sources cooler-climate parcels for site expression. Top V'yd Selection CAB SAUV **00'** 01 03 04' 05 06, Syrah, and oak-fermented SAUV BL. Premium range inc v.gd CAB SAUV, PINOTAGE, SHIRAZ, SAUV BL, and CHARDS from ST'BOSCH and ELGIN.

Newton Johnson Wines Upper Hemel-en-Aarde r w ★★→★★★ Cellar and restaurant with breathtaking view. One of few v.gd Cape PINOT NS; *outstanding Chard; intense Sauv Bl*; peppery SHIRAZ/Mourvèdre; food-style rosé and new SAUV BL/SEM blend. See also FIRSTCAPE.

Nitida Cellars Durbanville r w ★★→★★★ Expanding v.gd range from sea-cooled v'yds; fresh, vital SAUV BLS and SEM. Also gd CAB SAUV, B'x-style red Calligraphy, elegant SAUV BL/SEM blend Coronata, new intense botrytis SEM.

Olifants River West Coast region. Warm valley floors, conducive to ORGANIC cultivation, and cooler, fine-wine-favouring sites in the mountain WARD of Piekenierskloof and, nr the Atlantic, BAMBOES BAY and Koekenaap.

Organic Quality variable but producers with track records include AVONDALE, BACKSBERG, Bon Cap, Goedvertrouw, Laibach, Mountain Oaks, Stellar, Tukulu, TULBAGH Mountain Vineyards, Upland, and Waverley. See also BIODYNAMIC.

Outeniqua See KLEIN KAROO.

Overgaauw Estate St'bosch r w ★★→★★★ Van Velden family team, now led by scion David. Dependable, classic style B'x blend Tria Corda: CAB SAUV; Cape's only bottling of Sylvaner. Everyday fare in Shepherd's Cottage line.

Paarl Town and demarcated wine region ±50 km NE of Cape Town. 16,000 ha. Diverse styles and approaches; best results with Mediterranean varieties (r and w), CAB SAUV. Leading producers: AVONDALE, BACKSBERG, BOLAND KELDER, BOSCHENDAL, DIEMERSFONTEIN, FAIRVIEW, GLEN CARLOU, KMV, NEDERBURG, PLAISIR DE MERLE, RUPERT & ROTHSCHILD, Schalk Burger, VEENWOUDEN, VILAFONTÉ.

Paul Cluver Wines Elgin r w sw ★★→★★★ Appellation's leading winery, on scenic De Rust estate; convincing PINOT N, esp new Seven Flags res; elegant CHARD, always gorgeous Gewurz and botrytis RIES 03' 04 05' 06' 07; unique forest amphitheatre for summer concerts.

Pinotage A 1920s cross between PINOT N and Cinsault (aka Hermitage), South Africa's "own" red grape can be sharp, astringent and a tad wild, but in sympathetic hands becomes accessible, harmonious, even profound. ASHBOURNE, BEYERSKLOOF, DEWAAL, DIEMERSFONTEIN, FAIRVIEW, GROOT CONSTANTIA, KANONKOP, L'AVENIR, Perdeberg, Scali, SIMONSIG, Springfontein.

Pinot Noir Inspires a passion inversely proportionate to its less than 1% share of the national v'yd. BOUCHARD FINLAYSON, CAPE CHAMONIX, Catherine Marshall, DE GRENDEL, DE TRAFFORD, GLEN CARLOU, HAMILTON RUSSELL, MEERLUST, NEWTON JOHNSON, Oak Valley, PAUL CLUVER, Shannon, VRIESENHOF.

Plaisir de Merle Paarl r w ★★★ Imposing DISTELL-owned cellar and v'yds. Much improved range headlined by outstanding Cab Fr 03' 04 05 06, Grand Plaisir B'x/SHIRAZ blend. Other reds and SAUV BL also excellent.

Pongràcz sp ★★ DISTELL-owned MCC brand; vintaged Desiderius and popular NV Pongràcz.

Quoin Rock Winery St'bosch r w (sw) ★★→★★★ Classically styled wines, some featuring grapes from southerly Cape Agulhas v'yds. Picks are elegant Syrah, MERLOT, white flagship Oculus, and new perfumed SAUV BL The Nicobar. Second label is Glenhurst.

Raats Family Wines St'bosch r w ★★★ Acclaimed, minerally Cab Franc, and two pure-fruited CHENIN BLS, oaked and unoaked, both worth keeping a few yrs.

Raka Klein River r w ★★→★★★ Run by seafaring Dryer family; powerful, personality-packed wines, inc Biography SHIRAZ, Figurehead CAPE BLEND, MERLOT and SAUV BL.

Remhoogte Estate St'bosch r w ★★→★★★ Boustred family partnered by international consultant Michel Rolland; trio of classically styled CAPE BLENDS: Bonne Nouvelle, Estate Blend and Aigle Noir.

Riesling Aficionados of the great German grape may continue to hope for a local revival, but a steadily contracting area under vine (to just 0.2% of total) tells its own story. BUITENVERWACHTING, DE WETSHOF, Jack & Knox, HARTENBERG, KLEIN CONSTANTIA, NEDERBURG, PAUL CLUVER and THELEMA keep the faith.

Rijk's Private Cellar Tulbagh r w ★★→★★★ Depth, intensity are hallmarks of this small-scale winery and country hotel. Recent emphasis on blends, though varietal bottlings such as CAB SAUV, SHIRAZ, PINOTAGE and new CHENIN BL Res remain as pillars of the offering.

Robertson District Low-rainfall inland valley; 13,400 ha; lime soils; historically gd CHARD, dessert styles (notably Muscat); more recently SAUV BL, SHIRAZ, CAB SAUV; proliferation of family-run boutiques (best include Quando, Arendsig); condusive climate for ORGANIC production (eg Bon Cap). Major cellars: BON COURAGE, DE WETSHOF, GRAHAM BECK, Rietvallei, ROBERTSON WINERY, Rooiberg, SPRINGFIELD, WELTEVREDE, Zandvliet.

Robertson Winery Robertson r w sw ★→★★ Gd value from co-op-scale winery. Best is No. 1 Constitution Rd SHIRAZ; also v.gd Vineyard Selection range: SHIRAZ, PINOTAGE, and CHARD. RIES Noble Late Harvest can be superb.

Rudera Wines St'bosch r w (sw) ★★★ New owners, new winemaker, big plans (own cellar, visitor facilities, v'yds) for winery hailed for consistently excellent

CHENIN BL (dry/semi-dry and botrytis), CAB SAUV, Syrah. New 2nd label Lula. Co-founder Teddy Hall now solo.

Rupert & Rothschild Vignerons r w ★★★ Top v'yds, cellar at Simondium nr PAARL. Joint owned by the Rothschilds and the Ruperts, two old French and South African wine families. Impressive B'x blend Baron Edmond 98 **00** 01 03' 04; CHARD Baroness Nadine is a deep-flavoured classic.

Rustenberg Wines St'bosch r w (sw) ★★★→★★★★ Prestigious family winery. Flagship is single-v'yd CAB SAUV Peter Barlow 99' 01' 03 04 05. Outstanding B'x blend John X Merriman; savoury Syrah; *single-v'yd Chard Five Soldiers*. MERLOT-based Red and Rhône-style White on the cards. 2nd label Brampton.

Rust en Vrede Estate St'bosch r ★★★ Revival underway thanks to owner Jean Engelbrecht (ERNIE ELS partner) and ex-DISTELL winemaker Coenie Snyman. Strong, individual offering now features pricey single-v'yd Syrah, and limited-release SHIRAZ/CAB SAUV blend "1694". Critically acclaimed new restaurant.

Sadie Family Swartland r w ★★★★ Organically grown, traditionally-made Columella (SHIRAZ/Mourvèdre) 01 02' **03** 04 05' 06 a Cape benchmark. Complex, intriguing CHENIN BL-based white Palladius. Star winemaker Eben Sadie also grows the rated Sequillo Red and White with Cornel Spies.

Saronsberg Cellar Tulbagh r w ★★→★★★ Growing following for Rhône varieties and blends, inc SHIRAZ and Viognier-seasoned Full Circle. Detour into B'x territory via red blend Rooi, in jazzily packaged Provenance range.

Sauvignon Blanc Plantings barely meet demand for South Africa's white grape du jour. Breakneck development, esp in ELGIN and WALKER BAY, sees a new generation: Benguela Cove, Constantia Glen, Creation, Crystallum, Domaine des Dieux, Elgin Heights, Herold, Highlands Road, La Vierge, Lomond, Nomada, Shannon, Sir Lambert, South Hill.

Saxenburg St'bosch r w (sp sw) ★★→★★★ Swiss-owned v'yds and winery jointly run with French Ch Capion. Roundly oaked reds, SAUV BL and CHARD in high-end Private Collection; flagship SHIRAZ Select 98 **00 01** 02 03'; well-flavoured easy-drinkers in Guinea Fowl range.

Semillon Enjoying renewed interest in blends. Likes of BOEKENHOUTSKLOOF, CAPE POINT VINEYARDS, CONSTANTIA UITSIG, Eikendal, FAIRVIEW, Landau du Val, NITIDA, RIJK'S, STEENBERG and STELLENZICHT still offer varietal bottlings worth sampling.

Ses'Fikile Somerset West r w ★★ Front-ranker among Cape's new black-controlled wine ventures; all-woman business in partnership with FLAGSTONE.

Shiraz Wins plaudits both as standalone and in blends. Top varietal bottlings (sometimes as "Syrah"): BOEKENHOUTSKLOOF, BON COURAGE, CEDERBERG, DE TRAFFORD, FAIRVIEW, GLEN CARLOU, GRAHAM BECK, HARTENBERG, Luddite, QUOIN ROCK, SADIE FAMILY, SARONSBERG, SIMONSIG, STELLENZICHT, WATERFORD.

Signal Hill Cape Town r w sw ★★→★★★ French flair in lively range; widely sourced grapes inc tiny parcels in/around Cape Town city-centre. SHIRAZ, Malbec, Petit Verdot, Furmint (in Tokaji lookalike Mathilde Aszú) and PINOTAGE all feature; several ageworthy desserts.

Simonsig Estate St'bosch r w sp sw ★★→★★★ Consistency and value among hallmarks of Malan family winery. Extensive but serious top end inc B'x blend Tiara, decorated Merindol Syrah 01' 02 03 04 05, Red Hill PINOTAGE 01 02 03' 04 05 06', CHENIN BL. First (30 yrs ago) with a *mcc*, *Kaapse Vonkel*, from CHARD/PINOT N; portfolio since expanded to 5 bubblies.

Solms-Delta Franschhoek r w ★★→★★★ Neuroscientist Mark Solms and veteran winemaker Hilko Hegewisch make intriguing and intelligent wines; best inc Amarone-style SHIRAZ Africana, sophisticated dry Rosé Lekkerwijn, scented RIES blend Koloni, new Cape Jazz series pétillant SHIRAZ, Rosé and White.

Southern Right See HAMILTON RUSSELL.

Spice Route Winery Swartland r w ★★★ Charles Back (FAIRVIEW)-owned cellar;

Rhône-style reds, esp new spicy Chakalaka blend; also scented Viognier. Non-Rhône offerings inc v.gd old-vines CHENIN BL and classy PINOTAGE.

Spier Wines St'bosch r w ★★→★★★ A serious player (500,000+ cases per annum), notably Spier and Savanha, each with tiers of quality. Most excitement in Spier's Private Collection and Vintage Selection ranges.

Springfield Estate Robertson r w ★★★ Cult wines, traditionally vinified, oozing personality. Exceptional softer-style CAB SAUV; B'x red Work of Time; opulent Méthode Ancienne CHARD; unwooded Wild Yeast CHARD; consistent SAUV BLS labelled Special Cuvée and Life From Stone.

The Stables Estate r w (sp) ★→★★ KwaZulu-Natal's first registered wine estate, family run, welcoming; mix of KwaZulu-Natal and Western Cape v'yds.

Steenberg Vineyards Constantia r w (sp) ★★★→★★★★ Top winery and v'yds, known for arresting SAUV BLS and SAUV BL/SEM mix Magna Carta. Reds inc fine Nebbiolo. Bubbly range recently expanded with PINOT N MCC.

Stellenbosch (St'bosch) Oak-shaded university town and demarcated wine district 50 km east of Cape Town. Heart of the wine industry – the Napa of the Cape. Many top estates, esp for reds, tucked into mountain valleys and foothills; extensive wine routes and increasing number of fine restaurants.

Stellenzicht Vineyards St'bosch r w ★★ DISTELL co-owned Helderberg winery and v'yds; excellent, sturdy Syrah; v.gd barrelled SEM Res; and, in Cellarmaster's Release range, CAB SAUV and new PINOTAGE and SHIRAZ.

Stormhoek r w ★★ UK/South African partnership, growth fuelled by clever use of the internet. Expanded range inc Couture Rosé, served on the rocks.

Thandi Wines St'bosch r w ★→★★ Black empowerment venture until recently under the COMPANY OF WINE PEOPLE aegis. Now provides shareholding/land ownership for over 240 farmworker families. Best: Cab Sauv, PINOT N, CHARD.

Thelema Mountain Vineyards St'bosch r w (sw) ★★★→★★★★ Pioneer of South Africa's modern wine revival. Top labels: CAB SAUV 00' 03 04 05 06; The Mint CAB SAUV 05 06'; MERLOT Res; SHIRAZ; CHARD; SAUV BL. Expansion of Sutherland range in ELGIN with new B'x-style red, Rhône-style red and white, and PINOT N.

Tokara St'bosch r w (sw) ★★★ Showcase cellar and v'yds. Best: CAB SAUV-based Red and SAUV BL/SEM White; elegant CHARDS and SAUV BLS, one each from young ELGIN vines. *Entry-level range Zondernaam* puts many top-tier labels to shame. Gd restaurant. Winemaker Miles Mossop's own label shows pedigree.

Tulbagh Inland district historically associated with white wine and bubbly, now also known for beefy reds, some sweeter styles and ORGANIC. 1,500 ha. Blue Crane, KRONE, RIJK'S, SARONSBERG, Tulbagh Mountain Vineyards, Waverley.

Twee Jonge Gezellen See KRONE.

Uva Mira Vineyards St'bosch r w ★★→★★★★ Lofty Helderberg sites yielding v.gd V'yd Selection CHARD and B'x/SHIRAZ Red Blend; v. fine SHIRAZ and SAUV BL.

Wineries to watch in 2010

AA Badenhorst Family Wines, Swartland. Unpretentious and downright delicious Rhône-style wines by Adi Badenhorst, ex-RUSTENBERG.

Creation Wines, Walker Bay. Auspicious site, cool climate, trendy varieties and the latest technology. Prepare to be exhilarated.

Mullineux Family Wines, Swartland. Chris and Andrea Mullineux, previously TULBAGH based, raise their game with a blended white, Syrah, and ambrosial Straw Wine.

Teddy Hall Wines, St'bosch. RUDERA co-founder and serially awarded CHENIN BL specialist Teddy Hall vinifying solo.

Shannon Vineyards, Elgin. SAUV BL, Viognier, PINOT N and MERLOT to match an exquisite location.

Veenwouden Private Cellar Paarl r (w) ★★→★★★★ Range recently revamped, but MERLOT and B'x-style red Classic remain first choices. New red and white blends in 2nd label Thornhill.

Vergelegen Somerset West r w (sw) ★★→★★★★ To many still the top South African winery. A great mansion, immaculate v'yds and wines, serially awarded cellar door. Flagship is powerful, luxury-priced "V" **01'** 03 04 (single-v'yd Cab); B'x blend Vergelegen Red is lower keyed but still sumptuous; ditto Cab Sauv, MERLOT, approachable SHIRAZ. "White" is minerally, oak-fermented SEM blend. Superb, lemony CHARD Res; standout, racy SAUV BL Res (aka Schaapenberg). Even quaffing Mill Race Red is rung above the norm.

Vilafonté Paarl r ★★★★ First US-South African joint venture; California's Zelma Long (ex-Simi) and Phil Freese (ex-Mondavi viticulturalist) partnering WARWICK's Mike Ratcliffe. Top international notices for B'x blends: firmly structured Series C, more accessible Series M.

Villiera Wines St'bosch r w sp sw ★★→★★★★ Grier family v'yds and winery with excellent quality/value range. Cream of crop: B'x red Monro; Bush Vine SAUV BL; CHENIN BL in serious Cellar Door range; 5 MCC bubblies (inc sulphur-free Brut Natural); 2 botrytis desserts from RIES and CHENIN BL. Boutique-scale Dom Grier nr Perpignan now has its own sparkling, mainly CHARD/Macabeo.

Vriesenhof Vineyards St'bosch r w (sw) ★★★ Three labels, vinified by veteran Jan Coetzee: Vriesenhof (inc flagship B'x blend Kallista; PINOT N; PINOTAGE-based Enthopio); Talana Hill (B'x red Royale and CHARD); and Paradyskloof easy-drinkers (PINOTAGE, CHARD, etc).

Walker Bay Small fast-developing and highly reputed district, with sub-appellations HEMEL-EN-AARDE, Bot River and Sunday's Glen. PINOT N, CHARD and SAUV BL are standouts; some top producers: ATARAXIA, BOUCHARD FINLAYSON, HAMILTON RUSSELL, Hermanuspietersfontein, La Vierge, Julien Schaal, RAKA, Springfontein.

Ward Geographically the smallest of the four main WINE OF ORIGIN demarcations (largest is Geographical Unit, followed by Region and District).

Warwick Estate St'bosch r w ★★→★★★ Steered by dynamic Ratcliffe family (scion Mike also partner VILAFONTÉ). Fine B'x reds Trilogy (aka Estate Res) and The First Lady; PINOTAGE blend Three Cape Ladies; Cab Fr; Bush Vine PINOTAGE; CHARD; Prof Black SAUV BL.

Waterford Estate St'bosch r w sw ★★→★★★ Outstanding v'yds and hewn-stone cellar, with top-rank status under veteran Kevin Arnold. SHIRAZ (01 02' 03 04 05) is Cape classic; minerally Cab Sauv (01 **02** 03' 04 05), and CHARD. Superb CAB SAUV-based flagship, The Jem, among South Africa's priciest wines.

Welgemeend Estate Paarl r ★★→★★★ Boutique winery, owned by Gauteng-based consortium. B'x blend (South Africa's first) Estate Res; Malbec-based Douelle.

Weltevrede Estate Robertson r w (sp) sw ★★ Well-crafted, individual CHARD, SAUV BL and Syrah emphasizing diverse soils. Expanded Philip Jonker Brut MCC sp range: Entheos (CHARD/PINOT N), The Ring (CHARD), Aletheia (PINOT N/CHARD).

Wine of Origin South Africa's "AC", but without French crop-yield etc restrictions. Certifies vintage, variety, area of origin. See also WARD.

The Winery of Good Hope St'bosch r w ★★→★★★ Australian-French-South African joint venture. Flagship range is Radford Dale with promising new Freedom PINOT N. First-rate CAB SAUV and CHENIN BL in Vinum range; Swartland opulence in Black Rock White and Red. New Land of Hope range (CAB SAUV and CHENIN BL) helps fund staff children's education.

Zorgvliet Wines St'bosch r w ★★→★★★ Vinous arm of diversified lifestyle group Zorgvliet Portfolio. 20+ labels in 4 ranges, topped by pricey B'x red Richelle.

Wine in South America

A continent comes alive

The past two decades have seen South America emerge from stagnation to become arguably the most dynamic wine continent in the world. The dominant forces are Chile and Argentina, and the rivalry between these two countries can be intense and at times even heated. Yet there's also a grudging respect, as seen in the growing number of South American producers who now have wineries on both sides of the Andes.

Both countries have a long history of enthusiastic domestic wine consumption that fell drastically in the 1990s at a time of major political unrest. Since then each has re-emerged in splendid fashion, and much to the delight of wine drinkers around the world.

With just a few exceptions, the wines lapped up by the people of Chile have been of very basic quality. With the move to develop higher quality wines for the international market, many Chilean producers simply started new wineries in which they developed entirely different ranges from those available on the home market.

In contrast, Argentina with its strong European heritage had a history of fine-wine production. Faced with falling domestic consumption, producers began to look to other markets in which to sell their wines. Argentinian wine-makers found, however, that there was little demand for the rather stolid, old-fashioned wines that went down well at home. It has taken time for the ocean liner that is the Argentine wine industry to change direction in order to cater to outside tastes, but the ship is finally pointing in a much more satisfactory direction.

Chile and Argentina aren't the only wine-making countries, however, in South America. Uruguay has also attracted international attention, but the place we're likely to hear much more of in the future is Brazil. It's early days here, but there are signs that the country has the potential and the desire to play a far more prominent role in the world of wine. Chile and Argentina had better watch out.

Previous page: Mendoza, Argentina   Opposite: Colchagua Valley, Chile

The best is yet to come

While South America has made a significant impact with its wines over the last ten years in particular, there is very much a feeling that the best is still to come. In the early 1990s, a visitor to the wine regions of Chile might drive through long stretches of vineyards to a gleaming new winery for a tour of shiny stainless-steel tanks and row upon row of oak barrels. Ten years later, a visit was more likely to be to a vineyard to be shown the new drip-irrigation system and experimental plots of new grape varieties. Today, you may find yourself standing in a hole in the ground, prodding the soil with a hammer or squeezing a bottle of hydrochloric acid onto the rock. The lessons learned from this exploration of terroir are not only helping the Chileans to develop new vineyards and new regions, and to match the right grape variety to particular sites, but they are also causing them to challenge some

Catena Zapata winery, Argentina

long-held assumptions. For example, Chilean winemakers have found that sporadic use of drip irrigation at times when the vines look thirsty isn't necessarily a good thing, since it means the vine's roots seldom need to dig deep for moisture. A better way of working is to give the vines a hefty dose of water early in the season, which will sink down through the soil. When the vines need a drink, their roots have to head downwards into the more interesting decomposed rock layers. The result is grapes and eventually wine in which the vineyard character comes through more strongly.

In Argentina, exploration of the vineyards lags behind that of Chile. When Chile's producers were experimenting with their gleaming new wineries, their Argentine counterparts were attempting to upgrade their old, and often unhygienic facilities. The fruit coming into the wineries was often finer, but the wines going out weren't always as good as they could have been. With the cellars now in a better condition, the Argentineans are starting to focus more on their vineyards, planting at high altitudes in established regions, and at higher latitudes in new ones.

There has also been an evolution in the style of the wines. In Argentina, the rather rustic reds and dull whites are now a thing of the past, replaced by cleaner, riper Malbecs and Cabernets, and finer, fresher whites. The reds went through a period around five years ago when the goal seemed to be power at the expense of drinkability, but today's wines are better balanced and finer in structure. And they're improving with each vintage. While Malbec and Cabernet remain the most successful grapes, there's renewed interest in the many other

varieties that are grown, particularly Tempranillo, Bonarda and Torrontés, which have been here for some years, and newcomers such as Syrah, Chardonnay and Sauvignon Blanc. The first Chilean wines to make an impression outside the country were the easy-drinking Cabernet Sauvignons and Merlots. Attempts in the 1990s to make more ambitious reds of these were often unsuccessful, with the wines being simply riper, oakier versions of the basic cuvées. But with better fruit coming from the vineyards, and with the winemakers also becoming more experienced, the wines have improved dramatically.

Fulfilling potential

Chile's main export market has been the UK rather than America, and perhaps this may be why winemakers haven't strayed too far down the "size at all cost" path. Cabernet Sauvignon remains the most widely planted variety, but it's far from being the only successful performer. For reds, Syrah, Pinot Noir and Carmenère can also be superb, while Grenache, Petit Verdot and Cabernet Franc should be among the stars of the future. In whites, Sauvignon Blanc is top dog, but Chardonnay from places like Limarí, Casablanca and Bio-Bio can also be terrific.

Whereas the wine industries in some countries are having a tough time at present, both Chile and Argentina have cause to be optimistic about the future. Neither is suffering from drought in the way that parts of Australia and southern Europe are, so while the major vineyard regions of today may not be the same as those of tomorrow, there should be no glitches in supply. For Argentina, the home market remains strong, but exports, particularly to the UK, have boomed in recent times. The stated aim of the trade organization Wines of Argentina to have 10 per cent of the world export market by 2020 does not look impossible.

The same goes for Uruguay, a small, well-watered country between two giants, often overlooked but deserving of greater attention. Tannat from Uruguay first appeared on foreign markets around ten years ago, and impressed with its flavours and balance – but its tannins were, frankly, a little rustic. That's not the case today. Now it's all about ripeness in the vineyard, and getting those tannins really silky. Add to that the natural acidity of the grape and you have a wine that not only has the body to tackle a steak but the lightness not to overwhelm it: we should never forget that wine needs to wear its weight lightly to be refreshing. And Uruguayan Tannat tends to be just that. Uruguay is also a source of Merlot with rather more character and appeal than most Merlot – again, it's a question of acidity rather than jamminess – and Viognier that combines exotic perfumes with perfect poise. South America in miniature, in fact. And what of Brazil whose modern wine industry is even younger, yet which already has world-class Merlot and some very promising sparkling wines?

Whatever happens in the future, South America's evolution as a source of world-beating wine will be a pleasure to watch.

The power of climate

The underlying story of South American wine is the same as California's and Australia's: a search for cool climates. This can mean going west, or it can mean climbing; and then climbing some more.

Chile

In the far north of Chile, it's too hot and dry. In the far south it's too cold and wet. Between these two extremes, there is a large expanse of land where, providing there's sufficient water, wine grapes will grow. Quite how large remains to be seen, as the country's producers are currently engaged in a vigorous programme of expansion into regions once deemed unsuitable for viticulture.

The bulk of the vineyards are in the Central Valley between the Andes and the coastal mountain range. You'd think that it would be warmer the further north you travelled, but here the east-west axis is the important one. The middle of the Central Valley is generally made

Chile's climate varies with altitude, latitude and proximity to the coast

Carmenere grape

up of fertile alluvial soils on which grapes will happily grow, irrigated by plentiful snowmelt from the Andes, but which seldom yield anything beyond basic wine. Head up into the Andean foothills or up the slopes of the coastal range and the picture changes. Not only do the soils become more rocky, but the extra altitude means cooler nights, which leads to grapes with higher acidity and fresher aromas.

The last decade has seen a general move off the valley floor up onto the steep slopes of places like Apalta and Ninequén, resulting in wines that, while still bold, have a little more elegance and aroma than was once the case. There has also been a drift westwards to cooler spots such as Lolol and Marchihue. Expect to hear more of these districts in the future, anad of Ucuquer, close to where the Rapel River flows into the sea.

Argentina

The majestic Andes cast a spell over the landscape in Argentina's main wine regions, and the impact of the mountains on the wines themselves is equally immense. In the west of the country where all the grapes are grown, the climate is dry, but thanks to the rivers flowing from the Andes, the grapes never lack water. The mountains also act as a buffer for cool breezes from the Pacific, which means that many places are far too warm for viticulture. However, the closer you get to the mountains, the cooler it becomes.

More than 80 per cent of Argentina's wine comes from the province of Mendoza. With an average height of 900m, it's one of the highest-altitude wine regions in the world. Indeed, altitude is the key to determining the style of wine. With vineyards in the region lying at every height from 450m up to 1,500m and beyond, the wines vary markedly, since a 100m rise lowers the average temperature by around 0.6°C. Moreover, as you travel up into the Andean foothills, the soils become less alluvial and more rocky. Experimentation is ongoing on to discover which is the optimum altitude for the various varieties. White varieties such as Chardonnay and Sauvignon Blanc tend to favour higher vineyards, but Malbec has also been shown to perform well in such sites, retaining a perfume not found at lower levels.

Many of Argentina's most famous wines come from the vineyards of Maipú and Luján de Cuyo in the Mendoza River area. Here the vineyards lie between 650m and 1,050m, and the well-drained soils are ideal for Cabernet at lower altitudes, Malbec at higher ones and

The Mendoza region is home to most of Argentina's vineyards

several other red varieties too. The Uco Valley is the "hot" region of Mendoza. With vineyards at between 900m and 1,500m (in the Tupungato district), the style tends to be lighter than in the River area.

But to reach Argentina's highest vineyards, you need to travel north to Salta, and in particular to Colomé which has vines planted at around 3,000m. Even in other parts of the province, there's little below 1,700m, and the combination of altitude and the power of the sun at this northerly latitude makes for intensely flavoured and aromatic reds and whites – Torrontés is a speciality here. There are also vineyards to the south in the Patagonian provinces of Rio Negro and Neuquén. The Andes exerts less of an influence here, and the vineyards lie at lower levels, but the southerly location means that temperatures are generally cooler than in Mendoza. This means that hail, a problem in the more northerly regions, especially close to harvest time, is seldom a problem here. Frost, however, can be, affecting entire vineyards in some vintages.

Brazil

The majority of Brazil's vineyards lie in the Serra Gaucha region of the most southerly province, Rio Grande del Sul. Currently the most impressive district is the Vale dos Vinhedos, which is the first region and so far the only region in the country to have its own official geographical indication. While grapes have been grown on the gently undulating slopes here (it resembles Beaujolais) for more than a century, the move to quality wine has only taken place in the last 15 years. In a climate that can suffer from excess humidity, Merlot is the most impressive variety so far. This humidity has led some producers to seek out drier zones, such as Encruzilhada del Sul close to the Serra zone in the northwest of the province, home to some of the coolest and highest (1,000m) vineyards in Brazil.

In the north, the sub-tropical climate of the São Francisco Valley means that vineyards can be controlled to yield grapes all year round, and so provide two or more crops per year. Such a climate may not be suitable for good quality wine, but it does mean that the producers can start experiments at any point in the year, rather than having to wait for the appropriate season. As a publicity stunt, the Miolo winery recently developed a vineyard in which successive rows of vines each at a different stage of the growing cycle, allowed visitors to see grapes from budburst to full maturity. With other countries such as Australia struggling to maintain a flow of good cheap wine, this could be a region with a promising future.

Uruguay

Uruguay's vineyards are mostly found in the south of the country in the provinces of Montevideo, San José and Canelones close to the capital Montevideo. With a maritime climate, the challenge to wine growers is to cope with the humidity and to restrain vigour in the soils which can be on the fertile side. But it is notable that Uruguay is notable in being able to produce ripe reds at relatively low alcohol levels – say 13 or 13.5 %. That maritime climate seems to be the reason: with more cloud cover than in either Chile or Argentina winegrowers here can get ripe tannins without the high sugar levels that can be such an inbalancing factor in other countries.

Malbec grapes

Movers & shakers

These are the people who will decide the style of the wine we may well be drinking in the next few years.

Chile
Rafael and Eduardo Guilisasti

You won't find their names on a wine label – but you may well know the name of their company. Concha y Toro, and Rafael and Eduardo Guilisasti are respectively vice president and CEO. C&T is Chile's largest wine company, so all credit to the brothers for giving something not far off a free rein to top winemakers such as Marcelo Papa, Adolfo Hurtado and Ignacio Recabarren, allowing them to put into practice innovative ideas about terroir and viticulture.

Eduardo Chadwick

A much more familiar figure to wine lovers, Eduardo Chadwick is head of Viña Errázuriz and one of Chile's most enthusiastic international ambassadors. In 2004, at what became known as The Berlin Tasting, that he pitted his top wines – Seña, Don Maximiano Founder's Reserve and Viñedo Chadwick – against Bordeaux First Growths and top Super-Tuscan reds. Viñedo Chadwick 00 came out top, followed by Seña 01, Château Lafite 00, Château Margaux 01 and Seña 00. Since then he has conducted similar tastings elsewhere, just to prove that Berlin wasn't a one-off.

Aurelio Montes

When Aurelio Montes first launched his Montes Alpha Cabernet Sauvignon 1987 a lot of people thought, hmmm: a serious wine from Chile? Really? Well, he made his point. He wanted to make an international impact, and this he did. He followed it with Montes Alpha M, and more recently Montes Folly, Chile's first ambitious Syrah, and Purple Angel Carmenère. In the last few years he's been exploring new sites higher up the slopes in Apalta and close to the coast in Marchihue, not to mention ventures in Mendoza, Argentina, and in California's Napa Valley.

Alvaro Espinoza

Remember when a lot of Chilean Merlot turned out to be Carmenère? Alvaro Espinoza was at the forefront of that discovery, and was the first to put Carmenère on a label – albeit under its pseudonym of Grande Vidure. That was when he was at Viña Carmen. In recent years he's set up on his own and turned to organic and biodynamic viticulture; he advises many companies and has his own label, Antiyal. Much of the transformation of Chile

from a country of winemakers to one of winegrowers can be traced back to Espinoza's door.

Pedro Parra

Soil specialist Pedro Parra is the least well-known in this line-up of renowned Chileans, but he is right at the forefront of the Chilean obsession with terroir. He has dug deep holes and examined the soil profiles in many of the world's finest vineyards, and is now in demand for his expertise both in realizing the full potential of existing vineyards and in seeking out unexplored regions that could be important in the future. Terroir comes to life when you see him standing in one of these holes, dressed in a scruffy t-shirt and wielding a small hammer. His advice has led to wineries rethinking their whole approach to irrigation, planting densities and much more.

Argentina
Nicolás Catena

If Argentina's image as a wine producer was created by any one person, Nicolás Catena is the man. In the 1980s, while visiting professor of economics at the University of California, he also visited Napa. Inspired by what he saw he returned to Mendoza and sold off the family bulk wine business in order to concentrate on fine wine. He started planting Malbec at higher altitudes than Mendoza had ever seen, and continues to go higher, and higher still.

Daniel Pi

Daniel Pi's arrival, in 2002, as chief winemaker of Peñaflor, Argentina's largest wine company, was a catalyst for change for what had been a slightly lumbering giant. Single-vineyard Malbecs were his weapon, and he galvanized his growers by putting their names on the bottles of the best. A simple enough idea, but enough to revolutionize the attitudes of a lot of people.

Susana Balbo

South America's starriest female winemaker runs her own winery and consults to many others, including some in Europe. She has a passion for the Torrontés grape – it was Torrontés which first inspired her to make wine, and the crisp, modern style of Torrontés is pretty much her invention. The hallmark of her wines is elegance: she eschews the opulent ripeness that many European palates find overwhelming.

Pedro Marchevsky

Even today, there are still several Argentine wineries who look on a vineyard as little more than a grape factory. If more don't, then a large proportion of the credit should go to Susana Balbo's

ex-husband, Pedro Marchevsky. He's a viticulturalist whose studies into matching vines to different terroirs, planting densities, methods of pruning and so on and so forth have been absorbed into a grape-growing system that he calls Precision Viticulture.

Michel Rolland

Okay, Michel Rolland is a Bordelais, but no outsider has embraced the Argentine cause in quite such an enthusiastic way as he. As a consultant winemaker he has championed Malbec and encouraged Argentines along the route of bold, ripe flavours. These can sometimes seem too bold, too ripe, but in the best wines, Rolland also gives the terroir and the aromatic character of Malbec a chance to shine through.

Brazil
Adriano Miolo

The Miolo family has been growing grapes in Brazil for several generations, but only established its own winery in 1989. Michel Rolland consults, which probably helps, but Adriano Miolo is turning Brazilian wine, hitherto rustic and frankly unappealing, into something with an international future.

Uruguay
The Pisano family

Uruguayans are nearly all of Italian or Spanish descent: the Italians came from the north of that country, and the Spaniards came from the Basque country. The Pisano family combine both heritages. Exuberant and moustachiod to a greater or lesser degree, the brothers make some of the most complex and elegant wines in the country. Arretexea Viognier is as good as that grape gets outside the Rhône, and RPF Petit Verdot would make the Bordelais weep.

Where to buy wine

El Mundo del Vino, Santiago, Chile: www.elmundodelvino.cl

The Vines Wine Shop & Vinoteca, Park Hyatt, Mendoza, Argentina: www.vinesofmendoza.com

The Winery, Chilé 898, Mendoza, Argentina: ww.winery.com.ar

Grand Cru Vinos, downtown Buenos Aires: www.grandcru.com.ar

South American food

How to describe the food of an entire continent? In Argentina you'll have an asado; in Chile some corn, and in Brazil flavours that come from the country's astonishing mix of cultures.

Argentina

Given the numbers of Italian and Spanish people that have made Argentina their home, it's not surprising that there is a European accent to much of the cuisine, especially in the cities. Pastas, here in the plural, is popular, as are polenta and pizzas, and fainá, a pancake-like bread made from chickpea flour. The Spanish influence comes through in the stews, tortillas and rice (arroz) dishes, both savoury and sweet. And despite having a considerable coastline, Argentina isn't a major consumer of fish and seafood. The country grows, on the other hand, marvellous fruit.

In Argentina and indeed Uruguay, the grass-fed beef is legendary and the classic Argentine meal is the asado. Many South American countries have a tradition of eating meat cooked on a grill or an open fire, but in Argentina it's close to being an art. Comparisons with a barbecue fall short of the mark: this is a celebration of meat in almost all its forms. Some meats demand long, slow cooking: they are started off early and not subjected to too much of the intense heat of the fire. Others require shorter, sharper cooking. The meats are then served straight from the grill. For a snack, try an empanada. These are semi-circular filled pastries which are either baked in the oven or deep-fried. Once again, there are examples in various parts of the continent, but the Argentina versions are as good as any.

Grilling meat outdoors is a tradition across South America

Fresh fish is a Chilean staple: farmed along its vast coastline

Chile

Chile isn't an especially large country, and its inhabitants tend to be a little more reserved than other South American nations. There can be no such thing as typical food in a country whose northern tip is desert, while its southern end is in a region where summer snow is common.

Where to eat in Santiago

Agua, Nueva Costanera 3467: reservas@aguarestaurant.cl

Akarana, Reyes Lavalle 3310: cafemelba@yahoo.com

Astrid y Gaston,Antonio Bellet 201:astridygaston@astridygaston.cl

Cuero de Vaca, El Mañio 1659, Vitacura:
gerencia@cuerovaca.com

Infante 51, Infante 51: restaurant@infante51.cl

Zully, Concha y Toro 34: kfugarte@yahoo.com

Where to eat in Mendoza and Buenos Aires

1884 Francis Mallman, Belgrano 1188, Mendoza:
www.1884restaurante.com.ar

Francesco, Chile 1268, Mendoza: www.francescoristorante.com.ar

Palacio Duhau Park Hyatt, Buenos Aires:
buenosaires.park@hyatt.com

A little learning...

A few technical words

The jargon of laboratory analysis is often seen on back-labels. It creeps menacingly into newspapers and magazines. What does it mean? This hard-edged wine-talk, unsympathetic as it is to most lovers of wine, is very briefly explained below.

Alcohol content (mainly ethyl alcohol) is expressed in per cent by volume of the total liquid. (Also known as "degrees".) Table wines are usually between 12.5° and 14.5°, though up to 16° is increasingly seen.

Acidity is both fixed and volatile. Fixed acidity consists principally of tartaric, malic and citric acids, all found in the grape, and lactic and succinic acids, produced during fermentation. Volatile acidity consists mainly of acetic acid, which is rapidly formed by bacteria in the presence of oxygen. A small amount of volatile acidity is inevitable and even attractive. With a larger amount the wine becomes "pricked" – to use the Shakespearian term. It turns to vinegar. Acidity may be natural, in warm regions it may also be added.

Total acidity is fixed and volatile acidity combined. As a rule of thumb, for a well-balanced wine it should be in the region of one gram per thousand for each 10° Oechsle (see above).

Barriques Vital to modern wine, either in ageing and/or for fermenting in barrels (the newer the barrel the stronger the influence) or from the addition of oak chips or – at worst – oak essence. Newcomers to wine can easily be beguiled by the vanilla-like scent and flavour into thinking they have bought something luxurious rather than something cosmetically flavoured. But barrels are expensive; real ones are only used for wines with the inherent quality to benefit long-term. French oak is classic and most expensive. American oak has a strong vanilla flavour.

Malolactic fermentation is often referred to as a secondary fermentation, and can occur naturally or be induced. The process involves converting tart malic acid into softer lactic acid. Unrelated to alcoholic fermentation, the "malo" can add complexity and flavour to both red and white wines. In hotter climates where natural acidity may be low canny operators avoid it.

Micro-oxygenation is a widely used technique that allows the wine controlled contact with oxygen during maturation. This mimics the effect of barrel-ageing, reduces the need for racking, and helps to stabilize the wine.

pH is a measure of the strength of the acidity: the lower the figure the more acid. Wine usually ranges from pH 2.8 to 3.8. High pH can be a problem in hot climates. Lower pH gives better colour, helps stop bacterial spoilage and allows more of the SO_2 to be free and active as a preservative.

Residual sugar is that left after fermentation has finished or been stopped, measured in grams per litre. A dry wine has virtually none.

Sulphur dioxide (SO_2) is added to prevent oxidation and other accidents in winemaking. Some of it combines with sugars etc and is "bound". Only the "free" SO_2 is effective as a preservative. Total SO_2 is controlled by law according to the level of residual sugar: the more sugar, the more SO_2 is needed.

Tannins are the focus of attention for red-winemakers intent on producing softer, more approachable wines. Later picking, and picking by tannin ripeness rather than sugar levels gives riper, silkier tannins.

Toast refers to the burning of the inside of the barrel. "High toast" gives the wine caramel-like flavours.

vast semi-arid plains, home to large number of cattle, while closer to the coast, there are fertile regions suitable for a wide range of crops. Rice, beans, coconut milk and chillies are widely used for dishes here. Beans and rice are also staple dishes in the southeast. The Portuguese influence comes through in the national dish, feijoada, a stew of black beans with beef and pork, typically served with rice, refried greens, farofa (toasted manioc) and hot pepper sauce.

Uruguay has absorbed the influences of its large neighbours in its cuisine. Empanadas, asados, and dulce de leche, a sweet paste used to fill pancakes or cakes, are widespread. Chivitos are sandwiches of grilled meat with bacon, cheese, and salad and pascualinas, pies filled with chard, spinach, cheese and eggs. Finally there is puchero, a Uruguayan version of a pot-au-feu. Meats, corn, beans and other vegetables are cooked together and the broth is served as a starter.

The Brazilian dish feijoada

Pupunha palm fruits from Brazil: native to the rainforest

What Chile does have in its favour is a coastline that stretches over 6,000 km. Unsurprisingly, the fish and seafood are both varied and terrific, especially at their freshest, cooked simply at a seafront restaurant. Meat isn't embraced here to the same extent it is in Argentina but one dish found in the many tourist traps is chorillana, which is basically a plate of chips topped with a steak and two fried eggs. Also popular are choripánes, a snack akin to a hot-dog involving a chorizo or longaniza served in crusty bread with a variety of sauces. For something more traditional, there's cazuela, a stew made by cooking meat (usually chicken or beef) with vegetables such as pumpkins and potatoes. The cooking broth is often served as a starter, followed by the solid ingredients as a main course. Corn is another major ingredient. You'll find it in empanadas and humitas, which see corn, onions and seasoning wrapped up in the corn husks and then baked, boiled or steamed.

Brazil and Uruguay

If there's a common thread to Brazilian cuisine, it's flavour. In the north, the native Indian influence comes through the strongest with the use of indigenous vegetables such as cassava, yams and peanuts. Thanks to the Amazon, fish and seafood are plentiful, and are used both fresh and dried in stews such as caruru do par, a melange of dried shrimp, okra, onion and toasted nuts. Food in the northeast sees the impact of both the Portuguese and the Africans. Inland are